FOUNDATION PRESS

IMMIGRATION STORIES

Edited By

DAVID A. MARTIN

Warner–Booker Distinguished Professor of International Law
Class of 1963 Research Professor
University of Virginia

PETER H. SCHUCK

Simeon E. Baldwin Professor of Law
Yale Law School

FOUNDATION PRESS
New York, New York
2005

THOMSON
———*———™
WEST

Cover image: Chinese Immigrants at the San Francisco Custom-House, Harper's Weekly, February 3, 1877.

© 2005 By FOUNDATION PRESS
    395 Hudson Street
    New York, NY 10014
    Phone Toll Free 1–877–888–1330
    Fax (212) 367–6799
    fdpress.com
Printed in the United States of America

ISBN 1–58778–873–X

TEXT IS PRINTED ON 10% POST CONSUMER RECYCLED PAPER

IMMIGRATION STORIES

Contents

FOUNDATION PRESS

IMMIGRATION STORIES

*

v

Introduction

David A. Martin and Peter H. Schuck

Immigration stories help shape how we conceive of ourselves as a nation. At the end of his noted history of multicultural America, Ronald Takaki reflects:

> As Americans, we originally came from many different shores, and our diversity has been at the center of the making of America. While our stories contain the memories of different communities, together they inscribe a larger narrative. Filled with what Walt Whitman celebrated as the "varied carols" of America, our history generously gives all of us our "mystic chords of memory."[1]

In an earlier generation, Oscar Handlin opened his Pulitzer Prize-winning book, *The Uprooted,* with these words: "Once I thought to write a history of the immigrants in America. Then I discovered that the immigrants *were* America."[2]

Although the American immigration narrative is sometimes rendered as a pure tale of hope, grit, and triumph, a truthful account would include its share of stories of tragedy, shame, conflict, and failure (as Takaki's and Handlin's works make manifest). This mixed picture of success and setback holds whether viewed from the perspective of the individuals who migrate, the society that receives them, or the government that seeks to regulate the process. And of course this complex story is still unfolding. Since September 11, 2001, we have seen a remarkable reaffirmation of inclusiveness alongside an increased fear of aliens from certain regions associated with terrorist threats.

Given the centrality of immigration to American self-understanding, it is wholly fitting that *Immigration Stories* should join a new series of vital teaching materials augmenting law school casebooks. The *Stories* series tells the tales behind leading cases, anchoring them in their historical contexts, revealing the political and litigation strategies that drove them forward, and humanizing the individuals caught up in their toils. (Immigration stories are particularly rich in this human element, owing to the distinctive aspirations and struggles bound up with a decision to migrate.) The series also is meant to analyze the ongoing significance of each of the judicial decisions, as the polity accepts, rejects, or modifies their legal implications.

It is no easy task to select a baker's dozen of the most important, representative, or revealing immigration cases to include in such a volume. As editors, we knew, of course, that we would include cases that depict the Supreme Court's broad deference to the political branches in the immigration realm, the so-called "plenary power doctrine." But which cases should we choose–concerning that seminal doctrine as well as others–and how should we array them, given that many of the most important immigration cases address multiple themes? Ultimately, we decided to present those we selected in chronological order; one who reads from start to finish can gain some sense of the ebb and flow of the immigration case law.

Our book begins, naturally, with the Supreme Court's consideration of the Chinese Exclusion Acts of the 1880s and 1890s, the first sustained assertions of federal immigration control authority. Gabriel Chin describes the fascinating litigation context and the continuing significance of the two cases—*Chae Chan Ping v. United States* (sometimes called the *Chinese Exclusion Case*) and *Fong Yue Ting v. United States*—that are regarded as the foundation stones for the plenary power doctrine. In later generations, it was usually war that tested the constitutional limits of the government's plenary power over immigration. We pick up that thread with the Cold War. In *Harisiades v. Shaughnessy*, in 1952, the government successfully relied on the doctrine to justify deportation of three former members of the Communist Party, all long-time lawful permanent residents, based on a retroactive application of a statute passed after all three had terminated their membership, at least formally. Burt Neuborne relates how various strategic decisions led to the Court's rejection of their constitutional claims under the Ex Post Facto and Due Process clauses and the First Amendment. Twenty years later, the Court in *Kleindienst v. Mandel* reaffirmed plenary power by overriding First Amendment challenges to the exclusion of a Marxist intellectual, despite the post-*Harisiades* liberalization of First Amendment doctrine. In recounting that litigation, Peter Schuck shows how the lower courts subsequently exploited a doctrinal loophole left by the Court, which helped give reformers the opening they needed to limit the government's visa-denying discretion. In the chapter on the 2003 case of *Demore v. Kim,* Margaret Taylor explains how elements of the plenary power doctrine–coupled with the national trauma created by September 11, 2001–may have led the Court to countenance an unnecessarily harsh mandatory detention provision despite a precedent from only two years earlier (*Zadvydas v. Davis*) that seemed to presage a more forceful judicial defense of the liberty claims of detained aliens.

Plenary power, however, is not the whole immigration law story. Perhaps influenced by the almost universal academic criticism of the doctrine, the Supreme Court has occasionally reined in the political branches, usually using a distinctively stingy form of statutory construction—what Hiroshi Motomura has labeled phantom constitutional norms[3]—to defeat the government's broadest claims. At other times, the Court has deployed the Constitution itself to protect aliens or their children against political branch overreaching. *INS v. St. Cyr*, recounted by Nancy Morawetz, reflects the former approach. Congress tried in 1996 to strip the courts of jurisdiction to consider challenges to removal filed by virtually any alien with a criminal conviction in the United States. The Supreme Court read the law quite narrowly, finding that it allowed the trial courts to entertain habeas corpus petitions filed by such aliens. The ruling resulted in thousands of new hearings.

The Court's use of constitutional provisions to protect immigrants, at least in some circumstances, actually began in the Chinese exclusion era. Not only did the Court apply a strong version of equal protection to shield resident Chinese merchants against discriminatory administration of a San Francisco ordinance in the great case of *Yick Wo v. Hopkins*[4] (a decision discussed briefly in several of the chapters in this book), but it also held unconstitutional a central provision of the federal Chinese exclusion laws themselves. In *Wong Wing v. United States*, analyzed here by Gerald Neuman, the Court ruled that Congress could not impose criminal punishment for immigration violations through summary procedures. Although the government had established the habeas corpus petitioners' unlawful presence, it could not imprison them at hard labor without affording them all the protections of the criminal justice process—a decision that the scholar Henry Hart lauded as "one of the bulwarks of the Constitution."[5]

The xenophobic impulse that produced the Chinese exclusion laws also found expression in a late 19th century effort—supported by prominent legal academics and ultimately the Solicitor General of the United States—to persuade the Supreme Court that children born in the United States to lawfully present Chinese were not entitled to automatic citizenship under the Fourteenth Amendment. Lucy Salyer recounts the litigation in *Wong Kim Ark v. United States* that led the Court to affirm a broad birthright citizenship rule. Peter Spiro tells the story of *Afroyim v. Rusk*, a 1967 decision that adopted an even more expansive reading of the Citizenship Clause of the Fourteenth Amendment. *Afroyim* and its progeny shield citizens from government attempts to enforce the loss of citizenship on the basis of such acts as voting in a foreign election or naturalizing elsewhere—unless the citizen actually intends to renounce that precious status.

Landon v. Plasencia presented the question of the procedural due process rights of lawful permanent residents, even if they were technically claiming admission at the border when returning to the United States after foreign travel. As Kevin Johnson details, the Court chose to apply a more protective line of precedents, reaffirming that rights should be measured based on the alien's true status and her stake in the decision, rather than lumping returning residents together with aliens seeking initial admission. The Court on one occasion has also protected those without legal status. *Plyler v. Doe* presented a challenge by undocumented children to a Texas statute that permitted local governments to charge them tuition for basic public schooling. Michael Olivas dissects the legal strategies that led the Court to apply equal protection doctrine to invalidate Texas' statute on behalf of this particularly vulnerable group.

The other three stories in this volume are harder to classify but nevertheless reveal the operations of our immigration enforcement system, and, in some cases, the difficulty of balancing the demands of enforcement against other important societal goals. Daniel Kanstroom provides a rich and compelling account of the organized crime leader Carlos Marcello, a lawful permanent resident since infancy, whom the government tried to deport for decades, without success. One of the key markers in Marcello's seemingly endless journey through the courts, *Marcello v. Bonds*, was an instance of plenary power-style deference that restricted procedural protections under the Constitution for persons facing deportation. Other rounds of the government's battles with Marcello and his extraordinarily resourceful lawyers led to changes in the laws governing judicial review—but not always with the impact that the government anticipated. David Martin's chapter addresses political asylum, an issue in an increasing percentage of modern removal cases. It is the only chapter that does not focus on Supreme Court rulings; instead, it addresses a widely noted landmark decision of the Board of Immigration Appeals, *Matter of Kasinga,* which held that the customary practice the BIA called female genital mutilation (FGM) could form the basis for an asylum claim. It also considers an important follow-on FGM case, *Abankwah v. INS*, which illustrates the enforcement difficulties and dilemmas raised by this nation's asylum law. The *Abankwah* account also provides a close-up look at how cases unfold in immigration court. Finally, Catherine Fisk and Michael Wishnie, analyzing the 2002 decision in *Hoffman Plastic Compounds v. NLRB*, consider how the enforcement of the immigration laws should be balanced with other policy objectives (there, labor law's protection of workers, including the undocumented).

Specialists may find it odd that *Immigration Stories* does not include chapter-length treatment of the *Knauff* and *Mezei* cases.[6] These landmark plenary power decisions from the early 1950s permitted the government to visit harsh consequences on two rather sympathetic prospective immigrants, based on secret information allegedly revealing their subversive character—information they had been wholly unable to challenge. Those stories, however, have been well told elsewhere, particularly in Charles Weisselberg's comprehensive account of the two cases, as well as in a book Ellen Knauff herself authored once she had won a full hearing and eventual admission through political intervention.[7] And those cases do receive some attention in this book, particularly in the chapters on *Demore v. Kim* and *Landon v. Plasencia.*

The reader will learn here that many of the stories did not end once the Supreme Court issued a decision decreeing judicial deference to a harsh congressional policy or executive branch ruling. *Marcello v. Bonds,* for example, blessed an administrative deportation process that would mix the roles of prosecutor and judge, and seemed to allow for other departures from standard due process requirements. Yet administrative needs and enlightened management led to an evolution over the next two decades toward exactly the kind of trial-type procedures that Marcello's lawyers had advocated. *Kleindienst v. Mandel* approved ideological exclusion of those who gave merely intellectual support to Marxist ideas, but within two decades Congress had removed those provisions from the statute books. *Plyler v. Doe* seemed to leave the door open to restricting the access of undocumented children to our schools if Congress explicitly blessed such a state-law policy. But when certain members of Congress pushed for such a law in 1996, they were beaten back by a concerted political effort. As Margaret Taylor explains, some lower courts have interpreted *Demore* in ways that narrow the categorical mandatory detention that the Court upheld. And of course (in a development not addressed here), Congress finally cleansed our laws of the national-origins quota system in 1965, even though numerous court decisions had previously upheld it against constitutional challenge.

In short, even in those areas where the plenary power doctrine reigns, the polity is not saddled forever with objectionable laws or practices. The doctrine is an invitation to roll up one's sleeves and become active in the political arena in order to amend bad laws or defend good ones against amendments that would erode the hard-won gains of earlier campaigns. There is room in these stories to find both worry and inspiration at a time when many propose to trim protections in the name of the war on terror. The long struggle to assure fair process and sound substantive law continues.

ENDNOTES

1. Ronald Takaki, A Different Mirror: A History of Multicultural America 428 (1992), quoting from Whitman's *The Leaves of Grass* 38 (Signet ed. 1958) ("I Hear America Singing") and Abraham Lincoln's First Inaugural Address.

2. Oscar Handlin, The Uprooted: The Epic Story of the Great Migrations That Made the American People 3 (1st ed. 1951). See also Oscar Handlin, The Americans: A New History of the People of the United States ix-x (1963).

3. Hiroshi Motomura, Immigration Law After a Century of Plenary Power: Phantom Constitutional Norms and Statutory Interpretation, 100 Yale L.J. 545 (1990).

4.118 U.S. 356 (1886).

5.Henry Hart, The Power of Congress to Limit the Jurisdiction of the Federal Courts: An Exercise in Dialectic, 66 Harv. L. Rev. 1362, 1387 (1952).

6.United States ex rel. Knauff v. Shaughnessy, 338 U.S. 537 (1950); Shaughnessy v. United States ex rel. Mezei, 345 U.S. 206 (1953).

7.Charles D. Weisselberg, The Exclusion and Detention of Aliens: Lessons from the Lives of Ellen Knauff and Ignatz Mezei, 143 U.Pa. L. Rev. 933 (1995); Ellen Knauff, The Ellen Knauff Story (1952).

1

Chae Chan Ping and *Fong Yue Ting*: The Origins of Plenary Power

Gabriel J. Chin

At the Founding, there was essentially no federal immigration policy.[1] States regulated entry of immigrants, particularly in major seaports like New York and later San Francisco, but once the newcomer had successfully landed, he or she was in. There were no green cards, no quotas, no caps, no Border Patrol or ICE. And there was no deportation.

Anxiety over Asian immigration led the federal government to assume regulatory authority over immigration.[2] Although the policy goal of dealing with the "Yellow Peril" no longer significantly influences the content of the Immigration and Nationality Act, this anxiety spawned a pair of late nineteenth century Supreme Court cases establishing the principle that Congress possesses plenary power to regulate immigration. More than a century later, these cases continue to shape federal constitutional authority over immigration.

In *Chae Chan Ping v. United States*,[3] sometimes called the *Chinese Exclusion Case*, the Court held that a returning resident non-citizen could be excluded if Congress determined that his race was undesirable—or for any other reason. In *Fong Yue Ting v. United States*,[4] the Court held that these non-citizens could be deported because of their race—or for any other reason. Under domestic law, of course, racial classifications are now suspect; indeed, racial discrimination is more likely to be illegal than discrimination on any other basis. The message from these cases, whose core holdings have not been overruled, then, is that where the status of immigrants is concerned, almost anything goes. Congressional power to determine who may come and stay, and who may not, is virtually unrestricted.

Background

The United States is a nation of immigrants, and early prospects for the development of a Chinese immigrant community in America were bright. Chinese came to the country they called "Gold Mountain" to participate in the California gold rush, and their numbers grew slowly. Between 1870 and 1880, 138,941 Chinese migrated to the United States (4.3% of all immigration); by 1880, the Chinese population totaled 105,465, 0.2% of the U.S. population of 50 million.[5]

This immigration was specifically authorized by the Burlingame Treaty, concluded between China and the United States in 1868.[6] The signatory nations recognized "the inherent and inalienable right of a man to change his home and allegiance, and also the mutual advantage of free migration and emigration of their citizens and subjects ... for purposes of curiosity, of trade, or as permanent residents." Travelers from one country to the other were entitled to "the same privileges, immunities, and exemptions in respect to travel or residence, as may there be enjoyed by the citizens or subjects of the most favored nation."[7]

By the mid–1870s, however, California and other western states demanded restriction of Chinese immigration, primarily because of racial hostility fueled by economic depression in California. The Burlingame Treaty was modified in 1880 to allow restriction of the immigration of Chinese laborers, but the rights of those already in the country on November 17, 1880 were to be protected, including their right to come and go.[8] Taking advantage of this modification, Congress passed the Chinese Exclusion Act[9] in 1882. The Act suspended immigration of Chinese laborers for ten years, excluding from entry any who were not in the United States on November 17, 1880, or who arrived within ninety days after the Act came into force. Merchants and government officials were exempted. The Act required registration documents for laborers, to serve as "proper evidence of their right to go from and come to the United States."[10] These documents were issued upon departure, certifying the identity of individuals who might later wish to return. Those present in violation of the Act could be deported.

The Chinese Exclusion Act worked. In 1882, before it took effect, over 39,000 Chinese came to America. In 1887, Chinese immigration bottomed out at ten![11] While America's population more than doubled between 1880 and 1920, the population of Chinese ancestry declined by over a third.[12]

The Chinese Exclusion Act solidified another element of U.S. citizenship policy. The first naturalization law of 1790 allowed naturalization of "free white persons"; by judicial decision, Chinese were not regarded as white.[13] The 1882 Act codified this rule, prohibiting any state or federal court from naturalizing Chinese.[14] Accordingly, new Chinese immigration was prohibited and those already here could not become citizens.

The Act was motivated in large part by the racist ideas that were then in vogue. Senator John F. Miller of California, a leader of the restriction movement, reasoned:

> It is not numbers that are needed; quality is of more importance than quantity. One complete man, the product of free institutions and a high civilization, is worth more to the world than hundreds of barbarians. Upon what other theory can we justify the almost complete extermination of the Indian, the original possessor of all these States? I believe that one such man as Washington, or Newton, or Franklin, or Lincoln glorifies the Creator of the world and benefits mankind more than all the Chinese who have lived, and struggled, and died on the banks of the Hoang Ho.[15]

Legislators were not concerned only with the Chinese; some viewed them as part of a larger racial problem. For example, Senator John P. Jones of Nevada reasoned: "What encouragement do we find in the history of our dealings with the negro race or in our dealings with the Indian race to induce us to permit another race-struggle in our midst?"[16]

Critical to understanding the legal situation of the Chinese in this period is that they were frequently represented by high quality legal counsel. In the 1880s, a federal constitutional right to appointed counsel even in capital criminal cases was still decades away,[17] and many Chinese immigrants were miners, manual laborers, laundrymen or in other occupations where the salaries would scarcely permit hiring even the most inexperienced counsel. Many immigrants, moreover, were on a boat or in federal custody; even an unskilled job was a dream for the future. Nevertheless, many immigrants and would-be immigrants were represented by counsel.[18]

Indeed, Chinese immigration cases making it to the Supreme Court were handled by a "Dream Team" of elite lawyers of the day. Chae Chan Ping, for example, was represented by leading Supreme Court advocates: George Hoadly was a former Governor of Ohio, and James C. Carter was "widely acknowledged as the leader of the American bar,"[19] based in large part on the many cases he argued in the Supreme Court. Chae Chan Ping was also represented by Thomas S. Riordan, winner of several Supreme Court interpretations of the Exclusion Act favorable to Chinese immigrants,[20] and Harvey S. Brown, who argued several Supreme Court cases for railroads and had already won a case there for a Chinese immigrant.[21]

Fong Yue Ting's attorneys were equally distinguished. Joseph H. Choate served as Ambassador to the Court of St. James and frequently argued before the Supreme Court.[22] J. Hubley Ashton, as Acting Attorney General, advised President Lincoln during the Civil War,[23] and later represented the Southern Pacific Company.[24] Maxwell Evarts won several important cases for the Chinese.[25] Fittingly, he was the son of William M. Evarts, who had served as Attorney General, Secretary of State, and U.S. Senator. The senior Evarts, as Secretary of State, oversaw the negotiation of the 1880 treaty protecting the rights of Chinese laborers already in the United States; in the Senate, he supported paying an indemnity to the families of twenty-eight Chinese who had been massacred in Rock Springs, Wyoming, and opposed the amendment to the Chinese Exclusion Act at issue in *Chae Chan Ping* on the ground that it violated treaty obligations.[26]

These lawyers were not working pro bono, nor were they what would now be called public interest lawyers; they represented trusts and railroads more often than humble toilers like their Chinese clients. The existence of a network of Chinese family and district organizations in California and New York, to which virtually all of the Chinese in America paid dues, made it possible to retain these distinguished men, and other lawyers in the much more common proceedings in the federal trial courts. At the top of the network was an organization of organizations, the Chinese Six Companies, which historian Lucy Salyer explains became "the advocate for the Chinese community in the white world."[27] Thomas S. Riordan was counsel to the Six Companies.

The 1882 Act left open many questions for lawyers and courts to address. Were the "Chinese" who were covered by the Act defined by racial ancestry, or nationality? Many persons, for example, were citizens or nationals of countries other than China, but of Chinese descent.[28] Who were the "laborers" covered by the Act? Did it mean unskilled laborers, or were those in skilled trades and crafts also covered?[29] Did the Act cover Chinese sailors on U.S.-flag ships when they returned to port?[30] And would the Act be applied retroactively to Chinese who left before the effective date of the Act, and who therefore could not possibly have obtained certificates?[31] Although the federal courts' decisions were not uniform, it is fair to say that they frequently took the interests of the Chinese seriously, and frequently ruled in their favor.

In 1884, Congress made clear that it regarded the legal defense of Chinese immigrants as too effective, and the resulting judicial decisions too lenient. A new statute provided that the Act would apply "to ... Chinese, whether subjects of China or any other foreign power,"[32] making explicit that exclusion was based on race, not nativity or citizenship, and that it also applied to "both skilled and unskilled laborers and Chinese employed in mining."[33] The Act narrowed eligibility for favored treatment as merchants. Finally, the Act made clear that the re-entry certificate was "the only evidence permissible to establish [a returning resident's] right of re-entry."[34]

The 1884 Act, like the 1882 law, raised the question of retroactivity. Chew Heong, a Chinese laborer, sought admission without a return certificate, claiming that he had left in 1881, before they were available. Thomas Riordan and Harvey Brown represented him; Justice Harlan wrote for the Court that under the Act, Chew Heong could show lawful residence with other evidence.[35] This construction, said the Court, would give full prospective effect to the 1882 and 1884 legislation, while protecting the treaty rights of Chinese laborers who left before exclusion went into effect. In a later case, but this time over the dissent of Justice Harlan, Riordan persuaded the Court that the government copy of the re-entry certificate could be examined in the case of a laborer who left the United States with a re-entry certificate but was unable to present it because it had been stolen by pirates.[36]

Virulent anti-Chinese activity, such as the 1885 massacre of the Chinese community of Rock Springs, Wyoming and the 1885–86 expulsion of the Chinese residents of Seattle and Tacoma, induced Congress to continue to tighten exclusion. Congress passed, and the President signed, a strengthened Chinese Exclusion Law in September 1888 but, by its terms, the new statute was to take effect only upon conclusion and ratification of treaty modifications.[37] When negotiations between the United States and China broke down, Congress provided in the so-called Scott Act that any Chinese laborer, resident in the United States, who left and had not returned by the effective date of the Act could not "return to, or remain in, the United States."[38] In effect, most persons of Chinese ancestry could leave the United States only on one-way trips.

As for the return certificates, the statute provided that no more could be issued, and that "every certificate heretofore issued ... is hereby declared void and of no effect, and the chinese laborer claiming admission by virtue thereof shall not be permitted to enter the United States."[39] Perhaps 30,000 Chinese, residents of the United States but temporarily overseas, held re-entry certificates that were now void.[40]

Chae Chan Ping had come to the United States in 1875, and lived here until June 2, 1887, when he returned for a visit to China after first having obtained a re-entry certificate. On September 7, 1888, before the Scott Act had even been introduced in Congress, he boarded a vessel bound for San Francisco. He arrived on October 7 or 8 (the court papers are inconsistent), with a re-entry certificate that had been declared void while he was at sea.

Prior Proceedings in Chae Chan Ping

The court proceedings in San Francisco were swift. A habeas corpus petition was filed on October 10, 1888; Chae Chan Ping was brought to court on October 12, where the petition was heard by Circuit Judge

Lorenzo Sawyer and District Judge Ogden Hoffman, who had wide experience with Chinese immigration, naturalization and discrimination cases.[41] The immigrant was represented by Thomas Riordan and two other lawyers. The circuit court ruled against him on October 15; that same day, a notice of appeal was filed and bail was granted.

The circuit court assumed that Chae Chan Ping was covered by the 1888 Act, making the unanswerable point that the Act covered "not every Chinese laborer who shall have departed and not yet have started on his return, but every Chinese laborer who shall have departed, and shall not in fact have returned before the passage of this act."[42] The court noted that "great hardship" to individuals may bear "upon the construction of an ambiguous statute," but there was no room, as there had been with respect to the 1882 and 1884 enactments, to deny the statute retroactive effect.[43] Accordingly, the central legal issue was whether for some other reason the Act could not be applied to Chae Chan Ping.

It was insufficient for him to show that he possessed a privilege that was later extinguished. No legal doctrine mandates that privileges once granted can never be withdrawn; the government can change the speed limit or close national parks. The question here was whether the government's power was restricted for some reason, whether a privilege had, in effect, matured into a right.

The circuit court held that the treaty did not represent a contract with individual Chinese immigrants which was binding on the government. "There was no meeting of two minds on the terms of an agreement. The Chinese laborers were not consulted at all in the matter."[44] But even in the absence of a contract, the court recognized, a privilege might have become "fully executed," so that it could not be arbitrarily taken away. "But we do not regard the privilege of going and coming from one country to another as of this class of rights. The being here with a right of remaining is one thing, but voluntarily going away with a right at the time to return is quite another."[45] Thus, the court seemed to recognize the possibility that accepting an invitation to move here might create a continuing right to remain, but an unaccepted offer or other expectancy could be withdrawn.

The court concluded that the 1888 law was not ex post facto, for it created no crime and imposed no penalty.[46] The court noted that in the past, it had discharged its duty, "however unpleasant," to protect the rights of the Chinese under the law: "[a]s we faithfully enforced the laws, as we found them, when they were in favor of the Chinese laborers, we deem it, equally, our duty to enforce them in all their parts, now that they are unfavorable to them."[47] Any redress for the violation of the treaty must be sought by "the nation with whom we have made the treaty."[48]

Proceedings in the Supreme Court

Four lawyers represented Chae Chan Ping in the Supreme Court. George Hoadly and James C. Carter filed the main brief; Carter also filed a shorter summary. Thomas Riordan and Harvey Brown argued. For the United States, the Solicitor General filed a brief; lawyers appointed for the state of California filed an amicus brief.[49] Among the lawyers was John F. Swift, one of the American commissioners who had negotiated the 1880 treaty with China. By supporting the United States, he was, in essence, arguing that the treaty he had helped negotiate was unenforceable.

The Court, in a unanimous opinion written by Justice Stephen Field, began by exploring the background of the exclusion law, and the reasons that Californians, in particular, had sought restriction on Chinese immigration. Californians claimed "that the presence of Chinese laborers had a baneful effect upon the material interests of the state, and upon public morals; that their immigration was in numbers approaching the character of an Oriental invasion, and was a menace to our civilization."[50] The Court also asserted that administration of the laws allowing the re-entry of returning residents had been afflicted with fraud; because of "the loose notions entertained by the witnesses of the obligation of an oath," some Chinese got in claiming to be returning residents "who, it was generally believed, had never visited our shores. To prevent the possibility of the policy excluding chinese laborers being evaded, the act of October 1, 1888 . . . was passed."[51]

There was no doubt that Chinese laborers could be prohibited prospectively, or that an otherwise valid treaty could be repudiated by subsequent legislation.[52] The Supreme Court, like the circuit court, recognized the uncontroversial proposition that later legislation could effectively invalidate an earlier, inconsistent treaty: "the last expression of the sovereign will must control."[53] The real issue was whether Chae Chan Ping was in a different situation because he had left with the assurance of the United States government that he could return.

The innovative ground of the Supreme Court's decision, which had not been focused on in the circuit court, was the breadth of federal power over immigration. The Constitution does not in so many words state that the federal government has any authority over immigration, much less plenary power. However, the Court concluded: "That the government of the United States, through the action of the legislative department, can exclude aliens from its territory is a proposition which we do not think open to controversy."[54] The Court recognized this authority not from any particular provision of the Constitution, but as inherent in sovereignty:

> While under our constitution and form of government the great mass of local matters is controlled by local authorities, the United States, in their relation to foreign countries and their subjects or citizens, are one nation, invested with powers which belong to independent nations, the exercise of which can be involved for the maintenance of its absolute independence and security throughout its entire territory.[55]

The Court's understanding of the scope of the power may have been influenced by the circumstances under which it was exercised. It regarded the exclusion of Chinese as almost a war measure:

> To preserve its independence, and give security against foreign aggression, is the highest duty of every nation, and to attain these ends nearly all other considerations are to be subordinated. It matters not in what form such aggression and encroachment come, whether from the foreign nation acting in its national character, or from vast hordes of its people crowding in upon us.... If, therefore, the government of the United States, through its legislative department, considers the presence of foreigners of a different race in this country, who will not assimilate with us, to be dangerous to its peace and security, their exclusion is not to be stayed because at the time there are no actual hostilities with the nation of which the foreigners are subjects. The existence of war would render the necessity only more obvious and pressing. The same necessity, in a less pressing degree, may exist when war does not exist, and the same authority which adjudges the necessity on one case must also determine it in the other. In both cases, its determination is conclusive upon the judiciary.[56]

The circuit court had reached the somewhat remarkable conclusion that the re-entry certificates "are mere instruments of evidence, issued to afford convenient proof of the identity of the party entitled to enjoy the privileges secured by the treaties, and to prevent frauds."[57] The Supreme Court seemed to recognize that the certificates were more than identification documents, quoting language from the statute providing that the certificate "shall entitle the Chinese laborer to whom the same is issued to return to and reenter the United States."[58] But that the certificates granted a "right" did not mean that they granted a right that could not be taken away. Even if there had been a bargained-for "contract" or other agreement that Chae Chan Ping could return, the power to exclude was an "incident of sovereignty" and thus "cannot be granted away or restrained on behalf of anyone. [Sovereign powers] cannot be abandoned or surrendered. . . . The exercise of these public trusts is not the subject of barter or contract."[59]

The Court agreed with the circuit court that certain rights under a treaty or other law would continue even if that law were superseded: "Of course, whatever of a permanent character had been executed or vested under the treaties was not affected by it. In that respect the abrogation of the obligations of a treaty operates, like the repeal of a law, only upon the future, leaving transactions executed under it to stand unaffected."[60] In 1823, a unanimous Supreme Court had held that "termination of a treaty cannot devest rights of property already vested under it. If real estate be purchased or secured under a treaty, it would be most mischievous to admit, that the extinguishment of the treaty extinguished the right to such estate."[61] However, the right to re-enter was not like the right to own real property; it did not survive cancellation of the law creating it. "Between property rights not affected by the termination or abrogation of a treaty, and the expectation of benefits from the continuance of existing legislation, there is as wide a difference as between realization and hopes."[62]

The Court stated that any objection to the violation of the treaty provision protecting the rights of those already present to come and go would have to come from the beneficiary of the treaty, i.e., the Chinese government. Although this was cold comfort to Chae Chan Ping, it was not completely meaningless. China took an active interest in its overseas subjects; their rights were the subject of diplomatic negotiations and consular attention in the United States. Congress could violate treaty rights only at a diplomatic cost. Indeed, American policy towards Asian immigration was liberalized during World War II, the Korean War and the Vietnam War, largely because of diplomatic and foreign policy concerns.[63]

From a modern perspective, an interesting aspect of the case is what was not argued or decided. There was no claim that the Chinese Exclusion Act was flawed because it was racially discriminatory; notwithstanding the recent Supreme Court success of Chinese litigants challenging racially discriminatory prosecutions by local authorities in Yick Wo v. Hopkins,[64] no equal protection challenge was made. Had such an argument been raised, it certainly would have failed. The Equal Protection Clause of the Fourteenth Amendment, by its terms, applied only to the states, not to the federal government. Although an equal protection principle was later read into the Due Process Clause of the Fifth Amendment, the Court then took the position that "the Fifth contains no equal protection clause and it provides no guaranty against discriminatory legislation by Congress."[65] Accordingly, "[g]iven in congress the absolute power to exclude aliens, it may exclude some and admit others, and the reasons for its discrimination are not open to challenge in the courts.''[66]

More fundamentally, *Chae Chan Ping* (as well as *Fong Yue Ting*) was decided a few short years before *Plessy v. Ferguson*;[67] racial classifications were not then suspect or subject to special scrutiny, and if "reasonable" racial classifications were acceptable with respect to citizens, they presumably were even more so for non-citizens. Also related was the Court's recognition of expanded federal authority other areas. In addition to its immigration decisions, in this era the Court held that the federal government had plenary power over the indian tribes, and territories such as Puerto Rico. Professor Sarah Cleveland demonstrates that these developments were related (many of the major cases cite each other), and stemmed at least in part from "nativist, nationalistic, and authoritarian impulses among the nation's political elites that justified the subjugation of 'inferior' peoples."[68]

On September 2, 1889, *The New York Times* reported that Chae Chan Ping had been deported.[69] Yet for Chinese immigrants as a group, and even for Chae Chan Ping, the Court's decision might have been regarded at the time as merely a bump in the road. After all, it was rendered more than seven years after the passage of the original Chinese Exclusion Act. Therefore, in less than three years, when the ten-year suspension under the Chinese Exclusion Act expired, Chinese immigration would be restored to the same basis as immigration of all other persons in the world. However, as the expiration drew closer, calls for continuation of exclusion grew more strident.

Background to Fong Yue Ting

On May 5, 1892, one day before the original act would have lapsed, President Harrison signed into law the Geary Act, a new and yet sterner measure.[70] The Act was entitled "An Act to prohibit the coming of Chinese persons into the United States;" by using the words "persons" instead of "laborer," the law signaled that it was intended to exclude all except those specifically permitted, rather than to admit all except those specifically excluded.[71] The Geary Act extended existing exclusion laws for ten years. It created a presumption that any Chinese person found in the United States was deportable "unless such person shall establish, by affirmative proof . . . his lawful right to remain in the United States."[72] It provided that persons found to be unlawfully present should be imprisoned at hard labor before deportation, and that no bail should be allowed during deportation proceedings.[73]

The most fundamental change imposed by the new law, however, was creation of a registration program. All Chinese laborers were given one year to obtain a certificate of residence from the collector of internal

revenue. After one year, any Chinese person "found within the jurisdiction of the United States without such certificate of residence, shall be
deemed and adjudged to be unlawfully within the United States," and
brought to a U.S. judge, who would order deportation.[74] The law created
an exception for those unable to procure the certificate "by reason of
accident, sickness, or other unavoidable cause" who could establish "by
at least one credible white witness that he was a resident of the United
States at the time of the passage of this act."[75]

Campaign of Resistance

The level of community organization that allowed the Chinese to
obtain legal counsel gave them the opportunity for organized resistance
to a law they detested. In California, the Chinese Six Companies organized a boycott of the registration program; nationally, perhaps 15% of
the eligible Chinese registered, leaving over 80,000 in violation of the
law.[76] Every Chinese person in America was asked to contribute a dollar
to a legal defense fund. Meanwhile, in New York, the Chinese Equal
Rights League was formed in part to organize resistance to the law.[77]
Thomas Riordan and distinguished co-counsel arranged a test case.

The litigants were laundrymen who had lived in New York for years.
Chinatown residents Fong Yue Ting and Wong Quan had failed to apply
for a residence certificate; Lee Joe, an upper East Sider, had applied for
one, but was refused because he had only Chinese witnesses who were
deemed not credible by the administrator.[78]

Proceedings Below

The Geary Act's validity was tested with a speed probably un-
matched by any other fully briefed, plenary decision of the Supreme
Court. The plaintiffs were arrested on May 6, 1893; Lee Joe and Wong
Quan were brought before a U.S. district judge in New York and ordered
deported. Later that day, petitions for writs of habeas corpus were filed
in the circuit court; the writs were issued, heard, and dismissed; applications for appeal to the Supreme Court were filed and granted; and the
immigrants were released on bail. Present at the circuit court proceedings were attorneys Joseph Choate and Maxwell Evarts,[79] and representatives of the Chinese Consulate in New York and the Chinese Legation
in Washington.[80] The circuit court record was filed in the Supreme Court
on May 8; briefs for the immigrants and for the United States were filed
and argument was heard on May 10; on May 15, 1893, the Supreme
Court issued a full written decision with three dissents. A total of nine
days elapsed from the initiation of the dispute to the final decision on
the merits by the highest court in the land.[81] The celerity of the
proceedings, of course, was prearranged; the Chinese Minister to the

United States successfully prevailed upon the Secretary of State to help expedite the case.[82]

The brief for the United States made the expected claims under domestic and international law. Most notable to the modern reader is the frank appeal to racial considerations. The Solicitor General's brief noted that England had expelled "Egyptians" and "Turks," argued that "[a]nalogies might also be drawn from the forcible removal by the United States of Indians, who, for this purpose, as well as in the exercise of the treaty-making power, are regarded as aliens,"[83] and noted that "Russia is now engaged in expelling the Jews, and laws looking to a limitation upon their rights and regulating their *status* have been in recent years a source of party strife in the German Empire."[84] To the argument that the Chinese had a vested right to remain, the United States had a telling rejoinder:

> In view of past experiences of civilized communities with hordes of barbarians, it does not seem possible that a rule never yet ingrafted upon this principle of self-preservation will have its origin in this court. Again, it is now generally conceded that the most insidious and dangerous enemies to the State are not the armed foes who invade our territory, but those alien races who are incapable of assimilation, and come among us to debase our labor and poison the health and morals of the communities in which they locate.[85]

Supreme Court Opinion

Fong Yue Ting, Wong Quan and Lee Joe were to be deported from the United States; Chae Chan Ping was excluded at the border. A five-justice majority,[86] through Justice Gray, held that this distinction made no constitutional difference: "The right of a nation to expel or deport foreigners who have not been naturalized, or taken any steps towards becoming citizens of the country, rests upon the same grounds, and is as absolute and unqualified, as the right to prohibit and prevent their entrance into the country."[87] According to the Court, Fong Yue Ting's rights as a resident were no more vested than Chae Chan Ping's as a returning resident who left with an assurance that he could return; after all, Chae Chan Ping had been admitted permanently under the terms of a treaty then in full force. As Chae Chan Ping's rights were defeasible, those of current residents had the same status: "it appears to be impossible to hold that a Chinese laborer acquired, under any of the treaties or acts of Congress, any right, as a denizen, or otherwise, to be and remain in this country, except by the license, permission and sufferance of Congress, to be withdrawn, whenever, in its opinion, the public welfare might require it."[88] After this conclusion, the rest of the case was relatively simple. The only question was whether the provisions of the Act for some reason violated another part of the Constitution. The Court was untroubled by the allocation of enforcement authority. Deportation or exclusion of aliens "may be exercised entirely through executive officers; or Congress may call in the aid of the judiciary to ascertain any contested facts."[89] Imposing the burden of proof on the Chinese person, and providing for testimony of white witnesses only "is within the acknowledged power of every legislature to prescribe the evidence which shall be received, and the effect of that evidence, in the courts of its own government."[90]

The Court's determination that deportation "is not a punishment for crime"[91] was pivotal, given that much of the Bill of Rights applies specifically to criminal punishment. Accordingly, "the provisions of the Constitution, securing the right of trial by jury, and prohibiting unreasonable searches and seizures and cruel and unusual punishments, have no application."[92] Finally, the Court held that immigration policy presented something close to a political question. "[W]hether, and upon what conditions, these aliens shall be permitted to remain within the United States being one to be determined by the political departments of the government, the judicial department cannot properly express an opinion upon the wisdom, the policy, or the justice of the measures enacted by Congress in the exercise of the powers confided to it by the constitution over this subject."[93]

Unlike *Chae Chan Ping*, there was substantial opposition to the majority's view. Justices Brewer, Fuller and Field (author of *Chae Chan Ping*) dissented in three separate opinions that ultimately made similar points. First, they rejected the idea of unlimited inherent sovereign powers. Justice Brewer argued that "[t]his doctrine of powers inherent in sovereignty is one both indefinite and dangerous. Where are the limits to such powers to be found, and by whom are they to be pronounced?"[94] Even if deportation were an implied power, "yet still it can be exercised only in subordination to the limitations and restrictions imposed by the constitution."[95] Field contended that "[a]s men having our common humanity, they are protected by all the guaranties of the constitution."[96] Fuller agreed.[97]

The dissenters also argued that permanent residents, even if aliens, were on a different footing than those seeking admission. Chief Justice Fuller argued that lawful immigrants had acquired a vested right: deportation amounts to "the deprivation of that which has been lawfully acquired."[98] Justice Field agreed that the power to exclude was plenary, but government "power to deport from the country persons lawfully domiciled therein by its consent, and engaged in the ordinary pursuits of life, has never been asserted ... except for crime, or as an act of war" other than in the discredited Alien and Sedition Acts.[99] Justice Brewer argued that "[w]hatever may be true as to exclusion ... I deny that there is any arbitrary and unrestrained power to banish residents, even resident aliens."[100]

In addition, the dissenters agreed that deportation is punishment. Justice Brewer explained: "Every one knows that to be forcibly taken away from home and family and friends and business and property, and sent across the ocean to a distant land, is punishment, and that often-times most severe and cruel."[101] Justice Field regarded deportation as "punishment for his neglect [in failing to obtain a certificate,] and that, being of an infamous character, can only be imposed after indictment, trial and conviction."[102] Chief Justice Fuller understood the statute to be "a legislative sentence of banishment, and, as such, absolutely void."[103]

The dissenters regarded the majority's decision as portentous. Field argued that the constitutional "guaranties are of priceless value to every one resident in this country, whether citizen or alien. I cannot but regard the decision as a blow against constitutional liberty."[104] To Fuller, the Geary Act "contains within it the germs of the assertion of an unlimited and arbitrary power, in general, incompatible with the immut-able principles of justice, inconsistent with the nature of our govern-ment, and in conflict with the written constitution by which that government was created, and those principles secured."[105] Brewer argued that "[t]he expulsion of a race may be within the inherent powers of a despotism," and warned "[i]t is true this statute is directed only against the obnoxious Chinese, but, if the power exists, who shall say it will not be exercised to-morrow against other classes and other people?"[106]

Lee Joe, Wong Quan and Fong Yue Ting paid the price for partici-pating in the test case. As undesirable as the Chinese might have been to Congress, the government chose not to take the opportunity to deport the Chinese community en masse. Because of a lack of funds, the Attorney General and the Secretary of the Treasury instructed their officers not to enforce the law.[107] In November 1893, Congress enacted the first immigration amnesty legislation, granting unregistered Chinese an additional six months to comply with the law.[108] But, of course, the deportation orders of Lee Joe, Fong Yue Ting and Wong Quan had long since become final.

The cancellation of the certificates at issue in *Chae Chan Ping* and the registration system at issue in *Fong Yue Ting* were based largely on the belief that the Chinese were fraudulently abusing the system. There was certainly some truth to this.[109] Because legal immigration was unavailable to most Chinese during the exclusion era, those determined to enter had to do so illegally—as so many immigrants from so many countries do today and have done in the past. Until the mid–1920s, many Chinese came in through Canada or Mexico,[110] which were easier to enter legally. Mexico encouraged Chinese immigration for a period and Canada while imposing a race-based head tax, had no outright exclusion until 1923.[111] In addition, the Canadian and Mexican borders with the United States were highly permeable compared to the seaports. Aided by organized smuggling operations, Chinese immigrants sometimes pretended to be of Mexican or African ancestry; despite the discrimination those groups experienced in the interior of the United States, they were better off than the Chinese at the border.

Government corruption also provided opportunities for illegal immigration. Consular officials and immigration officers were bribed; for a fee, clerks would provide documentation or interpreters would provide the right answers regardless of what the applicant had said. Professor Lee reports that "U.S. marshals in charge of Chinese deportation cases routinely substituted Chinese who had been ordered back to China with other Chinese who wanted to make visits or return permanently."[112] In addition, "[i]mmigration inspectors commonly substituted the photographs in Chinese files" or sold "immigration papers belonging to Chinese who had returned to China permanently."[113] Some Chinese falsely claimed to be in classes eligible to return to the United States, such as U.S. citizens, merchants or students. The destruction of the public records of San Francisco in the 1906 earthquake and fire facilitated fraudulent claims, and applications for admission based on citizenship could be supported with the testimony of Chinese.[114] For almost a century, litigation over claims that Chinese admitted as relatives of citizens were in fact "paper sons" continued.[115]

Otherwise law-abiding Chinese Americans were willing to oppose the exclusion policy, reasoning, as did Martin Luther King, Jr., that there was no duty to obey unjust laws.[116] Professor Wigmore sympathetically noted that the law excluding Chinese testimony "was itself breaking solemn treaty-faith with the very nation whose members it thus condemned as oath-breakers; and that the supposed special danger of perjury by Chinese attempting to evade those statutes of exile was precisely what might be expected from the people of any country when a hostile measure is attempted to be enforced by the harshest means."[117]

The Continuing Importance of Chae Chan Ping and Fong Yue Ting

In a long line of decisions fairly regarded as the progeny of *Chae Chan Ping* and *Fong Yue Ting*, the Court has used very broad language affirming that substantive decisions about who may be admitted are virtually immune to judicial review.[118] Even the Court in the era of *Chae Chan Ping* and *Fong Yue Ting* may not have thought judicial review was precluded entirely; as Justice Field noted in his *Fong Yue Ting* dissent, if administrative officers, having determined that applicants for admission were ineligible, were authorized to drown or shoot them (not as punishment, but to save the expense of removal), probably some judicial intervention would have been deemed available.[119] In addition, with respect to the procedures used to determine whether a non-citizen present in the United States is eligible to remain, the Court has long ruled—beginning in cases involving Asian immigrants decided early in the twentieth century—that the basic elements of due process apply.[120]

The critical question is whether there is any classification, even one based on race, religion, sex or political grounds, which the Supreme Court might deem beyond the power of Congress to use in order to determine who may be admitted to or remain in the country. Language in some of the early and modern cases seems to support the idea that judicial review of such determinations is available,[121] and this may ripen one day into a judicial standard that would strike down a modern re-incarnation of the Chinese Exclusion Act. But it remains true today that in its actual decisions, "The Court without exception has sustained Congress' 'plenary power to make rules for the admission of aliens.' "[122]

Accordingly, the holding of *Chae Chan Ping* and *Fong Yue Ting* that for noncitizens, living in the United States is a privilege rather than a right, continues to accurately state the law. As Justice Frankfurter explained, if federal immigration law has been "based . . . in part on discredited racial theories [and] whether immigration laws have been crude and cruel, whether they may have reflected xenophobia in general or anti-Semitism or anti-Catholicism, the responsibility belongs to Congress."[123]

Related to the idea that non-citizens have no right to remain in the United States is the principle recognized in *Chae Chan Ping* and *Fong Yue Ting* that deportation is not punishment. The Court reinforced the point in *Wong Wing v. United States,*[124] which was decided three years after *Fong Yue Ting* and explored an aspect of the Geary Act that was not at issue in the earlier case. Under the statute, Chinese found without a certificate and ordered deported were first to be summarily "imprisoned at hard labor for a period not exceeding one year."[125] The Court held that summary imprisonment was unconstitutional, but its opinion emphasized the powers of Congress to control immigration by methods falling short of summary imprisonment: "[p]roceedings to exclude or expel would be vain if those accused could not be held in custody pending the inquiry into their true character, and while arrangements were being made for their deportation."[126] An immigration violation could also be made "an offense punishable by fine or imprisonment, if such offense were to be established by a judicial trial."[127]

Although imprisonment of the latter type may be punishment, nothing else associated with deportation is.[128] Many constitutional provisions apply exclusively to government action constituting punishment.

United States residence is a valuable right, deprivation of which, the Supreme Court has recognized, may mean "loss of both property and life, or of all that makes life worth living."[129] Nevertheless, the Ex Post Facto clause is inapplicable, and Congress is free to deport resident non-citizens for conduct that was perfectly legal when it occurred.[130] The constitutional requirements of reasonable bail,[131] speedy trial[132] and jury trial[133] are also inapplicable, and deportation does not constitute cruel and unusual punishment.

Chae Chan Ping and Fong Yue Ting gave Congress essentially a free hand with respect to non-citizens outside or inside the United States. Chinese immigrants permitted to enter were prohibited by law from becoming naturalized citizens—a ban that ended only in 1943—so they would remain perpetually foreign. The last open constitutional question was the citizenship status of those born here. In United States v. Wong Kim Ark,[134] the Justice Department took the position that Chinese born in the United States were not citizens, the Fourteenth Amendment[135] notwithstanding. "There certainly should be some honor and dignity in American citizenship," they argued, "that would be sacred from the foul and corrupting taint of a debasing alienage."[136]

Wong Kim Ark was represented by Thomas Riordan, who lost in Chae Chan Ping, and Maxwell Evarts, and J. Hubley Ashton, who lost in Fong Yue Ting, but this time, the outcome was different. By a vote of 7 to 2, the Court held that even persons of Chinese racial ancestry born in the United States were citizens, under "the peremptory and explicit language of the fourteenth amendment."[137] Wong Kim Ark preserved the possibility of the growth of an Asian–American community in the United States; a contrary holding would have left Asians without a vested right to remain no matter how many generations their families had been in this country.

However, the policy of exclusion continued. The Geary Act upheld in Fong Yue Ting extended Chinese exclusion for ten years, to 1902 and then indefinitely, but over time Chinese exclusion became Asian exclusion, which was a feature of American immigration policy until 1965.[138] In 1907–08, an exchange of diplomatic notes called the "Gentlemen's Agreement" restricted the immigration of Japanese; in 1917, Congress created the Asiatic barred zone, marking out a geographical area from which no Asians could immigrate. In 1924, the right to immigrate was tied to racial eligibility for naturalization; all aliens ineligible to citizenship were excluded. Because Asians remained racially ineligible for naturalization, they were kept out. These policies were modified over time, but, as late as 1965, federal courts upheld laws classifying Asian immigrants by race, while all others were classified by nativity.[139] In 1965, for the first time in United States history, immigration policy was put on an entirely race-neutral basis.

ENDNOTES

1. Gerald L. Neuman, The Lost Century of American Immigration Law (1776–1875), 93 Colum. L. Rev. 1833 (1993).

2. The Supreme Court dates the beginning of federal immigration regulation to 1875, with the passage of the Page Law, Act of Mar. 3, 1875, 18 Stat. 477, designed to regulate allegedly involuntary immigration of Asian men as "coolies" and women as prostitutes. INS v. St. Cyr, 533 U.S. 289, 305 (2001). An 1862 law also addressed immigration of coolies. Act of Feb. 19, 1862, 12 Stat. 340 (repealed 1974).

3. 130 U.S. 581 (1889).

4. 149 U.S. 698 (1893).

5. Bill Ong Hing, Making and Remaking Asian America Through Immigration Policy, 1850–1990, at 48 (1993); Erika Lee, At America's Gates, Chinese Immigration During the Exclusion Era, 1882–1943, at 25 (2003); Lucy E. Salyer, Laws Harsh as Tigers 8 (1995).

6. 16 Stat. 739 (July 28, 1868).

7. Id. at 740.

8. Treaty between the United States and China concerning immigration, 22 Stat. 826, 827, Art. II (Nov. 17, 1880) ("Chinese laborers who are now in the United States shall be allowed to come and go of their own free will and accord, and shall be accorded all the rights, privileges, immunities, and exemptions which are accorded to the citizens and subjects of the most favored nation.").

9. Chinese Exclusion Act, Act of May 6, 1882, ch. 126, 22 Stat. 58.

10. Id. § 4, 22 Stat. 59.

11. Lee, At Americas Gates at 43–44 (cited in note 5).

12. Id. at 238.

13. In re Ah Yup, 1 F. Cas. 223 (C.C.D. Cal. 1878) ("Mongolian" ineligible for naturalization).

14. Chinese Exclusion Act § 14, 22 Stat. 61.

15. 13 Cong. Rec. 1487 (1882).

16. Id. at 1745.

17. It remains the law that "there is no Sixth Amendment right to appointed counsel at a deportation hearing." United States v. Torres–Sanchez, 68 F.3d 227, 231 (8th Cir. 1995) (quoting United States v. Campos–Asencio, 822 F.2d 506, 509 (5th Cir. 1987)).

18. Lee, At America's Gates at 138–40 (cited in note 5); Salyer, Laws Harsh as Tigers at 70–72 (cited in note 5).

19. Ullmann v. United States, 350 U.S. 422, 437 (1956). Remarkably, in Williams v. North Carolina, 325 U.S. 226, 228 n.4 (1945), decided forty years after Carter's death, the Court quoted as authority a *brief* Carter had written in an earlier case. Carter's life and jurisprudence are explored in Lewis A. Grossman, James Coolidge Carter and Mugwump Jurisprudence, 20 Law & Hist. Rev. 577 (2002).

20. Lau Ow Bew v. United States, 144 U.S. 47 (1892) (merchants resident in the United States returning from brief overseas trips did not have to have certificate from Chinese government showing that they were merchants); United States v. Jung Ah Lung, 124 U.S. 621 (1888) (right to re-enter may be proved through government records if certificate lost); Chew Heong v. United States, 112 U.S. 536 (1884) (re-entry certificate requirement inapplicable to Chinese laborer who left before effective date of Act).

21. Chew Heong v. United States, 112 U.S. 536 (1884).

22. Only for other people's clients were taxes certain; in Pollock v. Farmers' Loan and Trust Co., 158 U.S. 601 (1895), Choate successfully argued that the federal income tax was unconstitutional, leading to the Sixteenth Amendment.

23. See 11 U.S. Op. Att'y Gen. 70 (Aug. 26, 1864).

24. Ashton later was co-counsel with Riordan in Lau Ow Bew v. United States, 144 U.S. 47 (1892).

25. See Chin Yow v. United States, 208 U.S. 8 (1908) (Holmes, J.) (habeas corpus may be granted if individual is ordered deported by administrative authority without due process); United States v. Wong Kim Ark, 169 U.S. 649 (1898) (persons of Chinese ancestry born in the United States are citizens), discussed in Chapter 3, this volume.

26. Chester L. Barrows, William M. Evarts: Lawyer, Diplomat, Statesman 476 (1941).

27. Salyer, Laws Harsh as Tigers at 40 (cited in note 5).

28. Compare In re Ah Lung, 18 F. 28 (C.C.D. Cal. 1883) (Field, J.) (Act applies to persons of Chinese race) with United States v. Douglas, 17 F. 634 (C.C.D. Mass. 1883) (Act applies only to subjects of China).

29. In re Ho King, 14 F. 724 (D. Or. 1883) (Chinese actor is not a laborer).

30. Justice Field on circuit ruled such sailors were not covered by the Act, and could land. Case of Chinese Laborers on Shipboard, 13 F. 291 (C.C.D. Cal. 1882).

31. The courts held that these Chinese were excused from the obligation to obtain certificates. In re Leong Yick Dew, 19 F. 490 (C.C.D. Cal. 1884) (counsel for the immigrant was Thomas Riordan); In re Chin A On, 18 F. 506 (D. Cal. 1883) (Hoffman, J.). But those who left after the Act, failed to get a certificate, and then changed their minds and wanted to return, were out of luck. See In re Pong Ah Chee, 18 F. 527 (D. Colo. 1883).

32. Act of July 5, 1884, ch. 220, 23 Stat. 115, 118.

33. Id.

34. Id. at 116.

35. Chew Heong v. United States, 112 U.S. 536 (1884).

36. United States v. Jung Ah Lung, 124 U.S. 621 (1888).

37. Act of Sept. 13, 1888, ch. 1015, 25 Stat. 476.

38. Act of Oct 1, 1888, ch. 1064, § 1, 25 Stat. 504.

39. Id. § 2.

40. Charles J. McClain, In Search of Equality: The Chinese Struggle Against Discrimination in Nineteenth Century America 194 (1994). Professor Lee puts the figure at 20,000. Lee, At America's Gates at 45 (cited in note 5).

41. See In re Baldwin, 27 F. 187 (C.C.D. Cal. 1886) (Sawyer, J.), rev'd as Baldwin v. Franks, 120 U.S. 678 (1887); In re Jung Ah Lung, 25 F. 141 (D. Cal. 1885) (Hoffman, J.), aff'd, 124 U.S. 621 (1888); In re Tiburcio Parrott, 1 F. 481 (C.C.D. Cal. 1880) (Hoffman, J.) (invalidating California constitutional prohibition on corporations employing Chinese or Mongolians); In re Ah Yup, 1 F. Cas. 223 (C.C.D. Cal. 1878) (Sawyer, J.) (Chinese not white and therefore ineligible for naturalization).

42. In re Chae Chan Ping, 36 F. 431, 432 (C.C.N.D. Cal. 1888).

43. Indeed, the court noted that in the Senate, while the bill was pending, a motion to reconsider was made "to provide an exception of this very class of cases, but that body refused to reconsider for that purpose. So the president, in his message accompanying his approval, ... suggested [legislation] making this very exception; but congress declined to act upon the suggestion." Id. at 433.

44. Id. at 434.

45. Id.

46. Id. at 436.

47. Id.

48. Id. at 435.

49. Brief By Counsel Appointed by the State of California in Support of the Contention of the United States, Chae Chan Ping v. United States, 130 U.S. 581 (1889), No. 88–1446 (filed Mar. 21, 1889).

50. Chae Chan Ping v. United States, 130 U.S. 581, 595 (1889).

51. Id. at 598, 599.

52. Chae Chan Ping's brief stated: "As to the treaty with China, we do not deny the plenary power of Congress at will to abrogate each and every one of its provisions." Brief for Appellant at 16, Chae Chan Ping v. United States, 130 U.S. 581 (1889), No. 88–1446 (filed Mar. 19, 1889). "We do not deny the plenary power of Congress over the treaty and over its own legislation so as to forbid the future immigration of Chinese laborers and the future issue of [re-entry] certificates." Id. at 18.

53. 130 U.S. at 600.

54. Id. at 603.

55. Id. at 604.

56. Id. at 606.

57. 36 F. 433–34.

58. 130 U.S. at 598.

59. Id. at 609.

60. Id. at 601.

61. Society for Propagation of the Gospel in Foreign Parts v. Town of New-Haven, 21 U.S. (8 Wheat.) 464, 493 (1823).

62. 130 U.S. at 610.

63. See Gabriel J. Chin, The Civil Rights Revolution Comes to Immigration Law: A New Look at the Immigration and Nationality Act of 1965, 75 N.C. L. Rev. 273 (1996).

64. 118 U.S. 356 (1886).

65. Detroit Bank v. United States, 317 U.S. 329, 337 (1943).

66. Lees v. United States, 150 U.S. 476, 480 (1893). See also In re Sing Lee, 54 F. 334 (W.D. Mich. 1893) (rejecting equal protection challenge). The federal government continues to enjoy greater power than the states to classify and categorize noncitizens. *See e.g.,* Toll v. Moreno, 458 U.S. 1, 10–13 (1982).

67. 163 U.S. 537 (1896).

68. Sarah H. Cleveland, *Powers Inherent In Sovereignty: Indians, Aliens, Territories, And The Nineteenth Century Origins Of Plenary Power Over Foreign Affairs*, 81 Tex. L. Rev. 1, 15 (2002).

69. Chan Ping Leaves Us, N.Y. Times 3 (Sept. 2, 1889).

70. Geary Act, Act of May 5, 1892, ch. 60, 27 Stat. 25.

71. See also United States v. Ah Fawn, 57 F. 591 (S.D. Cal. 1893) (holding "laborer" means any immigrant other than one coming for teaching, trade, travel, study, or curiosity).

72. Geary Act § 3, 27 Stat. 25.

73. Id. §§ 4–5, 27 Stat. 25.

74. Id. § 6, 27 Stat. 25–26.

75. Id.

76. Salyer, Laws Harsh as Tigers at 46–48 (cited in note 5).

77. Qingsong Zhang, The Origins of the Chinese Americanization Movement, in K. Scott Wong and Sucheng Chan, eds., Claiming America 52 (1998).

78. The statutory disqualification of non-white witnesses applied only to judicial proceedings.

79. Thomas Riordan's name also appears on the circuit court papers, but he apparently did not sign the Supreme Court briefs.

80. Ready for the Supreme Court, N.Y. Times 8 (May 7, 1893).

81. The litigation surrounding the 2000 presidential election took a comparatively leisurely two weeks to make its way from trial court to Supreme Court decision. Gore v. Harris, 772 So.2d 1243, 1247 (Fla. 2000) (per curiam) (noting that trial court action filed Nov. 27, 2000), rev'd as Bush v. Gore, 531 U.S. 98 (Dec. 12, 2000).

82. McClain, In Search of Equality at 207–08 (cited in note 40).

83. Brief for the Respondents at 28, 29, 30, Fong Yue Ting v. United States, 149 U.S. 698 (1893), No. 92–1345, 92–1346, 92–1347 (May 10, 1893).

84. Id. at 54.

85. Id. at 55.

86. The Court was one person short; Justice Harlan was absent serving as U.S. representative to the Bering Sea Arbitration. 149 U.S. iii n.1.

87. Fong Yue Ting v. United States, 149 U.S. 698, 707 (1893).

88. Id. at 723–24.

89. Id. at 714.

90. Id. at 729.

91. Id. at 730.

92. Id.

93. Id. at 731.

94. Id. at 737 (Brewer, J., dissenting).

95. Id. at 738.

96. Id. at 754 (Field, J., dissenting). Field added: "According to this theory, Congress might have ordered executive officers to take the Chinese laborers to the ocean, and put them into a boat, and set them adrift, or to take them to the borders of Mexico, and turn them loose there, and in both cases without any means of support." Id. at 756.

97. Id. at 761–62 (Fuller, C.J., dissenting).

98. Id. at 762.

99. Id. at 746 (Field, J., dissenting).

100. Id. at 738 (Brewer, J., dissenting).

101. Id. at 740.

102. Id. at 758–59 (Field, J., dissenting).

103. Id. at 763 (Fuller, C.J., dissenting).

104. Id. at 760 (Field, J., dissenting).

105. Id. at 763 (Fuller, C.J., dissenting).

106. Id. at 743 (Brewer, J., dissenting).

107. Salyer, Laws Harsh as Tigers at 55–57 (cited in note 5); see also United States v. Chum Shang Yuen, 57 F. 588 (S.D. Cal. 1893).

108. Act of Nov. 3, 1893, ch. 14, 28 Stat. 7.

109. Salyer, Laws Harsh as Tigers at 44–45 (cited in note 5); Lee, At America's Gates Part III (cited in note 5).

110. Lee, At America's Gates at 152–60 (cited in note 5).

111. Id. at 153–54.

112. Id. at 199.

113. Id. at 200.

114. E.g., In re Jew Wong Loy, 91 F. 240, 243 (N.D. Cal. 1898).

115. Lim v. Mitchell, 431 F.2d 197 (9th Cir. 1970). See also Pon v. Esperdy, 296 F. Supp. 726, 727 (S.D.N.Y. 1969) (discussing "Chinese confession" program under which paper sons were urged to confess).

116. Lee, At America's Gates at 192 (cited in note 5). In his Letter from a Birmingham Jail, Dr. King explained: "Thus it is that I can urge men to obey the 1954 decision of the Supreme Court, for it is morally right; and I can urge them to disobey segregation ordinances, for they are morally wrong." Martin Luther King Jr., Why We Can't Wait 85 (1964).

117. John H. Wigmore, 1 Evidence in Trials at Common Law § 516, at 646 (1904).

118. In upholding discrimination based on sex and out-of-wedlock birth in 1977, the Court explained: "This Court has repeatedly emphasized that 'over no conceivable subject is the legislative power of Congress more complete than it is over' the admission of aliens." Fiallo v. Bell, 430 U.S. 787, 792 (1977) (quoting Oceanic Steam Navigation Co. v. Stranahan, 214 U.S. 320, 339 (1909)). In upholding exclusion based on political beliefs in 1972, the Court stated that "an unadmitted and nonresident alien, ha[s] no constitutional right of entry to this country as a nonimmigrant or otherwise." Kleindienst v. Mandel, 408 U.S. 753, 762 (1972). In 2003, the Court observed: "In the exercise of its broad power over naturalization and immigration, Congress regularly makes rules that would be unacceptable if applied to citizens." Demore v. Hyung Joon Kim, 538 U.S. 510, 521 (2003) (quoting Mathews v. Diaz, 426 U.S. 67, 79–80 (1976)). See also Galvan v. Press, 347 U.S. 522, 531 (1954) ("[T]hat the formulation of [policies pertaining to the entry of aliens and their right to remain here] is entrusted exclusively to Congress has become about as firmly imbedded in the legislative and judicial tissues of our body politic as any aspect of our government.").

119. Cf. Zadvydas v. Davis, 533 U.S. 678 (2001) (holding that method of deportation, indefinite detention, after a deportation order that the government has been unable to carry out, was subject to due process scrutiny).

120. Kwock Jan Fat v. White, 253 U.S. 454 (1920); Chin Yow v. United States, 208 U.S. 8 (1908); Yamataya v. Fisher, 189 U.S. 86 (1903).

121. For example, in Zadvydas v. Davis, 533 U.S. 678, 695 (2001), the Court said:

The Government also looks for support to cases holding that Congress has "plenary power" to create immigration law, and that the Judicial Branch must defer to Executive and Legislative Branch decisionmaking in that area. Brief for Respondents in No. 99–7791, at 17, 20 (citing Harisiades v. Shaughnessy, 342 U.S. 580, 588–589 (1952)). But that power is subject to important constitutional limitations. See INS v. Chadha, 462 U.S. 919, 941–942 (1983) (Congress must choose "a constitutionally permissible means of implementing" that power); The Chinese Exclusion Case, 130 U.S. 581, 604 (1889) (congressional authority limited "by the Constitution itself and considerations of public policy and justice which control, more or less, the conduct of all civilized nations").

122. United States v. Valenzuela–Bernal, 458 U.S. 858, 864 (1982) (quoting Kleindienst v. Mandel, 408 U.S. 753, 766 (1972), quoting Boutilier v. INS, 387 U.S. 118, 123 (1967)).

123. Harisiades v. Shaughnessy, 342 U.S. 580, 597 (1952) (Frankfurter, J., concurring). See also Gabriel J. Chin, Segregation's Last Stronghold: Race Discrimination and the Constitutional Law of Immigration, 46 UCLA L.Rev. 1 (1998).

124. 163 U.S. 228 (1896). The case is discussed in detail in Chapter 2 of this volume.

125. Geary Act § 4, 27 Stat. 25.

126. 163 U.S. at 235.

127. Id.

128. Even deportation for a criminal conviction is not punishment; according to the Court, "[t]he coincidence of the local penal law with the policy of Congress is an accident." Bugajewitz v. Adams, 228 U.S. 585, 592 (1913).

129. Ng Fung Ho v. White, 259 U.S. 276, 284 (1922).

130. Galvan v. Press, 347 U.S. 522 (1954) (non-citizens' membership in Communist Party at a time when membership was not grounds for deportation could retroactively be made a ground for deportation).

131. Carlson v. Landon, 342 U.S. 524, 544–46 (1952).

132. Prieto v. Gluch, 913 F.2d 1159 (6th Cir. 1990).

133. Sabino v. Reno, 8 F. Supp. 2d 622, 624 (S.D. Tex. 1998).

134. 169 U.S. 649 (1898). This case is discussed in detail in Chapter 3 of this volume.

135. US Const. amend. XIV § 1 ("All persons born or naturalized in the United States, and subject to the jurisdiction thereof, are citizens of the United States and of the state wherein they reside.").

136. Brief for the United States at 37, United States v. Wong Kim Ark, 169 U.S. 649 (1898) (No. 95–904).

137. 169 U.S. at 694.

138. See Hing, Making and Remaking Asian America (cited in note 5).

139. Hitai v. INS, 343 F.2d 466 (2d Cir. 1965).

*

2

Wong Wing v. United States: The Bill of Rights Protects Illegal Aliens

Gerald L. Neuman[1]

As Justice Felix Frankfurter once wrote, "The history of liberty has largely been the history of observance of procedural safeguards."[2] The case of *Wong Wing v. United States*[3] offers a superb illustration of this proposition. Congress' disregard of procedural safeguards enshrined in the Bill of Rights led to a unanimous affirmation of constitutional principles, including their applicability to immigration statutes and to all non-citizens within the territory of the United States. The decision was a major landmark in constitutional jurisprudence, making explicit some truths that should have been self-evident.

The Hard Labor Provision of the Geary Act

The *Wong Wing* decision arose out of the Geary Act of 1892, "An act to prohibit the coming of Chinese persons into the United States,"[4] the same statute involved in *Fong Yue Ting v. United States*.[5] Thomas J. Geary, a California congressman, proposed the legislation in the House of Representatives. Vehemently opposed to the presence of Chinese immigrants in California, he aimed to extend the Chinese exclusion laws enacted since 1882, and to make their enforcement far more stringent. The Supreme Court upheld the basic policy of the Geary Act, its requirements for registration of Chinese residents, and its procedures for deportation without criminal trial, in *Fong Yue Ting*. But Geary had not been content with deporting Chinese immigrants. He also insisted on deterring future arrivals by imprisoning Chinese deportees at hard labor for a period preceding their deportation. This separate provision of the Geary Act ran afoul of the Constitution.

The congressional debate in the spring of 1892 focused primarily on other issues, but the legislative history does shed some light on the purpose of the hard labor provision. Geary's bill in the House, originally adopted without significant debate, included a variety of harsh enforcement measures against Chinese immigrants violating the exclusion laws

and those who aided them. Any Chinese person accused of being unlawfully in the United States could be taken before a federal judge or
commissioner, and if found to be unlawfully present "shall be imprisoned in a penitentiary for a term of not exceeding five years, and at the
expiration of such term of imprisonment be removed from the United
States."[6] The five-year term was one of the many defects the Senate
Foreign Relations Committee saw in the House bill. The Senate's substi-
tute bill modified this provision by limiting the maximum term of
imprisonment before deportation to six months, while specifying that it
should be served "at hard labor," and imposing it only on repeat
offenders, Chinese who returned to the United States unlawfully after
having been removed.[7] The two provisions were then compromised in the
conference committee to produce a maximum term of one year at hard
labor before removal, but applying it to the first violation as well.[8]

The goal of the hard labor provision was emphasized several times
in the Senate debate, for example by Senator William E. Chandler of
New Hampshire, chairman of the Committee on Immigration:

> It may be thought a harsh proceeding to imprison China-
> men coming here unlawfully and after their terms of imprison-
> ment to send them to China. The necessity, however, is a very
> evident one. Unless the Chinamen coming here unlawfully into
> the country are placed in prison, the penalty of a return to
> China or across the border is of no value whatever. The China-
> man can move easily; he gets transportation at the expense of
> the United States about the time that he is ready to go across
> the border or is ready to go to China again. When he wishes to
> return to this country once more, there is no difficulty in his
> coming here, and therefore practically, as has been shown by
> the testimony which I have read and as will appear from much
> other testimony that is accessible, there is no way of keeping
> Chinese out of this country except by imposing a term of
> imprisonment upon them. Put them in prison for a limited
> period of time and deport them after they have served the term
> of imprisonment, and this penalty will be effective, and no other
> will be effective.[9]

Notably, Chandler referred to deportation as a penalty, in contrast to the
Supreme Court's subsequent characterization of deportation as non-
punitive in *Fong Yue Ting*, and he justified the hard labor provision on
the ground that mere deportation was too light a penalty.

The Geary Act authorized this punishment after a hearing before a
federal judge or commissioner—that is, a subordinate judicial magistrate
without the tenure protections of Article III of the Constitution—
bypassing the procedures of ordinary criminal prosecution. That choice

was intentional. Senator Frank Hiscock of New York defended the procedural approach of the Geary Act, insisting that "we have the right to make precisely the same laws, establish the same rules and regulations in respect to the immigration of foreigners that we have in respect to the importation of foreign manufactured goods, and we do not put them under our criminal laws."[10] He continued:

> To me, sir, it does not seem quite the thing to provide that a Chinese laborer coming here is either to be indicted or to be subjected to a long investigation, to give bail and to have thrown around him those provisions of law which from their very cumbersomeness involve in their execution an invitation to attempt to evade the law and violate its provisions. So far as the Chinese laborers who are here are concerned I am in favor of there being an investigation in reference to each particular case that will develop the fact whether he is here lawfully or not. But I do not believe that it is necessary that we should construct a law upon that palladium of our liberties, the grand jury, or the right to bail, or any of the provisions which have been accustomed to be enacted in respect to criminals, either in regard to delay or punishment. . . .[11]

As a result, Section 3 of the Geary Act established deportation proceedings before a federal judge or commissioner, and Section 4 decreed:

> That any such Chinese person or person of Chinese descent convicted and adjudged to be not lawfully entitled to be or remain in the United States, shall be imprisoned at hard labor for a period of not exceeding one year and thereafter removed from the United States, as hereinbefore provided.[12]

This detention policy applied only to Chinese migrants, and not to other unlawful migrants. One of the Chinese government's many objections to the Geary Act addressed this discrimination, which it viewed as yet another violation of the most-favored-nation provision of the Burlingame Treaty.[13]

Unlike the registration provisions of the Geary Act, which had delayed effect after a year, the hard labor provision came into force immediately. The lower federal courts were troubled by Section 4, and they differed in their responses. Some judges concluded that imprisonment at hard labor was unavoidably a form of criminal punishment, even "infamous" punishment. The Constitution did not prohibit imposition of hard labor after conviction, but the Bill of Rights required a set of procedural protections in federal criminal trials, including indictment or presentment by grand jury under the Fifth Amendment, and trial by jury under the Sixth. The grand jury issue was particularly salient because the Supreme Court had held a few years earlier, in *Ex parte Wilson*,[14] that imprisonment at hard labor amounted to infamous punishment triggering the grand jury guarantee.

If Section 4 made imprisonment at hard labor a necessary feature of every deportation proceeding under the Chinese exclusion laws, and if the Constitution required a full criminal trial before such imprisonment, then the Geary Act would have increased the obstacles to enforcing federal immigration policy rather than eased them. Some courts responded by treating Section 4 as an alternative, optional procedure. The government could seek simple deportation by proceeding civilly before a commissioner or judge under Section 3, or it could seek deportation preceded by hard labor under Section 4, subject to normal criminal process.[15]

Other judges denied that Section 4 necessitated criminal proceedings. One judge in Louisiana actually rejected a United States Attorney's attempt to prosecute by indictment under Section 4.[16] Instead, the judge construed Section 4 as part of a method for removing aliens deemed injurious, which "to be effective of its object, must be summary in its methods, and political in its character." While awaiting deportation, the alien must be detained, and "[t]o prevent expense to the government, and as a sanitary matter, he is to be made to work."

Judge Erskine Ross of the Southern District of California directly confronted the constitutionality of Section 4 in *United States v. Wong Dep Ken*.[17] Distinguishing the recent decision in *Fong Yue Ting*, he concluded that imprisonment at hard labor required a normal criminal trial, and that Section 4 was invalid but severable. He rejected the U.S. Attorney's argument that constitutional protections did not extend to aliens who had entered the United States unlawfully. Rather, "the constitution, which has potency everywhere within the limits of our territory, covers alike with its protection every human being within it."[18] These were the principles that the Supreme Court would vindicate in *Wong Wing*.

The Wong Wing *Case*

Into the midst of this constitutional controversy stepped four Chinese immigrants, Wong Wing and his compatriots Lee Poy, Lee Yon Tong, and Chan Wah Dong. The surviving court records tell little about them as individuals. They were arrested in Detroit on July 15, 1892, only two months after the passage of the Geary Act, and taken before U.S. commissioner John Graves. After a hearing at which both sides presented testimony (whose content is now unknown), Graves found them to be unlawfully in the United States, and sentenced them to sixty days at hard labor, followed by deportation to China. The order could not have been based on failure to comply with the registration requirements of the Geary Act, subsequently upheld in *Fong Yue Ting*, because the registration period had barely begun. Their counsel later mentioned that they were "poor men,"[19] and that they had entered the United States from Canada,[20] but even those facts remained outside the formal record. They also used other names: John Ling, Jung Sang, Hong Jo, and Chin Lee, respectively. Their cases were consolidated at all stages of proceeding, and it will be convenient to personify them in the lead petitioner, Wong Wing.

Crucially, fortunately, they were represented by counsel. The record does not explain why, but the context makes it likely that their representation was funded by the Chinese Six Companies or by some other organization as part of a series of challenges to the Geary Act.[21] As in similar cases, these poor men had a distinguished attorney arguing on their behalf. Frank Henry Canfield (1837–1916) was an experienced Supreme Court advocate, and a cousin of Supreme Court Justice Henry Billings Brown. At the time, he shared an office with his son, George Lewis Canfield (1866–1928), who later became a founding partner in the leading Detroit law firm of Miller Canfield.[22] Their litigation practice included a specialty in admiralty, and the Canfields became "perhaps the foremost admiralty practitioners in the Midwest."[23] George Canfield would lecture on that subject at the University of Michigan Law School from 1911 to 1920, and write a treatise in the field.[24] Thus, their participation in the *Wong Wing* case was hardly routine. In the early stages of the litigation, the Canfields were joined by Harrison D. Paul, an attorney from Chicago, who represented Wong Wing at the hearing before the commissioner, and co-signed the notice of appeal to the Supreme Court.

The Litigation

At first the proceedings moved swiftly. Wong Wing was arrested by a deputy customs collector on July 15, examined before Commissioner Graves on July 19, and committed to the Detroit House of Correction for sixty days on July 20. He filed a habeas corpus petition with the Circuit Court for the Eastern District of Michigan on July 21, leading to a hearing on July 26, and an order rejecting his claim for release on August 1. The next day, Frank Canfield and Harrison Paul took an appeal to the Supreme Court, and the circuit court admitted Wong Wing to bail pending appeal.

On August 26, Frank Canfield wrote to the Clerk of the Supreme Court to clarify the applicable procedures. He pointed out that the appellants "have appealed to [the] Supreme Court in order to test the constitutionality of the law," and maintained that the proceedings "were in the nature of criminal cases."[25] He expressed the hope "to bring the causes to a hearing as soon as possible in October." But that was not to be. The case remained on the normal slow pace of the Supreme Court's crowded docket in that period of broad mandatory appellate jurisdiction.[26] The delay presumably did not harm Wong Wing, who was free on bail, and whose deportation to China was postponed.

Canfield wrote again in May 1893, having learned that the later litigation in *Fong Yue Ting* was being advanced on the Court's docket.[27] Although he described the cases as "similar," the special arrangement to expedite the challenge to the registration system did not extend to Wong Wing's situation, and three more years passed before the Court reached him. That interval gave Canfield the opportunity to analyze and distinguish the Court's decision in *Fong Yue Ting*, and to cite favorable intervening lower court precedent.

Frank Canfield's brief on behalf of Wong Wing was concise and forceful. Wong Wing's case differed importantly from *Fong Yue Ting*, he argued, because the sentence imposed on Wong Wing included both deportation and a definite term of imprisonment at hard labor. Section 4 of the Geary Act violated both the Fifth and Sixth Amendments, because it imposed infamous punishment without indictment and criminal punishment without jury trial. The imprisonment was intended as punishment and operated as punishment. The government could have deported Wong Wing from Detroit to Canada in thirty minutes, and sixty days' confinement at hard labor could not be regarded as incident to deportation. If Congress could subject aliens to hard labor without criminal trial, it could subject them to the death penalty in the same manner.

Moreover, the sentence to hard labor violated the Thirteenth Amendment, which prohibited involuntary servitude except after conviction for crime.[28]

The protection of the Fifth, Sixth, and Thirteenth Amendments extended to Chinese aliens as well as American citizens; indeed the Fifth Amendment covered "any and every person within the jurisdiction of the republic."[29] An alien resident "owes obedience to the laws of the country in which he is domiciled, and, as a consequence, he is entitled to the equal protection of those laws." Canfield described this proposition as well-established—too established to require argument—but he could cite no Supreme Court precedent directly holding that the Fifth Amendment protected aliens against the federal government.[30]

Finally, Canfield argued that the commissioner's lack of jurisdiction entitled Wong Wing to full release on habeas corpus. If the government wanted to pursue deportation, it should commence new proceedings.[31]

Canfield spent less than a page arguing that the Constitution protected Wong Wing, but the response of the United States gave that issue the bulk of its attention. Assistant Attorney General J.M. Dickin-

son argued that because Wong Wing was unlawfully within the United
States, therefore he had no constitutional rights. Indeed, neither aliens
who entered unlawfully nor aliens who entered lawfully but remained
unlawfully could raise constitutional objections to their treatment.[32]

Although Supreme Court precedent protected lawfully resident
aliens, "[n]one of these cases decided that an alien could sneak or force
his way into the United States against their will, and stand under the
protection of the Constitution."[33] The Constitution "was not made nor
intended for all humanity, nor to operate as a restriction on the Government to protect foreigners against its action in political matters, but was
ordained and established by the people of the United States for their
own benefit and the benefit of those lawfully within their Territory."[34]
The Court should not hold "that aliens can, *against the will of the
United States*, acquire or hold the Constitutional guaranties to personal
liberty and rights of property."[35]

Dickinson pointed out the practical consequences of accepting Wong
Wing's claim. The total population of China was over 400 million, and
the total number of non-Christians in the world was over one billion. If
only 1% of these aliens decided to come to the United States, and
Congress found it necessary to deter them with a penalty of confinement
at hard labor, then there would be four million or ten million candidates
for trial by jury. The country would be impoverished and the courts
overwhelmed.[36] Yet penalizing unlawful entrants was necessary. "It is
rather a pleasant experience than otherwise for a Chinaman to come to
the United States at a small expense and then be sent back to China at
the cost of the United States, he being also fed and lodged as a guest of
the Government. . . . If they be sent back without any punishment, it is a
game at which they win in any event."[37]

Assuming, arguendo, that the Constitution might apply, Dickinson
denied that imprisonment with hard labor necessarily amounted to
infamous punishment. State courts had upheld short terms of confinement at hard labor, after summary trials, for vagrants and disorderly
persons.[38]

Finally, Dickinson maintained that if the order for imprisonment
were void, it should be severed from the order of deportation, which the
Court should uphold.[39]

The Ruling of the Court

The Supreme Court held oral argument in *Wong Wing* on April 1
and April 2, 1896, and issued its unanimous decision on May 18.[40] Justice
George Shiras wrote the opinion of the Court. He began by reviewing the
Chinese exclusion acts and the Court's prior decisions upholding them.
He reaffirmed these precedents, approving both the power of Congress to

exclude or expel classes of aliens, and the power to assign exclusion or expulsion proceedings to executive officers. But Section 4 of the Geary Act raised a different issue.

Shiras observed that the Chinese exclusion laws "operate upon two classes,—one consisting of those who came into the country with its consent, the other of those who have come into the United States without their consent, and in disregard of the law."[41] Both classes could be expelled, and aliens allegedly within either class could be detained during the course of proceedings:

> We think it clear that detention or temporary confinement, as part of the means necessary to give effect to the provisions for the exclusion or expulsion of aliens, would be valid. Proceedings to exclude or expel would be vain if those accused could not be held in custody pending the inquiry into their true character, and while arrangements were being made for their deportation.[42]

The hard labor provision of the Geary Act, however, decreed imprisonment in addition to, and not necessary for, deportation.

> But when Congress sees fit to further promote such a policy by subjecting the persons of such aliens to infamous punishment at hard labor, or by confiscating their property, we think such legislation, to be valid, must provide for a judicial trial to establish the guilt of the accused.[43]

The Court had held in *Ex parte Wilson* that imprisonment at hard labor was infamous punishment, and that it amounted to involuntary servitude that could not be imposed under the Thirteenth Amendment without prior criminal conviction.[44]

Shiras quoted the Court's holding in *Yick Wo v. Hopkins*, that the due process and equal protection clauses of the Fourteenth Amendment were "universal in their application to all persons within the territorial jurisdiction, without regard to any differences of race, of color, or nationality."[45] He continued:

> Applying this reasoning to the Fifth and Sixth Amendments, it must be concluded that all persons within the territory of the United States are entitled to the protection guaranteed by those amendments, and that even aliens shall not be held to answer for a capital or other infamous crime, unless on a presentment or indictment of a grand jury, nor be deprived of life, liberty, or property without due process of law.[46]

Accordingly, Wong Wing should have been discharged from the Detroit House of Correction, "without prejudice to [his] detention according to law for deportation."[47]

Justice Stephen Field added an unusual opinion of his own, described as "concurring in part and dissenting in part."[48] In fact, he concurred with his fellow Justices, and "dissented" from the arguments of the government:

> But I do not concur, but dissent entirely from what seemed to me to be harsh and illegal assertions, made by counsel of the Government, on the argument of this case, as to the right of the court to deny to the accused the full protection of the law and Constitution against every form of oppression and cruelty to them.[49]

That may seem a peculiar choice of wording, but by that date Field's tenure on the Court was peculiar. He had suffered serious mental decline, though still capable of great lucidity, and remained on the Court because of his determination to break Chief Justice Marshall's record for length of service. The Court assigned him few opinions in the 1894 and 1895 terms, and his concurrence in *Wong Wing* was the last opinion of his career.[50] He ultimately retired as of December 1, 1897, technically surpassing Marshall's longevity.[51]

The main virtue of Field's opinion lay in its emphasis on the government's effort to exclude unlawfully present aliens from constitutional protection. Field copied much of the opinion essentially verbatim from the appellants' brief, including the entire section of Canfield's argument confirming that the Fifth Amendment included "any and every human being within the jurisdiction of the republic."[52] He then added his own comment:

> The contention that persons within the territorial jurisdiction of this republic might be beyond the protection of the law was heard with pain on the argument at the bar,—in face of the great constitutional amendment which declares that no state shall deny to any person within its jurisdiction the equal protection of the laws.[53]

Field went on to express his agreement with the main propositions of the majority opinion, including the power of Congress to expel classes of aliens and to delegate the authority to deport them to executive officials.[54] His acceptance of the propriety of executive deportation is surprising, given the vehemence of his earlier dissent from that principle in *Fong Yue Ting*.[55] Field had been so opposed to the decision that he wrote to the Attorney General proposing a scheme for having it reargued and overruled.[56] He had insisted that a new Justice should be appointed for the purpose, whether by replacing an ailing colleague or by expanding the size of the Court if necessary.[57] Field's acquiescence three years later probably reflected the weakness of his concentration as much as the force of stare decisis.

Thus, the Supreme Court in *Wong Wing* held that constitutional rights protected unlawfully present aliens even against the exercise of Congress' power to control immigration. For the first time in its history, the Court expressly invalidated a federal statute for violating the constitutional rights of an alien. And it did so despite the government's argument that unlawfully present aliens should not be recognized as possessing constitutional rights.

What benefit Wong Wing gained from this decision is unclear from the surviving court records. Presumably, he avoided the term of imprisonment at hard labor, or its unexpired remainder. Still, the Court's ruling left him vulnerable to deportation to China. There is no record, however, that any proceedings were held on remand. Wong Wing had been free on bail while his appeal languished on the Supreme Court's docket, and immigration bail often provided worthless security to the government. It is possible that the deportation order was never enforced.

A Decision Taken In Stride

The Supreme Court decided *Wong Wing* on May 18, 1896, along with thirty-two other cases resolved by written opinions. The most famous of those cases was *Plessy v. Ferguson*, rejecting the claim that state-imposed racial segregation on private railways violated the Equal Protection Clause.[58] Another historic opinion issued that day in *Talton v. Mayes,* holding that the Bill of Rights did not restrict the exercise of governmental power by Indian Tribes.[59] The Court struck down a Kansas statute expanding rights of redemption under pre-existing mortgages as a violation of the Contracts Clause, and upheld a Georgia statute forbidding the running of freight trains on Sundays as consistent with the Commerce Clause.[60]

In this company, the *Wong Wing* decision received only limited media attention. *The New York Times* and the *Washington Post* each printed a list of the cases the Court had decided, but did not describe the content of *Wong Wing*.[61] Both covered *Plessy*, and other cases deemed more newsworthy, including a jurisdictional victory by "the richest woman in America."[62] Closer to home, the Detroit *Evening News* summarized this "Michigan case" as affirming the deportation law, but ruling that the penalties must be imposed by courts. The initial headline read "Upholds the Law."[63] The *Detroit Free Press*, in contrast, overlooked the case, reporting only on *Plessy*, the Kansas and Georgia decisions, and a decision on infringement of the trademark for Singer sewing machines.[64] The *San Francisco Chronicle* understandably gave prominence to *Wong Wing*,[65] as well as to another case decided that day concerning the reimbursement of U.S. attorneys for litigating cases under the Chinese exclusion laws.[66] The *Los Angeles Times* added a summary of *Wong Wing* at the bottom of a column of miscellaneous wire reports.[67] The *Evening News*, the *Chronicle* and the *Los Angeles Times* supplied matter-of-fact accounts of *Wong Wing* as legal news. They expressed neither approval nor alarm.

The Attorney General's Annual Report for 1896 listed *Wong Wing* in its summary of Supreme Court litigation involving the federal government, but only as a case that "presented interesting questions," and did not "call for special mention."[68] The report passed in silence over its content, while describing and commenting on other government wins and losses.

The response of the law reviews was equally bland. The *Albany Law Journal* reported the decision in a short squib, and the *Yale Law Journal* described it in a longer, and less accurate, paragraph.[69] *Wong Wing* figured marginally in the turn of the century debates about the application of the Constitution to overseas territories, cited as authority that the Bill of Rights protected all persons within U.S. borders regardless of their status, and for dictum suggesting that this principle extended to territories as well as states.[70] In 1904, an author surveying the instances in which the Supreme Court had invalidated acts of Congress included *Wong Wing* in his generalization that most such cases "were decided and the judgments passed into the archives of the country and into the jurisprudence of the world, without arousing serious public interest or comment."[71]

The Legacy of Wong Wing

Wong Wing stands at the intersection of several lines of Supreme Court precedent. It addresses congressional power over migration, constitutional protection of aliens against the federal government, the rights of *illegal* aliens, the distinction between civil detention and criminal punishment, and the character of hard labor as punishment. The landmark significance of *Wong Wing* arises from a series of firsts: it was the first Supreme Court decision invalidating a federal immigration statute, the first Supreme Court holding that the Bill of Rights protects aliens against the federal government, and the first Supreme Court confirmation of the constitutional rights of illegal aliens.

Congressional Power over Immigration

The Court upheld much of the Geary Act in *Wong Wing*, and the decision has been cited for what it permits as well as for what it forbids.[72] Justice Shiras reaffirmed basic propositions announced in *Chae Chan Ping* and *Fong Yue Ting*. Congress has power to control immigration. Congress can decide which categories of aliens should be excluded or expelled from the United States. Congress can assign the enforcement of the immigration laws to executive officers. *Wong Wing* added two important corollaries to these propositions: the civil enforcement of deportation policies includes physical detention necessary to ensure successful deportation, and Congress can also impose criminal sanctions for violations of the immigration laws *if* it affords appropriate criminal procedures. The progeny of *Wong Wing* therefore include later cases delineating the scope of Congress' power to detain aliens in civil immigration proceedings, such as *Zadvydas v. Davis* and *Demore v. Kim*.[73]

The Court in *Wong Wing* did not reject the main policy concern that underlay Section 4 of the Geary Act, that the prospect of deportation might give some categories of aliens insufficient incentive for compliance with the federal immigration laws. The Court explained that the Constitution authorized Congress to supplement the administrative enforcement model with a criminal enforcement model. Today we have a wide variety of federal criminal statutes punishing aliens with fine or imprisonment for illegal entry, marriage fraud, return after prior deportation, refusal to comply with registration requirements, refusal to comply with a removal order, and other immigration offenses.[74] But the Court refused to facilitate criminal prosecution by circumventing the constitutional protections that the Fifth and Sixth Amendments afford to criminal defendants. Thus *Wong Wing* also stands for the crucial proposition that the "plenary" congressional power over immigration must be exercised in compliance with constitutional limitations.[75]

Hard Labor as Infamous Punishment

Wong Wing did not hold that immigration violations could not be punished by imprisonment at hard labor, but only that such punishment required a prior criminal trial. Hard labor amounted to an infamous punishment triggering the grand jury provision of the Fifth Amendment, not the cruel and unusual punishment ban of the Eighth Amendment.[76] The Court followed its precedent in *Ex parte Wilson*,[77] which invalidated a federal sentence of fifteen years at hard labor for counterfeiting because the prosecution had bypassed the grand jury. In *Wilson*, Justice Horace Gray reviewed the history of penal policy in England and America, and concluded that imprisonment at hard labor had been considered infamous for over a century. The Due Process Clause of the Fourteenth Amendment did not compel the states to employ grand juries, but the Fifth Amendment expressly demanded grand jury proceedings before the federal government could inflict infamous punishment.

The government had tried to distinguish *Wilson* in *Wong Wing* by arguing that brief sentences including hard labor had been traditionally imposed without indictment for minor offenses like vagrancy. Justice Shiras treated this argument as foreclosed by the breadth of the Court's conclusions in *Wilson*.[78] Years later, the federal government tried to reopen this question, defending the procedures of the family court in the

District of Columbia. In *United States v. Moreland*,[79] the defendant had been sentenced to six months at hard labor in the workhouse for willfully neglecting to support his minor children. The government tried to cast doubt on the validity of *Wong Wing*, and to limit it to hard labor *in a penitentiary*. But the majority reaffirmed *Wilson* and *Wong Wing*, and interpreted them as depending on the infamous character of compulsory hard labor as such. This rigid traditionalism provoked a dissent from Justice Louis Brandeis, joined by Chief Justice William Howard Taft and Justice Oliver Wendell Holmes. Brandeis praised the industrial farm at Occoquan as an institution for rehabilitation and education of delinquent fathers.[80] Brandeis invoked both the historical pedigree of the workhouse and the progressive notion that constitutional principles adapt to modern conditions as support for his conclusion that hard labor at the workhouse should not be regarded as infamous.[81]

Thus *Wong Wing* has benefited citizens as well as immigrants, protecting them against streamlined procedures leading to re-educative labor.

The Constitutional Rights of Aliens

The government's argument in *Wong Wing* took advantage of a fundamental ambiguity in the drafting of the federal Bill of Rights, which did not identify the category of persons to whom it guaranteed rights. In the 1790s, that ambiguity had fueled debate over the constitutionality of the Alien and Sedition Acts.[82] Some of the Federalist defenders of those statutes had argued that the Constitution protected only citizens, the people by whom and for whom it was made. The Jeffersonians responded that subjection to U.S. law justified corresponding safeguards of aliens' rights. The controversy over the Alien Act of 1798 never received definitive resolution. The Supreme Court under Chief Justices John Marshall and Roger Brooke Taney protected statutory and treaty rights of European immigrants, but never found occasion to hold that their constitutional rights had been violated. The maintenance of slavery, and the dismissive approach to the status of free African–Americans expressed in the *Dred Scott* decision,[83] prevented the antebellum Court from reading the Bill of Rights as broadly as its language permitted.

Once the Civil War led to the abolition of slavery, the Fourteenth Amendment could offer constitutional protection to all persons. The wording of the Due Process and Equal Protection Clauses calls attention to the rights of aliens as "persons," and the legislative history of the Amendment reflected explicit attention to mistreatment of the Chinese on the Pacific coast.[84] The Supreme Court interpreted the Amendment accordingly in 1886 in *Yick Wo v. Hopkins*, its first decision invalidating a state statute for violating the constitutional rights of aliens. It described those clauses as "universal in their application, to all persons within the territorial jurisdiction, without regard to any differences of race, of color, or of nationality."[85]

The federal immigration statutes of the 1890s gave the Supreme Court the opportunity to confirm that the language of the Bill of Rights should apply as broadly in limiting the federal government. The dissenters in *Fong Yue Ting* argued that the deportation provisions of the Geary Act violated the Fourth, Fifth, Sixth and Eighth Amendments, and echoed the Jeffersonian arguments against the Alien Act of 1798.[86] The majority in *Fong Yue Ting* did not deny that aliens possessed constitutional rights, but held that the deportation provisions were consistent with those Amendments.[87] The weight of analogy and dictum thus favored the recognition of aliens' rights in *Wong Wing*, which explains the government's effort in its brief to distinguish the situation of unlawfully present aliens. Nonetheless, the Court quoted the universal scope attributed to the Fourteenth Amendment in *Yick Wo*, and unanimously applied it to the Fifth and Sixth Amendments.

The influence of *Wong Wing* can be seen seven years later in Justice John Marshall Harlan's opinion in *Yamataya v. Fisher*,[88] insisting that executive deportation procedures must be conducted in accordance with due process. Although Harlan expressly cited *Wong Wing* only as support for executive deportation,[89] he recalled its spirit in maintaining that "this court has never held ... that administrative officers, when executing the provisions of a statute involving the liberty of persons, may disregard the fundamental principles that inhere in 'due process of law' as understood at the time of the adoption of the Constitution.... No such arbitrary power can exist where the principles involved in due process of law are recognized."[90]

A quarter century later, Chief Justice Charles Evans Hughes cited *Wong Wing* while further expanding the reach of its principle in *Russian Volunteer Fleet v. United States*.[91] There the Court confirmed that the Takings Clause protects property rights within the United States acquired by a foreign corporation outside the United States. The plaintiff was a Russian corporation based in St. Petersburg,[92] to which a Norwegian company had assigned contractual rights to ships being constructed in the United States. The United States had requisitioned the vessels for use in the First World War. The situation was further complicated by the intervening October Revolution in Russia, and the lack of diplomatic relations between the Soviet Union and the United States. But the Supreme Court still viewed the Russian corporation as an "alien friend" entitled to just compensation for its property at the time of its expropriation.[93]

In 1976, Justice John Paul Stevens summarized the legacy of *Wong Wing* as follows in *Mathews v. Diaz*:

> There are literally millions of aliens within the jurisdiction of the United States. The Fifth Amendment, as well as the Fourteenth Amendment, protects every one of these persons from deprivation of life, liberty, or property without due process of law. Even one whose presence in this country is unlawful, involuntary, or transitory is entitled to that constitutional protection.[94]

Although that summary occurred in dictum, because the plaintiffs in *Diaz* were lawfully present, the Court reaffirmed this proposition in *Plyler v. Doe*, applying a form of heightened equal protection scrutiny to protect illegal alien children against invidious discrimination by a state government. Justice William Brennan's majority opinion emphasized *Wong Wing*'s guarantee of Fifth and Sixth Amendment rights to unlawfully present aliens, and insisted that the Equal Protection Clause of the Fourteenth Amendment also applied to everyone within a state's territory, regardless of legal status.[95]

It would be unrealistic, however, to suggest that Justices have never tried to retreat from the principle that the Bill of Rights protects all persons within the territorial jurisdiction of the United States. Even in *Yamataya*, Justice Harlan claimed to "[leave] on one side the question whether an alien can rightfully invoke the due process clause of the Constitution who has entered the country clandestinely, and who has been here for too brief a period to have become, in any real sense, a part of our population, before his right to remain is disputed."[96] More recently, Chief Justice William Rehnquist included dicta in his opinion in *United States v. Verdugo–Urquidez*, attempting to reopen the question whether unlawfully present aliens were entitled to Fourth Amendment protection against unreasonable searches and seizures.[97] He distinguished the Fourth Amendment from the Fifth Amendment because the former spoke of a "right of the people." He pointed out that earlier cases had assumed without analysis that the Fourth Amendment limited searches of illegal aliens within the United States. And he cited *Wong Wing* as protecting only "resident aliens."[98]

Conclusion

In the judiciary-centered system of U.S. constitutional law, holdings have special force. Even widely recognized principles need to be fortified by being embodied in rulings with precedential effect. We may consider ourselves fortunate that Thomas Geary's lack of restraint led so quickly to a Supreme Court decision drawing the line and affirming that the Bill of Rights protected Chinese aliens unlawfully within the country against the federal government. Coming as it did in the formative period of federal immigration law, at the height of Sinophobic racism, *Wong Wing v. United States* stands as a striking demonstration that the "plenary" immigration power must be reconciled with the constitutional framework of human liberty.

ENDNOTES

1. Herbert Wechsler Professor of Federal Jurisprudence, Columbia Law School. The author is grateful for advice and help from Marian Smith, Lucy Salyer, Dana Neacsu, and Barbara Silkworth, and especially wishes to thank William B. Canfield for sharing information about family history.

2. McNabb v. United States, 318 U.S. 332, 347 (1943).

3. 163 U.S. 228 (1896).

4. Act of May 5, 1892, ch. 60, 27 Stat. 25.

5. 149 U.S. 698 (1893). See Chapter 1 of this volume.

6. 23 Cong. Rec. 2911 (1892).

7. 23 Cong. Rec. 3476 (1892) ("That any such Chinese person or person of Chinese descent, once convicted and adjudged to be not lawfully entitled to be or remain in the United States, and having been once removed from the United States in pursuance of such conviction, who shall be subsequently convicted for a like offense, shall be imprisoned at hard labor for a period of not exceeding six months, and thereafter removed from the United States as hereinbefore provided.").

8. 23 Cong. Rec. 3831 (1892).

9. 23 Cong. Rec. 3524 (1892) (remarks of Sen. Chandler).

10. 23 Cong. Rec. 3878 (1892) (remarks of Sen. Hiscock).

11. Id. at 3878–79.

12. Act of May 5, 1892, ch. 60, § 4, 27 Stat. 25.

14. 114 U.S. 417 (1885).

13. See Letter, The Tsung-li Yamên to Charles Denby, Aug. 5, 1892, reprinted in Papers Relating to the Foreign Relations of the United States, H.R. Exec. Doc. 1, 52d Cong., 2d Sess. 127, 128 (1893).

15. United States v. Wong Sing, 51 F. 79 (W.D. Wash. 1892); In re Ng Loy Hoe, 53 F. 914 (N.D. Cal. 1892); In re Ah Yuk, 53 F. 781 (D. Minn. 1893); In re Sing Lee, 54 F. 334 (W.D. Mich. 1893).

16. United States v. Hing Quong Chow, 53 F. 233, 234–35 (E.D. La. 1892).

17. 57 F. 206 (S.D. Cal. 1893). Counsel appearing for Wong Dep Ken included Thomas J. Riordan, the attorney for the Chinese Six Companies.

18. Id. at 211.

19. See Letter, Frank H. Canfield to John H. McKenney, Aug. 26, 1892 (contained in the Supreme Court case file). McKenney was the Clerk of the Supreme Court.

20. See Brief for the United States at 8, Wong Wing v. United States, 163 U.S. 228 (1896) (noting counsel's statement at argument).

21. See Lucy E. Salyer, Laws Harsh as Tigers: Chinese Immigrants and the Shaping of Modern Immigration Law 40–48 (1995).

22. See James E. Tobin, Jr., Miller Canfield at 150: An Informal History 25–27 (2002).

23. Id. at 27.

24. Elizabeth Gasper Brown, Legal Education at Michigan, 1859–1959, at 471 (1959); George L. Canfield and George W. Dalzell, The Law of the Sea: A Manual on the Principles of Admiralty Law for Students, Mariners, and Ship Operators (1921).

25. Letter, Frank H. Canfield to John H. McKenney, Aug. 26, 1892 (contained in the Supreme Court case file). Under Section 5 of the Evarts Act, ch. 517, 26 Stat. 826, cases in the circuit courts raising constitutional issues were subject to direct appeal to the Supreme Court, skipping the new circuit courts of appeals.

26. See James W. Ely, Jr., The Chief Justiceship of Melville W. Fuller, 1888–1910, at 40–44 (1995); cf. Charles Fairman, Reconstruction and Reunion 1864–88, Part One, at 69–70 (1971) ("After docketing, a case would wait some two or three years before in turn it was called for oral argument.... While this waiting was too long, the process of consideration was too cursory. Ordinarily the interval between argument and announcement of the decision was about a month....").

27. Letter, Frank H. Canfield to John H. McKenney, May 8, 1893.

28. U.S. Const., amend. XIII ("Neither slavery nor involuntary servitude, *except as a punishment for crime whereof the party shall have been duly convicted*, shall exist within the United States, or any place subject to their jurisdiction.") (emphasis added).

29. Brief for Appellants at 11.

30. Id. The brief cited Yick Wo v. Hopkins, 118 U.S. 356, 369 (1886), a Fourteenth Amendment case involving discrimination by the state of California; Carlisle v. United States, 83 U.S. (16 Wall.) 147 (1873), discussing resident aliens' obligations of obedience to law and construing a congressional statute to avoid conflict with the President's power to pardon Confederate supporters; and some lower court cases, mostly involving the Fourteenth Amendment.

31. Brief for Appellants at 12. Canfield lost on this issue. See infra.

32. Dickinson observed that the record did not clearly establish which category Wong Wing was in, but the burden would have been on him to demonstrate a more favorable status, and that anyway, at the time of his proceedings, he would have been deportable only if he had entered unlawfully. Brief for the United States at 5–6 (cited in note 20).

33. Id. at 9.

34. Id. at 19.

35. Id. at 21.

36. Id. at 22.

37. Id. at 23.

38. Id. at 25.

39. Id. at 28.

40. In those days, despite the crowded docket, the Court permitted counsel two hours per side. Supreme Court Rule No. 22, 108 U.S. 573, 586 (1884).

41. 163 U.S. at 234–35.

42. 163 U.S. at 235.

43. 163 U.S. at 237.

44. Id. at 237–38.

45. Id. at 238 (quoting Yick Wo v. Hopkins, 118 U.S. 356, 369 (1886)).

46. Id. at 238.

47. Id.

48. 163 U.S. at 238 (opinion of Field, J.). The Reporter gave the opinion the neutral running head "Mr. Justice Field's Opinion."

49. Id. at 239.

50. See Willard L. King, Melville Weston Fuller: Chief Justice of the United States 1888–1910, at 222–24 (1950). More fully, Field delivered his last two opinions on May 18, the *Wong Wing* concurrence and a brief opinion denying a motion for rehearing in Telfener v. Russ, 163 U.S. 100 (1896), correcting omissions in his final opinion for the Court, Telfener v. Russ, 162 U.S. 170 (1896); see King at 222.

51. Id. at 226–27. Field died in 1899.

52. 163 U.S. at 242. Field substituted "human being" here for Canfield's repetition of "person." Field also copied Canfield's string citation of authority, but someone corrected the misprinting of one case name in the list, Ho Ah Kow v. Nunan, 12 F. Cas. 252 (C.C.D. Cal. 1879) (No. 6,546) (Field, Circuit Justice) (invalidating San Francisco "queue ordinance" as violation of the Fourteenth Amendment).

53. 163 U.S. at 242–43.

54. Id. at 243.

55. 149 U.S. 698, 742 (1893) (Field, J., dissenting); See Chapter 1 of this volume.

56. See Alan F. Westin, Stephen J. Field and the Headnote to O'Neil v. Vermont: A Snapshot of the Fuller Court at Work, 67 Yale L.J. 363, 381–83 (1958).

57. Id. at 382. Field's court-packing plan may have been inspired by his experience on the losing side when an expansion of the Court reversed the Legal Tender Cases. See Knox v. Lee, 79 U.S. (12 Wall.) 457 (1871) (overruling Hepburn v. Griswold, 75 U.S. (8 Wall.) 603 (1870)).

58. 163 U.S. 537 (1896).

59. 163 U.S. 376 (1896) (holding that the Fifth Amendment right to grand jury proceedings did not apply to the Cherokee Nation).

60. Barnitz v. Beverly, 163 U.S. 118 (1896); Hennington v. Georgia, 163 U.S. 299 (1896).

61. See Federal Courts: United States Supreme Court, N.Y. Times 3 (May 19, 1896); Legal Record: Supreme Court of the United States, Wash. Post 9 (May 19, 1896).

62. See Louisiana's Separate Car Law, N.Y. Times 3 (May 19, 1896); A Victory for Hetty Green, id. at 1 (reporting on Cornell v. Green, 163 U.S. 75 (1896) (dismissing appeal for want of jurisdiction)); Separate Coach Law Upheld, Wash. Post 6 (May 19, 1896); Hetty Green Wins Her Suit: She Secures Chicago Property Valued at Five Million Dollars, id. at 2.

63. Upholds the Law: Supreme Court on Chinese Deportation Statute, The Evening News, Detroit 6 (Monday, May 18, 1896).

64. Supreme Court Decisions: Opinions Handed Down by Federal Justices at Washington, Detroit Free Press 2 (Tuesday, May 19, 1896); Singer Mfg. Co. v. June Mfg. Co., 163 U.S. 169 (1896).

65. Opinions of the Supreme Court: Decisions in Interesting Cases: Punishment of a Chinese, San Francisco Chronicle 3 (Tuesday, May 19, 1896). The *Chronicle* went on to discuss the Georgia case and *Plessy* (combined under the heading, Two Railroad Cases), the trademark case, and the Kansas case. It also reported the dismissal for want of jurisdiction in a theatrical copyright case, Webster v. Daly, 163 U.S. 155 (1896).

66. Hilborn v. United States, 163 U.S. 342 (1896) (denying additional reimbursement for defending against challenges to exclusion or deportation). The local interest of the case was no doubt increased by the fact that Hilborn had been elected to Congress from Oakland.

67. Flashes from the Wires, Los Angeles Times 2 (May 19, 1896). The Los Angeles Times gave greater prominence to the trademark case and the case on reimbursement of U.S. Attorneys. The Singer Trade Mark, id. at 1; Hilborn Loses His Fees, id. at 2.

68. Annual Report of the Attorney–General of the United States for The Year 1896, at xiv (1896).

69. Notes of American Decisions, 54 Alb. L. J. 80 (1896/97); Comment, 5 Yale L.J. 269 (1896). The Yale author counted three rather than four appellants, and claimed that the decision "turned upon the question of 'due process of law,' under the well-known provision of the Fourteenth Amendment." Id.

70. See Simeon E. Baldwin, Constitutional Questions Incident to the Acquisition and Government by the United States of Island Territory, 12 Harv. L. Rev. 393, 404 (1899) ("shared by every foreigner who may be found within our jurisdiction"); Abbott Lawrence Lowell, The Status of Our New Possessions: A Third View, 13 Harv. L. Rev. 155, 167 (1899); Edward B. Whitney, Porto Rico Tariffs of 1899 and 1900, 9 Yale L.J. 297, 300 (1900). Justice Brown then cited *Wong Wing* in his opinion in Downes v. Bidwell, 182 U.S. 244, 283 (1901), for the proposition that aliens are "entitled under the principles of the Constitution to be protected in life, liberty and property."

71. Blackburn Esterline, Acts of Congress Declared Unconstitutional by the Supreme Court of the United States, 38 Am. L. Rev. 21, 38, 40 (1904).

72. See, e.g., Bugajewitz v. Adams, 228 U.S. 585, 592 (1913); United States v. Gue Lim, 176 U.S. 459, 464 (1900).

73. See Demore v. Kim, 538 U.S. 510 (2003); Zadvydas v. Davis, 533 U.S. 678 (2001); Reno v. Flores, 507 U.S. 292 (1993); United States v. Sing Tuck, 194 U.S. 161 (1904). Chapter 13 of this volume is devoted to *Demore v. Kim.*

74. See, e.g., Immigration and Nationality Act of 1952, as amended, §§ 275(a), 275(c), 276, 266, 243(a), 8 U.S.C. §§ 1325(a), 1325(c), 1326, 1306, 1253(a).

75. See, e.g., Carlson v. Landon, 342 U.S. 524, 533 (1952); Li Sing v. United States, 180 U.S. 486, 495 (1901); see also Louisville Joint Stock Land Bank v. Radford, 295 U.S. 555, 590 (1935) ("The bankruptcy power, like the other great powers of Congress, is subject to the Fifth Amendment.") (citing *Wong Wing*).

76. But see Weems v. United States, 217 U.S. 349 (1910) (holding that the particular form of "hard and painful labor," combined with other penalties, imposed under Spanish tradition in the Philippines, amounted to cruel and unusual punishment for the crime of falsifying public accounts).

77. 114 U.S. 417 (1885).

78. *Wong Wing*, 163 U.S. at 237–38.

79. 258 U.S. 433, 434 (1922).

80. 258 U.S. at 444–45 (Brandeis, J., dissenting).

81. Id. at 449–51.

82. See Gerald L. Neuman, Strangers to the Constitution: Immigrants, Borders, and Fundamental Law 52–60 (1996). The Alien Act (or Alien Friends Act), ch. 58, 1 Stat. 570 (1798), authorized the President to arrest and deport aliens he deemed dangerous.

83. Scott v. Sandford, 60 U.S. (18 How.) 393, 407 (1857) ("They had for more than a century before been regarded as beings [who] had no rights which the white man was bound to respect. . . .").

84. See Cong. Globe, 39th Cong., 1st Sess. 2891–92 (1866) (remarks of Sen. Conness); see also id. at 497–98 (colloquy); id. at 1757 (remarks of Sen. Trumbull).

85. 118 U.S. 356, 369 (1886).

86. Fong Yue Ting v. United States, 149 U.S. 698, 733, 740–41 (1893) (Brewer, J., dissenting); id. at 759–60 (Field, J., dissenting); id. at 761–62 (Fuller, C.J., dissenting).

87. Id. at 730.

88. 189 U.S. 86 (1903).

89. Id. at 97.

90. Id. at 100–01.

91. 282 U.S. 481, 489 (1931).

92. In fact, the Russian Volunteer Fleet was originally a government-owned company operating merchant vessels that could be converted into war vessels in time of war, initially funded by private donations. See Amos S. Hershey, Some Questions of International Law Arising from the Russo–Japanese War, Part VI, 16 Green Bag 659, 664 & n.3 (1904). After the Russian Revolution of 1917, emigrés and Soviet officials disputed control of the corporation. The Supreme Court found it unnecessary to address the current status of the Fleet, for purposes of the phase of the litigation then before it. See *Russian Volunteer Fleet*, 282 U.S. at 489; Brief for the United States at 13 (reserving the status question for remand). The Fleet's compensation claim was later included in the comprehensive settlement between the United States and the Soviet Union known as the Litvinov Assignment. See United States v. Pink, 315 U.S. 203, 212–13 (1942).

93. 282 U.S. at 489. Ultimately, the Court interpreted the relevant statute as permitting suit in the Court of Claims, in light of the constitutional background. Id. at 491–92.

94. 426 U.S. 67, 77 (1976) (citations omitted).

95. Plyler v. Doe, 457 U.S. 202, 210–12 (1982), discussed in Chapter 8 of this volume. See also Zadvydas v. Davis, 533 U.S. 678, 693–94 (2001).

96. *Yamataya*, 189 U.S. at 100. Presumably Harlan was leaving open a question concerning the application of due process in administrative removal proceedings, not in criminal trials.

97. 494 U.S. 259, 272 (1990). The discussion was dictum, because the case really involved the inapplicability of the Fourth Amendment to a search of property in Mexico. Moreover, Justice Kennedy's concurring opinion in that case suggests that the Chief Justice was speaking only for a plurality of four. Id. at 275 (Kennedy, J., concurring).

98. 494 U.S. at 271.

3

Wong Kim Ark: The Contest Over Birthright Citizenship

Lucy E. Salyer

In August 1895, Wong Kim Ark sailed into San Francisco harbor aboard the steamship *Coptic*, returning to the city of his birth after a visit to China. His journey did not end there, however, as Wong Kim Ark's right to enter and remain in the United States, the country of his birth, became embroiled in a fierce legal battle that was not resolved until the U.S. Supreme Court finally decided in his favor in 1898.[1] The legal question was deceptively simple: Under the Fourteenth Amendment, are all persons born in the United States American citizens? As one legal commentator at the time noted, the "commonly accepted notion" was that birth conferred citizenship.[2] The uncommon length of the attorneys' briefs and the Court's divided opinion suggest, however, that the issue was not so straightforward, especially in an era of growing immigration and American imperial expansion. If the United States had long recognized birthright citizenship as a core organizing principle for determining membership in the polity, it had also made significant exceptions to that rule, especially for African Americans and Native Americans who were often excluded from citizenship. Although many thought the Fourteenth Amendment, adopted in the aftermath of the nation's bloodiest war, had created a more inclusive democracy with its bold declaration that "all persons born ... in the United States, and subject to the jurisdiction thereof, are citizens of the United States," the *Wong Kim Ark* case revealed that the United States in the late nineteenth century continued to be deeply divided over the relationship among race, culture, and citizenship.

Birthright Citizenship and Race in U.S. Law

The Legal and Conceptual Background

The Constitution, as originally ratified, had not defined citizenship. It gave Congress the power to create uniform laws for the naturalization of aliens, limited the office of the presidency to "natural born" citizens, and spoke of the "privileges and immunities" of "citizens of each state."

But nowhere did it define "citizen." In that absence, American jurists had turned unhesitatingly to the British common law as the authoritative source in determining who were citizens of the United States.[3] Under the common law, *jus soli* or the "law of the soil" provided that anyone born within the nation's territory was its citizen. This contrasted with the Roman civil law definition of citizenship, *jus sanguinis*, or the law of descent. Under *jus sanguinis*, adopted by most of Europe by the nineteenth century, a child's nationality was determined by that of the parents, regardless of the place of birth. In England, however, *jus soli* became the dominant rule. In *Calvin's Case* in 1608, the famous jurist Sir Edward Coke provided the most thorough justification for this rule. All persons born within the king's dominion, and thus under his protection, he wrote, were subjects of the king and owed him allegiance. The relationship between king and subject, defined by reciprocal duties of allegiance and protection, was, according to Coke, part of the hierarchical natural order divined by God, and could not be changed. Once a subject of the king, always a subject.[4]

With the Enlightenment and the American Revolution came new concepts of citizenship, emphasizing the contractual nature of civil society and the choice individuals had in deciding to become citizens. As historian James Kettner argues, naturalization—the process by which an alien voluntarily and affirmatively decides to become a citizen of another country—provided the model of republican citizenship. In this model, foreigners took up residence in the United States, learned republican principles of governance, became part of the social and economic life of the community, and eventually, through taking an oath of allegiance, were adopted into the polity as full citizens. If naturalization reflected the republican ideal, however, birthright citizenship remained the primary path of citizenship for most Americans, even though it seemed at odds with the ideal's emphasis on the voluntary consent of the citizen as manifested in an explicit declaration of allegiance. As Kettner explains, "No one appeared to reexamine and justify Coke's idea of the 'natural-born citizen.' Americans merely continued to assume that 'birth within the allegiance' conferred the status and its accompanying rights. Natives were presumably educated from infancy in the values and habits necessary for self-government and there was no need to worry about their qualifications for membership." Another noted commentator explained in somewhat circular fashion: "The principle of birth within a country is a natural principle, because resulting from birth, itself a natural process."[5] Those aliens who became U.S. citizens as adults were "made natural" through "naturalization," a term which indicates that the benchmark for citizenship remained birth in the country.[6]

Just as birthright citizenship was accepted into American jurisprudence with little debate, so, too, was the notion that America was a white

man's republic.[7] To be sure, the Revolution had unleashed potent principles of equality and freedom, but citizenship remained constrained by
racial and sexual hierarchies. Women born in the United States were
considered citizens, for example, but could not vote and, if married, had
few civil rights over their property, earnings, or children. African Americans born into slavery were considered property and thus objects, not
subjects capable of being citizens. Free blacks were often treated as
citizens, particularly before 1830, but, like women, often could not vote,
serve on juries or in militias, or even, in some cases, move freely
throughout the country.[8] Race also colored *who* could become a citizen,
as well as the rights one could wield. When Congress exercised its power
over naturalization, for example, it adopted the Act of 1790 which
extended the privilege to all "free white persons." As historian Matthew
Frye Jacobson notes, the act sparked debate on several fronts—over, for
example, how long an alien should live in the United States before
naturalization, whether Jews and Catholics should be eligible, what the
naturalization process should entail—but none over whether race should
be a requirement. "So natural was the relationship of whiteness to
citizenship," observes Jacobson, "that ... the racial dimension of the act
remained unquestioned."[9] Being white—or, after 1870, of African descent—would remain a requirement for naturalization until 1952, meaning that for most of its history, the United States has linked citizenship
with race.

Even birthright citizenship, a seemingly natural and automatic
status, would only be guaranteed for those deemed white. Before the
1830s, state courts in the North and the South had regarded free native-
born African Americans as U.S. citizens, even as the judges upheld laws
and practices that discriminated against them. As slavery became a more
divisive issue, however, southern courts began to deny the citizenship of
free blacks, arguing that not everyone born within the nation was a
member of the political community. Those courts used blacks' lack of
equal rights against them, as marks that they were not actually citizens,
but rather more akin to aliens or denizens. Chief Justice Roger B. Taney
used similar reasoning when, in *The Dred Scott Case* in 1857, he
concluded that free blacks could never be considered U.S. citizens,
regardless of their free status or their birth within the national territory.
Taney argued that only the "class and description of persons, who were
at the time of the adoption of the Constitution recognized as citizens in
the several states ... and their posterity" became citizens of "the new
political body; but none other." Were blacks considered citizens at the
time the Constitution was adopted? Taney concluded that African Americans had been regarded at that time as "beings of an inferior order ...
altogether unfit to associate with the white race, either in social or
political rights; and so far inferior, that they had no rights which the

white man was bound to respect."[10] Not being part of "we the people of the United States" at the time the Constitution was ratified, free blacks were not citizens of the United States, Taney held, leaving them in the anomalous position of being neither citizens nor aliens.

The *Dred Scott* decision regarding citizenship would not stand long, however, as the ensuing Civil War brought fundamental changes in the nation's understanding of citizenship and of the federal government's responsibility in protecting citizens' rights. After the war, the Republican-dominated Congress embarked on a flurry of reform, of such sweeping proportions that historians have referred to Reconstruction as the "second American revolution."[11] In a decade, Congress had added three new amendments to the Constitution—the Thirteenth, Fourteenth, and Fifteenth—and passed six major civil rights statutes. The "new Constitution" was striking in several respects. Not only did it explicitly outlaw slavery and, in President Abraham Lincoln's words, dedicate the nation to "a new birth of freedom," but it also defined citizenship explicitly for the first time.[12] In a conscious repudiation of the *Dred Scott* decision, the Fourteenth Amendment began with the seemingly unequivocal statement: "All persons born or naturalized in the United States and subject to the jurisdiction thereof, are citizens of the United States and of the State wherein they reside."[13] The Reconstruction Amendments and statutes went even further in defining what rights citizens had and committing the federal government to protecting its citizens' rights. This was a key shift. Before the Civil War, the *states* had primary power to decide who were citizens and what rights they had. After the war, congressional Republicans did not believe that the rights of citizens— particularly those of the newly freed African Americans—could be trusted to states, especially in light of southern resistance to Reconstruction and efforts to restrain black freedom. Increasingly, Republicans in Congress came to believe that only a strong federal government could ensure that the black man had rights which all were bound to respect.

In November 1869, the political cartoonist Thomas Nast conveyed the ideals and hopes of an inclusive reconstructed nation in his drawing, "Uncle Sam's Thanksgiving Dinner." Nast portrayed Uncle Sam carving the turkey at the head of a table, surrounded by a dignified gathering of diverse families: Irish, Spanish, German, Native American, and East Indian share the table's bounty. The American hostess, perhaps the iconic figure of Columbia, sits between a Chinese and an African American man, and their families. The centerpiece of the table proclaims "self-government" and "universal suffrage." Portraits of Presidents Lincoln, Washington, and Grant grace the wall as does a picture of Castle Garden, the immigration station in New York, with "Welcome" written above the top. In case a reader missed the point, Nast included "Come One Come All" and "Free and Equal" at the bottom of the cartoon.[14]

In practice, however, the revolutionary promise of Reconstruction fell flat by the 1870s, and the commitment to universal and equal citizenship flagged as well. A failure of national will, the turn in Republican interests to economic issues, the persistence of southern resistance and violence, and the refusal of the Supreme Court to read the Reconstruction Amendments and legislation broadly all played a role in Reconstruction's demise. Booming immigration in the late nineteenth century also energized efforts to narrow the conception of citizenship. By 1900, a third of the American population was either foreign-born or had at least one foreign-born parent.[15] Immigration was certainly not a new phenomenon for the United States, but the numbers—and the immigrants' diverse origins and cultural backgrounds—made the post-Civil War migration distinctive, as people increasingly arrived from Southern and Eastern Europe, and also from Asia. Many "oldcomer" Americans saw the newcomers as peculiar, and often inferior, members of distinct cultures who threatened to undermine American social and political institutions.

The new mood is aptly revealed in another cartoon entitled "Uncle Sam's Thanksgiving Dinner," printed in 1877 in *The Wasp*, a satirical weekly magazine published in San Francisco. Apparently parodying Nast's cartoon of 1869, *The Wasp*'s version portrayed Uncle Sam, in his stereotypical red and white striped pants, lounging at the head of the table, while a black waiter carries in his huge turkey. Nast's dignified gathering of diverse families, joined together by American principles of self-government and equality, has been replaced by a random group of distinct caricatures, sharing nothing in common and absorbed in their own cultures. As a throng of people wait to be seated, a motley assortment of men of various nationalities—without families—sit around the table, eating their (bizarre) native foods: the German his sausage, the Italian a big bowl of pasta, the Frenchman a plateful of frogs with his glass of wine. A Native American squats, rather than sits, and gnaws on a leg of venison. The Chinese man sitting to the right of Uncle Sam captures the greatest attention and disgust from the other diners, however, as he pierces a rat with his fork.[16]

UNCLE SAM'S THANKSGIVING DINNER.

Chinese Immigration and Anti–Chinese Sentiments

The focus on the Chinese man as particularly shocking in his different cultural habits was not accidental, for Chinese immigrants became the first, and most despised, targets of post-Civil War nativism. Like many other immigrants, Chinese came to the United States to improve their economic situation and escape an unstable political situation in the homeland. Drawn initially by the Gold Rush in California in 1849, Chinese immigrated primarily to the West Coast, moving from mining in the 1850s to railroad construction in the 1860s to farm labor and urban occupations by the 1880s. In comparison to European immigration, their numbers were quite small, totaling only 105,465 in 1880, or less than 2% of the total foreign-born population.[17] Yet, almost from the beginning of their arrival in the United States, Chinese became the periodic targets of discriminatory legislation by California and other western states and, by 1876, the object of a congressional investigation. In 1882, the United States Congress passed the first Chinese Exclusion Act, forbidding further immigration by Chinese laborers and strictly regulating the entry of other Chinese. It also explicitly prohibited Chinese from becoming naturalized citizens.[18]

In justifying the exclusion of Chinese from the nation as immigrants and from the polity as citizens, nineteenth century policymakers typically resorted to racial and cultural rationales, arguing repeatedly that Chinese were a race apart, so distinct in their history, biology and culture, that they could never assimilate.[19] Not only would they remain strangers to American ideas and culture, but, nativists argued, they also posed a distinct threat to the country's republican principles and institutions. Americans, the inheritors of the "Anglo–Saxon civilization," loved freedom and embraced self-government. In contrast, Senator John F. Miller and other exclusionists asserted, Chinese were servile drudges with limited intellectual and political capacities, so accustomed to thousands of years of rule by a despotic imperial government that they could never understand, much less participate in, republican self-government. To admit the Chinese to citizenship, they warned, "would be to begin the wreck of the Republic" for "there would be a new element introduced into the governing power of this nation, which would be the most venal, irresponsible, ignorant, and vicious of all the bad elements which have been infused into the body-politic—an element disloyal to American intuitions, inimical to republican liberty, scornful of American civilization, not fit for self-government and unfit to participate in the government of others—a people destitute of conscience or the moral sense."[20] Such sentiments were voiced by judges and politicians, and became common fodder in popular culture.[21]

Even before the 1882 Chinese Exclusion Act, Congress had taken steps to ensure that Chinese would not become American citizens. When the Reconstruction Congress discussed eliminating any further bars to citizenship for African Americans, Radical Republican Charles Sumner of Massachusetts proposed eliminating all racial requirements for naturalization by striking out "white" from the 1790 law. His plan sparked a determined opposition from Westerners such as Senator William Stewart of Nevada who declared, "I do not propose to hand over our institutions to any foreigners who have no sympathy with us, who do not profess to make this country their home, who do not propose to subscribe to republican institutions."[22] Consequently, the 1870 law expanded naturalization, but only reached aliens of "African descent."[23] The law had not explicitly prohibited Chinese from becoming naturalized, however, and several did seek to become citizens, with varying degrees of success. A

federal circuit court decision in the 1878 case *In re Ah Yup*, holding that
Chinese were not "white" and thus were ineligible for naturalization,
severely hampered their efforts. The explicit prohibition on Chinese
naturalization in 1882 resolved any ambiguity in the 1870 law. Naturalization would not be possible for Chinese until 1943.[24]

Attacks on Birthright Citizenship

Perhaps emboldened by the success in barring Chinese from naturalization, exclusionists in the 1880s and 1890s would also target those
born in the United States of Chinese immigrant parents, the so-called
"native born," arguing they should not be considered citizens by birth.
Although the Chinese immigrant community was overwhelmingly male,
the number of children born in the United States to Chinese parents
grew steadily in the late nineteenth century, from only 1% of the
population of Chinese ancestry in 1880 to a purported 11% in 1900.[25]
Chinese American children were a favorite subject of photographers, who
portrayed them as rare curiosities of Chinatowns, but they struck alarm,
rather than amusement, in the minds of exclusionists. The rising number of native-born Chinese Americans foiled expectations that the Chinese Exclusion Act would eventually eliminate Chinese from America's
shores. As the Act proved more difficult to enforce than expected and
Chinese Americans began to organize politically in the 1890s, a campaign developed to deny Chinese Americans their birthright citizenship
claims. But undermining birthright citizenship would prove to be a
daunting task.

Legal scholars began the assault on birthright citizenship by laying
the intellectual foundation for the central argument. Although *jus soli*
had been the practice in the United States, they contended, birthright
citizenship was neither a wise policy nor a correct interpretation of the
law binding the country. George D. Collins, a young lawyer from San
Francisco, precipitated a flurry of exchanges in legal journals when, in
1884 (while still a law student at California State University Law School,
now Hastings College of the Law), he boldly challenged the common law
rule as wrong and "manifestly impolitic." *Jus sanguinis*, the law of
descent, he argued, was the rule the United States should follow. Collins
and other critics acknowledged the long line of precedents to the contrary, the most prominent being *Lynch v. Clark*, a New York decision in
1844.[26] There, the court had held that in the absence of explicit congressional or constitutional provisions, the principles of the common law
should govern; hence, the English common law rule of *jus soli* applied in
the United States. Here, Collins argued, was the beginning of a long line
of bad law. The New York court was wrong, Collins and others argued,
because the federal government *had* no common law, but rather was
governed either by the explicit provisions of Congress or the Constitution, or, in their absence, by the law of nations, which followed the rule

of descent. Failing to grasp the errors of the New York court's opinion in *Lynch*, judges and administrators had followed its ruling with little critical reflection, leading the nation to a rather desperate situation by the 1880s, defenseless to protect itself against the citizenship claims of those, particularly the children of Chinese immigrants, who were unworthy and even dangerous citizens.[27]

Other legal scholars agreed with Collins' criticism of the doctrine of *jus soli*, though not necessarily because they opposed Chinese immigration and citizenship. Alexander Porter Morse of Louisiana, for example, challenged a broad reading of the Fourteenth Amendment, in bestowing citizenship on anyone born in the United States, upon federalism grounds. He and others objected to the expansion of the federal government's power in the Reconstruction amendments and sought to leave the definition of citizenship and its rights to the states.[28] Others believed that *jus sanguinis* was the more logical and more widely adopted rule among nations. They worried that birthright citizenship would encourage the "absurd" and "untenable" doctrine of dual citizenship, which they tellingly referred to as "double allegiance." The child of alien parents born in the United States would be considered an American citizen, but the parents' native country might also claim the child as a citizen, under the rule of *jus sanguinis*.[29] Such a situation could provoke confusion and diplomatic crises among nations, but also created a divided allegiance that was, for many Americans, worrisome and even morally repugnant, akin to polygamy. In an age of mass immigration and the emergence of the United States as a world power in competition with other nation states, many Americans thought it all the more important to ensure that their fellow citizens have only one nation they called home.[30]

If the issue was sometimes broader than Chinese exclusion, authors frequently referred to children of Chinese descent becoming citizens to illustrate the perceived dangers and folly of the *jus soli* doctrine. Collins argued that children of Chinese descent "born upon American soil are Chinese from their very birth in all respects, just as much so as though they had been born and reared in China; they inherit the same prejudices, the same customs, habits, and methods of their ancestors." "It is evident," Collins asserted, "that such persons are utterly unfit, wholly incompetent, to exercise the important privileges of an American citizen . . . ; and yet under the common-law rule they would be citizens."[31]

The Battle in the Courts

In re Look Tin Sing: *the First Federal Court Ruling on Birthright Citizenship*

While commentators debated the issue of birthright citizenship in the pages of legal journals, courts began to hear legal challenges to the citizenship of Chinese Americans. In 1884—the same year Collins published his first attack on *jus soli*—the federal circuit court in northern California provided a victory for Chinese American citizens in a case that Supreme Court Justice Stephen J. Field, who presided at the hearing, dubbed "the case of the Chinese Boy Citizen." The facts of the case were undisputed: Look Tin Sing had been born in Mendocino, California, in 1870 to a Chinese father and mother who had lived in the United States for twenty years and owned a general merchandise store. When Look Tin Sing was nine, his parents sent him to China, presumably to be educated. After he left, Congress adopted the Chinese Exclusion Act, and when Look Tin Sing returned to the United States at age fourteen in September 1884, he was denied entry on the grounds that he did not have a certificate, as required under the acts of 1882 and 1884, to prove he was exempt from exclusion. The issues at stake were momentous and, not surprisingly, captured the attention of both the public and the bar. Justice Field, according to historian Charles J. McClain, Jr., issued an open invitation to all lawyers in the area to give their opinions on the constitutional questions involved. Possibly for that reason, "the array of legal lights both for and against the petitioner was dazzling," according to the San Francisco *Morning Call*.[32]

The U.S. Attorney drew on the expert assistance of John Norton Pomeroy, a renowned treatise writer, distinguished professor at Hastings College of Law, and friend of Justice Field. In his oral argument, Pomeroy voiced many of the doctrinal contentions made by Collins and others, including that *jus sanguinis* was the preferred doctrine, because it avoided the problem of "double allegiance." His remarks signaled that Pomeroy was less concerned about the double allegiance that might occur if, for example, a child of British aliens living in the United States could claim both British and American citizenship. Such aliens, at least, belonged to the "free Caucasian races of the world, such peoples as have so near an origin that they can assimilate." Rather, he focused concern on "all yellow and brown races," who had been traditionally barred from naturalization, yet who would seem to fall under the Fourteenth Amendment's guarantee of citizenship to "all persons born within the United States, and subject to the jurisdiction thereof." Pomeroy warned that "some limitation [should be] placed on [the] broad language" of the Fourteenth Amendment "for the safety of the country" and found that limitation in the clause "subject to the jurisdiction thereof." That language, Pomeroy argued, should be interpreted to require those claiming birthright citizenship to be *fully* subject to U.S. jurisdiction, without competing allegiances, whether they be political, cultural or racial. Simply being born within the geographic limits of the United States and entitled to some protection from the nation did not suffice to show that one owed complete allegiance to the country. The U.S. Assistant Attorney, Carroll Cook, went even further. He argued that even if Look Tin Sing *was* a citizen by virtue of his birth in the United States, he was still barred from admission under the Chinese exclusion laws, because the Fourteenth Amendment prohibited only the *states* from abridging the rights of citizens. The federal government, not explicitly mentioned, "reserved to itself the right to abridge such rights."[33]

Attorneys for Look Tin Sing resorted to the clear language of the first sentence of the Amendment, which contains the Citizenship Clause, and looked askance at Cook's proposition that the federal government was not bound by it. (Only the second sentence contains language that is plainly limited to states' obligations.) A.P. Van Duzer sought to dispel the image of alien Chinese, unable and unwilling to assimilate and subverting the republic, by emphasizing that Look Tin Sing's parents had "lived here for twenty years, paying taxes, abandoning Chinese garments, and conforming to the customs of the country." To deny citizenship to their son was "the height of foolishness and like going back to the dark ages," he declared. Finally, the petitioners' attorneys warned that, in attacking birthright citizenship, exclusionists were reaching too far and would end up endangering the very policies they were trying so hard to protect. William M. Stewart, who, as a U.S. Senator from Nevada had strenuously objected in 1870 to Sumner's proposal to drop the racial bar to naturalization, now argued on behalf of Look Tin Sing's citizenship. A decision against Look Tin Sing, throwing birthright citizenship into question, would have ramifications far beyond the Chinese and put at risk the citizenship of "millions of children born in the United States" to alien parents. When exclusionists returned to Congress for further legislation, "they would find that they had placed an element in the Chinese controversy which would go far toward preventing further Chinese legislation."[34]

The circuit court, in an opinion by Justice Field, unanimously ruled that Look Tin Sing was a citizen of the United States and thus could not be barred from the country by the exclusion laws. The key issue was the meaning of the Fourteenth Amendment, particularly the qualifying clause, "all persons born ... in the United States, *and subject to the jurisdiction thereof*, are citizens." Did the clause refer to those born within the territorial limits of the United States? Or within its political or even cultural jurisdiction? Historically, American courts had assumed that geography determined the boundaries of U.S. sovereignty as well as the citizenship of those born within territorial limits. They expanded upon the principle in *Calvin's Case*, reasoning that those born within the U.S. territorial boundaries came under the nation's protection, and, in turn, owed it their obedience and allegiance. Justice Field agreed with that formulation, noting that "it has always been the doctrine of this country"—one embraced uniformly by legislators, lawyers, and the public as well as by judges—that "birth within the dominions and jurisdiction of the United States of itself creates citizenship." The Fourteenth Amendment incorporated, authoritatively, "the generally recognized law of the country" and explicitly extended it to "all persons" to "overrule the doctrine of the *Dred Scott Case.*" The clause "subject to the jurisdiction thereof," according to Field, excluded only the children of foreign diplomats or those born on foreign vessels while in U.S. waters who, though technically within the physical jurisdiction of the United States, were considered to be "born in the country of their parents." The clause also exempted those who had been born in the United States but had voluntarily expatriated themselves and become citizens of other countries. All others born in the United States, including Look Tin Sing, were citizens. Attorneys had argued that the legal bar to the naturalization of Chinese, as racially undesirable, should weigh against the birthright citizenship of their children, but Field ruled that the status of the parents was irrelevant to the citizenship claims of the children. Finally, Field curtly dismissed the government's argument that even if Look Tin Sing was a citizen, he should be denied entry under the Chinese exclusion law. Field declared: "no citizen can be excluded from this country except in punishment for crime. Exclusion for any other cause is unknown to our laws, and beyond the power of congress."[35]

Chinese American Mobilization

The *Look Tin Sing* opinion represented a significant victory for Chinese Americans, but it would be only the first skirmish in the legal battle over birthright citizenship. The case was decided in the midst of a bitter fight over the enforcement of the Chinese exclusion laws. Though Congress had severely limited the immigration of Chinese laborers, the Chinese American community had made skillful use of litigation to limit the reach of the exclusion law and to keep avenues open to their immigration. Congress responded with successive laws in 1884, 1888, 1892, and 1893 to tighten the exclusion laws, and the Department of Justice pursued a litigation strategy to restrict Chinese access to the federal courts, which had proven to be unexpectedly favorable arenas for the Chinese litigants.[36] Though Congress and the Department of Justice succeeded in making the laws more onerous and difficult to evade, they found the claims of Chinese American citizens to be particularly difficult to contest. Justice Field had ruled that the exclusion laws did not apply to American citizens of Chinese descent. Not only were those born in the United States exempt, but, also, any children fathered in China by Chinese American citizens were considered derivative citizens with the right to enter the United States.[37] As other routes into the United States became more difficult while the pressures to emigrate continued, more Chinese resorted to fraudulent claims of native-born or derivative citizenship to gain entry. As the population of Chinese American citizens and illegal "paper sons" grew over the years, officials and exclusionists saw the citizenship exemption as a major obstacle to their goal of eradicating Chinese from the United States.

As early as 1888, the Department of Justice began to consider a test case in the Supreme Court to challenge the birthright citizenship of Chinese Americans. On October 27, 1888, U.S. Attorney John T. Carey reported to the Attorney General, with evident satisfaction, that the circuit court in San Francisco had upheld the Chinese Exclusion Act of 1888 in *In re Chae Chan Ping*. The case would be appealed to the U.S. Supreme Court and the exclusion law would be upheld in the strongest terms possible, in an unanimous opinion written by Justice Field.[38] While glowing with his several successes in his battle to close perceived loopholes in exclusion, Carey warned of a new phenomenon:

> The remarkable increase in the per cent of those claiming to be citizens is portentous of the desperate resorts that will be made to defeat the objects of the Exclusion Bill. Most of them range from 15 to 20 years of age, claiming that they had returned to China for purposes of education, and most of them leaving so young that they could not have known anything about the country. Their statements show that they were born in Chinese quarters and in places, the surrounds of which are all Chinese, cutting off all hope of getting any white testimony to contradict them and putting the government absolutely in the power of the Chinese. They are all from the highest to the lowest, utterly regardless of the truth and have no appreciation of an oath; and while you feel that you are being imposed upon you are power-less to contradict them.[39]

Carey urged that a test case be prepared for the consideration of the Supreme Court as soon as possible, with the hopes of cutting off this avenue of immigration as well. In the mid–1890s, a special commissioner appointed by Attorney General Richard Olney confirmed Carey's report in his finding that "large numbers of Chinese were landing" in San Francisco as "native sons," and the federal courts continued to rule that they had a right to a judicial hearing regarding their admission.[40]

At the same time, Chinese American citizens made their presence felt more keenly as they sought to organize to protect their civil and political rights. With their actions and their words, Chinese Americans refuted the exclusionists' claims that Chinese neither desired nor de-served full citizenship. Chinese Americans began to form associations as early as 1884 to lobby for continued access to citizenship and to protest discrimination against Chinese, using the same rhetoric of allegiance and republicanism as was embraced by their opponents. For example, the Chinese American Equal Rights League was formed in New York in 1892 under the leadership of Wong Chin Foo, initially to resist the enforcement of the Geary Act, which required all Chinese to register with the government or face deportation. The League also emphasized broader goals, however, such as to secure the rights of those of Chinese descent who were citizens by birth or who desired to become citizens but faced legal bars. The League purported to speak for the "Americanized and American-born Chinese of the United States," claiming to have "no sympathy for those of our countrymen who persist in their own civilization and refuse to become Americanized." The League required every member to "adopt American customs, to cut off his queue, and wear the regulation clothing used in the United States." The League emphasized that many Chinese, who could not become naturalized citizens, nonetheless considered the United States their home. In a circular published in 1897, the League proclaimed the great distress of the Chinese Americans "that notwithstanding the love we cherish in our hearts for the home and country in which we live, but cannot legally call it our own, we are not permitted to share with you its glories and responsibilities." In the racialized context of citizenship in the 1890s, the League drew comparisons, complaining of the favored position of African Americans:

> We feel grieved and humiliated every time we behold our colored brethren, even from the wilds of African jungles, sit and eat from the National family table, while we, the descendants of the oldest race on earth, are not even allowed to pick up the crumbs from under the table.

"Who will help us?" the League plaintively asked. "Where are the country's Washingtons, Sumners, Beechers, Lincolns and Grants?"[41]

Opponents of Chinese American citizenship refused to admit the possibility of Chinese American allegiance and viewed attempts to lay claim to citizenship and its rights with alarm. "There is a good deal of cunning" in the League's appeal, warned the *San Francisco Call*, as "it is well known that a Chinaman never becomes Americanized." Even the more tolerant *New York Times* reprimanded the League for putting its case "rather too strongly" and asking "too much."[42] When native-born Chinese Americans in major cities began in the 1890s to assert their rights as citizens, primarily through an organized suffrage campaign, the *Call* warned of the "dawn of danger."[43] Both exclusionists and Chinese American activists understood that the success of the exclusion policy had rested, in part, on the lack of representation and political power of Chinese in the United States. Without the right to vote, Chinese could be sacrificed by both parties. With it, Chinese Americans would become the object of their affections, or, at least, of their attention. Wong Chin Foo, a pioneer in civil rights struggles for Chinese, focused on suffrage as essential for Chinese American men to assume their rightful place in the republic. He remarked, "When you don't vote and don't wish to vote, they denounce you as a reptile; the moment you appear at the ballot box you are a man and a brother and are treated to cigars, whiskeys and beers. Why can't we make our mark in politics as well as any of our brother races?"[44] Despite Wong Chin Foo's hopes, the potential numbers of Chinese American voters were quite small and posed no serious political threat to the exclusionists' policies. Nonetheless, the slightest suggestion that Chinese Americans deserved equal treatment and would exercise the right to vote rankled their opponents and fueled efforts to obtain a Supreme Court ruling against their claim to birthright citizenship.[45]

Searching For a Test Case: the Road to Wong Kim Ark

As more Chinese Americans claimed native-born citizenship and sought to exercise their political rights, the Department of Justice came under increased pressure to bring a test case for an ultimate determination by the Supreme Court. George Collins, the brash lawyer who had led the charge against *jus soli* in the legal journals in 1884, lobbied the Department with special zeal. Collins had continued to make his legal case against birthright citizenship, in the words of U.S. Attorney Henry S. Foote, "a special hobby," publishing a new article attacking birthright citizenship in the *American Law Review* in 1895 and engaging in a verbal sparring match with Justice Field in the San Francisco newspapers. In local newspaper interviews, Collins denounced Justice Field's decision in *Look Tin Sing* as "very poor law." "The evil effects of Justice Field's decision have now become so virulent and diffusive," declared Collins, "that the necessity for a ruling by the Supreme Court defining what constitutes a native-born citizen has become one of pressing urgency." Justice Field retorted that Collins' views did not possess "any merit" and that the only value of Collins' articles on citizenship was to please "the vanity of the writer ... by seeing his crudities in print." Collins responded that he was not surprised by Field's dismissive insults, as Field's "supreme veneration for his own opinion is a matter of common knowledge, and of course he brooks no dissent from his views."[46]

Collins' contentious personality led him to deluge the Attorney General with letters, urging him to authorize a test case and, with equal fervor, to appoint Collins as special counsel to "see to it that no essential fact and no essential procedure be omitted." "No more momentous question has ever arisen," he argued, and a failure to act would have unfavorable political ramifications for the administration in California. Acting Attorney General Holmes Conrad readily agreed to the test case but hesitated to appoint Collins as special counsel. U.S. Attorney Foote had reacted to Collin's request with alarm, cautioning the Attorney General that while Collins was "a man of no mean ability," he "has

rather a bad reputation as regards professional ethics'' and ''I would not
employ [him] in any matter whatsoever.'' As a compromise, Collins
grudgingly agreed to serve as amicus curiae in lieu of a position as
special counsel.[47]

Wong Kim Ark, c. 1895

U.S. Attorney Henry Foote searched for a viable test case and
settled on Wong Kim Ark. Wong Kim Ark was a cook from California, in
his early twenties, when he became caught up in the legal dispute which
would eventually make Supreme Court history. He had been born in San
Francisco in 1873 to Wong Li Ping, a merchant, and Wee Lee, his
mother, who had made the United States their home for at least
seventeen years. Wong Kim Ark lived in California his entire life, leaving
only for two trips to China, one in 1890 and the other in 1894. When he
returned from his second trip in 1895, the Collector of the Port admitted
that Wong Kim Ark's ''papers were all straight;'' he had the required
''certificate of identity,'' bearing his photograph and the signature of
three ''white'' witnesses, attesting to his birth in California. But the
collector denied Wong Kim Ark admission on the grounds that his birth
in the United States did not make him a citizen.

The collector's refusal set the legal wheels in motion. Wong Kim Ark had at his disposal a well-organized legal network, developed by the Chinese American community over the years in its efforts to contest discriminatory legislation and the enforcement of the exclusion laws. Thomas Riordan, the lawyer held on retainer by the Chinese Consolidated Benevolent Association, who had extensive experience in litigating Chinese exclusion cases, would represent Wong Kim Ark in the Federal District Court for the Northern District of California.[48] Riordan filed a petition for a writ of habeas corpus, charging that his client was being wrongfully detained on board the steamship *Coptic*.[49]

In their arguments, Wong Kim Ark's lawyers contended that the Fourteenth Amendment extended citizenship to all born within the *territorial* boundaries of the United States, a view supported by a long line of judicial precedents and official practices. The government, represented by Henry S. Foote and George Collins, milked whatever precedents and legislative history they could find, which were precious few, to support their claim that "subject to the jurisdiction" referred to those born within the *political* as opposed to the *territorial* jurisdiction of the United States.

The government emphasized two cases: the *Slaughter-House Cases* of 1873 and *Elk v. Wilkins* of 1884.[50] In the former, the majority opinion by Justice Miller had remarked that "subject to its jurisdiction' was intended to exclude from its operation children of ministers, consuls, and *citizens or subjects of foreign states born within the United States.*"[51] Children of diplomats had always been exempt from the common law rule of birthright citizenship, in recognition of their fathers' residence in the United States as official representatives of another country. The government argued that children of aliens should be viewed in the same light; the alien parents were only partially and temporarily subject to the local jurisdiction of the United States. While in residence, they had to comply with American law; yet, they owed only obedience, not necessarily allegiance. The parents' ultimate political allegiance remained with their native countries and, relying on the theory that a child's allegiances followed that of the parent, so did the children's.[52]

Miller's comment was an incidental observation and had not been critical to the decision in the *Slaughter-House Cases*. So the government turned to *Elk v. Wilkins*, which dealt explicitly with the interpretation of the jurisdiction clause. In that well-known case, John Elk sued the registrar of voters, Charles Wilkins, in Omaha, Nebraska, who had refused to allow Elk to register on the grounds he was an Indian and thus not a citizen. The Court held that Indians, even those like Elk who had left their native tribes and assimilated into white American society, were not citizens under the Fourteenth Amendment. Though born within the geographical boundaries of the United States, Indians remained at least partially subject to the political jurisdiction of their tribes and could not, on their own volition, become U.S. citizens without the explicit consent of the American government. The case, as scholars have documented, drew on a long jurisprudential tradition of viewing Indian tribes as quasi-foreign nations, exercising jurisdiction over internal tribal affairs, even while under the paternal supervision and control of the United States, but also upon perceptions of Indians as culturally distinct and inferior, at best merely in training for inclusion in the American polity.[53] The government sought to draw parallels between Elk and the child of alien parents; neither was subject to the "full and complete jurisdiction" of the United States, but rather remained subject to foreign powers. As such, Wong Kim Ark could not be considered a citizen by birth.[54]

The heart of the government's argument, however, rested on policy grounds, stressing the inability of birthright citizenship to ensure the allegiance of those it made citizens. Collins, carrying the weight of the policy arguments, argued that the common law of birthright citizenship was "anti-republican, anti-national, ... anti-American, and antagonistic to the principles of the Revolution." He stressed the feudal origins of the English common law, in which allegiance bound the subject forever in obedience to the King in exchange for protection and the ability to hold lands in tenure. Such a law had no place in a republic, thundered Collins. In a republican nation such as the United States, allegiance was neither natural nor compulsory, but rather a voluntary and conscious declaration of one's loyalty to the nation, made after a period of education. A child's allegiance did not attach immediately to the soil upon which he was born; national identity and affection depended on the teachings of the parent: "the enthusiastic ardor which fires the zeal of the loyal citizen in support of his country's cause, must be inculcated in the mind of the child by the teachings of the parent ... , else there will be no patriotism, no true citizenship."[55] In an era of rising immigration, Collins warned, one could not trust alien parents, attached to their own native lands, to foster in their U.S.-born children the type of allegiance required for republican citizenship. Only a law of citizenship based on descent, Collins argued, would protect the nation against "the rag tag and bob tail of humanity, who happen to be deposited on our soil by the accident of birth, and whose education and political affiliations are entirely alien." Collins protested against the continued adherence to "a foreign and incompatible system of law, the jurisprudence of the very nation that we revolted against," which would "force upon us as natural born citizens, persons who must necessarily be a constant menace to the welfare of our Country."[56]

Judge William W. Morrow, hearing the case in the district court, expressed sympathy with Collins' arguments, but nonetheless ruled

against the government in January, 1896.[57] Under circuit court precedent, Morrow ruled, Wong Kim Ark was a U.S. citizen, illegally detained
on board ship, and should be released.[58] The holding did not come as a
surprise. While "there was great rejoicing in Chinatown ... after Judge
Morrow's decision," the *San Francisco Call* noted that "this ruling has
by no means settled the question. It was, in truth, merely a technical
ruling on a test case." For Wong Kim Ark, Morrow's decision meant he
could finally walk on firm ground after four to five months' detention on
board ship in San Francisco harbor, but only on $250 bond while the
government pursued its appeal. All eyes turned to the U.S. Supreme
Court as the ultimate arbiter of this "question of vast importance."[59]

Wong Kim Ark *before the Supreme Court*

The question was of great importance, not just to Chinese Americans, but to all American citizens who had been born to alien parents.
The *Call* observed that "one sees at a glance that many thousands of
voters all over the United States are deeply interested in the knotty legal
problem," for, as Judge Morrow had pointed out, the government's
proposed rule of descent would have the inevitable result "that thousands of persons of both sexes, who have been considered as citizens of
the United States, and have always been treated as such, will be, to all
intents and purposes, denationalized and remanded to a state of alienage." The government, well aware of this pragmatic difficulty and its
political ramifications, attempted to schedule the timing of their Supreme Court appeal to avoid a decision just before the major presidential
election of 1896. Collins explained the necessity of avoiding an election
year decision in which "a decree might be rendered not so much upon
the bare merits of the case" but rather be influenced by a "question of
policy." Nonetheless Collins had continually downplayed the pragmatic
concerns, calling them "entirely chimerical" and only posing a "supposed inconvenience." In his view, Congress could easily provide for a
summary naturalization procedure to ensure that those racially quali-
fied—Caucasians—could be naturalized in time to vote in later elections.[60] The government succeeded in its efforts to avoid an election year
decision; the Supreme Court did not issue its opinion until 1898.

In the Supreme Court, the question of birthright citizenship would
have its fullest debate, argued by eminent appellate attorneys. The
government's case was argued by the Solicitor–General, Holmes Conrad,
a distinguished lawyer from Virginia who, as acting Attorney General,
had authorized the test case, and George D. Collins. Wong Kim Ark had
as his advocates two eminent attorneys from the Northeast, Maxwell
Evarts and J. Hubley Ashton, who had represented Chinese in previous
litigation, in particular the *Fong Yue Ting* case.[61] The lengthy briefs not
only recapitulated the essential arguments made in the lower federal

courts, which focused on the jurisdiction clause of the Fourteenth Amendment, but also engaged in vigorous and often rancorous debate about the nature of allegiance, about the nation's commitment to racial equality, and even more, about the boundaries of national power.

These were not rarified, abstract legal questions, but rather lay at the heart of many of the most contentious issues of late nineteenth century America. As many historians have elucidated, the Reconstruction Amendments wrought a change in U.S. federalism that remained controversial, especially in debates over civil rights. If the Fourteenth Amendment's framers sought to nationalize citizenship and provide federal protection for citizens' rights, subsequent judicial opinions, legislative actions, and political debates continued to struggle over the proper locus of citizenship—whether it be national or state—and the rights guaranteed to citizens under the Constitution.[62] Eventually, as Reconstruction came to an end, North and South sought reconciliation, in part by sacrificing the civil rights of African Americans and the national commitment to racial equality. By 1896, when the Supreme Court endorsed state-sanctioned racial segregation in *Plessy v. Ferguson*, the Fourteenth Amendment's national protection of citizens' rights had been whittled away and states had regained substantial control over defining the rights of citizens—a resolution that had disastrous results for African Americans.[63] In that context, *Wong Kim Ark* posed the stark question of whether the Fourteenth Amendment's guarantee of national birthright citizenship would succumb to similar racialist constructions.[64]

U.S. Solicitor General Holmes Conrad, representing the government in its challenge to Wong Kim Ark's citizenship, took a dim view of the Fourteenth Amendment and did his best to argue that it had neither expanded national power over citizenship nor extended birthright citizenship to those deemed racially or culturally unfit. Conrad was a southerner, and, judging from the tone and focus of his argument, an unreconstructed southerner. Born to a prominent family in Winchester, Virginia, in 1840, Conrad had served in the Virginia cavalry throughout the Civil War, reaching the rank of major, and continued to fight the outcome of the war long after it was over.[65] In his brief to the Supreme Court, Conrad began by contesting the very premise of birthright citizenship—that it was based on common law adopted by the national government. Like Collins and Pomeroy, Conrad asserted that "there can be no common law of the United States," but his objection came from the viewpoint of a southerner who rejected any hint of a body of law that might expand national power. For Conrad, a powerful national government brought distasteful memories of Reconstruction, described in the brief as "that unhappy period of rabid rage and malevolent zeal when corrupt ignorance and debauched patriotism held high carnival in the halls of Congress." Conrad acknowledged that the framers of the Fourteenth Amendment had tried to expand federal control over citizenship, but he disparaged their efforts and challenged the very legality of the Fourteenth Amendment, arguing that southerners had been coerced into ratifying it. Fortunately, Conrad continued, the Supreme Court in the *Slaughter-House Cases* had "forever shattered the idol of national citizenship which the 'reconstruction Congress' had placed upon so lofty a pedestal." The Court there had interpreted the Amendment in light of the true constitutional principles of the United States, by insisting that the states retained primary responsibility for defining citizenship and its rights.[66] Conrad's diatribe against Reconstruction sought to counter the argument that birth within the nation had always been considered to confer citizenship. States, he contended, had always retained primary responsibility for deciding issues relating to citizenship, aside from naturalization.[67] Ultimately, Conrad sought to argue that much of the popular perception about birthright citizenship was based on erroneous assumptions, thus leaving open the possibility for adopting the law of descent as the better rule.

In his interpretation of the jurisdiction clause of the Fourteenth Amendment, Solicitor General Conrad relied on cases that expressed cultural concepts of citizenship, in which citizens shared something more than mere birth in the same territorial boundaries. That shared characteristic was usually race. Perhaps most striking was his extensive quotation from an antebellum Kentucky case, one of several before *Dred Scott* in which the citizenship status of free blacks was denied. There, the Kentucky judge had suggested that blacks might be subjects, but not citizens, stating: "It is, in fact, not the place of a man's birth, but the rights and privileges he may be entitled to enjoy which make him a citizen." Conrad further relied on a comment in *United States v. Cruikshank* that "citizens ... are the people who compose the community." Buoyed by these references, Conrad sought to draw cultural and social boundaries around citizenship, which in his opinion would keep out those like the Chinese who were not recognized as part of the community, deserving of rights. He argued that Chinese residents, already shunned as unworthy of naturalized citizenship, passed their outsider status to their children.[68]

He drew heavily, as earlier opponents of birthright citizenship had, on court cases like *Elk v. Wilkins* denying citizenship to Native Americans on the grounds they were not fully subject to the political jurisdiction of the United States. The comparison of Chinese with Indians evoked implicit messages about the extent to which jurisdiction connoted cultural as well as political factors. Though exclusionists argued that Chinese maintained a secret, internal government—usually referring to the perceived control of the Chinese Consolidated Benevolent Association, an immigrant aid association—over the Chinese immigrant community, it was difficult for the government to equate that organization's structure or authority with that of tribes, explicitly recognized by the U.S. government for years as "dependent nations" and the legal governing bodies for Indians. Nor was the hold of the Chinese government over its subjects in the United States comparable, in a political sense. The argument, rather, was that both Indians and Chinese were subject to foreign powers, in terms of their cultural and social allegiance, no matter what the countervailing evidence might be.

In their response to the government's case, Wong Kim Ark's attorneys, Maxwell Evarts and J. Hubley Ashton, sought to empty "allegiance" of its cultural and racial content and return to the basic understanding of that concept under the common law as connoting obedience to the law. They relied on Justice Story's formulation in 1830 that "allegiance is nothing more than the tie or duty of obedience of a subject to the sovereign under whose protection he is." They emphasized the "remarkable unanimity of opinion in every quarter" in American jurisprudence that birth within the territorial jurisdiction created citizenship and that allegiance naturally followed. The law of descent had never been accepted, nor, argued the attorneys in their own republican rhetoric, did it suit American principles. "A man cannot inherit his citizenship from his father as he does his property. It is something between himself and the country of his birth, and in no way connected with the relations of the family as distinct from the State." Ashton warned that adopting the government's "new-fangled theory" of the law of descent would create a "race of aliens, all born in the United States," but without citizenship, "doomed by the Constitution to perpetual alienage in the country of their birth, their homes, and their affections." That, he suggested, would generate greater problems, not only in barring those with natural allegiance from membership, but also in potentially alienating their affections and creating an "alien nation."[69]

While the heart of Wong Kim Ark's case rested on the long-standing acceptance of the common law, Evarts and Ashton could not let Conrad's attack on the Fourteenth Amendment and Reconstruction stand without rebuttal. The lawyers' briefs, in this respect, waved the bloody shirt of the Civil War and revealed continuing sectional divides. Such divisions split the government's attorneys as well. George Collins, ostensibly working with Conrad on the government's case, was so appalled by Conrad's brief in its endorsement of the "political doctrines ... of the Democratic Party," its "preposterous position that there is no national citizenship," and his "inexcusable assault upon the sterling and exalted patriotism" of the framers of the Fourteenth Amendment that he urged the Attorney General to repudiate "the very objectionable Brief of Mr. Conrad."[70]

Evarts and Ashton argued that the Fourteenth Amendment's Citizenship Clause did more than just affirm the traditional common law rule of birthright citizenship; its framers intended to set aside "prejudice by *race* and pretension by *caste*." On the heels of a war "for which the country had paid so dearly in costly treasure and still more costly blood," argued Ashton, the framers of the Fourteenth Amendment understood the far-reaching nature of the Citizenship Clause and had no desire to retain any restrictions on race, color, or descent which might create future discord of the type leading to the Civil War. Conrad had turned to antebellum Southern jurists and politicians to bolster his cause. Evarts, a New Englander, ended his brief with a rousing quote from Charles Sumner, the abolitionist and Radical Republican, on the meaning of the "great Amendment": "Here is the great charter of every human being, *drawing vital breath upon this soil*, whatever may be his condition and *whoever may be his parents*. He may be poor, weak, humble, or black—he may be Caucasian, Jewish, Indian or Ethiopian race—he may be of French, German, English or Irish extraction; but before the Constitution all these distinctions disappear.... He is one of the children of the State, which like an impartial parent, regards all its offspring with an equal care."[71]

Though they made impassioned appeals to principles of equality, Evarts and Ashton homed in on another issue they thought of greater importance in the *Wong Kim Ark* case: the impact different citizenship rules would have on national power. Conrad's brief had sought to limit national power, in the interest of preserving traditional understandings of federalism. Evarts and Ashton, however, spoke as men of the future, concerned to shore up the sovereign power of the United States at a time when it was on the brink of becoming a major player in world affairs. By the 1890s, the United States was emerging as one of the world's leading economic powers and, by 1900, an imperial power with increasing influence in the Pacific and Latin America. In the cultural and political realm, the new nationalism led to the creation of patriotic rites, such as the flag salute in public schools, as well as to a rush to war with Spain in 1898.[72] In the legal arena, the Supreme Court bolstered national power through several decisions upholding congressional authority to police the national borders, to exercise greater unilateral control over Indians, and to deny suffrage to polygamists in Utah Territory as part of the congressional campaign against the Mormons.[73]

This nationalistic approach by Evarts and Ashton may seem surprising, for it echoed arguments made earlier by exclusionists to *deny* rights to Chinese residents, though to a much different end—here to *defend* the rights of the aliens' children. Though we cannot know their specific intent, this choice may have been for strategic reasons. Evarts and Ashton certainly knew firsthand, from representing Chinese in the *Fong*

Yue Ting and *Lem Moon Sing* cases, that the Supreme Court was committed to broad national power when it came to immigrants and resident aliens. In those earlier cases, they had personally argued—unsuccessfully—that Congress did not have unfettered power to exclude or deport resident aliens. But the Court had consistently upheld Congress' plenary control over immigration policy and its enforcement, on the grounds that the nation had an inherent sovereign power to "preserve its independence and give security against foreign aggression and encroachment."[74]

Building on this approach, Evarts and Ashton took umbrage at the suggestion of Collins and Conrad that the United States would have to bow to another country's decisions on membership. Acceding to the law of descent, which would compel the United States to recognize residents born here as foreign nationals subject to foreign jurisdictions, was tantamount to allowing another country to meddle in American affairs. Why have the Monroe Doctrine, limiting foreign interference in the Western Hemisphere, if the government was going to hand over the definition of citizenship—the very heart of sovereign power—to foreign countries? Evarts and Ashton trumpeted, instead, the absolute sovereign power of the United States—and all nations—"to determine the condition of persons, as citizens or aliens, within the territory of the State."[75]

The two sides thus posed a distinct choice for the Supreme Court justices. The government emphasized the problem of allegiance in an era of growing ethnic and racial diversity. Wong Kim Ark's attorneys stressed the challenge of the national government to police its territorial and political borders at a time of growing international competition. The attorneys would wait a full year before hearing the Court's final judgment.

The Supreme Court's Decision

Finally, on March 28, 1898, a divided Supreme Court ruled in favor of Wong Kim Ark, by a vote of 6–2.[76] Both the majority and dissenting opinions were lengthy and thorough, revealing, as legal scholar Bernadette Meyler argues, that the outcome in *Wong Kim Ark* "did not appear inevitable" to the Justices, nor "to contemporary commentators."[77] The unusual delay between argument and decision may have resulted from special efforts by Chief Justice Melville W. Fuller, who ultimately dissented, to persuade a majority to rule for the government.[78]

Justice Horace Gray, writing for the Court, followed the essential arguments laid out by Wong Kim Ark's attorneys on three major points. First, he found the common law precedent of birthright citizenship too well-rooted to abandon at that point of the nation's history. The Court held that the persistent and widespread application of the *jus soli* "irresistibly" led to the conclusion that the Fourteenth Amendment intended to reaffirm "the ancient and fundamental rule" of birthright citizenship.[79] Second, the Court worried about the substantial practical difficulties of a government victory in *Wong Kim Ark*, noting that it would "deny citizenship to thousands of persons of English, Scotch, Irish, German or other European parentage, who have always been considered and treated as citizens of the United States."[80] Despite efforts by Conrad and other legal commentators to argue that Chinese could be singled out as the only group affected by the adoption of *jus sanguinis*, the Court found such a result neither practical nor consistent with earlier cases which had held that Chinese have the same rights as other aliens.[81] The Court endorsed the more inclusive vision of the polity, noting that the framers had explicitly considered and accepted the possibility that the Fourteenth Amendment would result in birthright citizenship for children of Chinese immigrants.

Finally, and perhaps most importantly, the Court acted to affirm the sovereign power of the national government over its territory and those who resided within. "It can not be doubted," wrote Justice Gray for the majority, "that it is the inherent right of every independent nation to determine for itself, and according to its own constitution and laws, what classes of persons shall be entitled to citizenship." Gray had been the author of the *Fong Yue Ting* decision which had upheld the sweeping power granted to Congress to deport aliens at will and by any process it thought proper. That decision had been controversial, but Gray, in *Wong Kim Ark*, remained committed to the doctrine of sovereign national power and responded to the arguments made by Evarts and Ashton about the importance of protecting national self-determination. Gray focused on obedience to the laws as the essential element of allegiance, and on the authority of the national government to compel the obedience of all within its geographical boundaries. In its analysis of the nature of national jurisdiction, the Court relied heavily on Chief Justice John Marshall's broad statement that "the jurisdiction of the nation within its own territory is necessarily exclusive and absolute," reaching aliens as well as citizens. It was a rule well suited to justifying the expansion of federal authority, especially over immigration, in the late nineteenth century.[82]

The government's attorneys did win over the dissenting justices, Chief Justice Fuller and John Marshall Harlan. While Gray championed the heritage of the common law and the power of the national government, Fuller and Harlan proved more susceptible to concerns about allegiance, despairing that the children of Chinese—of "a distinct race and religion, remaining strangers in the land"—could become citizens by mere "accident of birth."[83] At first glance, Harlan's participation in the dissent seems odd, given his previously stated views on racial equality

before the law and his endorsement of the Fourteenth Amendment as a
revolutionary expansion of national power. Justice Harlan, only two
years earlier in his stinging dissent to *Plessy v. Ferguson*, had pronounced that "our Constitution is color-blind" and should not be read to
endorse racial inequality. He had also dissented in *Elk v. Wilkins*, on the
grounds that Native Americans who had left their tribes and assimilated
into white American society should be considered American citizens
under the Fourteenth Amendment. But, as historian Linda Przybyszewski argues, Harlan saw the Chinese as fundamentally different, in terms
of their racial and cultural identities and their ability to be part of
America's unique republican experience.[84] Neither Fuller, the author of
the dissent, nor Harlan believed that the American law of citizenship
should be read to make citizens of individuals who, in their opinion,
would never be able to develop a true allegiance to the country.

Picking up on George Collins' arguments about the feudal roots of
birthright citizenship, Fuller emphasized that the common law rule of
jus soli insisted upon perpetual and involuntary allegiance, a notion at
direct odds with the American republican emphasis that individuals
chose to become part of political communities and could also opt out of
them through expatriation. Fuller insisted that the United States had
always recognized the right to change one's nationality through expatriation, even in the absence of direct statutory provisions—a factor which
proved that the common law rule had not been adopted in the United
States.[85] The recognition of expatriation rested on the country's experience as an immigrant nation. "Expatriation included not simply the
leaving of one's native country, but the becoming naturalized in the
country adopted as a future residence," explained Fuller. But only
certain types of immigrants were desired: "The emigration which the
United States encouraged was that of those who could become incorporate with its people; make its flag their own; and aid in the accomplish-
ment of a common destiny."[86]

Children born in the United States of Chinese residents presented
two difficulties. First, their parents' native country did not recognize the
right of expatriation, thus raising the abhorrent specter of "double
allegiance," or dual citizenship, in today's parlance. Second, Chinese did
not fit the American model of immigration, as they were perceived as
remaining a separate people, and had thus been excluded from the polity
as immigrants and as potential citizens. For these reasons, Wong Kim
Ark's parents could never be fully "subject to the jurisdiction of the
United States" as required by the Fourteenth Amendment, Fuller argued. Their children likewise remained, in Fuller's opinion, "pilgrims
and sojourners" in the United States, "subject to the same sovereignty
as their parents."[87] The dissenters' culturalist interpretation of the

Fourteenth Amendment would remain part of the political dialogue on citizenship.

Thus, the journey of Wong Kim Ark through the courts came to an end—a relief, no doubt, to him but also to the Justices, as a poem penned by Justice David Brewer and circulated privately at the Court suggests:

> At last the end of Wong!
>
> We've studied, written long,
>
> And may be wholly wrong;
>
> Yet join the happy song,
>
> Goodby, goodby to Wong.[88]

The Legacy of Wong Kim Ark

The fate of Wong Kim Ark, the litigant, is difficult to discern from the historical records. Having been declared a citizen by the U.S. Supreme Court, he does not reappear in the immigration records nor can his subsequent life be traced with any certainty through census or other government registers. We do not know whether he married, what occupation he pursued, where he lived, or when he died. Nor do we know what significance he attached to his American citizenship, whether he viewed it strategically, primarily as a shield from the discriminatory exclusion laws, or, like those Chinese Americans who belonged to the Native Sons of the Golden State, embraced his American citizenship as an essential aspect of his personal and political identity.[89]

Although Wong Kim Ark and his attorneys won the battle and established the "color-blind" principle of birthright citizenship, the allegiance of Chinese Americans—and, indeed, of Asian Americans generally—would continually be called into question. Asian Americans would face ongoing challenges to their legal status as citizens on the grounds that they were not "real" citizens. Immigration officials referred to Chinese Americans as "accidental" or "technical" citizens and subjected their cases to more searching scrutiny. Exclusionists would regularly propose constitutional amendments to deny children of Asian residents birthright citizenship or the right to vote. By 1924, Congress had also extended the exclusion policy to all Asians, and courts had denied naturalization to Japanese and Asian Indians, as well as to Chinese.[90] Nor were the rights of Asian American citizens secure. Even though the Court had insisted on a national definition of citizenship, for decades it also left it up to the states to determine what rights citizens would have in practice.[91] Just as African Americans experienced "second-class citizenship," Asian Americans confronted such local discriminatory measures as residential and school segregation. When World War II broke out, thousands of Japanese Americans would be interned by the federal government, on the grounds that they belonged to an "enemy race" whose "racial strains are undiluted," despite their birth in the United States. Throughout much of modern American history, then, Asian Americans would remain, in Mae Ngai's words, "alien citizens," citizens by birth, but alien in the eyes of the dominant society.[92]

If *Wong Kim Ark* did not immediately secure the position of Asian Americans in the polity, the Court's ruling nonetheless did provide a rare legal toehold for their tenuous position in American society and for sustaining and expanding Asian American communities. When, for example, California passed the Alien Land Laws of 1920, forbidding those who were "ineligible for citizenship"—i.e., Asians—from owning or leasing land, Japanese farmers protected their property and livelihoods by placing the deeds in the names of their citizen children. *Wong Kim Ark* provided a strategic buffer for Asians and their American-born children, as well as an important symbolic victory in its "affirmation of the legal rights of an unpopular racial minority in the face of powerful opposition and hostility."[93] More generally, the principle of birthright citizenship established by *Wong Kim Ark* became the settled doctrine, though it certainly did not resolve many thorny questions that arose in the next century in response to the expansion of American imperial power and the resurgence of global migration.

Ironically, on the day that the Supreme Court handed down its long-awaited opinion in *Wong Kim Ark*, *The New York Times* gave it scant attention, reporting its decision in a brief paragraph buried on its back pages. Instead, Americans' eyes were on Congress, as crowds "stormed the galleries" of the House and Senate to hear the President's report on the sinking of the battleship *Maine* in Havana, Cuba, an incident which would be used to justify the United States' declaration of war on Spain a month later. The Spanish–American War would lead to the American acquisition of the insular territories of the Philippines and Puerto Rico, and to new disputes about race, culture and American citizenship as legislators and judges debated the political status of the territorial inhabitants.[94]

In the late twentieth century, the globalization of the economy and the accompanying surge in immigration to the United States and other countries raised a host of issues, both familiar and novel, about citizenship, ranging from the acceptability of dual nationality to new challenges to birthright citizenship. In 1985, for example, Peter Schuck and Rogers Smith argued that the Fourteenth Amendment, because grounded on a consensual idea of citizenship, did not require birthright citizenship for the native-born children of undocumented aliens. Their proposal sparked a contentious contemporary debate about the theoretical and practical implications of American citizenship rules.[95] More recently, a growing number of scholars have challenged the coherence of the very premise of *Wong Kim Ark*, which grounded birthright citizenship upon the nation state's sovereign power over its territorial boundaries. They argue that a plural, transnational citizenship, transcending geopolitical borders, better fits the realities and needs of a global order.[96] Yet the birthright citizenship doctrine of *Wong Kim Ark* has remained intact for over a century, still perceived by most to be a natural and well-established rule in accordance with American principles and practice. It is unlikely to be uprooted easily.

ENDNOTES

1.   United States v. Wong Kim Ark, 169 U.S. 649 (1898).

2.   Marshall B. Woodworth, Who are Citizens of the United States?, 32 Am. L. Rev. 554 (July–Aug. 1898).

3.   Rogers M. Smith, Civic Ideals: Conflicting Visions of Citizenship in U.S. History 115–16 (1997); Bernadette Meyler, The Gestation of Birthright Citizenship, 1868–1898: States' Rights, the Law of Nations, and Mutual Consent, 15 Geo. Immigr. L. Rev. 519, 526–27 (2001); James H. Kettner, The Development of American Citizenship, 1608–1870, at 224–32, 287–88, 317–18 (1978).

4.   Calvin's Case, 7 Co. Rep. 1 (1608). On *Calvin's Case,* see Kettner, Development of American Citizenship at 16–28 (cited in note 3); Smith, Civic Ideals, 44–49 (cited in note 3); Polly J. Price, Natural Law and Birthright Citizenship in Calvin's Case, 9 Yale J. L. & Human. 73 (Winter 1997).

5.   Kettner, Development of American Citizenship at 173–209, 287 (cited in note 3); James Brown Scott, Nationality: *Jus Soli* or *Jus Sanguinis*?, 24 Am. J. Int'l L. 58, 59 (1930).

6.   Benedict R. o'G. Anderson, Imagined Communities 145 (1983); Smith, Civic Ideals at 13–14, 15 (cited in note 3); Jonathan C. Drimmer, The Nephews of Uncle Sam: The History, Evolution, and Application of Birthright Citizenship in the United States, 9 Geo. Immigr. L.J. 667 (Fall 1995); Kettner, Development of American Citizenship at 8–9 (cited in note 3).

7.   See, e.g., Matthew Frye Jacobson, Whiteness of a Different Color 15–38 (1998); David Roediger, The Wages of Whiteness (1991); Reginald Horsman, Race and Manifest Destiny (1981).

8.   Linda K. Kerber, No Constitutional Right to be Ladies (1998); Leon F. Litwack, North of Slavery (1961).

9.   Matthew Frye Jacobson, Whiteness of a Different Color 22 (cited in note 7); see generally id. at 15–38; Gary B. Nash, Race and Revolution (1990).

10.   Scott v. Sandford, 60 U.S. 393, 406–07, 404–05 (1857). Such a rationale was not limited to southern courts, nor to southern justices, however. Litwack, North of Slavery at 85–86 (cited in note 8).

11.   Charles A. Beard and Mary A. Beard, II The Rise of American Civilization 52, 53–54, 99–105 (1927).

12.   Address at Gettysburg, Nov. 19, 1863.

13.   U.S. Const., amend. XIV, sec. 1. The Civil Rights Act of 1866 foreshadowed the Fourteenth Amendment in its provision that all persons born in the United States, but not subject to a "foreign power," nor those Indians "not taxed," were citizens. The Fourteenth Amendment sought to give the act a constitutional foundation. On the revolutionary

nature of Reconstruction, see Robert J. Kaczorowski, To Begin the Nation Anew: Congress, Citizenship, and Civil Rights after the Civil War, 92 Am. Hist. Rev. 45 (Feb. 1987); Eric Foner, Reconstruction: America's Unfinished Revolution, 1863–1877 (1988); and Rogers Smith, Civic Ideals at 305 (cited in note 3). For contrary historical interpretations of Reconstruction, see Kaczorowski, supra, To Begin the Nation Anew at 45–47, and William E. Nelson, The Fourteenth Amendment 1–12 (1988).

14. Thomas Nast, Uncle Sam's Thanksgiving Dinner, 13 Harpers Weekly 745 (Nov. 20, 1869).

15. Statistics derived from U.S. Department of Commerce, Bureau of the Census, Historical Statistics of the United States, Colonial Times to 1970, Part 1, Series C228–295, C195–227 (1975).

16. G. Frederick Keller, Uncle Sam's Thanksgiving Dinner, 2 The Wasp (Nov. 24, 1877).

17. Campbell J. Gibson and Emily Lennon, Historical Census Statistics on the Foreign–Born Population of the United States: 1850–1990, tables 1 and 2 (U.S. Bureau of the Census, Population Division, Working Paper no. 25, 1999), available at <http://www.census.gov/population/www/documentation/twps0029/twps0029.html>; Shih–Shan Henry Tsai, The Chinese Experience in America, map II (1986).

18. Chinese Exclusion Act of 1882, 22 Stat. 54, ch. 126.

19. For a useful overview of historians' explanations for exclusion, see Andrew Gyory, Closing the Gate 3–16 (1998). On racial and cultural arguments, see Stuart Creighton Miller, The Unwelcome Immigrant (1969); Jacobson, Whiteness of a Different Color at 39–46, 158–61 (cited in note 9); Thomas F. Gossett, Race: The History of an Idea in America 289–94 (1963).

20. Cong. Rec., 47th Cong. 1st Sess. 1486 (1882).

21. See H. Bruce Franklin, War Stars 33–34 (1988); William F. Wu, The Yellow Peril 34–37 (1982). As early as 1854, for example, the California Supreme Court relied on similar arguments and fears in reaching its decision to deny Chinese the right to testify against white persons in legal proceedings, warning that if the state granted Chinese the right to testify as witnesses, they might soon exercise "all the equal rights of citizenship, and we might soon see them at the polls, in the jury box, upon the bench, and in our legislative halls." People v. Hall, 4 Cal. 399, 404 (1854).

22. Quoted in John Hayakawa Torok, Reconstruction and Racial Nativism, 3 Asian L.J. 55, 92 (May 1996).

23. Act of July 14, 1870, ch. 254, sec. 7, 16 Stat. 256.

24. Naturalization of Chinese, Sacramento Union 2 (April 18, 1878); Charles J. McClain, In Search of Equality 70–73 (1994); In re Ah Yup, 1 F. Cas. 223 (C.C.D. Cal. 1878); Act of May 6, 1882, 22 Stat. 58, sec. 14. In 1943, Congress repealed the Chinese exclusion law and also extended the privilege of naturalization to Chinese—a belated conciliation toward a wartime ally. Act of Dec. 17, 1943, ch. 344, sec. 3, 57 Stat. 601. In 1952, the Immigration and Naturalization Act eliminated race as a requirement for naturalization altogether. Act of June 27, 1952, tit. 3, ch. 2, sec. 311, 66 Stat. 163, 239. For useful overviews of Asians and U.S. citizenship policy, see Charles J. McClain, Tortuous Path, Elusive Goal, 2 Asian L.J. 33 (May 1995); Leti Volpp, "Obnoxious to Their Very Nature": Asian Americans and Constitutional Citizenship, 5 Citizenship Stud. 57 (2001).

25. The figures are approximate, drawn from the U.S. census. They reflect those who *claimed* birth in U.S., including those who were actually born here and those who had been born in China but sought to evade the Chinese exclusion laws through false citizenship claims. For figures and discussions of the extent to which they include fraudulent claims, see Sue Fawn Chung, Fighting for Their American Rights, in K. Scott Wong and Sucheng

Chan, eds., Claiming America: Constructing Chinese American Identities during the Exclusion Era 95–97 (1998); Madeline Yuan-Yin Hsu, Dreaming of Gold, Dreaming of Home 74–85 (2000); Yong Chen, Chinese San Francisco, 1850–1943, 52–60 (2000).

26. 1 Sand. 583 (N.Y. 1844).

27. George D. Collins, Are Persons Born within the United States Ipso Facto Citizens Thereof?, 18 Am. L. Rev. 831, 836 (1884).

28. See Meyler, Gestation of Birthright Citizenship at 538–45 (cited in note 3). Morse would successfully argue for Louisiana, in *Plessy v. Ferguson* in 1896, that states retained primary control over defining the substantive rights of their citizens. Plessy v. Ferguson, 163 U.S. 537 (1896).

29. Prentiss Webster, Acquisition of Citizenship, 23 Am. L. Rev. 759 (1889); Meyler, The Gestation of Birthright Citizenship at 545–548 (cited in note 3). On Collins, see The Bay of San Francisco 456–57 (Lewis Pub'g Co. 1892).

30. See Peter J. Spiro, Dual Nationality and the Meaning of Citizenship, 46 Emory L.J. 1411 (Fall 1997).

31. Collins at 834 (cited in note 27). Even some who supported *jus soli* in general sought to find a rationale to deny birthright citizenship to Chinese. One such argument asserted that Chinese could be treated differently because they were not truly domiciled in the United States; they remained sojourners, and would "return, sooner or later, to China." Henry C. Ides, Citizenship by Birth—Another View, 30 Am. L. Rev. 241, 246, 247, 250 (1896).

32. In re Look Tin Sing, No. 3477 (1884), Circuit Court Casefiles, U.S. Circuit Court for the Northern District of California, Records of the District Courts of the United States, RG 21, National Archives, San Francisco Branch; McClain, In Search of Equality 163–64 (cited in note 24); A Chinese Lad, San Francisco Morning Call 1 (Sept. 28, 1884).

33. The oral arguments are reported in Agreed to Disagree, San Francisco Evening Bulletin 3 (Sept. 29, 1884); A Chinese Lad, San Francisco Morning Call 1 (Sept. 28, 1884). George Collins was probably a student of Professor Pomeroy's. He attended Hastings College at the time of the *Look Tin Sing* case, and reported later that he and Pomeroy had discussed the case with Judge Sawyer, a member of the panel deciding the case.

34. Agreed to Disagree, San Francisco Evening Bulletin at 3 (cited in note 33). On Stewart's shifting positions regarding the Chinese, see McClain, In Search of Equality at 37–40 (cited in note 24).

35. In re Look Tin Sing, 21 F. 905, 909, 906, 910–11 (C.C.D. Cal. 1884).

36. Lucy E. Salyer, Laws Harsh as Tigers (1995).

37. For a variety of reasons—Chinese cultural preferences as well as the hostility of Americans to intermarriage manifested in miscegenation laws—Chinese American men often married Chinese wives, who remained in China. See Hsu, Dreaming of Gold, Dreaming of Home at 90–123 (cited in note 25).

38. In re Chae Chan Ping, 36 F. 431 (C.C.D. Cal. 1888), aff'd as The Chinese Exclusion Case, 130 U.S. 581 (1889). See Chapter 1 in this volume.

39. John T. Carey to Attorney General, Oct. 27, 1888, File 980–84, Letters Received, Year File, Central File, Records of the Department of Justice, RG 60, National Archives and Records Administration.

40. Salyer, Laws Harsh as Tigers at 97–99 (cited in note 36); Chinese Triumph—The Collector Cannot Exclude the Native Sons!, San Francisco Call 8 (Nov. 16, 1894); The Question of Citizenship, San Francisco Call 9 (Feb. 8, 1896).

41. A Chinese League, San Francisco Call 6 (May 26, 1897); To Americanize Chinamen, New York Times 1 (Apr. 4, 1897); Qingsong Zhang, The Origins of the Chinese

Americanization Movement: Wong Chin Foo and the Chinese Equal Rights League, in K. Scott Wong and Sucheng Chan, eds., Claiming America at 41–63 (cited in note 25).

42. A Chinese League, San Francisco Call at 6 (cited in note 41); Editorial, New York Times 4 (Dec. 18, 1892).

43. Dawn of Danger, San Francisco Call 3 (Nov. 12, 1894); Sue Fawn Chung, Fighting for Their American Rights: A History of the Chinese American Citizens Alliance, in Wong and Chan, eds., Claiming America at 95–126 (cited in note 25).

44. Wong Chin Foo quoted in Zhang, Origins of the Chinese Americanization Movement at 48 (cited in note 41).

45. A Chinese League, San Francisco Call at 6 (cited in note 41); The Wong Kim Ark Case, San Francisco Call 19 (Mar. 29, 1896).

46. Henry S. Foote to Holmes Conrad, Nov. 6, 1895, File 10613, Box 857, Letters Received, Straight Numerical Files, Department of Justice, RG 60; Attorney Collins' Part, San Francisco Call 11 (Nov. 14, 1895); Judge Field Criticized, San Francisco Call 10 (June 21, 1895).

47. See correspondence in File 10613, especially Collins to Secretary of Treasury, July 11, 1895; Collins to Holmes Conrad, Aug. 19, 1895; Foote to Conrad, Nov. 6, 1895; Foote to Attorney General, Aug. 8, 1895, Letters Received, Department of Justice (cited in note 46).

48. The Chinese Consolidated Benevolent Association (CCBA) was better known to the white American community as the "Chinese Six Companies." It provided service and informal governance for the Chinese immigrant community. As hostility to Chinese in the United States grew, the CCBA took a leading role in opposing anti-Chinese sentiment. See, e.g., McClain, Search for Equality at 14–15 (cited in note 24); Chen, Chinese San Francisco at 71–73 (cited in note 25). On administrative procedures in Chinese exclusion cases, see Salyer, Laws Harsh as Tigers at 17–23, 37–45, 58–68 (cited in note 36); Erika Lee, At America's Gates 77–109 (2003). On Chinese hiring of American lawyers to challenge discriminatory laws, see McClain, The Search for Equality at 102 (cited in note 24); Salyer, Laws Harsh as Tigers at 70–72 (cited in note 36).

49. Petition for Writ of Habeas Corpus, In re Wong Kim Ark, No. 11198, Admiralty Casefiles, 1891–1924, U.S. District Court for the Northern District of California, Records of the District Courts of the United States, RG 21, National Archives, San Francisco Branch.

50. Slaughter–House Cases, 83 U.S. 36 (1873); Elk v. Wilkins, 112 U.S. 94 (1884).

51. 83 U.S. at 73 (emphasis added).

52. The lawyers' arguments are outlined in their briefs, filed in the district court. See Brief on Behalf of the United States, submitted by George D. Collins, and Points and Authorities of the United States, submitted by Henry S. Foote, in In re Wong Kim Ark, No. 11198, Admiralty Casefiles (cited in note 49). See also Chinese as Citizens, San Francisco Call 5 (Jan. 4, 1896). Similar arguments were made on appeal in the Supreme Court. See, e.g., Brief for the United States at 41 and Reply Brief for the United States at 6–10, United States v. Wong Kim Ark, 169 U.S. 649 (1898).

53. See, e.g., Frederick E. Hoxie, A Final Promise (1984); Sandra L. Cadwalader and Vine Deloria, Jr., The Aggressions of Civilization (1984). Later statutes did extend citizenship to Native Americans, but without calling into question the constitutional ruling of *Elk v. Wilkins.*

54. Points and Authorities of United States [Foote], In re Wong Kim Ark, Admiralty Casefiles at 3–5, 6–7 (Cited in note 49). For similar arguments in the Supreme Court, see Brief for the United States [Conrad] at 37–41, and Brief on Behalf of the Appellant [Collins] at 22–26, United States v. Wong Kim Ark (cited in note 52).

55. Brief on Behalf of the United States [Collins], In re Wong Kim Ark, Admiralty Casefiles, at 7, 5. 4, 6 (cited in note 49).

56. Id. At 4, 6.

57. Henry C. Ides, Citizenship by Birth—Another View, 30 *Amer.L.R.* 241 (Mar–Apr 1896), 246, 247, 250. Morrow supported the policy of Chinese exclusion and, as a congressional representative before his appointment as a federal judge, had sponsored legislation to strengthen those laws. Salyer, Laws Harsh as Tigers at 33–34, 72, 86–87, 96–99, 109 (cited in note 36).

58. In re Wong Kim Ark, 71 F. 382, 392 (N.D. Cal. 1896).

59. The Question of Citizenship, San Francisco Call 9 (Feb. 8, 1896); Chinese as Citizens, San Francisco Call at 5 (cited in note 52).

60. The Wong Kim Ark Case, San Francisco Call 19 (Mar. 29, 1896); Judge Field Criticized, San Francisco Call 10 (June 21, 1895); The Question of Citizenship, San Francisco Call 9 (Feb. 8, 1896); Citizenship by Birth, San Francisco Call 12 (June 18, 1895); Brief on Behalf of the Appellant [Collins], United States v. Wong Kim Ark at 32–33 (cited in note 52); Brief on Behalf of the United States [Collins] at 8–9, In re Wong Kim Ark, Admiralty Casefiles (cited in note 49).

61. 149 U.S. 698 (1893) (discussed in Chapter 1 of this volume).

62. See, e.g., Kaczorowski, To Begin the Nation Anew, (cited in note 13); Foner, Reconstruction: America's Unfinished Revolution (cited in note 13).

63. Plessy v. Ferguson, 163 U.S. 537 (1896).

64. On reconciliation and racism, see Nina Silber, The Romance of Reunion 124–58 (1993); Cecilia Elizabeth O'Leary, To Die For 112–28 (2000).

65. Conrad, Holmes, in 4 Dictionary of American Biography, 1928–1936, at 354–55 (base set 1930). Conrad participated in the "rituals of reconciliation," traveling to Chicago to deliver a speech entitled "Our United Country" at the dedication of a Confederate War Memorial in 1895 but his brief suggested that he continued to contest certain outcomes of the war. See The Blue and the Gray, New York Times (June 2, 1895); Silber, Romance of Reunion at 172–73 (cited in note 64).

66. Brief for the United States [Conrad], United States v. Wong Kim Ark at 8–9, 15–17, 46–50 (cited in note 52). Conrad included in a footnote a several-page excerpt from George Ticknor Curtis, Constitutional History of the United States, to support his point that the ratification of the Fourteenth Amendment was accomplished through an unconstitutional procedure.

67. His arguments were not unlike those of Alexander Porter Morse, a treatise writer who later defended Louisiana's segregation law in *Plessy v. Ferguson* (discussed in note 28 and accompanying text).

68. Brief for the United States [Conrad], United States v. Wong Kim Ark at 11–12, 13 (cited in note 52); United States v. Cruikshank, 92 U.S. 542, 549 (1876); Amy v. Smith, 11 Ky. 326 (1822).

69. Brief for the Appellee, [submitted by J. Hubley Ashton], United States v. Wong Kim Ark, 169 U.S. 649 (1898), at 16, 93–94 ("Ashton Brief"); Brief of the Appellee [submitted by Maxwell Evarts] at 65, 28 ("Evarts Brief"); Inglis v. Trustees of the Sailor's Snug Harbor, 28 U.S. 99, 155 (1830).

70. Collins to Attorney General, March 6, 1897, File 10613, Box 857, Letters Received, Straight Numerical Files, Department of Justice.

71. Ashton Brief at 8, 12; Evarts Brief at 66 (emphasis added by the brief-writer) (cited in note 69).

72. O'Leary, To Die For at 150–93 (cited in note 64).

73. United States v. Kagama, 118 U.S. 375, 379–80 (1886); Murphy v. Ramsey, 114 U.S. 15 (1885); Sarah Barringer Gordon, The Mormon Question 149–64 (2002); Sarah H. Cleveland, Powers Inherent in Sovereignty, 81 Tex. L. Rev. 1 (2002).

74. Chae Chan Ping v. United States, 130 U.S. 581, 606 (1889); Fong Yue Ting v. United States, 149 U.S. 698 (1893); Nishimura Ekiu v. United States, 142 U.S. 651 (1891); Lem Moon Sing v. United States, 158 U.S. 538 (1895). See Chapter 1 of this volume. Both Evarts and Ashton served as appellate attorneys in *Fong Yue Ting*; Evarts represented Lem Moon Sing on his own.

75. Ashton Brief at 69, 66 (cited in note 69). Evarts stressed that the recognition of Indian tribes as sovereign nations was exceptional, an acknowledgment that "they were the original inhabitants of the country." Evarts Brief at 27 (cited in note 69).

76. Justice Joseph McKenna did not participate in the decision, probably because he was appointed in 1898, after the case had been argued.

77. Meyler, Gestation of Birthright Citizenship at 519 (cited in note 3).

78. James W. Ely, Jr., mentions that the "justices debated the matter for nearly two years," and that the Chief Justice "worked hard for his position" that Wong Kim Ark was *not* a citizen. Quoting another biographer, Ely says that "Fuller's inability to persuade his colleagues in *Wong Kim Ark* 'was perhaps his worst defeat on the Court.'. " James W. Ely, Jr., The Chief Justiceship of Melville W. Fuller 164–65 (1995); quoting Willard L. King, Melville Weston Fuller 235 (1950).

79. United States v. Wong Kim Ark, 169 U.S. 649, 655–66, 693 (1898).

80. Id. at 694.

81. Id. at 694–704.

82. Id. at 668, 683–88, 690, 693, quoting Justice Marshall in The Schooner Exchange v. M'Fadden, 11 U.S. 116, 136 (1812).

83. *Wong Kim Ark*, 169 U.S. at 731 (Fuller, C.J., dissenting).

84. In his dissent to *Plessy*, Harlan had referred to the Chinese, "a race so different from our own that we do not permit those belonging to it to become citizens of the United States," to highlight the injustice to done to "citizens of the black race" by the Louisiana statute providing for segregation in train cars. Chinese could ride "in the same passenger coach" with white citizens, while black citizens, "any of whom, perhaps, risked their lives for the preservation of the Union [and] are entitled, by law to participate in the political control of the State and nation, . . . are yet declared to be criminals, liable to imprisonment, if they ride in a public coach occupied by citizens of the white race." Linda Przybyszewski, The Republic According to John Marshall Harlan 118–22 (1999); Plessy v. Ferguson, 163 U.S. at 559, 561 (Harlan, J., dissenting); Elk v. Wilkins, 112 U.S. at 110–123; Gabriel J. Chin, The *Plessy* Myth, 82 Iowa L. Rev. 151 (Oct. 1996).

85. *Wong Kim Ark*, 169 U.S. at 731 (Fuller, C.J., dissenting). Although there was considerable support for expatriation, in principle, courts proved more ambivalent about recognizing expatriation in practice. Expatriation was not explicitly recognized until Congress passed the Act of July 27, 1868, ch. 249, 15 Stat. 223. Kettner, Development of American Citizenship, 267–84, 343–44 (cited in note 3).

86. *Wong Kim Ark*, 169 U.S. at 712 (Fuller, C.J., dissenting).

87. Id. at 720–32, especially 725, 726.

88. Scrapbooks on Court's History, vol. I, Clerks Office, Entry 56, Records of the Supreme Court of the United States, RG 267, National Archives and Records Administration, Washington, D.C. The poem contains two more verses in similar style ("No more, no more of Kim!" and "The last, the last of Ark!").

89. A search through the online manuscript census records for California turned up a couple of possible matches, but nothing definitive. The 1910 federal census lists a "Kim Wong" born in 1872, living in San Francisco, and an "Ark Wong," born in 1876, living in Los Angeles. Neither are exact matches. 1910 United States Federal Census, searchable at www.ancestry.com (2004).

90. Immigration Act of 1924, ch. 190, 43 Stat. 153 (1924); Ozawa v. United States, 260 U.S. 178 (1922); United States v. Thind, 261 U.S. 204 (1923) (holding that Japanese and Asian Indians, respectively, were not "white" within the meaning of the naturalization laws).

91. See, e.g., Plessy v. Ferguson, 163 U.S. 537 (1897).

92. Salyer, Laws Harsh as Tigers at 207–12 (cited in note 36); Mae Ngai, Impossible Subjects 8, 170, 175 (2004); Lucy E. Salyer, Baptism by Fire, J. Am. Hist. 847–76 (December 2004); Korematsu v. United States, 323 U.S. 214, 236 (1944); John S.W. Park, Elusive Citizenship (2004); Lisa Lowe, Immigrant Acts (1998).

93. Joseph H. Carens, Who Belongs?: Theoretical and Legal Questions about Birthright Citizenship in the United States, 37 U. Toronto L.J. 413, 436 (1987); Yuji Ichioka, The Issei: The World of the First–Generation Japanese Immigrant, 1885–1924 (1988); Roger Daniels, Politics of Prejudice (1973); David Yoo, Growing Up Nisei (2000); Xiaojian Zhao, Remaking Chinese America (2002); Shehong Chen, Being Chinese, Becoming Chinese American (2002).

94. Chinese Born Here are Citizens, New York Times 7 (Mar. 29, 1898); Congress Hears the News, New York Times 2 (Mar. 29, 1898); Christina Duffy Burnett and Burke Marshall, eds., Foreign in a Domestic Sense (2001).

95. Peter H. Schuck and Rogers M. Smith, Citizenship without Consent: Illegal Aliens in the American Polity (1985). The response to their proposal was enormous and varied. For examples, see Joseph Carens, Who Belongs? (cited in note 93); Bernadette Meyler, The Gestation of Birthright Citizenship (cited in note 3); Gerald L. Neuman, Back to Dred Scott?, 24 San Diego L. Rev. 485 (1987); David A. Martin, Membership and Consent: Abstract or Organic?, 11 Yale J. Int'l L. 278 (1985); Adam C. Abrahms, Closing the Immigration Loophole, 12 Geo. Immigr. L.J. 469 (Spring 1998).

96. Ngai, Impossible Subjects, 265–70 (cited in note 92) Linda Bosniak, Citizenship Denationalized, 7 Ind. J. Global Leg. Stud. 447 (Spring 2000); Noah M.J. Pickus, ed., Immigration and Citizenship in the Twenty–First Century (1998).

*

4

Harisiades v. Shaughnessy: A Case Study in the Vulnerability of Resident Aliens

Burt Neuborne

We owe the ancient Greeks a great debt for inventing the *polis*—a geographically-defined community of citizens who regard themselves as members of a self-contained political unit. When, at the close of the *Oresteia*, Orestes, guilty of matricide with an explanation,[1] is delivered from the Furies to the citizens of Athens for human judgment, notions of man-made law and the *polis* merge, paving the way for the modern state. Ever since, although we have argued bitterly about how law should be made and what it should say, the intellectual partnership between law and the *polis* has remained almost as constant as sex and the city.

But the very idea of the *polis* has a darker side. The concept of an inclusionary community of citizens with legal rights and duties linked to a shared political unit necessarily carries with it the seeds of the "alien-other" who lives outside the charmed circle that defines the political unit.

The limits of the circle can be conceptual or physical. The Athenians drew the conceptual circle relatively narrowly, including enough people to qualify Athens as the first experiment in democratic rule, but excluding women, slaves, paupers and aliens. Ever since, political theory has been dominated by a struggle to define and re-define the contours of that circle, ranging from efforts to draw it narrowly on the basis of divine right, physical strength, intellect, race, religion, ethnicity, gender, and wealth to efforts to enlarge the circle to encompass all who live in the community or under its rule.

The story of American law has been an ever-expanding circle of political membership, characterized by the establishment of democracy, relatively generous naturalization, the end of slavery, the banning of racial discrimination in access to the ballot, the political emancipation of women, the enfranchisement of eighteen-year-olds, the abolition of literacy tests for voting, and the elimination of all vestiges of property qualifications for full citizenship.

One group—aliens—has remained outside. Since the *polis* needs the counterpoint of the alien-other for its continued coherence, excluding aliens residing abroad from the circle is understandable, perhaps inevitable. Expanding it to include aliens living outside the geographical boundary of the *polis* challenges the very idea of a self-contained, inclusionary political unit; witness the halting efforts to build the European community, the agony of the American Civil War, the fight over the International Criminal Court, the contested status of the United Nations, and the contemporary disagreement over the judicial enforceability of customary international law.

But no such conceptual problem complicates the status of lawful permanent resident aliens (LPRs), persons who have been admitted to the *polis* for long-term residence, but who have not acquired citizenship. Should they be treated as being inside or outside the circle? The answer is of enormous practical importance to LPRs, ultimately defining the level of legal security they enjoy in their new homes. If LPRs are placed outside the circle, their status is fragile and vulnerable. In the chilling words of the distinguished panel of the Second Circuit in *Harisiades*, their "license to remain is revocable at the sovereign's will."[2]

If, on the other hand, LPRs are invited into the circle, they share many, if not all, the legal protections available to full citizens, including constitutional protection against banishment for controversial political or religious beliefs and associations.

Finally, as we shall see, if the circle is drawn in an irregular, arbitrary manner, the lives of LPRs exhibit a baffling mixture of legal protection and extreme vulnerability. This is the story of how the Supreme Court drew the circle very narrowly in *Harisiades v. Shaughnessy*, so narrowly that LPRs residing in the United States remain exposed to banishment during recurrent outbreaks of fear and mistrust.

The Holding in Harisiades: *The Court Draws a Small Circle*

Harisiades upheld the deportation, in 1952, of three LPRs, Peter Harisiades, Luigi Mascitti, and Dora Coleman, who had lived in the United States for a total of 106 years, had married United States citizens, and were parents of citizen-children.[3] Peter Harisiades had lived in the United States for thirty-six years since arriving from Greece at age thirteen with his father in 1916.[4] Luigi Mascitti had lived in the United States for thirty-two years since arriving from Italy at age sixteen in 1920. Dora Coleman had lived in the United States for thirty-eight years since arriving from Russia in 1914 at age thirteen. None of the three had ever been convicted of a crime.[5]

In each case, the sole basis for deportation was a long-terminated membership in the American Communist Party. Mascitti joined the precursor of the American Communist Party in 1923 when he was nineteen, but had resigned from the party by 1929 because he lost sympathy with it. Coleman joined the precursor of the American Communist Party in 1919, at age eighteen. She left the party after about a year, and re-joined twice for short periods during the 1930s, until finally terminating her membership in 1937 or 1938.

Harisiades, the most committed of the three to communism, joined the party in 1922, at age twenty-two. An active labor organizer, Harisiades held minor party office during the 1930s as Second Secretary of the New Jersey branch of the American Communist Party. He was a staff writer for the Greek ethnic Communist Party newspaper, *Empros/Forward*, and served as Secretary of the Greek Bureau of the American Communist Party from 1933–37.

Harisiades apparently came to the attention of federal authorities for the first time in April 1930, after he had been arrested a month earlier in connection with a textile strike in New Bedford, Massachusetts. During his interrogation at police headquarters, Harisiades admitted that he belonged to the Communist Party, but disclaimed any commitment to violence. He told the police that the communists wished to overthrow the government by politics, not violence. Criminal charges were eventually dismissed.

The immigration warrant for his deportation was issued one month after his arrest in 1930, but no effort appears to have been made to serve it until 1944, when Harisiades applied for citizenship for the second time.[6] The rather lame explanation offered by the government for the failure to have moved on the outstanding deportation warrant for at least fourteen years was that Harisiades had used a number of aliases during those years. No serious effort was made, however, to show that Harisiades had sought to avoid arrest between 1930–1944. Since his Greek birth-name was Panagiotis Hadjielas, the use of an anglicizing alias, then a common practice by Eastern European immigrants, was hardly surprising.

Harisiades never voluntarily terminated his association with the American Communist Party. In 1939, in a strategic move designed to take advantage of *Kessler v. Strecker*, a Supreme Court decision construing the governing statute to bar deportation for past Communist Party membership, the American Communist Party terminated the membership of all non-citizens, including Harisiades.[7]

At that point, Harisiades joined the International Workers Order, where he headed the Greek–American section of the IWO, which had between 1,000 and 1,600 members. He also worked during WW II as a propagandist for the Greek Resistance Movement, serving as General Manager of the *Greek-American Tribune*, the official newspaper of the Greek–American section of the IWO.[8] He organized bi-monthly meetings during the war, at which American and Soviet propaganda movies were shown, speakers calling for a second front in Europe were presented, and, perhaps most importantly, refreshments were served.

Harisiades was working at the IWO when he applied for citizenship in 1944. The government responded to the citizenship application by serving the 1930 deportation warrant. On May 2, 1946, Harisiades was arrested on the deportation warrant, and briefly jailed. The government quickly released him on his own recognizance pending deportation proceedings.

The government sought to deport Harisiades under a 1918 statute authorizing the deportation of "aliens who believe in, advise, advocate, or teach, or who are members of or affiliated with any organization, association, society or group that believes in, advises, advocates, or teaches the overthrow by force of violence of the Government of the United States." In *Kessler v. Strecker*,[9] the Supreme Court in 1939 had initially construed this statute narrowly to require proof of current, as opposed to past, membership in the proscribed organization in order to justify deportation. When the Communist Party responded to *Kessler* by terminating the membership of all non-citizens in order to shield them from deportation, Congress promptly overruled *Kessler*, explicitly authorizing deportation proceedings for past membership in a proscribed organization.

On October 15, 1946, Harisiades' deportation hearing commenced before a single INS inspector, Gilbert Zimmerman, who was expected— in accordance with the inquisitorial-type process then in place—both to introduce the government's case, and to render a decision on the merits. Harisiades was represented by Carol King, a noted immigration lawyer and civil rights advocate, who had represented him in connection with his application for citizenship. King, an active member of the National Lawyers' Guild,[10] and a General Counsel of the American Committee to Protect the Foreign Born, had defended a number of Communist Party members and sympathizers against deportation, including Harry Bridges, the leader of the West Coast Maritime Union.[11] King called two witnesses. Harisiades acknowledged a continuing commitment to communism, but disavowed any belief in violence, and denied that the Communist Party advocated the violent overthrow of the government. William Schneiderman, Chairman of the California Communist Party and its principal voice for peaceful political change, argued that American communists would come to power through electoral means, not violence. He explained that violence would be used only if the capitalist class refused to turn over power. The hearing was then adjourned until January, 1947.[12]

On January 21, 1947, with deportation proceedings pending against more than 100 aliens on the basis of former ties with the Communist Party, King persuaded the American Committee to Protect the Foreign Born (ACPFB)[13] to select Harisiades as a First Amendment test case to challenge the government's right to deport aliens for past Communist Party membership. Unlike Mascitti and Coleman, who appear to have voluntarily ended their relationship with the Communist Party long before deportation proceedings were commenced, Harisiades publicly proclaimed his continued allegiance to the party, and stated that he would have remained a Communist Party member if the party had not terminated the memberships of non-citizens in 1939.[14] Forty of Harisiades' Flatbush neighbors formed a Neighbors' Defense Committee, wrote letters on his behalf, and made small contributions to a legal defense fund. A nationwide group of clergy, the Committee for Clemency for Peter Harisiades, unsuccessfully petitioned Attorney General Tom Clark on his behalf. Union leaders throughout the United States rallied to his support. At one point, the ACPFB generated 50,000 post cards addressed to the Attorney General supporting Harisiades.

Harisiades' deportation hearing continued on January 30–31, 1947, when hearing officer Zimmerman introduced the government's case, a huge compendium of communist writings, designed to demonstrate that the Communist Party did, in fact, advocate the overthrow of the government by force and violence. On March 11, 1947, Zimmerman issued a sixty-five-page memorandum opinion recommending that Harisiades be deported to Greece on the basis of past membership in the Communist Party, but making a highly favorable factual finding that Harisiades was not currently a party member and had never personally advocated violence.

King had fought hard to retain Zimmerman as the INS hearing officer, apparently because she detected some sympathy in his actions. In a strategic move that would haunt the defense, King sought to keep Zimmerman in the case by explicitly waiving any claim that Zimmerman was violating the newly enacted Administrative Procedure Act (APA) by acting as both the prosecutor and the judge.[15] On May 13, 1947, the Board of Immigration Appeals denied Harisiades' appeal, recognizing that no charges could be sustained on the basis of personal belief or current membership, but finding that past membership alone was a sufficient ground for deportation. When King filed objections, the Commissioner decided on August 5, 1947 to re-open the proceedings to verify existing evidence and to present new evidence.

In October 1947, the government formally re-opened proceedings, seeking, over King's objections, to replace Zimmerman with two immigration examiners who had worked on the Harry Bridges case. The parties split the difference, with Zimmerman remaining as hearing officer, but with one of the examiners, Inspector Phelan, acting as prosecutor. On February 18, 1948, an FBI informant, identified as a former member of the Communist Party, testified that Stalin had urged the destruction of the United States in 1932, that 30,000 party members were receiving military training in upstate New York in preparation for the revolution, and that he had seen 300 men being trained in the basement of Communist Party headquarters to cause demonstrations and set up barricades. On March 9, 1948, the hearing concluded with additional testimony by William Schneiderman that "socialism can be instituted here by democratic means."

On June 24, 1948, Phelan, presenting the government's case, filed a 300–page report recommending deportation. On December 16, 1948, Zimmerman, as the hearing examiner, accepted the report and recommended deportation to Greece. On May 13, 1949, the Board of Immigration Appeals upheld the deportation order, although it reinstated the favorable findings about Harisiades' personal beliefs that Zimmerman had initially announced. After being held on Ellis Island for sixty-four days without bail at the direction of Attorney General Tom Clark, Harisiades was released pending habeas corpus review of his deportation order, which became final on December 16, 1949.

On February 9, 1950, the district court denied the habeas corpus application, applying a deferential "some evidence" standard of review that upheld Zimmerman's finding that the Communist Party advocated and taught the violent overthrow of the United States government.[16] The district court also held that mere membership in the Party at any time sufficed for deportation, regardless of Harisiades' personal views. The district court relied on Supreme Court dissents in *Kessler* and *Schneiderman* to support the argument that the Party is dedicated to the overthrow of the government by force and violence.

The Second Circuit affirmed, holding that Harisiades' deportation proceedings had commenced before the effective date of the APA, and that mere membership in the Communist Party was grounds for deportation, regardless of personal belief.[17] Judge Swan, writing for Learned Hand and Augustus Hand, held that "there is nothing in the Constitution which imposes on deportation officials the difficult and uncertain task of distinguishing between those members of a subversive group who individually advocate a forbidden course and those who do not.... Nor is it a valid objection that the ground for deportation is an act that occurred before the statute was adopted."[18] Significantly, however, the Second Circuit modified the deportation order to permit deportation to a country other than Greece, in order to avoid the possibility of physical persecution there.

On March 10, 1952, the Supreme Court affirmed the deportation orders, noting that Harisiades, Mascitti and Coleman had each disclaimed any personal belief in the use of force or violence, were not charged with any unlawful act, and had not been Communist Party members for between fourteen and twenty-three years. Nevertheless, the Court, in a 6–2 decision[19] authored by Justice Robert Jackson, upheld the deportations. In the Court's view, LPRs have no substantive constitutional right to remain in the United States, no matter how long they live among us, and no matter how flimsy the justification for banishment may be.[20] Echoing the Second Circuit panel in *Harisiades*, Justice Jackson noted that LPRs' "domicile here is held by precarious tenure," and found that deporting them solely for past membership in the American Communist Party, while harsh, did not violate the First Amendment, or constitute an unconstitutional ex post facto law.

Justices Douglas and Black dissented, noting that the deportations were premised, not on the LPRs' actions, or even on their current beliefs, but on what their political views once were. Constitutional protection against deportation solely for past beliefs should, argued Douglas and Black, be available to LPRs under the First Amendment because their long-time lawful residence here warranted protection against banishment based solely on past Party membership.

On November 12, 1952, Harisiades, accompanied by his wife Esther and his two children, was deported to Poland, where he had been offered political asylum. Esther, who was the American-born child of a naturalized citizen, lost her American citizenship. Settling in Warsaw, Harisiades worked as a broadcaster for the Polish state radio. On May Day, 1955, Harisiades personally offered radio greetings to the Polish people on behalf of "progressive American workers struggling against American imperialism." He never returned to the United States and remained a devoted communist until his death from cancer in 1973 in Warsaw at age seventy. Poland awarded Harisiades "The Golden Cross of Merit," and a ranking member of the Polish Communist Party delivered his eulogy.

The Road to Harisiades

The Supreme Court's decision in *Harisiades* stands at the confluence of two broad currents in American life and law: (1) a recurrent nativist tendency to fear the foreign-born as bearers of alien beliefs and customs that jeopardize "American" values; and (2) an intense fear, bordering on hysteria, during the late 1940s and the 1950s that domestic communists would succeed in subverting or violently overthrowing the American government.

Fear of Foreigners Bearing Dangerous Ideas

When Harisiades, Mascitti, and Coleman appeared before the Supreme Court in 1952, they did so against the background of 150 years of recurrent suspicion and persecution of aliens. Fear of foreigners bearing dangerous ideas begins early in American political history, despite the fact that everyone living in the American *polis*, including American Indians, either emigrated from abroad or is descended from immigrants. The French Revolution's death spiral into violence, bloody vengeance, and dictatorship triggered intense concern in the United States, especially among the propertied class. The Adams administration, confronted by propaganda efforts on behalf of the French government often accompanied by support for Thomas Jefferson in the upcoming presidential election of 1800, singled out foreign-born supporters of the French Revolution for special concern, pushing the Alien and Sedition Acts through the Federalist Congress in 1798 over the opposition of John Marshall, then Federalist leader in the House of Representatives.

The Alien Act of 1798 authorized the summary arrest and immediate deportation of aliens judged by the President as "dangerous to the peace and safety of the United States." No provision existed for judicial review. The passage of the statute caused a number of prominent supporters of the French Revolution to leave the country or go into hiding. The Alien Act expired in 1800, with no formal proceedings having been initiated under it.[21]

Mistrust of foreign ideas, fueled by an open-door immigration policy that encouraged large-scale immigration of cheap labor from Ireland and China, flared again between 1825 and 1860 in a series of political movements culminating in the "Know Nothings," a national political movement aimed at suppressing foreign influence. Briefly quite powerful, Know Nothings instigated widespread mob attacks on Masons, Catholics and Mormons.

As efforts increased to organize a nascent American labor movement, fear of aliens intensified, triggering a number of efforts to punish the foreign-born for spreading alien ideas. The Haymarket Riot of 1886, a violent confrontation between supporters of the Knights of Labor and the Chicago police, escalated after an unknown person threw a bomb, leaving eight policemen dead. Eight anarchist speakers and writers were convicted of murder based largely on their inflammatory speeches and writings in German and English;[22] one of them committed suicide in prison and four others were hanged. The remaining three were pardoned three years later by Governor Altgeld.

The economic depressions of the 1880s and 1890s triggered a surge of nativism that led to restrictions on immigration and the first summary, non-judicial deportation mechanism since the Alien Act of 1798.

The assassination of President McKinley in 1901 by a foreign-born anarchist cemented a volatile connection in the public's mind between foreigners, radical ideas, and violence, ushering in intense pressure to combat alien subversion that culminated in the Immigration Act of 1903, expressly aimed at excluding subversive and undesirable aliens.[23] The emergence in 1905 of the Industrial Workers of the World, an aggressive labor organization celebrating anarchism, led to violent clashes with state and local authorities, often couched as efforts to protect American institutions against overthrow by alien ideas.

America's entry into the First World War in 1917 led to a massive crackdown on anti-war speech.[24] Aliens were caught up in the general effort to suppress radical political activity. The Immigration Act of 1917, as amended in 1918, broadened efforts to exclude subversive ideas. With the establishment in 1918 of a communist regime in the Soviet Union, fear swept the United States that Bolshevik agitators would strike at American institutions. The post-war depression that began in 1919 led to a series of bitter strikes, and a nationwide wave of more than thirty bombings and attempted assassinations of public figures culminating in an unsuccessful bombing attempt on the life of Attorney General A. Mitchell Palmer. In 1920, Palmer, aided by a young FBI official named J. Edgar Hoover, invoked the 1918 immigration statute used in *Harisiades* to launch a series of raids against alien communists and political radicals, eventually arresting more than 4,000 aliens, often under disturbing circumstances that ignored warrants and due process of law. Although the number of formal deportations arising from the Palmer raids was relatively small, the impact on the foreign-born community was enormous, causing many thousands of aliens to leave the country or to avoid politics.

With the passing of this "Red Scare" in the early 1920s, the threat of deportation under the 1918 Act continued to be used against aliens engaged in radical political behavior. Indeed, the formal deportation order against Peter Harisiades was issued in 1930 in response to his labor organizing activity.

The tensions generated by the drift toward the Second World War resulted in the passage of the Alien Registration Act of 1940, which included the Smith Act, the first federal peacetime sedition law since the Alien and Sedition Acts of 1798.

The final stage for *Harisiades* was set by Congress' prompt overruling in 1940 of the Supreme Court's 1939 effort in *Kessler* to limit the 1918 deportation statute used in *Harisiades* to current, as opposed to past, political activity. Ironically, Congress' overruling of *Kessler* was almost certainly triggered by the Communist Party's obvious effort to exploit *Kessler* by terminating the formal membership of all non-citizens, thereby insulating them from deportation. If the Party had not sought to turn *Kessler* into a de facto amnesty from deportation, it is unlikely that Congress would have struck back by making the statute retroactive. Thus, the deportations of Coleman, Mascitti and people like them who had genuinely severed ties with the Party before 1939 may well have been caused by the Party's effort to protect aliens like Harisiades with continuing allegiance to the Party.

The McCarthy Era: Fear of Subversion by Domestic Communists

During the Cold War with the Soviet Union that followed WW II, the American Communist Party and its supporters occupied a highly ambivalent status in the minds of many Americans. The Party claimed to be a garden-variety, if intensely controversial, political organization engaged in electoral politics and political agitation. Large numbers of Americans were drawn to it because of its positions on particular social issues, especially its opposition to fascism, capital punishment, and racial discrimination, and its sustained critique of unfair working conditions which it claimed were endemic in a capitalist society. At its peak, the Party boasted some 60,000 members,[25] contested elections throughout the United States, and publicly proclaimed its intention of coming to power through democratic means. Vito Marcantonio, an avowed defender of the Communist Party, was repeatedly elected to Congress between 1935 and 1950 from East Harlem.[26] But many suspected the Party, or elements of the Party, of organizing a vast criminal conspiracy directed from Moscow bent on the subversion of American institutions and the violent overthrow of the government at the earliest opportunity.

The result in *Harisiades*, as well as the outcome of most of the McCarthy-era attacks on domestic communists, turned in large part on which of those views was accepted as correct, and how and by whom that knotty question was to be determined. In case after case, the crucial legal issue boiled down to whether the mere fact of past or present membership in the Party could be used as a proxy for persons posing an unacceptable current risk to American institutions.

In retrospect, this intense fear of domestic subversion and violent overthrow seems to have been hugely exaggerated. Before it ran its course, overreaction to the threat posed by domestic communism, often called McCarthyism, after Senator Joseph R. McCarthy of Wisconsin, whose repeated high decibel charges of communist subversion fueled the nation's anxiety attack,[27] blighted the lives of many thousands of persons who suffered loss of livelihood, prison and banishment merely because they once were too close to the Party. Recent scholarship made possible by the opening of Soviet archives has documented the post-WW II activities of Soviet intelligence agents in the United States.[28] Thus, the issue is not whether a communist threat existed during the McCarthy years, but whether the nation's response was disproportionate to the risk.

Why did we fear domestic communists so much during the McCarthy-era? One reason for the fear was the communist canon itself. The *Communist Manifesto*, written by Marx and Engels in 1848, is a summons to the violent overthrow of capitalist rule. Marx's later writings, and Lenin's additions to the communist scriptures, are replete with calls for violent action. Not surprisingly, given the inflammatory rhetoric favored by party spokesmen, and the secret, hierarchical nature of the Party's organization, American communists were feared by many as committed revolutionaries, taking orders from Moscow and cladestinely plotting the violent overthrow of American institutions at the first opportunity, just as the Nazis had overthrown the Weimar Republic by attaining power legitimately in 1933, and then dismantling the democratic process by force and violence.

While the WW II years saw an uneasy truce with American communists caused by the temporary wartime alliance with the Soviet Union against Nazi Germany, the end of WW II signaled an intense increase in the level of concern over domestic subversion by American communists. In part, the increased concern was a reaction to aggressive efforts by Stalin to impose communist regimes in Greece and Eastern Europe—a concern reflected in Winston Churchill's famous "Iron Curtain" speech at Fulton, Missouri in 1952. The concern also flowed from the expansion of communism into Asia, with the emergence of a communist-controlled China, the outbreak of a shooting war against communist expansion on the Korean peninsula, and the collapse of the French position in Indo-China. Finally, it flowed from anxiety over the Soviet Union's acquisition of nuclear weapons, an anxiety inflamed by the Rosenberg espionage trial, where three American communists, Julius and Ethel Rosenberg and Morton Sobell, were convicted of supplying the Soviet Union with what the government claimed was the secret of the atom bomb. The Rosenbergs were executed in 1952. Sobell was sentenced to thirty years in prison.

The most direct McCarthy-era assault on the Party was the successful effort to convict its leadership under the 1940 Smith Act for conspiracy to "knowingly or willfully" advocate or teach the propriety or desirability of overthrowing the government by force or violence. In July 1948, during the pendency of Harisiades' deportation hearing, twelve leaders of the Party were indicted, charged with teaching or advocating the violent overthrow of the government. One defendant's trial was severed because of ill health. The remaining eleven were convicted and sentenced to prison.[29] Their convictions were affirmed in an influential Second Circuit opinion authored by Learned Hand that deferred to the jury's judgment concerning the true nature of the Party, and treated exhortations to violence in the communist canon as a set of literal instructions, not rhetoric.[30] Influenced heavily by Hand's opinion, which required a jury finding of intent to use force and violence as speedily as circumstances would permit, the Supreme Court sustained the convictions in *Dennis v. United States*.[31] Justices Black and Douglas dissented.

In *Dennis*, the Court ducked the crucial question of whether the Party was really a giant criminal conspiracy, or was just an intensely controversial political organization addicted to angry rhetoric. Instead, the Court elected to treat the issue as closed because the trial jury had found that the Party was in fact advocating and preparing for the violent overthrow of the government as soon as possible, although that moment might be far in the future, and because the Second Circuit had ruled that sufficient evidence existed in the communist canon to support the jury's finding. The Court was able to do this because it had limited its review to legal issues,[32] explicitly denying review of the key factual findings upheld by the Second Circuit.[33]

Having accepted these findings, the *Dennis* opinion went on to hold that assessing the level of risk of a future overthrow was an issue for Congress, not the courts, and rejected the argument that the government was obliged to show a clear and present danger of imminent lawless action by someone in order to punish the leadership of the party. Justices Black and Douglas dissented, arguing that the defendants were not charged with specific wrongdoing, and that merely teaching and advocating the advisability of overthrowing the government at a time in the indefinite future could not be made a crime.

Since the defendants were the conceded leaders of the party, and since the lower courts had required proof of personal intent to overthrow the government,[34] the question raised in *Harisiades* of whether mere membership in the Party, especially past membership, could justify sanctions was clearly not before the Court in *Dennis*.

Dennis was quickly followed by fifteen prosecutions of second-level leaders of the party involving 121 additional defendants, but the combined impact of two 1957 Supreme Court opinions virtually ended the Smith Act prosecutions. In *Yates v. United States*,[35] the convictions of fourteen second-tier California communists were reversed when the Court, in an effort to limit *Dennis*, construed the Smith Act narrowly to require proof that the defendants had actually incited forcible overthrow, instead of merely teaching its advisability as abstract doctrine. Perhaps more importantly, two weeks prior to *Yates*, the Court had ruled in *Jencks v. United States*,[36] that criminal defendants were entitled to inspect statements made to the FBI by informants, and to use those statements in cross-examination of government witnesses. In the wake of *Yates* and *Jencks*, all pending prosecutions of party leaders were vacated or dismissed.

The line between "innocent" and "guilty" membership in the Communist Party was further refined in *Scales v. United States*[37] and *Noto v. United States*.[38] In *Scales*, the Court affirmed the convictions based on a showing that the defendants were members of the Party with full knowledge of its illegal purposes, and with the specific intent to accomplish violent overthrow as quickly as circumstances would permit. In *Noto*, the convictions were reversed because the government had failed to prove that defendants were anything more than Party members.

When the dust had settled on the Smith Act prosecutions, 141 persons had been indicted, and twenty-nine had served prison terms for the crime of being an official of the Party. The Supreme Court had established a bright-line distinction between "guilty" members of the Party who saw it as an engine for the violent overthrow of the government and who worked with the specific intent of achieving violent overthrow at the earliest date, and members who either failed to embrace its revolutionary rhetoric, or failed to act with a specific intent to carry the revolutionary purpose into effect.

The identical distinction between "guilty" and "innocent" membership was applied by the Supreme Court when the government attempted to use Communist Party membership as a basis for denying passports,[39] denying the right to work in a defense plant,[40] barring communists from serving as labor union officials,[41] preventing communists from becoming lawyers,[42] and barring communists from working for the government.[43] In each setting, the Court refused to permit mere membership to be the basis of sanctions.[44]

The Supreme Court eventually provided a watered-down version of the "guilty-innocent" distinction to LPRs, but it was far less protective than the version applied to citizens. And it came too late to save Luigi Mascitti or Dora Coleman, the innocent passengers on Peter Harisiades' doomed ship.

In *Galvan v. Press*,[45] Justice Frankfurter, writing for the Supreme Court two years after *Harisiades*, expressed concern over the harshness of deportations based on past activities without any showing that the LPR had personally espoused any unlawful aims of the Party. Nevertheless, he upheld the provisions of the newly-enacted Internal Security Act of 1950, which mandated deportation for past membership in the Communist Party without proof of personal knowledge or espousal of the Party's unlawful objectives.[46] As Justice Frankfurter noted, "[i]t is enough that the alien joined the Party, aware that he was joining an organization known as the Communist Party which operates as a distinct and active political organization, and that he did so of his own free will."

Three years later, in *Rowoldt v. Perfetto*,[47] confronted by an effort to deport "an old man who had lived in this country for forty years," Justice Frankfurter had a partial change of heart. His opinion for the Court construed the term "member" in the 1950 Act as requiring "meaningful association" with the Party, something far short of knowing espousal, but greater than casual "non-political" membership. Justice Harlan, writing for four Justices, dissented, arguing that the literal language of the Act required deportation for formal membership alone. The tiny opening in *Rowoldt* was applied in *Gastelum-Quinones v. Kennedy*,[48] another 5-4 decision, to block the deportation of an ex-Party member. Justice Goldberg, writing for the Court's majority, held that while proof of personal advocacy or espousal of the Party's unlawful aims was not required, something more than temporary membership without knowledge of the Party's international status was needed to make an LPR into a "member" within the meaning of the 1950 statute.

While *Rowoldt* and *Gastelum-Quinones* slightly ameliorated the plight of LPRs, the difference between the treatment of citizens and the treatment of LPRs is unmistakable. In order to punish citizens for Party membership, the government was required to prove current personal knowledge and espousal of the Party's unlawful aims. LPRs, on the other hand, were subject to banishment for past Party membership without any showing of personal adherence to an unlawful creed. For LPRs it was enough that they had joined the Party with a rudimentary understanding of its political status. Moreover, while the cases protecting citizens noted constitutional limits on the government's power, neither *Rowoldt* nor *Gastelum-Quinones* questioned Congress's power to eliminate even the minimal protections provided by the Court to those few LPRs who had joined the Party in total ignorance of its character.

Thus, although the McCarthy era was characterized by efforts to impose a broad array of sanctions on citizen-members of the Communist Party, in each instance the Supreme Court eventually required both current membership and proof of personal espousal of the unlawful aims of the Party, before permitting membership alone to trigger punishment of a citizen. LPR members of the Communist Party, however, were deported under a lower standard triggered by past or present membership, without any requirement of proof of knowing espousal of the Party's unlawful tenets. While *Rowoldt* and *Gastelum-Quinones* provided some relief to a small number of LPRs who had formally joined the Party knowing virtually nothing about it, the "meaningful association" test was much less protective than the "knowing espousal" standard applied to citizens.[49] Is it possible to justify such differential treatment of LPRs when the consequences are banishment? A majority of the Supreme Court believed so in *Harisiades*.

The Opinion in Harisiades

Justice Jackson's opinion for the Court in *Harisiades* does not persuasively explain the differential treatment. The opinion has four components.

First, Justice Jackson adopted the technique used by the *Dennis* Court of refusing to decide whether the Party was an intensely controversial political party adorned with revolutionary rhetoric, or a revolutionary conspiracy bent on the overthrow of the government by force.

Before *Dennis*, the Court had debated this issue vigorously, most notably in connection with the government's unsuccessful effort to revoke the naturalized citizenship of William Schneiderman. Justice Murphy argued that the *Communist Manifesto* was rhetoric; Chief Justice Stone insisted that it meant exactly what it said. In *Schneiderman v. United States*,[50] a majority of the Court, swayed by Wendell Wilkie's[51] pro bono representation of Schneiderman in the Supreme Court, rejected the government's argument that one could not simultaneously adhere to Communist Party principles and swear a naturalization oath in good faith to support and defend the American Constitution. Given the government's onerous burden of proof in a denaturalization case,[52] the majority found that Schneiderman's adherence to communist principles could not be treated as conclusive proof of fraud in swearing allegiance to the Constitution in the naturalization ceremony.[53] Thus, a narrow majority of the Supreme Court in *Schneiderman* appeared to reject the argument that mere membership in the Communist Party was grounds for sanction because the Party was really a criminal conspiracy.

The *Dennis* majority had side-stepped this issue. The *Harisiades* majority likewise spent virtually no time on that crucial issue, noting merely that findings had been made by an immigration examiner that the Party taught and advocated the overthrow of the government by force and violence, and that the lower courts had ruled that those findings were supported by "some evidence."

In fact, the Supreme Court declined to rule on the precise nature of the Communist Party in either *Dennis* or *Harisiades*. One of the unresolved institutional issues of the McCarthy era is whether the Supreme Court had a duty to rule for itself on this question.[54] What institution should decide it: Congress; the Supreme Court; an administrative agency; a jury? In *Harisiades*, the decision as to the nature of the Communist Party was made by a single immigration hearing officer, subject to toothless review under a "some evidence" standard in the district court. In *Dennis*, the issue was decided by a jury. Later cases substituted Congressional findings. In all cases, the principal "evidence" was the revolutionary writings of Marx and Lenin.

Once Justice Jackson disposed of the "true" nature of the Communist Party, he turned to a classic description of the status of LPRs under Supreme Court precedent, accurately noting that they are entitled to important constitutional protections, including equal economic opportunity,[55] protection under the Fifth and Sixth Amendments when charged with a crime,[56] access to the writ of habeas corpus,[57] compensation for the taking of private property,[58] and basic procedural fairness.[58] Moreover, although Justice Jackson omitted it from his list, Justice Douglas observed in his dissent that aliens had also been granted free speech protection in *Bridges v. California*,[59] reversing the contempt citation of a non-citizen union leader for threatening to strike if a court decision were enforced.

Justice Jackson also accurately observed that the Supreme Court had recognized no limits on the government's plenary power to "terminate its hospitality" to LPRs.[61] Most opinions involving deportation stop at this point, relying on the presumably self-evident nature of the *polis* to explain why LPRs are outside the circle. But Jackson felt compelled to justify the Court's refusal to grant them substantive protection against Congress' decision to deport them for past membership in the Party. In a painful passage bristling with hostility to LPRs, Justice Jackson blamed their legal plight on their failure to have sought American citizenship.[62] By electing to remain aliens, he argued, they were able to derive benefits from two sources of law, American and international, thereby retaining benefits and avoiding burdens that fell on citizens. But, the so-called benefits of remaining an LPR are strictly formal. According to Justice Jackson, the principal "benefit" retained by an enemy LPR is the right not to be conscripted and forced to wage war against his native land. But enemy LPRs hardly enjoy a favorable legal status under international law. They are subject to conscription as long as they are not forced to engage in combat operations directed against their country of citizenship. They are also subject to internment,[63] and confiscation of their property without compensation.[64] Another benefit cited by the Court is the right to call on one's country of origin for diplomatic assistance against deportation, hardly a viable option for Harisiades, who was deported to Poland because the Second Circuit found that he would have been subject to physical danger, even execution, in his native Greece.[65]

Justice Jackson closed by defending the unfettered power to expel LPRs as a "weapon of defense and reprisal confirmed by international law as a power inherent in every sovereign state." Apart from Justice Jackson's unpersuasive reliance on the alleged benefits resident aliens derive from international law, though, he makes no principled case for the status quo. "[I]n the present state of the world," according to Justice

Jackson, it would be "rash" to provide additional rights to aliens, without extracting additional protections for Americans. In the end, Jackson's rationale is all a matter of international *realpolitik*.

Once Justice Jackson had dealt with the status of the Party and attempted to justify the precarious legal status of LPRs, he held that *Dennis* disposed of the First Amendment challenge. He failed even to acknowledge that *Dennis* dealt with the eleven ranking leaders of the Party and rested on proof of specific intent to foment revolution by force and violence, while *Harisiades* involved three persons whose Party memberships had ended many years ago, two of whom had no current connection with it, and all three of whom had firmly rejected violence as a means of governmental change. In fact, Coleman, Mascitti, and perhaps Harisiades were exactly the type of persons who would benefit from the Supreme Court's later effort to distinguish "innocent" from "guilty" Party members. The combined force of Jackson's evident irritation with LPRs who do not seek citizenship, and his deep concern over possible communist subversion, seemed to erase the Court's willingness to distinguish between efforts to punish the Party's current leadership, and efforts to deport LPRs who rejected violence and had long-since severed Party ties.

Finally, Justice Jackson disposed of the ex post facto challenge by asserting, first, that the Ex Post Facto Clause governs only criminal proceedings, while deportation is a civil proceeding. In fact, the Ex Post Facto Clause had been invoked in a civil context by the Court in the wake of the Civil War to strike down efforts to punish Confederate loyalists.[66] Justice Jackson sought to distinguish the Civil War cases, calling the treatment of Confederate sympathizers punitive, but he failed to explain why the treatment of Harisiades, Coleman and Mascitti was not equally punitive.

More significantly, he argued that the decision of the Party in 1939 to terminate the membership of all non-citizens in order to take full advantage of *Kessler* stripped the notion of current non-membership of real meaning, since many alien non-members, like Harisiades, remained fully committed to the Party. While such an analysis might well apply to Harisiades, who publicly professed continuing allegiance to the Party, it had no relevance to Mascitti or Coleman, both of whom had ended their association before *Kessler*, before the Party attempted to take advantage of *Kessler*, and before Congress responded in 1940 by giving the statute retroactive effect.[67]

In short, at every stage of Justice Jackson's *Harisiades* opinion, from the Court's refusal to opine on the nature of the Party, allowing that crucial judgment to be made by a single immigration official; to the effort to justify the precarious legal status of LPRs; to the cavalier First

Amendment analysis, using long terminated "innocent" membership in the Party as a proxy for current dangerousness (a position that the Court would reject in all later cases); to the unsatisfactory effort to rebut the LPR's ex post facto argument, especially as applied to Mascitti and Coleman, the Jackson opinion reads more like a brief for the government than the resolution of a difficult case by a great jurist who wrote *Barnette*[68] in the midst of the Second World War, dissented in *Korematsu*,[69] warning of the danger of military abuse, and concurred in *Youngstown Steel*[70] in the midst of the Korean War.

What Went Wrong?

What went wrong? Maybe nothing. Given the long tradition of treating LPRs as lacking significant substantive legal defenses to banishment, the intense fear of communist subversion that gripped the country in 1952, and the relatively undeveloped First Amendment protections available to citizens, much less to LPRs, during the McCarthy years, the outcome in *Harisiades* may well have been a foregone conclusion.

But the Communist Party and it supporters did not make the task any easier. The Party's strategic decision in 1939 to terminate the formal membership of non-citizen members in order to maximize the impact of the Court's *Kessler* decision limiting the 1918 deportation statute to current party members backfired in several ways. Congress immediately reacted to the ploy by overruling *Kessler*, explicitly authorizing deportation for past membership in the Party, and the Supreme Court, whose already deep suspicion of the Party was only reinforced by the ploy, refused to give any weight to the fact that Harisiades, Coleman and Mascitti were no longer members.

Moreover, concentration on Peter Harisiades as the principal test case was ill-advised. Harisiades seemed an attractive choice because he had consistently rejected violence as a means of taking power, but several factors argued strongly against choosing him. Most importantly, he continued to work closely with the Party after 1939, publicly stating that he would have remained a member if it had not terminated his membership. His long record of labor activism confronted the Supreme Court with a second-tier Party official with thirty arrests whom the Party pretended was no longer a formal member, even though he continued to profess allegiance to it.

The choice of counsel was also problematic. Instead of an establishment lawyer like Wendell Wilkie, who had argued and won in *Schneiderman*, Harisiades was represented by lawyers provided by an organization perceived by the Court as very close to the Communist Party.[71] Things might have been different if Wilkie had argued a test case for the

American Civil Liberties Union confined to Luigi Mascitti or Dora Coleman.[72]

Is Harisiades *Still Good Law?*

The exclusionary circle drawn in *Harisiades* continues to place LPRs in an intensely vulnerable position, subject to banishment for behavior that for a citizen would be constitutionally protected. Unlike *Dennis*, which was merely the first in a series of decisions that ultimately forged a nuanced Smith Act jurisprudence that refused to equate mere membership in the Party with dangerousness, the broad constitutional principles of *Harisiades* were never the subject of clarifying, narrowing decisions by the Supreme Court. Although *Rowoldt* and *Gastellum-Quinones* provided minimal protection, today's circle is essentially where the *Harisiades* Court drew it—with long-time resident aliens on the outside looking in. What would happen today if *Harisiades* were challenged?

If recent cases like *INS v. St. Cyr*[73] are any guide, the Court would go beyond *Rowoldt* and use its power to read statutes narrowly to distinguish between "innocent" and "guilty" Party members, much as it read the Smith Act narrowly in *Yates*. If Congress insisted on deporting "innocent" party members, especially people who had long since terminated their party memberships, the First Amendment would pose a far greater obstacle to the government's position today than it did in 1952. *Dennis* has effectively been overruled, or at least substantially eroded by *Brandenburg v. Ohio*,[74] requiring the government to demonstrate something more than a theoretical future risk of violent overthrow before punishing someone for political association.

Moreover, the separation of powers concerns that impeded the *Harisiades* Court from interfering with the political branches' plenary power to deport LPRs have been substantially eased by generations of cases asserting judicial power in settings that the Court once thought beyond its power. Justice Frankfurter's separate opinions in *Dennis* and *Harisiades*, his dissent in *West Virginia v. Barnette*, and his opinion for the Court in *Communist Party v. SACB*, reflect a narrow vision of judicial power that compelled the Court to defer to congressional and executive judgments in many settings where important constitutional rights were in play. This narrow vision began to widen in *Baker v. Carr* when the Court refused to dismiss reapportionment cases under the political question doctrine.[75] The modern, expansive view of judicial responsibility to preserve constitutional rights would almost certainly provide the current Court with a greater field of action in cases like *Harisiades*. In short, *Harisiades* is ripe for overruling.

ENDNOTES

   1. In Aeschylus' trilogy, Orestes murders Clytemnestra to avenge the murder of Agamemnon for having sacrificed Iphigenia to secure fair winds for the voyage to Troy. According to Aeschylus, divine punishment for matricide was administered by the Furies. The *Oresteia* ends with the transfer by the gods of responsibility for dealing justly with Orestes' crime to the people of Athens. See Richard Posner, Law and Literature: A Misunderstood Relation (1988), for a discussion of the *Oresteia* as a parable of the birth of law.

   2. United States ex rel. Harisiades v. Shaughnessy, 187 F.2d 137, 141 (2d Cir. 1951), affirmed, 342 U.S. 580 (1952). The three Second Circuit judges in *Harisiades*, Learned Hand, Augustus Hand, and Thomas Swan, constituted one of the most respected appellate panels in American legal history.

   3. In 1937, Harisiades married Esther, the American-born daughter of a naturalized American citizen who had been born in Poland. They had two children, George and Irene. Dora Coleman was also married to an American citizen, and had three children. Luigi Mascitti married a resident alien and had one American-born child.

   4. Harisiades' father returned to Greece in 1923.

   5. Harisiades had been arrested approximately 30 times in connection with labor organizing activity and during protests over the execution of Sacco and Vanzetti. Apparently, none of the arrests resulted in convictions. Neither Mascitti, nor Coleman had had any brush with the law.

   6. Harisiades had initially applied for citizenship in 1922 when he lived in Canton, Ohio, but the application lapsed because he moved away.

   7. In 1940, Congress responded by amending the statute to permit deportation for past political activity. The disastrous consequences of the Party's effort to maximize the impact of the *Kessler* decision by terminating the memberships of all non-citizens is discussed infra.

   8. The FBI estimated that 75% of the members of the IWO were communists.

   9. 307 U.S. 22 (1939).

   10. The National Lawyers' Guild Immigration Project currently bestows an annual Carol King Award for excellence in the practice of immigration law. King, a college friend of Alger Hiss, was apparently not a member of the Communist Party. Unbeknownst to King, however, the FBI apparently targeted her clients for special attention because they were thought to be unacknowledged communists. Carol King died suddenly in 1952. See Ann Fagan Ginger, Carol Weiss King: Human Rights Lawyer, 1895–1952 (1993).

   11. The effort to deport Bridges failed when the government was unable to prove that he was a member of the Communist Party.

   12. The government had attempted to revoke Schneiderman's naturalized American citizenship on the grounds that, as an active party member, he must have committed fraud in taking the citizenship oath to support and defend the constitution. The effort failed in Schneiderman v. United States, 320 U.S. 118 (1943), when the Supreme Court rejected the government's argument that Communist Party membership was so inconsistent with attachment to constitutional principles that it amounted to fraud for a communist leader to take the naturalization oath.

   13. The American Committee to Protect the Foreign Born was founded in the mid–1930s by Roger Baldwin, the man who had founded the American Civil Liberties Union in 1917. The ACPFB, as it was known, initially flourished, receiving congratulations from President Roosevelt in 1940 at its Fourth Annual Conference. The organization successfully defended union leader Harry Bridges against deportation, and spearheaded the defense of Communist Party leader William Schneiderman against denaturalization. During WW II, the ACPFB hewed closely to the Stalinist line, refusing to challenge the Japanese internments, and vigorously criticizing the ACLU for representing Fred Korematsu. After WW II, the organization became increasingly identified with the Communist Party, eventually being listed by the Subversive Activities Control Board as a communist front organization. American Committee for the Protection of the Foreign Born v. Subversive Activities Control Board, 331 F.2d 53 (D.C. Cir. 1963). Judge Bazelon dissented, arguing that the government had not proved that the organization was "primarily operated for the purpose of giving aid and support to the Communist party." See John W. Sherman, A Communist Front at Mid–Century: The American Committee for the Protection of the Foreign Born, 1933–1959.

14. If you were structuring a test case challenging the right of the government to deport aliens for past membership in the Communist Party, would you have selected Peter Harisiades as your primary challenger? Wouldn't it have been wiser to concentrate initially on challengers like Luigi Mascitti and Dora Coleman, who had broken with the party?

15. In Wong Yang Sung v. McGrath, 339 U.S. 33 (1950), decided the day Harisiades filed his appeal to the Second Circuit from an unsuccessful district court challenge to his deportation order, the Supreme Court ruled that the recently enacted Administrative Procedure Act applied to deportation proceedings. Since Zimmerman had performed both prosecutorial and adjudicative functions in apparent violation of the APA, Harisiades' deportation hearing suddenly appeared vulnerable to procedural attack. The district court entertained a second habeas corpus petition on the procedural point. Since the APA did not apply to proceedings commenced prior to September 11, 1946, the APA issue initially turned on whether Harisiades' hearing had commenced in 1930, when the deportation warrant was issued; May, 1946, when the deportation warrant was served; or October, 1946, when the hearing proceedings commenced. Eventually, despite the fact that new charges were added after September, 1946, all three courts found that the APA was inapplicable because the hearing had commenced prior to September, 1946. 90 F. Supp. 431 (S.D.N.Y. 1950), aff'd, 187 F.2d 137 (2d Cir. 1951), aff'd, 342 U.S. 580 n.4 (1952).

In the Supreme Court, Harisiades argued that the use of a single hearing officer to play both a prosecutorial and adjudicative role violated the Due Process Clause. The Supreme Court rejected the argument, holding that King had explicitly waived the issue in an effort to keep Zimmerman in the case. No explanation was given why Harisiades' waiver precluded Coleman, who had raised a similar APA challenge, from raising the due process issue. In the end, the APA issue was a tease, since the Supreme Court eventually held that the APA did not apply to deportation proceedings under the 1917–18 statute. Heikkila v. Barber, 345 U.S. 229, 235–36 (1953). After the 1918 statute was re-enacted in expanded form in 1952, the APA was held applicable to post–1952 political deportation proceedings. Shaughnessy v. Pedreiro, 349 U.S. 48 (1955). The Court ultimately ruled that the mixture of prosecutorial and adjudicative functions in immigration proceedings did not violate the Due Process Clause. Marcello v. Bonds, 349 U.S. 302 (1955) discussed in Chapter 5 of this volume.

16.   90 F. Supp. 397 (S.D.N.Y. 1950).

17.   187 F.2d 137 (2d Cir. 1951).

18.   187 F.2d at 141–42.

19.   Newly-appointed Justice Tom Clark, who had played a major role in deciding to deport Harisiades, recused himself.

20.   Justice Jackson was no government pushover. He had recently returned to the Court from distinguished service as the chief American prosecutor at the Nuremberg War Crime Trials. See notes 64–66.

21.   Its companion, the Sedition Act, was broadly invoked against vigorous critics of the Adams administration, resulting in at least 25 arrests and 15 indictments. One of the more celebrated cases was the conviction of Congressman Matthew Lyons of Vermont, and his sentencing to four months in prison. Lyons was re-elected to the House during his incarceration. The Sedition Act expired in 1801, and President Jefferson pardoned all defendants. Not to be outdone, when the Jefferson administration came to power, it brought common law seditious libel prosecutions against vitriolic Federalist critics in Connecticut. The Supreme Court rejected the prosecutions, ruling that federal courts have no power to try common law crimes. United States v. Hudson & Goodwin, 11 U.S. (7 Cranch.) 32 (1812).

22. The convictions, premised on a theory that the defendants had aided and abetted the lethal violence, were affirmed by the Illinois Supreme Court. Spies v. People, 122 Ill. 1 (1887). The United States Supreme Court denied a writ or error without considering whether general writing about the desirability of revolution could constitute the aiding and abetting of violence. Spies v. Illinois, 123 U.S. 131 (1887). The issue would, of course, re-surface with a vengeance during the McCarthy era in the context of efforts to suppress the Communist Party and its members.

23. McKinley's assassination led, in 1902, to the passage of the first state sedition law, New York's so-called criminal anarchy statute, making it a crime to join any organization advocating the overthrow of organized government by force or violence. N.Y. Laws of 1902, ch. 371. The New York statute was the model for the 1918 federal deportation statute in *Harisiades*, and was the statute before the Court in Gitlow v. New York, 268 U.S. 652 (1925).

24. The classic description of WW I censorship is Zechariah Chaffee, Free Speech in the United States 37–41, 51–52, 100–101 (1941). The Supreme Court sustained the convictions. Schenck v. United States, 249 U.S. 47 (1919); and Abrams v. United States, 250 U.S. 616 (1919); but the cases spawned the Holmes–Brandeis opinions that paved the way for the modern First Amendment. See also Whitney v. California, 274 U.S. 357, 372 (1927) (Brandeis, J., concurring).

25. The number of ostensible members who were really law enforcement infiltrators remains unknown.

26. Marcantonio was not a member of the Communist Party, but he steadfastly defended it as a genuine political party devoted to working people. By 1948, when he was re-elected for the last time, he was opposed by a coalition of the Republican, Democratic and Liberal Parties. He ran under the banner of the American Labor Party. Marcantonio was defeated for re-election in 1950, after the gerrymandering of his congressional district had merged his East Harlem constituency with the much more conservative Yorkville area.

27. The vast literature on Senator McCarthy includes Robert Griffith, The Politics of Fear: Joseph R. McCarthy and the Senate (1970), and Fred J. Cook, The Nightmare Decade: The Life and Times of Senator Joe McCarthy (1971).

28. See John Earl Haynes & Harvey Klehr, Venona: Decoding Soviet Espionage in America (1999).

29. The jury trial in *Dennis* lasted nine months, from January 17, 1949–October 14, 1949, and generated a record of 16,000 pages.

30. United States v. Dennis, 183 F.2d 201 (2d Cir. 1950). Learned Hand's opinion was particularly influential both because of his reputation and his general commitment to free speech principles.

31. 341 U.S. 494 (1951).

32. The Court's limited certiorari order is reported at 340 U.S. 863 (1950). The Court noted in *Dennis* that:

> [O]ur limited grant of the writ of certiorari has removed from our consideration
> any question as to the sufficiency of the evidence to support the jury's determina-
> tion that petitioners are guilty of the offense charged. Whether on this record
> petitioners did in fact advocate the overthrow of the Government by force or

violence is not before us, and we must base any discussion of this point of the conclusions stated in the opinion of the Court of Appeals ... 341 U.S. at 497.

33. That left the First Amendment issue of whether the distant, contingent nature of the future violence was too uncertain to satisfy the clear and present danger test. Following the advice of Learned Hand, the *Dennis* Court deferred to Congress' assessment of the imminence of the risk. Many contemporary observers believe that the *Dennis* Court erred both in failing to grapple with the true nature of the American Communist Party, leaving that volatile issue to a jury in the grip of Cold War anxiety, and in failing to make an independent assessment of the imminence of the risk of violent overthrow.

34. The issue is somewhat circular, since virtually the only evidence against the defendants was their leadership role in an entity with an avowed purpose of overthrowing the government at some indefinite point in the future.

35. 354 U.S. 298 (1957).

36. 353 U.S. 657 (1957).

37. 367 U.S. 203 (1961).

38. 367 U.S. 290 (1961).

39. Aptheker v. Secretary of State, 378 U.S. 500 (1964) (invalidating indiscriminate denial of passports to members of Communist Party).

40. United States v. Robel, 389 U.S. 258 (1967) (invalidating indiscriminate ban on defense work while member of Communist Party).

41. American Communications Association v. Douds, 339 U.S. 382 (1950) (narrowly construing affidavit of non-membership in Communist party required of labor union officials to require knowing efforts to foment political strikes); United States v. Brown, 381 U.S. 437 (1965) (holding that statute making it a crime for a member of Communist Party to hold office in a labor union is a Bill of Attainder).

42. Schware v. Board of Bar Examiners, 353 U.S. 232 (1957) (past membership in Communist Party insufficient basis to deny admission to bar).

43. Weiman v. Updegraff, 344 U.S. 183 (1952) (invalidating oath for public employment that disqualifies all members of Communist Party without distinguishing personal beliefs); Greene v. McElroy, 360 U.S. 474 (1959) (invalidating denial of security clearance based on sympathetic association with communist supporters).

44. In addition to the Smith Act prosecutions, Congress enacted the Internal Security Act of 1950, requiring the registration of "communist action" organizations, and disclosure of their members and finances. No groups voluntarily registered. The government moved to compel the registration of the Communist Party. After an epic 10–year legal battle, the Supreme Court upheld the designation of the Communist Party by the Subversive Activities Control Board as a communist action organization directed from abroad, with the objective of overthrowing the United States government. Communist Party v. SACB, 367 U.S. 1 (1961). Justice Frankfurter's opinion for the Court in *SACB* sounded the familiar theme of deference to the findings of Congress and the administrative agency charged with carrying out the law. Chief Justice Warren, and Justices Black, Douglas and Brennan dissented, accepting judicial responsibility to make independent assessments of the evidence, and arguing the now familiar point that a difference exists between embracing abstract doctrine and actual efforts to overthrow the government. In the wake of *SACB*, party leaders declined to register, claiming that registration was the equivalent of self-incrimination. In Albertson v. SACB, 382 U.S. 70 (1965), the Court recognized that registration was tantamount to self-incrimination. Just as *Yates* had ended the Smith Act prosecutions, *Albertson* spelled the end of the effort to force the registration of communists.

45. 347 U.S. 522 (1954).

46. The 1950 Act dispensed with the requirement under the 1918 Act that each deportation be accompanied by proof of the Communist Party's unlawful aims, substituting a legislative finding that the Party was dedicated to the overthrow of the government by force and violence.

47. 355 U.S. 115 (1957).

48. 374 U.S. 469 (1963).

49. The Court continued to uphold the imposition of sanctions on LPRs for mere membership in the Communist Party even after the decisions in *Rowoldt* and *Gastelum-Quinones*. See *Flemming v. Nestor*, 363 U.S. 603 (1960) (upholding denial of Social Security benefits to LPRs deported because of Party membership).

50. 320 U.S. 118 (1943).

51. Wendell Wilkie, a pillar of the Establishment, was the Republican candidate for the Presidency in 1940.

52. The contrast between *Schneiderman* and *Harisiades* illustrates how important it is to be inside the circle. When Schneiderman became a naturalized citizen, he became a full member of the *polis*. Thus, the government's effort to expel him from the *polis* triggered legal protections, including a burden of proof rule that required the government to prove that it was impossible to be both a communist and a supporter of the Constitution. *Harisiades*, outside the circle, was faced with a procedure that required a court to affirm the deportation order as long as "some evidence" of Party's unlawful aims had been presented to the immigration examiner.

53. Communist spokespersons sought to explain the violent rhetoric in the canon by arguing that the party sought power solely through lawful, parliamentary means, and that violence was contemplated only if the ruling capitalist class sought to pre-empt the workings of democracy by refusing to recognize a communist victory.

54. Arguably, by developing the concept of "innocent" and "guilty" party membership in *Dennis, Yates, Scales* and *Noto*, the Court found that there were two Communist Parties—an ordinary political organization encompassing the bulk of the membership, and a smaller revolutionary core.

55. Yick Wo v. Hopkins, 118 U.S. 356 (1886) (invalidating racially discriminatory licensing system for laundries); Truax v. Raich, 239 U.S. 33 (1915) (invalidating ban on fishing license for aliens ineligible for citizenship); Takahashi v. Fish & Game Comm'n, 334 U.S. 410 (1948) (invalidating ban on fishing license for aliens); Graham v. Richardson, 403 U.S. 365 (1971) (invalidating exclusion of aliens from federal welfare program); In re Giffiths, 413 U.S. 717 (1973) (invalidating denial of bar membership to aliens); Sugarman v. Dougall, 413 U.S. 634 (1973) (invalidating ban on state civil service jobs for aliens); Hampton v. Mow Sung Wong, 426 U.S. 88 (1976) (invalidating ban on federal civil service jobs for aliens); Plyler v. Doe, 457 U.S. 202 (1982) (requiring access to school for children of undocumented aliens). But see Foley v. Connelie, 435 U.S. 291 (1978) (upholding ban on aliens serving as state troopers); Ambach v. Norwick, 441 U.S. 68 (1979) (upholding ban on aliens serving as public school teachers); Mathews v. Diaz, 426 U.S. 67 (1976) (upholding five-year permanent residence requirement on Medicare for aliens).

56. Wong Wing v. United States, 163 U.S. 228 (1896) (jury trial; burden of proof; self-incrimination). See Chapter 2 in this volume.

57. Nishimura Ekiu v. United States, 142 U.S. 651 (1892).

58. Russian Volunteer Fleet v. United States, 282 U.S. 481 (1931) (just compensation for seizure of property).

59. Ng Fung Ho v. White, 259 U.S. 276 (1922).

60. 314 U.S. 252 (1941).

61. Fong Yue Ting v. United States, 149 U.S. 698 (1893) (Congress has plenary power over deportation). Justice Fields, speaking for three Justices, dissented in *Fong Yue Ting*, arguing that resident aliens should be protected against arbitrary deportation. See Chapter 1 in this volume.

62. The irony is that Harisiades came to the government's attention only because he filed an application for citizenship in 1944. His earlier application for citizenship in 1922 had lapsed.

63. International law was of precious little value to the Japanese LPRs, and the American citizens of Japanese ancestry, who were interned during WW II. See Korematsu v. United States, 323 U.S. 214 (1944).

64. Justice Jackson was careful to exempt enemy aliens when he observed that LPRs were entitled to just compensation for seizure of their property.

65. Justice Jackson displayed a mastery of international law during his service as chief American war crime prosecutor at Nuremberg. But his deployment of international law in *Harisiades* as a justification for the banishment of LPRs on flimsy grounds betrayed the very purpose of international law, which exists to protect the weak, not to reinforce their vulnerability.

66. Cummings v. Missouri, 71 U.S. (4 Wall.) 277 (1867); Ex parte Garland, 71 U.S. (4 Wall.) 333 (1867).

67. This is the second instance in the *Harisiades* opinion where the rejection of an argument by Harisiades ended the matter even as to Coleman and Mascitti, despite the distinguishable nature of their positions. The first instance was the Court's rejection of Harisiades' due process argument that the immigration hearing officer had unconstitutionally performed both prosecutorial and adjudicative duties. The Court found that Harisiades' lawyer had explicitly waived the issue. Coleman had raised the APA issue with no question of waiver, but the Court ignored the due process issue latent in Coleman's challenge.

68. West Virginia State Board of Education v. Barnette, 319 U.S. 624 (1943), invalidated compulsory flag salutes in the schools. Justice Jackson's soaring rhetoric in *Barnette* remains a classic restatement of First Amendment values:

> If there is any fixed star in our constitutional constellation, it is that no official, high or petty, can prescribe what shall be orthodox in politics, nationalism, religion, or other matters of opinion or force *citizens* to confess by word or act their faith therein. If there are any circumstances which permit an exception, they do not now occur to us.

319 U.S. at 642 (emphasis added).

69. 323 U.S. 214, 242 (1944) (Jackson, J. dissenting).

70. Youngstown Sheet & Tube Co. v. Sawyer, 343 U.S. 579 (1952), rejected President Truman's assertion of inherent presidential power to seize the nation's steel mills to prevent a strike during the Korean War.

71. The trajectory of the American Committee for the Protection of the Foreign Born (ACPFB), which was founded by Roger Baldwin, should be contrasted with another organization founded by Baldwin, the American Civil Liberties Union. In 1940, the ACLU expelled Elizabeth Gurley Flynn, a prominent member of the Communist Party, from the ACLU Board of Directors, and barred communists from positions of influence in the organization. The ACLU also declined to represent communists directly during the McCarthy era, expressing itself solely as amicus curiae. Modern critics of the ACLU have argued that the organization erred in expelling Flynn, and in declining to provide direct representation to people like Harisiades, but the decline of the ACPFB provides a cautionary tale.

72. *Rowoldt v. Perfetto* and *Gastelum-Quinones,* the two cases that snatched a scintilla of protection for LPRs, were both argued by David Rein, a brilliant member of the D.C. bar.

73. 533 U.S. 289 (2001). *St Cyr* narrowly construed Congress' efforts to deport LPRs who had committed crimes to avoid giving the statute retroactive effect. See Chapter 11 in the volume.

74. 395 U.S. 444 (1969).

75. See Baker v. Carr, 369 U.S. 186 (1962), overruling Colegrove v. Green, 328 U.S. 549 (1946).

5

The Long, Complex, and Futile Deportation Saga of Carlos Marcello

Daniel Kanstroom*

If you want to know the law and nothing else, you must look at it as a bad man, who cares only for the material consequences which such knowledge enables him to predict, not as a good one, who finds his reasons for conduct, whether inside the law or outside of it, in the vaguer sanctions of conscience.[1]

—Oliver Wendell Holmes

Everybody in the United States knowed I was kidnapped, that what they done was illegal. I didn't have to discuss it with nobody. I told the whole world it was unfair....[2]

—Carlos Marcello

Introduction: Young Carlos Marcello and the Mob

The deportation story of Carlos Marcello offers a new perspective on Holmes' famous axiom. With its many twists and turns, it is, without doubt, the story of a bad man; indeed, it involves many bad men. Dark tales of the Mafia, public corruption, murder, robbery, drug-dealing, and fraud abound. But it is also a cautionary tale about law. Around its edges lurk allegations of quasi-legal skulduggery by Attorney General Robert Kennedy, and shadowy activities by all sorts of people in Dallas, Italy, Guatemala, and even Formosa. We will find hints of how one of the longest, costliest, and ultimately most futile deportation cases in U.S. history was possibly connected to the assassinations of President Kennedy and Dr. Martin Luther King, Jr. As if all that weren't enough, Marcello's deportation led to a fascinating Supreme Court case involving the Administrative Procedure Act, the Ex Post Facto Clause, due pro-

* Thanks to Mark Brodin for helpful comments and to Julie Dahlstrom, Renee Latour, Moira Smith and Sydney Urbach for outstanding research assistance.

cess, judicial review of agency discretion, and the Immigration and Nationality Act of 1952. His lawyers' skill at forestalling deportation for many years also played a major role in Congress' 1961 efforts to reshape judicial review of deportation orders, and it is cited to this day in debates over the availability and scope of habeas corpus review. Simply put, this is one wild ride.

Let us begin with a pastoral scene from the Old World. Giuseppe and Luigia Minacore were Sicilian peasants from a small village called Ravanusa.[3] Seeking a better life than the endless *malafortuna* of their homeland, they emigrated, as did many thousands of their compatriots. Their first stop, in 1908, was the ancient city of Carthage, in Tunisia. Within a year, however, Giuseppe determined to leave the Old World behind and to make his way to New Orleans, already home to a well-established Sicilian community. Luigia, pregnant with their first child, stayed behind. The baby, whom she named Calogero, was born on February 6, 1910.

In October 1910, Luigia and Calogero traveled to New Orleans on the Italian steamship *Liguria*. Like many other immigrants, Giuseppe adopted a new name for the New World. He chose Marcello, a less Sicilian, more typically north Italian name, for the family. He also anglicized his first name: to Joseph. Luigia became Louise and young Calogero became Carlos.[4]

Joseph was a small-time farmer, having purchased a rather ramshackle property in Algiers, near New Orleans. The family, with eight additional children born in the United States, grew fruit and vegetables, which they sold in a farmer's market near the *Vieux Carré*, the famous French Quarter of New Orleans. For reasons that remain mysterious to this day, both of Carlos' parents eventually naturalized as U.S. citizens but he did not.

Carlos Marcello was, by all accounts, a tough kid. Short and muscular, he was not an academically gifted student, and he dropped out of school at the age of fourteen. But he was apparently quite clever and seems to have shown initiative and sought authority at an early age. It was in this *milieu* that he likely encountered the Mafia. There had been a well-established Sicilian immigrant criminal network in New Orleans for nearly a half-century. Though the full extent of their operations has never been precisely determined, they were a significant force from the 1860s onward. Like many other immigrant groups during this dynamic immigration period in U.S. history, the Sicilian immigrants in New Orleans faced hyperbolic over-generalizations. New Orleans Mayor Joseph A. Shakespeare reportedly spoke of the newcomers as, "the most idle, vicious and worthless among us ... without courage, honour, truth, pride, religion or any quality that goes to make good citizens...."[5]

Three decades before the Marcellos arrived, New Orleans had witnessed one of the uglier incidents of mob violence in U.S. history. The New Orleans police chief, David Peter Hennessey, who had begun to crack down on expatriate gangs, was ambushed while walking home from a police board meeting. As he approached his house, an Italian boy skipped past him and whistled loudly into the night. Suddenly, gunmen opened fire, some with sawed-off shotguns, others with revolvers. According to apocryphal history, Hennessey's final words to Captain Billy O'Conner were, "Oh Billy, Billy they have given it to me and I gave them back the best I could! The Dagos did it."[6]

Public outrage (and a considerable anti-Italian hysteria) arose in New Orleans and spread around the nation. The police soon rounded up more than 100 Italian suspects. When the jury returned verdicts of not guilty against the most important defendants (and mistrials were declared against others), an armed mob stormed the prison, hunted down the terrified Italians, and killed several, hanging one from a lamp-post as the crowd took shots at him.

By the time Carlos Marcello arrived as a child into this environment, some of the violent anti-Italian, anti-immigrant animus had diminished. Young Marcello came of age in the 1920s in a city known for corruption, widespread lawlessness, open prostitution and gambling, as well as an entrenched, Sicilian-led organized crime operation. Marcello apparently began his criminal career rather early—leaving home at eighteen to live in the French Quarter and making his living from a string of petty burglaries. He was, by all accounts, a young man of considerable ambition and certain talents. In 1929, he successfully led a bank robbery with a group of teenage boys. They made off with some $7,000. Apparently, they went to Carlos' father's house with the loot, where the elder Marcello offered to hide it for a $400 payoff. Unfortunately, Carlos' brother Peter went to the police and reported the entire incident to them. All three Marcellos were arrested and Carlos achieved some fame when the *New Orleans Times–Picayune* published his photograph along with a story describing him as the mastermind of the operation. When all charges were ultimately dropped, Carlos was inspired to continue in this line of work. He reportedly organized a gang of teenage accomplices to plan more bank robberies. But one thirteen-year-old was caught by the police, lost his nerve, and turned on Carlos. The newspapers described Marcello as a "Fagin" criminal mastermind, and he was convicted and sentenced to nine-to-twelve years in the state penitentiary at the age of twenty.[7]

Prison provided a multi-faceted education for Carlos Marcello. Perhaps most importantly, he learned how to obtain and use information against those in power. When he discovered that the warden was engaged in an affair with a female cook, he was able to blackmail the warden with this information. He obtained a series of special favors, including not only better food but, reportedly, the romantic attentions of the cook herself.[8] He also learned the power of political influence. His father worked assiduously to get his son freed from prison, using connections to state officials that ultimately resulted in a governor's pardon after Carlos had served only four years.[9]

Upon his release from prison, Carlos was poised to begin what ultimately became one of the most successful criminal careers in U.S. history. He accomplished this by combining shrewd tactical and strategic sense, a deep appreciation for secrecy, ruthlessness, a deceptive demeanor, good luck, and—perhaps most importantly—the wisdom to hire a brilliant and energetic immigration lawyer named Jack Wasserman.[10]

Marcello Comes of Age and Meets the INS

Marcello's adult criminal career began with the purchase of a run-down "colored" bar in the town of Gretna, which he re-named *The Brown Bomber* after heavyweight champion Joe Louis. Gretna was a famously criminal town—largely controlled by the Mafia in conjunction with corrupt police—and a haven for gambling, prostitution, and marijuana and other drug-dealing.[11] Marcello reportedly achieved success as a drug dealer during this period. By the mid–1930s, he had also become close to the Louisiana Mafia, led by Sam "Silver Dollar" Carolla. In 1936, Marcello married Jacqueline Todaro, the sister of one of Carolla's *capos*. With his connections to the Louisiana mob secure, Marcello prospered. Unfortunately, however, his stewardship of one of the major marijuana selling operations in the region led to federal attention. In March 1938, Marcello allegedly sold some twenty-three pounds of marijuana to an undercover FBI agent. He pled guilty and was sentenced to a year and a day. This drug conviction later formed the basis for deportation proceedings against him.

Through his connections with Sam Carolla, Marcello became involved with a large slot machine operation that was to be set up in Louisiana by New York Mafia boss Frank Costello. Marcello was quite successful in this enterprise, which involved extensive payoffs to local public officials. He was later caught on a federal wiretap saying: "I used to give [Gretna Police Chief] Miller $50,000 in cash every few months. I used to stuff [the] cash in a suitcase and carry it over to his office."[12] By the early 1940s, Marcello also was involved in the large-scale, war-related black-market activities for which New Orleans became infamous. His lack of U.S. citizenship turned out to be a temporary advantage during this time, as it may have helped him to avoid the draft, unlike his native-born brothers, Peter and Vincent. His reputation as a ruthlessly efficient operator solidified. As John H. Davis has put it:

Carlos always brought back the bacon. He could be relied on.
There were rumors of fierce battles, brutal assaults, and an
occasional murder along the way, but these were to be expected.
The police ... were taken care of. The important thing was the
money. Carlos could always be counted on to bring back the
money.[13]

Indeed, Marcello's reputation was sufficiently solid by 1944 to in-
spire Frank Costello and Meyer Lansky to accept him as a 12.5% partner
in a large, new Las Vegas-style gambling establishment in Jefferson
Parish. During this period, the government's use of deportation as a tool
in J. Edgar Hoover's trumpeted war on crime at first worked to Marcello's advantage. The federal government had obtained a deportation order
against Sam Carolla. Although the proceedings were interrupted by
World War II,[14] by May 1947, Carolla's deportation was accomplished,[15]
and Marcello was positioned to take over his role. Marcello became
increasingly powerful and successful. In 1950, Washington columnist
Drew Pearson featured a nationally syndicated story about Marcello in
which he referred to him as "the crime czar of New Orleans."[16]

Marcello's rise to national prominence was enhanced by a *virtuoso*
performance before the Senate's famous Special Committee to Investigate Organized Crime in Interstate Commerce, chaired by Senator Estes
Kefauver of Tennessee. Kefauver, referring to Marcello as "the evil
genius of organized crime in Louisiana,"[17] alleged that his empire rivaled
that of the Capone gang.[18] This characterization might have seemed a bit
overblown to those who encountered Marcello's drawl and rough man-
ners in the Senate's New Orleans hearings. But he was well-advised by
counsel—as shrewd and tight-lipped as any witness who has ever appeared before any government body. Invoking the Fifth Amendment 152
times, he seemed true to the motto posted over his headquarters in the
Town & Country Motel in New Orleans Parish: "Three can keep a secret
if two are dead."

Senator Kefauver formed a clear opinion of Marcello:

The record is long, the connections are bad, the implications ...
are most sinister, and we wanted to find out among other things
what was the trouble with naturalization and immigration laws
that a man who is apparently having such a detrimental effect
on law enforcement and to decency in the community, how can
he continue to stay here.[19]

Kefauver recommended to the Attorney General that deportation proceedings be initiated as soon as possible.[20] Those proceedings, which
began promptly in 1952, lasted more than thirty years without government success.

Marcello was arrested on December 30, 1952 pursuant to an immi-gration warrant, but was soon released on bail. The charge was a violation of Section 241(a)(11) of the Immigration and Nationality Act of 1952 (INA), which mandated deportation for drug offenses. The proceed-ings were based on Marcello's 1938 marijuana convictions.[21] He had a full hearing before a special inquiry officer, a senior officer of the Immigration and Naturalization Service (INS), who found him to be deportable on February 20, 1953. Marcello was advised of his right to apply for the discretionary relief of suspension of deportation, then available to non-citizens with criminal records like Marcello's if they could prove that they had been present for more than ten years since the criminal act, that they exhibited good moral character during the most recent ten years, and that deportation would cause exceptional and extremely unusual hardship.[22] For reasons that do not appear in the record, Marcello's counsel at first stated that he did not wish to apply for such relief. (Marcello may well have been reluctant to open up his life for purposes of applying for discretionary relief, especially since—given his history—the likelihood of success would have been rather low.) Later, however, Marcello and counsel changed their minds and filed a motion to re-open the hearing for that purpose. The special inquiry officer denied the motion.[23] The Board of Immigration Appeals affirmed the order, rejecting several legal claims and going on to consider the merits of the relief application, though it had never been formally filed. The Board assumed, arguendo, that Marcello met the statutory requirements, but still denied suspension in the exercise of discretion, citing multiple negative factors, including his "prior convictions, arrests, newspaper clippings naming him the 'number one mobster in Louisiana,' and his refusal to testify before the Kefauver Committee. . . ."[24] The appeal had been speedily dispatched, and Marcello was arrested the next day, June 2, 1953.

Marcello appealed the Board's decision through a habeas corpus petition. At the time, this was the accepted method for federal court challenges to administrative orders of the Board. His attorneys argued, inter alia, that the deportation procedures of the Immigration and Nationality Act conflicted with the Administrative Procedure Act and violated his right to due process and to a fair and impartial hearing. To appreciate the full significance of these arguments, we will detour to consider the history of the Administrative Procedure Act and one of the first major cases to analyze it: *Wong Yang Sung v. McGrath.*[25]

The Administrative Procedure Act and **Wong Yang Sung**

The antecedents of the modern administrative state may be traced at least as far back as Progressive Era agencies.[26] But administrative law rose to the top of the national agenda from the beginning of the New

Deal through the end of World War II, eventually leading to the passage of the Administrative Procedure Act in 1946.[27] Federal government intervention had gradually gained acceptance as an essential protection against inevitable market failures, but controversy continued over *how* agencies did their work and whether their actions undermined the rule of law.[28] In May 1933, the ABA created a Special Committee on Administrative Law,[29] which expressed great concern about the "judicial function" being exercised by administrative agencies.[30]

It is difficult, more than half a century later, to appreciate the passion aroused by these issues at the time. But passion is undoubtedly the right word.[31] Indeed, the president-elect of the American Bar Association called on lawyers to join the "titanic struggle" against those " 'progressives,' 'liberals,' or 'radicals' who desire to invest the national Government with totalitarian powers in the teeth of Constitutional democracy...."[32]

In early 1939, President Roosevelt instructed Attorney General Murphy to appoint a new committee to investigate "the need for procedural reform" and to make a "thorough and comprehensive study" of "existing practices and procedures."[33] Following public hearings, the committee published twenty-seven monographs. The committee's final report paved the way for the federal Administrative Procedure Act of 1946.[34] Enjoying both government and ABA support, the bill easily passed both the House and the Senate.[35] Thus, for the first time in U.S. history, the huge and multi-faceted federal administrative process was to be subject to one procedural law. Although many of the Act's broad terms spawned decades of litigation and judicial construction, the APA clearly subjected adjudicative processes to important constraints, requiring relative independence for hearing officers, and providing for judicial oversight.[36]

By 1950, the APA had been mentioned in twelve Supreme Court cases.[37] But it was the deportation case of Wong Yang Sung[38] that offered the Court its first real opportunity to construe the deeper implications of the 1946 statute. Among the lawyers on the brief for Wong Yang Sung was Jack Wasserman, who was soon to represent Marcello. Wong Yang Sung, a citizen of China, was arrested for having overstayed his admission period. An immigration officer, after a hearing, recommended deportation. Per standard procedures, the Acting Commissioner approved, and the Board of Immigration Appeals later affirmed. Wong then filed a habeas corpus petition in which he argued that his deportation hearing was "not conducted in conformity with §§ 5 and 11 of the Administrative Procedure Act."[39] Those sections contained strict requirements for the independence of hearing examiners, including a provision barring officers "engaged in the performance of investigative or prosecuting functions" from participating in or rendering decisions. Examiners, said the APA, "shall perform no duties inconsistent with their duties and responsibilities as examiners." The government admitted that the immigration system deviated from the APA, but argued that the APA did not apply to immigration matters.

Justice Jackson began the Supreme Court's majority opinion by noting that the APA was "a new, basic and comprehensive regulation of procedures in many agencies" and warning that many agencies might argue for exemptions from its requirements. The Court's early, supportive view of the APA has been often quoted since: "The Act thus represents a long period of study and strife; it settles long-continued and hard-fought contentions, and enacts a formula upon which opposing social and political forces have come to rest. . . ."

Wong alleged two related, but distinct "evils." The first concerned the nature of immigration hearing officers' jobs. In those days, they performed various tasks: interviewing people seeking to enter the country, investigating non-citizens for possible deportation, and, as in this case, actually presiding in a relatively formal judicial capacity over the deportation proceedings. This last role required, among other things, developing the record and making a recommendation for final action by the Commissioner. Regulations prohibited an officer from combining these functions *in any particular case*. But concerns were raised about the realities of the system in practice. All such officers worked out of a common office under common supervision. An officer would sit in judgment on a case that his colleague had investigated, and vice versa. The conflict between the immigration hearing system and the APA was obvious. "Hearing examiners," who preside over such hearings under the APA, were required to be hired and supervised so that they were systematically separated from colleagues involved with investigation and prosecution. Thus, if the APA applied, the INS procedures were inadequate.

The second issue was that the proceedings themselves were inquisitorial in character. Although in some cases, an immigration "prosecutor"—a second officer who would present the government's case—was assigned, in many cases, as in this one, the presiding INS officer would conduct the proceedings on his own. Thus, this officer would present the case, cross-examine the respondent, interrogate other witnesses, if any, and then rule on evidentiary matters and certify the record with a recommendation to the Commissioner. The requirements of the APA as to the inquisitorial process were a little less clear. The APA *could* be understood to forbid a hearing examiner from protecting the government's interests while adjudicating. But the language could also be construed more narrowly—forbidding only a behind-the-scenes role for a clearly designated "prosecutor" in advising or influencing a hearing examiner in a particular case.

The Court had to grapple with two threshold questions. First, the APA hearing examiner provisions applied only to those hearings which were "required by statute to be determined on the record after an opportunity for an agency hearing." Strange though it may seem, at that time no statute required deportation hearings at all. The Supreme Court had, however, long required hearings as matter of due process.[40] Second, did APA § 7(a) exempt deportation hearings? Section 7(a) provided, in relevant part, that "nothing in this Act shall be deemed to supersede the conduct of specified classes of proceedings in whole or part by or before boards or other officers specially provided for by or designated pursuant to statute...."[41]

Today it has become familiar to speak of "immigration exceptionalism," treating immigration law as a highly specialized field where many of the normal constitutional and administrative rules do not hold, because of the Supreme Court's deference to the "plenary power" of the political branches. In that light, the *Wong Yang Sung* Court's recitation of the importance of uniformity in administrative proceedings is particularly striking.[42] Whether this was due to the Court's desire to say something important about the recently enacted APA or its reluctance to struggle with the constitutionally minimal requirements for deportation hearings is a tricky question. In any case, the Court saw that a fundamental purpose of the APA was "to curtail and change the practice of embodying in one person or agency the duties of prosecutor and judge." Indeed, Justice Jackson quoted extensively from a government report[43] that had said that such practice "not only undermines judicial fairness; it weakens public confidence in that fairness."[44] The Court also cited a 1940 government report about the INS that said: "A genuinely impartial hearing ... is psychologically improbable if not impossible, when the presiding officer has at once the responsibility of appraising the strength of the case and of seeking to make it as strong as possible...."[45]

The Court found that the immigration system specifically was "a perfect exemplification of the practices so unanimously condemned."[46] Moreover, in what by current standards seems a remarkably warm appreciation of the harshness of deportation, the Court noted that:

> [T]his commingling, if objectionable anywhere, would seem to
> be particularly so in the deportation proceeding, where we
> frequently meet with a voteless class of litigants who not only
> lack the influence of citizens, but who are strangers to the laws
> and customs in which they find themselves involved and who
> often do not even understand the tongue in which they are
> accused.[47]

But did the APA apply? The government had argued that, since there was no express requirement for any hearing or adjudication in the statute authorizing deportation,[48] these proceedings were not covered. But hearings had been required by the Court as a matter of constitutional interpretation. In the end, the Court relied on a complex sort of constitutional logic—and an implicit extension of its own authority— noting that even though the statute did not require a hearing, deportation without one would be unconstitutional. In other words, as the Court famously put it:

> When the Constitution requires a hearing, it requires a fair one, one before a tribunal which meets at least currently prevailing standards of impartiality. A deportation hearing involves issues basic to human liberty and happiness and, in the present upheavals in lands to which aliens may be returned, perhaps to life itself.[49]

And what of the argument that the immigration system was outside the APA under Section 7? The Court concluded that nothing in the immigration statute "specifically provides that immigrant inspectors shall conduct deportation hearings or be designated to do so."[50] Thus, the APA controlled.

Wong Yang Sung thus affirmed three basic, intertwined propositions of immense importance:

- The new APA applied to deportation proceedings;
- The constitutional protections of due process applied to deportation proceedings; but
- The Court would save for another day the question of what due process would require in the event of specific congressional exemption of deportation cases from the APA.

There were two major legal developments in the two years between the decision in *Wong Yang Sung* and the commencement of deportation proceedings against Carlos Marcello. Reacting to *Wong Yang Sung,* Congress adopted a rider to the Justice Department's supplemental appropriation in 1950 that specifically exempted exclusion and deportation proceedings from APA requirements.[51] If matters had stayed there, the Court might have had to confront directly the due process question it had avoided in *Wong Yang Sung.* But there was more to come. In 1952, Congress enacted a new and comprehensive immigration statute—the Immigration and Nationality Act (INA), also known as the McCarran– Walter Act. Its deportation hearing provision was not as procedurally restrictive as the APA. The INA only prohibited a hearing officer from conducting a proceeding in a particular case in which he or she had performed either investigative or prosecuting functions.[52] It permitted the hearing officer to "present and receive evidence, interrogate, examine, and cross-examine the alien or witnesses." Moreover, special inquiry officers were subject to supervision by the Attorney General.[53] In practice, this meant supervision by INS district directors and other officials with enforcement responsibilities. Finally, in what may have been a direct swipe at the *Wong Yang Sung* decision, the INA was to be "the sole and exclusive" deportation procedure.[54]

Marcello and the Courts

Carlos Marcello's deportation proceedings had been conducted under this new statute. After he was ordered deported, his habeas petition raised three issues: that the proceedings violated due process, that they did not conform to the APA, and that his deportation violated the Ex Post Facto Clause. He lost on all points in the Eastern District of Louisiana. As before, the process moved quickly. The court decision was dated June 8, 1953, a mere six days after Marcello had been re-arrested following the BIA dismissal of his appeal.

The district court was unimpressed by the due process and APA claims, which were somewhat confusingly intertwined at this early stage. The court held that the new INA guaranteed a fair hearing "before an executive tribunal which meets currently prevailing standards of impartiality." The mere fact that the deportation procedure deviated from the APA was not a due process concern, because the APA "is not the sole criterion of due process of law."[55] Moreover, the court held that Marcello's procedural claim "would seem to be largely academic," as he did not deny his conviction under the Marijuana Tax Act.[56] Thus, "no amount of due process would help him."[57] Furthermore, said the court, the Ex Post Facto Clause of the Constitution applies only to criminal proceedings.

At the very end of this decision, the court reported that the government did not oppose Marcello's release on bail. Thus, after posting $10,000 bond, he was released.[58] Marcello may have been an early beneficiary of a more lenient detention policy that was publicly announced by Attorney General Brownell in 1954. The new rules mandated detention only of those who were deemed likely to abscond or who were dangerous to national security or public safety.[59] Surprisingly, given the BIA's recitation of Marcello's criminal background and its reliance on indications that he was the leading racketeer in Louisiana, the government apparently did not consider that Marcello met these criteria. One wonders whether the years of litigation that were to follow would have taken place had Marcello remained in custody.

The Fifth Circuit affirmed the district court decision.[60] Marcello lost again on both of his APA claims. The Fifth Circuit now determined that *Wong Yang Sung* was no longer applicable because "Congress has provided [in the new Immigration and Nationality Act] a 'sole and exclusive' procedure for determining the deportability of an alien."

Although the court conceded that deportation could not proceed in violation of procedural due process, it agreed with the district court that the APA was not synonymous with due process.[61] It then rejected all of Marcello's due process claims, which ranged from the separation of functions issue, to the fact that the rules of evidence did not apply in deportation proceedings, to allegations that his case had been prejudged by the Board. The prejudgment argument was based upon the recently decided case of *United States ex rel. Accardi v. Shaughnessy*,[62] in which the Supreme Court had held that Accardi was entitled to a hearing to try and prove his allegations that his name had appeared on a list of "unsavory characters" whom the Attorney General wished to have deported. The Court held that the BIA was required to use its own discretion, independently of any views of the Attorney General privately communicated to its members. If the allegations were true, it was therefore likely that such discretion was compromised by the Attorney General's list.[63] Counsel of record in *Accardi* had been none other than Jack Wasserman.

Marcello argued that the Attorney General had made a public statement announcing his arrest as "the first major deportation move undertaken since the new Immigration and Nationality Act became effective." He further alleged that the Attorney General had said that he "was an undesirable citizen [sic] and had been guilty of many crimes, and that the proceedings were specially designed to deport [him] and that such publicity was bound to have great effect upon the special inquiry officer."[64] Marcello also claimed that he believed that the Attorney General had prepared a list of 152 persons whom he desired to deport, and that his name was on this list.[65] The court, however, noted that there was no evidence in the record of any such list, though there was evidence of unfavorable publicity. Nevertheless, said the court, even if the Attorney General had made such a statement, it could not have prejudiced Marcello or influenced the special inquiry officer because this was not a case with closely contested factual issues.[66] Although there were disputed factual issues relating to the suspension claim, the court found no flaw in the BIA's ruling denying relief. The fact that some of his initial convictions had been reversed or had resulted in a pardon did not preclude the Board from considering them as a matter of discretion.[67] The Ex Post Facto Clause argument was rejected, based on Supreme Court precedent to the contrary. The court noted that "Congress has plenary power over aliens and may deport them from this country at any time for any reason, even on grounds nonexistent at the time of their entry."[68]

When the case reached the Supreme Court, Marcello's legal theories, refined by Jack Wasserman, were presented in somewhat more subtle form. He argued that there were several significant discrepancies between the APA and the INA, particularly involving the separation of functions provisions, and that the APA should prevail, unless the INA expressly negated its application.[69] Wasserman vigorously attacked the supervision of the special inquiry officer by INS investigators and prosecutors.

Justice Clark wrote for a 5–3 majority in *Marcello v. Bonds*, rejecting the appeal. Strong dissents were written by Justices Black and Frankfurter on the APA and due process issues, and by Justice Douglas on the Ex Post Facto Clause issue. For the majority, the APA question was "whether the Congress had reversed itself [after the 1950 appropriations rider] in the 1952 Immigration Act and in effect reinstated the *Sung* case. . . ." A comparison of the pertinent provisions of the two statutes seemed to the Court "perhaps the strongest indication that the Congress had no such intention."[70] Citing many points of convergence, the Court concluded that it was "clear that Congress was setting up a specialized administrative procedure applicable to deportation hearings, drawing liberally on the analogous provisions of the Administrative Procedure Act and adapting them to the particular needs of the deportation process."[71] Although the Court conceded that exemptions from the terms of the APA are not lightly to be presumed,[72] stated that it could

> not ignore the background of the 1952 immigration legislation, its laborious adaptation of the [APA] to the deportation process, the specific points at which deviations from the [APA] were made, the recognition in the legislative history of this adaptive technique and of the particular deviations, and the direction in the statute that the methods therein prescribed shall be the sole and exclusive procedure for deportation proceedings.[73]

Eschewing the requirement of "magical passwords" to effectuate an exemption from the APA, the Court thus held that the INA expressly superseded its hearing provisions. This was an immensely important conclusion for the functioning of the immigration system. Had the Court held otherwise—and had Congress failed to respond—virtually every deportation hearing that had been conducted in the preceding couple of years would have been subject to collateral attack.

The logic of the majority opinion as to the APA seems convincing until one reads the dissent authored by Justice Black and joined by Justice Frankfurter, arguably the leading expert on administrative law on the Court at that time. The dissent began its analysis from a starkly different basic principle: "A fair hearing necessarily includes an impartial tribunal." From this fundamental idea, which, as we have seen, was a key concern dating back to the 1930s, the dissenters proceeded in a rather simple, functional way. The officer who had conducted Marcello's hearings, who had decided his case, and who had made recommendations for his deportation was inextricably connected to the INS. He was subject to the supervision, direction and control of the Attorney General and his subordinates in the Immigration Service who performed investigative and prosecutorial functions. Thus, the hearing officer adjudicated the case against Marcello that his own superiors had initiated and prosecuted. The dissenters found it unnecessary to resolve the profound due process questions this system posed. There was a patent violation of the APA, which controlled, particularly in view of its § 12: "No subsequent legislation shall be held to supersede or modify the provisions of this Act except to the extent that such legislation shall do so expressly." The 1950 appropriation rider had been an express modification, but the 1952 INA was not.[74]

The legislative history of the INA was instructive. The original proposals for the 1952 Act *had* expressly stated that the APA should not control immigration proceedings. Hearings on these proposals brought strong protests from some organizations, including the ABA, against the provision making the APA inapplicable to deportation proceedings.[75] The sponsors of the immigration measures thereupon introduced new bills that omitted the targeted words. Indeed, Senator McCarran had specifically stated: "The Administrative Procedure Act is made applicable to the bill. The Administrative Procedure Act prevails now.... The bill provides for administrative procedures and makes the Administrative Procedure Act applicable insofar as the administration of the bill is concerned."[76] The key for the dissenters was that no language in the 1952 Immigration Act *expressly* authorized deportation cases to be heard by hearing officers "who are the dependent subordinates of the immigration agency's prosecutorial staff."[77] The very idea was seen to be "wholly inconsistent with our concepts of justice." And, indeed, it had been the general motivating principle behind the APA itself.[78] "Human nature," wrote Justices Black and Frankfurter, "has not put an impassable barrier between subjection and subserviency, particularly when job security is at stake. That Congress was aware of this is shown by the Procedure Act, and we should not construe the Immigration Act on a contrary assumption."[79]

Marcello's other major claims fell more easily. As to prejudgment, the Court noted that Marcello did not even allege that either the inquiry officer or the BIA had seen the Attorney General's alleged list, had known of its existence, or had been influenced in their decisions by the inclusion of his name on it. Nor did the unfavorable publicity impress the Court. The sole issue as to deportability had required a mechanical application of the new immigration statute to the undisputed facts of Marcello's drug conviction. The Board had considered the question of suspending deportation on the merits even though it was not bound to do so, owing to Marcello's waiver below.[80]

The Court also disposed of the technical ex post facto issue rather blithely, citing recent precedent.[81] Nonetheless, the retroactive deportation of long-term residents raises profound concerns. Indeed, Justices Black and Frankfurter, although not focusing on the ex post facto issue, began their dissent in a way that highlighted the unfairness of such practice: "Petitioner was lawfully brought to this country forty-four years ago when he was eight months old and has resided here ever since. He is married and has four children. His wife and children are American citizens."

Justice Douglas, in his dissent, confronted the retroactivity problem head-on: "The Constitution places a ban on all ex post facto laws. There are no qualifications or exceptions."[82] Noting that there was a "school of thought that the ex post facto clause includes all retroactive legislation, civil as well as criminal,"[83] Douglas conceded that the Court had repeatedly stated, since the 1798 case of *Calder v. Bull*,[84] that the Ex Post Facto Clause applies only in criminal cases. But he also noted a parallel line of cases, dating back to Chief Justice Marshall's opinion in *Fletcher v. Peck*,[85] that had refused to construe the Ex Post Facto Clause narrowly and restrict it to criminal prosecutions. Rejecting formalist descriptions of deportation as a merely civil proceeding, Douglas reiterated that deportation may be as severe a punishment as loss of livelihood.[86] Quoting Justice Brandeis, he stated that deportation may result "in loss of both property and life; or of all that makes life worth living."[87] There was no finding that Marcello was "undesirable for continued residence here." Therefore, according to Douglas,

> In the absence of a rational connection between the imposition of the penalty of deportation and the *present* desirability of the alien as a resident in this country, the conclusion is inescapable that the Act merely adds a new punishment for a past offense. That is the very injustice that the Ex Post Facto Clause was designed to prevent.[88]

In the end, however, Marcello lost on every theory. The case, not much of a bombshell at the time, did have at least two important consequences. First, it apparently put to rest the broader due process implications of *Wong Yang Sung*. The *Marcello* Court essentially ignored the argument that there was any constitutional problem with the deportation system in the 1952 Act. Indeed, the *Marcello* Court had not even mentioned *Wong Yang Sung* in its breathtakingly short analysis of the constitutional questions: "The contention is without substance when considered against the long-standing practice in deportation proceedings ... and against the special considerations applicable to deportation which the Congress may take into account in exercising its particularly broad discretion in immigration matters."[89] Second—and clearly related to the first point—it reinforced the exceptionalism of immigration law, rendering it outside many of the most important protections contained in the APA.

But judicial rejection was not the final word on this subject. There was widespread criticism of the harsh deportation laws and of the INS throughout the mid–1950s. President Eisenhower had supported various liberalizations, some of which were enacted. Attorney General Brownell eased detention practices, as noted, in late 1954.[90] Special inquiry officers were also targeted.[91] In 1955, the Hoover Commission Task Force reported that "These officers for the most part are unqualified to perform legal or judicial functions."[92]

The questions raised by Marcello and others were thus not ignored,[93] and they eventually led to reforms achieving most of what Wasserman had advocated. The INS promulgated regulations in 1955 and 1956 requiring the use of a separate prosecuting officer in cases involving disputed factual issues.[94] In later years, the INS required all special inquiry officers to have law degrees, assigned INS trial attorneys to represent the government in all deportation cases, and redesignated hearing officers as immigration judges. In 1983, the new Executive Office for Immigration Review separated immigration judges entirely from the INS and placed them in a special adjudication unit of the Department of Justice.[95] Since then, deportation hearings generally conform to the procedural requirements for formal adjudication under the APA. All of this could be seen as a positive contribution to the law from Carlos Marcello's early legal battles, even though he narrowly lost the crucial Supreme Court decision.

Attempts to Deport: Judicial Review and the Kennedy Connection

The INS moved quickly to effectuate Marcello's deportation order. But it encountered a knotty problem. Where exactly could he be sent? The INA listed the countries to which a non-citizen could be deported,[96] ostensibly presenting a variety of options, obviously designed to accord considerable leeway to the government.[97] It provided, first, that the deportation should be to a country designated by the non-citizen, if that country was willing to accept him into its territory, unless the Attorney General concluded that deportation to that country would be prejudicial to the interests of the United States. It permitted only one such designation. On June 29, 1955, Marcello designated France. This was not a frivolous choice on his part, as Tunisia had been under French control at the time of his birth there. The government of France, however, was apparently not anxious to welcome Marcello to its bosom. On July 21, 1955, the INS received a formal refusal to accept him from the government of France.

The law also provided that deportation might be directed to any country of which the deportee was "a subject, national, or citizen, if that country is willing to accept him into its territory." Failing that, the Attorney General, in his discretion, was authorized to designate certain other countries, including the country from which "the alien last entered the United States" and the country in which he was born. The statute offered a total of seven different choices, the last of which—a poignantly ironic combination of hospitality and rejection—was to any country willing to accept the person into its territory.

After France refused to accept Marcello, the government turned to the next logical candidate: Italy. But the Italian government suddenly withdrew the permission that it had previously granted to Marcello to enter its territory. Exactly why this was so remains mysterious. It appears that Marcello undertook legal proceedings in the courts of Italy to secure a cancellation of his own permission to enter. Robert Blakey alleges that Marcello paid a $25,000 bribe to "a high ranking official of the Italian court."[98] In light of his record, one can appreciate the reluctance of his parents' homeland to welcome him back, but whether that concern, corruption, or the legal merits led to Italy's refusal to accept him remains uncertain.

This seems to have left the U.S. government in a bit of a pickle. And there matters stewed for some six years until what is probably the most incredible part of our tale began to unfold. The government had exerted strenuous efforts to deport Marcello. But Jack Wasserman had used the system brilliantly to keep his client in the United States. Indeed, in 1959, Attorney General Rogers wrote a letter to Senator Sam Ervin, a member of the McClellan committee who had already expressed considerable concern about Marcello. The letter recounted how Marcello's attorneys had instituted lawsuits on at least six different occasions, challenging various aspects of his deportation proceedings and leading to several trips to the court of appeals and three to the U.S. Supreme Court. (There had also been extensive legal measures undertaken in Italian courts.) For example, immediately following the Supreme Court's dismissal of Marcello's appeal of his deportation order on May 31, 1955, a suit for a declaratory judgment was filed in the U.S. District Court for the District of Columbia, again challenging the deportation order and seeking to restrain the government from deporting Marcello.[99] The declaratory judgment action was dismissed on October 25, 1955, thereby permitting deportation. However, the government was apparently unable to accomplish this during the statutorily allowed six-month period due to its inability to obtain travel documents.[100] Marcello was then released from custody on supervised release as required by the INA.[101] On October 31, 1956, fearing that he might be summarily deported, Marcello filed an action for a preliminary injunction that he not be deported without at least three days' notice.[102] The district court issued a temporary restraining order against the government, but Marcello was served the very next day with a "notice of intention to take him into custody and deport him after the expiration of 72 hours."[103] Thus, his motion for a preliminary injunction was denied. Wasserman, however, appealed the denial to the D.C. Circuit and obtained, as a result, a stay of deportation pending appeal.[104] These cases held off deportation for more than eight more months, before being finally denied and remanded to the district court in August 1957. When deportation again seemed imminent, in October 1957, Wasserman filed yet another suit for declaratory and injunctive relief in the district court, alleging that Marcello had sought a stay on the grounds of fear of physical persecution if deported to Italy and that his request had been denied due to "bias and prejudice, unfair hearings, and the application of improper statutory standards."[105] Seven days later, Wasserman also filed a *certiorari* petition in the Supreme Court, relating to the final action taken in August by the D.C. Circuit. These two proceedings delayed deportation for another year. Indeed, in October 1958, the court of appeals remanded the case to the district court, with directions that the court send the case back to the INS for further proceedings in which Marcello would be allowed a reasonable period of time to gather and present further evidence in support of his stay application.[106]

According to Attorney General Rogers, these suits, though mostly resolved in favor of the government, resulted in a "court-imposed restraint from deporting Marcello during most of this time." At the end of the letter, Rogers opined that, "[o]n the basis of past experience it is expected that Marcello will attempt other delaying tactics in the courts."[107]

Now begins the strangest part of our story. A Senate committee had been formed to investigate labor and corruption, chaired by Senator John McClellan. Its chief counsel was young Robert F. Kennedy. His brother, then-Senator John F. Kennedy, was also a member. In March 1959, Marcello was called as a witness before the McClellan committee, where he was accompanied by Jack Wasserman. Before Marcello took the stand, former FBI agent Aaron Kohn, who had been the principal investigator looking at the Marcello organization, provided the committee with extensive testimony about the history of the Mafia in New Orleans and the rise of Marcello to his current position of power. No fan of understatement, Kohn asserted that he believed that the Marcello organization was poised to achieve virtually complete control of the political and law enforcement machinery of the state of Louisiana.[108] When committee counsel Robert Kennedy interrogated the witness Carlos Marcello, however, he obtained only some seventy recitations of refusal to testify on grounds that "it may intend [sic] to incriminate

me." By all accounts, the committee members, and especially Robert
Kennedy, were exasperated by Marcello's arrogance and his repeated
reliance upon the Fifth Amendment.

Attorney Jack Wasserman sits between Carlos Marcello (left) and his brother
Vincent Marcello at the 1959 Senate hearings. (AP/Wide World Photos)

Less than two years later, when Robert Kennedy became Attorney
General in 1961, he undoubtedly remembered this interchange and was
determined to act decisively against Marcello. Indeed, the *New Orleans
States–Item* reported on December 28, 1960 a promise by Attorney–
General designate Kennedy to expedite Marcello's deportation.[109] This fit
perfectly with one of his main priorities: to wage war on organized crime.
He had written in his book, *The Enemy Within*: "If we do not attack
organized criminals with weapons and techniques as effective as their
own, they will destroy us."[110]

One idea, incredible though it may seem in retrospect, was to deport
Marcello to Formosa (now known as Taiwan). Justice Department documents obtained by John H. Davis state that,

> The General advised in extreme confidence that he had already
> secured authority from Formosa to deport Marcello there but he
> was seeking to arrange deportation to a closer country so that
> Marcello could be put on an Immigration and Naturalization

Service plane and his deportation effected before Marcello's attorney could institute court action to delay this.[111]

Such a swift removal, as it turned out, was exactly what happened— but not to Formosa. Apparently, in 1956, Carlos Marcello had obtained a false birth certificate from Guatemala by paying a large bribe to the law partner of the Guatemalan President.[112] It is not entirely clear why he would have done this, but it was perhaps a kind of deportation insurance policy. He was well-connected in Guatemala, seems to have traveled there with some regularity, and probably thought he could live there—a mere four-hour flight from New Orleans—if worse came to worst. His misfortune was that the birth certificate came to the attention and into the hands of the INS. Officials of the United States asked officials of Guatemala to accept Marcello if he were deported there. Permission for Marcello to enter was issued by the Guatemalan government (which, it should be noted, had been put into power less than a decade earlier through a CIA-supported *coup d'etat*).[113]

On April 4, 1961, Marcello made his way from home to the INS office in New Orleans for a regular check-in as required by the terms of his supervised release. He was accompanied to the building by a lawyer, Phillip Smith, who waited outside while Marcello went in.[114] All seemed normal until the INS agent suddenly began reading to him from a statement that said he was a citizen of Guatemala and would be immediately deported there. Marcello has described what happened next:

> I said what for. He say well you been overdue on your visa. I couldn't understand it myself. I just, I just couldn't believe it. So by that time two immigration officers that I have never seen before, they came up and they put the handcuffs on me. Two of them, about six foot something. So I say, could I use the telephone. I say I'd like to call to talk to my attorney. They say no. I say, can I call my wife to get a toothbrush and some money. They said no, let's go.[115]

Marcello was handcuffed and taken quickly out of the building to a waiting car. By all accounts, he did not go easily. He demanded to call Wasserman. Denied. He asked to be allowed to get some clothes and some money. Denied. He claimed he was being kidnapped. He said that the deportation was a violation of an order issued by Justice Hugo Black that he be given seventy-two hours' notice before being deported.[116] Less than one hour later, Marcello found himself to be the only passenger, along with two immigration agents, a pilot and co-pilot, on a seventy-eight-passenger plane bound for Guatemala. As he described the scene, "You would have thought it was the President going in instead of me going out."[117]

There is little doubt that the Justice Department knew that the Guatemalan birth certificate was fraudulent. Indeed, on April 6, 1961, two days after Marcello's deportation, Herbert J. Miller, Jr., assistant attorney general in the criminal division, received a communiqué from Edward Silberling, chief of the organized crime and racketeering section:

> In light of the information contained in our intelligence file the United States Government may be placed in the embarrassing legal position of having made certain representations to the Guatemalan government about Marcello's birth record while it was in possession of information indicating that the birth record was a forgery.[118]

Marcello's later description of the incident is uncomfortably close to the legal truth: "They just snatched me, and that is it, actually kidnapped me . . . and dumped me in Guatemala."[119]

Soon after Marcello's deportation, his attorneys filed an action in federal court for a declaratory judgment that the Guatemala deportation was invalid.[120] The court was told that, subsequent to his arrival in that country, the Guatemalan government had cancelled its prior permission and was now seeking to expel him. This, however, did not help him in a U.S. court. The judge professed no power to "intrude into any negotiations between the Government of the United States and the government of a foreign country." His reason? "The conduct of foreign relations is left solely to the President and his subordinates." The validity of the birth certificate was "not material," because "[t]he Government of Guatemala has accepted the plaintiff, and once the acceptance was acted on and the plaintiff was brought by our Government to Guatemala and landed there, the transaction is at an end."[121]

After he was, in fact, expelled from Guatemala, Marcello's lawyers tried again, with a motion to vacate the summary judgment. Again, however, the court declined to consider the matter:

> Once a foreign country informs this Government that it would accept a deportee from this country and he is actually permitted to land in that country pursuant to such acceptance, the matter is at an end so far as this country is concerned. . . . What the other country does thereafter does not affect the validity of the legality of the deportation.[122]

So we know that Marcello lost in court. But what actually happened on the ground? One version of the story, told by Frank Ragano, former attorney for Santo Trafficante, Jr.,[123] and Jimmy Hoffa, and also told by Robert Blakey, is that Marcello was deported from Guatemala to El Salvador, where he was held in a military barracks in the jungle for four or five days before being put on a bus, together with Michael Maroun, a visiting lawyer from Shreveport, Louisiana (one cannot help but wonder how this lawyer billed for his time). When the bus stopped at the Honduran border, the two were forced to cross on foot and were abandoned there in a remote area. Marcello, at that time fifty-one years old, "paunchy," and dressed in a business suit and tie, had to trek some seventeen miles in the hot sun before reaching "a peasant village" from which he and his attorney were able to get a ride to Tegucigalpa. Somehow from there, they managed to get a flight and to re-enter the United States through Miami, "illegally but unhindered."[124] At least the last part of this story seems likely, as Marcello was soon indicted for illegal entry and using an invalid passport.

Others tell a less exciting tale. Ed Reid, the Pulitzer Prize-winning author of one of the first Mafia exposés,[125] reports that Marcello was actually wined and dined by the upper crust of Guatemalan society. He was then flown to a resort area in a private plane belonging to the President of Guatemala, where he was photographed at a racetrack with an old friend who owned the largest shrimp boat fleet in the Gulf of Mexico. According to this version, Marcello made his way to Honduras in comfort and was then escorted home on one of his friend's boats.[126]

In any case, things now get really interesting. Unfortunately, they also get murkier.[127] Edward Becker, who testified before the House Select Committee on Assassinations,[128] reported that during a September 1962 Mafia business meeting in a country barn in the Louisiana marshes, Marcello cried out: *"Livarsi na petra di la scarpa!"* a Mafia cry of revenge: "Take the stone out of my shoe!" "Don't worry about that little Bobby son of a bitch," he then reportedly shouted, "He's going to be taken care of!"[129]

According to Ed Reid, Marcello knew that to rid himself of Robert Kennedy, he would first have to deal with his brother, the President. As Marcello reportedly put it, "The dog will keep biting you if you only cut off its tail."[130] Becker testified that Marcello had explained that he would likely use someone not affiliated with his organization to do the job. Reportedly, the use of "a nut," as John H. Davis later phrased it, was a venerable Mafia tradition.[131]

Frank Ragano reports a conversation with Marcello that he had in March, 1962. Ragano claims that Marcello said to him, "You, Jimmy, and me are in for hard times as long as Bobby Kennedy is in office. Someone ought to kill that son-of-a-bitch.... Someone ought to kill all those goddamn Kennedys."[132] Ragano offers various anecdotes about the rage building in Hoffa, Trafficante, and Marcello against the Kennedys, including an incident in which Jimmy Hoffa allegedly had physically assaulted Robert Kennedy during a meeting at the Justice Department.[133] In September 1962, Santo Trafficante reportedly told Jose Aleman, a leader of the Cuban expatriate community in Miami, that

John F. Kennedy was "going to be hit."[134] Soon thereafter, in July 1963, Ragano claims that he had lunch with Jimmy Hoffa to prepare for a meeting that he was going to have later with Carlos Marcello and Santo Trafficante. Ragano says that Hoffa told him, "Something has to be done. The time has come for your friend [Trafficante] and Carlos to get rid of him, kill that son-of-a-bitch John Kennedy.... This has got to be done.... We're running out of time—something has got to be done."[135] Ragano asserts that he communicated this instruction to Trafficante and Marcello, thinking it was a joke. Ragano says that he waited for the laughter but there was only silence and "[t]heir facial expressions were icy." Then, when the news came from Dallas on November 22, 1963, Ragano says that Hoffa called him and said "Did you hear the good news? They killed the son-of-a-bitch bastard. Yeah, he's dead.... Lyndon Johnson is going to be sworn in as president. You know he'll get rid of Booby [sic]."[136]

Later, according to Ragano, Marcello told him to tell Hoffa that, "he owes me and he owes me big." Ragano also asserts that Hoffa said to him, with a grin, "I told you they could do it. I'll never forget what Carlos and Santo did for me."[137] Thirty years after that, according to Ragano, Santo Trafficante, on his deathbed, told his lawyer, "Carlos fucked up. We shouldn't have killed Giovanni. We should have killed Bobby."[138]

The assertion that Carlos Marcello was a leader of a successful Mafia conspiracy to assassinate President Kennedy is far from universally accepted.[139] The House Assassinations Committee Report did state, however, that the most likely organized crime figures to have participated in a unilateral assassination plan were Carlos Marcello and Santo Trafficante. Marcello, according to the committee, had the motive, means and opportunity to have President Kennedy assassinated.[140] In addition to Marcello's status as a prime target of the Kennedy Justice Department, the committee stated that "Marcello exhibited an intense dislike for Robert Kennedy ... claiming that he had been illegally 'kidnapped' by Government agents during the deportation." Marcello was also found to have had "credible associations" with both Lee Harvey Oswald and Jack Ruby[141] as well as with one David W. Ferrie, a shadowy figure with links to Oswald, who was also likely a pilot for Marcello.[142] Ferrie, interviewed after the assassination, stated that he himself may have spoken "in an offhand manner of the desirability of having President Kennedy shot," though he denied actually wanting it to be done. On the morning of the day of the assassination, Ferrie and Marcello were together at a courthouse in New Orleans, awaiting a jury verdict in Marcello's criminal trial on conspiracy and perjury charges.[143]

Marcello categorically denied any involvement in organized crime or the assassination of President Kennedy or even making any kind of threat against the President's life. Unfortunately, as a former FBI official told the committee, "With Marcello, . . . [t]here was just no way of penetrating. . . . He was too smart." Still, the committee noted that Marcello had been "endowed with special powers and privileges not accorded to any other La Cosa Nostra members." He had the extraordinary privilege of conducting syndicate operations without having to seek the approval of the national commission.

Finally, though, the committee cautioned that Marcello's "uniquely successful career in organized crime" was based to a large extent on "a policy of prudence." He was not reckless. Thus, on the basis of the available evidence, the committee stated that it is "unlikely that Marcello was in fact involved in the assassination of the President." On the other hand, "the evidence that he had the motive and the evidence of links through associates to both Oswald and Ruby, coupled with the failure of the 1963–64 investigation by the Warren Commission to explore adequately possible conspiratorial activity in the assassination, precluded a judgment by the committee that Marcello and his associates were not involved."

Other conspiracy theories have also swirled around Marcello, who was well-known to have had rather racist attitudes[144] and to have supported the Ku Klux Klan.[145] Four days after the assassination of Dr. Martin Luther King, Jr., a man went to the FBI in Memphis and reported that he had overheard a white man telling someone on the phone to "kill the S.O.B. on the balcony" and to "get the job done. . . . You will get your $5000.00." The white man continued, "Don't come here. Go to New Orleans and get your money. You know my brother."[146] The FBI determined that the owner of the store, believed to be the caller, was one Frank Liberto. His brother, Salvatore, was a New Orleans associate of Carlos Marcello.[147] The House Assassinations Committee determined in 1978 that the King assassination was likely the result of a conspiracy. James Earl Ray had stayed at a New Orleans motel, known as a Mafia hangout, in December 1967. Ray's brother had told the FBI, "My brother would never do anything unless he was richly paid."

Marcello and Judicial Review

In one of the many ironies of his story, just as Marcello was experiencing an illegal deportation, he was inspiring new laws intended to make legal deportation easier for the government. Indeed, in his 1959 letter to Senator Ervin about Carlos Marcello, Attorney General Rogers had stated that for the previous five years, the administration had sought legislation to limit judicial review of deportation orders, "so as to avoid its repeated use as a delaying tactic."[148]

Stories such as Marcello's ultimately had powerful effects.[149] In 1961, Congress added a new Section 106 to the INA that dramatically changed judicial review procedures.[150] Among its major provisions, the new law imposed stricter requirements for exhaustion of administrative remedies and channeled most review of deportation orders away from district courts.[151] Review generally was expected to occur through a petition for review filed in the appropriate court of appeals, thus eliminating one potential layer of proceedings. Although persons in custody could still file habeas corpus petitions in district courts, new restrictions on repetitive filings were expected to minimize any chance for manipulation or delay. Congress undoubtedly also thought it would expedite cases such as Marcello's in the future by preventing declaratory judgment actions such as those utilized by Wasserman. As it turned out, the success of this attempt to channel and contain judicial review was rather mixed.

A 1981 ruling that also involved Marcello came to stand as an example of the continued possibilities for prolonged review proceedings even under the 1961 amendments.[152] The case involved a new application for suspension of deportation that Marcello had been allowed to file in 1972. Marcello's attorney, for various tactical reasons, challenged the BIA's 1976 denial through a district court habeas corpus petition well after the time had expired for filing a petition for review in the court of appeals. The district court ruled in 1979 and found several defects in the BIA ruling.[153] The government appealed, arguing first that the district court lacked jurisdiction. The court of appeals disagreed. It relied on evolving case law that had expanded the meaning of "custody" in the context of federal habeas review of state criminal convictions to find a similar expansion for purposes of deportation review. Though Marcello was not then physically detained under the deportation order, the court ruled that the restrictions on liberty that accompany the entry of a final order of deportation amount to "custody" for immigration habeas purposes. The 1961 limits on repetitive filings also did not stand as an obstacle to habeas review, largely because the time for the normal petition for review in the court of appeals had expired and the government had not seasonably argued that Marcello "deliberately bypassed" that avenue into the courts. On the merits, however, the government prevailed. The court of appeals reversed the district court and reinstated the BIA's deportation order against Marcello. This ruling, however, came nearly nine years after the 1972 application. Unsuccessful petitions for rehearing and for *certiorari* consumed another five months.

This case, like Marcello's multifarious earlier appeals and petitions, undoubtedly played some role in inspiring further congressional efforts to streamline judicial review, especially habeas corpus. The most extreme examples of this trend, the 1996 laws known as AEDPA[154] and IIRIRA,[155] contained a welter of provisions designed to eliminate judicial review of various immigration decisions, including matters of discretion and deportations based on criminal convictions.[156] The Supreme Court considered these provisions in the 2001 case of *INS v. St. Cyr*,[157] and its ruling offered a powerful admonition to the government. The Court held that the complete preclusion of judicial review in deportation cases would present, at the very least, a "serious constitutional question." As a result, it construed the 1996 amendments in such a way that habeas corpus review remained available, at least to consider "questions of law."[158] The full implications of *St. Cyr* for the reach of the 1996 restrictions on judicial review remain to be worked out.

Conclusion

Throughout the 1960s, 1970s and 1980s, Marcello faced sustained federal law enforcement attention. The INS could not deport him, in part because of complications caused by the illegal 1961 deportation, in part perhaps due to behind-the-scenes influence,[159] but mostly owing to the sustained efforts of Jack Wasserman—who received an estimated two million dollars in legal fees for his work[160]—and the complexity of U.S. immigration law.

Criminal prosecutors, however, eventually had better success, though they faced a long struggle. Although acquitted by a jury of perjury and conspiracy charges on the very day of John Kennedy's assassination, Marcello was again indicted in 1964 for "conspiring to obstruct justice" by "fixing a juror" and seeking the murder of a government witness.[161] The case was tried in 1965, and Marcello was represented, again, by Jack Wasserman. Verdict: not guilty. He was tried in 1968 for assaulting a federal agent (the background story seems to be that the agent was having an affair with Marcello's daughter). He was convicted on this charge but served less than six months in a federal prison medical center.[162]

In the 1970s it was said that, like the medieval understanding of God, "all that there is to know about the Mafia is known by now except whether it actually exists."[163] This was less true of Carlos Marcello: he was famous. *Life* magazine, in 1970, described him as "the second most powerful Mafia leader in the United States ... after Carlo Gambino of New York."[164] The House Select Committee on Crime determined in 1972 that Marcello "has become a formidable menace to the institutions of government and the people of the United States."[165]

Marcello was again indicted in New Orleans on racketeering (RICO) charges, mail and wire fraud and conspiracy charges in 1980, following an elaborate FBI sting operation.[166] Before a packed courtroom, he was convicted in 1981 of RICO conspiracy and three other counts. He was indicted the next day in Los Angeles for conspiring to bribe a U.S.

district court judge. On January 25, 1982, the seventy-two-year-old Marcello was sentenced to seven years. He was, however, released on $300,000 bond, having described himself to the sentencing judge as "a salesman for the Pelican Tomato Company."[167] In April 1982, the Los Angeles case resulted in a ten-year sentence. The judge, echoing the epigraph with which this chapter begins, noted, "I think it's fair to say you're a very bad man."[168]

Marcello entered prison in 1983, facing seventeen years behind bars. The Justice Department had sought and obtained an emergency order for his immediate imprisonment, based on a sealed affidavit stating that he planned to flee the country rather than serve his sentence.[169] One wonders if the aging Marcello appreciated the irony. Robert Kennedy's Justice Department had stretched legal boundaries to avoid judicial interference in its efforts to get him out of the country. But the Reagan Justice Department hastily sought court assistance to prevent that very result—which it might instead have treated as the culmination of a quarter-century deportation effort. By this point, however, Marcello may not have noticed much. He suffered from Alzheimer's disease and had also experienced more than one major stroke. He was released from prison in 1989 and was never seen again in public. He died in 1993, in his mansion in the New Orleans suburb of Metairie, cared for by relatives and private nurses, at the age of eighty-three.

ENDNOTES

1. Oliver Wendell Holmes, The Path of the Law, 10 Harv. L. Rev. 457, 459 (1897).

2. Carlos Marcello, testifying before the House Select Committee on Assassinations 1978 (quoted in John H. Davis, Mafia Kingfish: Carlos Marcello and the Assassination of John F. Kennedy 386 (1989) ("Mafia Kingfish")). I have slightly modified Davis's transcription of this quotation by replacing phonetics such as "de" and "dat" with "the" and "that," in order to maintain the distinctive pattern of Marcello's speech and unique *persona,* without being offensive about it.

3. See generally Davis, Mafia Kingfish; see also Thomas L. Jones, Carlos Marcello: Big Daddy in the Big Easy, available at http://www.crimelibrary.com/gangsters/marcello/ ("Jones").

4. Jones, ch. 1:2.

5. Id., ch. 2:2.

6. Id., ch. 3:2. Another reported version is slightly different. Davis, Mafia Kingfish at 18 (cited in note 2). For more scholarly treatments, see generally John E. Coxe, The New Orleans Mafia Incident, 20 La. Hist. Q. 1067–10 (Oct. 1937); J. Alexander Karlan, The New Orleans Lynchings of 1890 and the American Press, 24 La. Hist. Q. 187–203 (Jan. 1941); John H. Kendall, Who Killa De Chief, 22 La. Hist. Q. 492–530 (April 1939).

7. Davis, Mafia Kingfish at 21–23 (cited in note 2).

8. Id.

9. Id.

10. Jack Wasserman was one of this country's leading immigration lawyers for many decades. In the 1940s, he served a term as a member of the Board of Immigration Appeals

before developing his private practice. In addition to his work for Carlos Marcello, he was involved in dozens of high-profile immigration cases including those of Wong Yang Sung, Ignatz Mezei, Peter Harisiades, Tom We Shung, and many others. He authored many well-regarded books and articles on immigration law from the 1940s through the 1970s (including one of the first texts in the field, entitled Immigration Law and Practice) and was a major figure in the American Immigration Lawyers Association (AILA). Indeed, AILA confers a Jack Wasserman Memorial Award for Excellence in the Field of Immigration Law.

11. Davis, Mafia Kingfish at 28 (cited in note 2).

12. Id. at 36.

13. Id. at 37.

14. And, perhaps, by the collaborative relationship that developed between the U.S. government and the Italian Mafia during that period as a part of the war effort.

15. Well, maybe. Carolla himself apparently re-entered the United States illegally at least once. He died in New Orleans in 1972. G. Robert Blakey and Richard N. Billings, The Plot to Kill the President 241 (1981).

16. Davis, Mafia Kingfish at 58 (cited in note 2).

17. Id.

18. See Inquiry Asks Term For 'Top Criminal, N.Y. Times (Jan. 30, 1951).

19. Davis, Mafia Kingfish at 60.

20. Id.

21. See United States ex rel. Marcello v. Ahrens, 113 F. Supp. 22 (E.D. La. 1953).

22. 66 Stat. 214, 8 U.S.C. § 1254(a)(5) (1952).

23. See Marcello v. Ahrens, 212 F.2d 830, 833 (5th Cir. 1954).

24. Matter of M——, 5 I & N Dec. 261, 270–71 (BIA 1953).

25. 339 U.S. 33 (1950).

26. See generally Stephen Skowronek, Building a New American State: The Expansion of National Administrative Capacities, 1877–1920 (1982).

27. Robert Rabin, Federal Regulation in Historical Perspective, 38 Stan. L. Rev. 1189 (1986).

28. Id.

29. See generally Walter Gellhorn, The Administrative Procedure Act: The Beginnings, 72 Va. L. Rev. 219 (1986) ("Gellhorn") (Professor Gellhorn served as Director of the Attorney General's Committee on Administrative Procedure from 1939–1941).

30. 58 A.B.A. Rep. 197, 203 (1933). The committee thought that such functions should either be transferred to an independent tribunal or that "judicial-type" agency decisions should be subject to full factual and legal review by an independent tribunal. 59 A.B.A. Rep. 539 (1934). Gellhorn at 220.

31. See, e.g., Louis L. Jaffe, Invective and Investigation in Administrative Law, 52 Harv. L. Rev. 1201, 1233–34 (1939).

32. Jacob M. Lashly, Administrative Law and the Bar, 25 Va. L. Rev. 641, 658 (1939).

33. Final Report of the Attorney General's Committee on Administrative Procedure, Administrative Procedure in Government Agencies, S. Doc. No. 8, 77th Cong., 1st Sess. 1 (1941) ("Final Committee Report"); Gellhorn 225 (cited in note 29).

34. See S. Rep. No. 752, 79th Cong., 1st Sess. 37–38 (1945), reprinted in Administrative Procedure Act: Legislative History, S. Doc. No. 248, 79th Cong., 2d Sess. 223–24 (1946). Gellhorn at 231.

35. 92 Cong. Rec. 2167 (1946) (passage by the Senate); 92 Cong. Rec. 5668 (1946) (amended version passed by House); 92 Cong. Rec. 5791 (1946) (House version agreed to by Senate); 92 Cong. Rec. 6706 (1946) (approved by the President).

36. Martin Shapiro, APA: Past, Present, and Future, 72 Va. L. Rev. 447 (1986).

37. See generally Peter L. Strauss, Changing Times: The APA at Fifty, 63 U. Chi. L. Rev. 1389 (1996).

38. 339 U.S. 33 (1950).

39. § 5(c), 60 Stat. 237, 240, 5 U.S.C. § 1004(c); § 11, 60 Stat. at 244, 5 U.S.C. § 1010.

40. See Yamataya v. Fisher, 189 U.S. 86, 100, 101 (1903); Kwock Jan Fat v. White, 253 U.S. 454, 459, 464 (1920); Bridges v. Wixon, 326 U.S. 135, 160 (1945) (concurring opinion).

41. 60 Stat. 237, 241, 5 U.S.C. § 1006 (1946).

42. "One purpose was to introduce greater uniformity of procedure and standardization of administrative practice among the diverse agencies whose customs had departed widely from each other." 339 U.S. at 41 (footnote omitted).

43. Report of the President's Committee on Administrative Management, Administrative Management in the Government of the United States, 36–37 (Govt. Printing Office 1937).

44. Id. at 42.

45. The Secretary of Labor's Committee on Administrative Procedure, The Immigration and Naturalization Service, 77, 81–82 (Mimeo. 1940) (cited in 339 U.S. at 43).

46. 339 U.S. at 45.

47. Id. at 47.

48. See Section 19(a) of the Immigration Act of February 5, 1917, 39 Stat. 874, 889, as amended, 8 U.S.C. § 155(a) (1946).

49. 339 U.S. at 49–50. The tricky part of this argument is that the Court had never quite said before that without a hearing there would be "no constitutional authority" for deportation. And it had certainly never said that such a hearing had to be identical to those mandated in other administrative settings. Indeed, *Yamataya v. Fisher* was essentially what in modern terms we would call a "clear statement" case—one in which the Court interpreted a statute in a certain way to avoid a constitutional problem. The *Yamataya* Court had said: "This is the *reasonable construction of the acts of Congress here in question*, and they need not be otherwise interpreted. In the case of all acts of Congress, such interpretation ought to be adopted as, without doing violence to the import of the words used, will bring them into harmony with the Constitution." 189 U.S. 86, 101 (1903) (emphasis added).

50. 339 U.S. at 52. The statutory language did "direct them to conduct border inspections of aliens seeking admission . . . [and to] administer oaths and take, record, and consider evidence." But, said the Court, Congress had not, by granting these powers, "specially constituted them or provided for their designation as hearing officers in deportation proceedings." Id.

51. Supplemental Appropriation Act of 1951, ch. 1052, 64 Stat. 1044, 1048 (1950) (exempting deportation and exclusion proceedings from the Administrative Procedure Act, ch. 324, §§ 5, 7–8 60 Stat. 237, 239 (1946), repealed by Immigration and Nationality Act of

1952, ch. 477, § 403(a)(47), 66 Stat. 163, 280). This was not the first attempt. Indeed, in the immediate aftermath of the passage of the APA, proposed legislation had sought to exempt the INS from the hearing requirements of APA § 5. See H.R. 6652, 80th Cong., 2d Sess., 94 Cong. Rec. 6374 (1948). The bill, H.R. 6652, was sent to the House Judiciary Committee, 94 Cong. Rec. 6374 (1948), which reported the bill out without amendment within two weeks. H.R. Rep. No. 2140, 80th Cong., 2d Sess. (1948). No further action was taken, however.

52. 66 Stat. 208 (1950). An alternative method was permitted by the statute, however, under which an additional immigration officer presented the evidence while the special inquiry officer presided. See 8 C.F.R. § 242.53 (1955).

53. 66 Stat. 171 (1950).

54. INA § 242(b) (1952).

55. 113 F. Supp. at 22.

56. The Marijuana Act of Aug. 2, 1937, Pub. L. No. 238, ch. 553, 75th Cong. (26 U.S.C. §§ 2590 et seq.).

57. 113 F. Supp. at 26.

58. Id.

59. See Text of U.S. Attorney General's Talk to New Citizens, N.Y. Times 14 (Nov. 12, 1954).

60. Marcello v. Ahrens, 212 F. 2d 830 (5th Cir. 1954).

61. Id., citing the rather different case of United States v. Morton Salt Co., 338 U.S. 632, 644 (1950) (the Administrative Procedure Act created safeguards even narrower than the constitutional ones, against arbitrary official encroachment on private rights).

62. 347 U.S. 260 (1954).

63. See Daniel Kanstroom, St. Cyr or Insincere: The Strange Quality of Supreme Court Victory, 16 Geo. Immigr. L.J. 413 (2002) ("St. Cyr or Insincere"). On remand, Accardi was judged unable to prove the allegations, but the case made it to the Supreme Court again, which affirmed. 349 U.S. 280 (1955).

64. For the text of the release, see Marcello v. Bonds, 349 U.S. 302, 312 (1955).

65. 212 F.2d at 838.

66. Id.

67. Id. at 840. See also Marcello v. United States, 196 F.2d 437 (5th Cir. 1952). See Kanstroom, St. Cyr or Insincere (cited in note 63) (discussing history of review of discretionary questions in habeas petitions).

68. Recalling Justice Jackson's opinion in *Harisiades v. Shaughnessy,* the court stated that "this power of deportation . . . is 'a weapon of defense and reprisal confirmed by international law as a power inherent in every sovereign state.' " 212 F.2d at 836 (citing Harisiades v. Shaughnessy, 342 U.S. 580, 587, 588 n.14 (1952)).

69. The only exception to this proposition would be situations in which the provisions of the Immigration Act "shall . . . *expressly*" negate their application. 349 U.S. 302, 305 (citing Administrative Procedure Act, § 12 [emphasis added]).

70. 349 U.S. at 307.

71. Id. at 308.

72. Section 12 of the APA states that modifications must be express. Cf. Shaughnessy v. Pedreiro, 349 U.S. 48 (1955).

73. 349 U.S. at 310.

74. Id. at 315–18 (Black, J., and Frankfurter, J., dissenting).

75. Id. at 317 (citing Joint hearings before the Subcommittees of the Committees on the Judiciary on S. 716, H.R. 2379, H.R. 2816, 82d Cong., 1st Sess. 526–37, 591, 691–92, 739).

76. 98 Cong. Rec. 5778, 5779.

77. 349 U.S. at 318 (Black, J., and Frankfurter, J., dissenting).

78. Id.

79. Id.

80. Id. at 314.

81. Id., citing Galvan v. Press, 347 U.S. 522 (1954); *Harisiades,* 342 U.S. 580. See Chapter 4 in this volume.

82. For a favorable review of Justice Douglas's position, see John Hart Ely, Legislative and Administrative Motivation in Constitutional Law, 79 Yale L.J. 1205, 1312 (1970).

83. 349 U.S. at 319 (Douglas, J., dissenting), citing Crosskey, Politics and the Constitution, Vol. I, c. XI, Vol. II at 1053; and Ogden v. Saunders, 12 Wheat. 213, 271, 286; Satterlee v. Matthewson, 2 Pet. 380, 416, 681 (Appendix) (opinions of Johnson, J.).

84. 3 U.S. (3 Dall.) 386 (1798).

85. 10 U.S. (6 Cranch) 87, 138–139 (1810).

86. See Bridges v. Wixon, 326 U.S. 135, 154 (1945); Delgadillo v. Carmichael, 332 U.S. 388, 391 (1947).

87. Ng Fung Ho v. White, 259 U.S. 276, 284 (1922).

88. 349 U.S. at 321 (Douglas, J., dissenting).

89. Id. at 311.

90. See note 59 above.

91. See, e.g., 2 Davis, Administrative Law Treatise § 10.02, at 5 (1958).

92. Commission on Organization of the Executive Branch of the Government, Task Force Report on Legal Services and Procedure 273 (1955). See Bernard Schwartz, Administrative Law, 1955 Ann. Surv. Am. L. 93 (1955).

93. See generally Will Maslow, Recasting Our Deportation Laws: Proposals For Reform, 56 Colum. L. Rev. 309, 352 (1956).

94. 20 Fed. Reg. 5729 (1955), amending 8 C.F.R. § 242 (1952). See generally Note, The Supreme Court, 1954 Term, 69 Harv. L. Rev. 165 (1955). In 1956, comprehensive regulations substantially revised deportation hearing procedures, provided for an examining officer to present the government's case, and made clear that the only role for the special inquiry officer was to hear and decide the case. 21 Fed. Reg. 97–102 (1956); see 1955–56 INS Ann. Rep. 15–16. See generally Note, The Special Inquiry Officer in Deportation Proceedings, 42 Va. L. Rev. 803 (1956).

95. 48 Fed. Reg. 3038–40 (Feb. 25, 1983).

96. 8 U.S.C. § 1253 (1952).

97. See Marcello v. Kennedy, 194 F. Supp. 750 (D.D.C. 1961).

98. Blakey and Billings, The Plot to Kill the President 242 (cited in note 15).

99. No. 2763–55, cited in H.R. Rep. No. 565, 87th Cong., 1st Sess. 7 (1961).

100. H.R. Rep. No. 565, 87th Cong., 1st Sess. 6–7 (1961).

101. Section 242(d) of the Immigration and Nationality Act of 1952.

102. No. 4277–56, cited in H.R. Rep. No. 565, 87th Cong., 1st Sess. 8 (1961).

103. See H.R. Rep. No. 565, 87th Cong., 1st Sess. 8 (1961).

104. C.A.D.C. No. 13,595 (Nov. 5, 1956), cited in H.R. Rep. No. 565, 87th Cong., 1st Sess. 9 (1961); see also C.A.D.C. No. 13,653 (appeal of district court grant of Government's Motion for Summary Judgment).

105. Cited in H.R. Rep. No. 565, 87th Cong., 1st Sess. 9 (1961).

106. See id.

107. Id.

108. Davis, Mafia Kingfish at 76 (cited in note 2).

109. Blakey and Billings, The Plot to Kill the President at 242 (cited in note 15).

110. Robert F. Kennedy, The Enemy Within 265 (1960).

111. Davis, Mafia Kingfish at 88.

112. Blakey and Billings, The Plot to Kill the President 242.

113. See generally David Wise, Covert Operations Abroad: An Overview in the CIA File 3, 24 (Robert L. Borosage & John Marks eds., 1976); Mark Gibney, U.S. Responsibility for Gross Level of Human Rights Violations in Guatemala from 1954–1996, 7 J. Transnat'l L. & Pol'y 77, 79 (1997).

114. Davis, Mafia Kingfish at 90 (cited in note 2).

115. Id. at 91.

116. See H.R. Rep. No. 565, 87th Cong., 1st Sess. 8 (1961), for the exact history of the three-day-notice issue in Marcello's many cases. See also Marcello v. Kennedy, 114 U.S. App. D.C. 147, 312 F.2d 874 (D.C. Cir. 1962).

117. Davis, Mafia Kingfish at 91 (cited in note 2).

118. Id. at 92.

119. Id. at 93 (Marcello before a congressional committee).

120. Marcello v. Kennedy, 194 F. Supp. 750 (D.D.C. 1961), vacated by Marcello v. Kennedy, 114 U.S. App. D.C. 147, 312 F.2d 874 (D.C. Cir. 1962).

121. 194 F. Supp. at 752–53.

122. Id. at 754.

123. Trafficante was a racketeer who had worked for Meyer Lansky in Cuba and then moved to Florida where he rose to prominence as a Mafia leader.

124. Frank Ragano and Selwyn Raab, Mob Lawyer 130 (1994).

125. Ed Reid, The Grim Reapers: The Anatomy of Organized Crime in America (1970).

126. Id. at 154–55.

127. Id. at 161.

128. The House Select Committee on Assassinations was established in September 1976 by House Resolution 1540, 94th Cong., 2d Sess., to conduct a full and complete investigation of the circumstances surrounding the deaths of President John F. Kennedy and Dr. Martin Luther King, Jr. The Committee's final report is available at http://www.archives.gov/research_room/jfk/house_select_committee/committee_report.html.

129. Reid, The Grim Reapers, at 161–62.

130. House Assassination Committee Hearings, vol. 9H at 82–83; David E. Scheim, Contract on America 80–81 (1988).

131. Davis, Mafia Kingfish at 110 (cited in note 2).

132. Ragano and Raab, Mob Lawyer at 135 (cited in note 124).

133. Id. at 143.

134. Seth Kantor, Who Was Jack Ruby? 136 (1978).

135. Id. at 144.

136. Id. at 146.

137. Id. at 150.

138. Ragano, Mob Lawyer, Epilogue at 356 (cited in note 124).

139. See, e.g., Gerald Posner, Case Closed (1993).

140. Report of the Select Committee on Assassinations of the U.S. House of Representatives, I.C. at 147 (1979).

141. See also Kantor, Who Was Jack Ruby? (1978) (concluding that Ruby was a Mafia hit man). Posner disputes this vigorously.

142. The committee established that Oswald and Ferrie apparently first came into contact with each other during Oswald's participation as a teenager in a Civil Air Patrol unit for which Ferrie served as an instructor, although Ferrie, when he was interviewed by the FBI after his detention as a suspect in the assassination, denied any past association with Oswald.

143. In his testimony before the committee, Marcello acknowledged that Ferrie did work for his lawyer, G. Wray Gill, on his case, but Marcello denied that Ferrie worked for him or that their relationship was close.

144. Davis, Mafia Kingfish at 337 (cited in note 2).

145. Id. at 338.

146. Id. at 339.

147. Id.

148. Reprinted in H.R. Rep. No. 565, 87th Cong., 1st Sess. 6–7 (1961).

149. See also H.R. Rep. 1086, 87th Cong., 1st Sess. 28–32 (1961).

150. Act of Sept. 26, 1961, Pub. L. No. 87–301, § 5, 75 Stat. 651, adding a new § 106 to the INA, 8 U.S.C. § 1105a (1964).

151. Persons at the border challenging an exclusion order, in contrast, had to proceed to district court via habeas corpus.

152. United States ex rel. Marcello v. District Director, 634 F.2d 964 (5th Cir. 1981).

153. United States ex rel. Marcello v. District Director, 472 F. Supp. 1199 (E.D. La. 1979).

154. Pub. L. No. 104–132, 110 Stat. 1214 (1996) (codified as amended in scattered sections of 8, 18, 22, 28, 40, 42 U.S.C.) (1999).

155. Pub. L. No. 104–208, Div. C, 110 Stat. 3009–546 (1996) (codified as amended in scattered sections of 8, 18 U.S.C.) (1999).

156. See Chapter 11 in this volume. The success of these legislative attempts to limit judicial review was profoundly undercut by the 2001 Supreme Court decision in *INS v. St. Cyr,* which confirmed the availability of habeas corpus review. See Kanstroom, St. Cyr or Insincere (cited in note 63).

157. 533 U.S. 289 (2001).

158. See generally Kanstroom, St. Cyr or Insincere (cited in note 63).

159. Davis, Mafia Kingfish at 432 (cited in note 2) (recounting an FBI wiretap in which Marcello was informed that then Commissioner of INS, Mario Noto, had agreed to lift travel restrictions against him).

160. Id.

161. Id. at 299.

162. Id. at 323.

163. Wilfred Sheed, "Everybody's Mafia," 19 New York Review of Books No. 1 (July 20, 1972) (reviewing Joseph L. Albini, The American Mafia: Genesis of a Legend; Nicholas Gage, The Mafia Is Not an Equal Opportunity Employer; Gay Talese, Honor Thy Father: The Inside Book on the Mafia; Mario Puzo, The Godfather; and "The Godfather," directed by Francis Ford Coppola).

164. Life Magazine, April 10, 1970

165. Davis, Mafia Kingfish at 375 (cited in note 2).

166. Id. at 471.

167. Id. at 501.

168. Id.

169. See N.Y. Times A6 (April 16, 1983). (Thanks to David Martin for bringing this to my attention.)

6

Afroyim: Vaunting Citizenship, Presaging Transnationality

Peter J. Spiro

Citizenship rules supply a lens for viewing the foundational assumptions of the global system. Strictly enforced mono-nationality accompanied the organization of the world into sovereign and intensely competitive nation-states, crystallized in the 1648 Treaty of Westphalia and dominant for over three centuries. Plural citizenship, in contrast, may come to be the mark of globalization, as state-based allegiances today diminish in importance relative to other affiliations. The Supreme Court's 1967 decision in *Afroyim v. Rusk* supplies an early glimpse of the transition.[1] The ruling found unconstitutional the forced expatriation of a United States citizen for voting in a foreign political election. But *Afroyim* counts for much more than that narrow holding. Although ostensibly elevating the place of citizenship status in the constitutional landscape, the decision laid the groundwork for citizenship's eventual demotion. Most importantly, *Afroyim* opened the door to the maintenance of multiple active national ties. It is to *Afroyim* that one can trace the genesis of the late modern edition of American citizenship, a version less jealous of alternative attachments.

Afroyim thus continues to resonate as those alternative attachments become more open and commonplace. It may have accelerated the rise of plural citizenship and now certainly stands as a constitutional barrier against political efforts to reverse the trend. But the *Afroyim* evolution also presents a fascinating example of constitutional litigation, the capstone of a campaign to reverse a ruling of the Court less than a decade old. The Nationality Act provision mandating the termination of citizenship on the ground of foreign voting had been squarely upheld against constitutional attack in the 1958 decision in *Perez v. Brownell*.[2] Beys Afroyim's carefully designed assault on *Perez* presents a model for successful counterattack against precedents set by a closely divided court.

In the end, Justice Hugo Black delivered an absolutist opinion maximally protecting individual control over citizenship decisions. Although the legal issue was narrowly presented, the decision was broad and emphatic, by its terms severely constraining the conditions for revoking citizenship and going beyond what Afroyim's lawyers themselves had sought. Although it took additional decades to solidify *Afroyim's* vision, the decision pointed the way to a U.S. citizenship that, once given, could not be taken away. *Afroyim's* citizenship ruling was thus protective of individual rights and autonomy, but in the longer perspective may have marked a critical turn towards the dilution of national identity and of the importance of citizenship itself.

The Legal Context

On the doctrinal landscape, *Afroyim v. Rusk* is readily situated in a line of cases confronting the government's authority to decree expatriation. These decisions started from the premise of a nearly unconstrained power to strip citizenship for specified voluntary conduct, notwithstanding an individual's desire to retain the status. The hotly contested decision in *Perez* represented the zenith of judicial deference to the expatriation regime as part of the latitude afforded the political branches in matters relating to foreign relations. But *Perez* was vulnerable from its inception, an overextension of both the statutory scheme and corresponding judicial affirmations.

Until the beginning of the twentieth century, expatriation against an individual's will had been addressed in administrative practice, rather than under any formally codified regime. Debates and litigation in the earliest decades of national life had focused on a sharply different question: whether a willing individual had the power to renounce citizenship (in the absence of specific consent by the sovereign), or whether the entrenched British doctrine of perpetual allegiance would govern U.S. law.[3] The dispute was settled only with an 1868 congressional declaration of the individual's right to expatriate.[4] As it became clear that loss of citizenship was possible, the question shifted to whether a person would as a matter of course lose his citizenship by performing certain acts that the Department of State regarded as inconsistent with U.S. allegiance.

Rather than confronting head-on the government's authority to force expatriation, the administrative practice was initially framed in more ambiguous terms, focusing on the individual's entitlement to the prerogatives of citizenship, in particular, the right to U.S. diplomatic protection *vis-a-vis* foreign governments. In response to decades of presidential entreaties to formalize this practice, in 1907 Congress passed an expatriation measure explicitly providing for the loss of U.S. nationality upon naturalization in a foreign country, a woman's marriage to a foreigner, or the taking of an oath of allegiance to a foreign state. The measure also mandated loss of citizenship where a naturalized citizen returned to a residence in his former homeland for more than two years.[5]

The 1907 Act presented the first opportunity for judicial consideration of the power to expatriate, reaching the Supreme Court in 1915. In *Mackenzie v. Hare*, the Court upheld the termination of a woman's citizenship upon marriage to a non-citizen husband. The decision situated expatriation among the "powers of nationality" and "attribute[s] of sovereignty ... [that the Court] should hesitate long before limiting or embarrassing."[6] The Court highlighted the voluntariness of the conduct (entering into a marriage) that triggered the statutory ground for expatriation. Although this reasoning made available a duress defense to expatriation where the underlying conduct was not voluntarily undertaken, it rendered irrelevant the individual's subjective intent with regard to the citizenship consequences. The *Mackenzie* Court did concede that expatriation could not be "arbitrarily imposed, that is, imposed without the concurrence of the citizen," but the Court inferred consent from the fact that the marriage had been "voluntarily entered into, with notice of the consequences."

The distinction between voluntary performance of an act listed in the statute as expatriating and the person's specific intent with regard to citizenship consequences continued to figure prominently in later decisions. In 1950, the Court confirmed the power to terminate citizenship against an individual's will in *Savorgnan v. United States*.[7] The Court sustained the expatriation of an American woman for obtaining Italian citizenship in order to marry an Italian diplomat, though she never intended to lose her citizenship thereby and did not understand the oath of allegiance:

> The petitioner's principal contention is that she did not intend to give up her American citizenship, although she applied for and accepted Italian citizenship, and that her intent should prevail. However, the acts upon which the statutes expressly condition the consent of our Government to the expatriation of its citizens are stated objectively. There is no suggestion in the statutory language that the effect of the specified overt acts, when voluntarily done, is conditioned upon the undisclosed intent of the person doing them.

Congress, meanwhile, expanded the grounds for expatriation in the Nationality Act of 1940, enacted as World War II was erupting in Europe.[8] On top of existing provisions relating to naturalization in a foreign state, Section 401 of the 1940 act added statutory grounds for expatriation based on service in the armed forces of a foreign state or other foreign government employment where coupled with nationality in that foreign state. The statute mandated loss of nationality for desertion from the armed forces or remaining outside the United States for purposes of evading military service during wartime.[9] As with the 1907 statute, the citizen's intent with regard to the consequences was irrelevant. The conduct alone precipitated expatriation, and the government's function in declaring loss of nationality was viewed as ministerial.

Perhaps most dramatically, however, Section 401(e) of the Nationality Act now deemed expatriative the act of merely voting in a political election in a foreign state. This provision found its legislative roots in U.S. citizen voting in the 1935 plebiscite to determine the future affiliation of the Saar territory (to either France or Germany), as mandated by the 1919 Versailles Peace Treaty. Eligibility to vote was set by residence in the Saar as of the time of the peace treaty; many former residents who had since naturalized as Americans were thus able to cast ballots. Several hundred U.S. citizens returned from the United States to the Saar to participate in the plebiscite, with expenses paid by the Nazi government.[10] Among those incensed by the spectacle of Americans doing Hitler's bidding was the chairman of the House immigration committee, Samuel Dickstein, who soon after introduced a bill under which such voting would result in loss of U.S. citizenship.[11] The substance of that bill found its way into President Roosevelt's 1939 proposal to overhaul the nationality laws,[12] and, in turn, into the 1940 legislation. The Saar connection was evident in the statutory language itself, providing for the loss of citizenship not only for the broad category of "[v]oting in a political election in a foreign state," but also for the very particular act of "participating in an election or plebiscite to determine the sovereignty over foreign territory."

Section 401(e) was put to the test in *Perez*. The facts there favored the government's case. Clemente Martinez Perez had been born in Texas in 1909 (and thus received U.S. citizenship at birth), but moved in his youth with his parents to Mexico, where he lived without interruption until 1943. He failed to register for the draft, as was required of U.S. citizens regardless of place of residence, and thereafter three times represented himself as a Mexican citizen upon temporary re-entry into the United States. In 1946, he voted in the Mexican presidential elections. Only when faced with deportation from the United States after a subsequent re-entry did he claim United States citizenship.

The Court, per Justice Frankfurter, found constitutional Perez's involuntary expatriation on the ground of foreign voting. Echoing the government's briefs, the Court squarely framed the issue as one of foreign relations. Requiring only a "rational nexus" between legislative action and the regulation of foreign affairs,[13] the opinion stressed the government's need to "be able to reduce to a minimum the frictions that are unavoidable in a world of sovereigns sensitive in matters touching their dignity and interests," and the Court's duty to give Congress "ample scope in selecting appropriate modes for accomplishing its purpose" under the Necessary and Proper Clause.[14] The Court recounted at length the legislative conception of the 1907 and 1940 acts as exercises of the foreign affairs power, including the apparent congressional displeasure with the participation of U.S. citizens in the Saar plebiscite as the motivation for Section 401(e).[15] Against that backdrop, Frankfurter sustained the withdrawal of citizenship on the ground of foreign voting:

> Experience amply attests that, in this day of extensive international travel, rapid communication and widespread use of propaganda, the activities of the citizens of one nation when in another country can easily cause serious embarrassments to the government of their own country as well as to their fellow citizens. We cannot deny to Congress the reasonable belief that these difficulties might well become acute, to the point of jeopardizing the successful conduct of international relations, when a citizen of one country chooses to participate in the political or governmental affairs of another country. The citizen may by his action unwittingly promote or encourage a course of conduct contrary to the interests of his own government; moreover, the people or government of the foreign country may regard his action to be the action of his government, or at least as a reflection if not an expression of its policy.[16]

Foreign voting, Frankfurter continued, might also evidence "elements of an allegiance to another country in some measure, at least, inconsistent with American citizenship."[17] As for the remedy, Frankfurter argued that it was appropriate insofar as "it is the possession of American citizenship by a person committing the act that makes the act potentially embarrassing to the American Government." For that reason, "[t]he termination of citizenship terminates the problem."[18] Though he would not concede the severity of the result, in Frankfurter's conception, the weighty government interest in the foreign relations realm justified the sanction.

But the *Perez* decision was not as firm as Frankfurter's confident reasoning would otherwise have suggested. The Court split 5–4, drawing a notably broad and vigorous dissent from Chief Justice Warren, joined by Justices Black and Douglas. Warren vaunted the citizenry as the ultimate source of all governmental power. Under this logic, the government "is without power to sever the relationship that gives rise to its existence."[19] For the Chief Justice, the stakes were high: "[c]itizenship *is* man's basic right for it is nothing less than the right to have rights."[20] Warren would have allowed for the loss of citizenship through conduct showing a voluntary transfer of allegiance, as with obtaining naturalization in another state: "[a]ny action by which [a citizen] manifests allegiance to a foreign state may be so inconsistent with the retention of citizenship as to result in loss of that status."[21] But he dismissed foreign voting as insufficient to evidence abandonment, at least not as a categorical matter.[22] Highlighting the case of a citizen who had been expatriated for participating in a local Canadian referendum on the sale of beer and wine, Warren deemed voting "a most equivocal act, giving rise to no implication that allegiance has been compromised." Justice Douglas dissented separately, joined by Justice Black, condemning the measure as a grave threat to First Amendment rights: "if the power to regulate foreign affairs can be used to deprive a person of his citizenship because he voted abroad, why may not it be used to deprive him of citizenship because his views on foreign policy are unorthodox or because he disputed the position of the Secretary of State."[23] The hapless Justice Whittaker, finally, issued a "memorandum" agreeing to the premise of an expatriation power but finding it too broadly conceived to stand on the ground of foreign voting.

Perez was further enervated at birth by contrary results in two companion decisions issued the same day. In *Trop v. Dulles*,[24] again voting 5–4, the Court found unconstitutional the involuntary expatriation of a wartime deserter. Distinguishing *Perez*, the two opinions comprising a majority found the expatriation in *Trop* invalid as punishment. Chief Justice Warren, writing for a plurality, went so far as to find the termination of citizenship to be cruel and unusual punishment, in violation of the Eighth Amendment. It was the newly installed Justice Brennan who supplied the swing vote, joining to uphold expatriation in *Perez* (echoing Frankfurter's concern for "embarrassing" foreign relations), while finding expatriation to lack a rational relation to the war power, which had been claimed as the basis for the desertion measure.[25]

Warren also wrote for the Court in a third companion case, *Nishikawa v. Dulles*, in which the Court barred the expatriation of a dual Japanese and American citizen who had been conscripted into the Japanese armed forces during World War II. The decision rested on statutory construction rather than constitutional grounds, but the Court in *Nishikawa* noted the "drastic" consequences of expatriation on the way to imposing a demanding burden on the government. The government, the Court held, had to prove the voluntariness of Nishikawa's service in the foreign army, once the voluntariness of the expatriating act was put at issue, and it had to do so by "clear, convincing and unequivocal evidence."[26] In concurrence, Justice Black punctuated his conception of strict constitutional constraints on expatriation, while acknowledging that the conduct specified in Section 401 "may be highly persuasive evidence in the particular case of a purpose to abandon citizenship."[27] As one commentary observes, "the results of these three

cases seem intuitively backwards. The rather innocent act of voting in a
Mexican election (about which Mexico had made no complaint) resulted
in forfeiture of citizenship. Yet a wartime deserter and a citizen who
served with an enemy army escaped the same fate."[28]

Nor did *Perez* look very secure in the wake of subsequent cases
relating to imposed expatriation not intended by the individual. In its
1963 decision in *Kennedy v. Mendoza–Martinez*,[29] the Court found unconstitutional the termination of citizenship based on territorial absence
with the intent to evade conscription. The decision produced a riff on
Trop, holding that this expatriation—the deprivation of a "most precious
right"—constituted punishment without due process. In concurrence,
while finding the result ordained under the reasoning of *Trop*, Justice
Brennan openly expressed "some felt doubts of the correctness of *Perez*."[30] The following term, in *Schneider v. Rusk*,[31] the Court continued to
chip away at the government's expatriation authority, striking down a
Nationality Act provision that had mandated the loss of citizenship for a
naturalized citizen who had returned to reside in his country of origin.
Although the decision rested on what the Court deemed an unacceptable
distinction between birthright and naturalized citizens, Justice Douglas's
opinion intimated a vindication of Warren's view in *Perez*, while conceding that this did not yet command a majority of the Court.[32]

The *Schneider* vote was 5–3, with the wavering Brennan recused.
On top of Brennan's apparent shift away from *Perez*, Frankfurter's
replacement, Arthur Goldberg, had penned the majority opinion in
Mendoza-Martinez and sided with the majority in *Schneider*. Irving
Kaufman, a prominent judge on the influential U.S. Court of Appeals for
the Second Circuit, openly questioned the vitality of *Perez* in *Schneider*'s
wake.[33] The *Perez* decision also came under attack in the law reviews;
most notably, University of Chicago Law Professor Philip Kurland
concluded that the "case is probably now moribund" in the 1964
Foreword to the annual Supreme Court issue of the *Harvard Law
Review*.[34] As precedent, it was clearly vulnerable.

Factual Background and Proceedings Below

The case of Beys Afroyim presented an ideal vehicle for the challenge. Born Ephraim Bernstein in 1893 in Riki, Poland, Afroyim had
immigrated to the United States in 1912 and naturalized as a U.S.
citizen in 1926. Described as a "radical modernist," he studied at the Art
Institute of Chicago and the National Academy of Design. He was
commissioned for portraits of George Bernard Shaw, Theodore Dreiser,
and Arnold Schoenberg, among others, and counted Alfred Stieglitz as a
patron. He directed his own "experimental" art school from 1927 until
1946.[35] In 1949, he and his wife (who had been his student) left the
United States, traveled through Europe, and settled in Israel. The

marriage did not last, and desiring to return to the United States, Afroyim applied to the U.S. consulate in Haifa in 1960 for a new passport. The consulate instead issued a Certificate of Loss of Nationality on the ground that he had expatriated himself under Section 401(e) by voting in an Israeli national election in November 1951. (This fact had been noted in his Israeli identification booklet, which apparently had been submitted to the consul as part of his passport application.) Afroyim challenged the revocation of citizenship in administrative proceedings, claiming that he had entered the polls not to vote, but rather to sketch the voters as they cast their ballots. The State Department's Board of Review on the Loss of Nationality affirmed the consul's decision in May 1965. Afroyim brought an action in the federal district court in Manhattan for a declaratory judgment, challenging the constitutionality of Section 401(e).[36]

By this time, Afroyim had secured the representation of Nanette Dembitz, general counsel of the New York Civil Liberties Union. From a distinguished legal family (both father and grandfather had been prominent attorneys, and Louis Dembitz Brandeis, the late Supreme Court justice, had been her second cousin), she brought a rich experience to the case from government service, as well as more than a decade at the NYCLU.[37] Dembitz had worked at the U.S. Department of Justice on issues relating to the control of alien enemies in the United States during World War II, and had been on the briefs in both the *Hirabayashi* and *Korematsu* cases, though she denounced those decisions soon after leaving the government in 1945.[38] Afroyim thus enjoyed the services of a savvy constitutional lawyer.

And, indeed, Dembitz deftly framed the case to maximize the possibility of reversing *Perez*. Abandoning the factual challenge pursued in administrative proceedings, Dembitz agreed to a stipulation that Afroyim had voluntarily voted in the 1951 election. For its part, the government stipulated that it had found Afroyim to have expatriated himself on the basis of that conduct alone.[39] This later stipulation was crucial to isolating the constitutionality of Section 401(e). As of 1951, in the early years of Israel's independence, there was as yet no such status as Israeli citizenship. Eligibility to vote was based on residence. As of 1951, then, there was no question of Afroyim holding dual citizenship. He had subsequently acquired Israeli citizenship, and voted as an Israeli citizen in at least two other elections, but the stipulation allowed Afroyim's lawyers to sequester those facts, which might otherwise have overshadowed the 401(e) issue. Afroyim was, moreover, a more attractive petitioner than his counterparts in other expatriation cases; he was not deploying a claim to citizenship as a defense to deportation, and had apparently never denied his U.S. citizenship or evaded any obligations attaching to the status. Although not conceded as relevant by the government, the joint stipulations included plaintiff's contention that "neither at the time of the election nor at any other time did he have any intention or desire to lose or abandon his American citizenship."

The case thus presented a head-on challenge to *Perez*. Before the district court, Afroyim's counsel was left to argue that *Perez* was no longer good law. The court gave that claim a serious response, distinguishing *Trop* and *Mendoza-Martinez* on the grounds that those instances of expatriation had been penal in purpose. The district court also noted that *Schneider* had conceded the absence of a majority on the Supreme Court for denying Congress' expatriation power altogether. "[T]he authority of *Perez v. Brownell*," Judge Frederick van Pelt Bryan concluded, "still stands and is controlling here."[40]

No doubt assuming that a lower court would shy from declaring the premature death of a superior court's precedent (not only the Supreme Court's, but also the Second Circuit's 1965 ruling in *Tanaka v. INS*[41]), Dembitz also rehearsed substantive arguments against Frankfurter's finding in *Perez* that foreign voting could pose a distinctive threat to U.S. foreign affairs. Again, while crediting the challenge as "not wholly unpersuasive," the district court found Section 401(e) constitutional (as had *Perez*) as a reasonable mechanism for achieving a sensitive foreign relations objective. To the extent that the foreign relations rationale required shoring up, the district court supplied the alternate ground that Congress might reasonably regard such voting as inconsistent with full allegiance to the United States.[42]

On appeal, a Second Circuit panel upheld the district court's ruling on essentially the same grounds.[43] In a brief concurrence, Judge Kaufman reiterated the "grave doubts" he had expressed in his dissent in *Tanaka* as to whether *Perez* in fact remained good law. Working from Frankfurter's test, Kaufman also asserted the lack of rational nexus between the expatriation ground and foreign relations where, as here, there had been no showing of any foreign relations consequences. He highlighted the fact that, unlike *Perez*, Afroyim's U.S. citizenship had been known to Israeli authorities prior to balloting and thus could hardly have "embarrassed" the United States before the foreign power.[44]

Dembitz's petition for a writ of *certiorari* launched a frontal attack on *Perez*, attempting to peg *Perez* as an outlier decision, both in the context of nationality decisions and constitutional rights jurisprudence more generally.[45] A supplemental memorandum sought to demonstrate the continuing impact of Section 401(e) and its successor provision, documenting that more than five thousand individuals had lost their U.S. citizenship as a result of foreign voting in the period 1961–65.[46]

Briefs and Arguments Before the Supreme Court

Dembitz's merits brief to the Supreme Court took three tacks. It first sketched a scaled-down *Perez*, limited by subsequent decisions to the proposition that any congressional expatriation power was contingent on conduct establishing diluted allegiance to the United States. The brief argued that, as a general matter, voting could not be taken necessarily to denote changed allegiance and that, in fact, Congress had not been so motivated in adopting 401(e). Rather, Dembitz held the legislative focus on the Saar episode as evidencing a penal purpose to the provision, invalid under *Trop*. The brief noted the lack of any corresponding provision in the nationality laws of any foreign state, and offered a theoretical justification for voting as "not an unnatural concomitant" of the acknowledged "temporary and local" allegiance that arises under international law from the simple reality of residence.[47] It then deployed the fact that Afroyim did not hold dual citizenship at the time of the 1951 ballot to assert that "his voting was unaccompanied by any indication of a change of allegiance," acknowledging (as had Warren in his *Perez* dissent) that some conduct might warrant expatriation even in the absence of intent to relinquish citizenship.[48] By irrebuttably presuming foreign voting to comprise diluted allegiance, Dembitz reasoned, the measure violated not only the Citizenship Clause of the Fourteenth Amendment but also the Due Process Clause of the Fifth.

Dembitz also confronted Justice Frankfurter's fixation on the possible embarrassment to U.S. foreign relations posed by U.S. citizen foreign voting. The brief highlighted the absence of any evidence before Congress to that effect; even the Saar episode, Dembitz noted, had not resulted in any foreign policy complications.[49] The provision thus lacked a rational basis, argued Dembitz, and certainly failed to satisfy the higher scrutiny applied to restrictions on political expression in the First Amendment context.

In response, Solicitor General Thurgood Marshall's brief offered a muscular defense of *Perez* on all fronts. Congress had reasonably concluded that foreign voting manifested an attachment to another country sufficient to warrant expatriation. Beyond the legislative history and the cases, the government's brief ruminated broadly on the nature of citizenship and the function of voting. "In a democracy, voting is, for most people, the highest form of involvement in the political processes of the state.... Like a solemn oath of allegiance, the ceremony of voting conveys the image of a purposeful act of political commitment to a foreign state."[50] Even without citizenship, voting "could well be thought to signify a settled attachment to the foreign country" inconsistent with undivided allegiance to the United States.[51] As for embarrassing foreign relations, the government hypothetically situated U.S. citizen voting in such trouble spots as West Germany, South Africa, or India, and speculated on how those votes might give rise to grave diplomatic disputes. "The foreign state in which the voting occurs may charge this country with meddling," the brief cautioned. "Justifiably or not, the vote of the citizen may be deemed to reflect the official views of the government."[52] Given the serious possible international repercussions, Congress' imposition of the blanket expatriation measure was reasonable.

At oral argument, in February 1967, Edward Ennis stepped in for Dembitz, who (after composing the briefs) had since been installed as a family court judge in New York City. Ennis, who had been Dembitz's boss as wartime Director of the Alien Control Unit at the Department of Justice and had also served as general counsel of the Immigration and Naturalization Service, was by now chairman of the American Civil Liberties Union. Ennis invoked the Fourteenth Amendment with broad strokes at the same time that he avoided reaching further than required to sustain the challenge. He asserted that Congress had no power under the Constitution to provide for forfeiture of U.S. citizenship, but conceded that naturalizing in another country would "normally connote[] a putting off of your United States allegiance" so as to permit expatriation even where the individual denied "that what I'm doing has that natural effect." This stance echoed Warren's position in his *Perez* dissent. Beyond principle, Ennis hit hard at the lack of factual grounding for Frankfurter's foreign relations rationale. Even American citizen voting in the Saar plebiscite, he noted, had not bothered any of the foreign governments implicated, nor, indeed, the Department of State.[53]

Representing the government was current INS general counsel Charles Gordon. On the one hand, Gordon was a logical choice to argue the case before the Court. Not only was he the government's top immigration lawyer, he had recently penned a lengthy treatment of expatriation issues, including those relating to Section 401(e).[54] He had also argued the government's case the previous term in *Woodby v. INS*,[55] regarding the burden of proof in the context of deportation. On the other hand, insofar as the *Afroyim* case had been framed in broad constitutional terms, the government may have blundered in assigning the argument to an immigration law expert rather than one of the more seasoned constitutional litigators of the Solicitor General's office (as had been and would be the circumstances in other major cases involving expatriation). Gordon, moreover, had not even been on the briefs in the case.

Whether or not the choice of Gordon as principal advocate was well-advised, he clearly got off on the wrong foot in his opening statement. In reciting the factual background for the case, Gordon made the mistake of alluding to the two subsequent Israeli elections in which Afroyim had voted, in 1955 and 1959, by which time Afroyim had acquired Israeli citizenship. Gordon apparently wanted to bring to the Court's attention additional evidence to support a finding of diminished attachment to the

United States: "the facts here, if fully developed, would demonstrate that the allegiance here is primarily to Israel." But this tactic badly misfired. Much of the rest of the questioning took Gordon to task for introducing facts at argument that had not been briefed or included in the record before the Court. There was at least one sigh from the bench audible enough to be included in the official argument transcript, and exasperation is even more evident in the audio version. Gordon was chastised for "trying to muddy the waters so that we can't decide it on that simple issue that was in the complaint." It was not the finest hour for Gordon, who would go on to establish himself as the nation's pre-eminent immigration law practitioner and the principal author of the field's leading treatise.[56]

The Decision

Though by a slim majority, the terms of Afroyim's victory could not have been more complete. Justice Black rejected outright the premise of *Perez* that "Congress has any general power, express or implied, to take away an American citizen's citizenship without his assent."[57] Black worked from his tendency to textual absolutism in finding in the Citizenship Clause of the Fourteenth Amendment "no indication . . . of a fleeting citizenship, good at the moment it is acquired but subject to destruction by the government at any time. . . . Once acquired, this Fourteenth Amendment citizenship was not to be shifted, canceled, or diluted" at the government's will.[58] The opinion did not even deign to address Frankfurter's theories relating to embarrassed foreign relations and divided allegiance. Rather, Black recited a string of legislative episodes, mostly involving earlier failed initiatives to codify involuntary expatriation, by way of supplying historical evidence for the holding. The opinion also loudly echoed the philosophical underpinnings of Chief Justice Warren's dissent in *Perez*. "Citizenship in this Nation is a part of a co-operative affair. Its citizenry is the country and the country is the citizenry," intoned Black, whose opinion was joined by Warren, Douglas, now Brennan, and newcomer Abe Fortas. "The very nature of our free government makes it completely incongruous to have a rule of law under which a group of citizens temporarily in office can deprive another group of citizens of their citizenship."[59]

Afroyim and his ACLU advocates could not have asked for a more embracing affirmation of citizenship as an individual right. Indeed, they hadn't asked for it. Dembitz and Ennis had been careful to isolate Afroyim's case from those involving dual citizenship, and they had conceded along the way that naturalization in a foreign country could support the termination of citizenship against the individual's subjective will. This concession seemed accurately to read the extent of objections to *Perez*. There was little indication that overturning *Perez* would nullify the expatriation power at its root. Warren's dissent there had allowed for expatriation in the wake of foreign naturalization, as an "action[] in derogation of undivided allegiance"; he appeared to accept the possibility that some forms of voluntary conduct would justify expatriation, while denying its propriety on the flimsy grounds of foreign voting. In his *Nishikawa* concurrence, Black himself appeared to acknowledge that some forms of conduct short of express renunciation could evidence an intent to relinquish citizenship, allowing that the statutory expatriation grounds "may be highly persuasive evidence in the particular case of a purpose to abandon citizenship."[60] But the *Afroyim* opinion on its face appeared to leave no room for expatriation against an individual's will, boldly affirming "a constitutional right to remain a citizen in a free country unless he voluntarily relinquishes that citizenship."

In dissent, Justice Harlan condemned the majority opinion for engaging in a "remarkable process of circumlocution, ... essentially content with the conclusory and quite unsubstantiated assertion" that Congress lacks the power to expatriate a citizen without his assent.[61] Joined by Justices Clark, Stewart, and White, the dissent noted Black's failure to dispute the reasoning of *Perez* and then took on the historical argument at length. It recited solid historical evidence showing that the Congress that adopted the Fourteenth Amendment assumed it had "the authority to expatriate unwilling citizens" and never regarded citizenship as an "absolute." Harlan also understood that the majority opinion was not simply a rewrite of Warren's *Perez* dissent, finding it to "adopt a substantially wider view of the restrictions upon Congress's authority in the area." In any case, Justice Harlan predicted, "today's opinion will surely cause still greater confusion in this area of the law."[62]

The Immediate Impact

Harlan's challenge was not without foundation, and Black's literalism was not taken literally in *Afroyim*'s wake. Although the decision on its face appeared to preclude unwilling expatriation in all cases, it would take more than twenty years for that vision fully to take hold. In the meantime, expatriation without the individual's overt consent, though more closely scrutinized, remained an option in some cases. As a formal matter, conduct alone could not supply a categoric basis for the termination of citizenship; the government was now also required to establish that the conduct evidenced an intent to relinquish citizenship. As a practical matter, in many cases—especially those involving naturalization in a foreign state—conduct continued to give the government all it thought it needed to sustain expatriation.

Afroyim garnered its first returns in the case of a dual Canadian–American citizen who faced expatriation under Section 401 for holding foreign government employment as a public schoolteacher in Ontario—a result upheld by the Board of Immigration Appeals in a 1965 decision. Attorney General Ramsey Clark, who had ultimate decisional authority in such matters, withheld final disposition of the case pending the resolution of *Afroyim*, and reversed the BIA soon after that case was decided in the summer of 1967. While finding that the record in that case failed to show the necessary intent to relinquish U.S. citizenship, the Attorney General did note that it was "not necessary to determine what the full reach of *Afroyim* may be, either in terms of its effect on each of the provisions of the present statute, or in terms of what kinds of conduct might validly be held to constitute voluntary relinquishment of United States citizenship." He also dropped a footnote reference to Harlan's forebodings along the way.[63]

Hence the motivation for Clark's decision to issue a "statement of interpretation" on the subject in early 1969. "The sweeping language of the *Afroyim* opinion," wrote the Attorney General, "raises questions as to its effect on the validity of expatriation provisions, other than those relating to voting." The statement focused on what might constitute "voluntary relinquishment" consistent with Justice Black's analysis. On this point, the Attorney General looked to the earlier Warren and Black opinions for clarification. Clark thus concluded that "voluntary relinquishment" was "not confined to a written renunciation" of citizenship, but could "also be manifested by other actions declared expatriative" under the successor statute to Section 401. An intent to relinquish citizenship so manifested, however, could be rebutted by the individual, and, as per *Nishikawa*, the burden with respect to intent would remain on the government.[64]

The Attorney General's opinion thus sustained the government's power to expatriate a citizen by virtue of conduct indicating an intent to abandon citizenship, even where the individual did not consciously intend that result. As a matter of process, the approach gave rise to a rebuttable presumption of an intent to expatriate upon the undertaking of specified conduct, including naturalization in another country, the taking of an oath of allegiance to another country, service in foreign armed forces, and foreign government employment. Intent thereafter became a primary point of contention in expatriation cases. In *Matter of Stanlake*, for instance, the BIA upheld the expatriation of an individual who had naturalized as a Canadian citizen. "When one voluntarily takes the nationality of another country and takes an oath of allegiance to that country, whether or not it contains a renunciation of former allegiance," the Board held, "the normal inference is that there has been a transfer of allegiance from the old country to the new."[65] In *Matter of Wayne*, by contrast, the Board reversed an expatriation order, notwithstanding Canadian naturalization, where an individual had questioned and been reassured by U.S. authorities that his U.S. citizenship would not be jeopardized.[66] In practice, the threat of involuntary expatriation appears to have remained very real. The violinist Yehudi Menuhin, for instance, was threatened with the loss of U.S. citizenship after accepting merely honorary Swiss citizenship in 1970, though in the end Secretary of State William Rogers apologized for the "misunderstanding."[67]

The Attorney General's middle road, meanwhile, was at least indirectly vindicated by the Supreme Court's 1971 decision in *Rogers v. Bellei*.[68] That decision upheld a statutory provision that decreed the loss of U.S. citizenship acquired at birth by a child born abroad to a U.S. citizen parent if the child did not take up U.S. residency of a specified length before reaching age twenty-eight. *Afroyim* had placed at least some reliance on the Citizenship Clause, the first sentence of the Fourteenth Amendment, which applies only to "persons born or naturalized in the United States." The *Bellei* majority distinguished *Afroyim* on this basis, given that the individual was neither born nor naturalized in the United States. In Justice Blackmun's infelicitous phrasing, Bellei "simply [was] not a Fourteenth Amendment-first-sentence citizen." Justice Black vigorously dissented, finding the majority's position inconsistent with "the holding in *Afroyim* that the Fourteenth Amendment has put citizenship, once conferred, beyond the power of Congress to revoke."[69] For Black, there could be no expatriation power where none was expressly granted by the constitutional letter. One of Black's last opinions, the *Bellei* dissent reads like a lonely last call to a strictly textualist logic in the determination of governmental power. But it also evidenced Black's apparent failure to pull along the rest of the Court for his broad conception of *Afroyim*'s reach.

By 1980, the Court had adopted something closer to the Clark approach as its own. In *Vance v. Terrazas*,[70] the Court considered expatriation for affirming allegiance to a foreign state. Terrazas, who had been born a dual Mexican and American national, had at age twenty-two executed an application with Mexican authorities not only swearing allegiance to Mexico but also "expressly renounc[ing] United States citizenship, as well as any submission, obedience, and loyalty to any foreign government, especially to that of the United States of America." Although it would not have seemed necessary, given the clarity of Terrazas's oath, the government used the case as an attempt to roll back *Afroyim*, arguing that conduct specified in the expatriation statute was inherently inconsistent with the retention of citizenship and should automatically result in its termination.

The Court's ruling sufficed to sustain the expatriation on remand, but it rejected so narrow an interpretation of *Afroyim*. Instead, the Court made clear that expatriation could only be undertaken where conduct evidenced a specific intent on the individual's part to relinquish citizenship. On the one hand, mere voluntary performance of a listed expatriating act by itself would not justify the involuntary termination of citizenship; in all cases, the government would also have to prove the requisite intent to shed U.S. citizenship. "In the last analysis," wrote Justice White, "expatriation depends on the will of the citizen rather thañ on the will of Congress and its assessment of his conduct."[71] On the other hand, formal renunciation was not a necessary predicate to expatriation. In that respect, the opinion appeared to retreat from *Afroyim*. (Only Justice Brennan, who had by now come full circle from his freshman year acceptance of the expatriation in *Perez*, dissented on that point, asserting that citizenship should only be terminated by formal renunciation before U.S. consular authorities.[72])

The specific intent requirement still left room for the government to police the boundaries of membership. Naturalization oaths before other sovereigns often included renunciatory language which, taken on its face, evidenced a specific intent to relinquish original citizenship. In the absence of evidence to the contrary, such conduct sufficed to justify expatriation under *Terrazas*.[73] The State Department's *Foreign Affairs Manual*—a sort of how-to for American diplomats—continued to flag other activity "potentially" giving rise to the loss of nationality.[74] Thus, expatriation without explicit consent continued in *Terrazas*'s wake. Even as of the late 1980s, the Department of State was initiating an average of 4,500 potential loss-of-citizenship cases annually, of which 600 resulted in expatriation.[75]

This understanding of *Terrazas* supplied a temporary equilibrium point. The opinion ostensibly put to rest *Afroyim*'s lofty denials of any governmental capacity to terminate citizenship, but it clarified the mechanisms for defeating that power. Where a contrary intent was otherwise established, expatriation was defeated. In guidance issued to consular posts in the wake of *Terrazas*, the Department of State broadly itemized actions evidencing an intention to retain citizenship, including payment of U.S. taxes, voting in American elections, and continued use of a U.S. passport after the potentially expatriating conduct.[76] The Department also thereafter accepted contemporaneous statements regarding intent. This gave rise to a practice under which an individual naturalizing elsewhere or undertaking other conduct specified in the expatriation provision would execute a memo to the files attesting to the lack of intent to relinquish citizenship, even where the words uttered would have indicated otherwise.[77] Meanwhile, Congress finally amended the Immigration and Nationality Act in 1986 to conform with *Afroyim* and *Terrazas*, requiring that the specified expatriating acts be undertaken "with the intention of relinquishing United States nationality" as a predicate to the loss of citizenship.[78]

The Lasting Impact

In the long run, *Afroyim*'s vision of an absolute right to retain citizenship has been largely, if quietly, vindicated. As a matter of practice, it is now virtually impossible to lose American citizenship without formally and expressly renouncing it. But that endpoint has transpired in a rather different context than Black, Warren, and other sacralizers of citizenship might have supposed. It is precisely because citizenship has become less salient that it is now more easily retained, and the fact that it is so easily retained inexorably reduces further its value.

Terrazas has proved the last major statement from the Supreme Court on the issue of expatriation. In 1990, the Department of State adopted new guidelines, under the guise of evidentiary standards, which greatly reduced the incidence of unconsented loss of citizenship. The revised approach eliminated presumptions of intent theretofore associated with potentially expatriating conduct. The government would now work from "the premise that U.S. citizens intend to retain United States citizenship when they obtain naturalization in a foreign state, subscribe to routine declarations of allegiance to a foreign state, or accept non-policy level employment with a foreign government."[79] According to the new guidelines, this premise would generally apply except where an individual was convicted of treason, formally renounced citizenship before an American consular officer, or took policy-level employment in a foreign state. Leaving aside for a moment the obsolescent ground relating to treason (there has been no conviction for treason in more than fifty years), even the acceptance of top-level foreign government employment has generally not resulted in loss of U.S. citizenship. Only where an individual becomes the head of a foreign state has the Department of State insisted on the relinquishment of U.S. citizenship, and then only on the basis of persuasion rather than adversarial process (usually with an assist from the laws or political realities of the country where the individual is serving). Valdas Adamkus renounced his citizenship in 1998 only *after* being elected president of Lithuania. A 1995 State Department cable stated that "[i]t is no longer possible to terminate [an] American's citizenship without the citizen's cooperation."[80]

Nor does there seem to be much prospect of reversing the trend. Even the extreme circumstances of the September 11 terrorist attacks appear not to have sustained attempts at expatriation without clear individual consent. The Department of Justice explored the possibility of expatriating John Walker Lindh, the so-called American Taliban who took up arms against U.S. forces in Afghanistan, but in the end pursued only ordinary criminal charges.[81] Nor did the government try to rule that Louisiana-born Yaser Hamdi, who was detained during the fighting in the Afghanistan theater and was held for over two years as an enemy combatant, had lost his citizenship.[82] Hamdi, who also held Saudi citizenship, appeared to have had no contact with the United States since he left with his parents at the age of three.

Finally, a proposal to amend the Immigration and Nationality Act to terminate the citizenship of those joining or providing support to terrorist organizations never got out of the legislative gates. Included in the draft Domestic Security Enhancement Act of 2003, a putative follow-up to the 2001 USA PATRIOT Act that circulated internally in the Department of Justice but was never formally introduced, the provision would have deemed such service or support "prima facie evidence" of an intent to relinquish citizenship. The amendment was drafted with constitutional strictures in mind (accompanying explanatory materials referenced *Terrazas*), in effect requiring the likes of Lindh to produce a contemporaneous memo to the file documenting their intent if they wanted to defeat expatriation.[83] As of this writing, there appears no serious prospect that political initiatives will work a reversal of the now entrenched administrative refusal (in the full spirit of *Afroyim*) to terminate citizenship in the absence of the express renunciation of citizenship, nor that Congress will attempt to use expatriation as punishment (precluded by *Trop v. Dulles*).

Far more important have been the implications of the *Afroyim* regime for the incidence of plural citizenship. The case of Beys Afroyim itself may have played so well to the Court precisely because it did not involve dual nationality, and thus did not directly raise the specter of divided allegiances. Even though the decision itself hardly opened the door to untrammeled multiple national attachments, it laid the groundwork for a citizenship regime in which Americans can freely attach themselves to other polities without risk of losing U.S. citizenship. Increasing numbers are availing themselves of the benefits of additional nationalities now that those benefits often come at little or no cost. Native-born U.S. citizens with a single Irish grandparent, for example, are eligible to acquire Irish citizenship through a fairly speedy procedure, with the accompanying privileges of European Union citizenship as an incentive. It is the *Afroyim* regime which in effect gives them the right to acquire the additional nationality without endangering their continuing status as Americans. Moreover, *Afroyim*'s constitutional underpinnings would severely constrain any attempt to police the incidence of plural nationality among naturalizing Americans, who increasingly retain their citizenship of origin (although formally renouncing it) as they acquire U.S. citizenship.

The likes of Justices Black, Warren, and Douglas would almost surely defend the practice as it has evolved. Their conception of citizenship made it both the right that enabled all other rights and the very source of sovereignty, of all governmental authority. At that foundational level, the demise of unintended expatriation seems a logical constitutional endpoint. But one can query whether that destination has been attained because citizenship is ever more valued. On the contrary, one might suggest that the traditional citizenship regime, first breached with the decision in *Afroyim,* has more recently eroded as the product of citizenship's decline, rather than its revival. Where sovereigns once fought fiercely over the loyalties of individuals, national allegiance is now a more pliable or capacious concept. Warren's dictum that citizenship "is nothing less than the right to have rights" no longer holds in the wake of the human rights revolution, under which rights are contingent on personhood rather than nationality. And where Warren and Black equated the nation with its formal membership, one might more persuasively argue, as does Alexander Aleinikoff, that today " 'the country' is plainly more than the 'citizenry' of the United States."[84]

Afroyim itself may have contributed to this decline. To the extent that it facilitated the maintenance of multiple nationalities, the Court undermined the institution before which it genuflected. A less jealous state makes for a less devout citizenry; the end of exclusive national attachments has inevitably weakened the intensity of the tie, as there will be some for whom membership in the American community will be subordinated to membership in another.[85] *Afroyim* may nonetheless have advanced rights otherwise conceived. Americans can now pursue associational activities in other polities without incurring the cost of losing their American citizenship. Even where such other associations more centrally define identity, an individual can remain a good citizen. Beys Afroyim was no doubt one such American. Dividing his time between Israel and a home on Staten Island, a dual U.S. and Israeli national, he continued his work as an artist until his death in 1984, a man at least somewhat ahead of his time.

ENDNOTES

1.   387 U.S. 253 (1967).

2.   356 U.S. 44 (1958).

3.   See Peter J. Spiro, Dual Nationality and the Meaning of Citizenship, 46 Emory L.J. 1411, 1419–30 (1997).

4.   See Act of July 27, 1868, ch. 249, 15 Stat. 223 (codified at 22 U.S.C. § 1732 (2003)).

5.   See Act of Mar. 2, 1907, ch. 2564, 34 Stat. 1228.

6.   239 U.S. 299, 311 (1915).

7.   338 U.S. 491 (1950).

8.   Nationality Act of 1940, ch. 876, 54 Stat. 1168.

9.   Id. at § 401(j).

10.   See 800 of 900 Eligibles Return, N.Y. Times 20 (Jan. 6, 1935) (reporting return of former Saar Germans to take part in plebiscite). One report estimated that 40% of those eligible had acquired U.S. citizenship since immigrating to the United States. See Americans in Basin Now Fear Vote to Cost Citizenship, Wash. Post 1 (Dec. 30, 1934). U.S. officials denied rumors that voting would result in loss of citizenship. See Immigration Heads Deny Vote Perils Citizenship, Wash. Post 2 (Dec. 30, 1934).

11.   See H.R. 5799, 74th Cong. (1935). See also American Voters Assailed, N.Y. Times 12 (Jan. 4, 1935) (reporting Dickstein's objections).

12.   See Nationality Law of the United States: Message from the President of the United States Transmitting a Report Proposing a Revision and Codification of the Nationality Laws of the United States, House Comm. Print, 76th Cong. at 67.

13.   356 U.S. 44, 58 (1958).

14.   Id. at 60.

15.   Id. at 54.

16.   Id. at 59.

17.   Id. at 61.

18.   Id. at 60.

19.   Id. at 64 (Warren, C.J., dissenting).

20.   Id.

21.   Id. at 68 ("Nearly all sovereignties recognize the acquisition of foreign nationality ordinarily shows a renunciation of citizenship. Nor is this the only act by which the citizen may show a voluntary abandonment of citizenship.").

22.   Id. at 75. Warren conceded that in some circumstances, foreign voting would involve "a dilution of allegiance sufficient to show a voluntary abandonment of citizenship." Id.

23.   Id. at 81 (Douglas, J., dissenting).

24.   356 U.S. 86 (1958).

25.   Id. at 105 (Brennan, J., concurring).

26.   356 U.S. 129, 136 (1958).

27.   Id. at 139 (Black, J., concurring).

28.   T. Alexander Aleinikoff, David A. Martin, & Hiroshi Motomura, Immigration and Citizenship: Process and Policy 123 (5th ed. 2003).

29.   372 U.S. 144 (1963).

30.   Id. at 187 (Brennan, J., concurring).

31.   377 U.S. 163 (1964).

32.   Id. at 166.

33.   See Tanaka v. INS, 346 F.2d 438, 447–48 (2d Cir. 1965) (Kaufman, J., dissenting).

34.   See Philip B. Kurland, Foreword: Equal in Origin and Equal in Title to the Legislative and Executive Branches of the Government, 78 Harv. L. Rev. 143, 174 (1964). The accompanying student-written characterization, prompted by the 1964 decision in *Schneider*, also questioned the continuing viability of *Perez*. See The Supreme Court 1963 Term, 78 Harv. L. Rev. 143, 195 (1964).

35.   These facts are drawn from Afroyim's obituary in the Staten Island Advance (May 20, 1984), as well as the entry in Who Was Who in American Art 6 (Peter Hastings Falk ed., 1985) and a biography on the web site for the Museum of the City of New York, whose collection includes a painting by Afroyim. See http://www.mcny.org/Collections/paint/Painting/pttcat87.htm.

36. See Afroyim v. Rusk, 250 F. Supp. 686 (S.D.N.Y. 1966).

37. See Philippa Strum, Nanette Dembitz, in 10 American National Biography 406 (John A. Garraty & Mark C. Carnes eds., 1999).

38. See Nanette Dembitz, Racial Discrimination and Military Judgment: The Supreme Court's *Korematsu* and *Endo* Decisions, 45 Colum. L. Rev. 175 (1945).

39. The stipulations to the district court are found in Transcript of Record before the Supreme Court, Afroyim v. Rusk, No. 456, at 11 (1966).

40. *Afroyim*, 250 F. Supp. at 690.

41. 346 F.2d 438 (2d Cir. 1965).

42. 250 F. Supp. at 689.

43. Afroyim v. Rusk, 361 F.2d 102 (2d Cir. 1966).

44. Id. at 105 (Kaufman, J., concurring).

45. See Petition for Writ of Certiorari to the U.S. Court of Appeals for the Second Circuit, Afroyim v. Rusk, No. 456 (S. Ct. filed Aug. 18, 1966).

46. See Memorandum Supplemental to Petition for a Writ of Certiorari to the United States Court of Appeals for the Second Circuit, Afroyim v. Rusk, No. 456 (S.Ct. filed Sept. 23 1966).

47. Brief for Petitioner at 14, Afroyim v. Rusk, No. 456 (S.Ct. filed Dec. 17, 1966).

48. Id. at 17.

49. Id. at 20–21.

50. Brief for Respondent at 12–13, Afroyim v. Rusk, No. 456 (S. Ct. filed Dec. 17, 1966).

51. Id. at 14.

52. Id. at 16–17.

53. On this point, Afroyim's argument was clearly well-founded. At the same time that the Saar episode had clearly motivated Congressman Dickstein, the sponsor of Section 401(e), it appears that he was motivated more by anti-Nazism than by any diplomatic complications that arose from U.S. citizen voting. See *Afroyim*, 356 U.S. at 76 (Warren, C. J., dissenting) (reproducing statement by Rep. Dickstein). A lengthy history of the Saar plebiscite makes only passing reference to those who traveled from the United States to vote. See Sarah Wambaugh, The Saar Plebiscite 297 (1940). U.S. voters could not possibly have made a difference in the result, which overwhelmingly approved union of the Saar territory with Germany. See id. at 304 (setting forth vote tallies, with approximately 90% favoring union with Germany).

54. See Charles Gordon, The Citizen and the State: Power of Congress to Expatriate American Citizens, 53 Geo. L.J. 315 (1964).

55. 385 U.S. 276 (1966).

56. For a sketch of Gordon's career, including 35 years at the INS and seven other cases argued before the Court, see Influential Immigration Attorney and Scholar Charles Gordon Dies, 76 Interp. Releases 760 (1999).

57. Afroyim v. Rusk, 387 U.S. 253, 257 (1967).

58. Id. at 262.

59. Id. at 268.

60. *Nishikawa*, 356 U.S. at 139 (Black, J., concurring).

61. 387 U.S. at 269 (Harlan, J., dissenting).

62. Id. at 269 n.1.

63. See Matter of Becher, 12 I. & N. Dec. 380, 388 (AG 1965).

64. See Expatriation of American Citizens Abroad—Attorney General's Statement of Interpretation, 34 Fed. Reg. 1079 (1969).

65. Matter of Stanlake, 13 I. & N. Dec. 517 (BIA 1970).

66. Matter of Wayne, 16 I. & N. Dec. 248 (BIA 1977).

67. See Tad Szulc, Menuhin Warned on Citizenship, N.Y. Times 63 (Dec. 4, 1970); Rogers Tells Menuhin It Was All a Mistake, N.Y. Times 70 (Dec. 6, 1970).

68. 401 U.S. 815 (1971).

69. Id. at 844 (Black, J., dissenting).

70. 444 U.S. 252 (1980).

71. Id. at 260.

72. Id. at 274 (Brennan, J., dissenting).

73. See the State Department Board of Appellate Review cases cited in Note, United States Loss Of Citizenship Law After *Terrazas*: Decisions of the Board of Appellate Review, 16 N.Y.U. J. Int'l L. & Pol. 829, 862–63 (1984).

74. 7 F.A.M. 1200 et seq. Inexplicably, though the practice appears long to have been overtaken by other directives, the Manual still included these directives as of 2004, not having been updated since 1984.

75. See State Dept. Explains New Evidentiary Standards for Expatriation, 67 Interp. Releases 1092, 1094–95 (1990).

76. See Gary Endelman, How to Prevent Loss of Citizenship: Part I, Immigr. Briefings (Nov. 1989).

77. See Note at 865 (cited in note 73).

78. Pub. L. No. 99–653, 100 Stat. 3658 (1986), amending INA § 349(a), 8 U.S.C. § 1481(a).

79. See 67 Interp. Releases at 1093 (cited in note 75) (reproducing State Department statement). This guidance has been incorporated in federal regulations governing loss of nationality. See 22 C.F.R. § 50.40(a) (2004) (noting "administrative presumption" that individual does not intend to relinquish citizenship with respect to those acts).

80. See State Department Discusses Loss of Nationality Provisions, 72 Interp. Releases 1618 (1995).

81. See Eric Lichtblau, U.S. Talib is Charged With Conspiracy, L.A. Times A1 (Jan. 16, 2002).

82. See Hamdi v. Rumsfeld, 124 S. Ct. 2633 (2004). Hamdi did later agree, in negotiations to secure his release from detention, to renounce his citizenship before a U.S. consular officer, and he completed that process upon his return to Saudi Arabia. Eric Lichtblau, U.S., Bowing to Court, to Free "Enemy Combatant," N.Y. Times A1 (Sept. 22, 2004); Joel Brinkley & Eric Lichtblau, U.S. Releases Saudi–American It Had Captured in Afghanistan, N.Y. Times A15 (Oct. 12, 2004).

83. Domestic Security Enhancement Act (internal draft dated Jan. 9, 2003), available at http://www.pbs.org/now/politics/patriot2-hi.pdf.

84. T. Alexander Aleinikoff, Semblances of Sovereignty: The Constitution, The State, and American Citizenship 192–93 (2002).

85. See Peter J. Spiro, Dual Nationality and the Meaning of Citizenship, 46 Emory L.J. 1411 (1997).

7

Kleindienst v. Mandel: Plenary Power v. the Professors

Peter H. Schuck*

What a difference a judicial phrase can make. In 1972, the United States Supreme Court flatly rejected the First Amendment claims of a group of professors who challenged the government's denial of a temporary visa to a Belgian Marxist intellectual whom they had invited to speak to them. It formulated a standard for testing such exclusions— "facially legitimate and bona fide reason"—that was as easy for the government to satisfy as any known to the law. No one, least of all the Court, suspected that within less than two decades, immigration advocates would manage to convert this apparent judicial surrender into a solid victory over ideological exclusion. The saga and sequel of *Kleindienst v. Mandel* teach a valuable lesson to would-be law reformers: good lawyering (and politicking) can exploit tiny openings in otherwise restrictive Supreme Court doctrine to create far-reaching legal change.[1]

The Prelude to Mandel: Ideological Struggle and Ideological Exclusion

Kleindienst v. Mandel is one landmark in a long American struggle against subversives (variously defined) that goes back to the first decade of the Republic. In 1798, a Congress agitated by threats to a new and fragile polity posed by sedition and espionage, particularly in the wake of the French Revolution, enacted the Alien and Sedition Acts. They gave the President wide power to deport people he deemed dangerous or involved in "secret machinations." Highly controversial at the time, they were allowed to lapse two years later.[2] At the turn of the twentieth century, Congress barred anarchists and other immigrants who supported violent revolution, and this exclusion was subsequently extended to other groups. With the Bolshevik Revolution, however, this ideological crusade gained new force in the face of a new enemy: international

* Celia Whitaker, Yale Law School Class of 2006, provided excellent research assistance in this Chapter.

communism. While President Wilson was supporting a military expedi-
tion of "White Russians" seeking to defeat the revolutionaries, the
Attorney General launched, domestically, the so-called "Palmer Raids"
against suspected radicals in 1919.[3] The FBI intensified the hunt for
alleged subversives during the next two decades, finding them in many
areas of American life. In 1940, Congress enacted the Smith Act, which,
among other things, imposed new restrictions on immigrants and others
defined by the Attorney General as subversive.[4]

But it was the swift breakdown of the U.S.-Soviet alliance at the end
of World War II that raised the stakes in the ideological exclusion of
immigrants. The Cold War that ensued spawned ideological restrictions
in various laws governing immigration and refugee admissions and
citizenship. Of greatest relevance to the *Mandel* case was the enactment
of the McCarran–Walter Act of 1952, also known as the Immigration and
Nationality Act, particularly its Section 212(a)(28), which excluded aliens
from receiving visas to enter the United States if they advocated or
published, inter alia, the "doctrines of world communism."[5] Another
provision, Section 212(d)(3), authorized the Attorney General, in his
discretion (no criteria were provided), to accept a recommendation by the
Secretary of State or the relevant consular officer to issue a temporary
nonimmigrant visa to an alien otherwise excludable under (a)(28). Waivers were not possible, however, for applicants excludable under related
provisions covering expected activities "prejudicial to the public interest" or such crimes as espionage or violent overthrow of the government.
Waivers were often used to admit nonimmigrants otherwise excludable
on ideological and political grounds. By the time of the *Mandel* case, as
we shall see, the vast majority of such aliens received (d)(3) waivers.[6]

McCarran–Walter, of course, was a product of its time. Passed at the
height of Cold War fears, it was seen as a powerful weapon in the U.S.
arsenal against the domestic and international communist threat. In
1948, a Gallup poll found that only 15% of Americans believed the
United States was losing the Cold War, but by 1951, 30% believed the
Soviets were prevailing. In 1950, 81% of Americans believed the Soviet
Union wanted war, and 29% believed war was likely in one year.[7] The
Act, then, reflected the mood of the country: the idea of communism as
un-American, as an alien ideology at war with the nation's constitutional
values, was "[d]eeply ingrained in the American psyche."[8] As George
Kennan recalls in his memoirs, the term "McCarthyism" is inadequate
to describe a phenomenon that pre-dated and outlasted the Senator's
crusade: "he was its creature, not its creator."[9] With the benefit of
recently released Soviet archives revealing active and sometimes successful espionage by American communists directed by Moscow, we now
know that international communism did indeed pose a genuine threat.[10]
Even so, the anti-communist campaign produced numerous excesses,

injustices, and constitutional violations against American citizens and non-citizens alike.

Given this historical context, it is hardly surprising that the McCarran–Walter Act was more restrictive than its predecessors with respect to ideological exclusion, even as it relaxed some long-standing restrictions in other areas, such as limits on Japanese immigration and naturalization. Insofar as (a)(28) excluded aliens on the basis of their beliefs, advocacy, and writings, it penalized them for states of mind and activities that, if engaged in by U.S. citizens, were clearly protected by the First Amendment. Indeed, this was among the reasons why President Harry Truman vetoed the Act, denouncing the ideological exclusion and waiver provisions as "thought control."[11] In overriding his veto, Congress rejected any distinction between protecting political thoughts and penalizing subversive acts; the Act's exclusion provisions penalized both. In the landmark Hart–Celler Act that fundamentally liberalized immigration law in 1965, Congress retained these exclusion provisions.[12] Nevertheless, the basic First Amendment distinction between beliefs and writings, on the one hand, and dangerous acts, on the other, did not die; the opponents of ideological exclusion continued to press for it in *Mandel* and its aftermath, and they would eventually prevail.

The Dispute

Ernest Mandel, a Belgian citizen, was a journalist and editor of the socialist *La Gauche* newspaper. In 1940, at the age of seventeen, he had joined the Socialist Fourth International founded by Leon Trotsky two years earlier to promote world revolution. After World War II, he led the Fourth International's Belgian section, and in the 1950s and 1960s gained a reputation among European Marxist intellectuals for his advocacy of "orthodox" Trotskyism.[13] According to Professor Norman Birnbaum, who would later join the lawsuit challenging Mandel's exclusion, Mandel was "a major and prominent figure in Europe," and American intellectuals of the "nascent new left" appreciated his "intellectual openness and ... his opposition to Stalinist or post-Stalinist rigidity and apologetics."[14] Mandel's major work, *Marxist Economic Theory*, was widely circulated in Europe in the 1960s, released in the United States in 1969, and praised by American intellectuals on the left, such as economist Robert Heilbroner, who, like Birnbaum, would later become a co-plaintiff in the *Mandel* case.[15]

In March 1962, Mandel conducted research in the United States under a "working journalist" visa. Although the immigration authorities did not inform Mandel at the time, he had been deemed ineligible for admission under Section (a)(28) but was admitted under a discretionary (d)(3) waiver. In 1968, he returned to the United States on a lecture tour of thirty American universities. Again, he was not informed that he had entered under a (d)(3) waiver.[16]

In the summer of 1969, Stanford University invited Mandel to debate the prominent Harvard economist John Kenneth Galbraith at a conference on "Technology and the Third World," to be held on October 17–18. The plan was for Professor Galbraith to deliver the keynote address on the 17th, and for Mandel to participate in a panel discussion afterward. Mandel was also asked to deliver the keynote speech on October 18th. Stanford's president endorsed the invitation.[17] Mandel then applied for a B–1 non-immigrant visa on September 8, seeking admission for six days.[18] On October 23—five days *after* the Stanford conference had ended—Mandel, still in Brussels, received the first word that his application had been denied. It came in a telephone call from the American consul in Brussels, Alta Fowler, who learned during the conversation that Mandel had been unaware of his statutory ineligibility, and the waivers he had received, in 1962 and 1968. In an October 30 letter to Mandel, Fowler expressed regret that he had not been informed of this at the time, but neither the telephone call nor the letter gave any specific reason for his exclusions, other than citing the State Department's exclusion authority under (a)(28).[19]

Mandel was not the only one left in the dark. In September and October, before anyone had heard of Mandel's exclusion, many other American scholars and student groups began inviting him to speak at their universities. Mandel accepted, among others, invitations from Princeton, Amherst, the New School, MIT, and Vassar, as well as a Socialist Scholars Conference in New York City. Dates were set for November and December. On October 22, 1969, one day before hearing from Fowler in Brussels, he applied for another non-immigrant visa to enable him to participate in these six November and December events.[20] After talking to Consul Fowler, Mandel sent two letters dated October 23 and 24 to her, detailing his proposed itinerary for the November–December trip, giving the dates that had already been confirmed, and pledging to inform her of the precise dates of all his engagements once arranged. He also promised that he would neither diverge from the itinerary nor make any other public appearances or speeches. Although he considered these pledges "out of place and contrary to the elementary principles of liberty," he explained that he gave them because he had heard "indirectly" that his exclusion was due to a purported deviation from his approved plans during his 1968 visit. A week later, Mandel wrote to Fowler promising, in addition, not to undertake any fundraising while in the country.[21] In the October 30 letter in which she apologized for the authorities' failure to inform Mandel of the conditions of his entry in 1962 and 1968, Fowler also told him that the consulate had asked the State Department to waive ineligibility for the proposed

November–December trip.[22] As promised, Mandel subsequently furnished a final proposed itinerary.

Meanwhile, criticism of ideological exclusion, being used on a wider scale during this first year of the Nixon administration, began to mount. In Professor Galbraith's keynote address to the Stanford conference at which Mandel could not appear, Galbraith publicly condemned the government's treatment of Mandel. Calling the exclusion "silly, stupid, irrational and also grievously bad politics," he urged the audience to write to the State Department to condemn "this stupid action."[23] The press also took notice. Earlier that year, in response to a highly publicized government attempt to exclude the well-known Latin American writer Carlos Fuentes, *The New York Times* had editorialized that "the immigration law on exclusion is a vestige of the restrictive era of the 1950s," and went on to note how ideological exclusions had tarnished the U.S. image abroad.[24] After Stanford announced Mandel's exclusion from its conference,[25] other newspapers and magazines attacked the Nixon administration's use of (a)(28) as a reversion to McCarthyism. In an October 28 editorial, *The New York Times* compared such exclusions to "censorship by visa" and, in an important augury of legal arguments to come, maintained that they potentially violated U.S. citizens' First Amendment rights: substituting audiotapes, telephone hookups, and books for face-to-face interaction "in no way offset[s] the senseless violation of" basic American principles.[26] Indeed, prefiguring the bureaucratic clash that would surface later in the month, *Newsweek*'s November 8 issue reported that Secretary of State William Rogers had remarked to an aide, "Why should we be afraid of this man and his ideas?"[27]

Sympathetic intellectuals and professors from more than fifty U.S. universities (some of whom would become Mandel's co-plaintiffs) also joined the outcry. In a November 20 letter published in the *New York Review of Books*, eight prominent intellectuals denounced Mandel's earlier exclusion and called on all Americans to petition Rogers to issue Mandel's visa for his November–December engagements. Noting the Nixon administration's growing use of ideological exclusions, the letter pointed out that Mandel had been admitted just a year earlier and cited his renown as an economist and intellectual. Like the *Times* editorial of October 28, the letter invoked citizens' First Amendment right to have aliens like Mandel admitted in order to hear their views.[28] Fearing a repeat of Stanford's experience, Mandel's sponsors for the November and December events decided to obtain legal representation in order to put pressure on the government, get an explanation of the Stanford visa denial, and ensure that Mandel could participate in their programs.[29]

Mandel Finds a Lawyer

Enter Leonard Boudin, then perhaps the most famous legal advocate
for radical causes in the country. Boudin had begun to practice in the
late 1930s with his uncle, Louis Boudin, an influential member of the
Socialist Party. This was the height of the industrial union movement,
and most of Boudin's work for his uncle involved representing labor
unions, many of which were connected with the political left and far left
and included many communists. According to Victor Rabinowitz, then a
young attorney in Louis Boudin's firm, the office in these years was in
the vanguard of a popular crusade committed to a socialist economy. But
by the end of World War II, the young Rabinowitz was restless. Passion-
ately engaged in radical politics as well as law (he had been a card-
carrying member of the Communist Party since 1942), Rabinowitz
wanted to run his own show. He convinced his good friend Leonard
Boudin to leave his uncle's office in 1947 to become partners in a new
labor law firm, a collaboration that would continue for forty years.[30]

Their timing was impeccable. With the Cold War heating up and
McCarthyism about to sweep the country, suspected communists, libertarians, immigrants, and civil rights activists, among others, needed
representation. Many lawyers did not want to represent alleged subversives and other political untouchables. Indeed, some groups established
specifically to protect civil liberties also backed away as the political
intimidation worsened in the 1950s and 1960s. Even the American Civil
Liberties Union, the nation's pre-eminent civil liberties organization,
demurred. According to Ellen Schrecker, a chronicler of this period, the
ACLU's "wishy-washy behavior" showed that the organization "was
paralyzed, its inaction indirectly reinforcing the reluctance of liberal
lawyers to defend politically unpopular clients." But the threat to
lawyers with clients under political attack was not imaginary; defenders
of alleged communists were often tainted.[31]

What threatened other lawyers created an attractive professional
opening for Rabinowitz and Boudin. During the McCarthy era, their firm
represented some 225 witnesses before the House Un–American Activities Committee and Senator McCarthy's Committee on Government
Operations, all of them "unfriendly" to the panels and many of them
impecunious. According to Rabinowitz, "we considered ourselves lucky
when we were able to get travel expenses for hearings out of New York,"
yet they never refused to represent a witness for lack of funds.[32] As
radical lawyer Bernardine Dohrn wrote in her review of Rabinowitz's
memoirs, "Rabinowitz's 50–year partnership with the late Leonard
Boudin and the law firm they created is unique in the nation for their
unswerving legal representation of the underdog.... No law firm approaches Rabinowitz–Boudin in representing the history of the struggle
against political repression in the U.S. over the past 50 years."[33]

Their work in the late 1960s had again brought these legal crusaders into conflict with the government, this time over the Vietnam War. In 1968, Boudin defended Dr. Benjamin Spock, the beloved child-care writer who had co-authored a document addressed to potential draftees protesting the Selective Service Act. Spock's conviction for conspiring to counsel violation of the draft system was overturned on appeal. Then in 1971, Boudin took on a case of much greater drama and importance—the defense of Daniel Ellsberg, charged with unauthorized disclosure of classified materials that quickly came to be known as the Pentagon Papers.[34]

Initial inquiries on Mandel's behalf were made to the National Emergency Civil Liberties Committee. The ECLC, as it was called, was a civil liberties defense and advocacy group that Boudin had helped to found in 1951, and for which he served as general counsel until his death in 1989. The ECLC had courageously represented communists during the 1950s and early 1960s, but its staff and resources were limited, so it referred Mandel's case to the Rabinowitz & Boudin firm.[35] The firm jumped into the fray, although Rabinowitz would later state that Boudin did not share his "romanticism" about socialist revolution.[36]

In late October, Boudin wrote to the State Department official in charge of the Bureau for Security and Consular Affairs, expressing the desire of an unnamed group of American scholars to have Mandel admitted for his November–December trip. Boudin also asked that a Bureau representative meet with his clients to discuss Mandel's situation. Two weeks later, a Bureau official, Barbara Watson, responded to Boudin that the State Department was aware of the academic community's concern, but that it would not hold such a meeting. Mandel's 1962 and 1968 waivers of ineligibility, she explained, had been granted on the condition that he would conform to his stated itinerary and activities. But because the Department had learned that Mandel had "engaged in activities beyond the stated purpose of his trip" in 1968, it had not recommended a waiver allowing him to attend the Stanford conference. Although Watson did not specify which activities were being referred to, her letter marked the first direct explanation for the denial of Mandel's September 8 visa request. Nevertheless, she reported, the Department had recently changed its mind about barring Mandel when it learned in late October that he had been unaware of the conditions attached to his 1962 and 1968 visas. Accordingly, and given his assurances to Consul Fowler that he would adhere to his stated itinerary and purposes, the Department was further discussing his case with the Department of Justice, which had final authority to grant or deny the waiver.[37]

With only three weeks remaining before Mandel's first U.S. engagement, his American hosts began to lobby actively for his admission, instigating repeated requests to both the Justice and State Departments for a status report on his visa application, and stressing the urgency of the situation. They received no response. On November 29, the day of Mandel's scheduled speech in New York, the U.S. consulate in Brussels telephoned Mandel to inform him that the State Department's request for a waiver had been denied. Two days later, Consul Fowler confirmed this denial, apologizing for the untimely notice and explaining that the embassy in Brussels had only learned of the decision on the 29th.[38] Neither Boudin nor any of the Americans who had inquired about Mandel's visa status had received any word from the government.

The audience of 1,200 at New York's Town Hall ultimately heard a tape recording of Mandel's speech, owing to the organizers' last-minute arrangements. At great expense, they had also arranged for a telephone hook-up so that Mandel could answer questions and engage with the other participants, but a circuit failure aborted this plan.[39] In his remarks, Mandel criticized the passivity and over-intellectualization of many of his fellow socialists. Citing the 1968 student uprisings in France, he applauded the "revolutionary upsurge" in the West, urging his audience to form a "revolutionary vanguard organization" that would lead to "the emancipation of labor and of all mankind!" Mandel also mocked the Nixon administration's refusal to confront his ideas rather than exclude them, particularly when Marxist books, including his own, were freely available in U.S. bookstores: "I would not be carrying any high explosives, if I had come, but only, as I did before, my revolutionary views which are well known to the public."[40]

The controversy over Mandel's exclusion took a new twist as stories emerged that State and Justice disagreed about the issue at the highest levels. A front-page article in *The New York Times* on November 27 maintained that Secretary of State Rogers had unsuccessfully urged Attorney General John Mitchell to grant the waiver in November on the ground that Mandel's admission would be "in the national interest." The *Times'* sources "took the unusual step of disassociating the Secretary of State from the decision" by the Attorney General, and indicated that State might renew its effort to reverse the decision.[41] Once again, a *Times* editorial inveighed against the exclusion of Mandel on ideological grounds and the law that made this possible.[42] Mandel, still in Brussels, noted in a late November interview that he still hoped to reschedule his cancelled engagements for the following year, and opined that the public interest in his admission showed that Americans were "very much alive to the dangers that threaten our basic freedom."[43]

In December, Boudin wrote two letters to Attorney General Mitchell inquiring about the reasons for Mandel's visa denial, but received no reply. In late January, Boudin sent a third request for an explanation, noting the academic community's continuing desire to see and hear Mandel in the flesh, adding that he would consider a non-response from

Mitchell as evidence of his continuing intent to defy Secretary Rogers' recommendation and reject any future visa application from Mandel. Two weeks later, Boudin received a letter from INS Commissioner James Greene, which emphasized the INS's complete discretion, as delegate of the Attorney General, to grant or refuse a State Department waiver request. Although Mandel had been admitted for an academic visit in 1968, Greene stated, his activities "were much reported in the press and went far beyond the stated purposes of his trip," a fact that led the Justice Department to view Mandel's behavior as a "flagrant abuse of the opportunities afforded him to express his views in this country." Finally, Greene stated the INS's view that "there is no basis for changing this determination."[44] Around this time, the State Department confirmed that it had urged the Justice Department to waive exclusion in light of Mandel's ignorance of his 1968 visa conditions and "in the interest of the free expression of opinion and ideas," and that the INS, acting for the Attorney General, had rejected this recommendation.[45] Mandel and his frustrated U.S. sponsors were eager to reschedule their events for the spring or fall of 1970, but the legal uncertainty regarding Mandel's visa status made this impossible. Mandel therefore accepted the new invitations on condition that he would receive the visa.[46] The government, however, refused to oblige. The stage for litigation was now set.

Conceptualizing the Lawsuit

Boudin faced a daunting task. Mandel was not only an alien without any constitutional right to enter the country;[47] he was an outspoken Marxist who advocated international socialist revolution and the destruction of the capitalist system cherished by almost all Americans. Boudin would have to take on a wartime government and one of its broadest, most impregnable powers, the power to regulate entry to the United States. The long-established "plenary power doctrine"[48] had already deterred many potential challenges to arbitrary immigration rules, and (a)(28) had discouraged numerous alien radicals from even trying to enter the country. Some Europeans had even dubbed the U.S. immigration laws the "Iron Curtain of the West."[49] All of this, however, simply whetted the appetite of Boudin, who specialized in test cases that pushed against the existing limits of constitutional law.[50]

At the outset, Boudin had to resolve a thorny strategic question. According to David Rosenberg, then a young associate with Boudin's firm and now a professor at Harvard Law School, Boudin was inclined to argue the case purely on the ground that Mandel's own legal rights were violated by (a)(28)'s clear discrimination against particular political viewpoints. Rosenberg, however, took a different view. A challenge based on *citizens'* First Amendment right to hear the excluded alien, he thought, might finesse the plenary power precedents denying aliens any constitutional right to enter, and would have the additional advantage of removing Mandel, an outspoken revolutionary socialist, from the lawsuit's focus. Rosenberg, who recalls an intra-firm "war" over which strategy should be employed, eventually prevailed[51] and ended up writing much of the brief for the Supreme Court. After his defeat in *Mandel*, Boudin continued to wonder whether the outcome would have been different had he followed his own strategy. (In hindsight, Rosenberg also asks himself the same question. Taking on Boudin must have been difficult. Rosenberg refers to him today as "the best at his craft," and considers Boudin and Rabinowitz to have been "the premier constitutional lawyers of the 1950s and 1960s.")[52]

Once Boudin settled on the litigation strategy, he needed to find willing citizens to serve as plaintiffs. This, however, was easy. Not only were many individuals already committed to Mandel's cause—eight prominent academics, including four of the ultimate plaintiffs, had protested his exclusion in the *New York Review of Books*—but Boudin also had a cohort of like-minded friends who would be happy to serve as test-case plaintiffs.[53] Then too, it was 1969, the end of a decade during which the ACLU's membership had almost tripled[54] as many baby boomers, influenced by the civil rights movement, anti-war protest, and left-leaning faculty in their universities, flocked to liberal causes challenging the despised Nixon administration. In any event, the eight professors whom Boudin selected were happy to serve as named plaintiffs—suing, as the Supreme Court later put it, "to enforce their rights, individually and as members of the American public." But as is usually the case in such litigation, they played no other role.[55]

Later, when the case was appealed to the Supreme Court, Boudin brought in the ACLU as an amicus curiae.[56] This was an interesting choice because, as noted above, the ACLU had shied away from representing communists during the 1950s. Although the organization's policies had begun to change in the 1960s, and certainly by the time of *Mandel*, the McCarthy years had created enmity between Boudin and the ECLC, on the one side, and the ACLU on the other. The ECLC condemned the ACLU for failing to challenge the anti-communist provisions of the Taft–Hartley Act,[57] and for purging radicals from its ranks. Indeed, one of the ECLC's founders was Corliss Lamont, who in 1947 had left the ACLU in disgust over its policies. By the early 1970s, this acrimony was largely behind them, but the rivalry persisted. The ECLC (and its counsel, Boudin) and the ACLU vied for the hottest cases at the forefront of the civil liberties struggle. Boudin's lawyers believed that they were superior attorneys; they usually "thought the ACLU wouldn't add anything to a case, and more often than not would detract."[58] On the other hand, Boudin enjoyed close personal relationships with both Mel

Wulf, then the ACLU's Legal Director, and Burt Neuborne, then staff counsel for the New York branch of the ACLU. Boudin thought that the *Mandel* case might foster a rapprochement between the ACLU and the ECLC.[59] The ACLU in 1970 was eager to make amends for its past, to reinvigorate itself, and to take on an immigration case raising First Amendment issues. *Mandel* represented an opportunity to do all three.

Doctrinally, Boudin hoped to exploit two recent Supreme Court developments that had significantly expanded the concept of protected speech. First, the Court had derived from the traditional First Amendment rights of speakers and writers a concomitant right of listeners and readers. The two leading cases were *Lamont v. Postmaster General* in 1965 and *Red Lion Broadcasting Co. v. FCC* in 1969. *Lamont* upheld a challenge to a federal statute that authorized the postal service to withhold delivery of communist materials unless and until the addressee explicitly requested them in writing. The Court viewed the statute's interference with "the flow of mail" as an impermissible attempt to "control the flow of ideas to the public," basing its holding not on the sender's right to have its materials delivered but on the addressee's First Amendment rights to receive information.[60] And in *Red Lion*, the Court held that "the right of the public to receive suitable access to social, political, esthetic, moral, and other ideas and experiences ... may not constitutionally be abridged either by Congress or by the FCC."[61]

The second development in First Amendment doctrine was the Court's growing willingness, which would expand even further during the 1970s, to protect commercial speech.[62] If the Court was protecting speech at the periphery of First Amendment values, Boudin and his ACLU collaborators reasoned, then Mandel's kind of political speech, which lay at the core of the First Amendment, should be protected a *fortiori*. Still missing from the Court's jurisprudence, however, was an explicit acknowledgment that a speaker's *physical presence* was a necessary component of the right of communication guaranteed by the First Amendment. *Mandel* represented an opportunity to take this next step.[63] The task of advocating this extension fell to Boudin. In the brief submitted to the Supreme Court, Boudin relied on the academic nature of Mandel's proposed visit, arguing that the Court had already acknowledged the importance to American scholarship and education of contact with foreign scholars. As he put it, "there is nothing comparable in academic study to the face to face discussion that takes place in a classroom." He also analogized the classroom to the courtroom, invoking the landmark 1970 *Goldberg v. Kelly* decision in which the Supreme Court ruled that due process requires the opportunity for a live hearing rather than just oral submissions to contest the cutoff of welfare benefits.[64]

Mandel *in the Lower Court*

Mandel and eight co-plaintiffs sought a declaratory judgment that two provisions of the McCarran–Walter Act were unconstitutional, both on their face and as applied.[65] The facial challenge, which had to confront Congress' plenary power over immigration, targeted two particular subsections of Section 212 of the Act. First, Boudin contended that (a)(28), by making aliens associated with certain political doctrines categorically ineligible for admission, and thus denying the American plaintiffs' right to free academic inquiry, imposed an unconstitutional prior restraint on free speech, denied equal protection by excluding only leftists, and denied due process by providing no safeguards against erroneous determinations. Second, the plaintiffs claimed that (d)(3), which gave the Attorney General the discretion to waive inadmissibility and grant temporary admission, failed to provide adequate due process protections against arbitrary waiver decisions. The "as applied" challenge emphasized that Attorney General Mitchell's decision to deny Mandel a waiver was "arbitrary and capricious," based on "neither substantial evidence, a basis in fact, nor a rational ground." They emphasized that the government had never articulated exactly how Mandel's activities in 1968 constituted an alleged "flagrant abuse" of his visa conditions; had never justified the government's refusal to believe Mandel's written pledges that he would abide by his stated itinerary for the November 1969 trip; and had offered no evidence to rebut Mandel's statement on his visa application that he had never been a member of the Communist Party.[66]

A divided three-judge federal court in New York upheld plaintiffs' position, declaring (a)(28) unconstitutional. The majority rejected the government's argument that (a)(28) imposed merely an incidental restriction on First Amendment rights in the pursuit of legitimate government aims. Refusing to apply a balancing test, it held that the infringement on those rights was not necessary to avert a grave evil within the sphere of legitimate governmental concern and did not constitute a "secondary or mediating exercise of power." Although "the power to exclude aliens is not questioned," the court reasoned, the challenged statute could not stand because "the substance of the exercise of the power is the restraint on interests protected by the First Amendment."[67] Vindicating Boudin's tactical decision to emphasize the Supreme Court's recent expansion of protected speech, the majority asserted that "the rights of the citizens of the country to have an alien enter and to hear him explain and seek to defend his views ... is of the essence of self-government," at least where the alien's speech does not constitute "incitement or conspiracy to initiate presently programmed violence." As for (d)(3), the waiver authority, the majority condemned the absence both of standards to govern the exercise of discretion and of procedures to assure that the decision comports with due process. It concluded, however, that the question was moot because the government could not properly exercise the (a)(28) exclusion power in the first place.[68] The dissenting judge argued that the majority had interpreted the First Amendment without regard to the government's plenary power over matters of national security and foreign policy, and had overridden Congress' considered legislative judgment that advocates of international communism threatened national security and were more likely "to engage in acts of sabotage, civil disruption, and illegal incitement to violence." He also was reluctant to extend *Lamont* to Mandel's case.[69]

Mandel *in the Supreme Court*

The *Mandel* plaintiffs' victory gave them hope, but it seemed highly vulnerable to reversal in the Supreme Court. The plenary power doctrine, of course, loomed over the case. The First Amendment right of listeners was gaining ground in legal doctrine, but had not yet been applied by the Court in the situation of a would-be immigrant speaker, and might well be unworkable in that context, where any disappointed applicant for a U.S. visa would be able to make a speech-based argument much like Mandel's. In addition, the Court might recognize the plaintiffs' right to engage with Mandel without holding that his physical presence in the United States was necessary. The ACLU's Burt Neuborne, who was otherwise optimistic about the case, feared that this physical presence feature was the most likely to sink it.[70]

By 1972, moreover, the plaintiffs faced a more pro-government Supreme Court than they would have just a few years earlier. President Nixon had already placed his stamp on the Court, appointing the conservative Warren Burger as Chief Justice in the expectation that Burger would roll back the judicial activism of his predecessor, Earl Warren. Then Harry Blackmun replaced the liberal Abe Fortas, and in 1972, William Rehnquist and Louis Powell joined the Court. These four new arrivals were among the six justices who would reverse the district court later that year, with Blackmun writing the opinion. Blackmun is best remembered today as the author of the controversial *Roe v. Wade* abortion decision, and in later years became a "regular voting partner" of Justices Thurgood Marshall and William Brennan, who dissented vehemently in *Mandel*.[71] But in 1970, Blackmun was viewed merely as the "third choice" after the Senate had rejected Nixon's first two nominees for the Fortas seat. To avoid further political embarrassment after those Senate defeats, Nixon needed someone like Blackmun, who then appeared to be relatively non-partisan, non-ideological, and non-controversial. In the event, Blackmun was confirmed 94–0. A lifelong Republican and a close friend of Burger—he was best man at Burger's wedding, and the two were often referred to in the early years of their tenure as the "Minnesota Twins"—Blackmun was not viewed as a legal innovator, and civil liberties lawyers dreaded his appointment.[72]

Initially, Blackmun did vote quite closely with Burger. *Mandel* was an early example.[73] There, he rallied a 6–3 majority to reject the plaintiffs' claims. Justice Blackmun began by reviewing the history of U.S. immigration law, emphasizing the steady expansion of grounds covering suspected subversives. He also recounted the numerous Supreme Court precedents upholding such exclusions on the basis of broad deference to Congress in defining threats to national security. With almost no analysis, he rejected the government's argument that no First Amendment right was implicated by the exclusion because the government was restricting Mandel's physical movement, not his ideas which were accessible in other forms. Instead, Blackmun insisted that a citizen's claimed right to engage with an excluded alien like Mandel must be weighed against Congress' plenary power over immigration, as consistently reaffirmed by the Court. Turning to the plaintiffs' First Amendment claim, Blackmun formulated the question before the Court as "the narrow issue whether the First Amendment confers upon the appellee professors ... the ability to ... compel the Attorney General to allow Mandel's admission."[74] This curious wording suggested, contrary to fact, that the plaintiffs sought a blanket rule that the First Amendment trumps immigration restrictions whenever U.S. citizens have an interest in hearing the foreign speaker. In a stinging dissent, Justice Marshall, picking up a point in plaintiffs' brief,[75] argued that plaintiffs did not request such an extreme ruling, and that it was unnecessary to their case because the government could still justify an exclusion on the basis of a "compelling governmental interest" such as "actual threats to the national security, public health needs, and genuine requirements of law enforcement." But neither Marshall nor the plaintiffs acknowledged that requiring the government to meet this test whenever the immigrant wanted to speak to an American—true, of course, of all immigrants— might seriously compromise the administration of the immigration laws.

Having set up this conflict as Blackmun did, he then chose to finesse it so as to avoid the need to balance the listeners' rights against the government's interests. Instead, he focused on the "as applied" challenge, deciding that the waiver provision, (d)(3), had been validly applied to Mandel because the Attorney General had presented a "facially legitimate and bona fide" reason for excluding him. This reason was Mandel's "flagrant abuse" of the conditions imposed on his 1968 visa, and the Court would neither look behind it (to see whether it had a factual basis) nor test it by balancing its rationale against the listeners' First Amendment interests.[76]

It did not trouble Blackmun that this "flagrant abuse" reason was almost certainly a sham and a pretext. Mandel received no notice in 1968 that he was being admitted under a discretionary waiver, nor was he ever told of the visa conditions. And the letter from the INS Commissioner citing "flagrant abuse" of the visa conditions offered no facts to support this conclusion. The government never sought to back up this assertion thereafter, and the government did not even rely on this argument either at trial or in the Supreme Court. Rather, the government told the trial court that the 1968 visit was "irrelevant," instead relying entirely on Congress' plenary power and the unfettered discretion over waivers delegated to the Attorney General.[77]

Blackmun's reliance on this "facially legitimate and bona fide reason" was also problematic because, as Marshall pointed out in dissent, "[t]he waiver question . . . is totally secondary and dependent, since it is triggered here only by a determination of (a)(28) ineligibility."[78] Since Blackmun decided the case on other grounds, moreover, his lengthy discursus on the government's plenary power over immigration—and his strong suggestion that (a)(28) was constitutional—amounted to dictum. His explicit holding was simply that the Attorney General's "facially legitimate and bona fide reason" sufficed to justify Mandel's exclusion.

Mandel's *Aftermath*

The *Mandel* decision dismayed immigration advocates, civil libertarians, and others who opposed ideological exclusion, and with good reason. The opinion had confirmed the government's constitutional power under (a)(28) to exclude even temporary, otherwise eligible visitors solely because of the political ideas they entertained. In addition, the Court had interpreted the waiver provision in (d)(3) to give the government apparently untrammeled discretion to deny waivers simply by giving a reason—even (as in *Mandel*) a reason seemingly invented post hoc. It had acknowledged the interests of Americans wanting to engage in person with aliens holding radical views, only to give those interests the back of the judicial hand. The spark of hope, born of *Lamont* and *Red Lion*, that the First Amendment would protect those interests in the immigration context was unceremoniously snuffed out.[79]

But never underestimate the ability of resourceful advocates to turn the tide by using unexpected events, government over-reaching, public opinion, and legal and political creativity to exploit seemingly unpromising doctrinal leeways and to get Congress to amend the law. By 1990, with *Mandel* still on the books, ideological exclusion was essentially eliminated. It is doubtful that even Leonard Boudin would have predicted this legal revolution and total vindication. Alas, he was not around to enjoy it. How did this remarkable *volte-face* happen? What was the recipe for reform?

First consider the unexpected events. During a very brief period of détente with the Soviet Union, the idea of freedom of movement found its way onto the international human rights agenda. In 1975, the United States signed the Helsinki Accords,[80] which committed the thirty-five signatories to increasing international freedom of movement. Congress followed up in 1977 with the so-called McGovern Amendment,[81] providing that when a nonimmigrant was deemed excludable solely "by reason of membership in or affiliation with a proscribed organization," the Secretary of State "should" recommend that the Attorney General grant a waiver, unless the Secretary of State certified to Congress that the alien's admission would harm national security interests. The Amendment thus limited ideology-based exclusions under (a)(28) while allowing those based on national security. Indeed, the total number of aliens excluded under (a)(28)—both by State Department visa officers who declined to recommend a waiver of ineligibility, and by the Attorney General after a favorable State Department recommendation—had been declining even before the *Mandel* decision. From a peak of 1,098 exclusions of alleged "subversive" or "anarchist" aliens during the 1950s (up from just sixty under different legislation in the preceding decade), the total dropped to 128 in the 1960s and dwindled to thirty-two in the 1970s.[82] As a further sign of this trend, during the years leading up to the *Mandel* litigation, the Attorney General regularly approved the vast majority of waiver applications.[83]

Now add some government over-reaching. Abraham Sofaer, Legal Adviser to the State Department in the Reagan administration, informed Congress in 1987 that the government was then denying between 600 and 700 waivers of excludability *annually*[84]—although this high number may include consular visa denials as well as denials of State Department waiver recommendations. In any event, many of these exclusions became *causes célèbres*, notorious as examples of official excess, irrationality, spitefulness, and Cold War "gotcha" aimed at trivial, transient tactical advantage. In 1980, President Carter's State Department denied a visa to the Italian playwright (and later Nobel laureate) Dario Fo on the ground that "Fo's record of performance with regard to the United States is not good. Dario Fo has never had a good word to say about [the United States]."[85] From the 1960s through the 1980s, the government excluded famous writers of the first rank, such as Primo Levi, Gabriel Garcia Marquez (1963–1971, 1984, 1986), Carlos Fuentes (perennial exclusions from 1961 onward), and Pablo Neruda (1960s). Political figures from Hortensia de Allende, the widow of Chilean president Salvador Allende (1983), to former Canadian Prime Minister Pierre Trudeau (1984) either were excluded or experienced major immigration obstacles because of their political views.[86] The Reagan administration, civil libertarians charged, was using the ideological exclusion provisions as "punitive ... symbolic gestures meant to express American displeasure with prominent individuals who have publicly disagreed with American policy," as well as to "structure domestic political debate."[87] In 1983, while Europe and the United States were bitterly debating the proposed deployment of American cruise missiles in Europe, the State Department denied a visa to Nino Pasti—an Italian general who had been stationed in the Pentagon and served as Vice–Supreme Allied Commander of NATO for Nuclear Affairs—thwarting his plans to address a disarmament rally in Boston opposing the deployment.[88] That same year, Secretary of State George Shultz defended the exclusion of Tomas Borge, Interior Minister of Nicaragua, from a U.S. speaking tour on the ground that free speech "can get abused by people who do not wish us well."[89] In seeking to justify such exclusions, the government was hobbled by the pesky McGovern Amendment. Frustrated, the Justice Department tried to circumvent it by excluding ideological opponents under a different provision, (a)(27), which barred aliens whose entry would be "prejudicial to the public interest"[90] and which had the virtue, from the government's perspective, that it could not be waived. Both Pasti and Borge, for example, were excluded under (a)(27) instead of (a)(28).

Then spice this mixture with a mobilized public opinion. During the 1980s, the editorial pages of leading newspapers attacked ideological exclusions, which were largely associated with the Reagan administration and its aggressive Cold War policies.[91] The congressionally chartered and bipartisan Select Commission on Immigration and Refugee Policy recommended in its 1981 report that Congress completely overhaul the system of ideological exclusion, although no legislative action was then taken.[92] Scholars almost uniformly depicted ideological exclusion and the plenary power doctrine as relics of the McCarthy era, retrograde doctrines increasingly isolated from contemporary public law.[93] Even Sofaer, the State Department's top lawyer, conceded in the 1987 congressional testimony mentioned above that (a)(28) exclusions "remain the target of strong and valid criticism as undemocratic and inconsistent with our national policy in favor of the free and open competition of ideas." He stated that Attorney General Edwin Meese and Secretary of State George Shultz had opposed exclusions that would constrict free speech rights in the U.S.[94]

Finally, toss in some creative lawyering. Counsel for ideologically excluded aliens developed a clever and ultimately successful litigation strategy, which consisted of two elements. First, they avoided the First Amendment arguments that had proved unavailing in *Mandel* and instead spotlighted the government's effort to shift ideological exclusions from (a)(28), to which the strictures of the McGovern Amendment applied, to (a)(27), to which they might not apply and for which no waiver was available. The lawyers argued that this disingenuous tactic in effect nullified the McGovern Amendment and avoided the pressure on Justice Department waiver decisions that Congress sought to exert through the Amendment. After lengthy litigation, the lawyers representing Pasti, Borges, and two others excluded under (a)(27) persuaded the influential U.S. Court of Appeals for the District of Columbia Circuit to accept this legal theory. In *Abourezk v. Reagan*, it held that the government must seek any exclusions based on political ideology under (a)(28), not (a)(27), reasoning that any other rule would render (a)(28) and the McGovern Amendment nullities and thus allow the Justice Department to evade the will of Congress. Even more important, the D.C. Circuit went on to distinguish between exclusions based on an alien's prejudicial *activities* in the United States (the province of (a)(27)) and exclusions based on the alien's mere "presence" or "entry" (the province of (a)(28)).[95] The government successfully petitioned for *certiorari*, but the Supreme Court divided evenly and so affirmed *Abourezk* without opinion. Two years later, the First Circuit followed this same reasoning in a high-profile ruling, invalidating the government's attempt to use (a)(27) to exclude Hortensia Allende, the widow of Chilean president Salvador Allende.[96] With these victories based on statutory interpretation, the immigrants' lawyers succeeded in side-stepping both the plenary power doctrine and the restrictive view of the First Amendment rights of would-be immigrants and the U.S. citizens who wished to engage with their ideas.

The second element of the reformers' litigation strategy was to press against the tiny opening that Blackmun had left in his *Mandel* opinion—the "facially legitimate and bona fide reason" standard—in order to put some teeth into judicial review of Justice Department exclusion decisions. Blackmun cited no precedent for this standard because none existed—nor (as Justice Marshall pointed out in dissent) did Blackmun offer any explanation.[97] Understandably, therefore, this ruling sowed confusion in the law reviews and in the courts. Some scholars saw *Mandel* as a "chink in the plenary power armor" that had previously been thought to preclude any judicial scrutiny of immigration legislation. Like *Harisiades v. Shaughnessy*, which held that immigration statutes are "*largely* immune from judicial inquiry or interference," *Mandel*'s "facially legitimate and bona fide reason" standard might have left the door to judicial review open a crack.[98] Under this view, *Mandel* deferred entirely to congressional immigration policy choices but required at least some minimal showing of rationality to sustain discretionary decisions by the Attorney General. This double standard is common enough in public law, where courts review agency actions more closely than they review congressional ones. After all, considerations of institutional competence, separation of powers, and plenary congressional power over immigration seem less compelling where *agency* choices are concerned. There, the reviewing court acts as a kind of agent of Congress in ensuring faithful execution of the legislative will. In addition, courts have often used statutory interpretation and review of executive decisions as ways to circumvent the constraints of the plenary power doctrine and give aliens more protection than it would otherwise allow. Professor Hiroshi Motomura shows this use of "phantom norms" to be a long-standing judicial tactic in immigration cases. This technique enables judges both to expand the reviewability of immigration decisions and to extend to aliens more of the protections that individuals—citizens and non-citizens alike—enjoy outside the immigration context.[99]

Five years after *Mandel*, the goal of limiting the plenary power doctrine by broadening the scope of judicial review suffered an apparent setback when the Supreme Court, in *Fiallo v. Bell*, rejected a facial challenge to a congressional statute that denied to a father and his child born out of wedlock the immigration benefits available to other parents or children of U.S. citizens. Citing *Mandel*, the Court held that "despite the impact of these classifications on the interests of those already within our borders, congressional determinations such as this one are subject only to limited judicial review."[100] The Court reaffirmed this limitation in its 1986 decision in another immigration case, *Jean v. Nelson*, where it affirmed the lower court's interpretation of the *Mandel* standard as being equivalent to the more familiar, but equally narrow "abuse of discretion" standard.[101]

That same year, a district court, in *Harvard Law School Forum v. Shultz*, applied the *Mandel* standard to precisely the kind of First Amendment claim that Blackmun brushed aside in *Mandel*. The State Department had permitted an alien who was ideologically excludable because of his membership in the Palestine Liberation Organization to travel within the United States for recreational purposes but not to speak in public about Middle East politics or to participate in public political discussions. Because he was the PLO's representative to the United Nations, such restrictions were authorized by the UN Headquarters Agreement. The State Department had the power to review his non-UN-related activities, and could recommend a waiver of his PLO-based exclusion. Citing *Abourezk* and *Allende* to reject the government's political question defense, the court contended that *Mandel* had held that waiver decisions were justiciable, albeit under a narrow standard of review.[102] On the merits, the court required granting of the waiver. Declaring that the First Amendment interest in robust public debate trumped even the government's foreign policy concerns, it went on to hold that the State Department's reason for denying permission to travel was not facially legitimate "within the context of the specific statutory provision on which the exclusion is based" because it suppressed protected political debate.[103] The *Harvard Law School Forum* decision, however, was vacated by the First Circuit, and its approach has never been followed or even cited in any subsequent immigration cases.[104] Nevertheless, it did strengthen the gathering forces during the 1980s that challenged ideological exclusion and *Mandel's* deference to government compromise of First Amendment values.

Here the *Mandel* doctrine rested until 1988 when the attack on ideological exclusion finally found a receptive audience in Congress, which suspended some ideological exclusions for a period of thirteen months. This stopgap measure provided that "no alien may be denied a visa or excluded from admission into the United States . . . or subjected to deportation because of any past, current, or expected beliefs, statements, or associations which, if engaged in by a United States citizen in the United States, would be protected under the Constitution of the United States."[105] Although this law was only temporary, it signaled Congress' growing resolve to reform exclusion law in general and ideological exclusion in particular. Moreover, congressional leaders agreed that the exclusion provisions would be revamped and updated in the next Congress.[106] Equally important, the 1988 law bore the stamp of the plaintiffs' argument in *Mandel*, which had focused on how ideological exclusion impaired U.S. *citizens'* rights, rather than the putative rights of the excluded aliens, and had proposed the protected activity of citizens as a test for such exclusions. "[T]he citizens of the United States," the Conference Committee explained, "have been denied the opportunity to have full access to the full spectrum of international opinion." Consequently, "the reputation of the United States as an open society, tolerant of divergent ideas, has suffered." It noted that "the United States is not fearful of foreign ideas or criticism or the individuals who espouse such ideas or advance such criticism," adding that "it is not in the interests of the United States to establish one standard of ideology for citizens and another for foreigners who wish to visit the United States."[107] Leonard Boudin could not have said it better.

The lawmakers kept their promises. Mindful of the fall of the Berlin Wall in 1989 and the imminent end of the Cold War, the very next Congress enacted the Immigration Act of 1990,[108] a sweeping measure that significantly reformed the law of exclusion by regrouping the thirty-three separate grounds into nine headings and altering the most controversial ones, especially the foreign policy, national security, and ideological grounds. The Act permitted "foreign policy" exclusions of aliens only when "the Secretary of State has reasonable ground to believe" that their entry or activities in the United States "would have *potentially serious adverse foreign policy consequences*"[109]—a more demanding standard than under previous law. It also borrowed from the approach of the 1988 provision by barring foreign policy exclusions of most aliens based on "the alien's past, current, or expected beliefs, statements, or associations, if such beliefs, statements, or associations would be lawful within the United States," unless the Secretary of State personally certifies to Congress that the alien's entry would *"compromise a compelling United States foreign policy interest."*[110] No longer could aliens be routinely excluded solely for past membership in a communist or totalitarian party; only aliens applying for immigrant visas (not temporary visas) could still be excluded for current membership.[111] The House conference committee report made clear that it intended the "foreign policy" exception to "be used sparingly and not merely because there is a likelihood that an alien will make critical remarks about the United States or its policies." The report added that "aliens who would previously have been excludable under section 212(a)(28)" because of communist ties "would not be excludable under the new foreign policy grounds established by [the 1990 Act] merely because of such membership or affiliation."[112] The new law also continued to permit waivers of excludability if the Attorney General deemed them to be "in the national interest"—except for aliens suspected of potential "espionage, sabotage, or violent overthrow" of the U.S. government, or for those excluded under "foreign policy" grounds.[113]

We can rejoice that Ernest Mandel's controversial political views would no longer bar him from coming to the United States to lecture on Marxism. It would be pushing paradox too far to say that his loss in the Supreme Court made this possible, but in a sense it did. By 1990, a variety of legal and other developments had broadened the wafer-thin opening left by Blackmun into a much wider portal for entry for individuals like Mandel.

But this larger victory does not necessarily mean that the courts will have much influence over how the government exercises its discretionary waiver authority in future cases. The reason is that Congress in 1996 eliminated almost all judicial review of discretionary immigration enforcement decisions by the Attorney General.[114] Accordingly, in cases (unlike Mandel's) in which Section 212(a) continues to authorize exclusion and the waiver issue thus remains pivotal, even Blackmun's limited concession to judicial review will no longer be available—unless either the courts find some legal basis for review (perhaps limited to claims raising constitutional issues),[115] or Congress decides to amend the statute to restore the courts' jurisdiction to review such discretionary decisions.

Kleindienst v. Mandel reminds us that in the domain of immigration law where Congress, the courts, and the agency are engaged in an endless struggle for influence, few principles—even judicial review of official decisions affecting individual rights—are settled permanently. This lesson is particularly important in light of the war on terrorism, whose legal expression is the USA PATRIOT Act of 2001.[116] The challenge presented by this war and that statute both to the tradition of judicial review preserved by *Mandel* (albeit narrowly) and to the congressional commitment to ideological diversity exhibited in the Immigration Act of 1990 confirms that the battle for these values is never fully or finally won.[117]

ENDNOTES

1. Kleindienst v. Mandel, 408 U.S. 753 (1972).

2. See generally Gerald L. Neuman, Strangers to the Constitution: Immigrants, Borders, and Fundamental Law 52–63 (1996).

3. Paul E. Dunscomb, U.S. Intervention in Siberia as Military Operations Other Than War, Military Review 98, 98–99 (Nov./Dec. 2002); Jeffrey Rosen, Law and Order, New Republic 17, 17–18 (Sept. 24, 2001).

4. Smith Act, ch. 439, 1–5, 54 Stat. 670 (1940) (codified as amended at 18 U.S.C. § 2387 (1964)).

5. Immigration and Nationality Act (INA), Pub. L. No. 82–414 § 212, 66 Stat. 163, 182–88 (1952) (current version at 8 U.S.C. § 1182 (2004)).

6. See note 83 infra and accompanying text.

7. George H. Gallup, The Gallup Poll: Public Opinion 1935–1971, vol. 2, 1948–1958 (1972).

8. John Scanlan, Aliens in the Marketplace of Ideas: The Government, the Academy, and the McCarran–Walter Act, 66 Tex. L. Rev. 1481, 1493 (1988) ("Scanlan"). See also Ellen Schrecker, Many Are the Crimes: McCarthyism in America 6–26 (1998) ("Schrecker").

9. George Kennan, Memoirs: 1950–1963, at 190 (1972).

10. Harvey Klehr, John Earl Haynes, & Kyrill M. Anderson, The Soviet World of American Communism (1998).

11. 98 Cong. Rec. H8084 (daily ed., June 25, 1952) (messages of President Truman).

12. Immigration and Nationality Act Amendments of 1965, Pub. L. No. 89–236, § 10, 79 Stat. 911, 917–918 (codified as amended in scattered sections of 8 U.S.C).

13. This school of thought revered internationalism and revolutionary socialism as matters of principle, and Mandel never ceased to advocate the maintenance of the Fourth International as the crucial forum for organized revolutionary socialism. John Molyneux, Contradictory States, Socialist Review 189 (Sept. 1995).

14. E-mail from Norman Birnbaum, University Professor Emeritus, Georgetown University Law Center, to Celia Whitaker (Oct. 30, 2003) ("Birnbaum E-mail (Oct. 30, 2003)").

15. Robert Heilbroner, Marxism: For and Against, New York Review of Books (June 5, 1969).

16. Plaintiffs' Complaint, ¶ ¶ 8–9, Mandel v. Mitchell, 325 F. Supp. 620 (E.D.N.Y. 1971) ("Complaint"), reprinted in Appendix at 8, Kleindienst v. Mandel, 408 U.S. 753 (1972) ("Appendix").

17. Letter from Richard B. Miles, Chairman, Stanford Graduate Student Association, to Ernest Mandel (Aug. 20, 1969); Letter from Frederic O. Glover, Executive Assistant to the University President, Stanford University, to Ernest Mandel (Aug. 20, 1969), reprinted in Appendix at 33–35 (cited in note 16).

18. Ernest Mandel, Non-immigrant B–1 visa application, Sept. 8, 1969 (translated from the French by Celia Whitaker), reprinted in Appendix at 40–41 (cited in note 16). The Supreme Court apparently misunderstood this issue, stating erroneously that he filed for an H–1 visa. *Mandel*, 408 U.S. at 757.

19. Letter from Alta Fowler, American Consul, Consular Section, Embassy of the United States of America, Brussels, Belgium, to Ernest Mandel (Oct. 30, 1969), reprinted in Appendix at 13–14 (cited in note 16) ("Fowler to Mandel (Oct. 30, 1969)").

20. Brief for the Appellees at 7, Kleindienst v. Mandel, 408 U.S. 753 (1972) (No. 71–16) ("Brief for the Appellees").

21. Letters from Ernest Mandel to Alta Fowler, American Consul, Consular Section, Embassy of the United States of America, Brussels, Belgium (Oct. 23, 24 & 30, 1969) (translated from the French by Celia Whitaker), reprinted in Appendix at 46–47 (cited in note 16).

22. Fowler to Mandel (Oct. 30, 1969) at 14 (cited in note 19).

23. George Novack, Introduction to Ernest Mandel, Revolutionary Strategy in the Imperialist Countries (1970), reprinted in Appendix at 50–54 (cited in note 16) ("Mandel, Revolutionary Strategy").

24. Editorial, The Fuentes Incident, N.Y. Times (Mar. 5, 1969). The Kennedy administration had refused to allow Fuentes to enter the country in 1961, after NBC invited him to participate in a debate on the Alliance for Progress. Steven R. Shapiro, Ideological Exclusion: Closing the Border to Political Dissidents, 100 Harv. L. Rev. 930, 930 n.4 (Feb. 1987) ("Shapiro").

25. Stanford Says U.S. Denies Visa to a Marxist Scholar, N.Y. Times (Oct. 15, 1969).

26. Editorial, . . . and Abroad, N.Y. Times (Oct. 28, 1969).

27. Novack, Introduction to Mandel, Revolutionary Strategy at 54 (cited in note 23).

28. Arno J. Mayer, Gabriel Kolko, Noam Chomsky, Richard A. Falk, Richard Poirier, Robert L. Heilbroner, Robert Paul Wolff, & Susan Sontag, Letter to the Editor, New York Review of Books (Nov. 20, 1969) ("Mayer et al., Letter to the Editor").

29. Brief for the Appellees at 8 (cited in note 20).

30. Victor Rabinowitz, Unrepentant Leftist: A Lawyer's Memoir 23, 25, 73 (Univ. of Ill. Press 1996) ("Rabinowitz"); Obit. of Leonard Boudin, L.A. Times (Nov. 27, 1989). Rabinowitz, like many communists, became disillusioned with the Party as Stalin's crimes were revealed, and he did not consider himself a communist from the early 1960s onward.

31. Schrecker at 303–05 (cited in note 8).

32. Rabinowitz at 117 (cited in note 30).

33. Bernardine Dohrn, A Life Devoted to the Law and the Left, Chic. Trib. (Aug. 10, 1997).

34. United States v. Spock, 416 F.2d 165 (1st Cir.1969); Ellsberg v. Mitchell, 709 F.2d 51 (D.C.Cir.1983), cert. denied 465 U.S. 1038 (1984).

35. Telephone Interview by Celia Whitaker with David Rosenberg, Professor of Law, Harvard Law School (Oct. 22, 2003) ("Rosenberg Interview (Oct. 22, 2003)").

36. As the two men contemplated representing Cuban interests in the United States after the Cuban Revolution, both felt confident that they could draw on their past experience and enter the political fray. "But to this professional outlook there was added, *at least for me,* a large element of romanticism. How could I resist the lure of a socialist state (maybe) in the Western Hemisphere?" Rabinowitz at 201 (cited in note 30) (emphasis added).

37. Boudin's letter is referenced in Letter from Barbara M. Watson, Bureau of Security and Consular Affairs, U.S. Department of State, to Leonard B. Boudin, Plaintiffs' Counsel (Nov. 6, 1969), reprinted in Appendix at 21–22 (cited in note 16).

38. Brief for the Appellees at 8 (cited in note 20); Letter from Alta Fowler, American Consul, Consular Section, Embassy of the United States of America, Brussels, Belgium, to Ernest Mandel (Dec. 1, 1969) (translated from the French by Celia Whitaker) reprinted in Appendix at 22–23 (cited in note 16).

39. Brief for the Appellees at 9 (cited in note 20); George Novack, Introduction to Mandel, Revolutionary Strategy at 51 (cited in note 23).

40. Ernest Mandel, Revolutionary Strategy in the Imperialist Countries: Address Prepared for Delivery to the Socialist Scholars Conference at New York Town Hall, Nov. 29, 1969, in Mandel, Revolutionary Strategy at 54 (cited in note 23).

41. Mitchell Bars Belgian Marxist from U.S. Visit, N.Y. Times (Nov. 27, 1969).

42. Editorial, McCarranism Revisited, N.Y. Times (Nov. 27, 1969).

43. Marxist Attributes Denial of U.S. Visa to Rules He Broke, N.Y. Times (Nov. 29, 1969). The following week, news of an additional McCarran Act exclusion brought further criticism. Pakistani Student is Denied Visa for Speech in U.S, N.Y. Times (Dec. 3, 1969).

44. Letter from James F. Greene, Associate Commissioner of Operations, U.S. Department of Justice, Immigration and Naturalization Service, to Leonard B. Boudin, Plaintiffs' Counsel (Feb. 13, 1970), reprinted in Appendix at 68 (cited in note 16) ("Greene to Mandel (Feb. 13, 1970)"). No further facts were offered to substantiate this claim, and the government appeared to back off from it during the litigation. For further discussion, see notes 76–77 infra and accompanying text.

45. Letter from M.J. Ortwein, Chief of the Domestic Services Division, Visa Office, U.S. Department of State, to Bertrand Russell Peace Foundation (Jan. 27, 1970), reprinted in Appendix at 48–49 (cited in note 16).

46. Complaint at ¶ 50 (cited in note 16).

47. Galvan v. Press, 347 U.S. 522, 530–32 (1954); United States ex rel. Knauff v. Shaughnessy, 338 U.S. 537, 542 (1950); United States ex rel. Turner v. Williams, 194 U.S. 279, 292 (1904).

48. The classic expression of judicial deference to the executive branch in immigration matters came in the *Chinese Exclusion Case:* "[If Congress] considers the presence of foreigners of a different race in this country, who will not assimilate with us, to be dangerous to its peace and security . . . its determination is conclusive upon the judiciary." 130 U.S. 581, 606 (1889).

49. David Caute, The Great Fear 257 (1978).

50. Rosenberg Interview (Oct. 22, 2003) (cited in note 35).

51. Generally, the firm decided policy questions, including whether to take a given case, democratically—through a vote by both partners and associates. Rabinowitz at 325 (cited in note 30).

52. Rosenberg Interview (Oct. 22, 2003) (cited in note 35).

53. Id.; Mayer et al., Letter to the Editor (cited in note 28). Chomsky, Falk, Heilbroner, and Wolff were named plaintiffs in the case.

54. William A. Donohue, The Politics of the American Civil Liberties Union 18–19 (1985).

55. E-mail from David Mermelstein, Professor, Polytechnic University, to Celia Whitaker (Nov. 5, 2003); Birnbaum E-mail (Oct. 30, 2003) (cited in note 14).

56. Burt Neuborne recalls that it was Boudin who asked the ACLU, not vice versa. Interview by Author and Celia Whitaker with Burt Neuborne, John Norton Pomeroy Professor of Law, New York University Law School, in New York, NY (Oct. 21, 2003) ("Neuborne Interview (Oct. 21, 2003)").

57. Labor Management Relations Act of 1947, Pub. L. No. 80–101, 61 Stat. 136, 1947 (codified as amended at 29 U.S.C. § 141).

58. Telephone Interview by Celia Whitaker with David Rosenberg, Professor of Law, Harvard Law School (Nov. 5, 2003).

59. Rosenberg Interview (Oct. 22, 2003) (cited in note 30); Interview by Celia Whitaker with Melvin Wulf, Of Counsel, Beldock, Levine & Hoffman, LLP, in New York, NY (Oct. 21, 2003). Neuborne served as Staff Counsel for NYCLU from 1967–1972; Assistant Legal Director of the ACLU from 1972–74; and Legal Director of the ACLU from 1982–86. During the 1971–72 period, although he was based in New York, he often worked on national issues. Melvin Wulf served as Legal Director of the ACLU from 1962 to 1977.

60. Lamont v. Postmaster General, 381 U.S. 301, 306 (1965). See also Griswold v. Connecticut, 381 U.S. 479, 482 (1965) (First Amendment protects "not only the right to utter or to print, but the right to distribute, *the right to receive, the right to read*," because "[w]ithout those peripheral rights the specific rights would be less secure") (emphasis added); Pierce v. Society of Sisters, 268 U.S. 510 (1925) (mandatory public school education unconstitutionally interferes with the freedom of parents and guardians to direct the upbringing and education of children).

61. Red Lion Broadcasting Co v. FCC, 395 U.S. 367, 390 (1969).

62. See N.Y. Times Co. v. Sullivan, 376 U.S. 254, 266 (1964) (political advertisement entitled to the same degree of protection as ordinary speech); Ginzburg v. United States, 383 U.S. 463, 474 (1966) (the existence of "commercial activity, in itself, is no justification for narrowing the protection of expression secured by the First Amendment"); Virginia State Bd. of Pharmacy v. Virginia Citizens Consumer Council, 425 U.S. 748, 761, 770 (1976) (completing the doctrinal shift, the Court held that "commercial speech, like other varieties, is protected").

63. Neuborne Interview (Oct. 21, 2003) (cited in note 56).

64. Brief for the Appellees at 20 (cited in note 20) (citing Goldberg v. Kelly, 397 U.S. 254, 289 (1970)). The brief also cites Kent v. Dulles, 357 U.S. 116, 126 (1958) ("Scientists and scholars gain greatly from consultations with colleagues in other countries.") (citation omitted); and Sweezy v. New Hampshire, 354 U.S. 234, 250 (1957) ("No one should underestimate the vital role in a democracy that is played by those who guide and train our youth. To impose any strait jacket upon the intellectual leaders in our colleges and universities would imperil the future of our Nation.").

65. David Rosenberg remembers that the as-applied argument was crucial, because the plenary power doctrine made facial challenges to immigration statutes highly vulnerable. In the event, the district court found the statute facially unconstitutional. But when the case was appealed to the Supreme Court, Boudin left the facial challenge to the ACLU as amicus, and chose to concentrate on the as-applied challenge. Rosenberg Interview (Oct. 22, 2003) (cited in note 30); Brief for the Appellees at 3–4, 16 (cited in note 20).

66. Mandel v. Mitchell, 325 F. Supp. 620, 622 (E.D.N.Y.1971); Complaint at ¶ 18(d) (cited in note 16); Leonard Boudin Affidavit, Mandel v. Mitchell, 325 F. Supp. 620 (E.D.N.Y.1971), reprinted in Appendix at 31–32 (cited in note 16) ("Boudin Affidavit (May 22, 1970)").

67. *Mandel*, 325 F.Supp. at 627. Judge Dooling cites United States v. Robel, 389 U.S. 258, 264–68 (1967), which he interpreted to require that the government show it had "no reasonable alternative" to the measures imposed and that they have the "least drastic impact on First Amendment rights" possible.

68. Id. at 632–33.

69. Id. at 637–38, 640, 641 (Bartels, J., dissenting opinion).

70. Neuborne Interview (Oct. 21, 2003) (cited in note 56).

71. Kermit L. Hall ed., Oxford Companion to the Supreme Court of the United States 76 (1992).

72. Id. at 76; Linda Greenhouse, Justice Blackmun, Author of Abortion Right, Dies, N.Y. Times (Mar. 5, 1999).

73. This was his twenty-first opinion as a Supreme Court Justice.

74. *Mandel,* 408 U.S. at 762.

75. Id. at 783 (Marshall, J., dissenting opinion); Brief for the Appellees at 16 (cited in note 20). Burt Neuborne also felt that the ACLU should have taken this angle, rather than argue a facial statutory challenge. Neuborne Interview (Oct. 21, 2003) (cited in note 56).

76. *Mandel,* 408 U.S. at 769–70. The "flagrant abuse" language came from the letter that the INS had sent Mandel in February. Greene to Mandel (Feb. 13, 1970) (cited in note 44).

77. Motion to the Supreme Court to Affirm the Judgment Below, Kleindienst v. Mandel, 408 U.S. 753 (1972) (No. 71–16) at 9; Mandel, 408 U.S. 753 at 764–65, 769.

78. *Mandel,* 408 U.S. at 779 (Marshall, J., dissenting opinion).

79. See, e.g., Shapiro at 935–36 (cited in note 24) (the "decision in *Kleindienst v. Mandel* raises as many questions as it answers"); Scanlan, at 1506–07 (cited in note 8) (after *Mandel,* "an alien's sponsors or advocates are unlikely to [succeed] when they raise their own first amendment challenge to the alien's exclusion or expulsion"). But see Hiroshi Motomura, The Curious Evolution of Immigration Law: Procedural Surrogates for Substantive Constitutional Rights, 92 Colum. L. Rev. 1625, 1694 (1992) (*Mandel*'s "very minimal judicial scrutiny to be sure still suggested some limits to plenary power"); Harvard Law School Forum v. Shultz, 633 F. Supp. 525 (D. Mass. 1986) (government's foreign-policy justification for refusal to allow speech by member of PLO "not facially legitimate because it is related to the suppression of protected political discussion"); Abourezk v. Reagan, 1988 WL 59640 (D.D.C. 1988) (rejecting the Reagan administration's attempts to prevent foreign speakers from entering the United States).

80. Conference on Security and Cooperation in Europe, Final Act, Aug. 1, 1975, 73 Dep't St. Bull. 323 (1975), reprinted in 14 I.L.M. 1292 (1975).

81. 91 Stat. 848 (1977). This act was amended in 1978 and 1979. See Pub. L. No. 95–426, § 119, 92 Stat. 963, 970 (Oct. 7, 1978); Pub. L. No. 96–60, § 109, 93 Stat. 395, 397–98 (Aug. 15, 1979).

82. U.S. Dept. of Justice, 1998 Statistical Yearbook of the Immigration and Naturalization Service 226, Table 67 (2000); Charles Gordon, Stanley Mailman, & Stephen Yale–Loehr, Immigration Law and Procedure § 63.04 n.27 and accompanying text ("Gordon et al., Immigration Law and Procedure").

83. The government provided the following statistics in its *Mandel* brief. 1971: 6,196 waivers granted; 14 denied. 1970: 6,189 waivers granted; 4 denied. 1969: 4,984 waivers granted; 9 denied. 1968: 4,176 waivers granted; 8 denied. 1967: 3,852 waivers granted; 8 denied. Brief for the Appellant at 18 n.24, Kleindienst v. Mandel, 408 U.S. 753 (1972) (No. 71–16).

84. Exclusion and Deportation of Aliens: Hearings Before the House Comm. on the Judiciary, Subcomm. on Immigration, Refugees, and International Law, 100th Cong., 1st

Sess. 29–30 (1987) (statement of Abraham Sofaer) ("Sofaer statement, House Judiciary Committee").

85. Cross Left, Village Voice (June 2, 1980) (quoting Vittorio Brode of the State Department's Italian Desk), cited in Philip Monrad, Comment: Ideological Exclusion, Plenary Power, and the PLO, 77 Calif. L. Rev. 831, 838 n.32 (1989).

86. Kristin Helmore, Would William Shakespeare Get a Visa?, Christian Sci. Monitor (May 30, 1984); John Blades, PEN Authors Ready to Unsheath Vocal Swords at Congress, Chicago Tribune (Jan. 12, 1986); Shapiro at 930 (cited in note 24); U.S. Still Blacklists 3,000 Canadians for Politics, N.Y. Times (Feb. 19, 1984); Scanlan at 1497–98 and n.75 (cited in note 8). For more on the *Allende* case, see note 106 infra and accompanying text.

87. Shapiro at 934–35 (cited in note 24).

88. Id. at 935.

89. Rick Atkinson, Congressmen, Others Denounce Denial of Visas to Critics of U.S., Wash. Post (Dec. 3, 1983). An unnamed White House official confirmed that "the Government did not want to give Mr. Borge 'a propaganda platform in the United States.' "Hedrick Smith, Salvadoran Rightist and Key Sandinista are Barred by U.S., N.Y. Times (Nov. 30, 1983).

90. INA § 1128(a)(27) (cited in note 5).

91. See, e.g., Editorial, Don't Let the Sun Set on Free Speech, N.Y. Times (Sept. 15, 1988); Editorial, Hysteria Dies Hard, L.A. Times (July 30, 1988); Editorial, The McCarran–Walter Mischief, N.Y. Times (Sept. 5, 1986) ("The law is preposterous and outmoded"); Editorial, Turned Back in Toronto, Wash. Post (Apr. 29, 1985).

92. United States Select Commission on Immigration and Refugee Policy, U.S. Immigration Policy and the National Interest, Final Report and Recommendations 282–83 (1981).

93. See, e.g., Scanlan (cited in note 8); Shapiro (cited in note 24); Mitchell C. Tilner, Ideological Exclusion of Aliens: The Evolution of a Policy, 2 Georgetown Immigration Law Journal 1, 2 (1987); Burt Neuborne and Steven R. Shapiro, The Nylon Curtain: America's National Border and the Free Flow of Ideas, 26 Wm. & Mary L. Rev. 719 (1985); Peter H. Schuck, The Transformation of Immigration Law, 84 Colum. L. Rev. 1 (1984) ("Schuck, The Transformation of Immigration Law").

94. Sofaer statement, House Judiciary Committee at 35 (cited in note 84).

95. Abourezk v. Reagan, 785 F.2d 1043, 1056–57 (D.C. Cir. 1986), aff'd, 484 U.S. 1 (1987). The cases were remanded to the district court for reconsideration in line with the Court of Appeals' ruling on the proper interpretation of Section (a)(27), and the relationship of Sections (a)(27) and (a)(28) after the McGovern Amendment. On remand, the district court ordered that the aliens be admitted, if they still wished to enter the United States. Abourezk v. Reagan, 1988 WL 59640 (D.D.C. 1988).

96. Allende v. Shultz, 845 F.2d 1111 (1st Cir. 1988). The courts upheld some visa denials during this period. See, e.g., Adams v. Baker, 909 F.2d 643 (1st Cir. 1990).

97. *Mandel,* 408 U.S. at 777–78 (Marshall, J., dissenting opinion).

98. Gordon et al., Immigration Law and Procedure § 9.09 (cited in note 82); Schuck, The Transformation of Immigration Law at 65–66 (cited in note 93); Harisiades v. Shaughnessy, 342 U.S. 580, 588–89 (1952) (emphasis added) (treated in Chapter 4 of this volume). See also Hampton v. Mow Sun Wong, 426 U.S. 88, 101 n.21 (1976) ("the power over aliens is of a political character and therefore subject only to narrow judicial review"); Mathews v. Diaz, 426 U.S. 67, 81–82 (1976) ("The reasons that preclude judicial review of political questions also dictate a narrow standard of review of decisions made by Congress or the President in the area of immigration and naturalization.").

99. Hiroshi Motomura, Immigration Law After a Century of Plenary Power, 100 YALE L.J. 545, 560–65, 581 (1990).

100. Fiallo v. Bell, 430 U.S. 787, 795 (1977). The challenged statutory provisions were INA § 1101(b)(1)(d) and 1101(b)(2) (cited in note 5).

101. Jean v. Nelson, 472 U.S. 846, 853, 857 (1985). Some lower courts portrayed the "facially legitimate and bona fide" standard of review as less stringent than the "abuse of discretion" standard. See, e.g., Garcia–Mir v. Smith, 766 F.2d 1478, 1485 (11th Cir. 1985).

102. Harvard Law School Forum v. Schultz, 633 F. Supp. at 526–29, vacated without published opinion, 852 F.2d 563 (1st Cir. 1986).

103. Id. at 531.

104. The sole court to cite *Harvard Law School Forum* was considering a challenge to the U.S. decision to close the PLO's permanent observer office in 1987. United States v. Palestine Liberation Organization, 695 F. Supp. 1456 (S.D.N.Y. 1988).

105. Foreign Relations Authorization Act, Fiscal Years 1988–1989, Pub. L. No. 100–204, § 901(a), (b) (1987).

106. Gordon et al., Immigration Law and Procedure § 63.66 (cited in note 82). See the colloquy between Senator Simpson and Senator Kennedy, 100th Cong., 2d Sess., in 134 Cong. Rec. S13800 (daily ed. Sept. 30, 1988).

107. H.R. Conf. Rep. No. 100–475, in 133 Cong. Rec. H11343 (1987).

108. Immigration Act of 1990, Pub. L. No. 101–649, 104 Stat. 4978 (codified as amended in scattered sections of 8 U.S.C).

109. INA § 1182(a)(3)(C)(i) (emphasis added) (cited in note 5).

110. INA § 212(a)(3)(C)(iii) (emphasis added) (cited in note 5). Congress apparently intended that this exception set a high standard. See H.R. Conf. Rep. No. 101–955, at 128–31 (1990).

111. INA § 1182(a)(3)(D) (cited in note 5).

112. H.R. Conf. Rep. No. 101–955, in 136 Cong. Rec. H13239 (1990).

113. INA § 1182(d)(1), (3) (cited in note 5).

114. Illegal Immigration Reform and Immigrant Responsibility Act of 1996, Pub. L. No. 104–208, 110 Stat. 3009–3546 (codified as amended in scattered sections of 8 U.S.C.). The relevant provision categorically bars judicial review of "any other [unenumerated] decision or action of the Attorney General the authority for which is specified under this title to be in the discretion of the Attorney General," except decisions on asylum claims. INA § 242(a)(2)(B)(ii), 8 U.S.C. § 1252(a)(2)(B)(ii).

115. The Court's decision in INS v. St. Cyr, 533 U.S. 289 (2001), which preserved judicial review in the face of language in the 1996 Act that seemed to preclude it, involved different provisions and different considerations than those involved in waiver decisions under Section 212(a). See Chapter 11 in this volume.

116. Pub.L.No. 107–56, 115 Stat. 272 (2001).

117. See, e.g., Helène Fouquet, Switzerland: Barred Islamic Scholar Gives up U.S. Teaching Post, N.Y. Times A16 (Dec. 15, 2004) (U.S. revokes visa on unspecified security grounds).

8

Plyler v. Doe, the Education of Undocumented Children, and the Polity

Michael A. Olivas*

It is hard to know how Supreme Court decisions will come to be regarded, but one thing is certain: none of them exists in a vacuum. Getting a case to federal or state court in the first place is a lightning strike, and very few make it all the way through the chute to the Supreme Court. Fewer still are genuinely memorable, even within the specialty area in which the case is situated. *Plyler v. Doe*[1] always stood for its resolution of the immediate issue in dispute: whether the State of Texas could enact laws denying undocumented children free access to its own public schools. But it also dealt with a larger, transcendent principle: how this society will treat its alien children. Thus, for the larger polity, *Plyler* has become an important case for key themes, such as fairness for children, how we guard our borders, how we constitute ourselves, and who gets to make these crucial decisions. To a large extent, *Plyler* may also be the apex of the Court's treatment of the undocumented, a concept that never truly existed until the 20th century.[2]

In this Chapter, I consider first how the controversy developed and was treated on the ground, in school districts in Texas. Second, once the

* Kristen D. Werner and Eric L. Munoz provided excellent research assistance on this project. In addition, I wish to thank Professors Richard Delgado and Kevin R. Johnson for expert comments, and Professors David A. Martin and Peter H. Schuck for their editorial assistance and for undertaking this book enterprise. I acknowledge the extraordinary resources of the Green Library of Stanford University, and its Special Collections staff, particularly Roberto Trujillo (Head, Department of Special Collections and Frances & Charles Field Curator of Special Collections), Steven Mandeville-Gamble (Assistant Head and Special Collections Principal Manuscripts Processing Librarian), and Polly Armstrong (Public Services Manager). The MALDEF files gathered there are a treasure, and being in such a great reading room reminded me of what all professors know—we lead a charmed and privileged life. Although I agreed not to reveal the names of the several attorneys and other participants who talked to me about the *Plyler* case, thanks to all of them for their confidences.

case quickened, it took on unusual procedural dimensions that warrant discussion. After the various strands of the cases were consolidated, its actual litigation strategy required case management, with complex back-stage maneuvers essential to gaining traction for the parties. Because the decision itself is one with "epochal significance" for the undocu-mented population generally, in Peter Schuck's evocative characteriza-tion,[3] the third section dissects the case and examines some of the extensive commentary it prompted. Finally, as a postscript, I examine the path *Plyler's* teachings followed, both in related Supreme Court cases on the same issue and in allied settings, such as debates over federal legislation that would have mimicked the Texas law struck down in *Plyler*, and in postsecondary education residency litigation and legisla-tion. Understanding *Plyler's* provenance ultimately sheds light on how important legal cases become recurring fugues, with themes that build and influence subsequent decisions and sometimes the polity at large.

On the Ground in Texas: Undocumented School Attendance and the Legislative Reaction

In 1975, the State of Texas enacted section 21.031 of the Texas Education Code, allowing its public school districts (called "Independent School Districts" or ISDs in Texas) to charge tuition to undocumented children.[4] The Legislature held no hearings on the matter, and no published record explains the origin of this revision to the school code. Discussions with legislators from that time have suggested that it was inserted into a larger, more routine education bill, simply at the request of some border-area superintendents who mentioned the issue to their representatives.[5] The statute, in pertinent part, read:

> (a) All children who are citizens of the United States or legally admitted aliens and who are over the age of five years and under the age of 21 years on the first day of September of any scholastic year shall be entitled to the benefits of the Available School Fund for that year.
>
> (b) Every child in this state who is a citizen of the United States or a legally admitted alien and who is over the age of five years and not over the age of 21 years on the first day of September of the year in which admission is sought shall be permitted to attend the public free schools of the district in which he resides or in which his parent, guardian, or the person having lawful control of him resides at the time he applies for admission.
>
> (c) The board of trustees of any public free school district of this state shall admit into the public free schools of the district free of tuition all persons who are either citizens of the United

States or legally admitted aliens and who are over five and not over 21 years of age at the beginning of the scholastic year if such person or his parent, guardian or person having lawful control resides within the school district.[6]

Although they were entitled under this statute to do so, not all ISDs in the State chose to charge tuition. In a 1980 random survey prepared by Houston's Gulf Coast Legal Foundation once litigation commenced, six of the ISDs polled with more than 10,000 students reported that their districts would admit undocumented students without charge, six would charge tuition, eleven would exclude them entirely, while the rest did not respond or did not know how they would respond to such an occurrence.[7] For ISDs with enrollments under 10,000 students, seven would not charge tuition, five would charge tuition, three would exclude entirely, and sixteen did not know or did not respond. The State's largest district, Houston ISD (with over 200,000 students), and a smaller one, Tyler (with approximately 16,000 students) would allow them to enroll, but required parents or guardians to pay $1000 annually for each child. In addition, several of the school districts nearest the border reported they excluded these children from enrolling, whether or not tuition were paid, such as Ysleta ISD (near El Paso and across the border from Ciudad Juarez) and Brownsville ISD (across the border from Matamoros), as did the State's second largest district, Dallas ISD, many hundreds of miles from the border.

The Litigation and the Principal Players

Prologue

The first case to challenge 21.031 was *Hernandez v. Houston Independent School District*, filed in spring 1977 in state courts, by a local Houston attorney, Peter Williamson. The district court and the court of civil appeals rejected his due process and equal protection arguments against the statute.[8] In November, 1977, the appeals court held that such legislation was reasonable: "The determination to share [the State's] bounty, in this instance tuition-free education, may take into account the character of the relationship between the alien and this country."[9]

MALDEF's Role

While observers of thirty years ago recall some localized resistance across the state to the practice of charging the families tuition for what were generally referred to as "free public schools," the issue appears to have come onto the national radar in the late 1970s, prompted by a September 26, 1977 letter from Joaquin G. Avila, director of the San Antonio office of the Mexican American Legal Defense and Educational Fund (MALDEF). It was addressed to the MALDEF National Director for Education Litigation, Peter Roos, located at the organization's national headquarters in San Francisco, California. Avila wrote:

> This statute was made effective on August 29, 1977. Basically, this statute seeks to regulate the number of students who move in with relatives to attend another school district. As the amended statute now provides (Section 21.031(a)), a student who lives apart from his parent, guardian, or other person having lawful control of him under an order of a court, must demonstrate that his presence in the school district was not based primarily on his or her desire to attend a particular school district. In other words, if a case of hardship can be established, a student will be able to attend the school district. Otherwise, the relatives will have to secure a court order of guardianship. This requirement will impose a hardship on those families who cannot afford an attorney to process a guardianship. So far we have not received any complaints only a request by Pete Tijerina, our first general counsel to launch a lawsuit.
>
> What are your feelings on the constitutionality of such a provision. What would we have to show to demonstrate a disparate impact. Please advise at your earliest convenience.[10]

This letter contains the spores of the *Plyler* case (without referencing the *Hernandez* litigation that was underway in the state courts in Houston at the same time), even though Avila does not appear to have appreciated the full dimensions of the matter that had been flagged by MALDEF board member (and one of the organization's founders in the mid–1960s) Pete Tijerina. To Avila, the issue kicked up to San Francisco was whether the revised Texas statute improperly affected the residency of undocumented students, by requiring the parents or formal legal guardians to reside in the district. This was a related issue, but one far less essential to the algebra of undocumented school attendance than the tuition issue presented eventually in *Plyler*, especially for school districts in the interior, away from the border. Indeed, a year after *Plyler* ruled in favor of the schoolchildren, the exact issue Avila noted in his letter reached the Supreme Court in *Martinez v. Bynum*,[11] where it was resolved in favor of the school districts involved. By that time, however, the more fundamental and important threshold issue had been settled; all else was detail.

But this was not clear in 1977, when Peter Roos began to sniff out the full extent of the practice in Texas and other states. He looked especially at the Southwestern and Western states, where most undocumented families resided, where undocumented Mexican immigration was most pronounced (as opposed to undocumented immigration from other countries and other hemispheres), and where MALDEF concentrated most of its program activities. MALDEF was in search of an appropriate federal-court vehicle to consolidate its modest victories in the many small state-court cases it had taken on in its first decade of existence. Unlike the laser-like focus of its role model the NAACP Legal Defense Fund, which had strategically targeted desegregation as its reason for being, MALDEF had been somewhat behind the curve, in part due to its representation of ethnic and national-origin interests for Mexican Americans and in part due to the diffuse focus that derived from representing the linguistic, immigration, and even class interests of its variegated clients.

After all, Mexican Americans were not African Americans, although their histories of oppression and exclusion from American Anglo life were more similar than they were dissimilar. Historian Steven White has noted the origins of the different litigation theories employed by the two groups to combat school segregation:

> The ... creation of MALDEF had less to do with the shift in thinking [about school desegregation strategies] than might be expected. The upheavals brought by the black civil rights struggle, the farm workers' movement, and antiwar protests inspired many disaffected Mexican-descended youths to adopt similar goals and direct action tactics—such as walkouts and other disruptive demonstrations—in order to combat the inequities they encountered. As a result, however, activists frequently found themselves sanctioned by school administrators or even law enforcement agencies. Instead of suing schools to change the rules of desegregation, therefore, MALDEF undertook a number of cases that established the new organization as something of an unofficial civil liberties bureau for militant Chicano students. Significantly, in these cases, MALDEF's attorneys did not argue—and in civil liberties cases had no reason to claim— that Mexican Americans were and ought to be considered a group distinct from Anglos. Nevertheless, MALDEF's early victories in this field helped to reestablish litigation as a tool for vindicating Mexican Americans' civil rights.[12]

My discussions with the various parties involved from the MALDEF side of this case clearly indicate that Roos and MALDEF President Vilma Martinez, a young Texas lawyer who had begun her civil rights career with the NAACP Legal Defense Fund, soon saw *Plyler* as the Mexican American *Brown v. Board of Education*: a vehicle for consolidating attention to the various strands of social exclusions that kept Mexican-origin persons in subordinate status. This case promised to decide issues affecting Mexican migrant workers, who had been in the American imagination due to the charismatic leadership of Cesar Chavez, head of the United Farm Workers union, who had organized a successful nationwide grape boycott.[13] It concerned education in Texas schools, long considered the most insensitive to Mexicans and Mexican Americans. It incorporated elements of school leadership and community relations, where the political powerlessness of Chicanos was evident even in geographic areas where they were the predominant population. The tuition dimension resurrected school finance and governance issues, which had earlier been raised by Chicano plaintiffs seeking to have the radically unequal school financing scheme in Texas declared unconstitutional. After initial success, they had lost in a controversial 1973 decision by the U.S. Supreme Court, *San Antonio Independent School District v. Rodriguez.*[14] The 5–4 ruling seemed designed to call a halt to any expansions in the use of the equal protection clause, and it specifically declared that education was not a fundamental right that would trigger strict scrutiny under that clause. And finally, *Plyler* implicated immigration status, often dividing families based merely on the side of the Rio Grande where the mother had given birth. *Plyler* even held out the promise to unite the class interests between immigrant Mexicans and the larger, more established Mexican American community in a way that earlier, important cases litigating jury selection, school finance, and desegregation had not been able to achieve.[15] Even though these cases all occurred in Texas over many years, and had even included some small victories, they had not appreciably improved the status of Chicanos or broken down the barriers for large numbers of the community.

In his pathbreaking study of Mexican American education litigation, historian Guadalupe San Miguel analyzed the law suits undertaken by MALDEF in Texas in the years 1970–1981, its earliest record.[16] It undertook 93 federal and state court cases in the state during those years, and compiled a substantial record across several areas: 71 cases in the area of desegregation (76.3%), four in employment (4.3%), three in school finance (3.2%), seven in political rights (7.5%), six in voting (6.5%), and two other education cases (2.2%). In addition, a number of the cases included collateral issues such as language rights and bilingual education.[17] As an example of these cases, MALDEF undertook *United States v. Texas*, a comprehensive assault upon the worst exclusionary practices by school districts, such as class assignment practices and inadequate bilingual education.[18] The judge in that district court decision noted with some bite: "Serious flaws permeate every aspect of the state's efforts.... Since the defendants have not remedied the serious deficiencies, meaningful relief for the victims of unlawful discrimination must be instituted by court decree."[19]

Over the years, MALDEF had joined forces with other Mexican American organizations, including more conservative groups such as the League of United Latin American Citizens (LULAC) and the GI Forum, organizations active over the years in assimilationist and citizenship issues and Latino military veteran issues. Thus, these national organizations, all founded in Texas to combat discrimination, merged their divergent interests in order to effect solidarity, and have since served as plaintiffs in cases filed by MALDEF.[20]

Just as Thurgood Marshall had traveled the South to execute the Legal Defense Fund's strategic approach toward dismantling segregated schooling and the American apartheid system, seeking out the proper cases and plaintiffs, Martinez, Roos, and other MALDEF lawyers and board members had been seeking just the right federal case. They wanted to have a larger impact than they could expect from dozens of smaller cases in various state courts in the Southwest. If Mexican American plaintiffs could not win the school finance case in *San Antonio Independent School District v. Rodriguez*, with such demonstrable economic disparities as had been evident in that trial, MALDEF needed to win a big one, both to establish its credibility within and without the Chicano community and to serve its clients. A case involving vulnerable schoolchildren in rural Texas being charged a thousand dollars for what was available to other children for free seemed to be that vehicle. The MALDEF lawyers found their Linda Brown in Tyler, Texas, where the brothers and sisters in the same family held different immigration status. Some had been born in Mexico, while those born in Texas held U.S. citizenship. Perhaps more importantly, they found their Earl Warren in federal district court judge William Wayne Justice, widely admired and reviled for his liberal views and progressive decisions.[21] Thus, in this small, rural setting in Tyler, Texas, the stage was set.

The Plyler Campaign

The first issue to arise after the case was filed was whether the children could be styled in anonymous fashion in the caption and conduct of the case, so that their identities and those of their families would not be divulged. Use of the actual names of the plaintiffs in the *Hernandez* case against the Houston schools had placed all of them at risk of deportation. In the Tyler case, even though Judge Justice permitted the case to proceed with "John Doe" plaintiffs, the risk persisted. The U.S. Attorney had apparently asked the Dallas district director of the Immigration and Naturalization Service (INS) to conduct immigration sweeps in the area, so as to intimidate the families into dropping their suit.[22] In response, Roos wrote to the head of the INS in Washington, requesting that he call off any planned raids and characterizing them as trial-tampering. As it happened, in this endeavor MALDEF enjoyed a run of luck, which is always an ingredient of successful trials. The INS Commissioner at the time was Leonel Castillo, a native of Houston and a prominent Mexican American politician with progressive politics, himself a former Peace Corps volunteer who was married to an immigrant.[23] At his direction, the INS ultimately made no such raids. After these initial skirmishes, Judge Justice issued a preliminary injunction on September 11, 1977, enjoining the Tyler ISD from enforcing 21.031 against any children on the basis of their immigration status.[24]

As a part of the overall trial strategy, Roos, Martinez, and other MALDEF officials began to press public opinion leaders to "support the schoolchildren" and to develop a backdrop of public acceptance of their immigration status. As an example, Roos wrote leaders of the National Education Association (NEA), the progressive national teachers union, in October, 1977, to request support and assistance; NEA later filed a brief and provided additional support to MALDEF.[25] In addition, MALDEF leaders traveled to meet with other Latino organizational leaders to enlist support and solicit resources, and to encourage legal organizations to file *amicus* briefs on behalf of the plaintiff children. They asked for people to write editorials and to host fundraisers. I recall being a law student in Washington, D.C., during this time and cutting class one night to attend a small fundraiser at a local hotel, an event sponsored by Latino organizations and Washington professionals.

On September 14, 1978, after a two day hearing, Judge Justice issued his opinion, striking down 21.031 as applied to the Tyler ISD. He found that the state's justifications for the statute were not rational and violated equal protection, and that the attempt to regulate immigration at the state level violated the doctrine of preemption, which holds immigration to be a function solely of federal law.[26] Immediately after, the state moved for leave to re-open the case, citing the decision's implications for other school districts in the state and seeking a chance to bolster the record. Observers have suggested that the state had simply underestimated the plaintiffs' case, inasmuch as the *Hernandez* case in state court had sustained the statute fairly readily. But Judge Justice overruled the motion, because the "amended complaint does not state a cause of action against any school district other than the Tyler Independent School District and since this court intends to order relief only against the Tyler Independent School District...." [27]

Case Management by MALDEF

During the federal trial, the issue of *Plyler*'s potential impact upon other Texas school districts arose, as word had spread to dozens of other communities, sparking many companion lawsuits. The original *Hernandez* decision had not spawned similar state court litigation; MALDEF and others turned to the federal courts so as to avoid having to litigate in hostile state venues. MALDEF now confronted questions about how best to mesh its efforts, including its response to the *Plyler* appeals filed by the Tyler ISD and the State of Texas, with proceedings in other venues. Some of the issues became clearer when the State's largest school district, Houston ISD, faced a lawsuit in federal court in September, 1978, by a group of local attorneys and another California-based public interest law firm, with civil rights lawyer (and South African immigrant) Peter Schey as lead counsel. By this time, with the good news spreading from the Tyler case, four cases raising these issues had been filed in the Southern District of Texas, and two in the Northern District. Moreover, the Eastern District court that had just decided *Plyler* faced six additional cases after the ruling. Rather than just suing the particular ISDs, these suits included as defendants the State of Texas, the Texas Governor, the Texas Education Agency (the state agency that governed K–12 public education in the State), and its Commissioner. Eventually, all these cases were consolidated into *In re Alien Children*, which was tried in the Southern District of Texas in Houston, before Judge Woodrow Seals. Judge Seals held a 24–day trial.[28]

These sprawling cases presented an even broader assault upon the system, whereas *Plyler* had been narrowly focused upon 21.031 and the Tyler ISD. The various cases were brought by several different attorneys on many fronts, relying upon several theories, hoping that they could replicate the victory Roos had carved out in his Tyler case. At this point, it became crucial that the various parties coordinate, because the defendants had deep pockets, legions of deputy attorneys general and private counsel, and other advantages, most importantly the staying power to mow down the plaintiffs at the trial and appellate levels. True, Roos had convinced the United States to intervene in his case on the side of the alien schoolchildren, but over the long haul, the federal government could not be wholly relied upon in civil rights cases, as its interests could change, depending upon the administration in office.[29]

In May, 1979, after *Plyler* was decided at the trial level but before *In re Alien Children* was to go to trial, the local Houston counsel for the plaintiffs in the case before Judge Seals wrote Peter Roos, requesting that MALDEF consolidate its efforts into their case, which was more complex and comprehensive than the original case against the Tyler ISD. Roos responded to attorney Isaias Torres, a Texas native who had just graduated from law school and was working for the Houston Center for Immigrants, Inc., that MALDEF felt "quite strongly that consolidation would not be in the best interests of our mutual efforts."[30] After all, MALDEF had carefully selected Tyler as the perfect federal venue for arguing its case: progressive judge, sympathetic clients, a rural area where the media glare would not be as great. In addition, in Tyler the case could be made that excluding the small number of undocumented children (the practical effect of charging $1000 tuition to each) would actually lose money for the district, inasmuch as the State school funding formulae based allocation amounts upon head count attendance. In a large urban school district or a border school district, the fact questions and statistical proofs would be more complex and expensive to litigate for both sides.[31] Moreover, because the Tyler trial had been a case of first impression at the federal level, the State's legal strategy had not been as sophisticated as it would be in another similar trial. The *Hernandez* case in state court had not involved the full panoply of legal and social science expertise and financial support available to a national effort such as that mounted by MALDEF.

Roos noted to Torres that the State had tried to make a late-in-the-day correction for its ineffective original efforts by seeking the leave to re-open the record, a request that Judge Justice had denied. State counsel would not likely make that mistake again, and would mount a more aggressive strategy in their second go-around. Roos wrote: "While no doubt you have been incrementally able to improve upon our record [developed in the Tyler trial], consolidation would allow the state and other parties to buttress their record. I believe that one could only expect a narrowing of the present one-sidedness [of the trial record in MAL-DEF's favor]. Consolidation would play right into th[e] hands of [the State's attorney] Mr. Arnett."

Torres, on the other hand, worried that unless the cases were consolidated, the relief in *Plyler* might not extend beyond that small district. Tyler had folded, but what about Houston, Dallas, and the more important border districts? After all, Texas had over 1000 ISDs, and many of them had the same policies towards undocumented students as had Tyler; it was a state statute that gave them such permission. To this understandable concern, Roos indicated that his original strategy was aimed at winning once and then later applying it elsewhere, not joining up with other pending actions and thereby increasing the risk of losing on appeal: "Most importantly, I believe that once we have a Tyler victory, we will have started down a slippery slope which will make it impossible for the court to legally or logistically limit the ruling to Tyler." This approach mirrors that of the NAACP on the road to *Brown*, where Thurgood Marshall and his colleagues carefully picked their fights, each case incrementally building upon the previous litigation.[32] Indeed, MALDEF General Counsel Vilma Martinez had worked at the Legal Defense Fund with Marshall's former colleague and successor, Jack Greenberg; she clearly understood the value of an overarching strategic vision.

But Roos had yet another reason for declining to join in the consolidated cases: he had drawn ineffective opposing local counsel, and wished to press his momentary advantage. He wrote, in a remarkable and candid assessment: "A final, but important reason for believing consolidation unwise is, frankly, the quality of opposing counsel. Our [local] opposing counsel in Tyler is frankly not very good." He went on to say that this would likely not be the case in Houston, where the defense would include experienced attorneys from the specialized education law department of a major law firm, and where other districts would also contribute their efforts and resources. He added, "I believe it is our mutual interest to isolate the worst counsel to argue the case against us. Consolidation works against that. For the above-stated reasons, I would urge you not to seek consolidation. I just don't believe that it serves our mutual interest of getting this statute knocked out."[33]

The Results

Although Roos did not agree to combine forces at the crucial early stages, this issue was eventually taken out of his hands at the U.S. Supreme Court. At the request of the State of Texas, the Judicial Panel on Multidistrict Litigation eventually did consolidate a number of the cases—but significantly, not *Plyler*—into the *In re Alien Children* litigation, and notwithstanding Roos' doubts about whether the Houston plaintiffs would succeed, Judge Seals rendered a favorable decision on the merits on July 21, 1980.[34] The plaintiff schoolchildren prevailed in a big way, most importantly on the issues of whether the State of Texas could enact a statute to discourage immigration and whether equal protection applied to the undocumented in such an instance. Judge Seals determined that strict scrutiny applied because the law worked an absolute deprivation of education. Texas' concern for fiscal integrity was not a compelling state interest, and charging tuition to the parents or removing the children from school had not been shown to be necessary to improve education within the State. Most importantly, he concluded that 21.031 had not been carefully tailored to advance the state interest in a constitutional manner.

In the Fifth Circuit, meanwhile, Judge Justice's *Plyler* decision was affirmed in October, 1980, and in May, 1981, the U.S. Supreme Court agreed to hear the matter.[35] The Fifth Circuit issued a summary affirmance of the consolidated Houston cases a few months later, and the Supreme Court combined the Texas appeals of both cases under the styling of *Plyler v. Doe,* handing Peter Roos the lead vehicle over Peter Schey's cases.[36] Having developed fuller records and armed with Fifth Circuit wins, the two Peters worked out a stiff and formal truce, dividing the oral arguments down the middle, but with MALDEF's case leading the way.

Roos spent the time until the Supreme Court arguments shoring up political support. In March, 1979, he had written to Drew Days, the Assistant Attorney General for Civil Rights, urging the government to join the litigation. Later he persuaded the Secretary of Health, Education, and Welfare, Joseph Califano, to write the Solicitor General urging him to enter into the fray on the side of the children, which the government did. Other MALDEF letters went to state officials in Califor-

nia and elsewhere, requesting their support. After the Reagan administration took office in January of 1981, Roos wrote William Clohan,
Under Secretary of the newly created Department of Education, to urge
him to continue the actions of the Carter administration. Fortunately for
Roos, the Reagan administration did not seek to overturn the lower
court decisions, although it did not formally enter its amicus brief on the
side of the plaintiffs (as had the Democrat lawyers), and it took no
position on the crucial equal protection issue. In fact, the brief stressed
the primacy of the federal government in immigration, a position that
favored the schoolchildren.[37]

The Supreme Court's Ruling

In June, 1982, the Supreme Court gave the schoolchildren their win
on all counts, by a 5–4 margin. Justice Brennan, in his majority opinion
striking down the statute, characterized the Texas argument for charging tuition as "nothing more than an assertion that illegal entry,
without more, prevents a person from becoming a resident for purposes
of enrolling his children in the public schools."[38] He employed an equal
protection analysis to find that a State could not enact a discriminatory
classification "merely by defining a disfavored group as non-resident."[39]

Justice Brennan dismissed the State's first argument that the classification or subclass of undocumented Mexican children was necessary to
preserve the State's "limited resources for the education of its lawful
residents."[40] This line of argumentation had been rejected in an earlier
case, *Graham v. Richardson,* where the court had held that the concern
for preservation of Arizona's resources alone could not justify an alienage classification used in allocating welfare benefits.[41] In addition, he
relied on the findings of fact from the *Plyler* trial: although the exclusion
of all undocumented children might eventually result in some small
savings to the state, those savings would be uncertain (given that federal
and state allocations depended primarily upon the number of children
enrolled),[42] and barring those children would "not necessarily improve
the quality of education."[43]

The State also argued that it had enacted the legislation in order to
protect itself from an influx of undocumented aliens.[44] The Court acknowledged the concern, but found that the statute was not tailored to
address it: "Charging tuition to undocumented children constitutes a
ludicrously ineffectual attempt to stem the tide of illegal immigration."[45]
The Court also noted that immigration and naturalization policy is
within the exclusive powers of federal government.[46]

Finally, the state maintained that it singled out undocumented
children because their unlawful presence rendered them less likely to
remain in the United States and therefore to be able to use the free

public education they received in order to contribute to the social and political goals of the United States community.[47] Brennan distinguished the subclass of undocumented aliens who had lived in the United States as a family and for all practical purposes, permanently, from the subclass of adult aliens who enter the country alone, temporarily, to earn money.[48] For those who remained with the intent of making the United States their home, "[i]t is difficult to understand precisely what the State hopes to achieve by promoting the creation and perpetuation of a subclass of illiterates within our boundaries, surely adding to the problems and costs of unemployment, welfare, and crime."[49]

Prior to *Plyler*, the Supreme Court had never taken up the question of whether undocumented aliens could seek Fourteenth Amendment equal protection.[50] The Supreme Court had long held that aliens are "persons" for purposes of the Fourteenth Amendment,[51] and that undocumented aliens are protected by the due process provisions of the Fifth Amendment.[52] However, Texas argued that because undocumented children were not "within its jurisdiction,"[53] they were not entitled to equal protection. Justice Brennan rejected this line of reasoning, concluding that there "is simply no support for [the] suggestion that 'due process' is somehow of greater stature than 'equal protection' and therefore available to a larger class of persons."[54]

After the *Rodriguez* school finance decision, Justice Brennan had to walk a fine line to apply what amounted to scrutiny more demanding than the usual rational basis review. Although he rejected treating undocumented alienage as a suspect classification,[55] he concluded that the children were not responsible for their own citizenship status and that treating them as Texas law envisioned would "not comport with fundamental conceptions of justice."[56] He was more emphatically concerned with education, however, carefully elaborating the nature of the entitlement to it. While he reaffirmed the earlier *Rodriguez* holding that public education was not a fundamental right (undoubtedly to attract the vote of Justice Powell, the author of the *Rodriguez* majority opinion), he recited a litany of cases holding education to occupy "a fundamental role in maintaining the fabric of our society."[57] He also noted that "[i]lliteracy is an enduring disability,"[58] one that would plague the individual and society. These observations enabled him to establish "the proper level of deference to be afforded § 21.031." He concluded, in light of the significant ongoing costs, that the measure "can hardly be considered rational unless it furthers some substantial goal of the State"—subtle and nuanced phrasing that nudged the level of scrutiny to what would be characterized as intermediate scrutiny.[59] Chief Justice Burger's dissent, in contrast, stuck with the customary formulation, requiring only "a rational relationship to a legitimate state purpose."[60] As a result of Brennan's careful construction, the Court rejected the claim, which the dissent had found persuasive, that the policy was sufficiently related to protecting the state's asserted interests.

Further, while the Court did not reach the claim of federal preemption,[61] it did draw a crucial distinction between what states and the federal government may do in legislating treatment of aliens.[62] The Court had upheld state statutes restricting alien employment[63] and access to welfare benefits,[64] largely because those state measures mirrored federal classifications and congressional action governing immigration. For example, in *DeCanas v. Bica*, the Supreme Court had held that a state statute punishing employers for hiring aliens not authorized to work in the United States was not preempted by federal immigration law.[65] In public education, however, Brennan wrote, distinguishing *DeCanas*, "we perceive no national policy that supports the State in denying these children an elementary education."[66]

Reactions

Much of the considerable scholarly response to the Court's reasoning in the case has evinced surprise that the majority went as far as it did in rejecting the state's sovereignty. Peter Schuck, for example, characterized the decision as a "conceptual watershed in immigration law, the most powerful rejection to date of classical immigration law's notion of plenary national sovereignty over our borders.... Courts are expositors of a constitutional tradition that increasingly emphasizes not the parochial and the situational, but the universal, transcendent values of equality and fairness immanent in the due process and equal protection principles. In that capacity, they have also asserted a larger role in the creation and distribution of opportunities and status in the administrative state. In *Plyler*, the Supreme Court moved boldly on both fronts."[67] Surveying the line of equal protection cases involving aliens from *Yick Wo* through *Graham* to *Plyler* and beyond, Linda Bosniak has summarized: "alienage as a legal status category means that the law of alienage discrimination is perennially burdened by the following questions: To what extent is such discrimination a legitimate expression, or extension, of the government's power to regulate the border and to control the composition of membership in the national community? On the other hand, how far does sovereignty reach before it must give way to equality; when, that is, does discrimination against aliens implicate a different kind of government power, subject to far more rigorous constraints? To what degree, in short, is the status of aliens to be understood as a matter of national borders, to what degree a matter of personhood, and how are we to tell the difference? These questions, I argue, shape the law's conflicted understandings of the difference that alienage makes."[68]

Although *Plyler's* incontestably bold reasoning has not substantially influenced subsequent Supreme Court immigration jurisprudence in the

twenty-plus years since it was decided, the educational significance of
the case is still clear, even if it is limited to this small subset of
schoolchildren—largely Latinos—in the United States. Given the poor
overall educational achievement evident in this population, even this one
success story has significance.[69] Again, the parallel to *Brown* is striking:
Brown's legacy is questioned even after fifty years, largely due to Anglo
racial intransigence and the failure of integration's promise.[70]

Postscript to Plyler—*The Education of the Polity*

In September of the same year, the Court denied petitions to rehear
the case, and the matter was over.[71] More than five years had passed
since the issue had first appeared on the MALDEF radar screen, and the
extraordinary skills and disciplined strategy of Roos and Martinez had
prevailed. Indeed, their overarching strategic vision had enabled them to
avoid the many centripetal forces that threatened *Plyler* at every turn.
To be sure, good fortune appeared to have intervened at all the key
times: sympathetic clients with a straightforward story to tell confronting an unpopular state statute that never had had its own compelling
story, flying under big-city legal radar and lucking into poor opposing
local counsel, federal and state officials at the early stages who were
responsive and helpful, continuity in federal support for the plaintiffs
despite a change in the national administration, the ability to keep the
Tyler case on track and for the Houston-based cases to prevail at their
own speed and upon their own legs, and the right array of judges hearing
the cases as they wended their way through the system. This issue could
have foundered at any one of the many turns, winding up like *Rodriguez*,
with a similar gravitational pull but a more complex statistical calculus
and worse luck. But the considerable legal and political skills of the
MALDEF lawyers served the schoolchildren well, as had lawyers of color
and Anglo lawyers on the path to *Brown*.

Soon after *Plyler*, both Vilma Martinez and Peter Roos left MAL-
DEF, she to a Los Angeles law firm and he to the San Francisco-based
public interest organization, META, where he continued education litigation on bilingual rights and immigrant rights. The original MALDEF
San Antonio lawyer who had written the first *Plyler* memo, Joaquin
Avila, succeeded Martinez as President and General Counsel. In 1996 he
won a MacArthur Foundation "genius" fellowship after several years in
private practice concentrating on voting rights; he now is a law teacher
at Seattle University. Whatever became of the undocumented schoolchildren from Tyler, Texas? According to a newspaper story following up on
them, nearly all of them graduated and, through various immigration
provisions, obtained permission to stay in the United States and regularize their status.[72]

The U.S. Supreme Court soon took up a related case, *Martinez v. Bynum*,[73] and upheld a different part of section 21.031, which provided that the parents or guardians of undocumented children had to reside in a school district before they could send their children to free public schools. Although this was the element of the statute that first drew Avila's attention and started the ball rolling towards MALDEF's filing of the *Plyler* lawsuit, *Martinez* does not amount to a significant narrowing of *Plyler*, where the parents actually resided in the school districts, albeit in unauthorized immigration status. The student in *Martinez* was the U.S. citizen child of undocumented parents who had returned to Mexico after his birth and left him in the care of his adult sister, who was not his legal guardian. The Court in *Martinez* sustained Texas' determination that the child did not reside in the district and thus did not qualify for free public schooling there, ruling that *Plyler* did not bar application of appropriately defined bona fide residence tests. Interestingly, in *Plyler*'s footnote 22, the Court had indicated that the undocumented may establish domicile in the country, a much larger issue than that presented in *Martinez*, where the child's parents had not established the requisite residence in the district. That footnote elaborated: "A State may not ... accomplish what would otherwise be prohibited by the Equal Protection Clause, merely by defining a disfavored group as nonresident. And illegal entry into the country would not, under traditional criteria, bar a person from obtaining domicile within a State."[74]

In 1994, an unpopular governor of California, Pete Wilson, revived his reelection campaign by backing a ballot initiative known as Proposition 187, which would have denied virtually all state-funded benefits, including public education, to undocumented aliens. Proposition 187 passed with nearly 60 percent of the vote and Wilson was re-elected, but the federal courts enjoined implementation of most of the ballot measure, relying prominently on *Plyler*.[75] During the congressional debates that eventually led to the enactment of the Illegal Immigration and Immigrant Responsibility Act of 1996, Representative Elton Gallegly (R.-Cal.) proposed an amendment that would have allowed states to charge tuition to undocumented students or exclude them from public schools. He was banking that, in the wake of such federal legislation, the courts would distinguish *Plyler* and sustain the state measure. The provision became quite politicized, receiving prominent support from Republican presidential candidate Robert Dole. Gallegly might have been right that the Constitution would not be read by the Court of the 1990s to nullify a federal enactment of the kind he proposed, but he never got a chance to find out, because *Plyler* proved to have considerable strength in the political arena. The Gallegly amendment drew heated opposition in Congress and in the media, and critics relied heavily on the values and arguments highlighted in *Plyler*—and often on the decision itself. After months of contentious debate, the amendment was dropped from the final legislation, and no provisions became law that restricted alien children's right to attend school. *Plyler* and the polity appear to have settled the question.[76]

Although *Plyler* had addressed the issue of public school children in the K–12 setting, questions arose almost immediately after the ruling about how far the decision could be extended, notably whether it would protect undocumented college students. Before long, Peter Roos was going for the long ball again, litigating postsecondary *Plyler* cases in California.[77] The cases have mostly denied relief, although the record is mixed. That history is for a companion volume, but I will say this: the ultimate irony is that in 2001, just after Governor George Bush left Texas to become President George Bush, the State enacted H.B. 1403, establishing the right of undocumented college students to establish resident status and pay in-state tuition in the State's public colleges.[78] In the 25 years since Texas had enacted 21.031, this was silent testimony to the idea that you reside where you live, quite apart from your immigration status. A dozen states have acted since the Texas innovation.[79] And in Congress, conservative Utah Senator Orrin Hatch co-authored the Development, Relief, and Education for Alien Minors (DREAM) Act.[80] If enacted, it would remove a provision from federal law that discourages states from providing in-state tuition status to undocumented college students, and would also allow the students the opportunity to regularize their federal immigration status—an enormous benefit that would go well beyond what a state could provide.[81] *Plyler* clearly is alive and well in its adolescence.

ENDNOTES

1. 457 U.S. 202 (1982).

2. The historian Mae M. Ngai, in a perceptive study concerning the history of undocumented immigration and the way in which different nationalities have been racialized by the immigration process, has concluded:

> [The process of how the nation constituted immigration] had an important racial dimension because the application and reform of deportation policy had disparate effects on Europeans and Canadians, on the one hand, and Mexicans, on the other hand. But, the disparity was not simply the result of existing racism. Rather, the processes of territorial redefinition and administrative enforcement informed divergent paths of immigrant racialization. Europeans and Canadians tended to be disassociated from the real and imagined category of illegal alien, which facilitated their national and racial assimilation as white American citizens. In contrast, Mexicans emerged as iconic illegal aliens. Illegal status became constitutive of a racialized Mexican identity and of Mexicans' exclusion from the national community and polity.

Her full-length book, Illegal Aliens and Alien Citizens: Immigration Restriction, Race, and Nation, 1924–1965, outlines these differentiated developments in considerable detail, and this background elaborates upon why "illegal alienage" has developed in immigration policy and practice as essentially a concept of guarding our Southern border (our "frontera") from undesirables. See also Mae M. Ngai, The Strange Career of the Illegal Alien: Immigration Restriction and Deportation Policy in the United States, 1924–1965, 21 L. and Hist. Rev. 145 (2003). See Note, Law, Race, and the Border: The El Paso Salt War of 1877, 117 Harv. L. Rev. 941 (2004); Carl Gutierrez–Jones, Rethinking the Borderlands: Between Chicano Culture and Legal Discourse (1995); Steven W. Bender, Greasers and Gringos: Latinos, Law, and the American Imagination (2003); Juan F. Perea, A Brief History of Race and the U.S.-Mexican Border: Tracing the Trajectories of Conquest, 51 UCLA L. Rev. 283 (2003).

3. Peter H. Schuck, The Transformation of Immigration Law, 84 Col. L. Rev. 1, 54 (1984).

4. Tex. Educ. Code Ann. § 21.031 (Vernon Supp.1981).

5. In the Houston case challenging this statute, the federal court trial judge found:

> The court cannot state with absolute certainty what the Legislature intended when passing the amendment to 21.031. Neither the court nor the parties have uncovered a shred of legislative history accompanying the 1975 amendment. There was no debate in the Legislature before the amendment was passed by a voice vote. There were no studies preceding the introduction of the legislation to determine the impact that undocumented children were having on the schools or to project the fiscal implications of the amendment.

In re Alien Children Education Litigation, 501 F. Supp. 544, 555, n.19 (1980). The record, such as it is, showed that the legislation likely arose after a Texas Attorney General Opinion held that prior to 1975, the Texas education law did not differentiate among children based upon their immigration status. Att'y Gen. Op. H–586 at 3 (1975).

6. Tex. Educ. Code Ann. § 21.031 (Vernon Supp.1981).

7. The *In re Alien Children* record included considerable statistical testimony, including the data in this paragraph, prepared by then-law student Laura Oren and Houston lawyer Joseph Vail; I found copies of the original hand-tabulated data in the Oren files on this subject. (Copies on file with author.) Both Professor Oren and Professor Vail are now my colleagues at the University of Houston Law Center, where both migrated after local law careers, including Professor Vail's later service as an immigration judge.

8. Hernandez v. Houston Independent School District, 558 S.W. 2d 121(1977). The case was tried in Austin rather than Houston because of the administrative proceedings required to challenge the state administrative agency.

9. Id. at 125.

10. I found a copy of the letter in the Stanford University Green Library special Collections Room, MALDEF files. The concordance to these records is Theresa Mesa Casey and Pedro Hernandez, comps. and eds., Research Guide to the Records of MAL-DEF/PRLDEF (1996). The Avila–Roos letter was located in MALDEF, M0673, Box 115, Folder 5 (Avila to Roos, September 26, 1977). Additional files from early MALDEF work in Houston are available in the archives of the Houston Metropolitan Research Center (HMRC), particularly the Abraham Ramirez collection, used extensively by Guadalupe San Miguel, Jr. to explain earlier Houston school desegregation cases and bilingual education issues in his excellent study, Brown, Not White: School Integration and the Chicano Movement in Houston (2001). Ramirez was a local civil rights attorney who was affiliated with MALDEF in its early years, although he was not an employee. For additional studies of Houston schooling, see William H. Kellar, Make Haste Slowly: Moderates, Conservatives, and School Desegregation in Houston (1999); Angela Valenzuela, Subtractive Schooling: U.S.-Mexican Youth and the Politics of Caring (1999).

11. 461 U.S. 321 (1983). In order to stop this practice, Congress in 1996 enacted what is now INA § 214(m), 8 U.S.C. § 1184(m).

12.   Steven H. Wilson, Brown Over "Other White": Mexican Americans' Legal Arguments and Litigation Strategy in School Desegregation Lawsuits, 21 Law and History Review 145, 193 (2003) (citations omitted). See Vicki L. Ruiz, "We Always Tell Our Children They Are Americans," Mendez v. Westminster and the California Road to Brown v. Board of Education, Coll. Bd. Rev. No. 200 (Fall, 2003), at 20; Margaret E. Montoya, A Brief History of Chicana/o School Segregation: One Rationale for Affirmative Action, 12 Berk. La Raza L. J. 159 (2001); Ian F. Haney Lopez, Race, Ethnicity, Erasure: The Salience of Race to LatCrit Theory, 85 Cal. L. Rev. 57 (1998); Ian F. Haney Lopez, White by Law: The Legal Construction of Race (1996); Clare Sheridan, "Another White Race": Mexican Americans and the Paradox of Whiteness in Jury Selection, 21 L. and Hist. Rev. 109 (2003).

13.   Richard Griswold de Castillo and Anthony Accardo, Cesar Chavez: The Struggle for Justice (2002).

14.   411 U.S. 1 (1973).

15.   George A. Martinez, Legal Indeterminacy, Judicial Discretion, and the Mexican American Litigation Experience: 1930–1980, 27 U.C. Davis L. Rev. 555 (1994). Mario T. Garcia, Mexican Americans: Leadership, Ideology, & Identity, 1930–1960 (1989). Gary A. Greenfield and Don B. Kates, Jr., Mexican Americans, Racial Discrimination, and the Civil Rights Act of 1866, 63 Calif. L. Rev. 662 (1975); Richard Delgado and Victoria Palacios, Mexican Americans as a Legally Cognizable Class Under Rule 23 and the Equal Protection Clause, 50 Notre Dame Lawyer 393 (1975); George J. Sanchez, Becoming Mexican American: Ethnicity, Culture and Identity in Chicano Los Angeles, 1900–1945 (1993); Christopher Arriola, Knocking On the Schoolhouse Door: Mendez v. Westminster, Equal Protection, Public Education and Mexican Americans in the 1940's, 8 La Raza L. J. 166 (1995); Neil Foley, The White Scourge: Mexicans, Blacks, and Poor Whites in Texas Cotton Culture (1997); Juan F. Perea, Buscando America: Why Integration and Equal Protection Fail to Protect Latinos, 117 Harv. L. Rev. 1420 (2004).

16.   Guadalupe San Miguel, "Let All of Them Take Heed": Mexican Americans and the Campaign for Educational Equality in Texas, 1910–1981 (1987).

17.   Id. at 174 (Table 10); see Jorge C. Rangel and Carlos M. Alcala, De Jure Segregation of Chicanos in Texas Schools, 7 Harv. C.R.–C. L. L. Rev. 307 (1972).

18.   United States v. Texas, 506 F. Supp. 405 (E.D. Tex. 1981), rev'd, 680 F.2d 356 (5th Cir. 1982). It is not surprising that such anti-Mexican legislation and practices would have originated in Texas, a jurisdiction widely regarded to be officially inhospitable to its Mexican-origin population. See Arnoldo De Leon, They Called Them Greasers: Anglo Attitudes Toward Mexicans in Texas, 1821–1900 (1983); David Montejano, Anglos and Mexicans in the Making of Texas, 1836–1986 (1987).

19.   506 F. Supp. at 428.

20.   For example, the U.S. v. Texas case was formally styled United States of America, Plaintiff, Mexican American Legal Defense Fund, LULAC, and G. I. Forum, Plaintiffs–Intervenors v. State of Texas et al., Defendants. For histories of these organizations, see Carl Allsup, The American G. I. Forum: Origins and Evolution, Monograph No. 6, University of Texas Mexican American Studies (1982); Benjamin Marquez, LULAC: The Evolution of a Mexican American Organization (1993); Henry A. J. Ramos, The American GI Forum: In Pursuit of the Dream, 1948–1983 (1998); Laura E. Gomez, The Birth of the "Hispanic" Generation: Attitudes of Mexican–American Political Elites Toward the Hispanic Label, 75 Lat. Am. Persp. 45 (1992); Suzanne Oboler, The Politics of Labeling: Latino/a Cultural Identities of Self and Others, 75 Lat. Am. Persp. 18 (1992); Suzanne Oboler, Ethnic Labels, Latino Lives (1995).

21.   For example, Judge Justice was the trial judge in U.S. v. Texas, in which he found Texas and the school districts to have been out of compliance with regard to school desegregation and English language instruction obligations under federal law. 506 F. Supp.

405 (E.D. Tex. 1981), rev'd, 680 F. 2d 356 (5th Cir. 1982). For examples of his long record of progressive decisions, see John J. DiIulio, Governing Prisons (1987) (longstanding prison litigation). For this record, he earned an impeachment bill, H. Res. 168 (97th Cong.), introduced on June 24, 1981. See Frank R. Kemerer, William Wayne Justice: A Judicial Biography (1991).

22. The plaintiff in that early case was named Carlos Hernandez. See the letter from Peter Roos to Leonel Castillo (September 13, 1977), where he warns, "We have been informed that the local United States Attorney, John Hannah, has requested the Director of [the Dallas INS] to take steps to deport the plaintiffs in this case and possibly to conduct a sweep in the Tyler region." M0673, Box 115, Folder 5. This issue arose in a recent case in which undocumented college students in Virginia who brought an action concerning a state statute that denied state college access to undocumented students sought to file their case anonymously. The judge ruled against them on this issue. *Doe v. Merten*, 219 F.R.D. 387, 184 Ed. Law Rep. 843 (E.D. Va., 2004). And then he ruled against them on the larger issue, once alternative plaintiff organizations were enlisted as substitutes, holding that the State of Virginia could enact practices which denied undocumented students admission or residency status. *Equal Access Education v. Merten*, 305 F.Supp.2d 585 (E.D.Va. 2004), and 325 F.Supp.2d 655 (E.D. Va. 2004) (finding that students did not have standing, absent evidence that institution denied admission on perceived immigration status).

23. In the *Plyler* trial court case and at the Fifth Circuit, the U.S. Department of Justice and the U.S. Attorney intervened on the side of the schoolchildren. After he left office, Castillo returned to Houston. In 1983, he wrote in a Foreword to a special immigration issue of a law review: "the authors are all persons of recognized ability and concern.... [Among others, Isaias Torres and Peter Schey] have all been involved in the daily battles of making the INA fit a particular individual's situation at a particular time. During the time that I served as Commissioner (1977–79), it was my privilege to be sued by some of these individuals. I knew that regardless of the outcome, the ultimate goal of justice for immigrants would prevail because effective advocates help cure improper procedures and faulty legislation." Leonel Castillo, Foreword, 5 Hou. J. Int'l L. 191 (1983).

24. See Doe v. Plyler, 628 F. 2d 448, 450 (5th Cir. 1980).

25. MALDEF files, M0673, Box 115, Folder 6 (Roos to Roy Fuentes, October 18, 1977). Roos was also trying at this time to address similar issues in California, as a series of letters in the MALDEF files revealed. He wrote California school districts that their attendance practices violated State guidelines for undocumented children: M0673, Box 61, Folder 8 (March 12, 1979); M0673, Box 62, Folder 1 (October 29, 1979); M0673, Box 62, Folder 1 (October 19, 1979).

26. Doe v. Plyler, 458 F. Supp. 569 (E.D. Tex. 1978).

27. Quoted in In re Alien Children Educ. Litigation, 501 F.Supp. 544, 552 (S.D. Tex. 1980).

28. In re Alien Children Educ. Litigation, 501 F. Supp. 544 (S.D. Tex 1980). The federal case became a veritable magnet, as various plaintiffs and defendants were added, requiring many pages of explanation for these procedural issues. A playbill would include: (1) from the Southern District: Martinez v. Reagen, C.A. No. H–78–1797, filed September 18, 1978; Cardenas v. Meyer, C.A. No. H–78–1862, filed September 27, 1978; Garza v. Reagen, C.A. No. H–78–2132, filed November 6, 1978; Mendoza v. Clark, C.A. No. H–78–1831, filed September 22, 1978; (2) from the Northern District: Doe v. Wright, C.A. No. 3–79–0440–D; (3) from the Western District: Roe v. Holm, MO–79–CA–49; Coe v. Holm, MO–78–CA–54. What the court termed "tag-along actions," originally filed in the Southern District were also consolidated: Cortes v. Wheeler, C.A. H–79–1926, filed September 20, 1979; Rodrigues v. Meyer, C.A. H–79–1927, filed September 20, 1979; Adamo v. Reagen, C.A. H–79–1928, filed September 20, 1979; Arguelles v. Meyer, C.A. H–79–2071, filed

October 4, 1979. Six additional cases originally filed in the Eastern District of Texas were likewise consolidated: Doe v. Sulphur Springs, P–79–31–CA, filed October 29, 1979; Doe v. Lodestro, B–79–618–CA, filed September 18, 1979; Doe v. Ford, TY–79–351–CA, filed September 28, 1979; Roe v. Horn, TY–79–338–CA, filed September 24, 1979; Roe v. Como–Pickton, P–79–234–CA, filed October 19, 1979; and Poe v. Chappel Hill, TY–79–449–CA, filed December 10, 1979.

Observers of this trial have reported that Judge Woodrow Seals committed an interesting gaffe during arguments when he asked, "whether anything of worldwide importance had ever been written in Spanish," or words to that effect. (Apparently he had not heard of the classic works by Miguel Cervantes, Octavio Paz, Juan Vasconcellos, Gabriel Garcia Marquez, Pablo Neruda, Sor Juana, or many other Latino or Latina writers.) Witnesses report that it was an electric moment, one he sensed, and after which he publicly apologized. See Juan R. Palomo, Judge Seals Calls Spanish Comment "Senseless, Dreadful," Houston Post, March 7, 1980, 3B.

29. See below, note 37 and accompanying text. A good example of this unreliability appeared in connection with a long-running dispute involving public colleges in Nashville, Tennessee. The U.S. Department of Justice supported the plaintiffs over the course of many years, and after working out the dispute among the many parties, the judge entered a final order that included racially specific remedies. Later, after the Reagan administration took office, the U.S. Department of Justice attempted to switch horses and get the court to strike down the agreement. The judge refused to accept this too-little-too-late intervention. Geier v. Alexander, 801 F. 2d 799 (6th Cir. 1986); see also Geier v. Blanton, 427 F. Supp. 644 (M.D.Tenn.1977). The original case finally wound down on June 18, 2004, when the issue of attorney fees was decided. Geier v. Sundquist, 372 F. 3d 784 (6th Cir. 2004).

30. Roos to Isaias Torres, May 17, 1979, MALDEF files, M0673, Box 61, Folder 10. In the interest of full disclosure, I note that Mr. Torres was a Georgetown University Law Center classmate of mine.

31. These were some of the problems that had doomed the educational finance case. See Michael Heise, State Constitutional Litigation, Educational Finance, and Legal Impact: An Empirical Analysis, 63 U. Cinn. L. Rev. 1735 (1995); Augustina H. Reyes, Does Money Make a Difference for Hispanic Students in Urban Schools?, 36 Educ. and Urb. Society 353 (2003).

32. Mark V. Tushnet, The NAACP's Legal Strategy Against Segregated Education, 1925–1950 (1987); Mark V. Tushnet, Making Civil Rights Law: Thurgood Marshall and the Supreme Court, 1936–1961 (1994); Robert J. Cottrol, Raymond T. Diamond, and Leland B. Ware, Brown v. Board of Education: Caste, Culture, and the Constitution (2003); Amilcar Shabazz, Advancing Democracy: African Americans and the Struggle for Access and Equity in Higher Education in Texas (2004); William C. Kidder, the Struggle for Access from Sweatt to Grutter: A History of African American, Latino, and American Indian Law School Admissions, 1950–2000, 19 Harv. Black Letter L. J. 1 (2003). For the history of earlier Mexican American trial strategies, see Lisa Lizette Barrera, Minorities and the University of Texas Law School (1950–1980), 4 Tex. Hisp. J. L & Pol'y 99 (1998); Guadalupe Salinas, Mexican–Americans and the Desegregation of Schools in the Southwest, 8 Hous. L. Rev. 929 (1971); Ricardo Romo, Southern California and the Origins of Latino Civil Rights Activism, 3 W. Legal Hist. 379 (1990); George Martinez, The Legal Construction of Race: Mexican–Americans and Whiteness, 2 Harv. Lat. L. Rev. 321 (1997).

33. Roos to Torres, MALDEF files, M0673, Box 61, Folder 10, page two (May 17, 1979).

34. 501 F. Supp. 544 (S. D. Tex. 1980). His remarks about the Spanish language had occurred on the final day of the plaintiffs' testimony.

35. 451 U.S. 968 (1981) (noting probable jurisdiction in the *Plyler* litigation).

36. 452 U.S. 937 (1981) (noting probable jurisdiction in *In re Alien Children*). The procedural sequence is more fully explained in the *Plyler* merits decision, 457 U.S. at 207–10.

37. Although the Carter administration officials had actually supported MALDEF and the Houston children's attorneys in the earlier stages of the cases, including both the trial court and Fifth Circuit phases, the Reagan administration did not side with the appellee children when the cases finally made their way to the Supreme Court, filing instead only as amicus curiae. 1981 WL 390001. As examples of the support MALDEF tried to line up for its side, the MALDEF files include letters Roos wrote to Peter Schilla (Western Center on Law and Poverty, Sacramento, May 19, 1981), M0673, Box 63, Folder 6; Norella Beni Hall (May 14, 1981) (urging her support, but focusing upon education issue), M0673, Box 63, Folder 6; California Board of Education member Lorenza Schmidt (June 25, 1981), M0673, Box 63, Folder 7; Associate AG Drew Days (March 28, 1979), M0673, Box 61, Folder 8; and William Clohan, Undersecretary, U.S. Dept. of Education, May 20, 1981, M0673, Box 63, Folder 6. The files also include a letter from HEW Secretary Joseph Califano to the U.S. Solicitor General Wade McCree, urging the United States to enter the case on behalf of the children plaintiffs (July 17, 1979), M0673 Box 907, Folder 9. These letters and dozens more show the extent to which Roos and MALDEF sought and then shored up support for their clients.

38. 457 U.S. at 227.

39. Id.

40. Id.

41. 403 U.S. 365, 375 (1971).

42. Doe v. Plyler, 458 F. Supp. at 576–77.

43. 457 U.S. at 229.

44. Id. at 229–30.

45. Id. at 228.

46. Id. at 225–26.

47. Id. at 229–30.

48. Id. at 230.

49. Id. at 230.

50. "No State shall ... deprive any person of life, liberty, or property, without due process of law; nor deny to any person within its jurisdiction the equal protection of the laws." U.S. CONST. amend. XIV § 1.

51. Yick Wo v. Hopkins, 118 U.S. 356, 369 (1886) (stating that Fourteenth amendment provisions "are universal in their application to all persons within the territorial jurisdiction, without regard to any differences of race, of color, or of nationality").

52. Wong Wing v. United States, 163 U.S. 228 (1896). See Chapter 2 in this volume.

53. 457 U.S. at 211.

54. Id. at 213. In the dissent, Chief Justice Burger concurred that the equal protection clause applies to undocumented aliens. Id. at 243.

55. 457 U.S at 219, n.19.

56. 457 U.S. at 220 (citing Trimble v. Gordon, 430 U.S. 762, 720 (1977), an important case applying greater scrutiny to classifications disadvantaging out-of-wedlock children).

57. 457 U.S. at 221 (citations omitted).

58. Id. at 222.

59. Id. at 223–24.

60. Id. at 248.

61. Id. at 210 n.8. In a postsecondary education alienage case decided soon after *Plyler, Toll v. Moreno*, the decision turned on preemption. 458 U.S. 1 (1982). See Michael A. Olivas, Plyler v. Doe and Postsecondary Admissions: Undocumented Adults and "Enduring Disability," J. L. & Ed. 19 (1986).

62. 457 U.S. at 224–26.

63. De Canas v. Bica, 424 U.S. 351 (1976).

64. Mathews v. Diaz, 426 U.S. 67 (1976).

65. 424 U.S. 351, 356 (1976).

66. 457 U.S. at 226. This sentence became the focus of efforts to change federal law in 1996, led by Representative Elton Gallegly (R. Calif.), to incorporate an explicit provision authorizing exclusion of undocumented children from public schools. These efforts are discussed in the final part of this Chapter.

67. Peter H. Schuck, The Transformation of Immigration Law, 84 Col. L. Rev. 1, 58 (1984).

68. Linda Bosniak, Membership, Equality, and the Difference That Alienage Makes, 69 N.Y.U. L. Rev. 1047, 1057 (1994). See also Kevin R. Johnson, Civil Rights and Immigration: Challenges for the Latino Community in the Twenty–First Century, 8 La Raza L. J. 42 (1995).

69. See Guadalupe San Miguel, "Let All of Them Take Heed": Mexican Americans and the Campaign for Educational Equality in Texas, 1910–1981 (1987); Jorge C. Rangel and Carlos M. Alcala, De Jure Segregation of Chicanos in Texas Schools, 7 Harv. C.R.–C. L. L. Rev. 307 (1972); Gilbert G. Gonzalez, Chicano Education in the Era of Segregation (1990). While there is an increasing amount of attention to this complex history of Latino/a schooling, there is still much that needs attention by future scholars. And if there is too little we know about the schooling of Chicanos, we know less yet of the education litigation undertaken by Puerto Ricans or of other Latino populations. See Antonia Pantoja, The Making of a Nuyorican: A Memoir (2002).

70. For critiques of *Brown*, citing its promise and the failure of white communities to implement its holding, see, among others, Alex M. Johnson, Jr., Bid Whist, Tonk, and United States v. Fordice: Why Integrationism Fails African–Americans Again, 81 Cal. L. Rev. 1401 (1993); Kimberle Williams Crenshaw, Race, Reform, and Retrenchment: Transformation and Legitimation in Antidiscrimination Law, 101 Harv. L. Rev. 1331 (1988); Richard Delgado and Jean Stefancic, The Social Construction of Brown v. Board of Education: Law Reform and the Reconstructive Paradox, 36 Wm. & Mary L. Rev. 547 (1995); Jack M. Balkin, What Brown v. Board of Education Should Have Said (2001).

71. 458 U.S. 1131 (1982).

72. See Paul Feldman, Texas Case Looms over Prop. 187's Legal Future Justice: U.S. High Court Voided that State's '75 Law on Illegal Immigrants,but Panel has Shifted to the Right, L.A. Times A1 (October 23, 1994). I thank Professor Maria Pabon Lopez for bringing this source to my attention.

73. 461 U.S. 321 (1983).

74. 457 U.S. at 227 n.22.

75. League of United Latin American Citizens v. Wilson, 997 F.Supp. 1244 (C.D. Cal. 1997).

76. Stephen Legomsky, Immigration and Refugee Law and Policy 1162 (3rd ed. 2002); Thomas Alexander Aleinikoff, David A. Martin, Hiroshi Motomura, Immigration and

Citizenship, Process and Policy 1166–69 (5th ed. 2003); see also 73 Interp. Rel. at 1111, 1209, 1255, 1281 (1996); Rebecca A. Maynard & Daniel J. McGrath, *Family Structure, Fertility and Child Welfare* in The Social Benefits of Education 125 (Jere Behrman & Never Stacey, eds. 1997); Sidney Weintraub, Francisco Alba, Rafael Fernandez de Castro, and Manuel Garcia y Griego, *Responses to Migration Issues in* Mexico–US Binational Migration Study Report 467 (United States Commission on Immigration Reform) (1997), available at http://www.utexas.edu/lbj/uscir/binpapers/v1–5weintraub.pdf, at 468 (last visited on September 10, 2004). For a thorough analysis of these issues and other restrictive legislative efforts, see Kevin R. Johnson, Public Benefits and Immigration: The Intersection of Immigration Status, Ethnicity, Gender, and Class, 42 UCLA L. Rev. 159 (1995).

77. Roos later litigated such cases as Leticia "A" v. Board of Regents of the University of California, Tentative Decision, No. 588982–5 (Cal. Super. Ct. Alameda Cty., April 3, 1985); Judgment (May 7, 1985); Statement of Decision (May 30, 1985) (Leticia "A" I); Clarification (May 19, 1982) (Leticia "A" II). Peter D. Roos, Postsecondary Plyler, IHELG Monograph 91–7 (1991); Michael A. Olivas, Storytelling Out of School: Undocumented College Residency, Race, and Reaction, 22 Hast. Con. L. Q'tly 1019 (1995).

78. Tex. Educ. Code Ann. § 54.052 (Vernon Supp.2001). See Clay Robinson, Budget Hits Include Judges' Pay Hike, Houston Chronicle (June 18, 2001), at 1A (describing tuition, revenue bill details). For insomniacs in the reading public, see Michael A. Olivas, IIRIRA, The DREAM Act, and Undocumented College Student Residency, 30 J. Coll. & Univ. L. 435 (2004).

79. Olivas, at Table One (cited in note 78).

80. S. 1545, 108th Cong. (2003).

81. Olivas at 461–63 (cited in note 78).

9

Maria and Joseph Plasencia's Lost Weekend: The Case of *Landon v. Plasencia*

Kevin R. Johnson

In the 1970s and 1980s, political violence in Central America, a region of poverty and civil war, resulted in tens of thousands of deaths. The 1980 assassination of Archbishop Oscar Romero by a right-wing death squad during Catholic mass in San Salvador commenced a decade of bloodshed. During roughly the same time period, El Salvador's neighbor, Guatemala, waged war against armed guerrillas and indigenous peoples in the name of fighting communism. As the result of these tumultuous events, thousands of Central Americans fled their war-torn nations and came to the United States. Many of them claimed a fear of political persecution if returned to their native country and applied for asylum under U.S. law.

Worried about a mass migration, the federal government sought to prevent a "flood" of poor undocumented immigrants from El Salvador and Guatemala from entering the United States. To that end, the Immigration and Naturalization Service (INS) adopted a policy of mass detention of Central Americans pending decisions on their asylum applications, hoping to discourage asylum seekers from pursuing their claims and instead to "voluntarily" return to their native countries. Courts at times intervened to enjoin these policies and practices.[1] Litigation claiming that the U.S. government unfairly denied the asylum claims of Salvadorans on foreign policy grounds, rather than their merits, ended in a landmark settlement in which the government agreed to reconsider thousands of their applications without taking impermissible factors into account.[2]

Despite the heightened immigration enforcement measures, undocumented migration from Central America continued. Newly filed asylum applications skyrocketed from almost 25,000 in 1984 to more than 147,000 in 1995. Long backlogs developed in the agencies responsible for adjudicating them. The federal government responded with reform to the asylum process, adopting measures seeking to discourage the filing of frivolous applications.[3]

Other events during this period also contributed to public concern about immigration to the United States. Approximately 300,000 Southeast Asians had been admitted as refugees in the four years after the end of the Vietnam war in 1975. Congress responded with the Refugee Act of 1980, which ensured greater congressional control over refugee admissions.[4] Only weeks after the new law's enactment, however, the "Mariel boatlift" brought 125,000 persons from Cuba on boats to South Florida. News reports describing the Marielitos as Fidel Castro's undesirables— criminals, homosexuals, and the mentally ill—aroused public fears. The federal government responded with mass detention of the Cuban immigrants.[5]

The U.S. government also aggressively responded to the thousands of Haitians who in ramshackle boats fled the political violence and extreme poverty that gripped their native country. In 1980, President Ronald Reagan ordered the U.S. Coast Guard to interdict Haitians on the high seas before they could make it to shore, and, based on a brief interview on the ship, to allow only those determined to have strong asylum claims to come to the United States. Immigrant rights advocates strongly criticized the asylum screening process as both inadequate and unlawful. Interdiction proved effective. Between 1981 and 1991, only about 25,000 Haitians were stopped en route to this country, a reduction from previous levels of migration from Haiti. A political coup in September 1991 dramatically increased Haitian migration, with the U.S. government interdicting 34,000 Haitians in the next six months. A harsh change in policy resulted. Coast Guard cutters continued interdicting Haitian boats but began to return all of the asylum seekers to Haiti immediately, with no attempt to determine whether any of them were bona fide refugees fleeing political persecution and thus eligible under international and domestic law to stay in the United States.[6]

Facing the perceived threat of mass migration, many Americans favored dramatically reducing the level of immigration to the United States. The Reagan administration vigorously advocated immigration reform in the 1980s. Attorney General William French Smith told Congress in 1981, a little more than a year before oral argument in the Supreme Court in the case of *Landon v. Plasencia*, that "[w]e have lost control of our borders. We have pursued unrealistic policies. We have failed to enforce our laws effectively."[7] Within five years, Congress would enact the Immigration Reform and Control Act[8] and the Immigrant Marriage Fraud Amendments,[9] two laws that together intensified immigration enforcement in hopes of reducing and controlling undocumented immigration.

Undocumented immigration continued after the 1986 legislation, ultimately inducing the government to make border enforcement a top priority in the 1990s. Militarization of the Mexican border, with massive infusions of manpower and technology, made illegal entry extremely difficult at the major border crossings. Would-be entrants seeking to evade inspection risked life and limb traveling through dangerous terrain and harsh conditions. Over the next decade, thousands of people—most of them undocumented immigrants from Mexico—died attempting to reach the United States.[10]

Long before the 1986 reform measures and the 1990 border buildup, the Supreme Court had decried undocumented immigration in a number of cases involving border stops. The Court characterized undocumented immigration as a "colossal problem"[11] posing "enormous difficulties"[12] and "formidable law enforcement problems."[13] As early as 1975, the Court had asserted unequivocally (although many informed observers would disagree) that undocumented immigrants "create significant economic and social problems, competing with citizens and legal resident aliens for jobs, and generating extra demand for social services."[14]

Given the difficulties in enforcing the immigration laws, the Supreme Court has tended to defer to the federal government's immigration policies and not interfere with immigration enforcement.[15] Deference to administrative agencies generally approached its highwater mark with the Court's 1984 decision in *Chevron U.S.A., Inc. v. Natural Resources Defense Council, Inc.*,[16] which required reviewing courts to accept any reasonable interpretation by an administrative agency of a statute that it was entrusted with enforcing.

It was against this backdrop of deep public and governmental concern about the inadequacy of immigration enforcement that the Supreme Court took up the case of *Landon v. Plasencia*.[17]

A Weekend Trip to a Border Town

The basic facts that led the U.S. immigration authorities to arrest Maria Plasencia can be gleaned from the court records, including the thirty-two-page transcript of her brief exclusion hearing.

Born in El Salvador, Maria Antonieta Plasencia was forty-one years old when the INS arrested her in 1975 at the San Ysidro crossing on the Mexican border due south of San Diego, California. Although a Salvadoran citizen, she had entered the United States from Canada in March 1970 as a lawful permanent resident after marrying a native-born U.S. citizen, Joseph Plasencia. In the five years that Maria Plasencia had lived in the United States, the Plasencias established a home in downtown Los Angeles that included four children who, like Maria, all had immigrated from El Salvador; Joseph Plasencia had adopted them after marrying Maria.

On Friday, June 27, 1975, Maria and Joseph Plasencia made the two-hour drive from Los Angeles to the border town of Tijuana, Mexico for the weekend. Maria later explained that she "wanted a dentist to see [her] teeth" and that her "husband wanted to see how much they would charge . . . for some dental work." This was not their first trip from Los Angeles to Mexico; the couple had visited at least once before. Maria also had returned to El Salvador for two weeks in order to bring one of her sons to this country—apparently all in compliance with the law. She experienced no immigration problems on these trips, which reflected the commonplace back-and-forth trans-border movement by people in the region.

During their weekend in Tijuana, Maria and Joseph met several Salvadoran nationals at the hotel where they were staying. The Plasencias later gave a ride back to Los Angeles to several Salvadorans. Before the attempted border crossing, Maria provided them with minor alien registration cards that belonged to her children. It is difficult to say for certain, but the Plasencias may have seen an opportunity to earn a little extra money or at least pay for the cost of gas for the trip home. They also might have felt sorry for the stranded Salvadorans, so far from home and so close to their ultimate destination.

At about 9:30 p.m. on Sunday night, INS agents arrested and detained Maria while she attempted to enter the United States by car with her husband and six undocumented immigrants—four young men and two women, from El Salvador and Mexico. The next morning, the INS served Maria, who did not read English, with a notice in English of the immigration charges against her. The notice stated that Maria was charged with being inadmissible under Section 212(a)(31) of the Immigration & Nationality Act,[18] which at the time allowed for the exclusion of any alien seeking admission into the country "who at any time shall have, knowingly and *for gain*, encouraged, induced, assisted, abetted, or aided any other alien to enter or to try to enter the United States in violation of law." The notice also stated that an exclusion hearing in the immigration court would be held at 11:00 a.m. *that same morning.*

At that time, a non-citizen seeking entry into the country at the border was given an exclusion hearing; persons who faced removal from the interior of the country were placed in deportation hearings. The two types of hearings differed in a number of significant ways. The government bore the burden of establishing that a non-citizen should be deported from the United States; in exclusion proceedings, the non-citizen had the burden of proving admissibility. Practically speaking, it always has been much more difficult to deport a non-citizen already in the country than to exclude one stopped at the border. In addition, certain types of relief—suspension of deportation, voluntary departure, designation of the country of deportation, withholding of deportation, and adjustment of status—were available at that time in deportation proceedings but not in exclusion proceedings.

Caught in a bureaucratic whirlwind, Maria Plasencia must have been tired, confused, and overwhelmed. Just hours after receiving notice—in a language she did not understand—of the hearing after a night in INS detention, and less than twenty-four hours after her arrest at the border, the immigration court ordered Plasencia, before she ever talked with an attorney, to be excluded from the United States, her home.

The Immigration Court

The vast majority of migrants arrested by immigration authorities at the southern border are undocumented entrants with no legal right to immigrate to the United States, not lawful permanent residents like Maria Plasencia. Most of them quickly agree to return to Mexico. They understand the futility of challenging their removal from the United States when they have no real defense, and they want to avoid detention while awaiting an almost inevitable outcome. In contrast, Maria and Joseph Plasencia were determined to fight for Maria's right to return to her home, family, and life in the United States.

The transcript begins routinely, leaving the reader with the impression that the immigration judge had been through the same drill many times before:

> This is John Williams conducting an exclusion hearing on June 30, 1975, at San Ysidro, California, in the matter of Maria Antonieta PLASENCIA, A30 738 083. This hearing is in Spahinish [sic] through the official interpreter, Adeline Buckelew, and is recorded in the IBM machine. The applicant is not represented by counsel, but she is accompanied by her husband. The Government is represented by Harold Neubauer, Esq., Immigration and Naturalization Service, San Diego, California 92104.

Although the transcript does not mention the time that the hearing started or ended, an educated guess from a review of the transcript is that the hearing probably took less than an hour.

Maria and Joseph Plasencia testified at the exclusion hearing but presented no other evidence about the weekend trip to Mexico—no corroboration that Maria hoped to obtain dental work there, no explanation of how she and her husband happened to bring a group of undocumented immigrants into the United States, and no evidence of her community ties in Los Angeles.

The immigration court accepted Maria Plasencia's waiver of the right to counsel at no expense to the government. Of modest means, the Plasencias may not have believed that they could afford an attorney, much less find one in a few hours. The immigration judge did not inform Maria that the hearing could be continued to a later date to provide her with the opportunity to attempt to locate counsel or otherwise prepare her case. Nor did he attempt to determine whether she understood what was truly at stake in the proceedings, to explain the complexities of refuting the serious alien smuggling charge made against her, or to inform her that free legal services were available. He failed even to explain who carried the burden of proof on the charges against her. The immigration judge did not take into account the fact that Maria Plasencia was unschooled in the law and had lived for five years in the United States as a lawful permanent resident. Instead, he treated her like someone seeking entry into the country for the very first time. And just like most non-citizens in exclusion proceedings, Maria lacked counsel and ultimately would be ordered removed from the country by the immigration court.

The primary question disputed before the immigration court was whether Maria Plasencia had agreed to bring the six undocumented immigrants into the United States "for gain" and thus had committed an offense rendering her excludable. No other legal grounds for exclusion appeared to apply to her nor did the INS charge her with any. Maria emphatically denied having offered transportation to the migrants "for gain":

Q Wasn't there a mention of money involved in gaining their entry into the United States?

A No, the man just told my husband that he would fill his gas tank.

Maria testified that her husband agreed to bring the Salvadorans across because he "just felt sorry for them" and "did it just for pity." When the INS trial attorney persisted with this line of questioning, she stood by her story: "[T]here was no mention of money, I swear it. There was only the mention of gasoline." When pressed another time, she relented a tiny bit and mentioned that some of the passengers took her and Joseph to dinner the night before the attempted border crossing.

The INS called three witnesses, all natives of El Salvador who had used the minor alien identification cards of Maria's children in attempting to enter the country. Anna Elsa Lopez[19] testified that the passengers each agreed to pay Maria $250 once they arrived in the United States and got a job. Maria aggressively cross-examined Lopez:

Q Young lady, when did I speak to you of money?

A Yesterday.

Q Do you swear to God that I spoke to you of money?

A Yes.

Later, Maria followed up with Lopez:

Q Your uncle told me that you paid him all the way to come from El Salvador clear to Tijuana, isn't this true?

A No, I have no family.

* * *

Q Isn't Arturo———your uncle that we met at the hotel?

A No.

The record does not indicate who the mysterious "Uncle Arturo" was. It would seem irrational for Maria to have pressed the issue if he did not play some role in the unsuccessful effort to bring the immigrants to the United States. Lopez's answer to Maria's question about the uncle could not literally have been true ("No, I have no family."). Perhaps the uncle had been paid for the Salvadorans' trip and had told Lopez that he would pay Maria. That loose end, however, was left hanging.

Plasencia also did not ask Lopez the all-important question whether the INS somehow rewarded her for testifying against Plasencia. Nor did she seek to elicit testimony that would have detailed how the Plasencias came to provide transportation to their undocumented passengers.

The INS trial attorney next called Jose Alfredo Santillana, another Salvadoran, as a witness. On their way back to Los Angeles, the Plasencias had picked Santillana up hitchhiking. A young man in his twenties, Santillana had used the identification card of another one of Maria Plasencia's children in attempting to enter the country. Santillana's testimony contradicted the INS's contention that the Plasencias transported him "for gain":

Q When Mr. and Mrs. Plasencia stop[ped] to pick you up, [what] kind of conversation took place?

A Only that they would just give me a ride to Los Angeles.

Q And was there any mention of money?

A No.

* * *

Q Did you agree to pay Mr. and Mrs., or either one of them, that is Mr. and Mrs. Plasencia anything at all for the transportation into the United States from Mexico?

A No.

Santillana's testimony undercut the INS argument that the Plasencias were bringing people to the United States for financial gain and, in fact, suggests that they did not provide him with transportation for money. The INS trial attorney presumably would not have put him on the witness stand if the substance of his testimony had been known in advance. The pressure of time and a heavy caseload must have hindered the attorney's preparation.

The INS next called Luis Polio–Medina, whose testimony can most generously be described as muddled. Polio–Medina first testified that, at the time that Maria provided him with the minor alien identification card, and apparently a Social Security card, of one of her children, there had not been any discussion of payment for the transportation. In a subsequent confusing exchange, Polio–Medina seemed to testify that he thought that an unidentified friend had made arrangements—the details about which he was wholly unaware—to pay the Plasencias.

The burden of proof greatly influenced the final outcome of Maria Plasencia's case in the immigration court. The testimony of the three witnesses probably would not have satisfied the government's burden of proof ("beyond a reasonable doubt") on any *criminal* smuggling charge. Not surprisingly, the government never brought criminal charges. The Plasencias obviously were not big-time alien smugglers and the evidence of payment was at best mixed. The government probably figured that a criminal prosecution just was not worth the time and effort.

Nor would the government probably have been able to meet its burden of proof ("clear and convincing evidence") if it had sought to deport her rather than bar her from entering the country. For that reason, it is not surprising that the INS at every turn resisted Plasencia's efforts to have her case decided in deportation proceedings.

In the exclusion proceedings, however, Plasencia bore the burden of proof that she was entitled to enter the country and was not excludable. Based on the evidence, she in all likelihood could not satisfy that burden. The immigration judge informed Plasencia that she had the right to call witnesses. She was not told, however, whether the other three passengers, who also were arrested but were not called as witnesses by the INS, were available to testify and whether they had provided statements to the INS. One might speculate that, because the government had arrested the witnesses but did not put them on the stand, their testimony would not have helped to prove the smuggling-for-financial-gain charge and might have helped Maria Plasencia's case.

Maria's case for admission into the United States, then, rested almost entirely on her and her husband's testimony. She admitted that she had agreed to transport the six undocumented immigrants and that she had furnished several of them with her childrens' identification cards. Maria, however, contended that the only payment involved was $25 given to her husband for gasoline. Although the Board of Immigration Appeals had previously concluded that the payment of gas money to an alien might be enough to constitute alien smuggling "for gain,"[20] Plasencia could claim that she herself received no money.

After the testimony of the three INS witnesses, Plasencia elaborated on the story that she had previously laid out for the immigration judge:

> They said that they had no money. The man who makes the arrangements for this trip, they pay him, and that trip is from El Salvador to Los Angeles.... *This lady that I know is the Grandmother of this little child, and she knew that I was coming to Tijuana. Since I was coming, this man who brings them across had this boy here with his birth certificate, and he brought this boy to me and told me it was his child, but he didn't come because he didn't have proper papers.* He said that this child was born in the United States and it was through this that we met these people. I made no arrangements with anybody.... My husband is my witness. They make arrangement [sic] with the person who is going to bring them all the way to the United States. He is an uncle. *They were covering up for the people who are in Los Angeles.* I swear that I have never done this before and I will never do it again. (emphasis added).

This testimony adds further complexity to the events of that weekend. It suggests that Maria Plasencia talked with someone's grandmother about bringing the Salvadorans, who apparently had family or friends waiting for them in Los Angeles, to the United States. A U.S. citizen child also apparently figured in the drama. These assertions were never explored further in the hearing and Plasencia's version of the events was left far from clear.

When his turn came to testify, Joseph Plasencia pleaded on his wife's behalf to the immigration court:

> She has never done this before in her life and [n]either have I and it will never happen again. We ask for your forgiveness, not only from you but also from this officer over here and this lady. We have the children to take care of, they're at home now—. We ask the court, your Honor, and also this officer if you could please forgive not only me but her and we could go home to our children. It will never happen again. I swear on my mother's grave, and I swear on my word of honor, too. It will never happen again.

* * *

This will never, never, this will never happen again as long as I live. Because I do love my wife, and I am very sorry that this incident happened. We do this as a favor to these people, and it turned out to be for the money. It wasn't—but my wife is a good kind hearted person.

Had Maria been represented by an attorney, her story almost certainly would have been developed in greater detail. We might have learned about the role of "Uncle Arturo" and the grandmother in arranging for the Plasencias to bring the Salvadorans to Los Angeles. An attorney could have emphasized that Maria Plasencia was a lawful permanent resident and with strong equities for being permitted to remain in the United States. The record contains little about her, her motives, or her family and community life. What had she done for five years in the United States in addition to setting up a household? What were her ties to the community? What hardships would the family, including a U.S. citizen husband and four lawful permanent resident children, suffer if she were denied re-admission? In essence, why should we want to allow her to return to the United States?

One important fact clearly emerges from the hearing: the Plasencias were by no means sophisticated smugglers of undocumented immigrants, much less part of one of the organized criminal human smuggling networks that later blossomed with the great increase in border enforcement in the 1990s. By all appearances, this was an inept first attempt at bringing undocumented immigrants into the United States. Experienced smugglers would have known that the mere sight of eight adults driving across the border in one car would be a red flag to the Border Patrol, a virtual invitation to stop and question the group.

Even with the holes in the evidence, the immigration judge ruled that "clear, convincing and unequivocal" evidence supported a finding that Plasencia did "knowingly and for gain encourage, induce, assist, abet, or aid nonresident aliens" to enter or try to enter the United States in violation of law. Despite its importance to the resolution of the case, he did not state which party bore the burden of proof. The judge found the testimony of Anna Elsa Lopez and Luis Polio–Medina to be credible, whereas Maria Plasencia's testimony was not. The immigration judge did not explain or justify his credibility determinations, nor did he mention that Santillana's testimony supported Plasencia's defense.

The immigration judge further ruled that, even if Plasencia's version of the events were true, the admitted payment for gasoline was sufficient evidence of gain to establish her excludability under two Board of Immigration Appeals (BIA) rulings,[21] and that her departure from the United States was "meaningfully interruptive" of her residence in this country. In the 1963 decision of *Rosenberg v. Fleuti*,[22] the Supreme Court had ruled that a lawful permanent resident seeking to return after an "innocent, casual, and brief" weekend trip to Mexico was not seeking "entry" or "re-entry" into the United States that could render him excludable under the immigration laws.[23] The immigration court ruled that because Plasencia's conduct was not "innocent" under *Rosenberg v. Fleuti*, her return to the United States constituted a new entry, triggering excludability and deportation.

Less than twenty-four hours after Maria Plasencia's arrest at the border, she had been ordered excluded from the United States. Stripped of her five-year lawful permanent residency, she faced the prospect of separation from her family.

The Board of Immigration Appeals

Despite losing in the immigration court, the Plasencias steadfastly refused to throw in the towel. At the end of her exclusion hearing, Maria filed a notice of appeal to the BIA, along with the $25 filing fee. In support of Maria's appeal, Joseph wrote straight from the heart, not from the law books:

> I feel that my wife is a very kind and considerate person. She is big hearted, and she likes to help people. She never says no to anything. I beg the Court of Appeals with all my heart, and with my word of honor that what I have said is true. I am now left with the children, and they need her. They need their mother. I need her too. I swear on my flag because I was born in the United States that she will never, ever do such a thing again. Due to what happened, it was a favor to start with, out of pity. Then they turned around and accused her of malicious lies. This is not true and never was true. We have been married seven years, and have never been in trouble of any kind before.

> Therefore again, I beg the Court, to please forgive her for the sake of the children and myself. All that these people from El Salvador said about my wife was untrue. Mind you, she has always been an honest person. I am also teaching her the commandments [sic] in order that she could become a United States citizen. In closing I would say that I and the children would appreciate very highly if you would pardon her, and permit her to be home with us again. Thank you very much.
> P.S. Thanks again with my heart, and the children's too.

On September 19, 1975, while her BIA appeal was pending, the INS generously granted Plasencia humanitarian parole without bond for six months, thus allowing her to return to live with her family pending review of the exclusion order. This is another indication that Maria Plasencia's was not the ordinary exclusion case. In seeking release of his wife from INS custody, Joseph Plasencia stated that he had become unemployed and could not support Maria if she was forced to live outside the country. Allowed to enter the United States, Maria and her family were spared forced separation and extended financial hardship. The record is not clear what happened to her between the exclusion hearing in June and her release in September. She may have remained in INS custody or perhaps returned to Mexico during this period; in either case, Maria Plasencia was separated from her family for over three months.

At the BIA, Plasencia was not represented by counsel and waived the right to file a brief. She did not request an oral argument. Not surprisingly, the BIA affirmed the immigration court's ruling and dismissed the appeal in a two-sentence per curiam order not giving any reasons for the decision.

Not long after the BIA dismissed her appeal, Plasencia retained Gary Manulkin, an attorney with, and director of, One Stop Immigration Center, Inc., in Los Angeles, which serves the low-income immigrant community. Manulkin still recalls today that, when he first met Joseph Plasencia, he was desperate to ensure that his wife could stay in the country.[24] Although Manulkin handled the case in the BIA, the district court, and later the Supreme Court, he remembers meeting Maria Plasencia only once.

As we saw, the exclusion hearing had left many evidentiary gaps and many facts far from clear. The first thing that Manulkin did was to move to reopen the proceedings to offer additional evidence to show that Plasencia (1) had not effected an "entry" and was entitled to a deportation hearing with the full panoply of due process protections; and (2) had not knowingly waived her right to counsel.

In a three-page opinion, the BIA rejected both contentions. It denied the motion, finding that Plasencia "was accorded due process of law at every stage of the proceedings." Although denying the motion, the BIA apparently took Maria Plasencia's arguments a good deal more seriously once she had an attorney and, this time, offered an explanation for its ruling.

Appeal to the Federal Courts

Having lost in the BIA, Plasencia filed a petition for a writ of habeas corpus—then the proper way of appealing an exclusion order—in the federal district court in Los Angeles where the Plasencias lived. One Stop Immigration, through Gary Manulkin, continued to represent her. On her behalf, Manulkin contended that Plasencia, as a lawful permanent resident, was entitled to a deportation hearing with its more extensive procedural protections than those afforded in exclusion hearings.

The magistrate assigned to the case issued a Report and Recommendation to the district court judge. Accepting Plasencia's argument, he proposed a finding that, on the basis of evidence adduced at the exclusion hearing, "a meaningful departure [from the country] did not occur . . . and that therefore [Plasencia] is entitled to a *deportation* hearing," rather than an *exclusion* hearing. In the case of a lawful permanent resident like Maria, he reasoned, entry and excludability could not be determined in an exclusion proceeding, which lacked the necessary procedural safeguards; the INS must litigate the "entry" question in a deportation hearing.

The district court adopted the recommendation without comment, and the INS appealed the decision to the U.S. Court of Appeals for the Ninth Circuit. The Ninth Circuit, which decides more immigration cases than any other circuit court, had a reputation in the 1980s and 1990s for being pro-immigrant.[25]

On the appeal to the Ninth Circuit, Denis Campbell of One Stop Immigration took over for Manulkin, who had left One Stop Immigration to go into private practice. The briefs submitted to the Ninth Circuit focused on whether, under *Rosenberg v. Fleuti*, Plasencia's trip had been "innocent, casual, and brief," so that it was not meaningfully interruptive of her presence in the United States and she would be subject to deportation, not exclusion, proceedings. In distinguishing *Fleuti*, the INS relied heavily on the Ninth Circuit's decision in *Palatian v. INS*,[26] which held that a lawful permanent resident who, after leaving the country, had returned with illegal drugs, was re-entering the country because the trip was not "innocent." Playing on the popular fears, the INS contended that "[i]f anything, Plasencia's illegal attempt to smuggle aliens into the country was an even greater affront to the policy of the immigration laws than was Palatian's offense [drug smuggling]."[27] Plasencia's brief argued that *Palatian* was bad law, had been undermined by more recent decisions, and that, in any event, it was distinguishable because (1) Plasencia had been in the United States for many years compared to Palatian's eleven months; and (2) Palatian was ordered removed from the country in exclusion proceedings after serving time for a criminal conviction while Plasencia had not been convicted of any crime.[28]

The Ninth Circuit panel that heard the case included Judges Clifford Wallace, Mary Schroeder, and U.S. District Court Judge Valdemar A. Cordova of the District of Arizona, sitting by designation.[29] In November 1980, the Ninth Circuit, in an opinion written by Judge Schroeder,[30] and joined by Judge Cordova, affirmed the district court's ruling and fully endorsed its reasoning.[31]

Consistent with his generally deferential approach to the executive branch in immigration matters[32] and his philosophy of judicial restraint,[33] Judge Wallace dissented. He would have deferred to the BIA's judgment; Plasencia's "attempt to smuggle illegal aliens across the border made her departure from the United States meaningfully interruptive of her permanent residence. She was thus subject to exclusion on her attempt to enter the country."[34] The INS's motion for rehearing and, in the alternative, petition for rehearing en banc, was denied.

The Supreme Court

The Supreme Court, more conservative in judicial philosophy than the Ninth Circuit, has reversed many of the circuit's decisions, including some immigration cases. *Landon v. Plasencia* turned out to be one of them.

The Solicitor General filed a petition for writ of certiorari with the Supreme Court on behalf of the U.S. government and sought reversal of the Ninth Circuit's decision. Elliott Schulder was the Assistant to the Solicitor General on the petition and later argued the case for the government before the Court. Today, Schulder, now with a prestigious Washington, D.C. law firm, recalls little about *Landon v. Plasencia*; it does not stand out in his mind among the cases that he handled in the Solicitor General's office.[35]

Besides emphasizing the legal and practical importance of the Ninth Circuit's ruling, the government's petition seeking review by the Supreme Court played on the fears of the day: that lax border enforcement was leading to a flood of immigrants and contraband moving across the Mexican border into the United States. It emphasized that the lower court ruling would significantly weaken immigration enforcement by requiring admission of all lawful permanent residents even if "excludable for engaging in such violations as smuggling drugs or aliens." The government further contended that if lawful permanent residents were entitled to deportation proceedings, they would be eligible to apply for the many forms of relief noted earlier, which were not available to those in exclusion proceedings.

Maria Plasencia opposed the petition for writ of certiorari in a brief filed by Denis Campbell of One Stop Immigration, immigration attorney Peter A. Schey, and a group of lawyers from the National Center for Immigrants' Rights (later renamed the National Immigration Law Center), a nationally known immigrant rights organization. The brief defended the Ninth Circuit decision.

The Court granted the certiorari petition on January 11, 1982.

The government's main brief quoted liberally from the Court's 1977 decision in *Fiallo v. Bell*,[36] affirming Congress' plenary power over the admission of immigrants, and contended that the immigration statute required that all aliens seeking to enter the United States, whether undocumented immigrants or lawful permanent residents, be subject to exclusion proceedings. The procedures available to lawful permanent residents in exclusion proceedings, the government maintained, were "substantially similar" to those in deportation proceedings and satisfied due process requirements. Importantly, the government did *not* contend that Plasencia had no due process rights.

Buried under immigration cases and lacking the time necessary for full briefing and argument in the highest court of the land, Denis Campbell, Maria Plasencia's attorney in the Ninth Circuit, had asked the former director of One Stop Immigration, Gary Manulkin, who had represented Plasencia before the BIA and the district court, but not in the Ninth Circuit, to take over the case.[37] Manulkin agreed and was the only attorney listed on Plasencia's brief on the merits. With the assistance of a law clerk interested in Plasencia's case, he handled the case on a pro bono basis.[38]

Plasencia's brief contended that (1) a returning lawful permanent resident was entitled to have the issue of entry and excludability determined in a deportation proceeding, with its greater procedural safeguards; and (2) the immigration court erred in finding that Plasencia was excludable because clear, convincing, and unequivocal evidence did not support the finding that she had smuggled non-citizens into the country for financial gain. More than twenty years later, Manulkin recalls the due process argument as a "throw-in"; he believed that the best bet at prevailing in the case was to convince the Supreme Court that, as the Ninth Circuit held, Plasencia had not been "re-entering" under the *Rosenberg v. Fleuti* doctrine and thus should have the smuggling charges against her decided in deportation proceedings.

In the first week of the 1982 Term, the Supreme Court heard oral argument in *Landon v. Plasencia*. For the government, Elliott Schulder contended that Plasencia's smuggling case must be decided in an exclusion hearing. Schulder, however, made a critical concession in responding to a question from Justice Sandra Day O'Connor:

QUESTION: Mr. Schulder, is it the government's position that assuming an exclusion proceeding is the proper proceeding, that the alien is entitled to due process at that hearing?

MR. SCHULDER: Absolutely, yes.

This concession, which also appeared in the government's brief, loomed large in the case. The government declined to embrace the extreme view staked out by the Supreme Court in two notorious Cold War era immigration decisions ruling that aliens, including lawful permanent residents like Maria Plasencia, had absolutely *no* due process rights in exclusion proceedings. In both *United States* ex rel. *Knauff v. Shaughnessy*[39] and *Shaughnessy v. United States* ex rel. *Mezei*,[40] the

Court affirmed this principle, despite the harsh consequences to the non-citizens in question. In *Knauff*, the government relied on secret evidence to refuse entry to a German citizen who sought to join her U.S. citizen husband under the War Brides Act. In *Mezei*, the government, also based on confidential evidence, denied a hearing to a lawful permanent resident who had lived for twenty-five years in the United States before leaving to visit his dying mother in Romania and who faced the prospect of indefinite detention on Ellis Island because no nation would accept him. As the Supreme Court famously stated in *Knauff*, "[w]hatever the procedure authorized by Congress is, it is due process as far as an alien denied entry is concerned."[41]

Why did the government make the concession about due process in Plasencia's case? Perhaps it saw the writing on the wall. A dramatic expansion of due process rights beginning in the 1960s made the wholesale denial of such rights to lawful permanent residents completely out of step with mainstream constitutional law.[42] *Knauff* and *Mezei* had not aged well; the decisions were initially subject to harsh criticism, which only increased over time.[43] The denial of due process to a long-term lawful permanent resident with a U.S. citizen husband and four children lawfully in the United States strikes modern sensibilities as nothing less than Draconian, the height of bureaucratic tyranny, and unfair. The government presumably decided that it was too risky, based on Maria Plasencia's sympathetic facts, to assert an extreme position based on *Knauff* and *Mezei*.

This strategic decision to concede due process rights even in exclusion proceedings proved to be wise. At oral argument, several justices expressed concern about how little notice Plasencia had received of her exclusion hearing. Notice of a few hours was simply too short a period of time to reasonably expect a lawful permanent resident without legal representation to prepare for a hearing whose outcome would determine whether she could re-join family, friends, and the life she had created during her five years in the United States. In contrast, an undocumented immigrant arrested in the interior of the country—even if only in the country for a single day—would be entitled to a deportation hearing with the full panoply of due process rights, including ample advance notice before the hearing.[44]

When questioned, Elliott Schulder readily accepted the suggestion from the bench that, if the Court held that Plasencia was only entitled to an exclusion proceeding, remand of the case would be appropriate to determine whether Plasencia's due process rights had been violated. This acceptance foreshadowed the Supreme Court's ultimate decision.

On November 15, 1982, about five weeks after oral argument, the Supreme Court issued its decision in *Landon v. Plasencia*, one of the

Court's first decisions of the new Term. In an opinion written by Justice Sandra Day O'Connor, who had been an active questioner in oral argument, the Court reversed the Ninth Circuit's decision and held that the question whether Plasencia had entered the country could be determined in an exclusion hearing, but also that this hearing must comport with due process. The Court adhered to its holding in *Rosenberg v. Fleuti*[45] that an "innocent, casual and brief excursion" outside the United States by a lawful permanent resident would not, upon her return, mean that she was engaged in a new "entry" into the country. This question, however, need not be resolved in a deportation hearing; the immigration statute "clearly reflect[s] a congressional intent that, whether or not the alien is a permanent resident, admissibility shall be determined in an exclusion hearing."[46] The Court reasoned that, although *Kwong Hai Chew v. Colding*[47] held "that a resident alien returning from a brief trip has a right to due process just as would a continuously present resident alien[, it did] not create a right to identical treatment for these two differently situated groups of aliens."[48] The issue of Plasencia's alleged "entry" could therefore be resolved in an exclusion hearing, so long as it provided her with due process.

The Court restated the essence of *Knauff/Mezei* that "an alien seeking initial admission has *no* constitutional rights regarding his application, for the power to admit or exclude aliens is a sovereign prerogative."[49] However, the Court went on to observe that "once an alien gains admission to our country and begins to develop the ties that go with permanent residence, his constitutional status changes accordingly. Our cases have frequently suggested that a continuously present resident alien is entitled to a fair hearing when threatened with deportation...."[50] It emphasized that "[w]e need not now decide the scope of *Mezei*; it does not govern this case, for Plasencia was absent from the country only a few days, and *the United States has conceded that she has a right to due process.*"[51]

The Court proceeded to state that the flexible *Mathews v. Eldridge* balancing test—the general test previously articulated by the Court for evaluating whether governmental procedures complied with due process—applied to determining the specific procedures that due process required in Plasencia's immigration case:

> [T]he courts must consider the interest at stake for the individual, the risk of an erroneous deprivation of the interest through the procedures used as well as the probable value of additional or different procedural safeguards, and the interest of the government in using the current procedures rather than additional or different procedures.[52]

Although declining to strike the balance itself in Plasencia's case, the Court noted that she had a "weighty" interest at stake because she "stands to lose the right 'to stay and live and work in this land of freedom'" and "may lose the right to rejoin her immediate family, a right that ranks high among the interests of the individual."[53] It further observed that "[t]he government's interest in efficient administration of the immigration laws at the border also is weighty."[54] The Court reminded the lower court that, on remand, it could only decide "whether the procedures meet the essential standard of fairness under the Due Process Clause and [could not impose] procedures that merely displace congressional choices of policy,"[55] thus paying homage to the cases in which the Court deferred to the decisions of administrative agencies.

The Court raised questions about whether it was fair to have placed the burden of proof on Plasencia in her exclusion hearing, provided the short notice that she was given. Hinting at the need for regulations in these areas, the Court emphasized that "[i]f the exclusion hearing is to ensure fairness, it must provide Plasencia an opportunity to present her case effectively."[56]

Justice Thurgood Marshall concurred in part and dissented in part. Although agreeing that the government could proceed against Maria Plasencia in exclusion proceedings, he concluded that the hearing had violated due process by not giving her adequate and timely notice of the charges against her and of her right to retain counsel and present a defense: "[i]t was not until the commencement of the hearing that she was given notice in her native language of the charges against her and of her right to retain counsel and to present evidence."[57]

The Aftermath

Despite the fanfare, *Landon v. Plasencia* ended with little more than a whimper. On remand from the Supreme Court, the Ninth Circuit sent the case back to the district court, where the case effectively ended. The INS appears never to have sought to remove Maria Plasencia from the country. Thus it never had to take on the unenviable task of trying to persuade a court that her due process rights had not been violated in the original exclusion hearing.

Neither of Plasencia's attorneys, Denis Campbell and Gary Manulkin, has been in touch with her since the Supreme Court decision in 1982. As far as they know, Maria, who had been paroled into the United States pending appeal of her case, simply continued her life as a lawful permanent resident. Campbell suspects that, given the smuggling charges made against her, Maria might have experienced legal problems had she tried to naturalize. Consequently, she may still be a lawful permanent resident even after living more than thirty years in the United States.

The government presumably decided not to proceed against Maria because of the pro-immigrant due process law that the courts might have created if they had addressed her due process claims. The hasty proceedings against a long-term lawful permanent resident with a citizen husband and four children lawfully in the United States, and who did not pose a serious risk of danger to the community, probably would not have survived constitutional scrutiny, as the Supreme Court strongly hinted. In any event, had the INS persisted in trying to exclude Maria Plasencia, she might have obtained discretionary relief under former Immigration & Nationality Act § 212(c), repealed in 1996, which required seven years of residence in the country. The time consumed by her appeals would have satisfied the time requirement for this form of relief.

More generally, the Supreme Court's decision in *Landon v. Plasencia* has had a mixed legacy. The courts dutifully abided by the Court's holding that, when seeking re-entry into the country, a lawful permanent resident's claim of admissibility must be determined in exclusion proceedings.[58] Some courts, however, also viewed *Landon v. Plasencia* as standing for the proposition that the rights of lawful permanent residents increased as the length of their time in the country grew and thus were greater than those of first-time entrants.[59] In contrast, some courts have taken language from the decision to support Congress' plenary power with respect to the procedures accorded certain non-citizens seeking initial entry into the country.[60]

Importantly, other cases understood *Landon v. Plasencia* to require that the *Mathews v. Eldridge* balancing test be applied to evaluate whether hearing procedures were consistent with due process.[61] In 1988, the BIA ruled that a returning lawful permanent resident like Plasencia in exclusion proceedings must be given reasonable notice of the charges, as well as a procedurally fair hearing with the INS bearing the burden of proof; the lawful permanent resident could be excluded only upon a showing by clear, unequivocal, and convincing evidence of excludability[62] —procedures that differed dramatically from those afforded to Maria Plasencia.

Some immigration law scholars read *Landon v. Plasencia* as opening the door for expanded constitutional rights for non-citizens seeking entry.[63] They see the decision as a "crack" in the plenary power doctrine, which scholars almost universally scorn.[64] Other commentators, however, are more circumspect, emphasizing that *Landon v. Plasencia* included strong plenary power doctrine language and failed to define the constitutional rights of lawful permanent residents, including Plasencia, with any specificity.[65] Importantly, the Supreme Court has passed up several subsequent opportunities to overrule plenary power doctrine decisions such as *Knauff* and *Mezei*, which remain good law.[66] Indeed, the federal government's justification for many of its security responses directed at immigration and immigrants after September 11, 2001 has relied on the doctrine.[67]

Prompted by *Landon v. Plasencia*, Congress in 1996 amended the immigration statute to provide that returning lawful permanent residents seeking to enter the country are generally not subject to the same procedures and inadmissibility grounds as first-time entrants. The new law provides that a lawful permanent resident stopped at the border generally is *not* treated as seeking admission into the country;[68] this shifts the legal focus to whether the alien has been admitted into the country previously rather than whether there has been an entry,[69] and entitles most lawful permanent residents at the border to a "removal" proceeding, the equivalent of the old deportation hearing, with broader procedural protections than they would have enjoyed in the exclusion proceedings to which Maria Plasencia had been subjected. A beneficial dialogue between the Supreme Court in *Landon v. Plasencia* and Congress thus secured greater rights for lawful permanent residents and arguably made immigration procedures more consistent with mainstream constitutional norms.

Conclusion

The story of Maria and Joseph Plasencia shows a rather ordinary couple—one an immigrant, the other a native-born U.S. citizen—caught up in larger national and international tides. Far from a passive observer, Maria Plasencia refused to concede removal, but pressed her claim to return to her family in the United States. Legally, the Supreme Court decision in the case was a partial loss for Maria, but, released pending appeal and never pursued by the INS after the Supreme Court's decision, she returned to normal life in the United States with her family. This at the time was not that uncommon in immigration cases, even those in which the government claimed legal victory. Uneven enforcement, and the ability of immigrants to delay removal from the United States, often worked to their advantage. Since 1982, however, the federal government has made the deportation of non-citizens subject to removal—particularly those with criminal convictions—a priority, with the result being that immigration enforcement has tightened and record numbers of non-citizens have been detained and deported.

The Supreme Court's decision in *Landon v. Plasencia* had more general ripple effects. It extended due process rights to certain lawful permanent residents seeking entry into the United States and marked the end of the blanket denial of rights to every non-citizen seeking entry.

The executive branch and Congress followed the Court's lead and lawful permanent residents returning to the country today generally have the right to fundamental procedural protections before they can be denied entry into the country. This is an example of the Court prodding the political process in a way that resulted in the expansion of rights to non-citizens.

ENDNOTES

1. See, for example, Orantes–Hernandez v. Thornburgh, 919 F.2d 549 (9th Cir. 1990).

2. See American Baptist Churches v. Thornburgh, 760 F. Supp. 796 (N.D. Cal. 1991).

3. See, for example, 8 C.F.R. § 208.7 (2004) (limiting work authorization for asylum applicants); Immigration & Nationality Act (INA) § 208(d)(2), 8 U.S.C. § 1158(d)(2) (amended in 1996) (same); INA § 235(b)(1), 8 U.S.C. § 1225(b)(1) (amended in 1996) (creating a new system of expedited removal at ports of entry).

4. See Pub. L. No. 96–212, 94 Stat. 102 (1980); Harvey Gee, The Refugee Burden: A Closer Look at the Refugee Act of 1980, 26 N.C. J. Int'l L. & Com. Reg. 559 (2001).

5. See Mark S. Hamm, The Abandoned Ones: The Imprisonment and Uprising of the Mariel Boat People (1995).

6. See Sale v. Haitian Centers Council, Inc., 509 U.S. 155 (1993).

7. See Administration's Proposals on Immigration and Refugee Policy: Joint Hearing Before the Subcomm. on Immigration, Refugees, and International Law of the House Comm. on the Judiciary and Subcomm. on Immigration and Refugee Policy of the Senate Comm. on the Judiciary, 97th Cong., 1st Sess. 6 (1981).

8. Pub. L. No. 99–603, 100 Stat. 3359 (1986).

9. Pub. L. No. 99–639, 100 Stat. 3537 (1986).

10. For discussion and statistics on the deaths, see Wayne A. Cornelius, Death at the Border: Efficacy and Unintended Consequences of US Immigration Control Policy, 1993–2000, 27 Population & Dev. Rev. 661 (2001); Karl Eschbach et al., Death at the Border, 33 Int'l Migration Rev. 430 (1999); Bill Ong Hing, The Dark Side of Operation Gatekeeper, 7 U.C. Davis J. Int'l L. & Pol'y 121 (2001). For accounts of the deaths of Mexican migrants attempting to cross the border, see Ken Ellingwood, Hard Line: Life and Death on the U.S.-Mexico Border (2004); Luis Alberto Urrea, The Devil's Highway: A True Story (2004).

11. United States v. Valenzuela–Bernal, 458 U.S. 858, 864 n.5 (1982).

12. United States v. Cortez, 449 U.S. 411, 418 (1981).

13. United States v. Martinez–Fuerte, 428 U.S. 543, 552 (1976).

14. United States v. Brignoni–Ponce, 422 U.S. 873, 878–89 (1975).

15. See, e.g., INS v. Wang, 450 U.S. 139, 144 (1981); INS v. Rios–Pineda, 471 U.S. 444, 451 (1985).

16. 467 U.S. 837 (1984).

17. 459 U.S. 21 (1982).

18. 8 U.S.C. § 1182(a)(31) (later amended).

19. Lopez also used the name Eugenia Linares–Moreno. See Landon v. Plasencia, 459 U.S. 21, 40 n.5 (1982) (Marshall, J., dissenting). Lopez testified that Anna Elsa Lopez was her legal name but that Maria Plasencia had told her to use an assumed name to cross the border.

20. See Matter of P–G–, 7 I. & N. Dec. 514 (BIA 1957); Matter of B–G–, 8 I. & N. Dec. 182 (BIA 1958).

21. See id.

22. 374 U.S. 449, 462 (1963). In *Rosenberg v. Fleuti*, the lawful permanent resident faced exclusion from the country, after a brief weekend trip across the Mexican border, on the ground that he was homosexual, a ground for exclusion under the immigration laws until 1990. See Kevin R. Johnson, The "Huddled Masses" Myth: Immigration and Civil Rights 140–51 (2004).

23. The version of INA § 101(a)(13), 8 U.S.C. § 1101(a)(13) in effect at the time defined "entry" as

> any coming of an alien into the United States ... except that an alien having a lawful permanent residence in the United States shall not be regarded as making an entry into the United States ... if the alien proves ... that his departure to a foreign port or place or to an outlying possession was not intended or reasonably to be expected by him....

Congress amended this section in 1996. See infra note 68.

24. Telephone interview with Gary H. Manulkin on Feb. 5, 2004.

25. At the time, the reversal of the Board of Immigration Appeals by the federal courts was not uncommon. See generally Peter H. Schuck & Theodore H. Wang, Continuity and Change: Patterns of Immigration Litigation in the Courts, 1979–1990, 45 Stan. L. Rev. 115 (1992) (providing data on federal court decisions in immigration cases from 1970–90).

26. 502 F.2d 1091 (9th Cir. 1974).

27. Appellant's (INS) Brief, Plasencia v. Sureck, 637 F.2d 1286 (9th Cir. 1980) (Case No. 78–2641), at 8.

28. See Appellant's [sic] (Plasencia) Brief, Plasencia v. Sureck, 637 F.2d 1286 (9th Cir. 1980) (Case No. 78–2641), at 4–5. Plasencia's attorney may have misnamed the brief as "Appellant's" because his immigrant clients ordinarily were appealing adverse rulings, and thus usually were appellants rather than appellees.

29. Cordova was the first Latino judge from Arizona appointed to the federal judiciary.

30. Judge Schroeder, who was appointed by President Jimmy Carter, later became Chief Judge of the Ninth Circuit. About a decade after writing the court of appeals opinion in *Plasencia v. Sureck*, Judge Schroeder wrote the landmark decision in Orantes–Hernandez v. Thornburgh, 919 F.2d 549 (9th Cir. 1990), which affirmed the entry of a permanent injunction prohibiting the INS from coercing, through detention and other means, Salvadorans to agree to "voluntarily" depart from the United States rather than pursue their claims to asylum.

31. Plasencia v. Sureck, 637 F.2d 1286 (9th Cir. 1980).

32. See, e.g., Fisher v. INS, 79 F.3d 955 (9th Cir. 1996); Ghaly v. INS, 58 F.3d 1425 (9th Cir. 1995); McMullen v. INS, 788 F.2d 591 (9th Cir. 1986).

33. See J. Clifford Wallace, The Jurisprudence of Judicial Restraint: A Return to the Moorings, 50 Geo. Wash. L. Rev. 1 (1981).

34. Plasencia v. Sureck, 637 F.3d at 1291 (Wallace, J., dissenting).

35. E–Mail message from Elliot Schulder to Kevin R. Johnson, dated May 4, 2004.

36. 430 U.S. 787, 792 (1977).

37. Telephone interview with Denis W. Campbell on Jan. 28, 2004.

38. Telephone interview with Gary H. Manulkin on Feb. 5, 2004.

39. 338 U.S. 537 (1950).

40. 345 U.S. 206 (1953).

41. *Knauff,* 338 U.S. at 544 (citations omitted). The cases of Ignatz Mezei and Ellen Knauff are analyzed in Charles D. Weisselberg, The Exclusion and Detention of Aliens: Lessons from the Lives of Ellen Knauff and Ignatz Mezei, 143 U. Pa. L. Rev. 933 (1995).

42. See, e.g., Goldberg v. Kelly, 397 U.S. 254 (1970).

43. See Henry Hart, The Power of Congress to Limit the Jurisdiction of Federal Courts: An Exercise in Dialectic, 66 Harv. L. Rev. 1362, 1391–96 (1953).

44. Under the regulation in place at the time of Plasencia's arrest, the INS generally required that an alien be afforded seven days' notice. See Landon v. Plasencia, 459 U.S. at 26 (citing 8 C.F.R. § 242.1(b) (1982)).

45. 374 U.S. 449, 462 (1963).

46. Landon v. Plasencia, 459 U.S. at 28.

47. 344 U.S. 590 (1953).

48. Landon v. Plasencia, 459 U.S. at 31 (footnote omitted).

49. Id. at 32 (emphasis added).

50. Id. (citations omitted). One of the authorities relied on by the Court for this proposition was Johnson v. Eisentrager, 339 U.S. 763, 770 (1950), a case that later was much-debated in connection with the indefinite detention after September 11, 2001 of two U.S. citizens, Jose Padilla and Yaser Hamdi, whom the Bush administration classified as "enemy combatants." In *Eisentrager,* the Court highlighted the fact that the rights of a non-citizen who had resided in the United States ordinarily increased with the length of residence, which stood in stark contrast to the rights of "enemy aliens" in times of war.

51. Landon v. Plasencia, 459 U.S. at 34 (citing transcript to Oral Argument at 6, 9, 14 and Brief for Petitioner at 9–10, 20–21) (emphasis added).

52. 459 U.S. at 34 (citing Mathews v. Eldridge, 424 U.S. 319, 334–35 (1976)).

53. 459 U.S. at 34 (citations omitted).

54. Id.

55. Id. at 34–35.

56. Id. at 36.

57. Id. at 37, 39 (Marshall, J., concurring in part, dissenting in part).

58. See, e.g., INS v. Phinpathya, 464 U.S. 183, 193 (1984); Ali v. Reno, 22 F.3d 442, 448 (2d Cir. 1994).

59. See, e.g., Rhoden v. United States, 55 F.3d 428, 432 (9th Cir. 1995); Campos v. INS, 961 F.2d 309, 316 (1st Cir. 1992).

60. See, e.g., Cuban Am. Bar Ass'n v. Christopher, 43 F.3d 1412, 1428 (11th Cir. 1995); Haitian Ctrs. Council v. McNary, 969 F.2d 1326, 1340 (2d Cir. 1992), vacated as moot sub nom. Sale v. Haitian Centers Council, Inc., 509 U.S. 918 (1993).

61. See, e.g., Zadvydas v. Davis, 533 U.S. 678, 694 (2001); Flores v. Meese, 934 F.2d 991, 1013 (9th Cir. 1990), rev'd on other grounds, 507 U.S. 292 (1993).

62. See Matter of Huang, 19 I. & N. Dec. 749, 753–54 (BIA 1988); see, e.g., Khodagholian v. Ashcroft, 335 F.3d 1003, 1006 (9th Cir. 2003); Rosendo–Ramirez v. INS, 32 F.3d 1085, 1090 (7th Cir. 1994).

63. See, e.g., David A. Martin, Due Process and Membership in the National Community: Political Asylum and Beyond, 44 U. Pitt. L. Rev. 165, 214–15 (1983); Hiroshi Motomura, The Curious Evolution of Immigration Law: Procedural Surrogates for Substantive Constitutional Rights, 92 Colum. L. Rev. 1625, 1652–56 (1992); Hiroshi Motomura, Immigration Law After a Century of Plenary Power: Phantom Constitutional Norms and Statutory Interpretation, 100 Yale L.J. 545, 578–780 (1990); Michael Scaperlanda, Partial Membership: Aliens and the Constitutional Community, 81 Iowa L. Rev. 707, 744–45 (1996).

64. See, e.g., T. Alexander Aleinikoff, Semblances of Sovereignty: The Constitution, the State, and American Citizenship 151–81 (2002); Gerald L. Neuman, Strangers to the Constitution: Immigrants, Borders, and Fundamental Law (1996); Gabriel J. Chin, Segregation's Last Stronghold: Race Discrimination and the Constitutional Law of Immigration, 46 UCLA L. Rev. 1 (1998).

65. See Stephen H. Legomsky, Immigration Law and the Principle of Plenary Congressional Power, 1984 S. Ct. Rev. 255, 260 nn.25–26; Peter H. Schuck, The Transformation of Immigration Law, 84 Colum. L. Rev. 1, 62–63 & n.342 (1984).

66. See, e.g., Nguyen v. INS, 533 U.S. 53 (2001); Miller v. Albright, 523 U.S. 420 (1998); Jean v. Nelson, 472 U.S. 846 (1985).

67. See Kif Augustine–Adams, The Plenary Power Doctrine after September 11, 38 U.C. Davis L. Rev. 701 (2005).

68. INA § 101(a)(13)(C), 8 U.S.C. § 1101(a)(13)(C) (as amended by § 301(a) of the Illegal Immigration Reform and Immigrant Responsibility Act of 1996, Pub. L. No. 104–208, 110 Stat. 3009–546—3009–575 (1996)), provides that a lawful permanent resident

> shall not be regarded as seeking admission into the United States for purposes of the immigration laws unless the alien
>
> (i) has abandoned or relinquished that status,
>
> (ii) has been absent from the United States for a continuous period in excess of 180 days,
>
> (iii) has engaged in illegal activity after having departed the United States,
>
> (iv) has departed from the United States while under legal process seeking removal of the alien from the United States . . . ,
>
> (v) has committed an offense identified in section 212(a)(2) . . . , or
>
> (vi) is attempting to enter at a time or place other than as designated by immigration officers or has not been admitted to the United States after inspection and authorization by an immigration officer.

The legislative history suggests that Congress sought to codify the portion of *Rosenberg v. Fleuti* ensuring that most lawful permanent residents who had left the country for a brief period would not be considered as seeking entry. See House Report No. 104–469, 104th Cong., 2d Sess. 225–26 (1996). This new law came into play in the much publicized case of Jesus Collado, a long-term permanent resident who had a criminal conviction as a young man, and who was subject to exclusion proceedings even though he had only briefly left the country to visit the Dominican Republic. See Matter of Jesus Collado, 21 I. & N. Dec. 1061 (BIA 1998).

69. See David A. Martin, Graduated Application of Constitutional Protections for Aliens: The Real Meaning of *Zadvydas v. Davis*, 2001 Sup. Ct. Rev. 47, 64–66.

10

Adelaide Abankwah, Fauziya Kasinga, and the Dilemmas of Political Asylum

David A. Martin[1]

The story of Adelaide Abankwah reveals both real strengths and disquieting weaknesses in the institution of political asylum and in the American system for receiving and resolving asylum claims. The revelations become particularly sharp when Abankwah's case is viewed against the backdrop of a precedent decision decided just nine months before she arrived in the United States, *Matter of Kasinga*.[2] Both Abankwah and Fauziya Kasinga[3] based their claims on the threat that they would be subjected to female genital mutilation (FGM)* in their home countries in West Africa.[4] Both applications for asylum encountered skepticism and resistance, on factual and legal grounds. Both women endured lengthy periods in detention while awaiting resolution of their cases, and both achieved a remarkable degree of public notoriety during the wait. Not until the Board of Immigration Appeals (BIA) decided to grant asylum to Kasinga in 1996 did the U.S. system fully come to grips, as a matter of doctrine, with asylum claims based on this sort of ingrained cultural practice. That ruling resolved several key legal issues, but it did not make the subsequent administrative and judicial decisions in the *Abankwah* case easy or straightforward. In fact, Abankwah's case ultimately reached an unexpected ending that required over six years to unfold.

American law, like that of most other nations, offers asylum to persons who demonstrate that they are unwilling to return to their home countries because of a "well-founded fear of persecution on account of race, religion, nationality, membership in a particular social group, or political opinion."[5] A successful claim ordinarily trumps other violations

---

* FGM involves the cutting away of some or all of a girl's or young woman's external genitalia, usually in the belief that it prepares her for adulthood or preserves her purity. Practices vary, but the cutting can range from removal of part or all of the clitoris to removal also of the labia minora and closure of most of the vaginal opening. Often performed under unsanitary conditions, the cutting can cause long-term physical as well as psychological harm. An estimated 80–140 million women now alive have been subjected to this procedure, in one or another form, mostly in Africa but also in some parts of Asia.

of immigration law, and can lead after a few years to full lawful permanent resident status and ultimately to U.S. citizenship. Asylum cases present significant challenges of both fact and law. How can adjudicators predict what would befall an individual upon return to a distant country? What proof should applicants offer? How can adjudicators tell if the applicant is embroidering the story, or making it up out of whole cloth? What sorts of harm amount to persecution? How great must the risk be to make the fear well-founded? When does persecution have an adequate nexus to one of the five grounds listed in the statute? What is one to make of the most vague or open-ended factor in that list, membership in a particular social group? How should asylum claimants be housed and cared for while their cases are adjudicated? Under what circumstances should they be detained? Each of these questions played a role in the Kasinga and Abankwah stories.

Abankwah's History

Arrival and Initial Proceedings

Adelaide Abankwah, a twenty-seven-year-old citizen of Ghana, arrived at New York's JFK airport on March 29, 1997, bearing what a forensic document expert later described as a "fairly sophisticated" altered passport.[6] According to one published account, she was initially cleared through the border inspection process and was searching for the proper exit when a different officer called her back for further checking.[7] After a closer interview, the inspector decided to hold her for a formal removal hearing before an immigration judge (IJ), meantime sending her to the Wackenhut detention facility near the airport, operated by a private corporation under contract with the Immigration and Naturalization Service (INS).[8] Wackenhut became her home for the next twenty-seven months.

She first appeared before an immigration judge four days later, at an abbreviated hearing known as "master calendar," analogous to a status call in a civil case or arraignment in a criminal case. The judge advised her about the charges, her rights, and the immigration court process that would unfold, in the normal course, over the next few weeks. He also provided her, as the regulations require, with a list of pro bono legal services potentially available in the New York area, urging her to get a lawyer: "[Y]ou better prepare, okay? And you'll need some help."[9]

These required advisories by the judge reflect certain key features of the U.S. immigration court system. Immigration cases often require sophisticated legal representation for full and fair presentation of any possible defenses, particularly asylum claims. The Immigration and Nationality Act guarantees the right to a lawyer, but—pointedly—"at no expense to the government."[10] As though out of embarrassment at the system's failure to provide appointed counsel when the stakes are potentially so high, administrative practice has generated a rough accommodation: aliens in removal proceedings are given a regularly updated list of local persons or organizations who provide pro bono legal services.[11] Pro bono attorneys, however, having limited resources, often insist on interviewing a caller in detail, usually in person, before deciding whether to accept the case. The attendant delays often frustrate both the individual and government officials wanting to move the caseload—and indeed Congress, particularly if INS is paying for detention costs in the meantime (which can run $50 to $200 per day). By statute, Congress has essentially signaled that it considers ten days long enough to secure counsel and that the individual should proceed pro se if no attorney has been arranged by then.[12] But immigration judges, more familiar with the human realities involved, regularly grant additional time.

Adelaide Abankwah received seven more continuances before she was able to appear with counsel. She made telephone calls but always seemed to encounter problems. In one of several confusing dialogues with the judge, on April 25, at the fourth master calendar, she said that after she explained her case over the phone, the lawyer "said my case, I have to go back. And I told her I cannot go back because I ran away with that passport. And she said she can't do anything about that." The attorney also told her that "asylum is supposed to be political. And I said mine is not political. It's my working place." The judge then seemingly tried to discourage her from continuing with an asylum claim, pointing out that problems with her employer would not fit the asylum standards. In response, Abankwah, for the first time, spoke of additional problems in her village, relating somehow to her mother's role as a former queen mother of the tribe. In the end, the judge pressed her to complete the asylum application form, Form I–589, on her own even if she had difficulty in getting an attorney.[13] On May 20, she said she had completed the form but had met new difficulties in nailing down the services of attorneys she had thought would help. Perhaps discouraged by these problems and the detention still awaiting her, she openly considered withdrawing the claim and going home. But the judge was patient, carefully pointing out that she could ask for asylum without an attorney, if necessary. She ultimately decided to persevere. The judge accepted the I–589 for filing, but did not at that time have her sign it.[14] Finally, on July 3, Abankwah appeared at a master calendar hearing with counsel: Olga Narymsky, staff attorney for the Hebrew Immigrant Aid Society, a well-established refugee assistance organization. But counsel needed additional time for preparation, costing Abankwah another two months at Wackenhut.[15]

Immigration Court Preliminaries: The Documentary Filings

On September 9, 1997, the merits hearing finally commenced before Immigration Judge Donn Livingston. He had previously ordered that

Abankwah have the assistance of a Fanti interpreter, although she had maintained in earlier hearings that she was capable of proceeding in English.[16] (This form of assistance, unlike legal representation, is provided at government expense.) The judge inquired whether Abankwah would rely on the I–589 form previously submitted. "With certain corrections," was Narymsky's reply. Abankwah had written "Biriwa" when asked for her religion, but that was her home village. The entry was accordingly corrected to "Christian." And Abankwah had listed a spouse and date of marriage in September 1996 on the form. But, Narymsky stated, "she's not married. The person she listed as her husband is her boyfriend." With those changes noted, the judge asked Abankwah to sign and formally swear to the truth of the information contained in the application form.[17] It was then entered into the record, along with a September 5 Abankwah affidavit elaborating on the claim, two State Department memoranda—one discussing in general asylum claims from Ghana, the other titled "Female Genital Mutilation (FGM) in Ghana"—and a variety of other supporting documents.

These documents reveal the value added by attorney representation. The application form, filled out in longhand by Abankwah without counsel and submitted in May, is hard to follow and mentions a grab-bag of concerns about what would happen to her if she returned to Ghana. In responding to the key questions concerning why she was applying for asylum and what she thought would happen to her if she returned to Ghana, Abankwah's reply first discusses at some length her Accra employer's pursuit of her for money lost while she was employed there. Only then does she begin to discuss the reasons for fear of returning to her village: primarily, that she could not accept the role of queen mother, succeeding her own mother who recently died. She mentions many objections to taking on that role. They seem to include certain ceremonial clothing requirements, an obligation to take part in a ceremony that involves pouring blood on her feet, and concern about what she might have to do during royal funerals: "[Y]ou have to attend the funeral with human head because they will do the same when you also die." At several points, the handwritten explanation also addresses her fear of what would happen to her because she had previously had sex with a man. "And the worst thing is when they will fine out that you are not virgin they will cut your [illegible] so that you wouldn't feel for men, and true that you can die."[18]

Asylum applications prepared with the assistance of skilled counsel from the beginning usually answer the questions on the Form I–589 far more concisely, and are then accompanied by a detailed affidavit executed by the applicant, stating in chronological narrative the key parts of the person's background history and the central reasons why she fears return. Such an affidavit is usually prepared after hours of interviews with the client, during which the attorney can identify those parts of the story that are legally relevant to the asylum claim and present them in a logical order. It is common for clients to have only a general idea of the meaning of asylum. Often the bad things most on their minds that might happen if they return to their homeland, such as crop failures or severe drought, are simply not grounds for protection. Abankwah's rambling handwritten application, highlighting the Accra dispute, shows this tendency. An attorney can help clients understand what is legally significant.

Narymsky chose not to file a new form, perhaps because the first one had already been filed with the court and shared with INS when she took up her role as counsel. Instead she asked only for the two limited modifications before Abankwah swore to it, and then filed a compact supplemental affidavit from Abankwah, consisting of seven paragraphs.[19] Providing a more logical account of Abankwah's background, the affidavit also focused on the core element of the claim—certainly the part that would capture public attention.

The first paragraph was crisp and to the point: "I am a native and citizen of Ghana. I fled my country to avoid the practice known as female genital mutilation (FGM)." The affidavit then skillfully wove in some of the less relevant material mentioned in the handwritten form, downplaying it in the process. For example, the ceremony that involves blood— now revealed as sheep's blood—running on the feet has shifted from a possible objectionable practice to simply an illustration, among several others, of the religious responsibilities of a queen mother. (No mention was made, however, of human heads at funerals, nor of the Accra financial dispute.) The affidavit then described Abankwah's conversion to Christianity when she went away to school.

The next three paragraphs set forth the central elements of the claim:

> 4. As an oldest daughter, I was supposed to become the "Queen Mother" after my mother's death. The tradition required that the woman who is next in line to become the "Queen Mother" must remain a virgin until she is enstooled. After she is enstooled, the village elders select a husband for her. I never wished to become the "Queen Mother" because it went against my Christian believes. I did not obey the tradition, and became secretly involved with a young men whom I loved. When my mother died, and it was my turn to become the "Queen Mother," I was no longer a virgin.

> 5. I knew that the elders would discover that I was not a virgin. Before being enstooled, the newly selected Queen Mother has to go through a ritual which is supposed to reveal whether

or not she is a virgin. She must hold a bowl filled with water, as the elders perform a ritual prayer. If the woman had known men before, she will start to shake and will drop the bowl. Even if she does not betray herself at this stage, once she is married, it will be discovered that she is not a virgin.

    6.   In my tribe, sex before marriage is condemned, and the woman is punished by being forced to undergo FGM. I personally knew three women who were mutilated for this reason. If I refuse to become the "Queen Mother," the people will know that something is wrong and will suspect that I must have had an affair. I will be mutilated, and my lover will be found and executed. After that, I will have to live the rest of my life in shame.

Narymsky, again following good practice in asylum representation, also provided additional documentary evidence to support her client's case, mindful of the BIA's recent insistence on corroboration wherever it might appear possible.[20] Narymsky located a Ghanaian-born U.S. citizen, Victoria Otumfuor, a Pentecostal minister who often traveled to Ghana, to provide a short affidavit that modestly bolstered some of the specific details in Abankwah's account.[21] Effective asylum attorneys also annex to the application form additional background information to provide context, including general information documenting human rights abuses in the country of origin. Narymsky submitted a collection of published studies, 140 pages in total. One report, done by an advocacy and research organization called Rainbo, provided a general description of FGM and its incidence. The other two were academic studies focused specifically on FGM in Ghana, sponsored by the Ghanaian Association for Women's Welfare.[22]

Direct Examination of Abankwah

    With the documents introduced, Narymsky called her client to the stand. Abankwah's testimony on direct examination, done this time with the services of the interpreter (and therefore far clearer than her testimony in English at the master calendar hearings), initially followed fairly closely the account sketched in her affidavit. Then counsel asked her to explain the problems she encountered in Accra, and why she did not feel she could safely return there. Perhaps Narymsky pursued this theme in order to ward off any INS effort to undermine Abankwah's credibility by noting that her earlier comments and filings had emphasized a different risk. This line of inquiry also helped counter one other possible reason for denying asylum, often called the "internal flight alternative"—the chance that she could find safety in a different part of her own country and therefore did not need refuge outside Ghana.[23] Abankwah explained that when she could not pay the money her employers demanded of her, they went to her home village to seek her. "Then the villagers got to know that I have been in Accra." She elaborated: "If I return to Accra, I don't know where to go in Accra at the moment. I have to return to my village, and when I go to my village, they will kill me. That's why I came over here."[24] On redirect she would speak twice more of the risk that they would kill her, thus escalating her description of the consequences of return.[25]

Narymsky also used direct examination for another bit of anticipatory defense, by asking about Abankwah's passport and why she did not admit under early INS questioning that her document was false. Case law makes it clear that the use of false documents as part of the immediate escape from the country of persecution should not count against the individual, but immigration judges are often wary of the credibility of such persons if they do not own up to the fraud and reveal the full story promptly after arriving in a safe country.[26] She conceded that she said several times to the border inspectors that the passport was really hers.[27] Only when assured that she would be taken to court if she told the truth did she relent. Some friends in Accra had offered to help her get the documents, she said; she only had to supply them with two pictures of herself.

Cross-examination of Abankwah

It was then time for cross-examination by the INS trial attorney, James Paoli. Trial attorneys carry heavy caseloads and typically have only an hour or two preparation time before a merits hearing in an asylum case, though complex or novel cases may give rise to longer allowances. Their research may consist only of reviewing the file and perhaps pulling together some readily accessible information about general conditions in the country of origin. Consequently, trial attorneys often must rely primarily on their litigator instincts, refined over the course of the numerous asylum cases each attorney handles, to develop their trial strategy on the spot. They probe for apparent inconsistencies in the story or other possible indications of falsehood, or home in on undeveloped issues that might call for a legal conclusion that the claim does not meet the standards. Properly trained and supervised trial attorneys, however, do not understand their mission to be to defeat the asylum claim at all costs. If the applicant's story holds up under scrutiny, they are authorized to tell the judge at the end that the government does not object to a grant.

In cross-examining Abankwah, Paoli pursued three main themes. First, he zeroed in on the exact nature of her FGM claim, to enable him to emphasize later how it differed in important respects from the pattern in *Matter of Kasinga* and in other FGM cases.

Q. Now you told us that if they find out you're not a virgin that they would perform circumcision. Is that coarct [correct]?

A. Yes, I did.

Q. So is this a form of punishment?

A. Yes, because they mean that you are disgraced the gods, so they will punish you. . . .

Q. Well, are there any—is the female circumcise used for other purposes in your tribe?

A. In my village, if they find you a man and then you marry that man, that means you are a good person; they wouldn't do that to you. But if you disobey them, and then they find out, they want to punish you, then they will do that to you as punishment.

Q. Do any people do it voluntarily in your village?

A. No.[28]

Second, Paoli sought to establish that Abankwah might be able to get government or private assistance in avoiding circumcision. The State Department documents in evidence stated that Ghana outlawed female circumcision in 1994 and had initiated at least two prosecutions,[29] but Abankwah testified that it was still practiced in her village. He pointed out that certain nongovernmental organizations (NGOs) offer refuge throughout Ghana. Couldn't she use those services? "I didn't know that before," she admitted. But she persisted, through several avenues of cross-examination, in stating that wherever she went in Ghana, she would be found. Trading people would notice her, or the chiefs would communicate.[30]

Third, Paoli focused on her name and on oddities in her documents connected with it. She had stated on her I–589 that she was known by another name, Kukwa, and he asked her about that. "It means I was born on a rainy day. And Adelaide is a Christian name they gave to me when I went to school." He continued "What's your last name?" "My other name is Kukwa Norman, but they never used that name Norman; they call me Kukwa."[31] Paoli then asked if she had any other ID documents from Ghana with the Abankwah name. She said no, but when pressed, offered that she might be able to get some through a woman she knew.

Paoli pursued the issue by asking how the name Abankwah got on the passport she carried on arrival. She didn't know; she just gave her name and photos to "those people" and they got it for her. "This is in February of 1997?," Paoli asked. "Yes, when I came to Accra."[32] He then showed her the passport she presented at the airport. A forensic document report already in evidence stated that the main passport photo had been carefully inserted into the spot where the original had been sliced out, but that the photo incorporated into the U.S. visa had merely been retouched to alter its appearance.[33] She essentially conceded that the main photo was of her, and the visa photo was not. Paoli continued:

> Q. Ma'am, this visa is a valid United States visa, according to [the forensic document report]. And this visa was issued to someone named Adelaide Abankwah. She has the same name as you. This was issued in August of 1996, before you gave them your name and your picture. So that means that this person right here is Adelaide Abankwah. So, ma'am. Ma'am. Can you explain, if you know, how there could be two people with the exact same name as you and how you ended up with her passport?
>
> A. I cannot tell how they got it. Maybe it belongs to somebody when they gave it to. But I don't know how they got it.
>
> Q. Ma'am, is it possible that your true name is Kukwa Norman and the name Adelaide Abankwah is just the name you got off this passport?
>
> A. No, my real name is Adelaide Abankwah. In my house, they call me Kukwa.[34]

Final Stages of the Hearing

Following a brief redirect examination, Narymsky stated to the IJ that she was waiting for some other documents, including Abankwah's birth certificate, which were being obtained through the efforts of Victoria Otumfuor, the affiant, who would also be available to testify within the next few weeks. The judge then held a brief colloquy with Narymsky, candidly revealing several questions that were on his mind as he looked ahead to resolving this case. One was "really troublesome," the name on the passport. It shows an Adelaide Abankwah born in 1973; the person in the court room was born in 1969, according to her I–589. "So it's an Adelaide Abankwah with a different birthday." Narymsky's responses suggest that she had not previously noticed the discrepancy.[35]

The hearing reconvened three weeks later, on October 1. One further affidavit was submitted, but no birth certificate or other ID documents. The affidavit was from the son of Victoria Otumfuor, still in Ghana and unavailable for cross-examination. It essentially reported statements Abankwah had made to him when he knew her there. Otumfuor then took the stand. She was a twenty-year U.S. resident and two-year citizen. As a Pentecostal minister and family counselor, she still made frequent trips back to her native Ghana. She had met Adelaide briefly in Ghana, at Otumfuor's daughter's funeral, and then came to see her in the detention center. But her testimony went primarily to practices in Ghana. She described the institution of queen mother and the consequences of refusing the position, which vary from place to place. FGM is practiced primarily in the north of Ghana, but she said she had heard of FGM being used as punishment in the central region, and she knew that Adelaide was from the central region (which, confusingly, lies along the south coast of Ghana). She was still trying to obtain Adelaide's birth certificate, thus far without success, but she did know that Adelaide Abankwah was her name.[36]

Paoli's cross-examination produced a candid statement that Otumfuor did not know much about Abankwah's tribe, the Nkumssa, and that she did not know specifically that it used FGM as punishment. He suggested gently that her knowledge of Ghana could be dated; she was unaware that the government was trying to eliminate FGM.[37]

When Paoli concluded, Judge Livingston then began a fairly lengthy questioning of the witness (a not uncommon practice in immigration court) that revealed his own struggles with this case. After a few questions covering the Ghanaian government's current efforts to eradicate FGM, he noted that there was no mention in any of the documents that FGM is used as a punishment. He then asked Otumfuor if she knew of such usage of FGM or only thought it possible. She said she had heard of one incident when it had been used to punish for premarital sex—which had occurred in the central region. But this was back in 1963 or 1964.[38]

Narymsky's closing statement focused on credibility. Otumfuor had been candid in owning up to her limited knowledge of Abankwah's tribe. This showed how careful her testimony was, and it supported the claim. "I also believe my client's testimony. And one of the main reason which—well, one of the reason which makes me believe her is because she's been in the detention center already for six months, and if that's not an indication of her fear of returning, obviously she has a fear; she has a subjective fear."[39]

Judge Livingston then engaged the attorney in a lengthy dialogue, again revealing his concerns. What about government protection, now that Ghana has outlawed FGM? Narymsky pointed out that the evidence still showed that 30% of Ghanaian women had been circumcised; obviously the protection is inadequate. In any event, Abankwah could be subjected to other sanctions. Which of the five grounds are involved here? Religion and particular social group: "not being a virgin, it's a social group. It's a female." But Abankwah had said her lover would be killed, the IJ pointed out: "I mean, it's even handed that way." Narym-

sky gave a somewhat startling reply: "Well, the female genital mutilation is on account of being a female, because the boy will not be
mutilated, he will just be killed." Could a society make a law against
extramarital sex, the judge asked, and then enforce it with punishments?
Answer: the punishment cannot be disproportionate to the crime, and
FGM is disproportionate.[40]

Paoli's closing statement for the government initially suggested that
this was not really an FGM case. It had not been established, he
contended, that FGM is practiced by Abankwah's tribe or is imposed as
punishment. The State Department profile said that FGM happens in
the north of Ghana. Otumfuor "was a very nice woman," but her
knowledge of FGM as punishment was double hearsay, "a friend telling
of a friend who had a friend 20 years ago who was punished. I don't
think that that's enough corroboration." The Ghanaian government by
now was actively prosecuting practitioners of FGM, at least if people
cooperated in reporting such incidents, and NGOs were providing refuge.
"I find it rather unbelievable that a small tribe is going to send their
elders or officers out to widespread Ghana to try to find somebody who
refuses to be queen mother. It's an honor."[41]

Immigration judges typically recess for a few minutes at the end of a
removal case, then reconvene on the record and immediately deliver
their rulings orally, incorporating a discussion of facts and law. If the
case is appealed, the judge's opinion is transcribed along with the rest of
the proceedings, in order to provide a full basis for the BIA to consider
the legal and factual issues.[42] (Immigration court proceedings are record-
ed on a tape recorder operated by the judge, not through the services of a
court reporter.) The judge can usually base part of his oral opinion on
standard paragraphs describing the relevant law, with citations, that he
has developed over the course of hearing dozens or hundreds of cases
involving similar legal questions. He can then weave in a summary and
assessment of the facts from his notes and his still-fresh recollection of
the proceedings that have just concluded.

Judge Livingston followed a variant of this practice here. Stating
that the case presented "an extremely difficult issue" and was "very
unusual in my experience," he indicated that he would take a week to
think about it and then reconvene in his courtroom for the oral decision.[43]

Kasinga's Case and the Background Legal Doctrine

One legal issue that had stirred widespread debate just eighteen
months earlier no longer needed to trouble Judge Livingston. Fauziya
Kasinga's case had settled that FGM can legally count as the type of
persecution that gives rise to a valid asylum claim.[44] This conclusion may

seem commonplace or unsurprising today, but it was an open issue for refugee status adjudicators worldwide in the early 1990s, and it is worth looking at the difficulties and how the Board resolved them. A brief outline of Kasinga's situation sets the stage. It had many remarkable parallels to Adelaide Abankwah's case, but also a few differences— including one major one that would not be fully revealed until years later.

Kasinga's Journey

Fauziya Kasinga grew up in Kpalimé, Togo. Her family belonged to the Tchamba-Kunsuntu tribe, which traditionally subjected its daughters to FGM at about age fifteen, as a regular ritual expected of all women. But her influential father did not believe in the practice, and he had shielded Fauziya and her sisters from it. Some of her older sisters had married successfully, despite this departure from custom, but Fauziya was only sixteen years old when her father died in 1993. A paternal aunt then took over authority in the family. Disapproving of the way the family was run, she forced Kasinga's mother to leave. She then arranged for Kasinga to marry a forty-five-year-old man who already had three wives. The wedding was performed in October 1994, but Kasinga refused to sign the marriage certificate. The aunt also scheduled an older woman to come a few days later, "to scrape my woman parts off," as Kasinga later explained it. After allowing forty days for healing, the marriage would then be consummated. Before the cutting took place, however, Kasinga's sister helped her escape the house and drove her to the Accra airport in neighboring Ghana, providing her with $3,000 sent by her mother (who had obtained it at some hardship by disposing of most of her inheritance). Kasinga flew to Germany, and was able to find housing with a German woman who had befriended her while she was wandering, confused and uncertain, in the Düsseldorf airport. Two months later, equipped with a false passport provided by an African she met in Germany, she flew to the United States, where a cousin lived. Upon her arrival at JFK airport, in December 1994, she immediately told the inspector the truth about her false documents (in contrast to Abankwah) and asked for asylum based on the threatened FGM.[45]

She was interviewed and then placed in detention—obviously a severe prospect for an eighteen-year-old, but she had the further misfortune of being assigned to the Esmor facility in Newark, a private prison run under contract with INS. There, as a frightened young woman barely of age, in a wholly alien culture, she suffered several humiliations and guard mistreatment. The conditions were so bad at Esmor that the inmates rioted six months after Kasinga arrived (she did not take part). INS then closed the Esmor facility and launched a hard-hitting investigation into what had gone wrong.[46] Kasinga was not released, however;

she was simply moved to another jail in York, Pennsylvania. The Esmor turmoil delayed her hearing well beyond the norm for detainees. Finally, in August 1995, she appeared before IJ Donald Ferlise, who rejected her claim after a hearing. "The court wonders then how absolute can this tribal law be with so many exceptions being allowed for that rule," he stated. But his key ruling rested on credibility: "I have taken into account the lack of rationality, the lack of internal consistency and the lack of inherent persuasiveness in her testimony, and have determined that this alien is not credible."[47] Kasinga's lawyers appealed to the BIA.

INS had opposed the grant of asylum in the immigration court, but the FGM issue gathered sustained high-level attention at headquarters as the appellate brief was being prepared.[48] After careful internal review, INS decided to support firmly the BIA's development of comprehensive legal standards that would recognize the risk of forcible subjection to FGM as a valid basis for asylum, but within certain limits and guidelines. Its brief, filed in February 1996, set forth a proposed framework, generally favorable to such claims, for analyzing FGM cases and similar applications based on cultural practices.[49] But INS argued against an outright grant of asylum, favoring instead a remand for further factual inquiry once the BIA had spelled out the legal doctrine in a manner more hospitable to Kasinga's claim than that which Judge Ferlise had considered. The BIA set the matter for oral argument—something that happens only a handful of times each year, out of the tens of thousands of cases the BIA decides—to be held before the twelve-member Board sitting en banc.

While that appeal was pending, Kasinga's case began to receive media attention. A few weeks before her appeal was argued at the BIA, *The New York Times* ran a page-one story.[50] Over the next several weeks, dozens of major news outlets, both print and broadcast, covered her case. Several accounts were harshly critical of Judge Ferlise's alleged insensitivity in finding that the claim lacked rationality. The BIA had to make unprecedented arrangements for media presence in the courtroom and for a bank of cameras outside the building to film comments of the parties immediately after the argument. Ted Koppel devoted his entire *Nightline* show on the evening after the BIA hearing to an interview with Kasinga, a graphic background piece on FGM, and a review of the legal arguments in the case. She also appeared on CBS and CNN, and was interviewed by dozens of newspapers.[51]

Why did her case claim such attention? In part the interest derived from sympathy for an appealing young woman who had endured humiliation and suffering during sixteen months of detention, including detention at the grossly mismanaged Esmor facility. But the media fascination probably resulted more from the total unfamiliarity of most Americans—and probably a great many journalists—with the very existence of FGM.

Kasinga personalized the story for Americans in a way that human rights activists trying to abolish the practice had never been able to accomplish. She faced a possible fate that most Americans simply could not imagine. Could it really be that eighty million women had been subjected to a cutting of their genitalia?

In the glare of this publicity, INS belatedly reversed its previous detention decision. (The INS General Counsel's office had urged her release months earlier in internal agency discussions, without success.[52]) On April 25, *The New York Times* reported, again on page one, Kasinga's release from the York jail.[53] She attended the BIA's oral argument in the suburbs of Washington on May 23, 1996.

The Legal Difficulties

Why did asylum claims based on FGM present difficult legal issues? Classic refugee law, as embodied in the 1951 Convention relating to the Status of Refugees, was initially designed to address state-sponsored persecution of political opponents or of populations targeted because of hatred for their race or religion. Nonetheless, the Convention's words could be interpreted more expansively. As a practical matter, the main limit on that expansion derives from concern about the numbers of people who might then come to qualify. But as a doctrinal matter, there were three main obstacles to finding that FGM amounts to cognizable persecution.

First, FGM is rarely imposed directly by the government. Instead, it is practiced by members of the community, usually specially designated older women, as part of a religious or cultural rite. (This was clearly the fact pattern presented in *Kasinga* and the literature, rather than the FGM-as-punishment scenario set forth in *Abankwah*.) In some haven countries, non-governmental persecution is not recognized as giving rise to a valid refugee claim under the Convention.[54] But U.S. refugee law had firmly accepted in the 1980s that refugee claims could be based on the risk of private persecution, if the claimant could show that the government was unable or unwilling to control the persecutor.[55] This acceptance left only a factual question, as in *Abankwah*, over the government's attitude and capabilities.

Second, could FGM really be considered persecution? After all, parents willingly sought to have their young girls circumcised, and in many locations, young women old enough to make the decision for themselves also chose to have the act performed. Professor Karen Musalo, the attorney who argued Kasinga's case at the BIA and a pioneer in working to expand protections in gender-related asylum cases, stated that she was often "asked what right I had to judge or condemn the cultural practices of polygamy and FGM. I was sometimes accused of being a 'cultural imperialist' by imposing my Western concept of human rights on a very different culture and country."[56] BIA case law posed this obstacle in a slightly different form. One of the Board's earliest land- mark decisions on asylum, *Matter of Acosta*, spoke of persecution in ways that equated it with intentional *punishment* imposed because of "a belief or characteristic a persecutor seeks to overcome." Many judicial deci- sions employed similar formulations.[57] But the direct practitioners of FGM ordinarily did not intend to punish. They thought, under the precepts of their own culture, that they were doing something deeply beneficial for the girl or woman involved—as is the case with male circumcision in Western societies.

Third, even if the practice is considered persecution, despite the subjectively benign intent of the practitioners, can it be said to be inflicted based on one of the five covered grounds? "Membership in a particular social group" seems the most relevant category, but exactly what is the group? Is it all women? All women of a particular tribe? All who oppose the practice? Moreover, a strong strand of refugee doctrine, both in the United States and elsewhere, has resisted defining a particu- lar social group solely on the basis of the persecutory act or practice itself, lest the nexus requirement become circular or redundant.[58]

The BIA Decision

The BIA, in an opinion written by Board Chairman Paul Schmidt, ruled overwhelmingly in favor of Kasinga, granting asylum without remand. Exercising a power it then had to reconsider the factual findings de novo, the Board found Kasinga to be credible. The majority went out of its way to say that it "specifically reject[ed] the Immigration Judge's findings" on certain matters and his conclusion that the testimony was irrational, unpersuasive, or inconsistent.[59] Addressing the second doctri- nal issue mentioned above, the Board distinguished earlier decisions and held that a "subjective 'punitive' or 'malignant' intent [on the part of the actor inflicting the harm] is not required for harm to constitute persecution." FGM, the Board wrote, is a severe bodily invasion lacking any legitimate reason.[60]

The majority then provided this description of the particular social group involved: "[y]oung women of the Tchamba–Kunsuntu Tribe who have not had FGM, as practiced by that tribe, and who oppose the practice." Invoking standards set in earlier precedents, the BIA stated that this is a group "defined by common characteristics that members of the group either cannot change, or should not be required to change because such characteristics are fundamental to their individual identi- ties. . . . The characteristic of having intact genitalia is . . . fundamental to the individual identity of a young woman. . . . " The nexus require- ment was satisfied because the record showed that "FGM is practiced, at least in some significant part, to overcome sexual characteristics of young women of the tribe who have not been, and do not wish to be, subjected to FGM." Because Togo was a small country with a poor human rights record, the Board also concluded that Kasinga could not find refuge elsewhere in that country.[61]

Decision and Appeals for Abankwah

The Immigration Judge's Ruling

The BIA's *Kasinga* ruling had cleared away many possible legal disputes regarding asylum claims based on FGM, but Judge Livingston still found several difficult issues with which he had to wrestle in *Abankwah*. He announced his conclusions in the courtroom on October 8, 1997, denying asylum and ordering that Abankwah be deported.

The judge first discussed Abankwah's credibility. He noted that she had initially misrepresented her identity and that identity questions persisted. Developing a point not addressed by either party, the judge noted that the passport and visa spell her first name as "Adelaide," but in numerous court filings she signed or spelled her name "Adeliade." The judge had asked her whether she ever used any other name, but she then mentioned only the name Kukwa Norman. "On the basis of these factors, the Court finds that the question of the applicant's identity is somewhat cloudy; however, the Court does not find her testimony given at the hearing to be incredible. Quite frankly, the Court is somewhat mystified as to these inconsistencies."[62]

After comprehensively summarizing the evidence, Judge Livingston then addressed the elements of the claim. Asylum requires both a subjectively genuine fear and a finding that the fear is reasonable. "She is clearly very fearful of returning to Ghana.... [It is] an intense fear." But the evidence showed that the Ghanaian government has outlawed the practice of FGM and "people have been prosecuted and convicted." Moreover, NGOs in Ghana have established shelters, and "the applicant may be able to take advantage of this resource. The Court believes that the applicant sincerely was not aware of these resources and these factors prior to leaving Ghana.... Accordingly, ... the Court cannot find that [her subjective] fear qualifies as a reasonable fear."[63]

Judge Livingston also addressed the risk of other possible harm, besides FGM, based on "her refusal to assume the position of queen mother." She initially seemed to be able to avoid these consequences by going to Accra, but after the incident where she was accused of stealing, this option was no longer available, and she could not go to other villages, in his view, for fear of being reported to her home village. "So the Court does not accept that there is a complete internal flight alternative which would solve the applicant's problems." Nonetheless, on

nexus grounds, he ruled, this branch of the asylum claim was insufficient. Counsel for Abankwah had argued that the harm qualifies, using a
social group defined as "candidates for the queen mother position who
are unable or unwilling to accept that position." In the judge's view, this
social group was "too narrowly drawn to be cognizable under the
Immigration Law. Rather, I think that the applicant is faced with
something that's properly characterized as an individual predicament.
She has a problem which is more kin to a personal problem than a
problem relating to social groups or other organizations."[64]

Finally, he found the case distinguishable from *Matter of Kasinga*.
Kasinga faced FGM "practiced routinely in her village, and imposed
uniformly on a particular class of people. In this case, it appears that the
practice of FGM is basically abolished in the applicant's area, . . . [but]
would be imposed as a matter of individual punishment rather than a
matter of a general practice imposed upon a particular social group."[65]

Proceedings at the Board of Immigration Appeals

Though Olga Narymsky filed Abankwah's appeal on October 29, for
some reason the record, including the IJ opinion, was not transcribed
until the following March. BIA briefing schedules are not normally
established until that transcript becomes available. Briefing continued
through early May, 1998.[66] The briefs reiterated and refined most of the
points made in the parties' closing arguments, but Narymsky did add
one new element.[67] She objected to the IJ's characterization of the
particular social group and advocated a different formulation. It should
be considered "women from the Nkumssa tribe who lost virginity prior
to marriage," a characterization that, she argued, was close to the
particular social group defined in *Kasinga*.[68]

A three-member panel of the BIA dismissed the appeal in a four-
page nonprecedent decision, written by member Lauren Mathon. After a
concise recounting of the evidence in the record and the IJ's ruling,
which duly noted that the judge found Abankwah credible, the Board
discussed the various strands of the case. "We first find the applicant's
claim that she will be killed because she fled from her village to avoid
becoming the Queen Mother is unbelievable. The applicant has offered
no evidence that the punishment for refusing to become the Queen
Mother is death," nor did the evidence show any negative consequences
from refusing such an honor. On the central FGM claim, "we do not find
that she has established that the failure to remain a virgin would result
in punishment amounting to persecution." The panel also discounted
Victoria Otumfuor's testimony. She did not have specific knowledge
about Abankwah's tribe and could not support the claim that the
Nkumssa "practiced FGM as punishment." None of the reports Abankwah had offered gave any indication that FGM is used as punishment.

The specific report on practices in southern Ghana, written by Professor P.A. Twumasi, listed multiple reasons why FGM was imposed, but "[t]here is no indication that FGM was ever used as punishment for lack of virginity." In the end, "we find that the applicant has failed to meet her burden of proof."[69]

This opinion was issued July 30, 1998, nine and a half months after the IJ's ruling. By then, Abankwah had been detained for sixteen months. The BIA's action meant that she would stay at Wackenhut while her lawyers appealed to the U.S Court of Appeals for the Second Circuit. Almost a year would pass before that court ruled.

The Publicity Campaign

While her lawyers prepared their briefs, Abankwah's supporters opened another front in the battle. Following a pattern similar to the *Kasinga* case, they began to generate publicity about her plight. Leonard Glickman, executive vice president of the Hebrew Immigrant Aid Society, for which Olga Narymsky worked, published an op-ed piece in the *Washington Times* on Christmas Day, 1998, decrying her suffering in detention at a time when most Americans would be indulging in holiday celebrations. "Her crime? Seeking asylum on U.S. shores to escape female circumcision in her home country."[70] The *Village Voice* highlighted her as the longest-held detainee in the women's unit at Wackenhut, as part of a longer article condemning the grim conditions of INS detention.[71] The New York-based human rights group, Equality Now, which had helped to publicize Kasinga's case while she was detained, took up Abankwah's cause, enlisting celebrities in the effort. Feminist leader Gloria Steinem and later Fauziya Kasinga visited Abankwah in jail. The actors Julia Roberts and Vanessa Redgrave voiced support, and First Lady Hillary Clinton reportedly also weighed in quietly in internal government deliberations. "There is no length that we would not go to free Adelaide," Steinem said, "We have met her, and there is a human bond between us."[72]

Equality Now organized a visit to Abankwah at Wackenhut for two prominent members of Congress, Sen. Charles Schumer and Rep. Carolyn Maloney, in April, about two weeks before the scheduled oral argument in the Second Circuit, followed by a news conference on the plaza in front of the INS offices in Manhattan. The lawmakers sent a letter to the INS Commissioner and the Attorney General calling for her release and a change in the way INS deals with cases of this sort, asserting heatedly that INS failed to follow its own guidelines for gender asylum cases. "If we do not step in to right the wrongs of our own actions," Schumer's letter said, "Ms. Abankwah may die."[73] In May, *Marie Claire*, the Hearst Corporation fashion magazine with extensive worldwide circulation, featured an article on Abankwah titled "Why are Women Who Escape Genital Mutilation Being Jailed in America?".[74]

The Court of Appeals

For the appeal to the Second Circuit, Abankwah's supporters arranged for the pro bono services of experienced appellate lawyers from the New York firm of Orrick, Herrington & Sutcliffe. Jon W. Rauchway conducted the oral argument. In light of *Kasinga,* there was no significant dispute over the governing substantive law. Instead, Abankwah's attorneys basically needed to persuade the court that the administrative findings were wrong. In this respect, they had their work cut out for them. Supreme Court doctrine prescribes extraordinary deference to BIA factual findings in asylum cases. In *INS v. Elias–Zacarias*, the Court held that one who "seeks to obtain judicial reversal of the BIA's determination ... must show that the evidence he presented was so compelling that no reasonable factfinder could fail to find the requisite fear of persecution."[75]

Abankwah's brief, however, wove a well-constructed argument that subtly sought to shift the burden to the Board.[76] Initially, the brief noted that the BIA did not rely on what it called the IJ's erroneous arguments that Abankwah had failed to articulate a cognizable social group, and that she could have sought the protection of the Ghanaian government. Instead, it based its decision "upon entirely different grounds than that of the Immigration Judge," namely, "that she had not presented sufficient evidence to demonstrate a well-founded fear of persecution."[77] The Board had not rejected the IJ's finding that Abankwah was credible, but it still insisted on greater corroboration. In doing so, the brief contended, the BIA was seemingly demanding a document that spoke in detail of FGM practices among the Nkumssa. Such a document "may not—and probably does not—exist.... Ms. Abankwah is from a small tribe in a rural area of Ghana. Furthermore, the practice of FGM in Ghana is particularly secretive [citing to the record]."[78] The documents introduced into evidence, including State Department reports that confirmed the presence of FGM in Ghana, provide "as much corroboration for Ms. Abankwah's testimony as could conceivably and reasonably be expected. In fact, the Board's determination begs the question: what sort of documentation could an asylum applicant supply that would satisfy this impossible standard, especially without the benefit of counsel, as is frequently the case?"[79] The section closed with a final, carefully framed passage, perhaps meant to remind the judges of themes that they might remember from news accounts of the publicity campaign: "Ms. Abankwah has demonstrated a well-founded fear that she will be subjected to horrific persecution if she is returned to Ghana. She has no criminal record of any kind, she has an exemplary record of behavior during her two years of detention in this country, and she is not in good health."[80]

The brief of the government's lawyer, Assistant U.S. Attorney Meredith Kotler, was far more businesslike and comprehensive, thoroughly reviewing the evidence in the record and highlighting inconsistencies in Abankwah's reasons for fearing return. Abankwah never produced ID documents other than the admittedly false passport, and she "was unable to explain . . . how she was able to buy a passport from someone with the same name as her."[81] Though the Board noted the IJ's positive credibility finding, it had specifically labeled one part of her testimony "unbelievable"—the portion relating to her claim that she would be killed for her actions. The rest of the testimony in support of her claim was entirely conclusory, "too attenuated to constitute a basis for reversing the BIA" under the *Elias-Zacarias* standard of review.[82] The brief closed by contrasting Abankwah's evidence with that in *Kasinga*, where the applicant's personal story was corroborated in detail by State Department information about FGM and human rights conditions in Togo and by an expert witness. Abankwah had only the "tepid testimony" of Victoria Otumfuor.[83]

The Second Circuit ruled within two months of the argument, adopting the approach urged in Abankwah's brief and reversing the BIA. Although an early passage dutifully recited the *Elias-Zacarias* standard, the rest of the opinion reflected a different orientation. "The BIA was too exacting," the court ruled, "both in the quantity and quality of evidence that it required. As an initial matter, INS regulations do not require that credible testimony . . . be corroborated by objective evidence." The IJ had found Abankwah credible, and the BIA did not disturb this finding. To be sure, it expressly found one part of her story "unbelievable," but, the court stated, "this is a rejection of merely one aspect of Abankwah's asylum claim." That ruling did not affect the underlying IJ finding of credibility, which covered the FGM portion of the claim.[84] And "[h]aving established that Abankwah is credible, we accept as fact her assertion that Nkumssa custom includes FGM as a punishment for premarital sex. Abankwah's position is particularly compelling in light of the general conditions present in Ghana," noting that 15 to 30% of the women had been subjected to FGM. The government's efforts to criminalize the practice were labeled "insignificant."[85]

The BIA was also too quick, in the court's view, to discount Otumfuor's testimony because of her lack of familiarity with the Nkumssa tribe. In fact, her affidavit did state that FGM was sometimes inflicted as punishment and that Abankwah's account was consistent with her knowledge of the situation in Ghana. "This evidence is sufficient to support Abankwah's claim." The court concluded with this passage:

Without discounting the importance of objective proof in asylum cases, it must be acknowledged that a genuine refugee does not flee her native country armed with affidavits, expert witnesses, and extensive documentation. In this case, Abankwah has presented ... strong evidence to demonstrate that her fear of FGM is objectively reasonable.

Abankwah's fear of FGM is thus sufficiently "grounded in reality" to satisfy the objective element of the test for well-founded fear of persecution. Given the customs of the Nkumssa tribe, a reasonable person who knew that she had disobeyed a tribal taboo and knew that discovery by the tribe of her disobedience was imminent would share Abankwah's fears.[86]

Evidence "sufficient to support" her claim and "grounded in reality" thus constituted enough to overturn the BIA's factual conclusions. Having found Abankwah eligible for asylum, the court remanded the case to the Board.

Aftermath

Although remand proceedings were still under way, INS paroled Abankwah from Wackenhut ten days later, on July 19, 1999, after twenty-seven months in detention. Victoria Otumfuor took her in to her home. A few weeks later, the BIA formally granted Abankwah asylum. She then appeared at a celebratory news conference held at the *Marie Claire* offices on West Broadway, flanked by Gloria Steinem and other supporters. "I am so happy to be free. I don't have to worry about being deported or dying in jail."[87] She began to work part-time selling French beauty products and also took up studies to obtain her high-school equivalency diploma.

Abankwah proved a poor prophet about her worries. Seventeen months later, and nearly two years to the day after Glickman's op-ed opened her publicity campaign, the *Washington Post* broke a stunningly different story on its front page. An INS investigation, confirmed by the *Post*'s own inquiries, had found that Abankwah was an impostor. There was a real Adelaide Abankwah, a Ghanaian whose passport had been stolen in Accra in 1996 and who had been living illegally in the United States for four years, but who had now surfaced, she said, to reclaim her name. The asylum applicant's real name was Regina Norman Danson. A hotel-owner in Biriwa, Danson's home town, had records showing that Danson had worked several years as a cook there. Biriwa's chief, Nana Kwa Bonko V, said to a *Post* reporter that there had been only one queen mother of the tribe in the last seventy years, and only for a brief period. Danson was not part of the royal family. Moreover, he said, FGM was not part of his tribe's tradition, and refusal to become queen mother would not provoke punishment. According to the INS investigative report, Ghanaian police had found Danson's mother buying fish in Biriwa, and she had picked out her daughter from a photo spread.[88] Having seen the INS report, but not revealing that fact, the *Post* had interviewed Danson in a New York coffee shop. She recounted her story, then disputed the chief's version of tribal practices. The *Post* article continued: "Informed that police reportedly had found her mother alive in Biriwa, her eyes widened and she fell silent. After a lengthy pause, she reaffirmed her story, ... [then] declined to discuss the matter further."[89]

INS's chief press officer, Russell Bergeron, commented: "The attorneys and advocates for the alleged Adelaide Abankwah used this case to lambaste the I.N.S. by charging that we opposed the concept of a woman gaining asylum based on female genital mutilation. The fact of the matter is, that was hype and spin and a smoke screen to conceal what was fundamentally a weak case."[90] In this respect, the case could not have been more different from Kasinga's. After the BIA's ruling there, *The New York Times* had sent a reporter to Togo to investigate the facts and the family's reaction to the outcome.[91] The resulting 5,000–word story had confirmed Kasinga's account in detail.**

Surprisingly, after unrefuted public revelations that "Abankwah" was really someone else, nothing further happened for over twenty months. On September 9, 2002, however, on the final day permitted by the statute of limitations, Regina Norman Danson was indicted for perjury, false statements, and passport fraud. She pleaded not guilty and was released on $200,000 bond.[92]

At trial the following January, the government presented several witnesses brought from Ghana, the kind of eyewitness testimony not possible to marshal in the thousands of asylum cases heard each year. They confirmed her identity as Regina Norman Danson, and that she had never been known as Adelaide Abankwah.[93] An official of the marriage registrar's office in Accra produced a copy of her marriage certificate and testified that Danson was married in Ghana in September 1996—contradicting the "correction" to her asylum application and, of course, undercutting a key part of the foundation for her claim of risk. Chief Bonko spoke at length from the witness stand, confirming his statements to the *Washington Post* two years earlier. Danson, he said,

---

** It also contained intriguing insights into how the family and the local community were reacting to the intense global interest in the case:

> Just as Miss Kassindja has brought an awareness of Togo to America, so America has begun to seep into the life of the Kassindja family. The patriarch has been shaken by the persistent queries about a tradition he himself had never questioned. "Don't say I'm a bad person," he pleaded. "This practice came from my forefathers." He said he would summon family elders to a council, where he said he would argue that genital cutting should end so that no more girls run away.

was definitely not a member of the royal family, and he had never seen any notice that her mother had died. His appearance in the New York courtroom was covered with interest in the Ghanaian press, including an article titled "We Are Not Savages—Chief Nana Kwa Bonko V." That article included the reaction of one Ghanaian from Biriwa then residing in New York, who had followed the trial closely: "I am proud of my chief, and today, I feel exonerated because tenants in my apartment complex have been teasing me and asking me whether I have a human head under my bed.... You have no idea how shameful we felt as Ghanaians when this woman's story broke, ... but today, they will all eat their words."[94]

One other witness at the trial betrayed some of this same emotion. It was Professor Patrick Twumasi, author of the study on FGM in southern Ghana that Abankwah's attorney had entered into the record at the asylum hearing. The elegantly loquacious professor was obviously proud of the scientific rigor of his studies and of the extensive efforts the Ghanaian government and NGOs had made to combat FGM in his home country. FGM, he testified, is simply not practiced by the ethnic group to which Danson belongs, and in those areas where it is practiced, it is never used as punishment.[95] He thus confirmed one persistent doubt that had nagged at Judge Livingston after his review of the FGM literature five years earlier, and that probably also played a role in the BIA's rejection of the asylum claim—though neither tribunal directly rested the denial of asylum on this ground.

In closing arguments, the prosecutor framed the case in this way: "By using FGM, by lying about FGM, ... [Danson] delegitimized the very real danger, that very real victims of FGM face. Regina Danson's lies were a slap in the face to the people who truly are at risk of this brutal practice."[96] Her attorney countered by focusing on Danson's naivete, as "a frightened young woman who is trying to tell the truth.... [T]he name here is not a significant issue.... I submit to you that ... whatever name she used, she was still eligible for asylum."[97]

The jury quickly found, on a special verdict form, that Danson had lied when she made all the statements underlying the nine counts the judge allowed them to consider.[98] She faced a possible ten years' imprisonment, but in August 2003, the judge sentenced her to the time she had already served in INS detention, plus a small fine and two years of supervised release.[99] After the verdict, her attorney offered an unintentionally ironic comment to reporters: "Her biggest fear is deportation.... There may be people in Ghana who feel angry about her being found to have slandered Ghana."[100]

The verdict did not itself terminate Danson's asylum status, however, and she apparently has continued living and working in New York.

INS did file with the BIA a motion to reopen the asylum proceedings in order to rescind the grant of asylum and enter a removal order, relying on the proof of fraud in the criminal case. But the BIA remanded the matter to the immigration court for further factual proceedings. In keeping with the epic delays that marked every stage of this ill-fated case, no hearing had yet been scheduled as of January 2005.

Lessons

Danson apparently fabricated her story based on what she heard during her first few weeks in the detention facility about the most highly publicized asylum case of the decade, *Matter of Kasinga*. But she added some twists that simply did not comport with the way FGM is practiced in the world. Her embellishments, designedly or not, tapped into an apparent willingness of many in the United States to believe that developing countries are brutal places of primitive customs uncomplicated by any modern developments. The Second Circuit's pronouncement that "Abankwah's position is particularly compelling in light of the general conditions present in Ghana"[101] unfortunately reflects what Susan Akram has labeled, in a slightly different context, "orientalism"— a form of negative stereotyping about source countries that may be well-intended but ultimately damages the cause of asylum seekers.[102] Jean Allman, professor of African history at the University of Illinois, who had lived in Ghana off and on for twenty-three years, wrote a letter of protest to *Marie Claire* after its coverage of the case, complaining about such glibness:

> Let me make it clear that my response to your coverage is not motivated by support for the antiquated and racist immigration policies of the United States government, but from a long-term association with and love for Adelaide's home country.... I am disgusted that your magazine has made Adelaide into a cause celebre when there is every indication that her story is contrived. Female genital mutilation is not only NOT practised in the area of Ghana from which Adelaide claims to come, but NEVER has been.... Nowhere in Ghana and, in fact, nowhere on the African continent, is [FGM] used as a punishment against those who have lost their virginity. Her claims are preposterous and any glance at any relevant literature ... would have made this clear.[103]

Danson also persisted in claiming that the name on the passport was really hers, when she probably would have raised fewer suspicions by giving her real name once the photo substitution was discovered. Perhaps she feared that INS would be able to investigate and expose her falsehoods if she provided that lead. If so, she was overly concerned. James Paoli, the INS trial attorney, testified at the criminal trial: "Just for an asylum hearing I wouldn't have an [overseas] investigation done. And additionally, there are thousands of asylum applications that are received in New York alone and we don't have the resources to send investigators out to investigate every single asylum case."[104] The 1999 inquiry in Ghana was triggered only because some veteran INS officers felt they had little other recourse after the Second Circuit's decision, which accepted factual claims they had regarded from the beginning as blatantly false.[105]

That limited governmental investigative capacity leads to a real weakness of the asylum system, one that has sometimes been exploited by organizers who craft false claims by the dozens that are more sophisticated than Danson's home-made tale, and who reap large fees as a result.[106] This feature also spotlights the crucial role in asylum proceedings of credibility determinations—at best, a highly inexact science.

The *Abankwah* record, viewed in retrospect, presented abundant signals that the asylum seeker was an unreliable witness. The reported reluctance of several attorneys to take the case after speaking with her now seems far more understandable, for example. But any such doubts were, at least in formal terms, downplayed or ignored. The immigration judge, who had even spotted Danson's consistent misspelling of her own alleged first name, stated that her identity was "somewhat cloudy" and that he was "mystified as to these inconsistencies." Yet he still ruled that he would not find her testimony "incredible."[107] Perhaps Judge Livingston was spooked by the public pillorying that Judge Ferlise had encountered in the press the year before, with special focus on his rather insensitive dismissal of Kasinga's credibility. The BIA did expressly find "unbelievable" Danson's story that she would be killed for refusing the queen mother position. But it never clearly connected that finding with a ruling on her credibility in general.[108]

Both administrative tribunals ruled against her claim, to be sure, but framed holdings that savor more of legal rulings than rejection of the factual account. In this respect, the case is representative of a great many asylum cases. Credibility is crucial, but many judges seem more comfortable accepting the alleged facts, at least arguendo, and then rejecting the claim as a matter of law—often relying on insufficient nexus to the five grounds, but sometimes on the definition of persecution, or on a rather mechanical application of the BIA's corroboration rules. Immigration judges in asylum cases often appear, whenever they smell a falsehood, to apply stringent versions of these legal doctrines. But why not own up more often to a negative credibility ruling? Perhaps it is simply a daunting and unpleasant task to issue a ruling that essentially calls the asylum seeker a liar, particularly when the judgment must usually be rendered in the applicant's presence in a small courtroom. After all, asylum cases offer few solid guideposts to the truth or falsity of the claimant's account, which concerns events in a distant country and an unfamiliar culture. It is more comfortable to stay on the familiar terrain of legal rulings.[109]

The federal courts also bear some responsibility for this administrative timidity. Several circuits impose daunting burdens on the BIA to justify a negative credibility finding.[110] The Second Circuit here did essentially what the Supreme Court forbade in *Elias-Zacarias,* second-guessing the BIA's findings, merely because it found that Danson's claims were "grounded in reality."[111] Sometimes such an appellate ruling is at least understandable, when the court is confronted with a record (unfortunately not a rare event) that reveals an insensitive IJ or obvious mistakes that thwarted the applicant's chance to make out her asylum claim.[112] But *Abankwah* was not such a case. Judge Livingston was polite and solicitous, always careful to give Danson and her attorney a full opportunity to present the claim. Nevertheless, the Second Circuit panel seemed so determined to find the applicant credible that it bulldozed the one solid statement about credibility that the BIA issued. After essentially agreeing with the BIA that Danson was "unbelievable" when she said she would be killed, the court then confined that ruling to its narrowest possible compass, saying that this finding "is a rejection of merely one aspect of Abankwah's asylum claim."[113] In any other sort of litigation, a proven lie of this magnitude would be sufficient to cast major doubt on the entire testimony.[114]

The system's susceptibility to fraud and stereotyping deserves greater attention, from refugee advocates as much as from government officials. But overreaction is also a danger. After all, Kasinga too was disbelieved. Yet she persevered in her claim, later amply vindicated, and thereby provided INS and the BIA the occasion to develop sound new doctrine to deal with issues that the drafters of classic refugee law did not foresee. The *Washington Post* story that first publicly revealed the Abankwah fraud nicely captured both the delicate balance that our political asylum system requires and the ongoing dilemmas it faces:

> With a forged passport, an innocent demeanor and her startling tale, Danson managed to exploit the weaknesses inherent in U.S. asylum policy. That policy is designed to accommodate people fleeing political persecution abroad, often with false documents or no papers at all. Over the years, it has allowed thousands of genuine refugees to start new lives here, but it is vulnerable to abuse by people whose stories are difficult, if not impossible, to verify.[115]

ENDNOTES

1 The author would like to thank Jon W. Rauchway and Meredith Kotler, the lawyers who argued the *Abankwah* case in the Second Circuit, for their help in obtaining the central records of the administrative and judicial proceedings. Kent Olson of the University of Virginia Law Library provided considerable assistance and encouragement in obtaining other needed information, and Thomas Wintner contributed timely research assistance and a useful perspective on the narrative. Elijah Swiney later provided skilled assistance in the final stages of production for this Chapter and for the entire volume.

2. The primary reported cases are Abankwah v. INS, 185 F.3d 18 (2d Cir. 1999), and Matter of Kasinga, 21 I & N Dec. 357 (BIA 1996).

3. Her name is properly spelled Fauziya Kassindja. One of the first U.S. inspectors she encountered at JFK airport misspelled the family name on an interview form, and the misspelling persisted throughout the immigration proceedings. See Fauziya Kassindja and Layli Miller Bashir, Do They Hear You When You Cry 165 (1998). Because the case has become so well-known globally under the name of "Kasinga," however, this chapter will use that spelling here.

4. The practice is also known as female circumcision or female genital cutting; the nomenclature itself provokes controversy. The former term is sometimes thought to impart an undeserved aura of legitimacy to the practice as a valid religious ritual, whereas the FGM appellation is viewed by some as needlessly insulting to those women who have been subjected to it in the past, willingly or unwillingly. "Female genital cutting" is thus sometimes offered as a middle ground, simply descriptive of the practice. This chapter, with some reservations, will usually use the FGM terminology because of its heavy predominance in both the litigation and the public discussion of the *Abankwah* and *Kasinga* cases. For general discussions, see World Health Organization, Female Genital Mutilation: Information Pack, available at <http://www.who.int/docstore/frh-whd/FGM/infopack/ English/fgm_infopack.htm>; Haseena Lockhat, Female Genital Mutilation: Treating the Tears (2004); Anika Rahman & Nahid Toubia, Female Genital Mutilation: A Practical Guide to Worldwide Laws and Policies (2000); Ellen Gruenbaum, The Female Circumcision Controversy: An Anthropological Perspective (2000).

5. Immigration and Nationality Act (INA) § 101(a)(42)(A), 8 U.S.C. § 1101(a)(42) (2000) (definition of "refugee"). See also id. §§ 208, 241(b)(3), 8 U.S.C. §§ 1158, 1231(b)(3) (provisions for asylum and withholding of removal). U.S. asylum law is directly based on Arts. 1 and 33 of the Convention relating to the Status of Refugees, done July 28, 1951, 189 U.N.T.S. 137—obligations to which the United States became bound when in 1968 it ratified the the Protocol relating to the Status of Refugees, done Jan. 31, 1967, 19 U.S.T. 6223, T.I.A.S. No. 6577, 606 U.N.T.S. 267.

6. United States v. Danson, CR–02–1052 (CPS) (E.D.N.Y. 2003), Transcript of Trial, Jan. 7–15, 2003, at 145 ("Danson transcript").

7. Gini Sikes, Why are Women Who Escape Genital Mutilation Being Jailed in America?, Marie Claire 52, 56 (May 1998).

8. Abankwah arrived three days before expedited removal took effect, a system that allows for speedy issuance, in many port of entry cases, of a removal order by an immigration officer, without the involvement of an IJ, when an arriving alien presents false or improper documents. Had she arrived later, she would have undergone preliminary screening by an asylum officer and would have gone on to immigration court only if that screening determined that she had a "credible fear of persecution." INA § 235(b)(1), 8 U.S.C. § 1225(b)(1). It should also be noted that in March 2003, INS was abolished and its functions were taken over by the Department of Homeland Security (DHS). For convenience, this chapter will generally use a reference to INS, the operative agency during most of the time relevant to these stories, even when speaking generically of immigration functions that are now handled by DHS.

9. Joint Appendix, Abankwah v. INS, No. 98–4304, at 80 (2d. Cir. 1998) ("J.A."). This Joint Appendix contains the full record of the case, including transcripts of the proceedings at all master calendar hearings and the merits hearings, Abankwah's asylum application and affidavit, plus all supporting materials and other exhibits, the IJ and BIA decisions, and counsel's briefs before the BIA. Citations here will refer only to the J.A., but the text generally makes clear what transcript or document is being cited. Quotations in this chapter are set forth exactly as printed in the Joint Appendix, usually without effort to note or correct misspellings or grammatical mistakes.

10.   INA § 292, 8 U.S.C. § 1362 (2000).

11.   Provision of the lists was initiated by regulation in 1979. 44 Fed. Reg. 4651, 4654 (1979). Since 1996 it has been required by statute. Pub. L. No. 104–208, Div. C, Title III, § 304(a)(3), 110 Stat. 3009–587 (Sept. 30, 1996), codified in INA § 239(b)(2), 8 U.S.C. § 1229(b)(2) (2000).

12.   INA § 239(b), 8 U.S.C. § 1229(b) (2000).

13.   J.A. at 95–101.

14.   J.A. at 111–20.

15.   J.A. at 133.

16.   J.A. at 123.

17.   J.A. at 143–44.

18.   J.A. at 418–20.

19.   J.A. at 391–92.

20.   See, e.g., Matter of M–D–, 21 I & N Dec. 1180, 1182–83 (BIA 1998) ("where it is reasonable to expect corroborating evidence for certain alleged facts pertaining to the specifics of an applicant's claim, such evidence should be provided . . . [or] an explanation should be given as to why such information was not presented"). Most courts have found this more demanding corroboration requirement to be valid as a general statement of doctrine, but many decisions have reversed BIA rulings based on what they have seen as an overly severe application. The Ninth Circuit appears to go further and generally reject the imposition of a corroboration requirement, but the case law is not wholly clear on these points. See Thomas Alexander Aleinikoff, David A. Martin, & Hiroshi Motomura, Immigration and Citizenship: Process and Policy 975–76 (5th ed. 2003).

21.   J.A. at 248.

22.   J.A. at 250–390.

23.   See, e.g., Matter of Fuentes, 19 I & N Dec. 658, 662–63 (BIA 1988); 8 C.F.R. § 208.13(b)(3) (2004); James Hathaway, International Refugee Law: The Michigan Guidelines on the Internal Protection Alternative, 21 U. Mich. J. Int'l L. 131 (1999).

24.   J.A. at 161–62.

25.   J.A. at 185, 186.

26.   On the significance of owning up to the use of false documents immediately upon arrival, see Matter of Y–G–, 20 I & N Dec. 794, 796–99 (BIA 1994); Matter of Kasinga, 21 I & N Dec. 357, 368 (BIA 1996).

27.   J.A. at 165.

28.   J.A. at 169–70.

29.   J.A. at 403.

30.   J.A. at 172–75.

31.   J.A. at 175–76. From later proceedings, it appears that "born on a rainy day" may have been a mistranscription by the court reporter. The name means "born on a Wednesday." Danson transcript at 445, 622, 624, 652 (cited in note 6).

32.   J.A. at 176–77.

33. J.A. at 396. The full passport, with visa, appears at J.A. at 397–401.

34. J.A. at 177–78.

35. J.A. at 189.

36. J.A. at 201–08.

37. J.A. at 208–13.

38. J.A. at 217–19.

39. J.A. at 223.

40. J.A. at 224–30.

41. J.A. at 230–35.

42. Because only 15% of IJ rulings are appealed, the dictating of oral decisions saves considerable time and resources, while still giving the parties immediate information about both outcome and reasons. Executive Office for Immigration Review, FY 2003 Statistical Yearbook at Y1 (April 2004). The 15% figure is a bit misleading, however, because it includes cases that are essentially uncontested and so are resolved at master calendar. A significantly higher percentage of cases that have gone to a merits hearing result in a BIA appeal.

43. J.A. at 235–36.

44. Matter of Kasinga, 21 I & N Dec. 357, 365, 368 (BIA 1996).

45. This account draws on the statement of facts in the BIA decision, id., and also on Celia W. Dugger, Woman's Plea for Asylum Puts Tribal Ritual on Trial, N.Y. Times 1 (April 15, 1996) ("Woman's Plea"), from which the quote is taken.

46. See Ashley Dunn, U.S. Inquiry Finds Detention Center was Poorly Run, N.Y. Times 1 (July 22, 1995).

47. Quoted in Woman's Plea (cited in note 45).

48. The INS Office of International Affairs had issued a progressive set of "gender guidelines" for asylum officers in May 1995, widely praised by NGOs and refugee advocates. Considerations for Asylum Officers Adjudicating Claims from Women (Memorandum from Phyllis Coven, May 26, 1995), reprinted in 72 Interpreter Releases 771 (1995). The guidelines had stated in general terms that rape, sexual abuse, domestic violence, and FGM "are forms of mistreatment primarily directed at girls and women and they may serve as evidence of past persecution on account of one or more of the five grounds," but they did not provide a detailed legal analysis for FGM cases. The INS General Counsel's office undertook that task in preparing the agency's brief in Kasinga.

49. The wider framework of analysis offered by INS is summarized in the concurring opinion of Board Member Lauri Steven Filppu, 21 I & N Dec. at 370–72. The Board stated that it did not need to consider most of the INS proposal because the framework went well beyond the facts of this particular case. (The author of this chapter was General Counsel of INS at the time of the Kasinga case. He played a significant role in developing the brief, and he argued the case for INS at the BIA.)

50. Woman's Plea (cited in note 45). The newspaper coverage had begun in the Washington Post, which ran a column by Judy Mann in January 1996, followed by a news account by Linda Burstyn in March—but it was The New York Times article in April that stimulated nationwide attention. Do They Hear You When You Cry 429, 454–55, 463–64 (cited in note 3).

51. Celia W. Dugger, Roots of Exile: A Special Report: A Refugee's Body is Intact but Her Family Is Torn, N.Y. Times 1 (Sept. 11, 1996) ("Roots of Exile"). After she won her case at the BIA, book publishers clamored for her story. She eventually received a $600,000 advance and produced, with a co-author, a highly engaging account of her life in Togo, her escape, detention, and eventual triumph in the legal process. Do They Hear You When You Cry (cited in note 3).

52. This effort is reported in the Reply Brief for the Respondent, at 3, Matter of Kasinga, 21 I & N Dec. 357 (No. A73 476 695) (BIA 1996); and in Do They Hear You When You Cry 454 (cited in note 3).

53. Celia W. Dugger, U.S. Frees African Fleeing Ritual Mutilation, N.Y. Times 1 (April 25, 1996).

54. See Jennifer Moore, From Nation State to Failed State: International Protection from Human Rights Abuses by Non–State Agents, 31 Colum. Human Rights L. Rev. 81, 106–09 (1999)

55. McMullen v. INS, 658 F.2d 1312, 1315 (9th Cir. 1981); Matter of O–Z–and I–Z–, 22 I & N Dec. 23 (BIA 1998).

56. Karen Musalo, When Rights and Cultures Collide, 8 Issues in Ethics, No. 3 (Summer 1997) (Markkula Center for Applied Ethics, Santa Clara University), available at <http://www.scu.edu/ethics/publications/iie/v8n3/rightsandcultures.html>.

57. Matter of Acosta, 19 I & N Dec. 211, 226 (BIA 1985). For a discussion of the federal court case law, see Government's Brief in Response to Applicant's Appeal from Decision of Immigration Judge at 15–17, Matter of Kasinga, 21 I & N Dec. 357 (No. A73 476 695) (BIA 1996).

58. See Islam v. Secretary of State for the Home Dep't, [1999] 2 A.C. 629, 653–54 (House of Lords); Applicant A. v. Minister for Immigration and Ethnic Affairs, 190 CLR 225, 142 ALR 331, 341 (High Ct. of Australia 1997); T. Alexander Aleinikoff, Protected Characteristics and Social Perceptions: An Analysis of the Meaning of "Membership of a Particular Social Group," in Erika Feller, Volker Türk and Frances Nicholson eds., Refugee Protection in International Law: UNHCR's Global Consultations on Refugee Protection 263, 286–89 (2003).

59. Matter of Kasinga, 21 I & N Dec. 357, 364 (BIA 1996).

60. Id. at 365–67.

61. Id. One member dissented without opinion—a rather baffling stance on such a significant and hotly contested issue. Board member Lory Rosenberg concurred specially, arguing that the particular social group was improperly described; the woman's opposition to the practice was "surplusage." The applicant's attitude or intent "is not relevant to our definition of the group to which she belongs, but rather to whether the harm or abuse she faces constitutes persecution." Id. at 376. The INS brief had offered a similar analysis, arguing that, as with surgery that amputates a limb, serious bodily invasion does not constitute persecution if done with consent. Government's Brief at 18 (cited in note 57).

62. J.A. at 64–65.

63. J.A. at 71–73.

64. J.A. at 74–76. The judge also ruled against her claim that she faced persecution on account of her Christian religion. She might incur the wrath of the leaders "if she disappoints them by not taking on what they feel is her responsibility of being queen mother. . . . Nevertheless, I cannot find that the motive of the village leaders is to punish her on account of her religion." J.A. at 73–74.

65. J.A. at 76.

66. J.A. at 50.

67. The briefs appear in J.A. at 6–37.

68. J.A. at 29–31.

69. J.A. at 2–5 (citations omitted).

70. Leonard Glickman, Without a Home for the Holidays, Wash. Times A19 (Dec. 25, 1998).

71. Alisa Solomon, A Dream Detained, Village Voice 46–50 (March 24–30, 1999).

72. Ginger Thompson, Lawmakers Want an Asylum Rule for Sex–Based Persecution, N.Y.Times B8 (Apr. 26, 1999). See also Equality Now, 1998–1999 Report 12–13; William Branigin & Douglas Farah, Asylum Seeker is Impostor, INS Says: Woman's Claim Had Powerful Support, Wash. Post A1 (Dec. 20, 2000).

73. Allen Salkin, Schumer Fears for Life of Detained Immigrant, N.Y Post 22 (Apr. 18, 1999). See also Ginger Thompson, No Asylum for a Woman Threatened with Genital Cutting, N.Y. Times, sec. 1 at 35 (Apr. 25, 1999).

74. Sikes (cited in note 7).

75. INS v. Elias–Zacarias, 502 U.S. 478, 483–84 (1992); see also id. at 481 n.1 ("To reverse the BIA finding we must find that the evidence not only supports [the contrary] conclusion, but *compels* it.") (emphasis in original). In 1996, Congress enshrined this standard in the statute to govern all review of administrative factfinding in removal cases. INA § 242(b)(4)(B), 8 U.S.C. § 1252(b)(4)(B) (2000).

76. Brief for Petitioner–Appellant at 12, Abankwah v. INS, 185 F.3d 18 (2d Cir. 1999) (No. 98–4304).

77. Id. at 11, 14–15.

78. Id. at 22.

79. Id. at 24–25.

80. Id. at 26.

81. Brief for Respondent at 9, Abankwah v. INS, 185 F.3d 18 (2d Cir. 1999) (No. 98–4304), reprinted at 1999 WL 33612026 (April 14, 1999).

82. Id. at 20, 26.

83. Id. at 39–41, 34.

84. Abankwah v. INS, 185 F.3d 18, 24 (2d Cir. 1999).

85. Id. at 25.

86. Id. at 26 (citations omitted).

87. Winnie Hu, Woman Fearing Mutilation Savors Freedom, N.Y. Times B4 (Aug. 20, 1999). See also Andrew Jacobs, Fugitive from Genital Cutting is Released from Jail, N.Y. Times B3 (July 20, 1999); Liz Leyden, Getting Ready to Savor Freedom, Wash. Post A3 (July 21, 1999).

88. William Branigin & Douglas Farah, Asylum Seeker is Impostor, INS Says: Woman's Plea Had Powerful Support, Wash. Post A1 (Dec. 20, 2000) ("Asylum Impostor").

89. Id.

90. Dean E. Murphy, I.N.S. Says African Woman Used Fraud in a Bid for Asylum, N.Y. Times B3 (Dec. 21, 2000).

91. Dugger, Roots of Exile (cited in note 51). Another sympathetic page-one asylum seeker story in the *Times* the following year, however, had resulted in a rather embarrassing revelation several weeks later that the profiled Nigerian was an impostor. The revelation, however, ran on page 24. Celia W. Dugger, After a "Kafkaesque" Ordeal, Seeker of Asylum Presses Case, N.Y. Times 1 (Apr. 1, 1997); Celia W. Dugger, Doubts Cast on Identity of Nigerian Who Says He's a Political Refugee, N.Y. Times 24 (May 24, 1997).

92. William Glaberson, Woman Who Sought U.S. Asylum Is Arrested, N.Y. Times B3 (Sept. 10, 2002). The indictment in United States v. Danson, CR–02–1052 (CPS) (E.D.N.Y. 2003) is reprinted at <http://news.findlaw.com/hdocs/docs/ins/usdanson90902ind.pdf>.

93. The real Adelaide Abankwah, who meantime had obtained permanent resident status based on her U.S. employment, Update: Immigrant Gets Permanent Residency, Wash. Post B2 (Jan. 14, 2002), had been listed as a government witness. But the prosecution learned during the criminal trial that she had gone back to Ghana, in violation of a subpoena. Danson Transcript at 240 (cited in note 6). The reason for her departure and her current whereabouts are unknown.

94. General News of Sunday, 19 January 2003, available at <www.ghana-web.com/GhanaHomePage/NewsArchive/printnews.php?ID=31766>.

95. Danson Transcript at 519–23.

96. Id. at 600.

97. Id. at 640–43.

98. Id. at 728–36.

99. United States v. Danson, CR–02–1052 (CPS) (E.D.N.Y. 2003), Criminal Docket, entry for Aug. 12, 2003. In November 2004, the Second Circuit rejected her appeal of the conviction in an unreported opinion. United States v. Danson, 115 Fed.Appx. 486 (2d Cir. 2004).

100. Ghanaian Found Guilty in Mutilation Hoax, General News of Thursday, Jan. 16, 2003, available at <www.ghanaweb.com/GhanaHomePage/NewsArchive/print-news.php?ID=31605>.

101. 185 F.3d at 25.

102. Susan Musarrat Akram, Orientalism Revisited in Asylum and Refugee Claims, 12 Int'l J. Refugee L. 7 (2000). Professor Akram's focus is on distorted portrayals depicting a monolithic and repressive Islam, but the article's insights fit any such stereotyping. She notes that, among other problems, the stereotype "put forward by these refugee advocates can be disproved by government research and expert testimony, thus undermining the credibility of the refugee's account." Id. at 10. For a further discussion of the effects of stereotyping and assumptions, see David A. Martin, Reforming Asylum Adjudication: On Navigating the Coast of Bohemia, 138 U. Pa. L. Rev. 1247, 1273–79 (1990).

103. *Marie Claire* did not publish the letter, but the *Ghanaian Chronicle*, which had closely covered the *Abankwah* case, did. US Professor exposes deceit on Ghana, General News of Monday, 4 October 1999, available at <http://www.ghanaweb.com/GhanaHome-Page/NewsArchive/printnews.php?ID=8748> (emphasis in original).

The lessons of the Abankwah saga have not penetrated very deeply into U.S. media consciousness. Remarkably, another Ghanaian tried a similar story in 2000 about FGM that would be inflicted because she was "a member of the Ghanian royalty." The IJ rejected her claim, but she attracted strong local editorial support during her lengthy detention in York, Pennsylvania, while awaiting appeal. Viewpoints, York Daily Record 3 (June 27, 2004); Woman Says She Fled Mutilation, id. at 1, 14 (June 24, 2004). The *Ghanaian Chronicle* ran the York news story verbatim, but under the caption, Another Ghanaian Woman Try the "FGM Trick," General News of Friday, 25 June 2004, available at <www.ghanaweb.com/GhanaHomePage/NewsArchive/printnews.php?ID=60420>.

104. Danson Transcript at 225.

105. Interview of Jan. 12, 2005, with a U.S. official who had been posted to the embassy in Accra during the time of the proceedings.

106. See, e.g., Jerry Markon, 26 Charged in Va. In Document Fraud, Wash. Post A4 (Nov. 23, 2004) (ring that produced false asylum applications for over 1000 Indonesians); Yvonne Ndege, Investigation: Harrowing Tale I Learnt to Tell as a Bogus "Refugee," The Independent (London) 13 (Jan. 13, 2000) (high-volume production of false claims at a London law firm).

107. J.A.at 65. See supra note 62 and accompanying text.

108. J.A. at 4–5. See supra note 69 and accompanying text. Because many appellate opinions have clearly signaled that courts will treat the applicant's story (or any element thereof) as believable in the absence of highly specific BIA findings, the BIA's frequent failure to provide such a connection (as in this case) is surprising. See, e.g., Aguilera–Cota v. INS, 914 F.2d 1375, 1383 (9th Cir. 1990); Krastev v. INS, 292 F.3d 1268, 1279 (10th Cir. 2002). The Board's parsimony placed the government attorney handling the *Abankwah* appeal in an awkward position, as is evident from the tape of the oral argument, because she could not then argue broadly that Abankwah was wholly unworthy of belief.

109. See Audrey Macklin, Truth and Consequences: Credibility Determination in the Refugee Context, in International Association of Refugee Law Judges, Realities of Refugee Determination on the Eve of a New Millennium 134, 134–36 (Haarlem: IARLJ 1999), available at <http://www.refugeelawreader.org/index.d2?target=open & id=71>. In this intriguing article, Professor Macklin, a former member of Canada's Immigration and Refugee Board, describes the same tendency to avoid explicit negative credibility rulings among Canadian adjudicators, offers some thoughtful reflections on why this might occur, and critiques the practice.

110. See Abovian v. INS, 257 F.3d 971 (9th Cir. 2001) (Kozinski, J., dissenting from the denial of rehearing en banc) (critiquing in detail circuit doctrine that severely limits the bases on which an IJ or the BIA can make an adverse credibility finding). See generally Immigration and Citizenship: Process and Policy 972–77 (cited in note 20). In the REAL ID Act of 2005, Congress responded to this tendency in the federal courts by amending the statutory provisions on credibility and corroboration in a manner intended to produce far more deferential judicial review for such findings in asylum cases. Pub. L. 109–13, Div. B, § 101(a)–(e), 119 Stat. 231 (May 11, 2005), amending, inter alia, INA §§ 208(b)(1)(B), 241(b)(3)(C), 242(b)(4), 8 U.S.C. §§ 1158(b)(1)(B), 1231(b)(3)(C), 1252(b)(4).

111. 185 F.3d at 26.

112. For an example of such a case, wherein the court of appeals reversed a questionable denial of asylum through a careful application of the substantial evidence standard, see Mukamusoni v. Ashcroft, 390 F.3d 110 (1st Cir. 2004).

113. 185 F.3d at 24.

114. Judge Kozinski's opinion in *Abovian* builds the case that his court has set forth evidentiary rules "that ha[ve] no ready analogue outside the immigration context." They leave virtually "nothing the BIA or the IJ can do to insulate its exercise of discretion from reversal by our court. The petitioner will be entitled to spin a tale that bears no resemblance to reality, and his most implausible explanations have to be accepted." 257 F.3d at 977, 979–80.

115. Asylum Impostor (cited in note 88).

*

11

INS v. St. Cyr: The Campaign to Preserve Court Review and Stop Retroactive Application of Deportation Laws

Nancy Morawetz[1]

On April 24, 1996, the anniversary of the Oklahoma City bombing, President Clinton signed the Antiterrorism and Effective Death Penalty Act of 1996 (AEDPA).[2] The bill was prompted by early hunches that noncitizen terrorists were responsible for the bombing of the federal building in Oklahoma City the previous year. But the discovery that an American was responsible for the bombing did nothing to stop the bill's new rules for noncitizens who could be labeled as terrorists. Nor had this discovery prevented Congress from adopting provisions that had nothing to do with terrorism or the death penalty. Section 440 of AEDPA—entitled "Criminal Alien Removal"—dramatically altered the rights of lawful permanent residents (LPRs) with criminal convictions. Instead of having a right to a hearing under section 212(c) of the Immigration and Nationality Act on the equities of deportation, section 440(d) subjected these long time residents to mandatory deportation. Furthermore, section 440(a) appeared to cut off judicial oversight of how the law was applied. LPRs faced mandatory deportation without review by any court.

Most of the people affected by this law had no idea that it had passed and that it threatened their families. Enrico St. Cyr, whose case would later reach the Supreme Court, was beginning a five-year sentence for a drug offense. Junior Earl Pottinger was looking forward to being released from jail after serving a few months for a drug offense. Many others had long ago finished serving any criminal sentence. Jesus Collado was running his restaurant in New York City, twenty two years after having served a probationary sentence for having a sexual relationship as a teenager with his underage girlfriend. Danny Kozuba was working installing kitchens, and awaiting word on the government's appeal to the Board of Immigration Appeals (BIA) of a grant of relief from deportation in a case arising out of convictions for drug possession. All were LPRs who either had long forgotten their brush with the criminal law or assumed that any deportation consequences would be measured against their individual equities.

Over the next five years the lives of these people and thousands of others would be dramatically affected by AEDPA and similar provisions enacted five months later in the Illegal Immigration Reform and Immigrant Responsibility Act of Immigrant of 1996 (IIRIRA).[3] *INS v. St. Cyr*[4] is the story of their ordeal and that of thousands of other LPRs. It is also the story of a remarkable litigation campaign to preserve judicial review and prevent the new laws from being applied retroactively. By 2001, when the Supreme Court issued its decision in *St. Cyr* finding jurisdiction and ruling against retroactive application of new bars to relief from deportation, thousands had been deported and would not reap the benefit of the decision. But for those who managed to prevent their deportation, *St. Cyr* provided a chance to pick up lives that had been ravaged by five years of litigation and uncertainty.

St. Cyr, like many immigration decisions, did not rule squarely on constitutional grounds.[5] Instead the Court based both its jurisdictional holding and its ruling on the merits on "clear statement" rules. Thus, *St. Cyr* presents a case study of the role that the litigation of statutory claims (against a strong backdrop of constitutional avoidance), can play in achieving change. But it also shows the limits of such a campaign, in the absence of class-action procedures to stop deportations from continuing while advocates lay the groundwork for Supreme Court review. In the end, *St Cyr* is both a remarkable story of the potential of a well-orchestrated litigation campaign and a sober reminder of how difficult it is to protect immigrants from harsh and illegal deportation laws and legislation that curbs access to the courts.

The Enactment of the 1996 Deportation Laws

In the mid–1990s there was enormous congressional interest in immigration reform. The congressionally-established Commission on Immigration Reform recommended vast changes in the country's immigration system. Virtually every important immigration policy was on the table, including the rules for family and employment-based immigration, asylum claims, the cap on refugee admissions, standards for relief from deportation, rules governing detention of immigrants in deportation proceedings, court review of immigration cases, and public benefits for immigrants. Comprehensive bills to alter the immigration laws were introduced in the House and Senate and all interested groups carefully followed the process of mark-up by which the bills were revised prior to the final committee votes.[6]

As the comprehensive bills moved forward, immigrant advocates knew that judicial review of immigration decisions was a potential casualty of the new laws. Under then-existing law, immigrants who were ordered deported could petition to the courts of appeals. In most cases, their deportation would be stayed automatically pending a decision from the court. Those who lost their petition for review could sometimes get back into court on a motion to reopen. These procedures allowed lawyers to challenge the government's arguments for deportation. But judicial review had its critics who saw litigation as the immigrant's way to prevent lawful deportation. Government lawyers caustically joked that "the litigation isn't over until the alien wins." Congress heard these criticisms and drafted bills to curb judicial review by eliminating petition for review jurisdiction for classes of individuals, such as those convicted of certain crimes, and for classes of claims, such as those concerning the grant of discretionary relief.

The American Civil Liberties Union (ACLU) and the American Bar Association (ABA) were particularly concerned about proposed court-stripping provisions. But the issue was largely considered a lawyers issue. Far more compelling for much of the immigrant advocacy community were the substantive issues of family reunification through immigration, asylum, and public benefits.

Meanwhile, immigrant advocates paid little attention to proposals to bar relief from deportation for LPRs with criminal convictions. Under then-existing law, relief under section 212(c) of the INA served as the principal defense for LPRs who faced deportation due to a criminal conviction. Under section 212(c), a lawful permanent resident who had resided in the United States for seven years could apply for a waiver of deportation. To obtain a waiver, the immigrant would present evidence at a hearing about the equities counseling against deportation. The immigration judge would then balance evidence of such facts as military service, family responsibilities, rehabilitation, and the hardship that would be caused by deportation against the criminal record in the case. The waiver was granted in about fifty percent of cases. This was the kind of hearing that Danny Kozuba, the veteran who installed kitchens, had received. Danny had immigrated from Canada at the age of six and had volunteered for the Army during the Vietnam War. Following a difficult divorce, he had a drug problem and was convicted of drug possession. He was placed in deportation proceedings, but succeeded in persuading an immigration judge to grant him relief under section 212(c).

Relief under section 212(c) had long been a target for reform. In 1990, Congress barred this relief for those LPRs who *served* five years in prison for crimes classified as "aggravated felonies."[7] In 1996, the main proposal on the table for restricting the 212(c) waiver was to limit relief to those *sentenced* to less than 5 years. Although this was a serious change from considering the time the person actually served in prison, it did not raise major alarms among immigrant advocates who were stretched thin and battling many harsh proposals to change immigration policy.

As the comprehensive immigration bills moved forward, advocates paid little attention to provisions in a separate anti-terrorism bill that had been introduced in the wake of the Oklahoma City bombing. They believed that irreconcilable debates about gun control provisions would prevent it from being enacted into law. On March 14, 1996, however, the House suddenly passed its antiterrorism bill. This bill then went to conference with a Senate bill that leading immigration advocates had assumed was going nowhere. When the conference committee issued its report, it incorporated highly restrictive provisions on relief from deportation and judicial review from the Senate bill. No lawful permanent resident convicted of any drug offense (including possession), firearm offense or an offense denominated an "aggravated felony" would be eligible for relief from deportation. On jurisdiction, the bill provided that no one convicted of those crimes could seek judicial review of the deportation order. With the anniversary of the bombing looming, the conference agreement was guaranteed to pass.

The conference committee provisions were surprising, since the comprehensive immigration reform legislation still moving through both houses preserved relief for those with "aggravated felony" convictions who were sentenced to less than five years. But the legislation could not be stopped. Both houses signed off on the agreement and AEDPA was signed into law on April 24, 1996.

Meanwhile, the comprehensive bills reached their final stage. In a major victory for immigrant advocates, a broad coalition of business and immigration groups succeeded in a "split-the-bill" strategy that separated issues concerning legal immigration from those concerning illegal immigration. But LPRs with convictions were casualties of this approach. Senator Spencer Abraham, an architect of the split-the-bill strategy and a hero to immigration groups, was also a staunch advocate of deporting any immigrant who had been convicted of a crime, no matter how compelling the individual's equities.

Between the time of the floor votes in the two houses and the conference report on the comprehensive bill, prosecutors began to make aggressive jurisdictional arguments about the effect of AEDPA in traditional post-conviction criminal habeas corpus actions. These arguments achieved an immediate hearing from the Supreme Court, which ordered highly expedited briefing in *Felker v. Turpin*[8] about the effects of AEDPA on habeas challenges in death penalty cases. Senator Hatch, who chaired the Judiciary Committee, closely followed this case. He appeared as counsel of record in a brief urging the Supreme Court to rule that AEDPA had repealed the Supreme Court's original jurisdiction to hear habeas actions, and he attended the argument as a guest of one of the Justices. At the end of June, the Supreme Court issued its ruling, finding that general habeas jurisdiction under 28 U.S.C. § 2241 could only be repealed by an express statement from Congress. Although *Felker* did not involve immigration habeas, it would later prove to be an important precedent for *St. Cyr.*

In September, in a highly partisan process, the conference committee on the comprehensive immigration bills issued its report.[9] The conference bill enacted wholesale changes to the judicial review provisions and, among other restrictions cut off petition for review jurisdiction for noncitizens whose convictions met the new "aggravated felony" definition as well as for those with drug and firearm convictions.[10] But despite the ruling in *Felker*, no language was inserted to expressly repeal habeas jurisdiction over immigration cases. With respect to the substantive provisions on the rights of noncitizens with convictions, the bill was redrafted to be even tougher in most respects than the antiterrorism law that had passed five months earlier. Section 212(c) relief was repealed and replaced by "cancellation of removal." Anyone convicted of an offense covered by a newly expanded definition of "aggravated felony"— irrespective of whether that person had been sentenced to serve a day in prison—was barred from cancellation relief. The final bill, known as IIRIRA, was rolled into an omnibus budget bill. No one doubted that this bill could pass, since failure to pass the bill would literally shut down the government, leading to a showdown with the President that the Republican Congress had tried and lost once before. IIRIRA was soon signed into law.

The Immediate Aftermath of AEDPA and IIRIRA

The Government's Litigation Position

Two days after AEDPA was signed, the Immigration and Naturalization Service (INS) instructed its attorneys to argue that section 440(d) of AEDPA eliminated 212(c) relief for all LPRs, including those whose 212(c) hearings had already been held, but were still pending as of 3:05 P. M. on April 24, 1996.[11] Meanwhile, the Justice Department's Office of Immigration Litigation, which defends deportation decisions in federal court, moved to dismiss all federal cases that fell within the categories of cases where the new laws eliminated petition for review jurisdiction in the courts of appeals.

The government's position meant LPRs in deportation proceedings and with court cases felt the immediate impact of the new law. In a case such as Danny Kozuba's, where an immigration judge had awarded

212(c) relief, the government urged the BIA to reverse. In cases in the federal courts, the government argued for dismissal. Thus the stage was set for a battle over the retroactive elimination of 212(c) relief and elimination of judicial review.

Government lawyers thought they had an airtight case. With respect to jurisdiction, the government lawyers saw the statute as being clear; by its terms, it barred petition for review jurisdiction. There seemed little basis for opposition to the government's docket-clearing motions to dismiss. With respect to 212(c), the government's confidence stemmed from its experience litigating the 1990 restrictions on 212(c) relief. In those cases, the government had succeeded in persuading most courts of appeals that application of a new bar on 212(c) relief to those in deportation proceedings did not constitute a retroactive effect and therefore did not trigger rules of statutory construction requiring a clear statement from Congress to support a retroactive effect. Having won cases about the 1990 law, the government expected similar success with the 1996 laws. And with respect to constitutional arguments about restrictions on 212(c), the government had no concerns at all. It could cite to a long line of Supreme Court precedent holding that deportation is not punishment and thus does not implicate Ex Post Facto limitations on retroactive rules.[12]

The Immigrant Advocates' Response—Jurisdiction

On the jurisdictional front, the immigrant advocates were ready. Soon after enactment of the 1996 changes to the law, Lucas Guttentag at the Immigrant Rights Project (IRP) of the ACLU identified restrictions on judicial review as a top litigation priority. IRP saw three possible constitutional arguments for preserving judicial review: due process, separation of powers, and the prohibition against suspension of the writ of habeas corpus. It viewed the habeas corpus argument as the strongest of the three. Under this argument, Congress can prescribe procedures for challenging a deportation order; but its power to eliminate judicial scrutiny of deportation orders is restricted by the Constitution's prohibition on suspension of the writ of habeas corpus. Thus, the restriction on petitions for review was legal only if it left noncitizens with another route—such as habeas—for challenging the legality of their deportation orders.

Once AEDPA had passed and the government started moving to dismiss petitions for review in immigration cases, IRP embarked on a national litigation campaign to preserve judicial review. But it faced a daunting logistical problem. There were numerous cases in which the government filed motions to dismiss. Although IRP became involved in some cases right away, it was simply impossible to keep track of every case so as to present the courts with legal arguments for preserving some judicial review. In addition, many petitions for review presented a difficult context for arguing against restrictions on jurisdiction because they concerned how discretion had been exercised in a particular case.

Before long, the courts began issuing decisions in cases that had not benefited from briefing on the constitutional implications of eliminating judicial review. In *Duldulao v. INS*, the Ninth Circuit summarily dismissed a petition for review.[13] The decision included broad language stating that AEDPA precluded any court from reviewing the legality of Duldulao's deportation.

The *Duldulao* decision prompted the IRP to employ a rehearing strategy to persuade the Ninth Circuit to fix its broadly worded decision. The IRP contacted Duldulao and made sure that a petition for rehearing would be filed and moved for leave to appear as amicus curiae in support of rehearing. It argued that the panel had unnecessarily and improperly reached out and addressed the habeas corpus issue.

The IRP obtained help from a law professor who had been following efforts to restrict judicial review in immigration cases. For a year, Professor Gerald Neuman had been researching the question of Congress' ability to eliminate federal court jurisdiction in immigration cases. Neuman believed that discussions of habeas corpus in immigration cases had been distorted by the role of habeas corpus in collateral attacks on criminal convictions. His research focused on the core of the writ: the right to review of the legality of executive detention.[14] Neuman's views on habeas coincided with IRP's efforts to persuade the *Duldulao* court that it had stumbled unnecessarily into commenting on a major issue that deserved much closer attention. Neuman volunteered to draft an amicus brief on behalf of law professors explaining the gravity of reading AEDPA 440(a) as eliminating habeas jurisdiction.

The IRP's strategy was successful. On October 8, 1996, the Ninth Circuit panel revised its opinion and added language stating that the issue of the availability of habeas under the Constitution was not before it.[15] This was what the ACLU wanted—an express reservation of the issues implicated by the Suspension Clause.

Meanwhile, the government continued to file motions to dismiss throughout the country in cases pending in the courts of appeals. The IRP was determined to learn about every case and file briefs either before decisions or in petitions for rehearing. In most circuits that concluded that AEDPA repealed petition for review jurisdiction, the IRP succeeded in obtaining language that expressly reserved the question of 440(a)'s effect on habeas jurisdiction.[16]

The Immigrant Advocate's Response—Retroactivity

Unlike the IRP, which had anticipated legislation to restrict jurisdiction, the immigration bar was caught unaware by the drastic change in

212(c) relief. Faced with government arguments that immigration judges should refuse to hear any 212(c) application and should vacate any award of relief under 212(c), lawyers for immigrants set to work to craft arguments why the new restrictions did not apply to their clients. Just after AEDPA was enacted, these arguments focused on the retroactive effect of eliminating relief in cases where it had been granted, or where the agency had begun proceedings. Later, as more noncitizens were placed in deportation proceedings after AEDPA based on old convictions, lawyers would refine their arguments and present arguments about the retroactive effect of changing the consequences of a conviction, or changing the consequences of the underlying criminal conduct.

Realizing the importance of the retroactivity issue, the BIA invited the American Immigration Lawyers Association (AILA) and the Federation for Immigration Reform (FAIR), a group favoring broad application of deportation rules, to brief whether the new law should apply to pending cases. In June 1996, the BIA issued an en banc decision in *In re Soriano,* concluding that the new law did not apply in cases where an LPR applied for 212(c) relief prior to the enactment date of AEDPA.[17] In a prescient dissent, Judge Lory Rosenberg argued that the majority's view failed to account for the well-established presumption against retroactive application of new laws.

The Attorney General's Decision in In re Soriano

Soriano presented the INS with a major tactical choice. It could accept the BIA's decision and allow 212(c) relief for those, like Danny Kozuba, who had applied for relief pre-AEDPA, while opposing relief for those whose proceedings had not commenced before AEDPA. Alternatively, the INS could refer the *Soriano* to the Attorney General Janet Reno and urge her to reverse the decision.

In debating this choice, the INS focused on what it saw as an inconsistency between the BIA's reasoning and a prior decision in *Matter of U.M.*[18] Each case seemed to set a different test for evaluating the applicability of a new law restricting relief. Having clear rules for new restrictions on relief was a significant concern for the INS, which had to instruct its employees about the scope of many new laws. The INS also believed that Congress was seeking maximum enforcement of AEDPA. Some INS officials had met with Congressional staff to soften some of the effects of the AEDPA and had found the staff to be very unsympathetic. In July, 1996, the INS decided to refer *Soriano* to the Attorney General.

The Justice Department also has a strong interest in retroactivity issues. In *Landgraf v. USI Film Products,*[19] a 1994 case, the Supreme Court ruled that Congress must provide a clear statement if a statute is to be applied retroactively. The Justice Department faced an array of cases affecting different agencies in which litigants argued that, under the *Landgraf* rule, they should not be affected by new legislation. The Justice Department consistently sought a narrow application of the *Landgraf* rule. In particular, it relied on portions of the *Landgraf* decision that supported a distinction between rules that were procedural or jurisdictional and those that were substantive. [20]

Tension between the Justice Department's litigation policy and *Soriano* came to a head in September 1996. As the Supreme Court prepared for arguments in the case of *INS v. Elramly*, it appears to have focused on Elramly's argument that *Soriano* supported his argument against retroactive application of AEDPA. The Court ordered the parties to submit briefs within a week on the implications of *Soriano* for *Elramly*.[21]

The request for briefing in *Elramly* forced the government's hand on the retroactive effect of AEDPA. *Elramly* was a dispute about the proper standards for reviewing a denial of 212(c) relief, which was a moot point if AEDPA eliminated such relief for a person with Elramly's conviction. On the due date for the supplemental brief, the Attorney General issued a one line order vacating the decision in *Soriano*. This enabled the government to argue that AEDPA mooted Elramly's appeal. The Court ducked this question by reversing and remanding *Elramly* for further consideration in light of AEDPA.

No one will reveal the discussions at the Justice Department, but they are easy to imagine. The Attorney General oversees nationwide litigation for the federal government. A body under her control, the BIA, was undermining positions she sought to advance in the Supreme Court. She should do something about it. And she did.

Immigrant advocates greeted the vacatur of *Soriano* with cynicism. It seemed inevitable that the Attorney General's opinion in *Soriano* would adopt the INS's position that AEDPA's restrictions on relief were fully retroactive. Five months later, the Attorney General confirmed those fears. She ruled that no 212(c) relief could be awarded in any case that was still pending at any stage. She created an exception only for people with cases that were pending on the date of AEDPA's enactment who had conceded deportability prior to applying for 212(c) relief. Soon thereafter, the BIA began issuing summary decisions reversing awards of 212(c) relief and denying appeals for those who had been unable to obtain relief. Laurie Kozuba, Danny's wife, recalls opening the letter with the summary order on Good Friday, over three years after the immigration judge had awarded Danny 212(c) relief.

Challenging Retroactivity in the Courts, Congress, and the Media

Turning to the Courts to Overturn **Soriano**

After the Attorney General's decision in *Soriano*, immigrant advocates turned to the courts. With the issue in the courts, the questions of retroactivity and of jurisdiction were merged. Lawyers who specialized on retroactivity issues began working closely with the IRP to reverse the *Soriano* decision. By that time the IRP lawyers were coping with a new set of jurisdiction-stripping laws. In IIRIRA, enacted in September 1996, Congress had revamped the INA and completely rewritten the judicial review provisions. A set of transitional jurisdiction rules took effect immediately, while a set of permanent rules affected cases initiated after April 1, 1997. Briefing each set of rules, like section 440(a) of AEDPA, required distinct arguments geared to the rules' text and legislative history. In each case, however, the IRP employed the same basic approach; it argued that the statute should not be read to eliminate the constitutional minimum of habeas corpus review. The IRP's strategy was to argue that habeas rights could be secured either through a petition for review or a district court habeas action.

As draconian as the *Soriano* ruling was on the merits, it was a gift to those litigating the jurisdictional issues. It presented a pure question of law—whether AEDPA section 440(d) retroactively eliminated eligibility for relief—on which the courts could decide the jurisdictional question. The government was arguing that no court could review this question—not the courts of appeals in petitions for review, and not the district courts in habeas. To maintain that no court could review this legal question was an extreme assertion of government power, rendering the government's position all the more vulnerable in the courts.

With the *Soriano* ruling, the IRP and immigration lawyers were no longer placed in the defensive posture of defending against motions to dismiss. Instead, they could affirmatively file petitions for review and habeas actions to challenge the Attorney General's legal conclusions in *Soriano*. In one of the first affirmative habeas petitions, immigration attorneys in New York teamed up with the IRP in *Mojica v. Reno*.[22] Lee Gelernt at the IRP handled the jurisdictional questions. Manny Vargas, a specialist on criminal immigration issues, drafted the briefs on the retroactivity issues. Alan Strauss, a private attorney, briefed the issues specific to his client, Guillermo Mojica. The division of labor reflected the IRP's objective of being counsel on jurisdictional issues alone, leaving it to the immigration attorneys to protect the specific interests of each particular client.

The *Mojica* briefing led to an early victory. In July, 1997, Judge Jack Weinstein, in the Eastern District of New York, issued a 106–page opinion finding habeas jurisdiction and concluding that section 440(d) should not be applied retroactively. In what would later become a factual foundation for all the post-*Soriano* cases, Judge Weinstein cited an appendix to the petitioners' brief showing that in fifty percent of cases, LPRs who sought 212(c) relief won their cases. That same month, Judge Denny Chin, in the Southern District of New York, also ruled against the government's claims. The government immediately appealed both cases to the Second Circuit.

As the retroactivity issue reached the appellate courts, the government's lawyers felt quite confident. They took to heart the implications of the plenary power doctrine and Supreme Court cases that had upheld retroactive deportation laws. Case law plainly supported Congress' power to enact retroactive laws, even as to a person's deportability.[23] Furthermore, they did not view any change in a form of relief to be a "retroactive" effect. They drew confidence from their experience with litigation around the 1990 restrictions on 212(c) relief, where courts had concluded that changes in eligibility for 212(c) relief did not trigger a presumption against retroactive application of the law because the relief was discretionary.

With respect to the jurisdictional issues, government lawyers began to recognize the consequences of their post-AEDPA motions to dismiss. These motions resulted in circuit precedent dismissing petitions for review but reserving the question of habeas jurisdiction. Now, as they faced district court habeas filings, government lawyers had second thoughts. District court habeas cases meant more litigation in more courts as well as stay motions filed throughout the country. In retrospect, some government lawyers saw their early motions as not being refined and limited to narrow issues, such as conceding habeas over such issues as mistaken identity. The government tried to undo the damage by suggesting that the circuit courts' petition for review jurisdiction could be read to encompass issues that might have to be heard to avoid any constitutional infirmity. But given precedent that had left district court habeas as the only potential avenue for judicial review, this was an uphill battle.

Judge Weinstein's case presented the jurisdictional issues in exactly the way the IRP wished. One of the petitioners, Saul Navas, had both petitioned for review in the court of appeals and filed a writ of habeas corpus in the district court. Thus, the issue before the court was whether any procedure existed to obtain a court ruling on the AEDPA's retroactivity. This purely legal question did not require the courts to consider the full reach of Congress's power to limit court review in immigration cases. In another case, the petitioner, Daniel Magana–Pizano, had both petitioned for review in the court of appeals and filed for a writ of habeas corpus. When his habeas petition was dismissed, the IRP and immigration attorney Marc Van der Hout joined forces to ensure that the case was well-briefed and argued in the Ninth Circuit.[24]

But assuring that all cases were properly presented to the courts was an impossible task. In the past, litigators could take advantage of the class action device to litigate on behalf of large numbers of immigrants and maintain control over litigation. But IIRIRA provisions could be read to eliminate class-wide injunctions in immigration cases. Any class action would face immediate procedural hurdles that would bog down litigation. Furthermore the class action device, with its modern overtones, clashed with arguments to preserve a form of habeas that dated back to the Magna Carta. The IRP concluded that the judicial review issue had to be litigated on a case-by-case basis. With thousands of people affected by the law, and just a handful of lawyers at the IRP, there was no possibility of the IRP appearing on all of the possible cases. Therefore, it sought to identify and appear in any case that might set an important jurisdictional precedent.

Merely keeping track of cases was a Herculean task. Thousands of LPRs were denied 212(c) hearings as a result of *Soriano*, and many would go to court, in district courts scattered all over the country. These immigrants were often represented by attorneys with little or no practice in federal court litigation, much less a sophisticated understanding of the complex jurisdictional and retroactivity issues at stake.

Once the IRP learned of a case, it sought to appear as "counsel on jurisdictional issues" or otherwise serve as the lawyers handling jurisdictional questions. For the most part, local lawyers readily agreed to have the IRP shoulder this burden. Although the IRP did not generally take on the merits briefing, it also helped lawyers develop the retroactivity arguments for their clients and directed them to lawyers who were more familiar with these issues. In this way, the IRP set out to take control of the jurisdictional issue as it was litigated around the country and to assure high quality briefing and argument in precedent-setting cases.

Some lawyers bristled at the IRP's refusal to share its briefs and its insistence in handling jurisdictional arguments. But the IRP saw this as essential to maintaining high quality legal arguments on complex jurisdictional issues.

No comparable central advocacy organization attempted to manage litigation on the merits. But early on, those of us specializing in these issues focused on the claims of those who pled guilty to their crimes, many of whom had not been placed in immigration proceedings before the new laws were passed. We could most easily show that these people had legitimate expectations that their pleas would not result in summary deportation. But control of the merits litigation was not possible and probably not desirable because the framing of the merits arguments depended on the circumstances of a particular client. Those who were in deportation proceedings when AEDPA was enacted and had received 212(c) relief made arguments about expectations rooted in the 212(c) awards they had received. Others, who had applied for but not yet received relief, made arguments based on their decision to concede deportability. Those who had not yet been placed in deportation proceedings made arguments based on the length of time that had elapsed since their conviction or their expectations at the time of their plea. Still others made arguments based on the lack of fair notice of the deportation consequences at the time of their criminal conduct.

While the lawyers drafted their briefs, immigrants affected by the new laws faced the painful decision whether to endure detention in order to pursue their legal argument that they had a right to remain in the United States. One such individual was Junior Earl Pottinger, an LPR from England who had lived in the United States since the age of three.[25] After his release from a short prison sentence on June 12, 1996, Pottinger thought he was going home to his mother and brother in New York. Instead, he was whisked away to an INS detention center in New York and then transported to a remote detention facility in Oakdale, Louisiana. When he sought 212(c) relief before an immigration judge, his request was denied based on the BIA's *Soriano* decision, and he was summarily ordered deported. He remained in detention while he fought for his right to a hearing in an appeal to the BIA. By January 1997, when the INS finally agreed to release him from detention, Pottinger had spent far more time in detention fighting for a 212(c) hearing than he had spent in prison serving the sentence for his crime. But his ordeal was far from over. When Pottinger's lawyers filed a habeas action to challenge application of the *Soriano* rule, the government demanded that Pottinger surrender for further detention. On what he describes as the most difficult day of his life, Pottinger boarded a plane to return to detention in Oakdale so that he could pursue his claim in court for his 212(c) hearing. Others found that cost too high to bear and simply accepted deportation, giving up their claims to remain with their families in the United States.

Advocacy Outside the Courts

While the litigation got underway, journalists, advocacy groups and affected families began to educate the public about the harshness of the 1996 deportation laws. In the fall of 1997, the Alliance for Justice organized showings of a film that highlighted the experience of Jesus Collado. Collado had lived in the United States since 1972, when he immigrated from the Dominican Republic at the age of seventeen. In

April 1997, as he returned from a trip abroad, Collado was stopped by immigration inspectors, handcuffed and placed into detention as a result of a 1974 misdemeanor conviction for which he had received probation. The 1974 conviction resulted from Collado's consensual sexual relationship with his girlfriend when both were teenagers. The film showed the consequences of detention and the draconian effects of a law that barred Collado, his wife and daughters from testifying before any judge about the unfairness of deportation. The film premiered on October 6, 1997 on Capitol Hill in a showing for legislators and the press, and was later shown in 150 events across the country.

The Collado story immediately caught the attention of the media. *The New York Times* ran several stories, and Collado was featured on *Dateline*, public radio, and fifty local newspaper stories outside the New York area. By the end of the month, the INS released him from custody. As attention centered on Collado's case, Senator Abraham criticized the INS for pursuing cases against a persons with twenty year old convictions and promised to hold hearings.[26]

INS officials were baffled. While the legislation was being debated, they were led to believe that Senator Abraham intended to strip all discretion from INS regarding the deportation of aliens with criminal convictions. In earlier discussions with Abraham's staff, INS officials had even described sympathetic hypotheticals, often involving ancient convictions of LPRs who had lived exemplary lives since then, in order to convey that that law needed discretion and a more flexible range of relief. Now that the Collado case presented a concrete example very like the hypotheticals of which INS had warned, Abraham suddenly was refusing to take responsibility.

Thus began several years of finger pointing. Some members of Congress would claim that the INS was overzealous in applying the new law, while at the same time requiring reports on the number of "criminal aliens" deported. The agency would reply that the laws left them with no discretion to look at individual circumstances.

Other stories also flooded the press. Anthony Lewis, a columnist with *The New York Times,* wrote about people caught in the web of the new law and explained the significance of judicial review. Each profile told the story of an individual, such as Collado, whom no reasonable person would want to deport. Lewis also used his columns to obtain access to members of Congress and often quoted promises to seek reform.

Senator Abraham never held his promised hearings. But legislators introduced bills on behalf of their constituents. Leading the way was Congressman Barney Frank, a liberal congressman from Massachusetts. He proposed legislation that tracked the provisions that had passed both houses in the 1996 comprehensive bills, before the amendments made by the conference committee. Frank sought to restore relief from removal for those who had sentences of less than five years. His proposal also included provisions to assure that those who had already been deported could return.

But more surprising was the support for reform from those who had been staunch supporters of the 1996 laws. Representative Bill McCullom, a conservative from Florida, introduced a private bill on behalf of one of his constituents. After substantial media attention to the discrepancy between the law he had supported and this private bill, McCullom introduced legislation that would have eliminated some of the law's retroactive effects.

Meanwhile, affected families were organizing to prevent deportation of their family members. Danny Kozuba's wife, Laurie Kozuba, set out in the spring of 1998 to organize a network of affected family members called Citizens and Immigrants for Equal Justice. Operating out of her living room in Texas, she used e-mail and her phone to develop contacts with affected families around the country. By the spring of 1999, she and others brought over eighty families (including Pottinger's mother) to Washington D.C., to educate their representatives about what was happening to their families. They galvanized attention to the issues and helped to prompt a "Fix–96" campaign by national immigration groups. Other events were organized in local communities, including vigils and Father's Day rallies, to keep the issue in the public eye.

By the fall of 2000, support for reform was very high. A broad spectrum of organizations, led by the National Immigration Forum in Washington, was working to change the laws. A reform bill was reported out of the Judiciary Committee and passed the full House. But its fate in the Senate illustrates the difficulty of obtaining Congressional reform of laws affecting criminal aliens. In the Senate, the leadership allowed Phil Gramm of Texas to effectively veto the bill. Gramm issued a press release suggesting that the bill "welcomed money launderers, tax evaders, perjurers, fugitives from justice, alien smugglers and an assortment of other scoundrels to live among us."[27] Frank issued a quick retort saying that Gramm had refused to meet to discuss any amendments and had ignored the fact that the bill simply allowed consideration of the equities of each case. But it was too late. The bill died when the congressional session ended.[28]

Post-Soriano *Cases in the Circuit Courts*

Back in the courts, the litigation continued. By the winter of 1998, immigrant advocates were cautiously optimistic about obtaining favorable circuit court precedent. Oral arguments in the First, Second and

Ninth circuits had gone well. It was crucial to get a good early decision from the courts of appeals. Although no circuit is bound by another circuit, it is always harder to get a court to split with its sister circuits. Now it was a question of waiting for those courts to rule.

Then, in April 1998, came a devastating decision in the Ninth Circuit. In *Hose v. INS*,[29] a case the IRP had not known about, a Ninth Circuit panel ruled that Congress had eliminated habeas review by enacting INA § 242(g) as part of IIRIRA, a broadly worded provision restricting judicial review. Although *Hose* did not involve 212(c) relief, its jurisdictional ruling was broad and threatened to foreclose any judicial review through habeas. The IRP, hoping to clear the slate of this bad precedent, immediately returned to its strategy from *Duldulao* and filed for rehearing.

The following month the First Circuit issued the first court of appeals decision in the post-*Soriano* line of cases. In *Goncalves v. INS*,[30] the court concluded that it had habeas jurisdiction under 28 U.S.C. § 2241 over the legal issue of retroactivity and ruled that there was no basis for applying the new law to the immigrant in that case. Four months later, the Ninth Circuit issued a decision in *Magana-Pizano*.[31] Still bound by *Hose* (which would later be reversed en banc) the *Magana-Pizano* court concluded that IIRIRA's repeal of habeas was unconstitutional and remanded for a decision on the merits. Two weeks later, the Second Circuit issued a favorable ruling in *Henderson v. INS*[32] (affirming Judge Weinstein's decision), finding habeas jurisdiction and ruling that AEDPA could not be applied to anyone who was in deportation proceedings at the time AEDPA was enacted. The momentum was on the side of those trying to overturn *Soriano* and preserve judicial review.

The First Round at the Supreme Court

The government, now represented by the Solicitor General sought certiorari in the three cases. It argued that IIRIRA eliminated habeas jurisdiction to review legal issues in deportation cases of lawful permanent residents convicted of crimes. The government approached its certiorari petition with confidence based on its solid track record of victories in the Supreme Court in immigration cases.

Immigrant advocates faced a difficult task. The Solicitor General receives substantial deference from the Court on its views of what is cert-worthy. Moreover, by the time the certiorari petitions were decided, the Eleventh Circuit had issued a decision suggesting that IIRIRA eliminated jurisdiction. This split in the circuits provided the government with a classic argument for certiorari.

Because the IRP appeared in all three circuit cases, it was well-positioned to coordinate the response to the petitions. Although it argued that there was no clear split in the circuits and that the decisions were correct, it primarily argued that the cases were simply not important enough to warrant review. In all of the cases, the jurisdictional issues arose under IIRIRA's transitional rules. The IRP urged the Court to await the permanent rule cases before taking up the weighty issues raised by any effort to eliminate habeas corpus review. It exploited the fact that the government had taken shifting positions on the meaning of the transitional rules. Early on, government lawyers had sought dismissal of petitions for review, leaving to another day the question of habeas review in the district courts. Later, as it refined its arguments, government lawyers argued that the transitional rules preserved review over constitutional issues in the courts of appeals. The Seventh Circuit, in a case decided after the government's certiorari petition was filed, agreed with this view.[33] But, as the IRP argued, the meaning of the transitional rules could not be so clear if the government itself had made two diametrically opposed arguments on the issue. On the merits, advocates feared that the Court might summarily reverse the court of appeals' decisions on retroactivity without even granting certiorari and permitting briefing on the question. The government's petition had spoken at length about the merits—which was not properly a basis for granting certiorari—and was very dismissive of the lower court decisions. The challenge was to present solid grounds for the lower courts' decisions.

While the Court was considering the certiorari petitions, it was also putting finishing touches on the opinions in another major immigration case, *Reno v. AADC*,[34] which concerned a longstanding challenge to selective enforcement of the immigration laws against immigrants sympathetic to Palestinian independence. Lower courts had enjoined the deportation proceedings. In the Supreme Court, the government argued that IIRIRA prevented any such injunction until the administrative deportation process was over. *AADC* did not directly concern the issue of jurisdiction over the *Soriano* issue, but it did concern the scope of INA § 242(g), a sweeping provision that appeared to limit court review to the cases specified in INA § 242's petition for review scheme—a scheme that barred review for those with specified criminal convictions.

The day before the Court's conference on certiorari in *Navas* and *Goncalves*, the Court issued its decision in *AADC*. As expected, it found no lower court jurisdiction to enjoin the deportation proceedings. But in a surprise to everyone, the Court interpreted the jurisdictional restrictions in IIRIRA very narrowly. This eliminated one of the arguments the government had been using for barring any jurisdiction over final deportation decisions.

Shortly afterwards, the Court denied certiorari in *Navas* and *Goncalves* and vacated and remanded *Magana-Pizano*. Advocates breathed a sigh of relief. Soon thereafter some LPRs—those who fell squarely under the First and Second Circuit decisions, who had managed not to be deported and who were not detained outside their circuits of residence and thus subject to government arguments that other circuit precedent governed their cases—began receiving their 212(c) hearings.

To government lawyers, the *AADC* decision significantly changed the legal landscape. Prior to *AADC*, they had made a two-pronged argument on jurisdiction—first, that Congress had been clear about eliminating jurisdiction for those with specified criminal convictions in the petition for review provisions (INA § 242(a)(2)(C)); and second, that section 242(g) barred any review that was not authorized in Section 242. *AADC* undermined this second prong.

Continued Litigation of the Transitional Cases

Litigation continued throughout the country on both the jurisdictional issues and retroactivity. In many cases, the district courts simply dismissed the habeas petitions, without an opinion. After filing an appeal, the lawyers often looked to the IRP for help. But sometimes they waited until just days before argument to ask it to come in and handle a case. Others never asked. Lee Gelernt, from the IRP, recalls appearing to argue a case that he expected to be the lead precedent-setting case, only to learn that the issue was already pending before another panel.

Between 1998 and the end of 1999, eleven circuits had weighed in— all in cases in which the IRP had argued the jurisdictional issues. Ten concluded that the district courts retained habeas jurisdiction. Of these, eight ruled that some forms of retroactive application were impermissible. Nonetheless, the tide was turning against LPRs like Pottinger, who had pled guilty to his crime prior to AEDPA's enactment, but was not yet in deportation proceedings on that date. Increasingly, courts either rejected these claims or required a specific factual showing that the individual pled guilty in reliance on the prospect of receiving a 212(c) waiver hearing. But the district judge in Pottinger's case saw the merit of his claim. In 1999, two years after he surrendered for additional detention, Judge Weinstein ruled that AEDPA could not be applied to an LPR who had pled guilty prior to the enactment date. The government appealed, but agreed to release Pottinger from detention while the issue continued to be litigated.

Despite many pro-immigrant lower court decisions, many immigrants challenging retroactivity continued to be deported. A major factor in deportation was where the person was detained. In Pottinger's case, his lawyers had filed a writ of habeas corpus in the Eastern District of

New York, the district that covered the area if his residence. Judge Weinstein had kept the case over government objections that the case should be transferred to Louisiana, where Pottinger was detained. Other immigrants were not so lucky. Some resided in circuits where the courts refused to exercise jurisdiction over either habeas petitions or petitions for review. Others had cases transferred to courts that would refuse to issue stays. Deportations continued.

The Permanent Rule Cases

The Initial Phase of St. Cyr v. Reno

While the Supreme Court was considering *Navas, Goncalves* and *Magana-Pizano*, litigation was underway in the lower courts on behalf of LPRs who were placed in deportation (now called removal) proceedings after April 1, 1997, and were thus subject to the permanent jurisdictional rules of IIRIRA. Some of them, such as Jesus Collado, had very old convictions. Once again, the IRP sought to persuade lawyers to file both petitions for review in the courts of appeals and habeas petitions in the district courts, thereby enabling the IRP to argue that the fundamental issue in the case was whether there would be *any* avenue of review.

But most lawyers who were seeing detainees on a daily basis did not understand these nuances of federal court advocacy. A majority of circuits had ruled that there was no petition for review jurisdiction in criminal immigration cases but that jurisdiction lay in district court habeas; lawyers who managed to file habeas actions followed this precedent and did not think about how to position their cases for possible Supreme Court review. One of those lawyers was Michael Moore, a solo practitioner with approximately 300 clients. Moore was approached by Enrico St. Cyr, who had immigrated from Haiti at the age of 19 and faced deportation due to a drug charge for which he was serving a five year prison sentence. St. Cyr had every reason to fight his deportation. He knew that deportation meant being sent to Haiti, a country where he had no family and where deportees with criminal convictions are jailed in harsh conditions on arrival.

Unlike most immigration attorneys, Moore was not shy about filing habeas claims. But he also did not worry about refining his papers. Including the caption, his petition for St. Cyr was barely more than one page.

Neither Moore nor District Judge Alan Nevas focused on which laws applied to St. Cyr's case. Judge Nevas consolidated St. Cyr's case with petitions for two of Moore's other clients and treated all three cases as falling under AEDPA. He then ruled that all three were entitled to section 212(c) relief.[35]

When the cases reached the Second Circuit, the IRP worked to have
St. Cyr's case separated from the others. At that time, three other
petitions for review under the permanent rules were working their way
towards argument and the IRP was anxious to present the court with
every jurisdictional option for judicial review. Its first choice would have
been to present the circuit with habeas petitions on behalf of these same
petitioners. It was not an option, however, because the habeas petitions
for those immigrants were bogged down in the district courts. A second-
best option was to consolidate St. Cyr's case—which was already in the
circuit—with the other cases that had pending petitions for review.
Through consolidation, the IRP could provide the court of appeals with
every jurisdictional avenue, even if one of these avenues was unavailable
for a particular litigant.

The IRP's efforts succeeded. The Second Circuit separated St. Cyr's
case from the AEDPA cases and consolidated it with the petitions of
Delores Calcano–Martinez and two other petitioners whose cases fell
under IIRIRA. The IRP then took over the briefing and argument in St.
Cyr. For the first time, IRP lawyers presented both the jurisdictional and
retroactivity arguments.

By this time, the federal courts were lining up against finding any
restriction on habeas jurisdiction. Furthermore, the tide was turning
once again on the merits. After a number of cases that limited 212(c)
relief to those who were in deportation proceedings on AEDPA's enactment date or who could show specific reliance on the pre-AEDPA state of
the law, the Fourth Circuit issued a pro-immigrant decision in *Tasios v.
Reno*.[36] The Fourth Circuit is generally known as a conservative court,
and advocates had not expected to it to be sympathetic to the rights of
immigrants. On issues of retroactive government legislation, however, it
is a mistake to presume that conservatives would support laws that
change past expectations. In *Tasios*, the Fourth Circuit issued an across-
the-board ruling that retroactive changes in the consequences of a plea
were impermissible without explicit approval from Congress. *Tasios*
breathed new life into the argument that changes in 212(c) relief can
constitute a retroactive effect. But the IRP also had another problem. It
had to show that the law that governed St. Cyr's case—IIRIRA—did not
explicitly approve retroactive application (because Congress has the
power to authorize such application, if it clearly states its retroactive
intent). This showing had been easier in cases under AEDPA, which the
Soriano decision had described as silent on the retroactivity issue. No
circuit court had ruled on the language of IIRIRA.

In September 2000, the Second Circuit issued its decision. In a 2–1
decision, the Court concluded that the district court had habeas jurisdiction over St. Cyr's legal claim. It further held that applying IIRIRA's
repeal of 212(c) to St. Cyr would constitute a retroactive effect and that

IIRIRA included no clear language expressing Congress' intent to have the law applied retroactively.[37] In Calcano–Martinez's case, the Second Circuit ruled that the new law barred a petition for review directly to the courts of appeals, but that she could proceed with a habeas petition.[38]

The Petitions for Certiorari and Briefing

No one involved in the *St. Cyr* litigation doubted that the Supreme Court would grant review. The cases presented a fundamentally important question about judicial power under permanent jurisdictional rules. Furthermore, the circuits were clearly split both on the jurisdictional issues and on the question whether new restrictions on relief from deportation constitute a retroactive effect.

The ball was in the government's court. If it waited 90 days to petition (as permitted under the rules) or sought any extensions of time, the cases probably could not be decided during the Court's 2000–2001 Term. In November, the Solicitor General filed an early petition for certiorari in *St. Cyr*. This presented a problem for the IRP's strategy. St. Cyr's lawyer had only filed a habeas petition. He had never filed a direct petition for review in the court of appeals. If the Court considered only his case, it might rule that habeas was unavailable without ensuring that some review through petitions for review to the courts of appeals remained available. Furthermore, it would present both the jurisdictional issues and the retroactivity question in a single case. The prospect of briefing both issues in one set of briefs was daunting. The IRP decided to petition for certiorari in the *Calcano-Martinez* cases, arguing that they presented the best vehicle for the court to decide the issues. This was a tricky argument. Calcano–Martinez had not really lost below. Instead the Second Circuit had said that her case should be heard in habeas rather than through a petition for review. She could have gone ahead and pursued her habeas. But the IRP and Calcano–Martinez's lawyers knew that the Supreme Court would intervene, so they had an interest in ensuring that the issues were as well-presented as possible. Making sure that all jurisdictional avenues were available to the Court provided the best chance for preserving some forum for judicial review. In its petition in *Calcano-Martinez*, the IRP argued that unlike St. Cyr, Calcano–Martinez and the other petitioners had filed both a petition for review and a habeas corpus petition and that their cases were a better vehicle for a comprehensive review of the cases.

The Solicitor General's office responded that *Calcano-Martinez* should merely be held in abeyance or that the two cases should both be taken and consolidated. Its primary concern was to assure that there would be a ruling as soon as possible on both the jurisdictional and retroactivity issues. The IRP replied that the cases were in different postures, had some different legal issues, and had some different lawyers. If the Court took the cases, IRP argued, it should designate both for full briefing, rather than require a single set of consolidated briefs.

On January 12, 2001, the Supreme Court agreed to take both cases and ordered expedited briefing to permit argument and a decision before the end of the Term. The IRP got what it wanted—the opportunity to have both potential jurisdictional avenues before the Court and the opportunity to submit two separate sets of briefs. The government got what it wanted—an opportunity for full resolution of the issues that were being litigated in the lower courts. Since each side was the petitioner in one case, the schedule meant non-stop work for the lawyers, who had a brief due for each of the next three months.

The IRP's opening brief was in *Calcano-Martinez*. It devoted the brief entirely to the jurisdictional issues, stressing that the fundamental issue before the Court was whether *any* court could hear the retroactivity issue. In keeping with its strategy from the previous five years, the IRP indicated no preference about whether jurisdiction should be in the courts of appeals or the district courts. Its claim was that *some* court must be able to review the legality of eliminating section 212(c) relief retroactively and that stripping the courts of that power would violate the Suspension Clause of the Constitution.

In remaining agnostic about whether review belonged in the district courts or the court of appeals, the IRP avoided reliance on the approach that prevailed in many circuit courts, namely that statutory habeas jurisdiction under 28 U.S.C. § 2241 remains unless it is repealed through clear and specific legislation. This approach had resonated in the circuit courts in part because the issue arose after the circuit courts had already dismissed petitions for review on the government's motions. Those courts therefore had not had the option to construe the jurisdictional limitations on petition for review jurisdiction in a way that preserved judicial review in the circuits.[39] The Supreme Court would not face these same constraints. Furthermore, if it embraced the idea that jurisdiction was in the district courts, the IRP faced counter-arguments that Congress could not have intended to grant "criminal aliens" a route to court that involved both district court decisions and later appeals to the circuit courts. The IRP brief therefore returned to basics, arguing that the core function of habeas—whether through "habeas" actions or through petitions for review that substituted for habeas—was to allow for review of the legality of executive detention and that this included review of the legal issue whether Congress had retroactively eliminated 212(c) relief. The brief showed how the Court had historically treated habeas jurisdiction over such legal questions as a constitutional minimum, even during periods when Congress had barred judicial review. Because section 212(c) relief is discretionary, the IRP brief emphasized that the issue in the case was not how discretion should be exercised but instead the basic legal question whether IIRIRA operated retroactively to preclude eligibility for relief under section 212(c). It sought to persuade the Court that this was a fundamental question of the rule of law and that the Court should not abdicate to the executive branch the sole power to decide whether Congress meant a statute to have retroactive effect.

The government's opening brief was in *St. Cyr*, where it argued that Congress had eliminated habeas jurisdiction and that all claims that could be heard must be presented in the courts of appeals through petitions for review. St. Cyr's claim, they argued, concerned *discretionary* relief and therefore was barred altogether. Moreover, there was nothing retroactive about changing rules for relief from deportation. The government argued that the award of discretionary relief was an "act of grace" which created no legitimate expectation of receiving relief. Even if there were such an expectation, the government continued, Congress had made it amply clear that it wished to take away section 212(c) relief as part of a broader effort to speed the deportation of criminal aliens.

In writing the next round of briefs, the government was replying to the jurisdiction-only filing in *Calcano-Martinez* while the IRP was replying to briefs that mixed jurisdictional and merits issues. The IRP chose to devote the bulk of the answering brief in *St. Cyr* to the retroactivity issue. It also used this brief to present a statutory argument for district court habeas jurisdiction.

On the merits the brief placed 212(c) relief in the context of an immigration process which requires two steps before anyone is deported. First, there must be a determination whether a person is deportable. Next there must be a determination whether the person is eligible for and deserving of any relief. Only after these two steps can a person be lawfully deported. In this way, the brief sought to make 212(c) relief concrete so that it would make sense that noncitizens would have expectations about their ability to seek that relief. Critical to this presentation was the fact cited by Judge Weinstein in the earliest of the *Soriano* decisions—that 50% of LPRs who sought 212(c) relief obtained it. The brief also parsed IIRIRA, showing that Congress had used far clearer language of retroactivity in other sections.

Identifying an appropriate date against which to judge retroactivity was a particularly tricky aspect of the brief. As with its jurisdictional argument, the IRP was agnostic. It argued that it did not matter whether the Court used the date of conduct, plea or conviction to measure retroactive effect; all three dates worked for St. Cyr. This allowed the brief to take advantage of arguments rooted in the contract-like expectations of a plea bargain, as well as arguments for fair notice of the legal consequences of the immigration consequences of the underlying conduct.

A wide range of amici filed briefs together with the IRP's answering brief in *St. Cyr*. Since the government's brief in *St. Cyr* addressed both jurisdictional and merits issues, these briefs were free to reply on all of these questions. One amicus, drafted by Professors Michael Wishnie and James Oldham, presented the views of leading legal historians about whether habeas was historically limited to constitutional questions. The amicus provided the Court with detailed citations to habeas cases in England and colonial America to show that, at the time of the Founding, habeas provided review of questions about the legality of detention. This brief supported the argument that denying St. Cyr a day in court would violate the Constitutional prohibition against suspension of the writ of habeas corpus. Another amicus, drafted by Manny Vargas of the Immigrant Defense Project of the New York State Defenders' Association, provided specific evidence of how criminal defense lawyers were trained to consider eligibility for 212(c) relief when negotiating a plea agreement. A third amicus, drafted by Becky Sharpless of the Florida Immigrant Advocacy Center, provided case examples of people affected by retroactive application of new deportation laws, and included citations to press accounts since 1996 about highly sympathetic people who had been trapped by retroactive application of the changes in 212(c) relief.

The final set of briefs was due just two weeks later. The government chose to ignore the bulk of the presentation in the amicus briefs, returning instead to its basic theme that Congress had properly sought to streamline the deportation of criminal aliens thorough elimination of discretionary waivers and restrictions on judicial review. The IRP offered a reprise of its arguments for preserving jurisdiction in some court. Argument was set less than two weeks after the final filings.

The Argument

On April 24, 2001, five years to the day from the enactment of AEDPA, the Supreme Court heard back-to-back arguments in *INS v. St. Cyr* and *Calcano-Martinez v. INS*. For two straight hours, the Court heard from Lucas Guttentag, head of the IRP, and Edwin Kneedler, Deputy Solictor General.

First up was Guttentag in the *Calcano* case. Together with his colleague Lee Gelernt, Guttentag had argued these issues for five years in the courts of appeals. Their message remained what it had been from the start: that the issue was whether a legal ruling of the Attorney General was reviewable by any court and that the judicial branch had never allowed the legality of a deportation order to be shielded from any form of judicial scrutiny. Guttentag's theme was that the rule of law demands some oversight of such pure legal questions. Justice Kennedy, who later provided the deciding vote, offered a statutory argument for reading the petition for review statute as preserving review. The IRP had not advanced this specific statutory interpretation and Justice Scalia soon jumped in to suggest that the argument had not been presented because it did not work. Guttentag stayed out of the fray and stuck to his theme: one way or the other, the statutory scheme had to be read to preserve the constitutional minimum level of review.

Kneedler began by reminding the Court of the context of years of congressional concern with noncitizens convicted of crimes. He suggested that the criminal proceedings that led to the convictions for which these noncitizens were being deported provided all the process that was due. He also explained why Justice Kennedy's proposed statutory interpretation was problematic. But Kneedler's position bothered at least some Justices. In one interplay, he was asked whether a constitutional claim could be heard by a court. He said that it could. But when asked whether a court could interpret a statute to avoid a constitutional problem (something the Court often does in immigration cases) he replied that no court would have jurisdiction to do so.

After Guttentag's rebuttal argument, Kneedler returned to the podium to argue the government's case in *St. Cyr*. Kneedler devoted half of his time to the jurisdictional question before turning to the merits. Picking up on a theme from the government's brief that resonated with how the government's lawyers had long viewed the issues, he argued that any noncitizen's ability to remain in the country is inherently prospective. Because Congress has the power to enact retroactive deportation laws, he argued, it followed that no noncitizen could have a settled expectation not to be deported. He also argued at a technical level that Congress had been clear about its imposition of the new scheme on any noncitizen placed in proceedings after the effective date of the statute.

Guttentag was next. He immediately confronted a question about how a decision finding jurisdiction could be confined. He readily agreed that his argument need not extend to those who challenged the exercise of discretion and reminded the Court that the cases before the Court involved an error of law. Eligibility for 212(c) relief, he stressed, was an essential part of the ultimate removal decision. Conceding Congress' sweeping power to enact retroactive laws, Guttentag argued that this power provided all the more reason to apply the Court's rigorous clear statement rule before imposing a harsh retroactive consequence.

The Decision and Its Aftermath

On June 25, 2001, the Court issued its decision.[40] Although the 5–4 vote was close, the decision was a resounding victory for St. Cyr and other immigrants who had managed not to be deported during the preceding five years of litigation. It was also a resounding victory for the preservation of judicial review and the principle that new laws should not be applied retroactively. And it was a resounding victory for the IRP's national strategy of tracking every case and litigating cases in every circuit.

The Court's opinion, written by Justice Stevens, rested on clear statement rules. On jurisdiction, the Court first considered the historical and constitutional foundation of habeas review of immigration orders. It concluded that in the interest of avoiding constitutional questions about suspension of the writ, the restrictions on judicial review should not be read as precluding habeas jurisdiction. The Court proceeded to follow the lower courts, which had applied *Felker* to preserve section 2241 jurisdiction in the absence of a clear congressional statement to the contrary. On the merits, the Supreme Court applied *Landgraf* and ruled that eliminating 212(c) relief retroactively was a new legal consequence for which Congress had not provided the necessary clear directive.

The dissenters addressed only the jurisdictional issues. Justice Scalia's dissent, which was joined in full by Justices Rehnquist and Thomas, concluded that the Suspension Clause did not restrict Congress' ability to eliminate habeas corpus over a class of claims. Justice O'Connor offered a narrower dissent, finding that whatever the meaning of the Suspension Clause, it did not limit Congress' power to eliminate review over the kind of legal issues presented in *St. Cyr*. Thus, the Court was just one vote shy of permitting Congress to bar any court from reviewing a purely legal question on eligibility for discretionary relief from deportation.

Although the decision discussed constitutional issues, the Court's analysis of both jurisdiction and the merits ultimately rested on statutory interpretation. Thus, at a technical level, the decision simply sent the issues back to Congress. But the Congress that could have considered the issues in 2001 was not the same Congress that had passed AEDPA and IIRIRA in 1996. Although the Republicans had gained even more legislative power, and there was a Republican in the White House, the politics of both deportation policy and judicial review had changed. On deportation policy, Congress was well informed about the harshness of the 1996 laws. On judicial review, it had to contend with the Court's serious discussion of the constitutionality of restraints on access to the courts.

When Congress returned from its summer break in September 2001, further easing of the 1996 laws seemed more likely than a legislative overruling of *St. Cyr*. Even after the September 11 attacks on the World Trade Center and the Pentagon, which totally transformed immigration politics, efforts to reform the 1996 laws continued. By the end of 2002, the House Judiciary Committee reported out a bipartisan reform bill to increase relief from deportation under the successor provision to 212(c). Similarly, with respect to jurisdiction, Congress appeared to take the reasoning of *St. Cyr* to heart when it debated new restrictions on judicial review in the USA PATRIOT Act.[41] Although early proposals would have barred habeas actions with specific reference to section 2241, they were removed from the final legislation in apparent recognition of the serious constitutional issues they raised.

The jurisdictional system created by the merging of 2241 jurisdiction and petition for review jurisdiction was complex. It required two levels of review—first in district court and later on appeal to the circuit—in cases that before 1996 would have been resolved in a petition for review, heard exclusively in the court of appeals. Furthermore, it raised many new procedural issues. What, for example, were courts to do when a person raised some claims that could be heard in a petition for review and others that could only be heard in habeas? Some courts answered this question by requiring "judicial exhaustion" of the petition for review claims before a habeas petition could be filed. These questions led to new splits in the circuits. Other splits developed about where habeas petitions should be filed.

In 2004 Senator Hatch, still the chair of the Senate Judiciary Committee, introduced legislation to repeal expressly habeas review under section 2241 while reinstating the power of courts of appeals to hear legal and constitutional issues in cases of persons who had been subject to bars on petition for review jurisdiction under the 1996 laws. In introducing this bill, he went out of his way to explain that he only sought to change the forum for review of cases, not to provide express authority for elimination of review.[42]

In the spring of 2005, in a process reminiscent of 1996, Congress rushed through a number of immigration reforms in what became the REAL ID Act.[43] As in 1996, the legislation was attached to a must-pass appropriation bill. And as in 1996, many issues were on the table and many of the immigration-related provisions were not even submitted to a committee mark-up process. One of the amendments thrown into this mix largely followed Senator Hatch's proposal on changes to the judicial review scheme. It expressly precludes habeas actions challenging removal orders under section 2241 while allowing for petition for review jurisdiction over legal and constitutional questions. Thus, despite the hardball political tactics of the REAL ID Act, and Republican control of Congress and the Presidency, the actual amendments included in the REAL ID Act did not come close to restricting judicial review in the way that *St. Cyr*'s four dissenting justices would have permitted.

In the years to come, courts will face questions about how to interpret restrictions on judicial review under the REAL ID Act and how to apply the petition for review rules to accommodate the Suspension Clause concerns that the Court recognized in the *St. Cyr* decision. Immediately after REAL ID became law, the IRP, together with the American Immigration Lawyers Foundation, renewed the effort to keep track of cases and present arguments to assure adequate access to courts. It remains to be seen how the government will litigate the latest round of changes to the judicial review scheme and whether some petitioners will be denied an adequate and effective forum for review of the legality of their removal orders.

Meanwhile, Enrico St. Cyr had his hearing and received relief under section 212(c). At his hearing, the immigration judge asked him if anyone had written to him to thank him for the role he had played in helping others fight deportation. The answer was no. But as he left the courtroom, some women waiting for their husbands' cases to be called approached him and thanked him for giving their husbands a chance to stay in the United States.

Junior Pottinger, Danny Kozuba and countless others also had their hearings and were awarded 212(c) relief. Some immigrants were denied relief and have since been deported. But for those who had already been deported, the government refused to provide an avenue for relief. The government argued that *St. Cyr* gave these people no right to return and ultimately issued regulations providing reopening only for those who had not been deported.[44]

With respect to retroactivity, the principal open issue is whether the Court's analysis in *St. Cyr* applies only to a person who pled guilty prior to the enactment date of the 1996 laws. Many courts have held that only the disruption of a *quid pro quo* exchange, such as giving up the right to trial in the hope of relief, could establish a retroactive effect. On this view, LPRs who went to trial in their underlying criminal cases believing that they were innocent have been denied the benefit of *St. Cyr*, even if their sentences would have left them eligible for 212(c) relief. But arguments about retroactivity continue to be pressed, and can be expected to continue as new Jesus Collados discover on returning from a trip that an old conviction is coming back to haunt them.

Lessons Learned

At the end of the day, the IRP's litigation strategy was a remarkable success. Over a five-year period, the IRP managed to keep abreast of complex litigation that was being pursued around the country on a case-by-case basis by lawyers of varying sophistication and by pro se litigants. Ironically, although the government was in a better position to coordinate its litigation, the immigrant advocates did a better job of identifying and presenting a single basic message about jurisdiction to the courts. Their argument at the end of the day was much the same as the argument they had identified at the start: that some court must have the power to determine the legality of the Attorney General's reading of the law. The government, which began by simply trying to dismiss cases, soon found itself presenting contradictory arguments about which courts could hear which claims. By the time the government settled on the position that only some claims could be heard and only through petitions for review in the circuit courts, it was too late. The courts of appeals had already moved the jurisdictional focus to the district courts' habeas powers under section 2241. And when the government turned to Congress after *St. Cyr*, it was not to endorse the view it had first presented to the courts, but to support legislation that would consolidate legal questions about removal orders in the courts of appeals.

But the IRP's litigation strategy could not prevent thousands from being detained and deported. The *St. Cyr* litigation reminds us how much justice is lost when every individual case must be litigated separately or not at all. Many immigrants never filed habeas actions and, even when they did, many courts refused to provide the stays of deportation that would have allowed those affected by the 1996 laws to remain in the United States until the victory in *St. Cyr*. Some people are lucky; their cases draw the attention of lawyers and the courts. Others are not, and their families remain permanently separated or are forced to follow the deportee to a country where they may be strangers. Fortunately for Enrico St. Cyr, Danny Kozuba and Junior Pottinger, legal representation and stays of deportation allowed for a happy ending.

ENDNOTES

1. In preparation of this chapter, I conducted interviews of Kerry Bretz, Lee Gelernt, Lucas Guttentag, Laurie Kozuba, David Martin, Michael Moore, Gerry Neuman, Enrico St. Cyr, Alan Strauss, Manny Vargas, Nadine Wettstein, Michael Wishnie and Carol Wolchok. In addition I drew from interviews with government counsel, some of whom requested anonymity. I also drew from my own experience, which included participation in the briefing and argument of retroactivity issues in *Mojica, Henderson, Navas, St. Cyr,* and *Pottinger,* and representation, through the Immigrant Rights Clinic at NYU School of Law, of Citizens and Immigrants for Equal Justice in advocacy concerning the 1996 deportation laws.

2. Pub. L. No. 104–132, 110 Stat. 1214 (1996).

3. Pub. L. No. 104–208, Div. C, 110 Stat. 3009–546 (1996).

4. 533 U.S. 289 (2001).

5. *See* Hiroshi Motomura, *Immigration Law After a Century of Plenary Power: Phantom Constitutional Norms and Plenary Power*, 100 Yale L. J. 545 (1990).

6. *See generally* Philip Schrag, A Well–Founded Fear: The Congressional Battle to Save Political Asylum in the United States (2000).

7. Immigration Act of 1990, Pub.L. No. 101–649, 104 Stat. 4978 (1990).

8.   518 U.S. 651 (1996).

9.   *See* Eric Schmitt, *Conferees Approve Tough Immigration Bill,* N.Y. Times, Sept. 25, 1996, at A15.

10.   *See generally,* Lucas Guttentag, *1996 Immigration Act: Federal Court Jurisdiction—Statutory Restrictions and Constitutional Rights,* 74 Interpreter Releases 245 (1997).

11.   Memorandum from David A. Martin, General Counsel, Immigration and Naturalization Service to all Regional Counsels and District Counsels, dated April 26, 1996.

12.   *See, e.g.,* Galvan v. Press, 347 U.S. 522 (1954).

13.   90 F.3d 396 (9th Cir. 1996).

14.   *See, e.g.,* Gerald L. Neuman, *Habeas Corpus, Executive Detention and the Removal of Aliens,* 98 Colum. L. Rev. 961 (1998).

15.   Duldulao v. INS, 90 F.3d at 400.

16.   *E.g.,* Kolster v. INS, 101 F.3d 785 (1st Cir. 1996); Salazar–Haro v. INS, 95 F.3d 309 (3d Cir. 1996).

17.   Matter of Soriano, 21 I & N Dec. 516 (BIA 1996; A.G. Feb. 21, 1997).

18.   Matter of U. M., 20 I & N Dec. 327 (BIA 1991).

19.   511 U.S. 244 (1994).

20.   For a discussion of the interplay of Justice Department interests and INS policy making, see Margaret Taylor, *Behind the Scenes of St. Cyr and Zadvydas: Making Policy in the Midst of Litigation,* 16 Geo. Immigr. L.J. 271 (2002).

21.   INS v. Elramly, 518 U.S. 1049 (1996).

22.   Mojica v. Reno, 970 F. Supp. 130 (E.D.N.Y. 1997), *aff'd,* Henderson v. INS, 157 F. 3d 106 (2d Cir. 1998), *cert. denied sub. nom* Reno v. Navas, 526 U.S. 1004 (1999).

23.   *But see* Nancy Morawetz, *Rethinking Retroactive Deportation Laws and the Due Process Clause,* 73 N.Y.U.L. Rev. 97 (1998); Daniel Kanstroom, *Deportation Social Control, and Punishment: Some Thoughts on Why Hard Laws Make Bad Cases,* 113 Harv. L. Rev. 1890 (2000).

24.   See Magana-Pizano v. INS, 200 F.3d 603 (9th Cir. 1999) (decision after remand).

25.   Pottinger v. Reno, 51 F.Supp. 2d 349 (E.D.N.Y. 1999), *aff'd,* 242 F.3d 367 (2d Cir. 2000).

26.   Mirta Ojito, *Old Crime Returns to Haunt an Immigrant,* N.Y. Times, Oct. 15, 1997, at B1.

27.   Joao Fereira, *Frank Criticizes Gramm for Death of Deportation Bill,* South Coast Today, Dec. 21, 2000.

28.   For a discussion of the role of race and class in the politics of extending relief from deportation, see Victor Romero, *The Child Citizenship Act and the Family Reunification Act: Valuing the Citizen Child as well as the Citizen Parent,* 55 Fla. L. Rev. 489 (2003).

29.   Hose v. INS, 141 F.3d 932 (9th Cir. 1998), opinion withdrawn and case decided by en banc court, 180 F.3d 992 (9th Cir. 1999).

30.   Goncalves v. INS, 144 F.3d 110, 127 (1st Cir.1998), *cert. denied,* 526 U.S. 1004 (1999).

31.   Magana-Pizano v. INS, 152 F.3d 1213 (9th Cir. 1998), *as amended,* 159 F.3d 1217, *vacated,* 526 U.S. 1001 (1999).

32.   Henderson v. INS, 157 F.3d 106 (2d Cir. 1998) *cert. denied sub nom.* Reno v. Navas, 526 U.S. 1004 (1999).

33. LaGuerre v. Reno, 164 F.3d 1035 (7th Cir.1998), cert. denied, 528 U.S. 1153 (2000).

34. Reno v. American-Arab Anti-Discrimination Committee, 525 U.S. 471 (1999).

35. Dunbar v. INS, 64 F.Supp.2d 47 (D. Conn. 1999), *aff'd sub nom.* St. Cyr v. INS, 229 F.3d 406 (2d Cir. 2000), *aff'd*, 533 U.S. 289 (2001).

36. Tasios v. Reno, 204 F.3d 544 (4th Cir. 2000).

37. St. Cyr v. INS, 229 F.3d 406 (2d Cir. 2000).

38. Calcano-Martinez v. INS, 232 F.3d 328 (2d Cir. 2000), *aff'd*, 533 U.S. 348 (2001).

39. One circuit had construed the provisions limiting petition for review jurisdiction in this manner, so as to preserve jurisdiction in the courts of appeals over issues constitutionally required to be subject to judicial review. LaGuerre v. Reno, 164 F.3d 1035 (7th Cir. 1998).

40. INS v. Cyr, 533 U.S. 289 (2001). The companion case was issued as Calcano-Martinez v. INS, 533 U.S. 348 (2001).

41. Pub. L. No. 107–56, 115 Stat. 272 (2001).

42. 150 Cong. Rec. S5803 (May 19, 2004).

43. Pub. L. No. 109–13, Div. B, 119 Stat. 231 (2005).

44. 69 Fed. Reg. 57826–01 (Sept. 28, 2004).

*

12

Hoffman Plastic Compounds, Inc. v. NLRB: The Rules of the Workplace for Undocumented Immigrants

Catherine L. Fisk & Michael J. Wishnie

Are there two sets of rules for the twenty-first century workplace, one for citizens and legal immigrants and the other for the millions of undocumented workers in the country? Are the employers of those undocumented workers free to ignore the mandates of the National Labor Relations Act (NLRA), Title VII of the Civil Rights Act of 1964, and other federal and state labor and employment laws, without fear of the liability they would face if their employees were documented?

To an immigration lawyer familiar with immigration law's "plenary power doctrine" and the notion of an ascending scale of rights that privileges legal immigrants over undocumented ones, the intuitive answer might be, "of course; there are frequently different rules for immigrants and citizens, and for legal immigrants and the undocumented."[1] To a labor lawyer familiar with labor law's embrace of collective action and private rights enforcement to achieve public deterrence, the instinctive response might be, "of course not; there are no statutory exceptions to labor law coverage based on immigration status, and the fate of all workers depends on the treatment of each."

The story of *Hoffman Plastic Compounds, Inc. v. NLRB*[2] reveals the efforts of unions, employers, civil rights advocates, legislatures, executive branch agencies, and ultimately the Supreme Court to reconcile immigration and labor laws, to make sense of the sometimes contradictory legislative impulses these twin regimes manifest, and to develop a framework for the humane and effective regulation of both borders and labor markets.

In important ways, laws regulating our nation's borders and its labor markets share an ancestry that traces to early colonial rules on slavery, the slave trade, and indentured servants. Although modern lawyers are accustomed to thinking of "labor law" and "immigration law" as separate fields, current proposals for mammoth new guestworker programs, "earned legalization," and a new paradigm for U.S.-Mexico relations reflect the deep connections between these two bodies of law. This common heritage is apparent as well in the competing political pressures embodied in both schemes—at times and in places protectionist, nativist, bigoted, and designed to favor the interests of management, at other times and in other places open, non-discriminatory, inclusive, and designed to favor the interests of working people.

In *Hoffman*, five justices of the U.S. Supreme Court viewed the labor and immigration laws as fundamentally at odds with one another. This majority held that an employer who unlawfully discharges a worker for union organizing activities is immune from ordinary labor law liability for backpay, if the worker lacks work authorization under immigration law and the employer learns this only after the illegal discharge. Four dissenting justices viewed the labor and immigration laws as fundamentally harmonious. They would have allowed the National Labor Relations Board (NLRB) to enforce its backpay award, notwithstanding an immigration law that prohibits employers from knowingly hiring or employing unauthorized workers.

Hoffman will not be the last word on the subject of labor rights for immigrants and labor obligations for their employers. It remains to be seen whether the decision helps spur broader legislative reform in this area, strengthening the right to organize for all workers and reducing an incentive for outlaw employers to prefer undocumented employees, or instead promotes an already-flourishing underground economy that stokes the demand for illegal immigration.

Social and Legal Background

The *Hoffman* case was litigated over thirteen years amidst three important social and legislative developments. One occurred in the labor movement, a second in Congress, and the last in the population as a whole.

First, the union movement has significantly withered, and today represents only approximately 8.5% of private-sector, non-agricultural employees. This is a fraction of union density in the post-World War II era and a figure so low as to raise fundamental questions about the capacity of unions to protect the interests of working people. Perhaps not coincidentally, through the 1990s and into the new century, organized labor's attitudes towards immigration continued to reflect, in large measure, traditional fears that immigrants would work for lower wages than long-time residents and thus drive down wages. In 1986, the AFL–CIO had supported congressional enactment of a new employment verification system, and important voices within the labor movement still oppose legalizing undocumented workers or repealing the 1986 "employer sanctions" provisions.[3] The labor movement is not monolithic, however, and other labor leaders have embraced immigrant rights and sought to organize non-citizen workforces; these latter views have led to successful organizing drives in some immigrant-intensive industries, the AFL–CIO's adoption of a pro-immigrant resolution in February 2000, and the Immigrant Worker Freedom Ride of 2003. Labor organizers have also frequently found low-wage immigrant workers more receptive than American workers to unionization drives, and a number of unions have concluded that organizing immigrants is essential to their success.[4]

Second, Congress enacted and President Clinton signed three major pieces of anti-immigrant legislation in the 1990s. The legislation slashed the public benefits eligibility of millions of indigent immigrants and their families, mandated detention and deportation for tens of thousands of legal permanent residents (LPRs), and restricted traditional forms of deportation relief such as political asylum.[5] The human consequences of these bills were dramatic. The draconian Personal Responsibility and Work Opportunity Reconciliation Act of 1996, for instance, sought to achieve nearly one-half of its estimated savings through elimination of benefits for immigrants, even though far fewer than half of welfare recipients were non-citizens. And the number of LPRs deported on the grounds of past criminal convictions, often minor, rose significantly, separating tens of thousands of long-time residents from their families, jobs, and communities. These laws also increased the risk to immigrant workers of participating in a union organizing drive. For undocumented workers, deportation in the event of a retaliatory employer call to the Immigration and Naturalization Service (INS) became more likely, and for legal immigrants, the availability of a social safety net, in the form of public assistance in the event of a retaliatory discharge, became far less likely.

Third, the number of non-citizens in the country increased substantially in the 1980s and 1990s. From 1970 to 2000, the overall foreign-born population in the United States grew from 9.7 million to 28.4 million persons.[6] While unprecedented in absolute terms, this figure was well below historic levels as percentages of the overall population: in 2000, 10.4% of the population was foreign-born, the highest proportion since 1930, but from 1860 to 1930, the percentage of foreign-born was higher still.[7] The increase in the non-citizen population was even more dramatic, rising from 3.5 million in 1970 to 17.8 million in 2000.[8] Data on the undocumented population are notoriously imprecise, but estimates have risen from approximately 5 million in the mid–1990s to perhaps 10 million in 2004.[9]

Nationwide, a large and crucial segment of the workforce is undocumented. There are millions of undocumented workers, representing approximately 5% of the total workforce (including 4% of the urban workforce and 48% of the agricultural workforce).[10] An employer group estimated in 2001 that immigrants (both legal and undocumented) contribute $1 trillion per year to GDP and account for 12% of total hours worked in the United States.[11] Not surprisingly, undocumented workers are concentrated in some of the lowest-paying and most dangerous jobs in the country.[12] In California, the effect of immigration on the workforce was particularly notable. By the year 2000, foreign-born Latinos constituted 17% of California's total workforce, 42% of its factory operatives, one-half of its laborers, and over one-third of its service workers. The dominance of Latino workers is especially apparent in Southern California, where the Hoffman Plastic plant is located.[13]

The legal background to the *Hoffman* case reflected some of these social developments. The NLRB's position since at least the late 1970s was that undocumented immigrants were "employees" covered by the NLRA. As employees, undocumented workers who were fired for union organizing would be entitled to all remedies available under the NLRA. The Board normally orders reinstatement and backpay from the date of discharge until the date of reinstatement, issues a cease-and-desist order proscribing similar conduct in the future, and directs the employer to post a notice announcing the Board's decision and promising to abide by it. The NLRB requires employees to mitigate damages by seeking interim employment. Therefore, a backpay award may be reduced by wages an employee earned in interim employment or, if the employee failed to make reasonable efforts to find employment, by the amount he or she would have earned. Eligibility for backpay depends on the employee being available for work; a backpay award is reduced for any period during which the employee is unavailable for work. The Board will not order reinstatement if the employee engaged in egregious misconduct, or if the employer shows that at some point after the unlawful discharge the employee would have been terminated in any event. Interest is computed on a backpay award.

In 1984, the Supreme Court endorsed the view that undocumented workers are employees under the NLRA. In *Sure-Tan, Inc. v. NLRB*,[14] an employer contacted the INS shortly after his employees voted for a union. The INS visited the factory and questioned its Spanish-speaking employees. The INS arrested five of them; by the end of the day, all were on a bus bound for Mexico. The Board found that the employer-initiated raid amounted to an unlawful constructive discharge of its unionizing employees and ordered reinstatement with backpay, leaving for the compliance hearing the question whether the deported workers were available for work, a requirement for eligibility for backpay. On review, the court of appeals held that the constructively discharged workers would likely have been employed for six more months absent the employer's unfair labor practice, and it modified the Board's order to award a minimum of six months' backpay. The Supreme Court upheld the Board's conclusion that undocumented immigrants are statutorily protected as employees under the NLRA, explaining: "Application of the NLRA helps to assure that the wages and employment conditions of lawful residents are not adversely affected by the competition of illegal alien employees who are not subject to the standard terms of employment."[15] But the Court reversed the court of appeals' mandatory minimum backpay award as too speculative. In particular, the Court was concerned that allowing the Board's backpay award could undermine "the objective of deterring unauthorized immigration that is embodied in the [immigration statutes]."[16] On remand, the Court stated that remedies "must be conditioned upon the employees' legal readmittance to the United States" and "in computing backpay, the employees must be deemed 'unavailable' for work (and the accrual of backpay tolled) during any period when they were not lawfully entitled to be present and employed in the United States."[17] When *Sure-Tan* was decided, it was not unlawful for an undocumented immigrant to be hired or to work in the United States.

Two years after the *Sure-Tan* decision, the Ninth Circuit appeared to limit the opinion to its facts, holding that immigrant workers who remain in this country after discharge are eligible for backpay regardless of their immigration status (as contrasted with the already-deported workers held ineligible in *Sure-Tan*).[18] Months later, Congress enacted the Immigration Reform and Control Act of 1986 (IRCA). IRCA embodied a bargain struck between legislators who favored increased immigration enforcement and those who favored a legalization program. The bill's two key provisions were a one-time amnesty for those who could demonstrate continuous residency since 1982 and "employer sanctions" provisions that prohibited employers from knowingly hiring or employing unauthorized workers.[19] Employer organizations such as the U.S. Chamber of Commerce opposed employer sanctions as a costly, burdensome, and inefficient strategy to compel the private sector to enforce public immigration laws. The AFL–CIO, on the other hand, supported employer sanctions on the ground that they would reduce wage competition by deterring employment of undocumented immigrants.

IRCA did not penalize unauthorized workers who accept employment; instead, Congress enacted a scheme of civil and criminal penalties for *employers* who knowingly hire or employ them. This deliberate legislative choice grew out of many years of congressional studies and commissions. Congress recognized it could not hope to influence the supply of undocumented workers—the wage discrepancies between the United States and Mexico were just too great—but could, through regulation, dampen employers' demand for such labor.[20] The employer sanctions regime obligates employers to check the work authorization status of all new employees within three days of hire by completing an INS Form I–9, indicating that the employee is either a U.S. citizen or an immigrant authorized to work in this country. Employers must retain their completed I–9s and make them available to immigration agents for inspection upon request. Finally, when Congress enacted IRCA, it provided for a slow phase-in. The Attorney General could neither fine employers in the first six months after enactment nor fine an employer for a first offense committed in a subsequent grace period of twelve months (to June 1, 1988).

After IRCA made it unlawful to hire undocumented workers, employers sought to revisit the question whether the NLRA still protected undocumented workers, renewing the argument that undocumented workers were ineligible for backpay because they could not legally work in the United States and were therefore not technically "available" for work as required. The first wave of post-IRCA cases involved pre-IRCA conduct, and courts uniformly concluded that undocumented workers were statutory employees and eligible for backpay if they remained present in the country after a wrongful discharge. As cases involving post-IRCA conduct began to reach the courts, a split emerged: the Seventh Circuit concluded that undocumented workers were ineligible for backpay, thus raising questions about the continuing viability of the contrary view asserted by the Second and Ninth Circuits before IRCA had gone into effect.[21]

The NLRB attempted to reconcile this split in its lengthy decision in *A.P.R.A. Fuel Oil Buyers Group*,[22] which reaffirmed that undocumented immigrants are employees protected by the NLRA, their immigration status is not a flat bar to backpay, and they are entitled to the same remedies as other employees so long as the remedies do not require the employer to violate IRCA. Thus, the employer could be ordered to reinstate employees so long as the employees could present verification of an immigration status enabling them to work in the U.S. at the time of reinstatement, and an employer must pay backpay from the date of discharge until either the date of reinstatement or the date when the employee failed to produce evidence of eligibility to work in the U.S. It was against this background that *Hoffman Plastic* arose.

Factual Background

In May 1988, not long after IRCA went into effect and prior to the expiration of IRCA's "first offense" grace period for employers, a man whose real name may have been Samuel Perez applied for a job under the name Jose Castro at Hoffman Plastic Compounds factory in Panorama, California.[23] He spoke little English, so someone helped him fill out the six-page application form. On the form, he answered "Yes" to the question, "Are you prevented from lawfully becoming employed in this country because of visa or immigration status?" As part of the application process, however, he also completed the I–9 Form establishing that his immigration status permitted him lawfully to work and presented a birth certificate stating he was born in El Paso, Texas, a California ID card with his name and photograph, and a Social Security card in his name. Reflecting on this discrepancy in the file, Peter Tovar, the NLRB Regional Attorney who litigated the case, suspected that a Hoffman office employee looked at the application and explained to Castro that he could not be hired until he produced certain documents, and that Castro went away and came back with the requested papers.[24] Or maybe Castro did not understand the question on the application when it was translated to him. In any event, Castro was hired and began work at the factory. While working there he lived with his niece, sleeping on the couch in her living room, as he had no home of his own.

Hoffman Plastic Compounds, a family-owned firm, produces a type of plastic, polyvinylchloride (PVC) pellets, on order for firms that use PVC to make pharmaceutical, construction, and household products. Jose Castro worked as a production employee, operating machines that mix, cook, and press the PVC into pellets.

Shortly before Christmas 1988, the United Rubber, Cork, Linoleum and Plastic Workers of America, an AFL–CIO union, began to organize the plant. A union organizer visited the plant frequently. Castro was one of the employees who passed out union cards. In January 1989, after supervisors learned of the organizing drive and unlawfully interrogated employees about their union activity, nine employees were laid off. One of them was Castro.

Why did Jose Castro, an undocumented minimum wage worker without a home of his own, take the risk of speaking up for the union? According to the NLRB's Peter Tovar, Castro had been considered a good, hard-working employee and was not a leader of the union organizing drive. He was just in the wrong place at the wrong time.[25] To the extent that he did actively support the union, we can only speculate about his reasons. Scholars who studied union organizing campaigns in Southern California in the 1980s and 1990s found little fear among the undocumented. Some explained that if they were deported, they would simply come back. Others said that the possibility of INS raids seemed remote. Some Mexican and Central American immigrants had had positive experiences of unionism in their home countries and believed that, in contrast to the death threats leveled against union organizers by right-wing groups in Central America, the worst that could happen in the United States would be the loss of a low-wage job and deportation home to one's family.[26]

According to Hoffman's lawyer, the organizing drive failed, there have been no other efforts to unionize the plant, and it remains non-union. Many of the employees fired for union activity were reinstated, although some were later terminated for other reasons.[27]

Prior Proceedings

One of the laid-off employees, Casimiro Arauz, filed an unfair labor practice charge with the NLRB. In April 1990, over a year after the layoffs, an administrative law judge (ALJ) for the NLRB held a hearing on the charge. The employees testified that the supervisors had told employees that the union was "cabron" (which the ALJ rather delicately described as "an expression in Spanish which meant 'bad' or 'something not good'") and that they "could get into trouble if management found out about [their] passing out union cards." Ron Hoffman, the company owner, denied that the layoffs had anything to do with union activity, insisting that they were due to a decline in orders and that employees were selected for layoff based on a combination of seniority, disciplinary record, and skills. The ALJ found, however, that Hoffman had hired new employees after firing the union employees and had required existing employees to work overtime to keep up production. The ALJ also found conflicting evidence as to whether Hoffman had laid off employees to rid itself of the union, for lack of work, or for both reasons. The ALJ concluded, however, that regardless of the cause for the layoffs, Hoffman had violated the NLRA by deciding *which* employees to lay off based on their union activity, given evidence that all union adherents were laid off and that supervisors had interrogated them about their support for the union.[28]

Both the General Counsel and the employer appealed to the full NLRB, which in January 1992 largely upheld the ALJ's findings and conclusions but found that one of the nine employees would have been laid off regardless of his union activity.[29] Because the other fired employees eventually settled their charges with Hoffman,[30] Castro was the only one whose immigration status became an issue.

In June 1993, an ALJ conducted a hearing to determine the amount of backpay owed to the fired employees who had not yet settled. Hoffman's lawyer, Ryan McCortney, had worked in the Los Angeles office of the Sheppard Mullin firm since graduating from the University of Southern California Law School in 1987. He stated later that he had no idea at the start of the hearing that Castro might be undocumented, but hit upon the possibility entirely by accident, based on something that Castro volunteered while testifying.[31] Castro had missed an earlier hearing, and McCortney inquired about his absence. According to McCortney, the NLRB attorney, Peter Tovar, replied that Castro was in jail in Texas. Thinking that the jail time would toll the backpay award, McCortney hired a private investigator to figure out where he was in jail and how long he had been there. The private investigator faxed Castro's birth certificate to the jail and was informed that there was no one by that name in the jail. Suspecting that the birth certificate was faked, the investigator went to the hospital where Castro had been born and learned that the birth certificate was valid. McCortney then asked for a background check to see whether Castro had been in jail at other times that would toll the backpay period. The check revealed that Castro had a trucker's license, which convinced McCortney that Castro could easily have mitigated his lost wages. The check also indicated that Castro had briefly been in jail in Los Angeles County. Armed with this information, McCortney went to the backpay hearing intending to impeach Castro's credibility about his mitigation efforts.

McCortney spent much of the first part of the hearing establishing where Castro had lived since the lay-offs, in an attempt to demonstrate that he had been outside California (and thus unavailable for work at the Hoffman plant) or had failed to make adequate efforts to find work. In addition, there was some dispute about whether Castro had received a letter from Hoffman offering him reinstatement (which would also have tolled the backpay award). Testifying through a translator, Castro said that he had worked at a variety of irregular and low-paying jobs as a gardener, carpenter's assistant, and mechanic's assistant since being fired by Hoffman, and that he had spent six or seven months in El Paso.

Tovar thought that Castro's limited education was the reason he had had difficulty finding work since his lay-off.[32] Thus, on cross-examination, Tovar asked about his schooling, and Castro replied that he had had only two years of formal education while a child in Mexico. That made no sense to McCortney—why would someone born and raised in Texas have left school in the second grade? It was not until Castro said he had attended school in Mexico that it occurred to McCortney that Castro had borrowed the birth certificate because he was not a legal immigrant. On redirect, McCortney asked how many years of education he had had, and Castro said two. McCortney then asked why he had stated on his employment application that he had eight years of education, and Castro replied, "So that I could obtain work." McCortney continued, "Now, you were born in El Paso, Texas, correct?" "No, I am Mexican," responded Castro. "You're not a citizen of the United States?" "No." Over the objection of Tovar, the ALJ permitted McCortney to ask Castro whether he had documents permitting him to work in the United States. Castro said he had the birth certificate but admitted that he had borrowed it from a friend so that he could get a job.

Much later, when the case reached the Supreme Court, McCortney had come to characterize Hoffman as entirely "innocent," unaware that Castro was undocumented, and thus not needing the sanction of an

NLRA backpay award to deter him from hiring undocumented workers in the future.[33] But earlier, in the post-hearing brief to the NLRB, McCortney did not take this strong position. There was no evidence in the record as to whether Hoffman Plastic had knowingly hired other undocumented workers or had a policy against their hiring. Nor, apart from the information on Castro's initial employment application and I–9 form, was there evidence regarding Hoffman's knowledge of Castro's immigration status. The most that McCortney could argue, then, was that the evidence about Castro's immigration status on his employment application and I–9 form conflicted, and that because the law prohibited hiring undocumented workers, it was unnecessary to show that Hoffman had a policy against hiring them.

Even though the case law of the NLRB and the Ninth Circuit at that time held that undocumented workers who, like Castro, remained physically present in the United States could be awarded backpay and conditional reinstatement, the ALJ held that Castro was ineligible for backpay. The ALJ distinguished or ignored the contrary NLRB and Ninth Circuit decisions and instead followed a Seventh Circuit opinion.[34]

McCortney was thrilled that the ALJ rejected the Board position that immigration status is irrelevant to backpay. He thought it a vindication of his view that it would be unfair to award backpay to an employee who could not legally have been hired and could not legally mitigate damages by seeking interim employment. In his view, backpay for Castro would be an unjust windfall. Peter Tovar, of course, saw the matter differently. In his view, it is simply unrealistic to think that undocumented immigrants will sit around rather than look for other work. "They are here to work and they do work. Castro reported to us every job he had after being fired from Hoffman, and we discounted the backpay request to reflect all his interim earnings. There was no unfairness to the employer."[35]

The Regional Director filed an appeal to the full NLRB in December 1993. An unexplained five-year delay in the case followed. Notably, William B. Gould, IV, a Stanford law professor who became Chair of the NLRB in December 1994, did not recall *Hoffman Plastic* as being the "big case" on the issue of the rights of undocumented workers.[36] Instead, the big case was *A.P.R.A. Fuel Oil Buyers Group,*[37] issued in December 1995 while the *Hoffman* decision was pending. In *A.P.R.A.*, four members of the Board, including Gould, exhaustively considered how to reconcile the NLRA's remedial provisions with IRCA's prohibition on employing unauthorized immigrants. The majority of the Board concluded that IRCA's major purpose was to deter the employment of undocumented workers, and that providing NLRA remedies furthered this purpose. The Board noted that in *A.P.R.A.*, the employer knew from the date of hire that its workers were undocumented. Because the workers would have remained employed but for their union activity and the employer's illegal retaliation for it, backpay was appropriate. The Board had awarded backpay from the dates of discharge to the date that the workers were offered reinstatement and either accepted or failed to produce documents evidencing work authorization.[38]

By September 1998, when the NLRB finally issued its decision in *Hoffman*, the Board's membership had changed. The new members seemed to have a slightly different view of the equities of remedies for undocumented workers. While following the decision in *A.P.R.A. Fuel Oil Buyers Group* that undocumented workers are entitled to some backpay, they found a significant difference between *Hoffman* and *A.P.R.A.*: in *A.P.R.A.*, it was undisputed that the employer knew its employees were undocumented, whereas the evidence about Hoffman's knowledge of Castro's status was, at best, conflicting. The Board noted in a footnote that Castro had answered "yes" to the question on the application whether his immigration status prevented him from lawfully becoming employed. But the Board rejected the contention that this showed that Hoffman knew of Castro's status "because the record clearly shows that the Respondent only hired Castro after he had supplied, as the Respondent required, documents that appeared to be genuine and relate to the person presenting them."[39]

Having found that Hoffman learned of Castro's status only at the time of the NLRB hearing, the Board ordered that Hoffman's backpay liability terminate effective as of the hearing date, June 14, 1993. The Board thus calculated that Castro was entitled to $66,951 in backpay plus interest for the four-and-a-half years from when he was fired in January 1989 until the June 1993 compliance hearing, including a reduction in the damages based on Castro's earnings in mitigation. Chairman Gould remembered *Hoffman* as a somewhat controversial decision, and in fact drafted an opinion in the case (which was never issued) in which he disagreed with other members of the Board about whether Hoffman knew of Castro's immigration status.[40] That unpublished dispute about Hoffman's knowledge was the last time the issue was raised; for the rest of the litigation, McCortney insisted without challenge that his client did not know Castro was undocumented and would not have hired him if the company had known.

McCortney informed Ron Hoffman that the costs of judicial review would be high and the chance of winning uncertain, but Hoffman wanted to fight on. When Regional Attorney Tovar insisted that if Hoffman refused to pay the award, the Region would seek enforcement in the Ninth Circuit, McCortney decided to act. He knew that while the Board must seek enforcement of its orders in the court of appeals where the labor dispute arises, a "person aggrieved" by a Board order may seek judicial review in either the court of appeals where the dispute arose or in the D.C. Circuit.[41] Believing the D.C. Circuit to be a more favorable forum, McCortney filed a petition for review in the D.C. Circuit that same day, beating the NLRB to the courthouse.

McCortney's forum-shopping was unsuccessful. The AFL–CIO filed a forceful amicus brief in support of the Board, and Marsha Berzon, then one of the nation's leading labor and employment attorneys and soon to be confirmed by the Senate as a member of the U.S. Court of Appeals for the Ninth Circuit, participated in oral argument on behalf of amici. Berzon was a skilled and experienced appellate advocate, and as one member of the panel later recalled, she presented the case for enforcement superbly.[42]

The D.C. Circuit panel, in a majority opinion by Judge David Tatel, canvassed the history and structure of IRCA and the relevant NLRB doctrines on remedies. The majority concluded that Congress' intention in enacting IRCA was plain that there should be "expanded enforcement of existing labor standards and practices in order to deter the employment of unauthorized aliens and to remove the economic incentives for employers to exploit and use such aliens."[43] Judge Tatel also emphasized that IRCA "does not make it unlawful for an *alien* to work; it makes it unlawful for an *employer* to hire an alien knowing the alien is ... unauthorized.... [A]t the time Hoffman hired Castro, it complied with IRCA, and from that date until it learned he is unauthorized, nothing prohibited his continued employment."[44]

Judge Tatel's opinion also analyzed the sentence in *Sure-Tan* stating that "in computing backpay, the employees must be deemed 'unavailable' for work (and the accrual of backpay therefore tolled) during any period when they were not lawfully entitled to be present and employed in the United States." That sentence was dicta, Tatel wrote, because the *Sure-Tan* employees were not physically present in the United States at the time; it addressed the Board's decision to award six months' backpay to the deported Sure–Tan workers, without tailoring the award to the actual length of time they were unemployed or the actual amount of their mitigation. Tatel also read the *Sure-Tan* sentence in context as indicating approval of the Seventh Circuit's limitation of the backpay award to only six months, so as to avoid encouraging the deported employees to re-enter the country unlawfully to claim their backpay.

Judge David Sentelle dissented. In his view, the case was quite simple. Since Hoffman could not lawfully employ Castro, the company was immune from ordinary backpay liability for wrongful discharge. Were it not for the Supreme Court's decision in *Sure-Tan*, which granted undocumented workers statutory rights, Judge Sentelle "would hold that by no theory of law or equity could the federal government compel an employer to employ an illegal alien to do nothing and pay him for doing nothing when it could not lawfully employ him to work and pay him for working."[45] Judge Sentelle believed further that the *Sure-Tan* sentence regarding employees "deemed 'unavailable' for work ... during any period when they were not lawfully entitled to be present and employed in the United States" definitively foreclosed Castro's claim.[46]

McCortney and his client then had another choice to make. A petition for rehearing en banc would be a long shot. But when McCortney heard that dissenting Judge Sentelle was a friend and hunting companion of Supreme Court Justice Antonin Scalia and an influential voice within the court of appeals, Hoffman gave the go-ahead.[47]

The D.C. Circuit agreed to re-hear the case en banc,[48] a strong sign that a majority of the active judges disagreed with the panel decision. To the surprise of prognosticators, however, the en banc court denied Hoffman's petition for review and enforced the Board's award, in a 5–4 decision that saw two prominent conservative judges join three of the court's more progressive members in the majority.[49] The majority opinion, again written by Tatel, largely repeated the analysis of the panel opinion, and the dissents by Sentelle and Ginsburg largely repeated Sentelle's earlier argument that the *Sure-Tan* footnote controlled the disposition of the case.

The Supreme Court Proceedings and Decision

Hoffman filed a petition for certiorari in the Supreme Court in the spring of 2001. McCortney thought it was another long shot. His brief argued that the D.C. Circuit's decision was in conflict with *Sure-Tan* and that the Supreme Court's intervention was necessary to resolve a "severe" circuit split.[50] In opposition, the Board argued that the D.C. Circuit opinion was fully consistent with *Sure-Tan*, that no circuit split existed since the Board's decision in *A.P.R.A. Fuel Oil Buyers Group* had addressed the divergent approaches of the Seventh and Ninth Circuits, and that in any event this case was a poor vehicle to resolve any uncertainties about the best interpretation of *Sure-Tan*.[51] And then came the attacks of September 11, 2001. The Court granted the cert petition two weeks later, and McCortney thought the crisis made all the difference.

In preparing his brief on the merits and for oral argument, McCortney pondered whether and how to raise the link between lax immigration enforcement and terrorism. One day when McCortney called the Supreme Court clerk's office, no one answered. The following week, a staffer returned his call from a van parked near the Court and explained that the Court had been evacuated due to an anthrax scare. McCortney decided he did not need to mention the security issues posed by illegal immigration—the Justices had had personal experience with the threat of terrorism. (No evidence was ever made public indicating that an immigrant was responsible for the anthrax mailed to the Court, but it was then widely believed that there may have been a connection to foreign terrorists.) McCortney concluded that he need do no more at argument than mention categories of visas that allow people to enter the United States without work authorization. The example he chose was student visas, because many people associated student visas with the September 11 terrorists.[52]

The NLRB's brief on the merits also avoided direct reference to the events of September 11, but it continued in some ways the cautious approach of its opposition to certiorari. Paul Wolfson, who argued the case for the Board in the Supreme Court, later recalled that the INS had some discomfort with the the Board's position and some phraseology in the draft brief, but that the agency accepted the proposition that border enforcement alone could not stop undocumented immigrants from entering the country in search of work, and it endorsed efforts to reduce the employment magnet. But unlike review of other agency actions, where the Solicitor General's office might sometimes facilitate internal discussions with the challenged agency that could lead to adoption of a more legally defensible position, the Solicitor General's office must defend the NLRB's decisions as they are issued. This left Wolfson unsure that *Hoffman* was winnable. He was concerned that the Court would treat the case as obviously controlled by *Sure-Tan* and dismiss the Board's opinion as practically frivolous, resting on a factual distinction—the continued physical presence of the workers after discharge—of no legal moment. In its merits brief, then, the Board spent nearly the first half of its argument discussing *Sure-Tan*. Only later did the Board address the remedial purposes of the NLRA, the goals of IRCA, and why the backpay award to Castro was consistent with both. Mitigation was treated in a paragraph, on the penultimate page of argument.[53]

Soon after the Supreme Court granted certiorari, attorneys for civil rights groups, the AFL–CIO, and others began to coordinate the preparation of amicus briefs. It was quickly agreed that the AFL–CIO and its outside counsel would approach the case from a labor law perspective, including a close analysis of the *Sure-Tan* case and an emphasis on the tradition of deference to the Board's broad remedial authority. The ACLU would analyze the case from an immigration law perspective, including an exhaustive examination of the legislative origins of IRCA, to argue that Congress did not intend IRCA to alter the outcome in *Sure-Tan,* nor to limit labor law remedies. If possible, the ACLU would also argue that IRCA only confirmed Congress' intent that undocumented workers be eligible for backpay. Several civil rights advocacy organizations would organize a "Brandeis brief," collecting stories of exploitation of immigrants in the workplace. Finally, the attorneys agreed that two less common briefs would be useful, one by state attorneys general emphasizing that, whatever the outcome in *Hoffman*, state labor, employment, workers' compensation, tort, contract, and insurance law must be left undisturbed. Last, if possible, would be a brief on behalf of mainstream employers frustrated by unfair competition from outlaw shops that regularly violate labor and immigration laws. All five briefs, including the states'[54] and employer association briefs,[55] were eventually filed. Tellingly, the U.S. Chamber of Commerce declined to file a brief on either side, which supporters of the Board considered a victory. But if McCortney or his client were dismayed that even employer organizations came in on the other side, he did not admit it (Ron Hoffman's response was "basically, to hell with them"[56]), and McCortney dismissed as "nonsense" the employers' substantive argument that denying Castro backpay would grant unethical employers a competitive advantage. Nor, despite the immigration issues in the case, did any representative of the immigration bar file briefs.

As oral argument approached, observers considered Justice Kennedy the pivotal vote. Chief Justice Rehnquist had dissented from *Sure-Tan*, arguing that undocumented workers were not even statutory "employees" under the NLRA, and, together with Justices Scalia and Thomas, seemed certain to reject the analysis of the Board and D.C. Circuit. Justice O'Connor, as the author of *Sure-Tan*, was assumed to be hostile to backpay for immigrants and might perceive the Board's decision as an unprincipled effort to limit *Sure-Tan* to its facts. On the other side, Justice Stevens had dissented in *Sure-Tan*, and Justices Ginsburg, Souter, and Breyer had displayed both a willingness to defer to reasonable Board decisions and a sympathy for immigrants and working people. That left Justice Kennedy who, while a member of the Ninth Circuit, had joined an opinion holding that the NLRA applied to undocumented immigrants, penning a short concurrence that declared, "If the NLRA were inapplicable to workers who are illegal aliens, we would leave helpless the very persons who most need protection from exploitative employer practices...."[57] Although considered generally conservative, Kennedy had at times cast important votes in favor of civil rights and immigrant rights, and he had also supplied a fifth vote to affirm the Board in at least one case in which the Justices might have come out differently were they judging the matter in the first instance.[58] Labor and immigration advocates hoped that Kennedy's sensitivity to the situation of exploited immigrant workers might combine with an understanding of the concerns of law-abiding small businesses about unfair competition to yield a fifth vote.

It was Ryan McCortney's first Supreme Court argument. He had been involved in the case since he was a junior associate, and by the time he stood before the justices he was a partner. A more senior lawyer had argued both times in the D.C. Circuit, but Ryan had told him, at a time when it was just talk, that if the case went to the Supreme Court, he wanted to argue it. So McCortney got his chance. It was a big day in his life—he said everyone expects to be really nervous, but that the morning of the argument he woke "as calm as I've ever been in my life." McCortney invited Wendy Delmendo, a former Sheppard Mullin associate who, while a stay-at-home mother, had drafted the briefs for McCortney, to come to the argument. Going into the argument, McCortney believed that the key votes were those of Justices O'Connor and Kennedy.

As counsel for petitioner, McCortney spoke first. At the beginning of the argument, Kennedy asked him a friendly question: "And is it correct that when *Sure-Tan* was argued, IRCA ... was being considered by Congress and the Government in its argument told us that if IRCA had been passed, back pay would not be available?" McCortney figured that he had Kennedy and needed only O'Connor's vote to win.[59] McCortney's theory was that he had to distinguish his client—who did not know that he had hired an undocumented worker—from employers who did know. He had decided to label his client as the "innocent employer" to distinguish him from "the unscrupulous employer." The problem was that the NLRB rule, which terminated backpay liability on the date the employer learns the employee was undocumented, might actually treat the employer who knew it hired undocumented workers more favorably than one who did not. As one Justice remarked, such a rule "seems ... absolutely upside down."[60] McCortney was forced to admit, "that's the problem with the rule, is that it in some ways rewards the unscrupulous employer in *Sure-Tan* and penalizes the innocent employer, as in *Hoffman*. If the unscrupulous employer knowingly hires an illegal alien, then whenever some kind of union organizing drive comes along and say gee, we can get rid of them, and we know they're illegal, and we're going to terminate them, then they can report them to the INS right from the outset ... get him dep[o]rted, and cut off back pay."[61] That prompted the following interchange:

> JUSTICE BREYER: Take an employer who, you know, all he does, he says, I've checked their cards, I've checked their cards, the cards say they're here legally, and he runs some God-awful sweat shop. Now, your theory, there is no remedy under any law against that employer but for a prospective remedy, and so everyone gets one bite at that apple.
>
> JUSTICE SCALIA: Well, he has to pay for the sweat, though, doesn't he?
>
> MR. McCORTNEY: Absolutely.

JUSTICE BREYER: And it's pretty low cost, because he's violating every labor law under the sun.[62]

Wolfson approached the oral argument with different concerns. A skillful, experienced Supreme Court advocate, Wolfson had clerked for Justice Byron White in 1989–90 and spent nearly the entire Clinton administration in the Solicitor General's Office, handling a number of ERISA, labor, and employment law matters. But Wolfson was apprehensive that the Court would "tear my head off in this case" because the Justices might conclude that the Board had impermissibly ignored *Sure-Tan*. The key vote of Justice Kennedy seemed to Wolfson "almost impossible" to secure. Wolfson also recognized that a hostile opinion reversing the D.C. Circuit could sweep more broadly than necessary, endangering cases involving knowing employers, state law regimes, and perhaps the Board's remedial authority generally. Wolfson also knew that when his colleague Edwin Kneedler had argued *Sure-Tan* before the Supreme Court, Kneedler had seemed to concede that were Congress to prohibit the employment of undocumented workers, then those workers would become ineligible for backpay.[63]

Despite these concerns, there were signs during McCortney's argument that not all was lost for Castro and the Board. Justices Scalia and Kennedy had both commented that the Court's *Sure-Tan* opinion did not decide the issues in *Hoffman*, signaling that a majority of the Court might agree with the D.C. Circuit and Board on this crucial threshold point. Yet Wolfson was challenged the moment he rose to speak, unable even to complete the traditional opening, "May it please the Court," before Justice Scalia interrupted. "What was the position of the Immigration and Naturalization Service—... in this matter when it was told that it—that you're going to argue that courts should pay illegal aliens money that it was unlawful for them to earn? What did the INS say to that?" Wolfson replied, "The INS has agreed with it and accepts it...." Scalia retorted, "well, I have no—it explains why we have a massive problem of illegal immigration, if that's how the INS feels about this."[64] Scalia then pushed Wolfson on whether undocumented immigrants should ever be eligible for backpay because they are unable lawfully to mitigate: "If he's smart he'd say, how can I mitigate, it's unlawful for me to get another job.... I can just sit home and eat chocolates and get my back pay."[65]

Even more devastating than Scalia's barbs, however, was the moment mid-way through Wolfson's argument when Justice Kennedy leaned forward to ask whether it is lawful if a union "knowingly uses an alien for organizing activity?" Wolfson answered that under *Sure-Tan* and Board precedent, undocumented immigrants are included in a bargaining unit. Kennedy pressed the unexpected, and unmistakably hostile, point: "And that doesn't induce illegal immigration? ... Here what you're saying is that a union can, I suppose even knowingly, use illegal aliens on the workforce to organize the employer.... That seems to me completely missing from ... any equitable calculus in your brief. I'm quite puzzled by it."[66] Kennedy's aversion to the very idea of undocumented immigrants participating in a union was an ominous portent and strongly suggested that the Board would lose.

McCortney had expected his "innocent employer" strategy to work, but only in the middle of the government's argument did he feel the strategy had truly succeeded. Justice O'Connor asked Wolfson, "What [the Board's rule is] doing, though, really is kind of odd, because the result is that back pay awards to illegal workers are likely to be greater than to legal ones under this board's policy, and that's so odd, and it gives the illegal alien an incentive to try to phony up more documents and to extend for the longest possible time the charade that the worker is here lawfully, and that's surely strongly against the policies of the immigration act at the very least."[67] At this question, McCortney suspected he had the fifth vote he needed.

Overall, Wolfson had wanted to present the case as a *labor* case in which deference to the Board was appropriate, but much of the argument treated it as an *immigration* case arising under IRCA. "I could hear the INS attorneys shifting nervously behind me," Wolfson remembers, during questioning about the Board's authority and expertise in considering IRCA when fashioning a remedial order. The justices' focus on IRCA also served to highlight Castro's wrongdoing in tendering false documents; had the argument centered more on the NLRA, Wolfson would have had more opportunities to discuss Hoffman's own misconduct in discharging Castro for his union activities. In a final reminder that behind the Court's theoretical discussion of national immigration and labor policies exist the lives and experiences of real people, the day after argument Wolfson received a call from the Office of the President of Mexico, offering to assist in locating the man still referred to as Jose Castro.

Many observers of the litigation had believed before argument that Hoffman would prevail, and the oral presentations seemed to confirm this prediction. Accordingly, the very afternoon of the argument, a small group of labor and immigration advocates met with staff to the Senate Labor Committee and Senate Immigration Subcommittee to begin developing a legislative strategy in the event that the Court overturned the Board's order.

The Supreme Court reversed the D.C. Circuit, 5–4. Chief Justice Rehnquist wrote the majority opinion, which was joined by Justices Scalia, Thomas, O'Connor, and Kennedy. Justice Breyer dissented, joined by Justices Stevens, Souter, and Ginsburg.[68] This was the same line-up that had decided many other politically controversial Rehnquist Court decisions, including civil rights, voting rights, and federalism decisions, as well as the election-determining *Bush v. Gore*. Chief Justice Rehnquist's opinion began by analogizing undocumented immigrants to employees who have "committed serious criminal acts" such as trespass or violence against the employer's property. The Court noted that in *Sure-Tan* it had held that the Board lacked authority to order reinstatement to employees who had departed to Mexico, even though the employer had violated § 8(a)(1) and § 8(a)(3) of the NLRA by reporting the employees to the INS in retaliation for union activity. Next, the Court distinguished *ABF Freight System, Inc. v. NLRB*,[69] which had held that the Board was not obligated to deny backpay to an employee who gave false testimony in a compliance proceeding. The Court said that perjury, "though serious, was not at all analogous to misconduct that renders an underlying employment relationship illegal."[70]

Then the Court came to the heart of its reasoning: the determination that a backpay award would undermine "a federal statute or policy outside the Board's competence to administer," namely, the immigration laws.[71] The Court explained that IRCA prohibits employers from hiring undocumented workers and obligates employers to discharge them upon discovery of the undocumented status. The Court also noted that the Immigration and Nationality Act prohibits non-citizens from using false documents. Repeatedly characterizing Castro's behavior as "criminal"— despite Castro's acknowledgment on his initial employment application that he was unauthorized to work in the United States and the absence of any criminal charge or conviction—the Court went on to explain that awarding backpay "condones and encourages future violations" of immigration law because the eligibility for backpay turns both on remaining (presumably illegally) in the United States and mitigating damages by finding other work (also presumably illegally).[72] Hoffman's own illegal conduct in firing Castro for his union activities received scant attention in the majority opinion. To the question whether denial of backpay would encourage or reward employers who hire unauthorized workers by allowing them to violate labor law with impunity, Rehnquist responded curtly that a cease and desist order and notice posting requirements are "sufficient to effectuate national labor policy."[73] Notably, Chief Justice Rehnquist's opinion did not attempt to reargue that undocumented workers are not statutory "employees" under the NLRA, the point on which he and Justice Powell had dissented in *Sure-Tan*.

Justice Breyer's dissent in *Hoffman Plastic* began by observing that all federal agencies responsible for enforcing immigration and labor policy had concluded that backpay was consistent with immigration policy and, indeed, "helps to deter unlawful activity that *both* labor laws *and* immigration laws seek to prevent."[74] Justice Breyer continued:

"Without the possibility of the deterrence that backpay provides," employers might conclude that they could violate the labor laws with impunity. Next, examining the text and history of the INA, Breyer noted that IRCA does not state how violation of its provisions should affect enforcement of other laws, but that the policy underlying IRCA—"to diminish the attractive force of employment, which like a 'magnet' pulls illegal immigrants toward the United States"—is undermined by denial of backpay, which reduces the cost of labor law violations for employers and thus "increases the employer's incentive to find and to hire illegal-alien employees."[75] Nor did Breyer credit the view that eligibility for backpay in the event of an unlawful discharge might increase illegal immigration, "for so speculative a future possibility could not realistically influence an individual's decision to migrate illegally."[76]

Justice Breyer also challenged the majority's analogy to cases in which backpay was denied because of an employee's serious criminal acts. In those cases, Breyer observed, reinstatement and backpay were denied because the employee *responded* to the employer's anti-union conduct with illegal conduct, and it was the employee's illegal conduct that both prompted and justified the employer in firing the employee. Here, in contrast, the employer's anti-union conduct was the firing, and it was neither motivated by nor justified by the employee's own conduct. After all, according to the uncontested factual finding, Hoffman had no idea that Castro was undocumented. Finally, Justice Breyer dismissed the majority's objection that a backpay award would represent "unlawfully earned wages" that could be obtained only through "criminal fraud." The same award "requires an employer who has violated the labor laws to make a meaningful monetary payment" for work that the employer believed the employee could lawfully have performed and that he would have performed absent the employer's illegal conduct.[77]

Ultimately, the Court confronted a choice. It could wholly exempt a law-breaking employer from all monetary sanction, as Hoffman urged, because the illegally discharged employee happened also to be an unauthorized immigrant. Or the Court could defer to the Board's conclusion and enforce a compromise remedy that awarded Castro *something*, though less than the traditional make-whole relief of full backpay and reinstatement. At a broader level, the Court faced a choice between reading the labor and immigration laws as contradictory or, as the legislative history of IRCA seemed to indicate, as part of a comprehensive congressional scheme to protect wage levels in the United States while diminishing the incentive for outlaw employers to prefer unauthorized immigrants to legal workers. Because Castro had in fact sought and obtained work after Hoffman illegally fired him, the precise operation of the duty to mitigate could be postponed to a future case. Instead, the majority chose a different path, convinced that the NLRA's compensatory and deterrence goals were either fully accomplished through a cease-and-desist order, or could not be reconciled with IRCA, or, more likely, that the NLRA's purposes were simply less important than those of the immigration law's document fraud provisions.

The Supreme Court handed down its opinion in *Hoffman* in March 2002, only two months after the argument. The rapid ruling caught advocates for both sides by surprise. McCortney and his client were delighted; labor and immigrant defense advocates were quick to condemn the decision and vowed to seek a legislative fix. McCortney heard about it on the radio on his way into work and by the time he spoke to his client, Ron Hoffman said: "There are five TV camera trucks in my parking lot. What should I do?" Hoffman insisted the case was less a matter of principle than of money. Indeed, he ultimately paid almost as much in legal fees ($45,000) as he would have paid in back wages had he simply followed the Board's initial order to offer reinstatement to Jose Castro.[78] If the backpay award going back to 1989 were upheld, the accumulated pay plus interest would have been a considerable sum. Hoffman had told the press after the case was argued that it was unfair that he should be forced to pay backpay to *any* worker whom he fired, regardless of immigration status. "I don't think it's right to pay backpay for anyone who doesn't earn it—whether they are here legally or illegally."[79] Both he and McCortney were upset that the long delays in the appellate process (the Supreme Court decided the case thirteen years after Castro had been fired) meant that the accumulated interest on the backpay award was substantial, and that the number of years for which Castro might have been eligible for backpay vastly exceeded the number of months that Castro had worked for Hoffman.

To organizers and workers watching the case, the thirteen-year delay sent an equally troubling message. A wait of more than a decade from termination to final adjudication, even if backpay relief were eventually ordered, is enough to dissuade many workers from bothering to pursue relief from the Board. Union organizers working in Los Angeles today agree. Lawyers for unions organizing the predominantly Latino, and heavily undocumented, low-wage work force in Southern California believe that the NLRB will do little to help protect workers who seek to join unions. They recognize that organizing campaigns are won based solely on the union's support among workers and the community, not based on legal protections for union elections. They regard *Hoffman Plastic* as just another nail in the coffin of labor law. As one union organizer said, "the law was bad before, but it's ridiculous now. But the strength of the union doesn't come from the law. . . . It comes from the power of the members."[80] A union lawyer had not noticed that the lack of NLRA protection for undocumented workers had any impact on their willingness to join a union.[81]

Wolfson was naturally disappointed by the result but also relieved that the Court had split 5–4 and found the case relatively difficult, and that Chief Justice Rehnquist's opinion had not been disdainful of the Board. From the perspective of the Solicitor General's Office, which represents the Board before the Court every Term, preserving the justices' respect for the NLRB as an institution is an important goal. *Hoffman Plastic*, although an important case, was only one of many the Board must defend before the Court. Wolfson felt that he had protected the Board's institutional reputation and its claim to deference in future cases.

Whatever the case meant to others, it seemed to have done little for Jose Castro. At the time of the compliance hearing in June 1993, Castro was living and working in Texas. By the time of the Supreme Court argument, according to an NLRB spokesperson, he was living in Mexico.[82] The case did trouble Dionisio Gonzalez, the organizer who first tried to help the Hoffman employees. When interviewed about the decision in April 2002, he was working as an organizer for the United Steelworkers. He said "It makes it real difficult to convince someone to sign a union card.... At Hoffman I told them they were protected under the law. I guess I was wrong."[83]

Impact of Hoffman Plastic Compounds, Inc. v. NLRB

Not surprisingly, the initial reaction to the decision by labor and immigrant rights advocates was extremely negative, and academic commentary was largely critical. One scholar labeled *Hoffman* as a revival of the infamous Bracero Program, a discredited form of guest-worker program that brought 4.6 million Mexicans to the United States for agricultural work between 1946 and 1962 under circumstances ensuring that they worked for low wages in poor conditions.[84] Others expressed dismay that the decision had encouraged employers to violate labor laws with impunity. While some of these concerns may be overstated, some employers did seek to take immediate advantage. In New York, a lawyer for an employer who had violated minimum wage laws threatened a group of protesters outside his client's store, citing *Hoffman* and claiming that the Supreme Court had ruled "illegal immigrants do not have the same rights as U.S. citizens." Immigrants reported fewer labor violations to the New York Attorney General's Office after the Court's decision.[85] Reflecting the lack of a uniform employer view during the litigation, however, employer responses to the decision were divided.

The decision had a number of immediate legal effects. At the Supreme Court, the lawyers and the justices seemed concerned about the implications of the ruling for remedies under labor and employment laws other than the NLRA. McCortney had argued that a ruling for Hoffman would affect only backpay for work not performed. Thus, he attempted to draw a line between laws like the Fair Labor Standards Act (FLSA) that require payment of wages for work performed—which would fully protect undocumented immigrants—and laws like the NLRA and Title VII that provide prospective remedies, such as backpay, for work that was not performed. Wolfson pointed out in his argument that most states have held that undocumented workers are entitled to workers' compensation benefits even though the benefits compensate in part for wages that were not earned.

The first wave of legal responses occurred in executive branch agencies and concerned just this question of remedies. Within months, the EEOC rescinded its prior directive that undocumented workers are eligible for backpay under Title VII and other federal anti-discrimination statutes, but reaffirmed that undocumented immigrants are statutory "employees" and remain eligible for compensatory and punitive damages.[86] The U.S. Department of Labor acted similarly, declaring that undocumented workers were still covered "employees" under the FLSA and the Migrant and Seasonal Agricultural Worker Protection Act, and that such workers remained eligible for minimum wage or overtime compensation for work already performed.[87] And the Board itself, in its first relevant post-*Hoffman* decision, agreed that undocumented workers were eligible for damages for work already performed, where the employer unlawfully reduced the employee's wages in retaliation for protected activity.[88] Only one agency explicitly grappled with the circumstance of the "knowing" employer, a distinction that had been crucial to McCortney in crafting his arguments and a case that Justice Breyer, in dissent, had maintained was not before the Court. Unfortunately for workers, the NLRB General Counsel concluded that all employers, innocent or knowing, were exempt from backpay liability for the wrongful discharge of undocumented workers. The General Counsel sets enforcement policy for the NLRB, and his determination that employers who deliberately hire undocumented workers are exempt from backpay liability was a blow for those who had hoped that the NLRB would take a more limited view of *Hoffman*.

But some state agencies, including in California and Washington, took a different view, concluding that nothing in the *Hoffman* decision pre-empted state laws allowing even backpay, the very remedy at issue in *Hoffman*, to undocumented workers. The Attorney General of New York went no further than the U.S. Department of Labor, agreeing that undocumented workers remained eligible for minimum wage and overtime damages for work already performed, but declining to express a view on backpay, punitive damages, or other state law remedies.

Litigation is only now testing the implications of *Hoffman*. To date, every federal court to consider the issue has endorsed the view, shared by all agencies, that immigration status is no bar to recovery of damages

for work already performed. As to other remedies, workers have succeeded in the earliest cases in pressing points rejected by the federal
agencies. For instance, the only court since *Hoffman* to publish an
opinion in a case involving a "knowing" employer agreed with the
Hoffman dissent that its resolution was not controlled by *Hoffman* itself
and, contrary to the NLRB General Counsel, determined that a "knowing" employer was not immune from post-discharge liability.[89] And the
first federal court of appeals to examine a post-*Hoffman* question rejected the EEOC's assumption that *Hoffman* even applies in Title VII
actions.[90] State courts have also generally held that *Hoffman* does not
preclude an undocumented immigrant from recovering for lost wages
under tort law or in workers' compensation cases.[91]

Courts have also generally barred discovery of immigration status in
labor and employment litigation, concluding that compelled disclosure of
a worker's status is irrelevant where remedies are available regardless of
status and would have an obvious *in terrorem* effect on the willingness of
immigrant workers to vindicate their labor law rights. The NLRB too
has concluded that discovery of immigration status is not relevant at the
merits stage of an unfair labor practice proceeding, and further, that at
the compliance (remedy) proceeding, it is the employer's burden to
establish an employee's lack of work authorization such that the backpay
period should be tolled.[92] Importantly, the Board has already rejected an
employer's tender of a Social Security Administration "no-match" letter
as sufficient to carry this burden.[93]

Labor and immigration advocates have pursued legislative strategies
to address the consequences of *Hoffman*. California enacted a law
directing that state labor and civil rights remedies, "except any reinstatement remedy prohibited by federal law, are available to all individuals regardless of immigration status."[94] In 2004, Sen. Ted Kennedy and
others introduced major immigration reform legislation that included a
"*Hoffman* fix."[95] It is notable, however, that the *Hoffman* fix was
incorporated in a lengthy immigration bill providing for an expanded
guestworker program and earned legalization—that is, a bill unlikely to
be acted on for several years, as wider debates about comprehensive
immigration reform unfold. The *Hoffman* fix provision was not, for
instance, attached to a "must-pass" bill essential to the AFL–CIO's
legislative agenda, suggesting that while the labor movement supports
the measure, it is not today among the AFL's highest priorities.

Finally, labor advocates have sought to attack *Hoffman* in international fora. In October 2002, the AFL–CIO and the Confederation of
Mexican Workers filed a complaint with the International Labor Organization, alleging that the decision impermissibly infringed on workers'
rights to organize and bargain collectively, and on freedom of association. After reviewing the U.S. government's response, the ILO concluded

that "the remedial measures left to the NLRB in cases of illegal dismissals of undocumented workers are inadequate to ensure effective protection against acts of anti-union discrimination" under international law.[96] Advocates also raised objections to the *Hoffman* opinion at the Inter–American Court of Human Rights, where in May 2002 the Government of Mexico had requested an Advisory Opinion on whether *Hoffman* was consistent with international human rights law. In 2003, the Inter–American Court advised that under international law, immigrant workers, regardless of their status, were entitled to the same basic labor protections as citizens—including backpay.[97] To date, however, condemnations of U.S. labor policy in international tribunals have produced little change in the U.S.

Conclusion

Hoffman did not break new doctrinal or theoretical ground. Nor is it likely to affect general labor or immigration jurisprudence significantly. But it stands as an important limit on the rights of undocumented workers, a substantial and vulnerable segment of the U.S. labor market. Rather than harmonize the two statutory regimes, the Court concluded that immigration policies trump labor policies, as divined by five justices. In many ways, the opinion appears anachronistic, out of step with a trend toward deeper integration of regional, if not global, labor markets. It is also out of step with emerging norms of international labor law and human rights, as reflected in the critical appraisals issued by the ILO and Inter–American Court.

Nor is the opinion certain to endure. With the U.S. Chamber of Commerce and the AFL–CIO now united in opposition to IRCA's employer sanctions provisions, there is a real prospect that the prohibition on employment of unauthorized immigrants may be lifted before long, perhaps as part of another grand bargain on comprehensive immigration reform. Beyond repeal of employer sanctions, the interest of the business community in expanding guestworker programs and its growing recognition of the inefficiencies of maintaining a vast underground economy in this country, together with the AFL–CIO's commitment to the cause of undocumented workers, have increased the prospects for broader reforms affecting immigrant workers. Behind the current policy discussions, too, looms the interest of both political parties in cultivating support among Latino voters. Moreover, newly important national security considerations favor creating a path to lawful status that will encourage undocumented immigrants to come forward, "instead of the current situation in which millions of people are unknown, unknown to the law."[98]

But whatever the prospects for eventual reform, *Hoffman* seems likely to embolden unscrupulous employers who would hire and exploit unauthorized immigrants, resulting in more unfair competition for businesses that play by the rules, lower terms and conditions of employment for citizens and legal immigrants, and a stronger "magnet" effect encouraging illegal immigration. For the *Hoffman* majority, Chief Justice Rehnquist wrote reassuringly that immunity from backpay liability "does not mean the employer gets off scot-free," because employers of undocumented workers remain subject to cease-and-desist orders and notice-posting requirements.[99] To millions of workers in this country like Jose Castro, who labor under a different set of workplace rules, those words are of little comfort.

ENDNOTES

1. See, for example, Johnson v. Eisentrager, 339 U.S. 763, 770–71 (1950) ("The alien, to whom the United States has been traditionally hospitable, has been accorded a generous and ascending scale of rights as he increases his identity with our society.").

2. 535 U.S. 137 (2002).

3. Immigration Reform and Control Act of 1986, Pub. L. No. 99–603, 101(a)(1), 100 Stat. 3359 (Nov. 6, 1986), adding § 274A to the Immigration and Nationality Act (INA), codified at 8 U.S.C. § 1324a.

4. Telephone interview, Muzaffar Chishti, Senior Policy Analyst, Migration Policy Institute and former Director, UNITE Immigration Project (June 3, 2004).

5. These laws were the Antiterrorism and Effective Death Penalty Act of 1996, Pub. L. No. 104–132, Title IV, 110 Stat. 1214; Personal Responsibility and Work Opportunity Reconciliation Act of 1996, Pub. L. No. 104–193, §§ 400–451, 110 Stat. 2105; and the Illegal Immigration Reform and Immigrant Responsibility Act of 1996, Pub. L. No. 104–208, Division C, 110 Stat. 3009–546.

6. U.S. Census Bureau, Profile of the Foreign–Born Population in the United States: 2000, at 3 (Dec. 2001).

7. Id. at 9 & Figure 1–1.

8. Id. at 20 & Table 7–1.

9. The INS estimated the undocumented population to be 5 million persons as of October 1996 and 7 million as of January 2000. U.S. INS, Estimates of the Unauthorized Immigrant Population Residing in the United States: 1990–2000 (2003). But other demographers have concluded the total undocumented population may be closer to 11 million. See Jeffrey S. Passel, Randy Capps, & Michael Fix, Undocumented Immigrants: Facts and Figures (2004) (estimating undocumented population at 9.3 million); Cindy Rodriguez, Census Bolsters Theory Illegal Immigrants Undercounted, Boston Globe A4 (Mar. 20, 2001) (noting estimates ranging from 6 to 11 million persons).

10. Passel et al., Undocumented Immigrants at 1; Orrin Bair, Undocumented Workers and the NLRA: Hoffman Plastic Compounds and Beyond, 19 Labor Lawyer 153, 160 (2003), citing How Many Undocumented: The Numbers Behind the U.S.-Mexico Migration Talk, PEW Hispanic Center 3 (May 21, 2002).

11. Passel et al., Undocumented Immigrants at 1, citing Immigration Is Critical to Future Growth and Competitiveness, Employment Policy Foundation, Policy Backgrounder 1 (June 11, 2001).

12. Passel et al., Undocumented Immigrants at 2.

13. David Lopez & Cynthia Feliciano, Who Does What? California's Emerging Plural Labor Force in Ruth Milkman, ed., Organizing Immigrants (2000).

14. 467 U.S. 883 (1984).

15. Id. at 893.

16. Id. at 903.

17. Id.

18. Local 512 Warehouse and Office Workers' Union v. NLRB (Felbro), 795 F.2d 705 (9th Cir. 1986) (wrongfully discharged undocumented worker who remains in country eligible for backpay).

19. See INA § 274A(a)(1), 8 U.S.C. § 1324a(a)(1).

20. See Brief Amici Curiae of ACLU et al., No. 00–1595, 2001 WL 1631648 (discussing legislative history, including congressional acknowledgment that legislation might influence employer behavior but could not overcome wage differentials motivating employee migration).

21. Compare Del Rey Tortilleria, Inc. v. NLRB, 976 F.2d 1115 (7th Cir. 1992) (undocumented workers who remain in the country ineligible for back pay) with EEOC v. Hacienda Hotel, 881 F.2d 1504 (9th Cir. 1989); NLRB v. Felbro, 795 F.2d 705 (9th Cir. 1986); Rios v. Enterprise Ass'n Steamfitters Local 638, 860 F.2d 1168 (2d Cir. 1988). In a sui generis Title VII case, the Fourth Circuit adopted the Seventh Circuit's approach, arguably deepening the split. See Egbuna v. Time–Life Libraries, Inc., 153 F.3d 184 (4th Cir. 1998) (en banc) (per curiam) (temporarily unauthorized worker refused reinstatement after resignation cannot state claim under Title VII, implying undocumented workers not covered by Title VII).

22. 320 NLRB 408 (1995).

23. Except where indicated otherwise, this account of Castro's employment at Hoffman Plastic Compounds and subsequent events is drawn from testimony of Castro, his niece, and other witnesses at the backpay hearing before the Administrative Law Judge of Region 21 in Los Angeles on March 4–5, 1993 and June 14, 1993. In the Matter of Hoffman Plastic Compounds, Inc. and Casimiro Arauz, Case No. 21–CA–26630, National Labor Relations Board (1993).

24. Telephone interview with Peter Tovar (Jan. 21, 2004).

25. Id.

26. Ruth Milkman, Introduction, in Ruth Milkman, ed., Organizing Immigrants 8–9 (2000). By contrast, for those who have traveled greater distances and at greater cost, such as undocumented Chinese immigrants who may incur upwards of $50,000 in debt to the "snakeheads" who smuggle them, with family members liable in the event of default, the consequences of deportation can be far more dire. See Peter Kwong, Forbidden Workers: Illegal Chinese Immigrants and American Labor (1997). Similarly, with the increased militarization of the U.S.-Mexico border since September 11, the prospects of illegal re-entry following deportation have dimmed, and the possibility of removal has become more frightening to many Mexican and Central American immigrants.

27. Interview with Ryan McCortney (Jan. 16, 2004).

28. Hoffman Plastic Compounds, Inc., 306 NLRB 100 (1992).

29. Id.

30. Petitioner's Brief at 3 n.1.

31. Telephone interview with Ryan McCortney (Jan. 16, 2004).

32. Telephone interview with Peter Tovar (Jan. 21, 2004).

33. Transcript of Oral Argument, 2002 U.S. Trans Lexis 11 at 14; Petitioner's Reply Brief at 12.

34. Del Rey Tortilleria, Inc. v. NLRB, 976 F.2d 1115 (7th Cir. 1992).

35. Telephone interview with Peter Tovar (Jan. 21, 2004).

36. Telephone interview with William B. Gould, IV (Jan. 21, 2004).

37. 320 NLRB 408 (1995).

38. Id. at 416.

39. Hoffman Plastic Compounds, Inc., 326 NLRB 1060, 1062 n.10 (1998).

40. Telephone interview with William B. Gould, IV (Mar. 3, 2004).

41. 29 U.S.C. § 160(e), (f).

42. Telephone interview with the Honorable David S. Tatel (June 8, 2004). Berzon's San Francisco firm, Altshuler, Berzon, Nussbaum, Berzon & Rubin, had particular expertise in these issues. Another member of the firm, Michael Rubin, had successfully litigated several of the leading post-*Sure-Tan* cases, including Patel v. Quality Inn South, 846 F.2d 700 (11th Cir. 1988) (undocumented worker is employee for purposes of Fair Labor Standards Act and may sue for unpaid wages and liquidated damages); and Local 512 Warehouse and Office Workers' Union v. NLRB (Felbro), 795 F.2d 705 (9th Cir. 1986) (wrongfully discharged undocumented worker who remains in country eligible for backpay). Earlier the same year that Berzon argued *Hoffman*, the firm had also unsuccessfully petitioned for certiorari in Egbuna v. Time–Life Libraries, Inc., 153 F.3d 184 (4th Cir. 1998) (en banc) (per curiam) (temporarily unauthorized worker refused reinstatement after resignation cannot state claim under Title VII, implying undocumented workers not covered by Title VII).

43. Hoffman Plastic Compounds, Inc. v. NLRB, 208 F.3d 229, 240 (D.C. Cir. 2000) at 240 (quoting Pub. L. No. 99–603 § 111(d), 100 Stat. 3359 (1986)).

44. Id. at 243 (quoting 8 U.S.C. § 1324a(a)(1)(A)).

45. Id. at 253.

46. Id. at 254 (quoting *Sure-Tan*, 467 U.S. at 903).

47. Telephone interview with Ryan McCortney (Jan. 16, 2004).

48. 2000 WL 985015, 164 L.R.R.M. (BNA) 2814 (D.C. Cir. June 16, 2000).

49. Hoffman Plastic Compounds, Inc. v. NLRB, 237 F.3d 639 (D.C. Cir. 2001).

50. The petition for certiorari failed to note the Fourth Circuit's decision in *Egbuna* but did contend a split existed between the Seventh and the D.C., Second, and Ninth Circuits. Petition for Certiorari, U.S. No. 00–1595, 2001 WL 34091948 (filed April 16, 2001).

51. Brief for the NLRB in Opposition, 2001 WL 34090274, at *23 (June 16, 2001).

52. Telephone interview with Ryan McCortney (Jan. 16, 2004).

53. Brief for the NLRB, No. 00–1595; telephone interview with Paul R.Q. Wolfson (March 1, 2004). Notably, neither the Board nor Hoffman nor any of the amici engaged Board precedent addressing the appropriate remedy for wrongful discharge where there is a legal impediment to reinstatement other than immigration status, such as wrongful discharge of underage workers or unlicensed drivers, neither of whom can lawfully be re-employed. See, e.g., NLRB v. Future Ambulette, Inc., 903 F.2d 140 (2d Cir. 1990) (crafting remedy of backpay and conditional reinstatement for wrongfully discharged driver with suspended license).

54. The amicus brief of the state attorneys general was drafted by attorneys in the office of Elliott Spitzer, Attorney General of New York, see 2001 WL 1636790. Signatories included the attorneys general from three of the states with the highest population of undocumented immigrants (California, New York, and Arizona). Despite last-minute efforts, attorneys working through state labor federations, bar associations, and personal contacts failed to persuade the attorneys general of Florida, Illinois, and Texas to sign on.

55. While notable for their endorsement of a Board decision favoring an employee, the employer associations applied a traditional economic analysis in arguing that a rule exempting employers of undocumented immigrants from ordinary backpay liability for wrongful discharge was "bad for business" and would allow outlaw shops to compete unfairly with mainstream businesses that honored labor and immigration laws. 2001 WL 1631729. One author of this chapter, Michael Wishnie, was counsel of record for the employer association amicus.

56. Telephone interview with Ryan McCortney (Jan. 16, 2004).

57. NLRB v. Apollo Tire Co., 604 F.2d 1180, 1184 (9th Cir. 1979) (Kennedy, J., concurring).

58. See Holly Farms Corp. v. NLRB, 517 U.S. 392 (1996) (upholding as reasonable Board determination that chicken catchers are NLRA "employees," not exempt agricultural workers).

59. The transcript of oral argument is available at 2002 WL 77224.

60. Id. at *16.

61. Id.

62. Id. at *17.

63. Sure–Tan, Inc. v. NLRB, Transcript of Oral Argument, 1983 Trans. Lexis 5 at 47–48 (government statement that if Congress barred employment of undocumented immigrants, the "employment relationship would then become illegal, and for the Board to order the reinstatement of the employee to an illegal relationship and to pay him inconsistent with such a statute would clearly be improper"). Wolfson does not recall any discussion in the Solicitor General's Office of the possibility that Kneedler, who had argued many recent immigration cases before the Court, would argue *Hoffman*. Telephone interview with Paul R.Q. Wolfson (March 1, 2004).

64. Transcript, 2002 WL 77224, at * 27. Wolfson recalled that Solicitor General Theodore Olson was dismayed by Scalia's question. Wolfson himself thought the inquiry an improper intrusion into the internal deliberations of the Executive Branch. Telephone interview with Paul R.Q. Wolfson (March 1, 2004).

65. Transcript, 2002 WL 77224, at * 32–33.

66. Id. at *34–35.

67. Id. at * 38.

68. Hoffman Plastic Compounds, Inc. v. NLRB, 535 U.S. 137 (2002).

69. 510 U.S. 317 (1994).

70. 535 U.S. at 146.

71. Id. at 147 (citing 8 U.S.C. §§ 1324a(a)(1), (2), 1324c).

72. Id. at 150.

73. Id. at 152.

74. Id. at 153 (Breyer, J., dissenting).

75. Id. at 155.

76. Id.

77. Id. at 160.

78. Steve Toloken, Supreme Court Hears Hoffman, Plastics News 3 (Jan. 21, 2002).

79. Thomas Maier, Pitting Labor Against INS Laws, Newsday (Feb. 19, 2002).

80. Interview with Leticia Salcedo (Sept. 24, 2003).

81. Interview with Monica Guizar (Sept. 26, 2003).

82. Steve Toloken, Plastics News 3 (Jan. 21, 2002).

83. Nancy Cleeland, Employers Test Ruling on Immigrants Labor; Some Firms are Trying to Use Supreme Court Decision as Basis for Avoiding Claims Over Workplace Violations, Los Angeles Times C1 (April 22, 2002).

84. Christopher David Ruiz Cameron, Borderline Decisions: Hoffman Plastic Compounds, the New Bracero Program, and the Supreme Court's Role in Making Federal Labor Policy, 51 UCLA L. Rev. 1, 2–4 (2003).

85. Telephone interview with M. Patricia Smith (July 21, 2004).

86. Nancy Montwieler, EEOC: EEOC Limits Undocumented Workers' Relief Based on Recent Supreme Court Decision, 126 Daily Lab. Rep. (BNA) A–2 (July 1, 2002).

87. U.S. Dep't of Labor, Fact Sheet #48, Application of US Labor Laws to Immigrant Workers: Effect of *Hoffman Plastics* decision on laws enforced by the Wage and Hour Division (Aug. 19, 2002).

88. Tuv Taam Corp., 340 NLRB No. 86, at 4 & n.4, 2003 WL 22295361 (2003).

89. Singh v. Jutla, 214 F. Supp. 2d 1056, 1061 (N.D. Cal. 2002). The *Singh* opinion was authored by Judge Charles Breyer, brother of Justice Stephen Breyer.

90. Rivera v. Nibco, 364 F.3d 1057, 1069 (9th Cir. 2004), cert. denied, 125 S.Ct. 1603 (2005).

91. See, e.g., Tyson Foods, Inc. v. Guzman, 116 S.W.3d 233, 242–44 (Tex. App. 2003) (undocumented worker may seek damages for lost wages in negligence action for injuries suffered in forklift collision); Cano v. Mallory Mgmt., 760 N.Y.S.2d 816 (Sup. Ct. Richmond Co. 2003) (same, for injuries caused by electric meter explosion during course of employment); Rajeh v. Steel City Corp., 2004 Ohio 3211, 813 N.E.2d 697 (Ohio App. 7 Dist. 2004) (undocumented immigrant under order of deportation eligible for Ohio workers' compensation benefits); Correa v. Waymouth Farms, Inc., 664 N.W.2d 324 (Minn. 2003) (undocumented worker eligible for benefits under Minnesota workers' compensation law); Safeharbor Employer Services I, Inc. v. Velazquez, 860 So. 2d 984 (Fla. Ct. App. 2003) (same); Cherokee Industries, Inc. v. Alvarez, 84 P.3d 798, 801 (Okla. Civ. App. 2003) (same); Wet Walls, Inc. v. Ledezma, 598 S.E.2d 60. (Ga. App.2004) (same). But see Sanago v. 200 E. 16th St. Housing Corp., 788 N.Y.S.2d 314 (N.Y. App. Div. 2004) (undocumented worker injured on job eligible for wage-loss damages only at prevailing wage rate in worker's country of origin); Balbuena v. IDR Realty LLC, 787 N.Y.S.2d 35 (N.Y. App. Div. 2004) (same); Reinforced Earth Co. v. Workers' Comp. Appeal Bd. (Astudillo), 810 A.2d 99, 108–09 & n.12 (Pa. 2002) (undocumented worker is statutory employee and eligible for medical compensation, but wage-loss benefits may be suspended due to immigration status); Sanchez v. Eagle Alloy Inc., 658 N.W.2d 510, 514–16 (Mich. Ct. App. 2003) (undocumented worker who tenders false documents ineligible for workers' compensation pursuant to state law "commission of crime" exception to coverage).

92. Tuv Taam Corp., 340 NLRB No. 86, 2003 WL 22295361 (2003).

93. "No-match" letters are correspondence from the Social Security Administration to employers "identifying discrepancies between SSA records" and employer filings, which are frequently used by employers as grounds to conclude particular employees are undocumented. The NLRB rejected an SSA no-match letter as not being "legally cognizable evidence regarding the immigration status" of listed employees. Id. at 5 & n. 7.

94. Cal. Lab. Code § 1171.5(a) (West 2003); Cal. Civ. Code § 3339(a) (West 2004); Cal. Govt. Code § 7285(a) (West 2004). All three provisions were amended by enactment of Cal. Senate Bill 1818, c. 1071.

95. Safe, Orderly, Legal Visas and Enforcement (SOLVE) Act of 2004, S. 2381 (introduced May 2004), H.R. 4262 (introduced May 2004), § 321 (providing backpay or other monetary relief for labor or employment violation not to be denied because of employer or employee INA violation).

96. See Complaints Against the United States by AFL–CIO and Confederation of Mexican Workers, Case No. 2227, ¶. 610 (2003).

97. Advisory Opinion No. 18, Inter–American Court of Human Rights (Sept. 2003).

98. President George W. Bush, New Temporary Worker Program: Remarks on Immigration Policy (Jan. 7, 2004) (transcript available at http://www.white-house.gov/news/releases/2004/01/20040107–3.html).

99. 535 U.S. at 152.

*

13

Demore v. Kim: Judicial Deference to Congressional Folly

Margaret H. Taylor

"The INS wouldn't mind losing this case." This assessment was offered by an Immigration and Naturalization Service official en route to the Supreme Court to hear oral argument in *Demore v. Kim*.[1] In *Demore*, the Court rejected a due process challenge to a statute mandating detention without bond during the pendency of removal proceedings for virtually all non-citizens convicted of a crime. Many inside the INS had opposed this provision. For two years, the agency had delayed implementing the statute by certifying that it did not have sufficient bed space to fulfill the detention mandate foisted upon it. During this time, the Clinton administration had urged Congress to repeal the measure before it took effect. And in a move that surely surprised some of their former government colleagues, four top-level officials who had recently left the INS filed an amicus brief before the Supreme Court supporting Hyung Joon Kim. The former INS officials argued that mandatory detention "is both unfair and inefficient" and "serves no legitimate law enforcement purpose."[2]

This criticism is aptly illustrated by Hyung Joon Kim's life story. The statute at issue in *Demore* required the INS to keep Kim in custody even though he was a lawful permanent resident with strong ties to the United States, who the agency readily concluded "would not present a threat" if released on bond.[3] Kim came to the United States with his family in 1984, when he was six years old. The family settled in California, where Kim and his brother attended public schools. In 1996, Kim was convicted of burglary after breaking into a tool shed with some high school friends. He was sentenced to a short jail term and probation, but then was caught shoplifting on two separate occasions. Kim's burglary and shoplifting offenses all occurred in a ten-month span when Kim was eighteen and nineteen years old.[4] "I was young and dumb," Kim later said, voicing remorse for his actions and the toll they had taken on his close-knit family.[5]

California authorities had prosecuted Kim's second shoplifting offense—for stealing less than a hundred dollars' worth of merchandise from Costco—as a "petty theft with priors," punishable under state law as a felony. Kim was sentenced to three years in prison, serving less than two years before he was released for good behavior. One day after he was released from prison, Kim was taken into INS custody and detained at a county jail.

There was a time when minor property crimes would rarely trigger deportation proceedings, and when the youthful mistakes of long-term residents could be forgiven by an immigration judge who had discretion to grant relief from deportation. But Kim was convicted shortly after Congress had amended the immigration law in 1996 to crack down on so-called "criminal aliens." He was charged with being deportable under a vastly expanded definition of an "aggravated felony" in the newly amended immigration statute. If the classification proved accurate, deportation would be automatic because an aggravated felony conviction bars discretionary relief from removal.[6]

Hyung Joon Kim was kept in INS custody because another provision of the amended statute, § 236(c) of the Immigration and Nationality Act (INA), eliminated bond hearings for non-citizen offenders facing deportation. INA § 236(c) mandates detention during the pendency of removal proceedings for virtually all criminal offenders, regardless of the seriousness of the underlying crime, the risk of flight, or the immigration status of the offender.[7] As will be detailed later in this chapter, there was ample precedent to support Kim's argument that this provision violated due process. First, the Supreme Court had repeatedly imposed due process limits on preventive detention based on dangerousness in other contexts; taken together, these cases suggested that "[d]ue process calls for an individual determination before someone is locked away."[8] In addition, just two years before *Demore,* the Court in *Zadvydas v. Davis* had concluded that this precedent applied to lawful permanent residents detained by the INS.[9] In the wake of *Zadvydas,* all the courts of appeals to decide the question—including the Ninth Circuit in Kim's case—struck down INA § 236(c) as unconstitutional when applied to lawful permanent residents.[10]

Thus, based on the Court's due process precedent and the trend in the courts of appeals, one might have predicted a Supreme Court victory for Hyung Joon Kim. Why then did a five-member majority reject the due process claim when the case was decided in April 2003? The most plausible answer, like the proverbial elephant in the room, looms large even though everyone involved in the case—justices and lawyers alike—avoided commenting on its presence. The September 11, 2001 terrorist attacks intervened between *Zadvydas* and *Demore.* On the surface, *Demore v. Kim* upheld mandatory detention without bond for criminal offenders facing deportation, and had nothing to do with government efforts to battle terrorism. But the case is best understood as a post–9/11 decision, rendered at a time when a majority of the Court was reluctant to scrutinize the political branches' claimed authority to detain non-citizens who are perceived as a threat. It is the historical context of *Demore v. Kim,* rather than Court's analysis of precedent, that explains the outcome.

This legal realist interpretation of *Demore* is supported by evidence that the majority ignored or obfuscated the details of Hyung Joon Kim's case, the history of the statute, and the considerable costs to the government and to individuals resulting from blanket mandatory detention under INA § 236(c). As it turned out, Hyung Joon Kim's fight to remain in the United States was not nearly as quixotic as the *Demore* majority made it seem. This chapter recounts the twists and turns in that battle. It also considers the impact of mandatory detention on lawful permanent residents like Kim, who must relinquish their freedom as the price of contesting deportation, and on the Department of Homeland Security, the INS's successor agency, which must devote scarce bed space to detain individuals who do not present a risk of flight or a danger to the community. Given these costs, it is difficult to understand why Congress would enact such a sweeping detention mandate. We turn now to that part of the story.

From Neglect to Overreaction: The History of the Statute

The majority opinion in *Demore v. Kim* is premised on an overly optimistic view of the legislative process and an incomplete account of the history of INA § 236(c). The Court recounted the details of several congressional reports and government investigations to establish that the INS had a poor record of deporting criminal offenders. The Court also suggested that Congress reacted cautiously, at first "making incremental changes to the immigration laws," before it decided to enact mandatory detention, which had emerged as the recommended option in a number of government studies.[11] Throughout its discussion of the history of the statute, the *Demore* majority depicted INA § 236(c) as a carefully considered and justified response to well-known weaknesses in the system for deporting criminal offenders.

These weaknesses were indeed amply documented by the time Congress enacted INA § 236(c). But Congress had only recently become attentive to the problem, and was not at all measured in its legislative response. In truth, the detention mandate that ultimately became INA § 236(c) was inserted without study into omnibus legislation that Congress was in a hurry to pass. And the statute was widely considered by experts inside and outside the government to be unduly harsh, unrealistic, and unwise.

The Unacknowledged Backdrop: An Era of Nonenforcement

If Hyung Joon Kim had been convicted before Congress amended the statute in 1996, his burglary and shoplifting offenses probably would not have generated any attention from the INS. In the unlikely event that the INS had tried to deport him, Kim would have been able to argue that his brushes with the law did not justify removal from the United States. And he would have had no occasion to file a habeas petition to challenge his detention, because Kim would certainly have remained at liberty while he contested deportation.

Until the 1990s, release was the norm and detention the rare exception for non-citizens facing deportation. This was true both under formal legal rules and as a matter of practical reality. The INA provided that individuals who were taken into custody and charged with being deportable "may, in the discretion of the Attorney General and pending such final determination of deportability, be continued in custody ... or be released under bond."[12] By regulation, the INS official who issued the charging documents made the initial custody determination. Individuals who were detained could then petition an immigration judge for release on bond. Governing administrative precedent established a presumption of release; the INS had to demonstrate flight risk or danger to the community in order to keep someone in custody while deportation proceedings were pending.[13]

Even after a final deportation order was entered, non-citizens generally remained at liberty until the INS could effectuate their removal from the United States. The INA granted discretion to detain for this purpose, but, as a matter of administrative practice, individuals who had been ordered deported were rarely kept in custody. Those who were detained were released once a removal order had been outstanding for six months, "subject to supervision under regulations prescribed by the Attorney General."[14] It is important to note that these rules favoring release also applied to individuals who were being deported for criminal convictions. Thus, in most cases, non-citizen offenders remained at large both during removal proceedings and after a final order was entered.

Did these liberal rules undercut INS efforts to deport criminal offenders? That question lies at the heart of the controversy surrounding the wisdom and constitutionality of INA § 236(c). To Congress, the answer seemed obvious—years of study had shown that "[d]etention is key to effective deportation."[15] For a majority of the justices, this apparent truism resolved the case. Congress was "justifiably concerned" that deportable criminal offenders were not being removed,[16] and therefore was justified in mandating detention without bond for all who fell into this category.

But this analysis ignores both the complex causes of the INS's previous failure to remove criminal offenders and the significant costs of a statutory mandate to detain. From the time the INA was enacted in 1952 until the early 1990s, the INS had neither a political mandate nor the practical ability to build an effective system to deport non-citizen offenders. Certainly, it had plenty of substantive authority; the INA has always contained a list of deportable criminal offenses. But the infrastructure was totally lacking. Until fairly recently, the INS did not have the capacity to: (1) identify and apprehend non-citizen criminal offenders; (2) keep tabs on those who were placed in deportation proceedings; or (3) enforce removal orders.[17] The fact that deportable non-citizens— including criminal offenders—remained at large during the pendency of proceedings and even after they had been ordered deported was just one intractable feature of this broken system.

Deportable criminals slipped through the cracks at every point in the removal process. Deportation proceedings were seldom commenced, even for serious offenses, because foreign-born offenders were released from prison or probation back into the community without investigation of their immigration status.[18] Those few whom the INS identified and placed in removal proceedings were, as already noted, seldom detained. In perhaps the most remarkable illustration of systemic failure, the INS often did not try to enforce deportation orders against individuals who were not detained. Even after Congress began to devote close attention to criminal deportations (as detailed below), one government study of cases sampled from fourteen locations found that almost 40% of the time, the INS never even bothered to ask that someone subject to a final order surrender for deportation.[19] When surrender notices were issued, very few non-citizens reported for deportation, and virtually none of the absconders who failed to surrender were pursued by the INS. As a result, the INS deported only about 11% of nondetained aliens who were subject to final deportation orders.[20]

For over three decades, the INS's "near-total inability to remove deportable criminal aliens"[21] was something of an insider's secret. Congress did not fund the agency at anything close to the levels needed to have an effective deportation system. But neither Congress nor the general public seemed to know much or care much about the issue. Certainly morale was low inside the INS, where the letters asking a non-citizen to surrender for deportation were known as "run letters," and requests to have an investigator try to find an absconder were viewed as "pointless."[22] Few people outside the agency, however, knew that most deportation orders were destined for the back of the filing cabinet.

A lack of detention capacity was central to this state of affairs. In the early 1980s, the INS had the capacity to detain roughly 2,200 non-citizens on any given day.[23] Around 90% of INS detainees were Mexican nationals who were never placed in formal proceedings, but rather were ushered back across the border in a matter of hours or days, under a procedure known as voluntary departure.[24] Because INS detention facilities "generally operated for short-term holding in quick turnaround cases,"[25] few beds for were available for non-citizens apprehended inside the United States who were contesting deportation. This meant that during proceedings few individuals were actually detained based on flight risk and dangerousness under the statutory framework and regulations discussed above. Instead, a chronic lack of detention space caused the INS to release even those individuals who were seen as a risk, a practice that contributed to the agency's dismal rates of success in removing criminal offenders.[26]

Thus, it is certainly true, as the *Demore* court stated, that "one of the major causes of the INS' failure to remove deportable criminal aliens was the agency's failure to detain those aliens during their deportation proceedings."[27] The majority invoked a number of studies and statistics to back up this statement, but did not consider the underlying causes of this failure to detain. It was not a lack of legal authority to keep non-citizens in custody, nor a history of making poor judgments about flight risk or dangerousness, that caused the INS to have such a weak record of deporting criminal offenders. Rather, the agency lacked the bed space to hold almost anyone being deported from the interior, and had no system in place to keep track of those who remained at liberty pending deportation or after a final order was entered against them. Moreover, these problems were merely one part of an overall lack of immigration enforcement in this era.

Congress Responds: Omnibus Legislation as the Vehicle for Immigration Reform

Things began to change in the late 1980s when—at the impetus of state officials and a few key congressional leaders—the "criminal alien problem" became a hot political issue. Over the next decade, numerous congressional hearings, government reports, and newspaper stories recounted the failures of the system for removing noncitizen offenders from the United States.* Those not inclined to wade through the details of these reports can (as surely most newspaper readers did at the time)

---

* A must-read for those interested in a full analysis of the failures of the criminal removal system is Peter H. Schuck and John Williams, Removing Criminal Aliens: The Pitfalls of Federalism, 22 Harv. J.L. & Pub. Pol'y 367 (1999). My account here relies heavily on this article, which details the manifest problems in removing serious criminal offenders and Congress' ineffectual responses, which culminated in the expansion of mandatory detention as detailed in this chapter. See also Margaret H. Taylor and Ronald F. Wright, The Sentencing Judge as Immigration Judge, 51 Emory L.J. 1131 (2002) (detailing the structural problems of the criminal removal system, and proposing a targeted merger of criminal sentencing and deportation decisions).

simply skim the headlines. "Moves to Deport Aliens for Drugs are not Pressed," *The New York Times* declared from its front page in 1986.[28] "Porous Deportation System Gives Criminals Little to Fear," proclaimed the *Times*, again on the front page, eight years later.[29] The issue gained political legs after the 1994 midterm elections, when Republicans gained control over both the House and Senate. Ridding the country of "criminal aliens" became a top legislative priority and a central campaign theme for critics of the Clinton administration.

And so several decades of neglect were followed by overreaction,with amendments to the immigration statute and an infusion of resources coming so quickly that few could keep up with the changes. The INS, an agency with little expertise in detention management, soon found itself presiding over the fastest growing detention operation within the federal government.[30] From a daily population of roughly 2,200 in 1985,[31] INS detention capacity tripled to 6,600 beds in 1995,[32] and then tripled again—to an average daily population of around 20,000—by 2001.[33] Resources also flowed to other components of the criminal removal system, including a program to identify non-citizen offenders and place them in deportation proceedings while they were still incarcerated, so that they could be removed immediately at the end of their prison term.[34]

The result was a dramatic rise in the number of criminal deportations, which took hold several years *before* the broad detention mandate at issue in *Demore* went into effect in 1998. In fiscal year 1995, the INS removed over 33,000 criminal offenders—exceeding in just one year the total deported during the 1980s. In fiscal year 1997, over 50,000 criminal offenders were removed.[35] As one sign of how much things had changed from the prior decade, when low deportation rates were a well-kept secret inside the INS in 1996 the agency began holding quarterly press conferences to announce the total number of removals, touting the figures as a marked increase over statistics from the prior year.[36]

Increased resources and detention capacity, however, were not the only things fueling the rise in criminal deportations. The INS was, in the words of one of its congressional critics, "moving steadily backward on a fast-moving treadmill"[37] as Congress added more and more non-citizens with minor convictions to the pipeline for removal by repeatedly amending the statute to expand the criminal deportation grounds and restrict relief. Much of this happened through piecemeal legislation, often in the context of omnibus bills devoted to crime control or appropriations rather than immigration policy. It was within this milieu, rather than after a period of careful study as depicted by the majority in *Demore,* that detention mandates worked their way into the immigration statute.[38]

Initially, mandatory detention was linked to the statutory definition of an aggravated felony. The Anti–Drug Abuse Act of 1988 created this new category of deportable offenses, which originally encompassed only murder, drug-trafficking, or trafficking in firearms. The statute imposed an array of harsh immigration consequences for aggravated felony convictions, including a mandate to detain aggravated felons without bond in both the pre-hearing and post-order contexts.[39] In cases that presaged the arguments raised in *Demore,* this provision was soon challenged by lawful permanent residents who contended that due process entitled them to individualized consideration of their custody status. A number of district courts agreed, concluding that "there is a liberty interest that is implicated when one is detained, which creates the right to a bail hearing."[40]

In response to these legal challenges, Congress amended the statute in 1990 to provide lawful permanent residents with a hearing to establish their eligibility for release. In 1991, this exemption was extended to any "lawfully admitted" aggravated felon.[41] (The latter amendment was introduced to permit Robert Probert, a Canadian hockey player for the Detroit Red Wings, to be released on bond while he awaited deportation after being convicted for importing cocaine for his personal use.[42]) The amended statute still required the INS to take anyone who had been convicted of an aggravated felony into custody. But those who had been lawfully admitted—including nonimmigrants admitted for short-term stays in the United States—were entitled to a bond hearing, and could be released upon a showing that they were not a flight risk or a danger to the community.[43] Only aggravated felons who had entered without inspection remained subject to detention without bond during deportation proceedings.

These amendments significantly narrowed the blanket mandate to detain aggravated felons. Still, the INS detention capacity was so limited and its deportation caseload was growing so rapidly that mandatory detention created real strains for the agency.[44] Looking at the problem in 1992, the General Accounting Office concluded that "[d]etaining all aliens until their cases are resolved is too costly," and "[w]e do not believe that it is feasible to expand INS' detention capabilities sufficiently to solve the problems" that plagued the deportation system.[45]

Nonetheless, the political gain to be had from cracking down on criminal aliens enticed Congress to ignore this reality. In 1994, Congress expanded the statutory definition of an aggravated felony to encompass a much wider range of crimes, which in turn increased the population of non-citizen offenders who could not be released on bond.[46] Even after these amendments, the statutory definition of an aggravated felony was still linked to the severity of the underlying offense, although that link was becoming more attenuated. A theft offense, for example, counted as an aggravated felony conviction only if the prison sentence imposed (regardless of any suspension of imprisonment) was at least five years.[47]

By early 1996, much bigger changes were looming on the horizon. Congress was engaged in intense debate over immigration reform legislation; almost every part of the INA was on the table and potentially subject to major overhaul. While a few controversial provisions had delayed action on the mammoth bill, there was consensus that tough enforcement provisions would be a central feature of legislation that both parties hoped to pass before the presidential election in November.[48]

A consultation on immigration detention hosted by the Commission on Immigration Reform on April 11, 1996 captures the moment. Congress had chartered the bipartisan Commission to make recommendations on immigration policy. Top INS officials and immigration advocates from across the country were gathered in a conference room at a Washington, D.C. hotel to brief the commissioners on detention concerns. Coincidentally, that very day *USA Today* reported on a recently released study by the Department of Justice Inspector General documenting the lack of enforcement of deportation orders.[49] (That same study later played a central role in the litigation over mandatory detention and in the *Demore* decision.) It was the first newspaper story to report the now infamous statistic that the INS actually removed only one out of every ten individuals not kept in custody who were subject to final deportation orders.

At the consultation, INS officials and advocates alike voiced concern that Congress was poised to expand yet again the definition of an aggravated felony, which would in turn expand the scope of mandatory detention. Of particular concern was the impact this would have on a planned project of the Vera Institute of Justice to test supervised release as an alternative to INS detention. At that moment, final details were being ironed out for the contract between Vera and the INS. (The resulting program was also debated in the majority and dissenting opinions of *Demore.*) Vera planned to target lawful permanent residents with criminal convictions for supervised release under its pilot project.[50]

Vera was a respected innovator in the criminal justice arena, with considerable expertise in the area of pre-trial supervision. Its proposal built on an insight that went directly against the tide of public opinion. The key to more effective and humane immigration enforcement was not to expand mandatory detention, Vera argued, but rather to identify individuals who were good candidates for release and to establish an effective program of supervision. This would enable the INS to reserve its scarce bed space for non-citizen offenders who did pose a danger or a flight risk, as well as for other enforcement priorities.[51]

Keeping tabs on those who are not detained, in order to ensure that they appear at their hearings and are available for deportation, was an idea that the INS had never tried. Despite overwhelming evidence that pre-trial supervision is effective for criminal defendants, to some this focus on *releasing* criminal offenders seemed an odd route to correct the culture of noncompliance in the immigration system. Nevertheless, top officials at INS were committed to the project. The agency had already invested considerable time, money, and political capital into what eventually became known as Vera's Appearance Assistance Program. Although participants in the April 11 consultation were closely monitoring pending immigration bills, no one anticipated that, in a matter of days, Congress would seriously undercut these plans to create a pilot project to test supervised release as an alternative to detention.

Less than two weeks later, however, Congress enacted an omnibus crime bill that had emerged from the conference committee as the Trojan horse of immigration reform. The Antiterrorism and Effective Death Penalty Act (AEDPA) was originally drafted to facilitate terrorism prosecutions and to limit death penalty appeals. AEDPA had been pending in Congress for almost a year, held up by disputes over so-called "secret trials" for deporting non-citizen terrorists. By late March, however, the logjam began to loosen because both Congress and the President wanted to enact an antiterrorism bill by April 19, the first anniversary of the bombing of the federal building in Oklahoma City. Republican members of Congress seized the opportunity to use AEPDA as a vehicle to amend the immigration statute. All of a sudden, controversial measures that were still being debated as part of the comprehensive immigration reform bill, expected later that year, passed by an overwhelming (and veto-resistant) majority because they had been inserted into the AEDPA legislation.[52]

At the signing ceremony for AEDPA on April 24, 1996, President Clinton expressed concern that its "ill-advised changes to our immigration laws, having nothing to do with terrorism . . . will produce extraordinary administrative burdens on the Immigration and Naturalization Service."[53] The most visible of these changes included an expansion of the deportation ground for crimes involving moral turpitude, a provision eliminating relief from removal for most criminal offenders, and new and controversial summary exclusion procedures. Lurking in the background, however, was a highly significant detail. While observers had expected that mandatory detention would expand via an expansion of the statutory definition of an aggravated felony, the AEDPA mandate went much further, requiring detention without bond for virtually all non-citizens with criminal convictions. And AEDPA eliminated the escape valve that had permitted release of non-citizen offenders who had been lawfully admitted to the United States.[54]

The INS was "caught off guard" by this unplanned overhaul of much of immigration law.[55] Congress had failed to specify an effective date for many of AEDPA's immigration provisions, and the agency immediately became embroiled in litigation over its decision to apply both the detention mandate and the provision eliminating relief from removal retroactively to all pending cases.[56] Congress also failed to account for the fact that the INS simply did not have sufficient bed space to carry out the new detention mandate. The Clinton administration immediately announced that it would ask Congress to revisit a number of AEDPA provisions by proposing changes to the still-pending immigration reform legislation. Repealing AEDPA's broad detention mandate was at the top of the administration's list of "must-fix" provisions.[57]

Five months later, Congress did indeed pass a second major immigration reform bill, the Illegal Immigration Reform and Immigrant Responsibility Act of 1996 (IIRIRA).[58] IIRIRA was an "on-again, off-again" bill whose prospects were uncertain as Congress was set to adjourn at the end of September. It was revived by a last-minute agreement to incorporate amendments to the immigration statute into a massive omnibus appropriations bill enacted just hours before the close of the fiscal year in order to avoid a government shutdown.[59]

IIRIRA amended some of AEDPA's most controversial immigration provisions, but overall made things worse for non-citizen criminal offenders. The new immigration bill vastly expanded the statutory definition of an aggravated felony, and it made these changes retroactive. As Hyung Joon Kim would soon discover, a theft offense or burglary offense is now an aggravated felony under immigration law if the term of imprisonment imposed is at least one year—replacing the former five-year threshold.[60] IIRIRA also eliminated relief from removal for permanent residents with an aggravated felony conviction, and for non-permanent residents who have been convicted of any crime listed in the inadmissibility grounds.[61] Finally, IIRIRA adopted—and even broadened—the provisions in AEDPA that had expanded mandatory detention during the pendency of deportation hearings.[62]

In a small concession to practical reality, IIRIRA provided that the INS could delay implementation of mandatory detention for a total of two years by notifying Congress that it had insufficient detention space to carry out the new requirement—a step the INS promptly took. During this two-year period, a provision known as the Transition Period Custody Rules restored discretion to release lawfully admitted criminal offenders who were not a flight risk or danger to the community.[63] Thus, the detention mandate of IIRIRA did not go into effect until October, 1998, four months before Hyung Joon Kim was released from California prison and taken into INS custody pursuant to INA § 236(c).

Vera was forced to redesign its Appearance Assistance Program to account for the legal changes brought about by AEDPA and then IIRIRA. Ultimately, Vera signed a contract with the INS to run a pilot supervision program in New York City from February 1997 to March 2000. Non-citizen criminal offenders who were contesting deportation were placed in the program while the transition rules were in effect. Once IIRIRA's detention mandate kicked in, however, very few members of this target population remained eligible for release under Vera's supervision. Vera also had difficulty implementing supervised release for arriving asylum applicants in the midst of the sea change brought about by IIRIRA's expedited removal provisions. In the end, the Appearance Assistance Program showed highly promising results, even though it operated in a turbulent legal environment that thwarted the original program design.[64]

In sum, Congress did not enact the statute that mandated detention without bond for Hyung Joon Kim and other non-citizen offenders with anything close to the careful consideration depicted in the *Demore* decision. With the one-two punch of AEDPA and IIRIRA, Congress circumvented the usual obstacles of the legislative process, which are designed to promote deliberation and debate, and instead secured the passage of controversial immigration reform measures by appending them to larger omnibus bills that were certain to be enacted.[65] Mandatory detention was one small piece of these massive bills; it was expanded without study of the wisdom or feasibility of this approach. Indeed, given the limited detention capacity of the INS, a requirement to detain virtually all criminal offenders during the pendency of deportation proceedings—without regard to the seriousness of the underlying offense, the flight risk, or the equities of their case—was hardly considered to be a viable policy option until it was enacted.

A "Clear, Strong" Case for Cancellation: Mandatory Detention as Applied to Hyung Joon Kim

The *Demore* majority obfuscated this history in part by ignoring the broad scope of INA § 236(c), implying that AEDPA and IIRIRA enacted changes that were in keeping with earlier, more limited mandatory detention provisions. Thus, the Court described the statute as applying only to a "limited class" or a "subset of deportable criminal aliens."[66] Other statements in *Demore* reflect similar misrepresentations or misunderstandings. The majority asserted, for example, that Hyung Joon Kim had bypassed administrative procedures that would have provided an "individualized review" of his detention.[67] The Court also repeatedly emphasized that the INS had charged Kim with being deportable as an aggravated felon—a classification that would render him ineligible for relief from removal—and concluded that he had conceded deportability on this charge.[68] The overall picture that emerges is of a narrowly tailored statute being applied to a serious criminal offender who was pressing a hopeless case—a picture that, to the justices in the majority and perhaps to some readers, made detention without bond pending deportation seem perfectly justifiable.

Each component of this picture is demonstrably false. Hyung Joon Kim was not detained without bond pending deportation because he was a serious offender, but rather because the statute was so broad that it encompassed lawful permanent residents who were deportable for minor property crimes. It may have seemed pointless for him to argue that his convictions did not fall within the scope of INA § 236(c), but it was not at all hopeless for him to contest his removal from the United States. In fact, the original INS charge that Kim was deportable as an aggravated felon was already crumbling by the time his challenge to mandatory detention reached the Supreme Court. And after *Demore v. Kim* was decided, an immigration judge concluded that Kim had established a "clear, strong" case for discretionary relief, known after IIRIRA as cancellation of removal.

Admissions, Concessions, Misrepresentations, and Misunderstandings

The *Demore* majority's misstatements of law are the easiest to debunk. The Court's assertion that INA § 236(c) applies only to a "limited class" or "a subset of deportable criminal aliens" has spawned considerable confusion because it is so at odds with what the statute actually provides. Indeed, at times it is not clear whether the justices in the majority actually understood that mandatory detention is no longer linked to an aggravated felony conviction. As already noted, detention without bond during the pendency of deportation proceedings has expanded far beyond its earliest incarnation as a requirement to detain the most serious criminal offenders. INA § 236(c) now provides that immigration authorities "shall take into custody" any non-citizen who is inadmissible on any criminal ground, or deportable for any criminal ground *except* a single crime involving moral turpitude committed within five years after admission for which a term of imprisonment of less than a year has been imposed.[69] In short, almost any offense that renders a non-citizen deportable—including crimes such as simple drug possession, a fight in a bar, or two shoplifting offenses—will trigger detention without bond for as long as it takes to resolve the deportation case.

Because mandatory detention under INA § 236(c) is virtually coextensive with the criminal removal grounds, it is often fruitless for a non-citizen who is charged as deportable on the basis of a criminal conviction to argue that § 236(c) should not apply in his case. Thus, the Court was mistaken in attaching any particular meaning to the fact that Hyung

Joon Kim "forwent" the limited administrative procedures available to bring such a challenge. Under the governing regulations, a non-citizen detained under INA § 236(c) can seek a determination by an immigration judge that he is "not properly included" in the mandatory detention categories listed in the statute.[70] The *Demore* majority suggested that this so-called *Joseph* hearing (named after the Board of Immigration Appeals decision interpreting the regulation) provided a robust check on mandatory detention. Echoing the language often used to describe bond determinations, the Court also mischaracterized this proceeding as an "individualized review" of detention under the statute.[71]

But the statute and regulations do not permit non-citizens detained pursuant to INA § 236(c) to argue that they should be released based on the individual equities of their cases. Moreover, the scope of review of in a *Joseph* hearing is quite narrow. In *Joseph* itself, the BIA rejected an argument that the government must demonstrate a likelihood of success on the merits of a criminal removal charge to trigger mandatory detention. Instead, the burden is on non-citizen detained under § 236(c) to show that the government is "substantially unlikely to establish a charge of deportability."[72] In essence, under the BIA interpretation, an immigration judge asks only whether the government has a nonfrivolous claim that an individual should be detained under the statute. This question is often answered by the routine concession of the underlying criminal conviction made when removal is sought on criminal grounds. In many cases, in other words, a *Joseph* hearing is not worth pursuing.[73]

It was this routine concession by Hyung Joon Kim, which the majority incorrectly interpreted as an admission that Kim was both deportable *and* ineligible for discretionary relief, that so thoroughly muddied the Supreme Court's analysis. As is almost always true when an individual is charged with being deportable on criminal grounds, Kim admitted that he had been convicted of the underlying offense. This concession is routine—unless there has been a mistake of identity or some error in the compilation of records—because the INS usually has the record of conviction on hand when it files charges.

Admission of the fact of the underlying conviction may be coupled with a concession of so-called "baseline deportability," which is made when the conviction indisputably falls within one of the criminal deportation grounds listed in INA § 237(a)(2). There are, of course, cases where baseline deportability can be contested, and the non-citizen argues that the conviction does not fit within any of the statutory grounds—for example, that the offense is neither a crime involving moral turpitude nor an aggravated felony, as defined in the INA. Indeed, after IIRIRA sharply narrowed the availability of relief from removal, contesting baseline deportability has become an increasingly important defense strategy. Nevertheless, it is still quite common to find cases where both sides agree that *some* criminal deportation ground will apply, and the outcome turns on whether the non-citizen is both eligible for and deserving of discretionary relief from removal. For long-term lawful permanent residents facing deportation on criminal grounds, eligibility for relief today hinges on whether the conviction is properly classified as an aggravated felony.

Hyung Joon Kim's deportation proceeding (which proceeded in immigration court entirely separate from his habeas corpus challenge to the legality of his detention) was primarily litigated over the question of relief. But the Supreme Court failed to appreciate that relief was very much a live issue in Kim's case. Instead, from the fact that Kim "does not dispute the validity of his prior convictions," the Court concluded that he had conceded baseline deportability, and then erroneously assumed that this meant he *was deportable as charged* for an aggravated felony conviction.[74] Stated differently, the *Demore* majority equated an apparent concession of baseline deportability—an admission that Kim's convictions fit within *some* deportation ground—with a concession that the government had properly classified him as an aggravated felon, rendering him ineligible for discretionary relief from removal.

A second error compounded this mistake. The *Demore* court also assumed that the governing law and the facts were static, so that Kim's deportation would be decided based on the theories of the case developed when the initial charges were filed. Two weeks before the Supreme Court granted *certiorari* in *Demore v. Kim*, however, the Ninth Circuit, sitting en banc, held that a California conviction for petty theft with priors is not an aggravated felony conviction in immigration law, even when a sentence of a year or longer has been imposed.[75] (The earlier panel decision had reached the opposite conclusion.) The INS had originally charged Kim as being deportable as an aggravated felon only on the basis of his conviction for petty theft with priors. Thus, the intervening Ninth Circuit precedent opened the door for Kim to argue at his next administrative hearing that he was not deportable as an aggravated felon and that he was eligible for cancellation of removal.[76]

Just before the government's brief was to be filed in the Supreme Court, however, the INS amended the charging documents to allege that Kim was also deportable for having been convicted of two crimes involving moral turpitude. The government's opening brief noted in passing that the underlying charges had been amended, but did not explain that the original charge was no longer valid because the Ninth Circuit had changed its interpretation of the statute. Instead, government lawyers continued to state (accurately if somewhat disingenuously) that Kim was charged with being deportable as an aggravated felon.[77]

The question of whether Kim could properly be classified as an aggravated felon was conclusively resolved only after the Supreme Court issued its decision. On May 14, 2003, Kim's attorneys secured post-conviction relief from the California criminal court that had convicted Kim of burglary and petty theft with priors. The state court vacated the concurrent two-and three-year prison terms that had been imposed upon (and indeed, had been served by) Kim, concluding that that the original sentence was constitutionally invalid because the sentencing judge, prosecutor, and defense attorney were all unaware that it likely would trigger automatic deportation. The court then resentenced Kim *nunc pro tunc* to a term of 364 days, with credit for time served.[78]

Two weeks later, Kim filed his application for cancellation of removal. The Department of Homeland Security (which by then had taken over the functions of the INS) did not contest the California court order. Instead, the government withdrew the aggravated felony charge, leaving only the charge that Kim was deportable for having committed two crimes involving moral turpitude, and conceded that this meant Kim was statutorily eligible for cancellation of removal. The Department nevertheless vigorously opposed Kim's application on the ground that he was a repeat offender who was not deserving of relief.[79]

It was around this time that Hyung Joon Kim, having lost his challenge to mandatory detention in the Supreme Court, was taken back into INS custody pursuant to INA § 236(c). It is ironic that just as Kim appeared poised to prevail in his long fight against deportation, he was thrown back into the county jail.

A Rehabilitated Life

Once statutory eligibility is established, cancellation of removal for lawful permanent residents is granted as a matter of discretion. The statute provides no particular formula for making this determination. In general, the immigration judge must conclude that the positive equities in the case outweigh the negative factors, and that the applicant is deserving of a favorable exercise of discretion.[80] In a nutshell, the record of Kim's cancellation proceeding discloses the following story.

Hyung Joon Kim came to the United States from South Korea at the age of six, and became a lawful permanent resident when he was eight years old. He recalled that he had difficulty making friends when he entered school because he did not speak English; this early experience heightened the usual teenaged insecurities about wanting to fit in with the crowd. As he grew older, Kim also rebelled against his authoritarian father, who later admitted that his strict rules and "hot temper" had alienated his son.[81] It was during this period that Kim, often in the company of friends, engaged in criminal activity.

Kim's first brush with the law came when he was seventeen; he was placed on juvenile probation for unlawful possession of a BB gun and ammunition on school property. Kim later explained he had been motivated by a desire to "show off," and was arrested after he had taken a friend out to his car to see the items.

In April 1996, while Kim was still on probation for this offense, he and two friends broke into a tool shed that was adjacent to a home. Kim's friends had broken into the same shed the day before; among the items stolen were three handguns. They gave the guns to Kim, who kept them, knowing they were stolen property. The following day, all three returned to the same shed to see what else they could steal, and were apprehended on the scene. Kim was convicted and sentenced to serve six months in county jail and five years' probation. He was incarcerated for two months before he was granted early release so that he could begin his freshman year of college at the University of California at Santa Barbara.

In November 1996, Kim was convicted of shoplifting four computer games, batteries, and an extension cord from the UCSB bookstore. He was sentenced to thirty days' custody, but granted court extensions so that he could remain in school. Just three months later, in February 1997, Kim—along with two accomplices—was caught shoplifting a computer game and three phone cards from a Costco store. The prosecutor charged the offense as a "petty theft with priors," punishable under state law as a felony, and Kim pleaded guilty to this charge. A presentence report prepared by Kim's probation officer argued that Kim "has been given innumerable opportunities by the judicial system and has continued to violate the law," and thus should be sentenced to prison.[82] The state court judge agreed, imposing concurrent prison terms of two years for violating probation stemming from the burglary conviction and three years for the petty theft. Kim served two years at the California state prison, received a year's credit for good behavior, and was released from prison and taken into INS custody in February 1999.

The time spent in prison had a profound effect on Hyung Joon Kim and his family. His parents were distraught, and his father sought counseling that helped to repair his relationship with his son. For Kim, incarceration for two years in the state penitentiary and the distress of his family were a grim "wake up call" to turn his life around.

If the district court in Kim's habeas case had not ruled that mandatory detention was unconstitutional, Kim would have languished in custody while he pursued his claim for relief from removal; it is difficult to develop positive equities and demonstrate rehabilitation from a jail cell. In August 1999, however, the district court ordered the INS to assess whether Kim was a flight risk or a danger to the community.[83] A deportation officer readily concluded that Kim "would not be considered a threat" and freed him on a minimal bond without even holding a hearing.[84] Kim faithfully attended all of his immigration hearings while he remained free from detention. And over the next four years, Kim amply demonstrated that he had outgrown the difficulties that flared up in his teenage years.

After being released from INS detention, Kim re-enrolled in college. He was a junior at San Jose State University when the Supreme Court decided his case. Apparently a skilled computer technician, Kim was also regularly employed. His most recent job was at DirecTV Broadband, where he had worked for a year and a half, earning twenty-seven dollars an hour. His tax records from 2001 indicate that Kim's earnings for the year exceeded the wages of many recent college graduates.

Hyung Joon Kim was twenty-five years old in 2003, when his application for cancellation of removal was filed. He had not engaged in any criminal activity since the minor property crimes committed when he was eighteen and nineteen. After a detailed psychological evaluation, a psychologist who was an expert in personality disorders concluded that Kim "had some defiance and authority issues" when he was a teenager, but showed "no indications of impulsiveness or other psychological problems."[85]

Against this strong evidence of rehabilitation, skillfully developed by some of the best immigration lawyers in the country,[86] the Department of Homeland Security (DHS) asserted two arguments. First, government lawyers suggested that Kim had an impulse control disorder (they hinted that his shoplifting might have been prompted by kleptomania). The immigration judge found that this argument was "unsupported by any authoritative evidence" and had been conclusively refuted by the psychologist who examined Kim.[87] Second, the DHS attempted to challenge the evidence of Kim's rehabilitation, and argued that his criminal convictions were so serious that they outweighed the positive equities of his case.

The immigration judge instead concluded that this was a slam-dunk case for granting cancellation of removal. He ruled that the "positive equities in this case far outweigh the negative factors.... It is furthermore in our nation's best interest to keep the Respondent here, after having invested so much time both in his education and his rehabilitation, which in the Court's view is genuine."[88] The intensity of the government's opposition, and the fact that "[t]he whole DHS brass turned out for [Kim's] hearing,"[89] prompted the immigration judge to observe that the attention devoted to this seemingly ordinary case was unusual. He remarked at the close of the hearing: "The Government in this case is like a blind old dog that has gotten hold of an old rotten bone and won't let go in spite of everything to the contrary, that this case is a clear, strong grant of cancellation."[90]

Wasted Lives and Wasted Money: The Broader Impact of the Statute

The background story of Hyung Joon Kim's convictions and rehabilitation exposes the misrepresentations and misunderstandings that clouded the Supreme Court's judgment in *Demore v. Kim*. In addition, the nature of Kim's crimes and the strength of his ties to the community are precisely what an immigration judge would consider (albeit in less detail) if the statute allowed for a bond hearing. Most importantly, Kim's story shows the steep human cost and the government waste incurred when detention is mandated for virtually all non-citizen offenders facing deportation, without an individualized assessment of whether any purpose is served by their continued incarceration.

Even though the Supreme Court did not have access to many of these details about the life of Hyung Joon Kim, it did have before it evidence of the harsh impact of the statute on long-term residents of the United States and their families. An amicus brief filed by Citizens and Immigrants for Equal Justice (CIEJ) and other advocacy groups related the stories of individuals who had been detained by the INS for months (and sometimes for over a year) only to prove in the end that they were citizens of the United States, or had not been convicted of a deportable offense, or had compelling cases for cancellation of removal.[91] The CIEJ brief highlighted the fact that government statistics showing that mandatory detention lasts *on average* only "a brief period" are misleading when assessing the statute's impact on lawful permanent residents. Indeed, it is precisely those individuals with strong ties to the United States, who have both the legal grounds and every incentive to contest their deportation, who are detained the longest under the statute.[92] The CIEJ brief's vivid portrait of the lives shattered by INA § 236(c) "la[id] bare the fiction that mandatory detention ... is simply a brief way station on the inevitable path to deportation."[93]

The costs of mandatory detention are also borne by individuals who in the end are deported from the United States. There is no right to appointed counsel in immigration proceedings, and detention deprives non-citizens and their families of the resources—both financial and emotional—needed to sustain a prolonged fight against deportation. Moreover, immigration detainees are frequently transferred to remote locations, which can make it impossible for them to secure legal representation and to develop their claim.[94] While the law adheres to a fiction that immigration detention is not punishment, non-citizens are confined in places that are indistinguishable from corrections facilities (and indeed, often in state and local jails).[95] An indeterminate sentence in

DHS custody is a high price to pay for contesting deportation, and it induces many to give up on viable claims.

Finally, even for individuals who have no basis to contest deportation, mandating detention without bond while they await a final order is unjust. Those who would otherwise be released without the operation of INA § 236(c) are deprived of the chance to wind down their affairs and to spend their last days in the United States in the company of family and friends. Moreover, the statute does not provide for release for humanitarian reasons, even in the most compelling of circumstances. Thus pregnant women, nursing mothers, people with chronic or even life-threatening medical conditions, and countless individuals who are the sole source of support for their U.S. citizen families are among the people that the DHS has no choice but to detain under the statute.[96]

Mandatory detention also imposes significant costs on the government. Under INA § 236(c), virtually all the beds available for immigration detention must be used to hold non-citizens who are being deported for crimes. This impairs the Department's ability to use detention resources for other purposes. Late in the summer of 2004, for example, a spate of newspaper stories reported that the southern border of the United States was ripe for exploitation by terrorists. The key concern was that immigration authorities along the border had no spare detention capacity, and thus were employing a "catch and release" policy that permitted individuals from countries other than Mexico who were apprehended at the border to remain at large inside the United States.[97] Plainly the inability to shift detention resources to other enforcement priorities is a significant downside to mandatory detention of criminal offenders under INA § 236(c).

The governmental costs of mandatory detention were pressed before the Supreme Court by the former Commissioner and three former General Counsels of the INS, who filed an amicus brief arguing *against* the statute they had recently been charged with implementing. The former INS officials emphasized that "[f]or aliens who do not present a flight risk or danger to the community, mandatory detention serves only one purpose: to drain INS resources."[98] And they argued that discretionary bond decisions, rather than inflexible detention mandates, provided the best method for allocating scarce bed space among competing enforcement priorities.[99]

These were, of course, the same arguments that fell on deaf ears when advocates and government officials lobbied Congress to repeal AEDPA's sudden expansion of mandatory detention without bond. And the *Demore* majority concluded that it was the prerogative of Congress to weigh these costs against the perceived benefits of INA § 236(c). Rather than apply careful due process scrutiny to the statute, the Court instead invoked a "fundamental premise of immigration law"—deference to the political branches' plenary power to control immigration.[100]

A *Legal Realist Reading of* Demore

Students of immigration law, who are accustomed to seeing constitutional challenges brushed aside under the so-called plenary power doctrine, may not be surprised by this outcome. But *Demore v. Kim* might nevertheless be called a surprising decision, because just two years earlier it had seemed that the Supreme Court was backing away from a strong version of plenary power deference identified with the Cold War era.[101] In addition, as the dissenting opinion in *Demore* argued, INA § 236(c) would not withstand scrutiny under a line of Supreme Court cases imposing due process limits on civil detention.

If the Court had chosen to apply this body of precedent to assess the constitutionality of INA § 236(c), Hyung Joon Kim's due process challenge to detention without bond would have been—as Justice Souter observed—an easy case.[102] Freedom from physical confinement lies at the heart of the liberty protected by the Due Process Clause.[103] Outside the immigration context, the Supreme Court has repeatedly recognized both substantive and procedural due process constraints on the government's ability to detain individuals because they are seen as a threat.

The centerpiece of this line of cases is *United States v. Salerno,*[104] where the Court upheld a provision of the federal Bail Reform Act permitting detention without bond in a narrow category of cases. The statute at issue in *Salerno* required the government to show by clear and convincing evidence that a criminal defendant would present a danger such that no conditions of pretrial supervision "will reasonably assure ... the safety of any other person and the community."[105] Acknowledging that the statute presented serious constitutional issues, the Court nonetheless found that due process was satisfied because of several protections embedded in the "no bail" statute. Pretrial detention without bond was subject to "stringent time limitations." In addition, the statute provided substantive criteria to limit its application to "the most serious of crimes," and careful procedures, built around a bond hearing before a judicial officer, to protect criminal defendants against erroneous decisions.[106]

In a host of similar cases, the Supreme Court has considered due process challenges to civil detention based on an assessment of future dangerousness.[107] In each instance, the Court has insisted on "a constitutionally adequate purpose for the confinement."[108] The Court has also required that the substantive criteria for detention be "sharply focused" and "carefully limited,"[109] that detention must be justified by an assessment of future dangerousness *plus* some other "special circumstance" (such as mental illness),[110] and that the statute must afford individuals who were being deprived of liberty all of the procedural safeguards of "a full-blown adversary hearing."[111] The detention scheme of INA § 236(c), which mandates pre-hearing detention for virtually all non-citizen offenders without *any* hearing to assess flight risk or dangerousness, indisputably does not meet the criteria of the *Salerno* line of cases.

The *Demore* majority adopted a curious strategy to address this body of precedent: they ignored it completely. This silence was all the more remarkable because, as previously noted, two years before *Demore* was decided, the Supreme Court invoked *Salerno* and its progeny to invalidate the indefinite detention of lawful permanent residents who had been ordered removed. The petitioners in *Zadvydas v. Davis* had challenged their continued incarceration under the post-order detention statute, INA § 241, which provides that non-citizens whose physical removal cannot be effectuated within ninety days after a deportation order becomes final "may" be continued in custody.[112] In a 5–4 decision, the *Zadvydas* Court held that this provision could not be read to authorize detention of lawful permanent residents "beyond a period reasonably necessary to secure removal," because of the serious constitutional concerns such an interpretation would create.[113]

Although the holding of *Zadvydas* was one of statutory interpretation, the rationale was one of constitutional law.[114] *Zadvydas v. Davis* rejected the argument that the decisions of Congress and the Executive Branch were owed special deference when immigration policy is at stake, asserting instead that the political branches' plenary power to create immigration law "is subject to important constitutional limitations."[115] Notably, the Court also reaffirmed that non-citizens detained by the INS were protected by due process, and invoked the *Salerno* line of cases to conclude that "[a] statute that permitted indefinite detention of an alien would raise a serious constitutional problem."[116]

The *Zadvydas* decision had important implications for pending constitutional challenges to INA § 236(c). By explicitly applying *Salerno* and its progeny to lawful permanent residents detained by the INS, *Zadvydas* seemed to neutralize plenary power arguments and bolster the claim that a blanket mandate to detain non-citizen offenders without bond was unconstitutional. Moreover, Kim and others like him were asserting a narrower claim, with a less risky remedy, than the successful petitioners in *Zadvydas*. The *Zadvydas* decision mandates release after roughly six months, unless the government shows that removal is reasonably foreseeable, even if the government has evidence that the person is likely to continue violent criminal activity. In contrast, lawful permanent residents detained pursuant to INA § 236(c) did not claim an absolute right of release, but rather sought a bond hearing where flight risk and dangerousness would be assessed. Anyone adjudged dangerous at that hearing would remain in custody. After *Zadvydas,* the courts of appeals uniformly concluded that due process requires precisely this scheme.[117]

When Kim's challenge to mandatory detention reached the Supreme Court, however, the *Demore* majority minimized the constitutional component of *Zadvydas.* Rather than acknowledge its recent conclusion that the *Salerno* line of cases protects INS detainees, the *Demore* Court simply distinguished *Zadvydas* on its facts, focusing on purported differences in the purpose and length of detention in the pre-hearing and post-order contexts.[118] And instead of considering whether INA § 236(c) fulfilled the requirements of due process, the Court repeated three times (as if repetition would make up for the lack of analysis) the familiar incantation that "[i]n the exercise of its broad power over naturalization and immigration, Congress regularly makes rules that would be unacceptable if applied to citizens."[119]

The *Demore* majority's refusal to link its analysis to the most salient due process precedent, both inside and outside the immigration law context, is striking. It also accounts for the frustrating disconnect between the majority and dissenting opinions. Five justices thought the case could be resolved by reciting plenary power platitudes. To the four dissenting justices, "the only reasonable starting point is the traditional doctrine concerning the Government's physical confinement of individuals."[120] (Justice O'Connor was the swing justice who voted with the majority in both *Zadvydas* and *Demore.*) The two approaches are starkly different, yet nothing explains why the majority misrepresented the history of the statute, along with its scope and its impact, and retreated to a strong version of plenary power deference that some observers thought had been buried by the *Zadvydas* decision.

But this result was not completely unexpected, for a reason never mentioned within the four corners of the *Demore* decision. *Demore v. Kim* was the first immigration case to reach the Supreme Court after September 11, 2001. It was decided against the backdrop of the detention of hundreds of Arab and Muslim non-citizens in connection with the 9/11 terrorism investigation, who were taken into INS custody and held without bond until they were cleared by the FBI.[121] Although the briefs filed in *Demore* focused only on the constitutionality of INA § 236(c) as applied to lawful permanent resident criminal offenders, both sides knew that the case could affect the government's claimed authority to detain without bond any non-citizen deemed "of interest" to the terrorism investigation. This understanding was also reflected in contemporaneous newspaper accounts, which reported that the impending Supreme Court decision "will have significant implications for the ability of the federal government to fight the war on terror."[122] And while the Court studiously avoided commenting on the social and political context of the case, surely the justices saw the connection as well.[123]

In short, *Demore v. Kim* asked the Supreme Court to consider whether the Constitution imposes limits on the preventive detention of non-citizens at a time when the post–9/11 detention sweeps were fresh in the public's memory, and when criticism of that effort—from both inside and outside of the government—had not yet taken hold. The resulting decision is inconsistent with *Zadvydas* and the *Salerno* line of cases, and thus may be unstable as precedent. Already the lower courts, when asked to reconcile *Demore* with the rest of due process jurisprudence, have read *Demore* narrowly while more readily embracing the *Zadvydas* approach.[124] This trend may be bolstered by the fact that in January 2005 the Supreme Court, in a 7–2 decision, reaffirmed its interpretation of the post-order detention statute announced in *Zadvydas*. *Clark v. Suarez Martinez*[125] resolved a long-standing dispute over indefinite detention of non-citizens who were *not* lawful permanent residents—and indeed had technically never been admitted to the country. It ruled that because the statute did not distinguish between categories of non-citizens, the *Zadvydas* interpretation prohibiting detention beyond a period reasonably necessary to effectuate removal controlled.

Clark was decided purely as a matter of statutory interpretation, but there are also intriguing signals in the Supreme Court's constitutional jurisprudence that suggest that the Court might eventually back away from the strong version of judicial deference it embraced in *Demore v. Kim*. In the summer of 2004, the Court showed renewed skepticism of claims that non-citizen detainees (this time, in military custody at Guantanamo Bay) and citizens who were declared enemy combatants were beyond the reach of the courts and outside the scope of due process protection. The decisions in *Rasul v. Bush* and *Hamdi v. Rumsfeld* came after heightened scrutiny of the post–9/11 detention sweeps, and in the immediate wake of the disclosure of torture by the U.S. military at Abu Ghraib prison in Iraq.[126] Consistent with the analysis of *Demore* offered here, some commentators have observed that these decisions, although surprising to some, were best explained by the fact that the Supreme Court "appears acutely aware of the broader political climate in its decisions."[127]

In the end, Hyung Joon Kim himself offered the most convincing explanation for why he lost his Supreme Court case, one that is more plausible than the analysis of the *Demore* majority. "I think it's the climate," Kim said when asked about the ruling.[128]

Epilogue

At the close of the hearing on Hyung Joon Kim's application for cancellation of removal, the immigration judge—expressing dismay at the government's dogged persistence in pursuing Kim's deportation—cautioned the DHS attorney that "you're not going to want my decision to go up to the Board."[129] Nevertheless, the Department did appeal the grant of cancellation to the Board of Immigration Appeals. And on January 15, 2004, the Board, in a nonprecedent decision, reversed the immigration judge's ruling.[130]

In contrast to the lengthy summary of evidence by the immigration judge, the BIA, after a brief discussion of the applicable precedent, disposed of Kim's claim in a single paragraph. The Board concluded that Kim was a repeat offender who had engaged in a "serious pattern of criminal misconduct." His crimes were deemed "serious" because "two of the respondent's convictions involved the possession and theft of firearms"—a reference to the fact that handguns were stolen from the tool shed, and that Kim had been placed on juvenile probation for having a BB gun in his car at school. Kim had a "substantial criminal history," according to the Board, because he had twice been convicted of shoplifting after his burglary offense. Moreover, in an effort to demonstrate that he accepted responsibility for his crimes (which is usually viewed as a favorable factor), Kim had also admitted, upon questioning from his attorney, that he had shoplifted on other occasions before he was sentenced to prison. The Board took this admission as further evidence that Kim was a recidivist. Finally, although it was undisputed that Kim's convictions all occurred within a ten-month span when he was a teenager, the Board also asserted—without any supporting evidence in the record—that after Kim had been sentenced to probation, "he continued to engage in criminal misconduct for three years."[131]

These mischaracterizations of Kim's criminal history are nothing short of bizarre when compared with the full record developed in Kim's cancellation proceeding. In addition, the Board's recounting of the evidence was completely one-sided. The BIA noted that Kim and his father had "sincerely testified that he has changed since his incarceration in state prison," but did not recount specific evidence of rehabilitation or any details of the life Kim had built after he was released from prison. The Board also allowed that Kim had not engaged in any further criminal conduct after this term of imprisonment, but its decision failed to note that almost seven years had passed since Kim had been convicted of a crime, and that the teenaged shoplifter was now a responsible adult who had enrolled in college and embarked on a successful career. At the end of its one-paragraph analysis of the facts, the Board weighed its embellished version of Kim's criminal history against a rote recitation of positive equities, and concluded that Kim's "serious criminal misconduct outweighs his rehabilitation, family ties, and long residence in the United States."[132]

When Congress enacted IIRIRA in 1996, it amended the INA to provide that "no court shall have jurisdiction" to review final orders against virtually any non-citizen who is deportable for having committed a criminal offense. IIRIRA also precludes judicial review of a decision to deny cancellation of removal. But habeas corpus jurisdiction remains to challenge legal and constitutional errors in removal proceedings.[133]

Hyung Joon Kim's attorneys filed a new petition for writ of habeas corpus on January 26, 2004. The petition alleges that the BIA decision violates due process because the Board acted arbitrarily by inexplicably departing from its own precedent and treating Kim's minor property offenses as serious crimes. The petition also claims that Kim was singled out for unfavorable treatment because he had litigated his challenge to mandatory detention all the way to the Supreme Court.[134]

After the BIA reversed the immigration judge's grant of cancellation of removal and Kim's removal order became final, he was again released from INS custody under the post-order detention provision. Kim's attorneys were granted a discovery motion to examine all cases granting or denying cancellation of removal or similar relief decided by the BIA over a two-year period. When granting this motion, the district court concluded that Kim's allegations of a deprivation of due process "are serious and they warrant resolution."[135] As this chapter went to press in 2005, the case was still pending before the same district judge who had granted Kim's original habeas petition.

ENDNOTES

1. This chapter draws on my ongoing work analyzing immigration detention policy, and reflects insights gained through conversations I have had over a number of years with immigration advocates and government officials. Some of these conversations—including the one reported in the opening paragraph—were not for attribution. My research also included interviews with Timothy Edgar, Greg Nojeim, and Judy Rabinovitz of the ACLU and David Martin, former General Counsel of the INS. I was present at the Commission on Immigration Reform Consultation on Detention in April 1996 recounted in this chapter. I also served on the Advisory Board of the Vera Institute of Justice Appearance Assistance Program. David Martin, Hiroshi Motomura, Judy Rabinovitz, and Ron Wright provided helpful comments on the manuscript. I remain responsible for any errors.

2. Brief for T. Alexander Aleinikoff, David A. Martin, Doris Meissner, and Paul W. Virtue as Amici Curiae in Support of Respondent at 3, 21, Demore v. Kim, 538 U.S. 510 (2003) (No. 01–1419) ("Former INS Officials Brief").

3. Notice of Custody Determination, Aug. 16, 1999, reprinted in the Joint Appendix filed with the Supreme Court at 13, Demore v. Kim, 538 U.S. 510 (2003) (No. 01–1491).

4. Unless otherwise noted, all of the details of Hyung Joon Kim's life recounted in this chapter come from the record in a habeas corpus petition that Kim filed challenging a Board of Immigration Appeals decision that ordered his removal from the United States. As this chapter goes to press in 2005, the case is pending in the Northern District of California. Kim v. Ridge, No. C–04–0341 (N.D. Cal. filed Jan. 26, 2004). The record in this habeas action includes Kim's application for cancellation of removal with extensive supporting documentation, the transcript of the removal hearing, and the immigration judge's ruling.

5. Bob Egelko, Justices to Rule on Detention of Immigrants, San Fran. Chron. A3 (Jan. 15, 2003).

6. INA § 240A(a)(3), 8 U.S.C. § 1229b(a)(3) (2000).

7. The statute provides that the Attorney General (now the Secretary of the Department of Homeland Security) "shall take into custody" any alien who is inadmissible or deportable on any of the grounds listed within INA § 236(c). As explained below, this provision encompasses virtually all of the criminal grounds of removal. INA § 236(c) provides discretion to release only if necessary to provide protection to a cooperating witness under the federal witness protection program. 8 U.S.C. § 1226(c) (2000).

8. Demore v. Kim, 538 U.S. 510, 551 (2003) (Souter, J. dissenting).

9. Zadvydas v. Davis, 533 U.S. 678, 688–94 (2001).

10. Kim v. Ziglar, 276 F.3d 523 (9th Cir. 2002); Welch v. Ashcroft, 293 F.3d 213 (4th Cir. 2002); Hoang v. Comfort, 282 F.3d 1247 (10th Cir. 2002); Patel v. Zemski, 275 F.3d 299 (3d Cir. 2001). The Seventh Circuit reached a contrary conclusion in Parra v. Perryman, 172 F.3d 954 (7th Cir. 1999), but that decision preceded the Supreme Court's decision in *Zadvydas*.

11. 538 U.S. at 520–21.

12. Former INA § 242(a)(1), 8 U.S.C. § 1252(a)(1) (1994).

13. Former 8 C.F.R. § 242.2(c) & (d) (1997); Matter of Patel, 15 I & N Dec. 666 (BIA 1976). For an explanation of how the former statute operated, see Margaret H. Taylor, The 1996 Immigration Act: Detention and Related Issues, 74 Interpreter Releases 209 (Feb. 3, 1997) ("Taylor, The 1996 Act: Detention").

14. Former INA § 242(c) & (d), 8 U.S.C. § 1252(c) & (d) (1994). Courts interpreted the statute to impose a strict six-month time limit on post-order detention. Balogun v. INS, 9 F.3d 347, 351 (5th Cir. 1993).

15. Department of Justice, Office of the Inspector General, Immigration and Naturalization Service, Deportation of Aliens After Final Orders Have Been Issued 17 (Mar. 1996) ("IG Report"). The Inspector General's Report was included in the Joint Appendix submitted to the Supreme Court, and this sentence was quoted in the *Demore* opinion. 538 U.S. at 519.

16. 538 U.S. at 513.

17. Margaret H. Taylor and Ronald F. Wright, The Sentencing Judge As Immigration Judge, 51 Emory L.J. 1131, 1135 (2002) ("Taylor and Wright"). These problems are analyzed in detail in Peter H. Schuck and John Williams, Removing Criminal Aliens: The Pitfalls of Federalism, 22 Harv. J. L. & Pub. Pol'y 367 (1999) ("Schuck and Williams"). They are also documented in the Inspector General's Report (cited in note 15), and in the various congressional hearings and government reports cited in the *Demore* decision.

18. In fiscal year 1980, for example, out of an estimated 31,000 non-citizens who were deportable for criminal offenses (see Schuck and Williams at 381, table 2), fewer than 500 individuals were removed on criminal grounds. 1997 Statistical Yearbook of the Immigration and Naturalization Service 187, table 67 (reporting 206 non-citizens deported for criminal violations and 188 for narcotics violations in fiscal year 1980). Schuck and Williams stress that their estimate—derived by first estimating the number of foreign-born inmates, parolees, and probationers in the federal and state systems, and then further estimating what percentage of these foreign-born populations would in fact be deportable— was made in the face of a "lack of reliable information" about the size of the deportable criminal alien population. Schuck and Williams at 376. Moreover, the early data on criminal removals did not include non-citizens with criminal convictions who were deported on other grounds (such as entering without inspection or overstaying a visa), and thus underestimate to some degree the total number of criminal offenders who were removed. In 1994, the INS updated its data from 1990 onward to incorporate a new definition of criminal removals that included individuals with criminal convictions who were removed on other grounds. 1994 Statistical Yearbook of the Immigration and Naturalization Service 159.

19. IG Report at 11 (cited in note 15).

20. Id. at 12–15.

21. *Demore*, 538 U.S. at 518.

22. IG Report at 12, 13.

23. Administration Presses Policy of Incarcerating Illegal Aliens, Cong. Q. (Feb. 16, 1985), reprinted in Oversight Hearing before the Subcommittee On Courts, Civil Liberties, and the Administration of Justice of the House Committee on the Judiciary, 99th Cong. 1st Sess. 53 (Mar. 28, 1985).

24. U.S. Department of Justice, Federal Detention Plan 1993–1997, at 15 (Dec. 1992) ("Five–Year Detention Plan").

25. Id.

26. Former INS Officials Brief at 14–16 (cited in note 2).

27. 538 U.S. at 519.

28. Peter Kerr, Moves to Deport Aliens for Drugs are not Pressed, N.Y. Times A1 (July 30, 1986).

29. Deborah Sontag, Porous Deportation System Gives Criminals Little to Fear, N.Y. Times A1 (Sept. 13, 1994).

30. Testimony of Doris Meissner, Commissioner, Immigration and Naturalization Service before the Subcommittee on Immigration of the Senate Judiciary Committee (Sept. 16, 1998). A more detailed account of the INS's expanding detention operations from 1980 to 1995 can be found in Margaret H. Taylor, Detained Aliens Challenging Conditions of Confinement and the Porous Border of the Plenary Power Doctrine, 22 Hastings Const. L.Q. 1087, 1099–1110 (1995) ("Taylor, Conditions of Confinement").

31. See note 23.

32. Taylor, Conditions of Confinement at 1107 n.101 (cited in note 30).

33. Hearing on Review of Department of Justice Immigration Detention Policies, Subcommittee on Immigration and Claims of the House Judiciary Committee (Dec. 19, 2001) (detention population of 19,533 in fiscal year 2001); U.S. Department of Justice, Office of the Federal Detention Trustee, Persons Admitted to Federal Detention, Fiscal Years 1994–2002, available at http://www.usdoj.gov/ofdt/stsref1.htm (table giving INS figures of 19,395 for fiscal year 2000 and 20,653 for fiscal year 2002).

34. The Institutional Removal Program (formerly known as the Institutional Hearing Program) is described in Schuck and Williams at 406–08 (cited in note 17).

35. Taylor and Wright at 1135–36 (cited in note 17) (compiling INS data). Removal statistics can be accessed via the enforcement sections of the monthly and yearly statistical reports published on the website of U.S. Citizenship and Immigration Services, www.uscis.gov.

36. See, for example, Christi Harlan, Beefed up INS Getting Results; More Illegal Immigrants Are Being Sent Home, Atlanta Journal–Constitution A6 (May 14, 1997) (reporting national deportation statistics for the first three months of 1997 as 28% higher than the prior year, with removals from the Atlanta district having "more than doubled").

37. Opening Statement of Lamar Smith, Chairman, Subcommittee on Immigration and Claims of the House Judiciary Committee, Hearing on Criminal and Illegal Aliens (Sept. 5, 1996).

38. For a comprehensive account of the 1996 milieu, see Margaret H. Taylor, Behind the Scenes of St. Cyr and Zadvydas: Making Policy in the Midst of Litigation, 16 Geo. Immigr. L.J. 271, 277–80 (2002) ("Taylor, Behind the Scenes").

39. Anti–Drug Abuse Act of 1988, Pub. L. No. 100–690, 102 Stat. 4181 (1988). See Schuck and Williams at 387–88, 434 (cited in note 17); Taylor, The 1996 Act: Detention at 215–16 (cited in note 13).

40. Leader v. Blackman, 744 F. Supp. 500, 509 (S.D.N.Y. 1990). *Leader* is representative of those cases striking down the statute. A leading case to the contrary is Davis v. Weiss, 749 F. Supp. 47 (D. Conn. 1990). Citations to decisions on both sides are collected in Don Kerwin, Detention of Newcomers: Constitutional Standards and New Legislation (Part One), Immigration Briefings 7–8 (Nov. 1996).

41. Immigration Act of 1990 § 504, Pub. L. No. 101–649, 104 Stat. 4978, 5049 (1990); Miscellaneous and Technical Immigration and Naturalization Amendments Act § 306, Pub. L. No. 102–232, 105 Stat. 1733, 1751 (1991).

42. See Probert v. INS, 954 F.2d 1253 (6th Cir. 1992); Bail Hearing for Robert Probert?, Toronto Star F2 (Nov. 20, 1991) (noting that the amendment was "sought on Probert's behalf" by Michigan Representative John Conyers).

43. Former INA § 242(a)(2)(A) & (B), 8 U.S.C. § 1252(a)(2)(A) & (B)(1994). Detention mandates remained in the statute for applicants for admission who had been convicted of an aggravated felony, including lawful permanent residents returning from a trip abroad. Former INA § 236(e) provided that excludable non-citizens who had been convicted of an aggravated felony could be released from custody only if the INS determined that their country of origin would not accept their return and they were not dangerous. 8 U.S.C. § 1227(e) (1994). This provision remained in effect until it was repealed by IIRIRA, and continued to spawn due process challenges. See Taylor, The 1996 Act: Detention at 217–18 (cited in note 13); St. John v. McElroy, 917 F. Supp. 243 (S.D.N.Y. 1996).

44. Taylor, Conditions of Confinement at 1106 (cited in note 30).

45. U.S. General Accounting Office, Immigration Control: Immigration Policies Affect INS Detention Efforts 41, 43 (June 1992).

46. Immigration and Nationality Technical Corrections Act of 1994 § 222, Pub. L. No. 103–416, 108 Stat. 4305, 4321–22 (1994).

47. Former INA § 101(a)(43)(G), 8 U.S.C. § 1101(a)(43)(G) (1994).

48. Immigration, Other Priorities on Congressional Agenda for 1996, 73 Interpreter Releases 133 (Jan. 29, 1996).

49. Paul Leavitt, Report Suggests INS Should Increase Detentions, USA Today 3A (Apr. 11, 1996).

50. Vera Institute of Justice, Plan for an Appearance Assistance Program, Submitted to the Immigration and Naturalization Service and the National Institute of Justice, Jan. 2, 1996.

51. See Christopher Stone, Supervised Release as an Alternative to Detention in Removal Proceedings: Some Promising Results of a Demonstration Project, 14 Geo. Immigr. L.J. 673 (2000). Vera's final report to the INS, analyzing the outcome of the project, is available in the publications section of the Vera Institute of Justice website: www.vera.org.

52. Antiterrorism and Effective Death Penalty Act, Pub. L. No. 104–132, 110 Stat. 1214 (Apr. 24, 1996). See Lena Williams, A Law Aimed At Terrorists Hits Legal Immigrants, N.Y. Times A1 (Jul. 17, 1996); Immigration, Other Priorities on Congressional Agenda for 1996, 73 Interpreter Releases 133, 135 (Jan. 29, 1996); House Passes Anti–Terrorism Bill After Deleting Immigration Provisions, 73 Interpreter Releases 317 (Mar.

18, 1996); Final Anti–Terrorism Bill Contains Major Immigration Changes, 73 Interpreter Releases 521 (Apr. 22, 1996).

53. President Signs Terrorism Bill Into Law, 73 Interpreter Releases 568 (Apr. 29, 1996).

54. AEDPA § 440(c), 110 Stat at 1277.

55. Eric Schmitt, Provision in Terrorism Bill Cuts Rights of Illegal Aliens, N.Y. Times B9 (Apr. 19, 1996).

56. Taylor, Behind the Scenes at 277–80 (cited in note 38).

57. Lena Williams, A Law Aimed At Terrorists Hits Legal Immigrants, N.Y. Times A1 (July 17, 1996). Internal agency "talking points" used by top INS officials who were meeting with members of Congress included "Change the Mandatory Detention Provisions to Restore the Flexibility Needed for Balanced Enforcement" at the top of the list of issues to discuss.

58. Pub. L. No. 104–208, 110 Stat. 3009 (Sept. 30, 1996).

59. Eleventh–Hour Agreement Folds Immigration Bill into Omnibus Spending Measure, 73 Interpreter Releases 1281 (Sept. 30, 1996). See also Education Bar Dispute Again Stalls Immigration Bill, 73 Interpreter Releases 1255 (Sept. 23, 1996); Jerry Gray, Senate Approves a Big Budget Bill, Beating Deadline, N.Y. Times A1 (Oct. 1, 1996).

60. INA § 101(a)(43)(G), 8 U.S.C. § 1101(a)(43)(G) (2000). See Nancy Morawetz, Understanding the Impact of the 1996 Deportation Laws and the Limited Scope of Proposed Reforms, 113 Harv. L. Rev. 1936, 1939–41 (2000).

61. INA § 240A(a)(3), 240A(b)(1)(C).

62. IIRIRA § 303(a). The scope of IIRIRA's mandatory detention provision, which is now codified at INA § 236(c), is explained in note 69 infra.

63. IIRIRA § 303(b). INS, State Dept. Begin Implementing New Law, 73 Interpreter Releases 1417, 1418–19 (Oct. 11, 1996); INS Commissioner Invokes Detention Transition Rules for Another Year, 74 Interpreter Releases 1552 (Oct. 10, 1997). For an explanation of the Transition Period Custody Rules, see Taylor, The 1996 Act: Detention at 216–17 (cited in note 13).

64. See Stone, 14 Geo. Immigr. L.J. 673 (cited in note 51).

65. This "unorthodox" route through the legislative process is quite common for immigration reform measures, and indeed has become a routine part of contemporary congressional procedures. See Barbara Sinclair, Unorthodox Lawmaking: New Legislative Processes in the U.S. Congress (2d ed. 2000).

66. 538 U.S. at 518, 521.

67. Id. at 514 n.3.

68. Id. at 514, 522 n.6, 531.

69. The statute is difficult to decipher because it is littered with cross-references. INA § 236(c)(1)(A) mandates detention for any individual who is inadmissible on any of the criminal inadmissibility grounds. INA § 236(c)(1)(B) covers all of the criminal removal grounds *except* a single crime involving moral turpitude (CIMT) committed within five years after date of admission. (A single CIMT committed more than five years after admission is not a deportable offense, unless it falls within the aggravated felony definition). INA § 236(c)(1)(C) provides that a single CIMT committed within five years after date of admission will trigger mandatory detention if a prison term of one year has been imposed. Finally, INA § 236(c)(1)(D) provides for detention without bond for individuals who are inadmissible or deportable under the terrorism grounds.

70. 8 C.F.R. § 1003.19(h)(2)(ii) (2004).

71. 538 U.S. at 514 n.3. The fact that a *Joseph* hearing was available was also central to Justice Kennedy's concurring opinion, although he noted that the government need only meet a "minimal threshold burden" to justify continued detention under the statute. Id. at 1722.

72. See Matter of Joseph, 22 I & N Dec. 799, 1999 WL 339053 (BIA 1999).

73. This general principle—that conviction for a criminal offense usually establishes a basis for the application of INA § 236(c)—has some important exceptions. First, in some cases, the government argues aggressively for deportation based on an interpretation of the statute that is not supported by existing law. Second, the government may appeal to the BIA after an immigration judge has concluded that an individual who has been charged on criminal grounds is not in fact deportable. A *Joseph* challenge may well succeed on these and similar facts. Even then, the government may petition for a stay of the immigration judge's release order, and in some circumstances, may obtain an automatic stay based solely on the filing of the appeal. See 8 C.F.R. § 1003.19(i) (2004).

74. 538 U.S. at 514, 515 (referring to "the aggravated felony classification triggering respondent's detention"), 517–18 (concluding the statute "mandates detention during removal proceedings for a limited class of deportable aliens—including those convicted of an aggravated felony"), 522 n.6 (discussing respondent's concession of deportability).

75. United States v. Corona–Sanchez, 291 F.3d 1201 (9th Cir. 2002).

76. Brief for the Respondent at 11–12, Demore v. Kim, 538 U.S. 510 (2003) (No. 01–1491); Transcript of Oral Argument in Demore v. Kim, 2003 U.S. Trans Lexis 6, 123 S. Ct. 1708 at 35–45 (Jan. 15, 2003).

77. Brief for the Petitioners at 4 n.2, Demore v. Kim, 538 U.S. 510 (2003) (No. 01–1491).

78. Order Granting Motion to Vacate, Superior Court of the State of California, Monterey County (Cal. Super. Ct. May 14, 2003) (No. SM970463B). All of the records of the state criminal proceedings involving Hyung Joon Kim are now part of the record in Kim's pending habeas action (cited in note 4).

79. Decision and Order of Immigration Judge Paul Grussendorf, In the Matter of Hyung Joon Kim at 1 (IJ June 27, 2003) (No. A27–144–740) ("IJ Decision") (noting the government had amended the charging document, so that "DHS's only remaining charge is for two CIMTs").

80. INA § 240A. See Matter of Marin, 16 I & N Dec. 581 (BIA 1978); Matter of Sotelo, 23 I & N Dec. 201 (BIA 2001).

81. Unless otherwise noted, quotations in this section come from the transcript of the hearing on Kim's application for cancellation of removal, held on June 11, 2003 ("Hearing Transcript"). The hearing transcript is part of the record in Kim's pending habeas action (cited in note 4).

82. Probation Officer's Report, Superior Court of California, Monterrey Co., State v. Hyung Joon Kim (Cal. Super. Ct. June 9, 1997) (No. SM970463B).

83. Kim v. Schiltgen, 1999 WL 33944060 (N.D. Cal.).

84. Notice of Custody Determination (cited in note 3).

85. Psychological Evaluation for Hyung Joon Kim by Daniel W. Edwards, Ph.D. (June 23, 2003).

86. The San Francisco law firm of Van Der Hout, Brigagliano & Nightingale represented Hyung Joon Kim when he applied for cancellation of removal. Kim's attorney, Zachary Nightingale, received the Jack Wasserman Memorial Award from the American Immigration Lawyers Association in 2003 for excellence in litigation.

87. IJ Decision at 7–8 (cited in note 80).

88. Id. at 8.

89. Id. at 6.

90. Hearing Transcript at 163 (cited in note 82).

91. Brief of Amici Curiae Citizens and Immigrants for Equal Justice et. al Supporting Respondent, Demore v. Kim, 538 U.S. 510 (2003) (No. 01–1491) ("CIEJ Brief").

92. Id. at 23–26.

93. Id. at 1.

94. See Margaret H. Taylor, Promoting Legal Representation for Detained Aliens: Litigation and Administrative Reform, 29 Conn. L. Rev. 1647, 1667–75 (1997) (detailing the obstacles faced by INS detainees seeking to secure legal representation).

95. See Taylor, Conditions of Confinement at 1111–27 (cited in note 30); Former INS Officials Brief at 10 (cited in note 2) (conditions are "largely indistinguishable from those in actual prisons").

96. CIEJ brief at 8 (Hawa Said, who was pregnant, was transferred to a detention facility over 2000 miles from her family; her claim to U.S. citizenship was later recognized), 21 (Max Ogando, who is deaf and is only able to communicate in Spanish sign language, was transferred away from his counsel and interpreter in New York to Etowah County Jail in Alabama). See also Monica Rhor, Unwelcome Turn: '99 Conviction Spurs Mother's Detention, Boston Globe B1 (Aug. 7, 2003) (Edna Borges was separated from her 10–day old infant and 2–year-old son when she was taken into custody after the Supreme Court upheld mandatory detention in *Demore;* she had been convicted four years earlier, at the age of 17, of two shoplifting offenses).

97. See Senator Jon Kyl, Terrorism Threat Along Our Border is Serious, Tucson Citizen 5B (Sept. 16, 2004) (op-ed piece including DHS statistics on non-citizens "from countries with significant terrorist operations" apprehended at the U.S.-Mexican border); Richard B. Schmitt, H.G. Reza, and Richard Boudreaux, U.S. Fears Terrorism Via Mexico's Time–Tested Smuggling Routes, L.A. Times A16 (Sept. 15, 2004); Ralph Blumenthal, New Strains and New Rules for Agents along Mexican Border, N.Y. Times A17 (Aug. 12, 2004); James Pinkerton, Border Policy Loses 400,000 Fugitives, Houston Chron. A1 (Aug. 8, 2004); Jerry Seper, Revolving Door at the Border; Aliens Often Freed for Lack of Detention Space, Wash. Times A1 (July 21, 2004). The Department of Homeland Security responded by announcing that it would expand expedited removal procedures, which were created by IIRIRA and originally employed only at ports of entry, to secure final removal orders against some categories of non-citizens—including "other than Mexicans"—who were apprehended within fourteen days of arrival and within one hundred miles of the border. 69 Fed. Reg. 48877 (Aug. 11, 2004).

98. Brief of Former INS Officials at 21 (cited in note 2).

99. Id. at 6–10.

100. 538 U.S. at 521.

101. See Peter J. Spiro, Explaining the End of Plenary Power, 16 Geo. Immigr. L.J. 339 (2002); T. Alexander Aleinikoff, Detaining Plenary Power: The Meaning and Impact of Zadvydas v. Davis, 16 Geo. Immigr. L.J. 365 (2002). See generally David A. Martin, Graduated Application of Constitutional Protection for Aliens: The Real Meaning of *Zadvydas v. Davis*, 2001 Sup. Ct. Rev. 47.

102. 538 U.S. at 558 (Souter, J., dissenting).

103. Id. at 541.

104. 481 U.S. 739 (1987).

105. 18 U.S.C. § 3142(e) (1982 ed., Supp. III).

106. 481 U.S. at 747–48.

107. See Kansas v. Hendricks, 521 U.S. 346 (1997) (upholding Kansas statute providing for confinement of violent sexual predators who suffer from "a mental abnormality or personality disorder"); Foucha v. Louisiana, 504 U.S. 71 (1992) (striking down Louisiana statute that permitted indefinite confinement of an individual who was deemed dangerous but was not mentally ill); Addington v. Texas, 441 U.S. 418 (1979) (in civil commitment proceeding, the government must establish mental illness and future dangerousness by a "clear and convincing" evidentiary standard).

108. O'Connor v. Donaldson, 422 U.S. 563, 574 (1975) (mental illness alone cannot justify indefinite confinement of a person who is not dangerous).

109. *Foucha,* 504 U.S. at 81.

110. Id. at 79 (person acquitted by reason of insanity cannot be held by the state based on dangerousness alone, if he is no longer mentally ill); Kansas v. Hendricks, 521 U.S. at 358 (civil commitment statute must couple proof of dangerousness with proof of some additional factor, such as mental illness or mental abnormality).

111. *Salerno,* 481 U.S. at 750; *Foucha,* 504 U.S. at 81–82 (invalidating statute that places burden on individual to prove that he is not dangerous); *Hendricks,* 521 U.S. at 353 (stressing procedural protections provided in statute).

112. INA § 241(a)(6).

113. Zadvydas v. Davis, 533 U.S. 678, 699–700 (2001).

114. See Hiroshi Motomura, Immigration Law after a Century of Plenary Power: Phantom Constitutional Norms and Statutory Interpretation, 100 Yale L.J. 545 (1990).

115. *Zadvydas,* 533 U.S. at 695.

116. Id. at 690.

117. See cases cited supra in note 10.

118. *Demore,* 538 U.S. at 526–31.

119. Id. at 521–22 (citing to different sources for each of its iterations).

120. Id. at 547 (Souter, J., dissenting).

121. See U.S. Dept. of Justice, Office of the Inspector General, The September 11 Detainees: A Review of the Treatment of Aliens Held on Immigration Charges in Connection with the Investigation of the September 11 Attacks (Apr. 2003).

122. Bob Egelko, Justices to Rule on Detention of Immigrants, San Fran. Chron. A3 (Jan. 15, 2003). See also David G. Savage, High Court Upholds Jailing of Immigrants, L.A. Times 1 (Apr. 30, 2003) (noting that "[t]he ruling also gives U.S. Atty Gen. John Ashcroft a stronger legal basis to hold detainees in the war on terrorism"); Linda Greenhouse, U.S. Can Hold Immigrants Set to be Deported, N.Y. Times A2 (Apr. 30, 2003); Bob Egelko, Jail with No Bail OKd for Legal Immigrants, San Fran. Chron. A3 (Apr. 30, 2003).

123. *Demore's* connection to the government's post–9/11 enforcement efforts was subtly underscored by the fact that Solicitor General Theodore Olson, whose wife was killed in the 9/11 attacks, personally argued the government's case. David A. Martin, Too Many Behind Bars: The INS Doesn't Need to Lock Up Everyone Facing a Deportation Hearing. And the Supreme Court Should Say So, Legal Times 51 (Jan. 27, 2003).

124. Gonzalez v. O'Connell, 355 F.3d 1010 (7th Cir. 2004) (stating in dicta that *Demore* left open the question of whether INA § 236(c) is constitutional when a detainee makes a good faith argument that he is not in fact deportable, but concluding that petitioner in this case could not meet that standard); Ly v. Hansen, 351 F.3d 263 (6th Cir. 2003) (holding that *Zadvydas,* not *Demore,* governs a challenge to pre-hearing detention under § 236(c) when removal is not foreseeable and the length of detention is unreasonable).

125. Clark v. Suarez Martinez, 125 S. Ct. 716 (2005).

126. Rasul v. Bush, 540 U.S. 1175 (2004); Hamdi v. Rumsfeld, 540 U.S. 1099 (2004). See Linda Greenhouse, Access to Courts, N.Y. Times A1 (June 29, 2004).

127. Jeffrey Rosen, One Eye on Principle, the Other on the People's Will, N.Y. Times § 4 at 3 (Jul. 4, 2004).

128. Bob Egelko, Jail with No Bond OKd for Legal Immigrants, San Fran. Chron. A3 (Apr. 30, 2003).

129. Hearing Transcript at 163 (cited in note 82).

130. In Re Kim, 2004 WL 1059647 (BIA 2004).

131. Id.

132. Id.

133. INA § 242(a)(2)(C), 242(a)(2)(B)(i), 8 U.S.C. § 1252 (2000). See INS v. St. Cyr, 121 S. Ct. 2271 (2001) (which is treated in detail in Chapter 11 of this volume).

134. Petition for Writ of Habeas Corpus, Kim v. Ridge (N.D. Cal. Jan. 26, 2004) (No. C 04–0341).

135. Order Granting Motion for Discovery at 5, Kim v. Ridge (N.D. Cal. Apr. 9, 2004) (No. C 04–0341).

Contributors

Gabriel "Jack" Chin is Chester H. Smith Professor of Law and Co–Director of the Law, Criminal Justice and Security Program at the University of Arizona James E. Rogers College of Law. A graduate of Wesleyan University and the Michigan and Yale law schools, Professor Chin clerked for the Honorable Richard P. Matsch of U.S. District Court for the District of Colorado. With his students, he has sought to eliminate Jim Crow-era racial segregation laws still on the books; their work led to repeal of statutes in Kansas and Wyoming designed to prevent Asians from owning real property, and school segregation laws in Georgia, Louisiana, Missouri and West Virginia. In 2003, their work persuaded the Ohio General Assembly to ratify the Fourteenth Amendment. Professor Chin received the Outstanding Scholarly Paper Award from the Association of American Law Schools for *Segregation's Last Stronghold: Race Discrimination and the Constitutional Law of Immigration*, 46 *UCLA Law Review* 1 (1998). He and his students edit the *Immigration and Nationality Law Review*.

Catherine L. Fisk is Professor of Law at Duke University, where she teaches civil procedure and a range of labor and employment law courses. She graduated *summa cum laude* from Princeton University and from the law school of the University of California at Berkeley (Boalt Hall). After clerking on the federal court of appeals, she practiced labor law in Washington, D.C., before joining the appellate staff of the civil division of the U.S. Department of Justice. She has previously taught at the University of Wisconsin, Loyola Law School in Los Angeles, UCLA Law School, and the University of Southern California Law School. She has published articles and book chapters on union organizing among immigrant janitors, on the role of union lawyers in providing legal representation to individual employees, on wage and hour and other individual rights claims, and on a variety of other labor and employment-related topics. Her writings are included in *Organizing Immigrants* (Ruth Milkman, ed., 2000) and in *The Changing Role of Unions: New Forms of Representation* (P.V. Wunnava, ed. 2004), and her work has appeared in the Stanford Law Review and the University of Chicago Law Review among other journals. She is the co-editor of *Labor Law Stories* (2005). She thanks Paytre Topp, University of Southern California Law School class of 2005, for her research assistance on the chapter on *Hoffman Plastic Compounds*.

Kevin R. Johnson is Associate Dean for Academic Affairs and Mabie–Apallas Public Interest Professor of Law and Chicana/o Studies at the University of California at Davis. He has published extensively on immigration law and policy, racial identity, and civil rights in national and international journals. Professor Johnson's latest book, *The "Huddled Masses" Myth: Immigration and Civil Rights,* was published in early 2005. A graduate of Harvard Law School, where he served as an editor of the *Harvard Law Review*, Johnson earned his undergraduate degree in economics from UC Berkeley. After graduation from law school, he clerked for the Honorable Stephen Reinhardt of the U.S. Court of Appeals for the Ninth Circuit in Los Angeles and worked as an attorney at Heller Ehrman White & McAuliffe in San Francisco. Professor Johnson has experience representing immigrants in removal cases and class actions. He joined the UC Davis law faculty in 1989 and was named Associate Dean for Academic Affairs in 1998. Professor Johnson has taught a wide array of classes, including immigration law and refugee law.

Daniel Kanstroom is the Director of the Boston College Law School International Human Rights Program and Clinical Professor of Law. He teaches Immigration and Refugee Law, International Human Rights Law, the BC London Program, and Administrative Law. He was the founder and is the current director of the Boston College Immigration and Asylum clinic in which students represent indigent noncitizens and asylum-seekers. Together with his students, he has won several high-profile immigration and asylum cases and has provided counsel for hundreds of clients over more than a decade. He and his students have also written amicus briefs for the U.S. Supreme Court, organized public presentations in schools, churches, community centers, courts and prisons, and have advised many community groups. Professor Kanstroom has published widely in the fields of U.S. immigration law, criminal law, and European citizenship and asylum law in such venues as the Harvard Law Review, the Yale Journal of International Law, the Georgetown Immigration Law Journal, and the French *Gazette du Palais*. He is a co-author of Massachusetts Criminal Practice (LEXIS) and is currently completing a book, *Good-Bye Rosalita: A Social and Legal History of Deportation* (Harvard University Press, forthcoming 2005.) Professor Kanstroom has long served on the Board of the Directors of the Political Asylum Immigrant Representation (PAIR) Project, was *rapporteur* for the American Branch of the Refugee Law Section of the International Law Association and has co-chaired immigration committees of the American Bar Association.

David A. Martin is the Warner–Booker Distinguished Professor of International Law at the University of Virginia, where he teaches immigration and refugee law, constitutional law, and international law. He is a graduate of DePauw University and the Yale Law School. Following clerkships with Judge J. Skelly Wright and Justice Lewis F. Powell, Jr., and a period of private practice in Washington, D.C., he served from 1978 to 1980 as special assistant in the human rights bureau of the U.S. Department of State. There he participated in drafting the Refugee Act of 1980. Since joining the Virginia faculty in 1980, he has published numerous works on immigration, refugees, international human rights, and constitutional law, including a leading casebook on U.S. immigration and citizenship law (coauthored with T. Alexander Aleinikoff and Hiroshi Motomura, Thomson West, 5th ed. 2003). He has served as Vice President of the American Society of International Law and is a member of the Board of Editors of the American Journal of International Law. As a consultant to the Department of Justice in 1993, he helped design major reforms for the U.S. political asylum system, and in 2003–2004 he prepared a lengthy report for the Department of State on reforms for the overseas refugee admissions program. From August 1995 to January 1998, he served as General Counsel of the Immigration and Naturalization Service.

Nancy Morawetz is a Professor of Clinical Law at New York University School of Law, where she has taught since 1987. She currently specializes in issues related to deportation and detention. Her primary areas of interest are the intersection of immigration and criminal law and issues related to changes in immigration enforcement in the wake of the attacks of 9/11. In addition to her scholarly work, Professor Morawetz is engaged in litigation and advocacy surrounding deportation and detention policy with students in NYU's Immigrant Rights Clinic. Professor Morawetz is a graduate of New York University School of Law, where she was a Root Tilden scholar and was Editor in Chief of the New York University Law Review. After clerking for the Hon. Patricia M. Wald on the United States Court of Appeals for the District of Columbia Circuit, Professor Morawetz served as a staff attorney at the Civil Appeals and Law Reform Unit of Legal Aid Society in New York City. In addition to the Immigrant Rights Clinic, Professor Morawetz has taught civil litigation, lawyering theory, government benefits, and public policy advocacy.

Burt Neuborne is the John Norton Pomeroy Professor of Law, and one of the nation's leading scholars in the areas of constitutional law, procedure, and evidence. As Legal Director of the Brennan Center, he is at the center of emerging legal issues affecting democracy, poverty and the criminal justice system. In addition to his scholarly duties involving the publication of numerous books and articles, for the past 30 years, Professor Neuborne has been one of the nation's most active civil liberties lawyers. Most recently he has been involved as principal lawyer in several cases that have secured a billion dollars of compensation for Holocaust victims from German corporations and Swiss banks. He was a member of the New York City Human Rights Commission from 1988 to 1992 and served as National Legal Director of the ACLU from 1982 to 1986. He became Associate Professor of Law at NYU in 1974 and full Professor in 1976. He served as Assistant Legal Director of the American Civil Liberties Union from 1972 to 1974 and worked as a tax lawyer on Wall Street until becoming staff counsel for the New York Civil Liberties Union in 1967. He studied at Cornell University, 1957–1961, and graduated Harvard Law School in 1964 (cum laude). Professor Neuborne received a Distinguished Teaching Medal from New York University in 1990. He has been elected to membership in the American Academy of Arts and Sciences.

Gerald L. Neuman is the Herbert Wechsler Professor of Federal Jurisprudence at Columbia Law School, where he teaches immigration and nationality law, constitutional law, comparative constitutional law and human rights. He is the author of *Strangers to the Constitution: Immigrants, Borders, and Fundamental Law* (Princeton University Press, 1996), and co-author of the casebook *Human Rights* (Foundation Press, 1999), as well as numerous articles on immigration and nationality law. His principal research interests include habeas corpus and the rule of law, and transnational dimensions of constitutionalism. He is a graduate of Harvard College, the Massachusetts Institute of Technology, and Harvard Law School.

Michael A. Olivas is the William B. Bates Distinguished Chair in Law at the University of Houston Law Center, where he directs the UHLC Institute for Higher Education Law & Governance. He has held visiting teaching positions at the University of Wisconsin and the University of Iowa. He is an elected member of the American Law Institute and the National Academy of Education, the only person to hold membership in both organizations. He has served as Chair of the Immigration Law Section of the AALS twice, and as Chair of the Education Law Section three times.

Lucy E. Salyer is an associate professor in the History Department of the University of New Hampshire. She earned her doctorate from the Jurisprudence & Social Policy Program at the University of California, Berkeley, in 1989. She has served on the editorial board of *Law & History Review* since 1995, on the Board of Directors for the American Society for Legal History, and on the Membership Committee of the Organization of American Historians. She has been awarded fellowships from the Radcliffe Institute for Advanced Study, National Endowment of the Humanities, and the American Council of Learned Societies. Her book, *Laws Harsh as Tigers: Chinese Immigrants and the Shaping of Modern Immigration Law* (University of North Carolina Press, 1995), received the Theodore Saloutos Memorial Prize from the Immigration History Society. More recent publications include "Baptism by Fire: Military Service, Race and U.S. Citizenship Policy, 1918–1935," 91 *Journal of American History* 847–876 (Dec. 2004), which was awarded the Law & Society Association Article Prize in June 2005. She has completed a history of the California Supreme Court between 1910 and 1940 and is currently working on a socio-legal history of citizenship policies in the 19th and 20th century entitled "Pledging Allegiance."

Peter H. Schuck is the Simeon E. Baldwin Professor of Law at Yale University, where he has taught since 1979. His major fields of teaching and research are torts; immigration, citizenship, and refugee law; and administrative law, and he has written on a broad range of public policy topics. His most recent books include *Meditations of a Militant Moderate: Cool Views on Hot Issues* (in press, 2005); *Foundations of Administrative Law* (editor, 2d ed., 2004); *Diversity in America: Keeping Government at a Safe Distance* (Harvard/Belknap, 2003); *The Limits of Law: Essays on Democratic Governance* (2000); *Citizens, Strangers, and In–Betweens: Essays on Immigration and Citizenship* (1998); and *Paths to Inclusion: The Integration of Migrants in the United States and Germany* (co-editor, 1998). Earlier books include *Suing Government: Citizen Remedies for Official Wrongs* (1983); *Citizenship Without Consent: Illegal Aliens in the American Policy* (with Rogers M. Smith, 1985); *Agent Orange on Trial: Mass Toxic Disasters in the Courts* (1987); *Tort Law and the Public Interest: Competition, Innovation, and Consumer Welfare* (editor, 1991*)*; and *The Judiciary Committees* (1974). He was awarded a Harvard Graduate Prize Fellowship (1968–70), a Guggenheim Fellowship (1984–85), and a Fulbright Senior Fellowship to lecture in India (2004). Prior to joining the Yale faculty, he was Principal Deputy Assistant Secretary for Planning and Evaluation in the U.S. Department of Health, Education, and Welfare (1977–79), Director of the Washington Office of Consumers Union (1972–77), and consultant to the Center for Study of Responsive Law (1971–72). He also practiced law in New York City (1965–68) and holds degrees from Cornell (B.A. 1962), Harvard Law School (J.D. 1965), NYU Law School (LL.M. 1966), and Harvard University (M.A. 1969). He lives in New York City where he has an office at NYU Law School.

Peter J. Spiro is Rusk Professor of International Law at the University of Georgia Law School. He is a former law clerk to Justice David H. Souter of the U.S. Supreme Court and to Judge Stephen F. Williams of the U.S. Court of Appeals for the District of Columbia

Circuit, and has also served as an Attorney–Adviser in the Office of the Legal Adviser in the U.S. Department of State. In 1993–94 he was a Council on Foreign Relations International Affairs Fellow, during which he served as Director for Democracy on the staff of the National Security Council. He was awarded a 1998–99 Open Society Institute Individual Project Fellowship to undertake an examination of the law of United States citizenship. Professor Spiro's research interests include citizenship law and theory, the intersection of constitutional and international law, and the role of non-state actors in international decisionmaking. In addition to academic writing, his work has also appeared in such publications as Foreign Affairs, The Wall Street Journal, and The New Republic. He is a graduate of Harvard College and the University of Virginia School of Law.

Margaret H. Taylor is a Professor of Law at Wake Forest University School of Law, where she teaches courses in immigration law, legislation, and administrative law. Professor Taylor's research focuses on immigration detention and the deportation of criminal offenders. She served as chair of the AALS Section on Immigration Law, was appointed to the American Bar Association's Commission on Immigration, and served on the Advisory Board of the Appearance Assistance Program of the Vera Institute of Justice. She was invited to testify on detention policy before Congress and the U.S. Commission on Immigration Reform. Professor Taylor is a recipient of the Joseph Branch Excellence in Teaching Award from Wake Forest University School of Law and the Elmer Fried Excellence in Teaching Award from the American Immigration Lawyers Association. She is a graduate of the University of Texas and Yale Law School.

Michael J. Wishnie is Professor of Clinical Law at New York University School of Law, where he co-directs the Immigrant Rights Clinic and the Arthur Garfield Hays Civil Liberties Program. Wishnie's teaching, scholarship, litigation, and advocacy have concentrated on immigration, labor, and civil rights issues. Before joining the NYU faculty, Wishnie was a staff attorney at The Legal Aid Society of New York and Skadden Fellow at the ACLU Immigrants Rights Project, as well as a law clerk to Judge H. Lee Sarokin and Justices Harry A. Blackmun and Stephen G. Breyer. In the *Hoffman Plastic* litigation, Wishnie was counsel of record for business groups in support of the NLRB, edited several other amicus briefs, and participated in one moot at the Solicitor General's office and various legislative advocacy activities. He gratefully acknowledges the financial support of the Filomen D'Agostino and Max E. Greenberg Research Fund at the New York University School of Law.

†